Social Psychology of the Self-Concept

Social Psychology of the Self-Concept

EDITED BY

MORRIS ROSENBERG
University of Maryland

HOWARD B. KAPLAN
Baylor College of Medicine

HARLAN DAVIDSON, INC.
Arlington Heights, Illinois 60004

 For information address the publisher, Harlan Davidson, Inc., *formerly* AHM Publishing Corporation, 3110 North Arlington Heights Road, Arlington Heights, Illinois 60004.

Printed in the United States of America

82 83 84 85MA7 6 5 4 3 2 1

Contents

TWO

PRINCIPLES OF SELF-CONCEPT FORMATION

THREE

SOCIAL IDENTITY AND SOCIAL CONTEXT

FIVE

DEVIANCE

SIX

DEFENSE MECHANISMS

Acknowledgements

We are grateful to the following people who helped us to bring this work to fruition: to Carl W. Backman, General Editor for Sociology of Harlan Davidson, Inc., for his advice and encouragement throughout this undertaking; to Maureen Trobec and Timothy Taylor of Harlan Davidson, Inc. for their excellent editorial and production work; and to Jane Deiter, whose secretarial and administrative skills were so superbly demonstrated throughout the course of this work. The editors are also pleased to acknowledge the support of the National Institute of Mental Health, whose grant (MH27747) helped to support the work of Morris Rosenberg, and to the National Institute on Drug Abuse, whose grant (DA02497) helped to support the work of Howard B. Kaplan.

General Introduction

Although the self-concept is currently recognized as an important area of research both in psychology and in sociology, systematic research on the topic has entered both fields very slowly. The entry of such research into psychology was influenced by the explicit introduction of the doctrine of *phenomenology*. Following MacLeod's exposition (1947) of a phenomenological approach to psychology, Snygg and Combs in 1949 proposed a new frame of reference for psychology. The proper subject matter, they held, was the individual's phenomenal field, that is, "the universe of naive experience in which each individual lives, the everyday situation of self and surroundings, which each person takes to be reality" (1949: 15).

This doctrine represented a radical departure from the dominant psychological views at the time, although it was consistent with Gestalt psychology, field theory, and personalistic psychology. Phenomenology represented a challenge to the influential theory of behaviorism. Guided by the classical theories of Hull and the experiments of Pavlov, American psychology during the '20s and '30s embraced the theory of behaviorism, elaborated as *Reinforcement Theory*. In simplest terms, psychology attempted to explain actual human behavior by means of objective observation. It could best do so by exposing subjects to certain stimuli and then observing their responses. This approach dominated the field for several decades and continues to play a prominent role in psychology even today.

Another important set of theoretical influences was the *depth psychologies* —particularly the work of Freud. *Psychoanalytic theory* contended that adult responses could best be explained by unconscious drives or impulses having their roots in earlier experience. A major focus of interest was the attempt to understand how current psychological disturbances actually represented the symbolic expression of childhood events. All this occurred below the level of consciousness and resulted from the operation of intricate psychodynamic forces. Although academic psychology looked askance at this approach, it nevertheless continued to exercise wide influence.

The *phenomenological approach* differed from both behaviorism and psychoanalysis. For the phenomenologist, the subject matter of psychology is the phenomenal datum, that is, the psychological experience of the individual at a particular moment in time.

According to MacLeod: "Just as color is not an array of light waves, so the person we perceive is not the person who may really exist. . . .Our first phenomenological task is to observe, describe, and analyze the structures, properties, dimensions, and interrelations of phenomena as they are naively apprehended" (1968: 69-70). In this view, it is the individual's direct perception of the external world, what he or she actually sees and feels, that constitutes the subject matter of psychology.

While acknowledging the value of behaviorism's contribution to psychology, Snygg and Combs nonetheless contended that behavior could best be understood by taking account of the world of immediate experience, of direct apprehension. In their view: "All behavior, without exception, is completely determined by and pertinent to the phenomenal field of the behaving organism. . . .By the phenomenal field we mean the entire universe, including himself, as it is experienced by the individual at the instant of action. . ." (1949: 15).

The phenomenological approach thus undertook to shift psychology from an external to an internal frame of reference—from overt behavior to inner perception. It sought to understand the behavior of individuals from their own point of view, to observe people, not as they seemed to outsiders, but as they seemed to themselves. Each individual's phenomenal field is his or her sole psychological reality.

The special relevance of the phenomenological doctrine in the present regard is that it opened the door for the entry of the self-concept into the field of psychology. If one was willing to accept the view that a legitimate concern of the psychologist was the individual's perceptions of the world, then this would include perceptions of himself or herself as well. Snygg and Combs referred to the self-concept as "those parts of the phenomenal field which the individual has differentiated as definite and fairly stable characteristics of himself" (1949: 112). To accept phenomenology was thus to accept the self-concept as an essential topic of psychological research.

The barriers to self-concept research among sociologists were of a different sort. Not sharing the psychologists' qualms about probing inner states, sociologists were not impeded by such theoretical obstacles to self-concept research; however, they faced a different intellectual hurdle. Although earlier sociologists (notably Charles Horton Cooley) had presented many interesting and valuable insights into the self-concept, undoubtedly the towering intellectual figure in this area was George Herbert Mead. Mead's lectures at the University of Chicago in the '20s and '30s exercised an important intellectual influence in sociology. These lectures became more available in 1934 with the posthumous publication of *Mind, Self and Society*. Mead's theories, though brilliant, were also subtle and elusive and did not lend themselves readily to the positivistic approach to science to which sociology, like psychology, aspired. The unpredictable and spontaneous nature of the "I," the constant interaction of "I" and "me," the internal conversation of gestures—the entire ongoing process of the self— could not, as Blumer (1956) subsequently stressed, be fully captured by examining the relationships among static variables. To the sociological researcher, the theories of Mead were at once tantalizing and forbidding.

This may be why 20 years elapsed between the publication of Mead's book (based on his earlier lectures) and the appearance of the first empirical sociological study of the subject. It was the work of Manford H. Kuhn (Kuhn and McPartland, 1954) who, dedicated to the examination of symbolic interactionism by means of the established methods of empirical research (instead of the intuitive, introspective methods recommended by some of Mead's other followers), studied the self-concept directly. Kuhn utilized the Twenty Statements Test (TST), attempting to enter the psychological interior of individuals by asking them to respond spontaneously to the question "Who Am I?" In so doing, Kuhn started the era of research on the sociology of the self-concept, particularly through his direct influence on an intellectually united body of students and followers who came to be known as the "Iowa school" of symbolic interactionism (in contrast to the "Chicago school"). Compared to the flood of studies that poured from psychology, the number of sociological studies proved to be modest; nevertheless, much has been learned from this research.

Systematic self-concept research in psychology and sociology thus began at nearly the same time in psychology and sociology under the impetus of phenomenology and the Iowa school. These two currents quickly joined and moved forward together in an effort to understand the social psychology of the self-concept. In the course of time, related fields, such as vocational counseling, political science, anthropology, education, and psychiatry, conducted research on the self-concept and contributed to the common pool of knowledge.

Investigators in these fields join in viewing the self-concept as an unequivocally subjective phenomenon, a component of the individual's phenomenal field. But at the same time, they accept the fact that the self-concept is a social product, arising out of social interaction and constantly influenced by social experience, and that it is a major influence on the individual's thoughts, feelings, and behavior. In the words of McGuire and Padawer-Singer, "What we think of ourselves is probably the central concept of our conscious lives" (1976: 743). Thus, whatever decision we make, whatever action we take, is inevitably predicated on some implicit assumption of what we are like. Without the ability to view ourselves as objects, to assess our dispositions or other characteristics, and to consider these in relation to the particular situation, we are virtually immobilized. If it is true, as Lecky (1945) holds, that the self-concept is the basic axiom of the individual's life theory, then any effort to account for social behavior without reference to the self-concept must inevitably be deficient. Social interaction, occupational choice, educational performance, political apathy, susceptibility to mass communications, choice of leisure activities, religious behavior, social deviance—there is probably no realm of social action in which the individual's self-concept is not somehow implicated.

Before one can examine the social psychology of the self-concept—the view of the self-concept as a social product and a social force—it is necessary to decide what it is and what it includes. In our view, the self-concept is the totality of the individual's thoughts and feelings with reference to himself or herself as an object. Section One, The Constituents of the Self-Concept, proposes a framework for self-concept analysis. The self-concept includes a multiplicity of specific components, is organized into a structure, can be characterized in terms of diverse dimensions, contains a number of different regions, exists on several different planes, and so on. By stressing the diverse ingredients of the self-concept, we attempt to underscore the point that the self-concept is a genuinely complex structure and that research must confront and grapple with this reality.

Section Two turns to a discussion of four principles of self-concept formation—reflected appraisals, social comparison processes, self-attribution, and psychological centrality. Most of the empirical findings in the literature dealing with the relationship of social phenomena and self-concepts are best explained by these principles. Unfortunately, these principles, though sound, have often been misapplied, frequently resulting in erroneous conclusions.

Section Three considers elements of social identity. Starting at birth and continuing throughout life, members of society are socially classified in terms of various statuses, groups, or social categories. These are termed sociodemographic characteristics or "social identity elements." This section centers attention on four of these: minority group status, gender, social class, and age. Not only do these social identity elements constitute components of the self-concept, but they are also responsible for exposing the individual to characteristic social experiences—for example, prejudice, stereotyping, labeling—experiences which may profoundly influence the shaping of his or her self-concept.

Section Three also examines the impact of social contexts on the self-concept. These contexts refer to the social environments in which the individual is ensconced. The social psychological relevance of such contexts is that they attempt to explain the individual's self-concept by reference to the characteristics of other people in his or her environment.

Section Four turns attention to the connection between *social institutions* and the self-concept. An institution is a set of norms centering around one or more major social functions. Five institutions are considered: the family, the educational system, the political system, the economy, and the military. Section Four describes some ways in which the self-concept makes contact with these institutional structures, sometimes as cause and sometimes as effect.

Section Five looks at the relationship between the self-concept and social deviance. By *deviance* we refer to such psychological and social problems as crime, delinquency, drug addiction, alcoholism and (until recently) homosexuality. Although the clinical psychologist is prone to view deviance from the perspective of individual psychopathology whereas the sociologist is more likely to center attention on societal reaction to deviance, both implicitly or explicitly take account of the self-concept, either as a cause or a consequence of deviance. Section Five provides evidence that the individual's self-concept may be at the root of the deviance, but that the deviance may also influence the self-concept.

As one examines the various social forces that enter into the formation of the self-concept, it is easy to fall into the trap of thinking of the individual as a lump of putty, assuming whatever shape various social influences dictate. Nothing could be farther from the truth. The various social influences—interactions, social identity elements, institutions, contexts and so on—do *impinge* on the individual, but they do not *construct* the individual. The individual, guided by a powerful system of motives, answers back, coping in a variety of ingenious ways with the forces to which he or she is exposed. These intrapsychic processes help us to understand why social influences so often fail to produce the effects which we would, on theoretical grounds, expect. It was Freud's genius that called attention to the importance of these defense mechanisms. Section Six demonstrates that such defense mechanisms are primarily directed toward the protection of the self-concept, enlarging the range of defense mechanisms originally proposed by Freud.

Although literally thousands of studies on the self-concept have been conducted, they have scarcely scratched the surface of this complex and fascinating subject. Nevertheless, the following selections from the growing literature on this subject do demonstrate that, despite its considerable complexity, the self-concept is amenable to systematic research and will yield up its mysteries if approached in an imaginative fashion.

REFERENCES

Blumer, H.
1956 "Sociological analysis and the 'variable'." American Sociological Review 21: 683-90.
Kuhn, M. H. and T. McPartland
1954 "An empirical investigation of self-attitudes." American Sociological Review 19: 68–76.
Lecky, P.
1945 Self-Consistency: A Theory of Personality. New York: Island Press.
MacLeod, R. B.
1947 "The phenomenological approach to social psychology." Psychological Review 54: 193–210.
1968 "Phenomenology." Pp. 68-72 in D. L. Sills (ed.), International Encyclopedia of the Social Sciences Vol. 12. New York: Macmillan and Free Press.
McGuire, W. J. and A. Padawer-Singer
1976 "Trait salience in the spontaneous self-concept." Journal of Personality and Social Psychology 33: 743–54.
Mead, G. H.
1934 Mind, Self and Society. Chicago: University of Chicago Press.
Snygg, D. and A. W. Combs
1949 Individual Behavior: A New Frame of Reference for Psychology, New York: Harper.

ONE

CONSTITUENTS OF THE SELF-CONCEPT

Although no one knows how many books and articles on the self-concept have appeared in print, Ruth Wylie, in her review and synthesis of the self-concept literature, reports that she has examined over 4,500 references (1979: 5). Despite this immense outpouring, self-concept research, throughout most of its history, has suffered from a narrowness of focus. Research attention has centered largely on global self-esteem and on selected components of the self-concept. Recent developments, fortunately, reflect a growing awareness of the intricate complexity of this structure, and encouraging conceptual and methodological progress in this area can be discerned. Section One directs attention to some of the important ingredients of the self-concept.

Viewing the self-concept as the totality of the individual's thoughts and feelings with reference to himself or herself as an object, we suggest the following primary constituents: (1) components, (2) structure, (3) dimensions, (4) foci of attention, (5) regions, (6) planes, and (7) motives.

Although space limitations bar us from examining any of these constituents in complete detail, we shall attempt to illustrate each.

COMPONENTS

The components of the self-concept are the parts, elements, or units which constitute it. They consist primarily of nouns (for example, American, male, student, black) and adjectives (such as intelligent, sensitive, and moral). These components have proved to be inordinately resistant to simple classification. One reason is their enormous number. Many years ago, Allport and Odbert (1936) listed all the adjectives they could discover in an unabridged dictionary; the sum was nearly 18,000. Not all these adjectives, of course, are applicable to people but many are. Classification is also difficult because the self-concept is expressed in natural language; hence, there is considerable ambiguity and overlap among the components.

From the earliest works on this subject by Bugental and Zelen (1950) and Kuhn and McPartland (1954), problems of classification have seriously plagued self-concept research. Where broad classifications have been used, the detailed richness of the data has been sacrificed; and where the richness has been retained, looseness and confusion have frequently resulted. The most successful effort to deal clearly and comprehensively with this complex body of material is that of Gordon (Selection 1) who has classified the responses to the question "Who Am I?" into 30 broad categories. In a subsequent work, Gordon (1974) developed a computer readable dictionary which recognized over 5,000 entries. This sophisticated classification scheme afforded vivid evidence of the multiplicity of elements of the self-concept.

STRUCTURE

The structure refers to the relationship among or arrangement of these elements. As important as the parts themselves is the way in which these components are ordered and arranged. Not all components are on an equal footing. Some stand out, whereas others remain in the background. It is thus important to know how salient each component is. In addition to the salience of the components (which stand out in the individual's mind), it is essential to know which are most important (or matter most to the individual). Although salience and importance overlap, they are conceptually distinct. Third, there is the issue of the consistency of the parts, described by Morse and Gergen (1970) as "the extent to which [the individual] sees the various components of the self-concept as forming a coherent whole, as being consistent with one another."

The structural concepts of importance and consistency will be discussed in Section Two of this volume (Selections 14 and 15). In this section, we shall restrict ourselves to the issue of salience, discussed by McGuire and Padawer-Singer (Selection 2). Which self-concept components are at the front of the individual's attention? Although a number of factors—some situational, others dispositional—influence the salience of self-concept components, McGuire and Padawer-Singer find that a component tends to be salient if it is distinctive in a given environment. Sixth-grade subjects were asked to "tell us about yourself" and were given seven minutes to write down everything that came to mind. McGuire and Padawer-Singer demonstrate that the likelihood that an element will be salient depends on the distinctiveness of that characteristic in the individual's environment. Just as an orange stands out in a bushel of apples but remains unnoticed in a bushel of oranges, a self-concept component is more prominent in the individual's mind if it is different from those surrounding it.

Such salience, McGuire points out, does not necessarily serve the self-esteem motive. Negative qualities (such as overweight or underweight) may be more salient than positive ones (such as ideal or average weight). The critical question is not whether the individual is good or bad in some respect, but whether he or she is different. A later article (see Selection 23) demonstrates that the salience of a social identity element will affect the individual's responses and behavior in a number of ways.

DIMENSIONS

The dimensions refer to certain abstract qualities characterizing either specific components of the self-concept or of the self as a totality. Self-esteem, self-concept stability, self-confidence, and self-crystallization are examples of dimensions. If we wished to learn about people's self-concepts, one thing we would probably want to know is how intelligent they consider themselves. Over and above this specific item of information, however, we would also wish to learn whether they accept and respect their intelligence (self-esteem); whether their ideas about their intelligence are variable or stable (stability); how sure they are of success in the intellectual realm (self-confidence); whether they have a clearly defined and firmly structured idea about their type and level of intelligence (self-crystallization); and so on. But the same dimensions apply to these individuals' feelings toward themselves as a whole. Thus, an understanding of the self-

concept would lead us to ask whether they have global positive self-esteem; whether their ideas about themselves are generally stable; whether they generally feel confident that they can master life challenges; and whether their self-concept is generally firm and crystallized. These dimensions refer not to what each individual thinks about him or herself but how each individual thinks and feels about him or herself.

Only two of these dimensions, self-confidence (efficacy) and self-crystallization, will be considered here.

The dimension of self-confidence—*the feeling that one can effect one's will, accomplish one's goals, succeed in one's efforts—has commanded a good deal of research attention. Rotter (1966) has suggested that people can either be classified into those with an internal or those with an external locus of control. People with an internal locus of control feel that the things that happen to them are a* consequence *of their own efforts and that they can effect their own ends. People with an external locus of control feel that the course of their life is largely guided by external forces over which they have scant control. Literally hundreds of studies on this subject have been conducted (Joe, 1971; Throop and MacDonald, 1971; Lefcourt, 1976). Subsequently Gurin, Gurin, and Morrison (1978) have demonstrated that the locus-of-control measure confounds two ideas: the individual's feeling that he or she personally is master of his or her destiny as distinguished from his or her general belief that effort and merit receive their just reward in life. In this tradition, Franks and Marolla (1976) have introduced the distinction between inner and outer self-esteem.* Inner self-esteem *refers to the feeling of efficacious action or the confidence that stems from the successful exercise of one's abilities; it reflects "the experience of self as an active agent—of making things happen and realizing one's intents in an impartial world." In a later selection, Pearlin and Radabaugh (Selection 38) refer to this dimension as* mastery.

Bandura (Selection 3) discusses the factors that instill in the individual strong feelings of efficacy. Although vicarious experience, persuasion, and emotional response may all influence confidence in effecting one's will, the most important factor is successful performance. Bandura's social learning theory holds that we learn behavior not only by observing and modeling others' behavior but also by observing our own.

Self-esteem and self-confidence are distinct dimensions. Self-esteem *refers to whether one accepts oneself, respects oneself, considers oneself a person of worth.* Self-confidence *refers to the individual's conviction that he or she can make things happen in accord with his or her values.* Self-confidence, *however, may contribute to self-esteem.*

As noted earlier, self-confidence may apply either to specific self-concept components or to the self as a whole. Most writers who speak of competence, internal locus of control, mastery, or efficacious action assume that there is a general self-confidence disposition that cuts across situations. But this is not necessarily the case. One can be confident of one's ability to master intellectual tasks but feel totally inept about making house repairs. At the same time, some people appear to be self-confident in most things they undertake, often quite out of keeping with their actual abilities. Although, as Bandura suggests, efficacious actions in specific realms may generalize to other realms, it is important to specify whether the specific trait or the global disposition is the subject at issue.

Another dimension is the crystallization or fixity of the elements. This is discussed by Hazel Markus (Selection 4), who describes clear, definite self-concept components as self-schemata. "Self-schemata are cognitive generalizations about the self, derived from past experience, that organize and guide the processing of self-related information contained in the individual's social experiences."

The importance of self-schemata rests in the fact that the individual's self-concept is his or her fundamental frame of reference, his or her main anchor for adjusting to the shifting sea of daily experience. People respond to the world in these terms. They pay attention to certain things and ignore others; interpret facts in one way rather than another; accept or reject information about themselves; and generally respond to the concrete experiences of life in terms of their preestablished ideas of what they are like. Such self-schemata, in Markus' terms, "organize, summarize, and explain behavior"—and this is true whether the self-concept component is positive or negative.

Crystallization bears directly on the issue of self-concept change. One question frequently raised is whether it is easy or hard to change the self-concept. Certainly ample evidence can be found to support both positions. How is it that psychologists appear to experience no difficulty in affecting a subject's self-concept, using some utterly trivial stimulus, whereas the most probing psychoanalytic efforts sustained over an extended period of time are impotent to do so? The answer does not lie in the differential effectiveness of the two methods but in the definiteness or certitude of the self-concept components. The psychologist can powerfully influence a subject's view of his or her "contrast sensitivity," "speed of closure," "convergent symbol transformation ability," and so on because people have no crystallized ideas about themselves on these subjects, but the psychologist cannot so easily change the subject's ideas about his or her own morality, intelligence, friendliness, and so on. If a self-concept component is firmly structured, efforts to change it are perceived as threatening. As Lecky (1945) observes, what the psychoanalyst interprets as resistance (that is, a refusal to accept the analyst's interpretation of what one is like) is simply the patient's effort to maintain his or her integrity and to be true to his or her self-concept.

FOCI OF ATTENTION

The foci of attention deal with the centrality of the self in the individual's field of consciousness, either in specific or in general situations. At any given moment, what are we thinking about: ourselves or something else? The distinction is familiar. Asked to address a group, our attention focuses on the self: How do we look, how do we sound, what impression are we making? But if we are involved in a book, a sports contest, a symphony, our thoughts are focused on the external event. The self is in the background of awareness. Duval and Wicklund (1972:2) have used the terms objective self-awareness and subjective self-awareness to express this distinction: " 'Subjective self-awareness' is a state of consciousness in which attention is focused on events external to the individual's consciousness, personal history, or body, whereas 'objective self-awareness' is exactly the opposite conscious state. Consciousness is focused exclusively upon the self and consequently the individual attends to his conscious state, his personal history, his body or other aspects of himself."

The concept of self-consciousness refers to whether the self or something else is the primary focus of the individual's attention. Since it is easy to make one self-conscious, this variable can be manipulated experimentally. In actual research, self-consciousness can be induced by having one sit in front of a mirror, listen to a tape-recording of one's voice, look at one's photograph, examine one's hand or foot, and so on; subjective self-awareness can be induced by assigning people tasks requiring concentration, such as anagrams, arithmetic tests, or manual tasks.

Such self-consciousness is situationally based; as the situation changes, so does the degree to which the self is in the forefront of attention. Duval and Wicklund (Selection 5) show how situationally induced self-consciousness affects one's tendency to attribute blame to oneself or to others in problematic situations. But self-consciousness may also be dispositional (a general characteristic), as is shown later by Rosenberg and Simmons (Selection 18).

REGIONS

Various theorists have classified the self-concept into broad areas, sectors, or domains. The regions refer to these broad sectors of the self-concept. Probably the most familiar distinction is that between the conscious and the unconscious self-concepts; through dreams or free associations, one may learn one's underlying thoughts and feelings about oneself. A second distinction is between interior and exterior self-components—whether one sees oneself in terms of an inner world of thoughts and feelings or in terms of a social exterior—of overt, public qualities.

In this section, we shall limit our discussion to two important regions. The first, discussed by Turner (Selection 6), deals with the authentic or inauthentic regions of the self. Certain aspects of ourselves do not reflect what we feel we really are. Some parts of the self are experienced as the "true self" or "real me," whereas others are viewed as more superficial, artificial, or alien elements. The behavior we manifest in playing our social role may not, in our own view, be truly expressive of what we think we really are. Or we cannot understand why we danced maniacally with a lampshade on our head after four or five drinks, concluding, in the cold light of sobriety, that we were not being ourselves. We build up conceptions of what we are like and experience qualities or actions contrary to these notions as "alien" or "inauthentic."

The question is: What parts of the self are experienced as more real, genuine, and authentic? Turner suggests that this may be dependent on historical circumstances. At an earlier time, people felt that the real self was expressed in fulfilling one's social roles, accepting responsibility for one's decisions, setting high standards, and living according to ethical principles. Today, on the other hand, the real self tends to be recognized in impulse; that which is spontaneous, unreflective, emotional, and free of facade is interpreted to be the real self. The proliferation of encounter groups and related movements concerned with self-discovery or self-realization during the past decade is evidence of this change;

what at an earlier time were viewed as dark and strange impulses are now regarded as the essence of authenticity. This historical change should not be misinterpreted to suggest that people actually are closer to their real selves than they once were but rather that they define the "real self" in different terms. Today, a person may feel as guilty about repressing a sexual urge or concealing an aggressive feeling as, at an earlier time, he or she might have felt about expressing them.

The second distinction is between those components of the self-concept encased within the skin and those extending beyond it. One mystery is where the boundaries of the self lie or how far the self extends. That the self stretches beyond the bounds of the skin has been explicitly noted in the earliest writings on the subject. Cooley used the term "to appropriate" to express the process by which the individual draws external objects into the self. The self, then, has no solid boundaries; rather, it expands and contracts in the course of experience. New external elements are incorporated into the self, some even becoming central to it, while others are shunted aside or extruded.

The term commonly assigned to those external elements which are experienced as part of the self is ego-extensions. *These ego-extensions are protected and defended with as much vigor as components of the self proper. In the words of William James (1890: 291): "Our fame, our children, the work of our hands may be as dear to us as our bodies are and arouse the same feelings and the same acts of reprisal if attacked."*

The incorporation of external elements into the self is, of course, motivated and hence tends to be selective. Cialdini et al. (Selection 7) show how the self-esteem motive governs the student's identification with his or her university. The university is much more likely to be experienced as a part of the self when its football team wins than when it loses. This process of BIRGing (basking in reflected glory) is familiar; but it is also the case that we must often share the shame of an ego-extension that we are unable to extrude. Our selves are bound up with objects or individuals external to the skin whose fates are experienced as our own.

PLANES

The planes are different levels of thought, each with its distinctive self-concept. Piaget (1951: 245) once observed that "we gradually build up within ourselves a plane of reality, a plane of possibility, a plane of fiction, and so on." This is as true of the self-concept as of any other aspect of reality. Not only are we able to think of ourselves as who we really are, but we can also imagine ourselves as what we might possibly be, what we would ideally like to be, what we should be, and how we appear to others. The self-concept, then, includes a plane of reality, a plane of possibility, a plane of fantasy, a plane of morality, and a plane of performance.

Several important issues arise in considering these planes. One issue deals with the dominance of certain planes either in specific circumstances or in general. In certain circumstances (for example, in daydreaming), the plane of fantasy may fill our thoughts; in others (such as completing a license application), the mind shifts to the plane of reality. What may be extremely important for us, however, is whether we live primarily in the world of fantasy or reality. A second issue deals with the concordance or discordance among the self-concepts residing on these several planes. The gap between the plane of reality and of imagination is characteristically described in the literature as a "self-ideal discrepancy" and is often equated with low self-esteem. A divergence between the performance and reality planes is sometimes described as front, facade, or putting on an act. A third question is whether the planes retain their distinctiveness or merge into one another. A feature of the neurotic idealized image, according to Horney, is that the neurotic comes to believe he or she actually is the idealized figure he or she wishes to be.

For this section, we have chosen articles describing two of these planes. The first is the plane of fantasy or imagination, described by Karen Horney (Selection 8) as the "idealized image." Horney describes how people characterized by a basic anxiety deal with this unbearable state by elaborating in their minds a picture of a glorious being—an "idealized image." This glorified vision comes to dominate their thoughts, providing a much needed feeling of security and worth. But the feeling of reassurance that comes from contemplation of this imaginative self-concept is accompanied by an increasing divorce from reality. Furthermore, when these individuals compare the actual self that they see with the glorified self they wish to see, their response is hatred for the actual self.

The other plane is that of performance or self-presentation. Learning to act out certain roles begins in early childhood; children who play cowboy, daddy, mommy, or baby know full well that they are not who they pretend to be. In the course of time, they learn that a certain self should be presented in the process of social interaction and that this presenting self may or may not correspond to their view of their actual self. Though the content changes with age, the principle remains the same in adulthood. Adults learn that there is a certain type of self that they wish to present to others. The point to keep in mind is that the presenting self is a product of intention; it is the self that we decide (consciously or unconsciously) to play in the given social situation.

The outstanding exposition of the presenting self is to be found in the work of Goffman, part of whose article, "On Face Work," is given here (Selection 9). Goffman demonstrates that the presenting self is a product of social learning and is acted out in accordance with the norms of the society.

Goffman's description makes clear that people adjust their behavior to suit the demands of the situation. Snyder's contribution (Selection 10) is to show that some people adjust more readily than others. The tendency to modify one's responses and behavior in accordance with the character of the other person or the nature of the situation has been called self-monitoring. *Since the high self-monitoring (as opposed to low self-monitoring) person is highly sensitive to varying situational demands, his or her behavior strikes the outsider as very inconsistent. As William James (1890: 294) observes: "Many a youth who is demure enough before his parents and teachers, swears and swaggers like a pirate among his 'tough' young friends. We do not show ourselves to our children as to our club companions, to our customers as to the laborers we employ, to our own masters and employers as to our intimate friends." Low self-monitoring people, on the other hand, are less likely to change their roles in different situations; they behave much the same way whatever the situation or whoever the others involved are. Whereas the high self-monitoring person is constantly changing the script to suit the play, the low self-monitoring person seems to be unaware that there is a performance.*

From a mental health viewpoint, there is no apparent difference between high and low self-monitoring people. Snyder and Tanke (1976) observe that the self-monitoring scale is not substantially related to such variables as self-esteem, need for approval, inner versus other-directedness, neuroticism, Machiavellianism, or related variables. Second, advantages and disadvantages are associated with each trait. The social and interpersonal adjustment of the high self-monitoring person is probably superior. Social interaction is largely based on the mutual expectations required by roles; the person who fails to play the role properly breaks down the expectations and introduces uncertainty into the interaction. At the same time, the high self-monitoring person is more likely to feel that he or she is presenting a false front, acting in a way that does not correspond to his or her actual thoughts and wishes. Society thus demands that we present certain selves; but the degree to which we do so is a matter of individual personality.

MOTIVES

Finally, it is important to stress that the self-concept includes not only cognitions and emotions but motives as well. These motives refer to certain impulses to act in the service of the self-concept. In fact, much of human striving represents an effort to achieve a satisfying self-concept. People have strong preferences about the various constituents of their self-concepts. They prefer high self-esteem to low; clear, crystallized self-pictures to vague and ambiguous ones; stable self-concepts to shifting ones; consistent self-concepts to inconsistent ones; high feelings of efficacy to feelings of ineffectuality; low self-consciousness to high; and so on. The self-concept, then, is an arena of passionate involvement, not detached neutrality. It motivates behavior, interaction, perception, attention, valuation, or virtually anything else that enters the human experience.

The most prominent, and possibly the most powerful, of the self-concept motives is self-esteem. In presenting his theory of sentiments, William McDougall (1932) assigned to the "sentiment of self-regard" the place of the "master sentiment," the sentiment to which all others were subordinated. Similarly, Maslow (1956: 243) included self-esteem as one of his five basic human needs. "We need to respect ourselves, to be strong, to have good sound self-esteem." William James, too, considered it a fundamental human motive. The chief self-feelings, according to James (1890: 305-6) are "Self-complacency and self-dissatisfaction. . . .Language has synonyms enough for both primary feelings. Thus pride, conceit, vanity, self-esteem, arrogance, vainglory, on the one hand; and on the other modesty, humility, confusion, diffidence, shame, mortification, contrition, the sense of obloquy and personal despair. These two opposite classes of affection seem to be direct and elementary endowments of our nature."

Although the assumption that self-esteem is important is widespread, evidence of this importance is rarely adduced. Kaplan (Selection 11) directs attention to four types of evidence. First, empirical data show that people are strikingly more likely to assess themselves favorably than unfavorably—as above average rather than below average, as very intelligent and attractive rather than as very unintelligent and unattractive, and so on. If, in the face of frequently ambiguous evidence, people draw such conclusions, it can only be because they prefer such beliefs. Second, people invest enormous effort and exercise astonishing ingenuity in the defense of self-esteem. As we shall see in Section Six, the creative imagination that the human mind brings to bear in the interests of self-esteem defense is awe-inspiring (see, for example, A. Freud, 1946; Allport, 1961; Rosenberg, 1967; Scott and Lyman, 1968; Hewitt and Stokes, 1975). Only a motive of immense power could command so much active effort in its behalf. Third, empirical evidence shows strong statistical associations between self-esteem and various measures of psychological disturbance—depression, anxiety (or somatic symptoms), "happiness," "impulse to aggression," or related signs of neurotic disturbance (Kaplan and Pokorny, 1969; Bachman, 1970). Finally, since low self-esteem tends to be unstable, this suggests that it is a disagreeable state that people struggle strenuously to change.

Another self-concept motive has been called the self-consistency motive. The basic idea, initially advanced by Lecky, is that people develop pictures of themselves which represent the basic axioms of their life theories. "We conceive of mind or personality as an organization of ideas which are felt to be consistent with one another. . . . The nucleus of the system, around which the rest of the system revolves, is the individual's idea or conception of himself. Any idea entering the system which is inconsistent with the individual's conception of himself cannot be assimilated" (Lecky, 1945: 263). In this view, then, individual behavior can best be understood as an effort to be true to one's self-concept. In contemporary terms, people strive to maintain their "self-schemata" or to live in accord with their "self-theories" (Epstein, 1973).

But if self-esteem and self-consistency are fundamental human motives, what happens when they conflict? For example, if one has a negative view of a particular quality—considers oneself manually inept, for example—does one seek evidence confirming one's negative self-assessment (in accordance with the self-consistency principle) or disconfirming it (in accordance with the self-esteem motive)? This is the question raised by Jones (Selection 12). In his examination of 16 studies, Jones finds that the data are more likely to support the self-esteem than the self-consistency motive. He notes, furthermore, that those subjects who respond favorably to current negative self-evaluations may do so in order to avoid future failure, thereby protecting self-esteem in the long run.

But these data do not justify the conclusion that the self-consistency motive is unimportant. First, the Jones article makes evident that in most cases the same response serves the interests both of self-esteem and of self-consistency; only in a minority of situations are the two counterposed. More important is the point, made by McGuire and Padawer-Singer, that a large proportion of self-concept components appear to be free of value-relevance. When their sixth-grade subjects are asked to "tell us about yourself," 93 percent of the descriptions are nonevaluative: They describe the children's hobbies and amusements, sports activities, daily schedule, places lived, jobs held; their mothers, fathers, siblings, pets; their likes and dislikes; demographic characteristics; and other factual information. If these components are not evaluated, then people may be powerfully motivated to be true to, or consistent with, them; such consistency would have *no bearing on self-esteem. However, it must be kept in mind that conclusions based on sixth graders may not be generalizable to their seniors. Furthermore, many of these self-descriptions may only be apparently, rather than actually, irrelevant to self-esteem. These issues will probably be debated for years to come. At present, it seems reasonable to conclude that both motives are powerful and that they usually co-exist peacefully. In those rare instances in which they conflict, there appears to be some tendency for the self-esteem motive to predominate.*

REFERENCES

Allport, G. W.
1961 Pattern and Growth in Personality. New York: Holt, Rinehart & Winston.
Allport, G. W. and H. S. Odbert
1936 "Trait-names: a psycho-lexical study." Psychological Monographs No. 211.
Bachman, J. G.
1970 "The Impact of Family Background and Intelligence on Tenth-Grade Boys." Vol. 2 in Youth in Transition. Ann Arbor, Mich.: Survey Research Center, Institute for Social Research.
Bugental, J. and S. L. Zelen
1950 "Investigations into the 'self-concept': I. The W-A-Y Technique." Journal of Personality 18: 483–98.
Duval, S. and R. A. Wicklund
1972 A Theory of Objective Self-Awareness. New York: Academic Press.
Epstein, S.
1973 "The self-concept revisited: or a theory of a theory." American Psychologist 28: 404–16.
Franks, D. D. and J. Marolla
1976 "Efficacious action and social approval as interacting dimensions of self-esteem: formulation through construct validation." Sociometry 39: 324–41.
Freud, A.
1946 The Ego and the Mechanisms of Defense. New York: International Universities Press.
Gordon, C.
1974 "Persons-conceptions analytic dictionary for the General Inquirer System of computer-aided content analysis." Unpublished paper.
Gurin, P., G. Gurin, and B. Morrison
1978 "Personal and ideological aspects of internal and external control." Social Psychology Quarterly 41: 275–96.
Hewitt, J. P. and R. Stokes
1975 "Disclaimers." American Sociological Review 40: 1–11.
James, W.
1890 The Principles of Psychology. New York: Henry Holt. Reprint: Dover 1950.
Joe, V. C.
1971 "Review of the internal-external construct as a personality variable." Psychological Reports 28: 619–40.
Kaplan, H. B. and A. D. Pokorny
1969 "Self-derogation and psycho-social adjustment." Journal of Nervous and Mental Disease 149: 421–34.
Kuhn, M. H. and T. McPartland
1954 "An empirical investigation of self-attitudes." American Sociological Review 19: 68–76.

Lecky, P.
1945 Self-Consistency: A Theory of Personality. New York: Island Press.
Lefcourt, H. M.
1976 Locus of Control: Current Trends in Theory and Research. Hilldale, N.J.: Erlbaum.
Maslow, A. H.
1956 "Personality problems and personality growth." In C. E. Moustakas (ed.), The Self: Explorations in Personal Growth. New York: Harper & Row.
McDougall, W.
1932 The Energies of Men. London: Methuen.
Morse, S. and K. J. Gergen
1970 "Social comparison, self-consistency, and the concept of self." Journal of Personality and Social Psychology 16: 148–56.
Piaget, J.
1951 The Child's Conception of the World. London: Routledge and Kegan Paul.
Rosenberg, M.
1967 "Psychological selectivity in self-esteem formation." Pp. 26–50 in C. W. Sherif and M. Sherif (eds.), Attitude, Ego-Involvement, and Change. New York: John Wiley & Sons.
Rotter, J. B.
1966 "Generalized expectancies for internal versus external control of reinforcement." Psychological Monographs 80 (Whole No. 609).
Scott, M. B. and S. M. Lyman
1968 "Accounts." American Sociological Review 33: 446–62.
Snyder, M. and E. D. Tanke
1976 "Behavior and attitude: some people are more consistent than others." Journal of Personality 44: 501–17.
Throop, W. and A. P. MacDonald
1971 "Internal-external locus of control: a bibliography." Psychological Reports: Monograph Supplement 1-V28: 175–90.
Wylie, R.
1979 The Self-Concept: Revised Edition. Vol. 2. Theory and Research on Selected Topics. Lincoln, Neb.: University of Nebraska Press.

Self-Conceptions: Configurations of Content

Chad Gordon

1

There is one method that has the required features of allowing the respondent to represent himself in any framework he pleases, in terms of noun-like categories or adjectival attributes, in any order, and in any tense. This solution, which also possesses at least a plausible face validity for operationalizing self-conceptions, involves eliciting repeated answers to the open question "Who am I?"

Bugental and Zelen[1] were among the first to suggest that the respondent simply be allowed to describe himself. They merely provided the respondent with a blank piece of paper and asked him to give three answers to the question "Who are you?" These answers were then classified by mention of name, status characteristics, affective quality, and the like. Somewhat later, Kuhn and McPartland offered techniques for analyzing an expanded version of this procedure.[2] They asked respondents to give 20 answers to the question "Who am I?" in a period of 12 minutes, calling this technique the Twenty Statements Test.

At this point I wish to focus on the actual content of the self-representations as they are typically given in the Who Am I protocols, with the goal of introducing a system of ordered coding categories with which to capture the main dimensions of the data's meaning.

Kuhn has used a five-category qualitative coding scheme,[3] and McPartland, Cumming, and Garretson have been able to predict some forms of behavior among psychiatric patients using a very interesting procedure based on discerning

Source: Chad Gordon, "Self-Conceptions: Configurations of Content," from The Self in Social Interaction, Chad Gordon and Kenneth J. Gergen (editors), 1968: 115–36.

the respondent's most frequently used type of response.[4] In a series of unpublished papers, Theodore Kemper (with Orville Brim and Leonard Cottrell) has been developing a much more comprehensive set of categories for manifest content of self-representations, and a psychologically oriented self-conception dictionary has recently been constructed at Harvard for use with the General Inquirer system of computer-assisted content analysis.[5] The method of analysis proposed here was designed to consolidate many of the features of this previous work to tap more fully the categories of social identity and to provide a theoretical rationale for some of the more important response attributes.

The system is intended to capture the major varieties of concrete self-representation, including four more general or systemic senses of self to be proposed shortly. The categories are organized into a series of major rubrics, moving from the basic elements of social identity (the ascribed social locators and other social types), through abstract allegiances and connections, to particular interests, activities, and objects, and finally up to the major personal characteristics of self and psyche.

In the course of analysis each meaning element in the respondent's Who Am I protocol is coded for four things: its category designation; its tense; its evaluation; and the importance rank assigned to it by the respondent [See EDITOR'S NOTE]. Some references inherently carry more than one categorical meaning. Thus the self-representation "a boy" is simultaneously a sex reference *and* an age reference, since the respondent could have said "a male" if he meant only gender. Similarly, "a son" is both a kinship role and a sex reference, and "a teenager" is both a reference to age and to an abstract category. Thus a single word of self-description may yield two or even three codable meaning elements.

The following sections describe the content of each coding dimension, indicate those typically composed of categorical rather than attributive references, and give the percentage of the 157 high school students who were coded as using a given dimension at least one time. In a subsequent section, the category-attribute designation will be related to other features of self-conception.

DETAILED CATEGORIES WITH TYPICAL EXAMPLES

A. Ascribed Characteristics

	Percent of High School Students Mentioning at least once (N=157)
Fundamental to the idea of social identity used in this chapter are the ascribed role and category designations conferred on the individual at birth, which typically remain with him throughout his lifetime. They may well be viewed as one set of major "structural locators" that serve to position the individual with regard to the major axes of differentiation in his society. The coding categories for the ascribed characteristics follow.	
1. Sex: a man, a boy, a son, clear name, etc. (almost always categorical).	74%
2. Age: 15-years old, a boy, young, a teenager, a freshman, etc. (at least public if not exactly categorical).	82%
3. Name: John Jones, Claire M., etc. (at least public and partly categorical).	17%
4. Racial or National Heritage: a Negro, white; a Chinese (meaning ancestry or race, not current citizenship); of Italian, Irish ancestry; an immigrant, etc. (usually categorical).	7%
5. Religious Categorization: a Catholic, Protestant, Methodist, Jewish,	

etc. (not just "Christian," "atheist," etc., must be definite religious group) (predominantly categorical). 11%

Two of these categories require further comment. An individual's current age is not strictly an ascribed aspect, but the date of his birth is; thus in relation to others he is always put into categories such as baby, child, teenager, adult, "old man," and the like. Here we have an interesting case of changing ascription. Second, an individual's name at first does not seem to represent a category. Yet at the same time that it serves as his more or less unique "identity peg," it also locates him in his family and serves as a handy indication of his sex. References to clearly one-sex names are also coded as a sex reference, since most respondents feel that they have already made clear their sex if they have given such a name.

B. Roles and Memberships

The other basic set of social identity elements is comprised of roles and categorical designations which are to an appreciable degree under the control of the individual. This element of choice is important because it implies that the person who has entered these categories or social types has voluntarily chosen to do so, and can thus be held accountable or responsible. Clarification is needed regarding territoriality category. Being "an American" is usually an ascribed characteristic and thus belongs in the first set. But among younger respondents there is a more common form of response regarding territoriality. Many protocols contain a reference to current residence locale, conveying a distinctly temporary flavor (now living in the Back Bay area, etc.). Others give a mixed heritage and current "turf" answer (a Bostonian, etc). The responses in this category are generally less "structural" and "fixed" than were those of the ascribed characteristics.

6. Kinship Role: a son, mother, sister, aunt, housewife, etc. (also coded as sex references), engaged, going steady, married, etc. (generally categorical). 17%

7. Occupational Role: Specific occupation, employed, working part-time, hoping to become a doctor, etc. (mainly categorical). 5%

8. Student Role: a student, at South Boston High, getting bad grades, going to Harvard, taking 4 courses, trying to get into a good college, etc. (mainly categorical). 80%

9. Political Affiliation: a Democrat, an Independent, other clear party (not liberal, conservative, etc.) (almost always categorical). 1%

10. Social Status: from a poor family, an elite neighborhood, middle class, an aristocrat, of an old-line family etc. (somewhat more frequently attributive). 1%

11. Territoriality, Citizenship: now a Cambridge resident, living on Oak St., a Bostonian, from Alabama, an American, a German (current citizenship, not "heritage"), a foreign student, etc. (usually categorical). 16%

12. Membership in Actual Interacting Group: on the football team, in the science club, at a specific school, a friend, in a clique or fraternity, member of a certain family, etc. (almost always categorical). 17%

C. Abstract Identifications

A very interesting set of three dimensions contains those that (although often categorical rather than attributive) are usually too abstract or too private to serve as distinct social identity elements. The first of these portrays the individual as a unique, irreducible particle of Being, not definable by reference to anything outside himself. The second type places the person in some universal or very large and abstract category, without implication of interaction among members. The third form associates the person with some relatively comprehensive idea system, whether theoretical, philosophical, ideological, religious, or more narrowly political.

13. Existential, Individuating: me, an individual, an existing being, myself, nothing, unique, undefinable, etc. (generally the denial of categories). 29%

14. Membership in an Abstract Category: a person, a human, a voter, a teenager (also an age reference), a speck in the cosmos, etc. (almost exclusively categorical by definition). 41%

15. Ideological and Belief References: a liberal, a conservative, a Christian, very religious, a Marxist, against the war in Viet Nam, a pacifist, not prejudiced, etc. (somewhat more frequently categorical). 18%

D. Interests and Activities

It is often very difficult to distinguish among the various forms of personal connection to objects outside the self, and the cognitive, cathectic, and active modes are frequently blurred. Nevertheless, there are good grounds for distinguishing references to judgments of quality, concern over intellectual questions of meaning and substance, and actual participation in activities. In particular, the separation of intellectual and artistic references from the others was an attempt to verify hypotheses relating these kinds of self-conceptions to school performance and the qualitative nature of the career chosen by the respondent.

16. Judgments, Tastes, Likes: one who likes abstract art, hates rock 'n' roll, jazz fan, loves Bach, etc. (usually attributive). 27%

17. Intellectual Concerns: interested in literature, trying to understand modern theater, a reader, getting an education, a thinker, an intellectual, etc. (generally the verb-form of an attribute). 1%

18. Artistic Activities: a dancer, painter, poet, musician, singer, cello player, etc. (usually a category reference, the noun form of a verb). 4%

19. Other Activities: a football player, a hiker, a stamp collector, a moviegoer, one who dates a lot, a good swimmer, etc. (categorical on the whole). 27%

E. Material References

There have always been references to the body as a primary object of self-conscious awareness, but William James was among the first to point out the importance of other material objects as elements of identification. I have included both varieties, but have preserved separate coding.

20. Possessions, Resources: a car owner, one who has pretty clothes, hoping for a secure future, one who never has enough money, etc. (usually categorical). 5%

21. Physical Self, Body Image: good-looking, pretty, strong, tall, 5'10", too thin, blonde, healthy, ugly, 112 lbs., etc. (preponderantly attributive). 36%

F. Four Systemic Senses of Self

Categories 1 to 21 of this coding scheme are designed to encapsulate the meaning of relatively specific self-representations. Yet the literature on self-conception contains a number of potentially very important theoretical dimensions that refer to levels of the person's functioning which are at middle levels of generality, being somewhat less global than such very comprehensive variables as self-esteem or the sense of autonomy.

Examination of relevant theory indicates that there is at least one conceptual framework that was designed to cope with this middle level of functioning of any kind of system: the general theory of action, as formulated principally by Talcott Parsons.[6] This framework asserts that every system (whether at the cultural, social, personality, or organismic level) must in some fashion solve four problems—adaptation, goal-attainment, integration, and pattern maintenance—if it is to function and survive.

The central argument of this section is that the action theory perspective can be extended to order in a meaningful manner some of the person's subjective experience at this middle level of self-conception. This extension is possible because each of the four functional problems has a corresponding "sense of self" available to consciousness—the individual's interpretation of his standing with regard to that system problem. To outline briefly, in the following analysis I suggest the correspondence of the sense of *competence* to the problem of adaptation, the sense of *self-determination* to goal-attainment, the sense of *unity* to integration, and the sense of *moral worth* to pattern maintenance.[7]

The Sense of Moral Worth: Pattern Maintenance at the Person Level There seems to be one essential feature of James' treatment of pride versus shame and mortification, Baldwin's formulation of the ethical socius, Cooley's discussion of self-feelings, Mead's idea of self-respect, and many recent treatments of guilt.[8] This is the person's sensed degree of adherence to a valued code of moral standards transcending him.

Now it is just this legitimation of standards for action by moral norms and values, institutionalized and shared in the person's social systems, which constitutes the core of the pattern maintenance problem at the person level.[9] As highly generalized cultural symbols, these universalistic value standards are used by others in morally evaluating the actions and attributes of the individual in particular social situations.

The point of articulation to self-conception is seen in the fact that the person generally evaluates his *own* attributes and actions in terms of these same moral standards and therefore has a continuingly available sense of greater or less moral worth. Thus I am suggesting that the individual's sense of *moral worth* may well be viewed as his subjective interpretation of how he stands in relation to the problem of pattern maintenance.

Once more it should be emphasized that this coding system records each of the respondent's utilizations of the particular dimensions, while the corresponding evaluation codes are used to retain these references as positive, neutral, or negative. The two may then be used together (or even with the tense and importance) to characterize the respondent's meanings more accurately.

22. The Sense of Moral Worth: self-respecting, a sinner, bad, good, honest, reliable, trustworthy, responsible, evil, a thief, etc. (preponderantly attributive). 22%

The Sense of Self-Determination: Goal Attainment at the Person Level Every system must provide at least minimal gratification of the basic requirements of its constituent elements if it is to remain in operation. Yet the interchange processes in specific situations make such heavy demands on the resources of the system that it is never able to provide continuous gratification for all elements. These disruptions of consummatory relations with objects in the environment plus the competing demands made by the internal elements concerning the plurality of goal objects add to the complexity of the goal-attainment problem. Fulfilling the goal-attainment function requires complex processes which establish priorities among the goal objects, allocate facilities, and distribute rewarding resources among the internal elements.

At the level of the person, there is a well-established tendency to optimize gratification through selecting goals and instrumental steps for their attainment. Parsons, among others, has also pointed out the additional importance of volition toward achievement in these interchanges between the psychological and social systems. He focuses on the concepts of agency, decision making, and commitment to attainment of high-priority goals.[10]

One of the most sensitive psychological analysts concerned with consummatory gratification at this more complex symbolic level is Abraham Maslow. His delineation of the characteristics of the "self-actualizing" person contains many features that the action theory perspective can subsume under the problem of goal attainment at the level of the individual:

So far as motivational status is concerned, healthy people have sufficiently gratified their basic needs for safety, belongingness, love, respect and self-esteem so that they are motivated primarily by trends to self-actualization (defined as ongoing actualization of potentials, capacities and talents), as fulfillment of mission (or call, fate, destiny, or vocation). . . .[11]

Yet, as Maslow clearly indicates, only a tiny fraction of any society's members are able to make much sense of Nietzsche's directive, "Become what thou art!" A concept is needed which does *not* have a built-in requirement that the person possess a superior degree of certainty and insight regarding his "true self" and inherent destiny. Yet it *must* remain the essential features of *sensed ability* to select one's own goals and determine their relative priorities, initiate and vigorously pursue necessary lines of action, and act with freedom from control by others. This second systemic sense of self might well be called *self-determination.*

23. The Sense of Self-Determination: trying to get ahead, deciding things for myself, ambitious, hardworking, not my own boss, a self-starter, etc. (almost always attributive). 23%

The Sense of Unity: Integration at the Person Level The problem of system integration concerns the internal harmony of the constituent elements. At the social system level this is the problem of solidarity or cohesion among units despite their differentiated functions. At the person level, we are concerned with the degree of conflict or inconsistency among personality dispositions, social roles, priorities or goal objects, loyalties, transcendent value standards, and the like.[12]

Erik Erikson's formulations of various aspects of identity are among the most subtle and insightful in the literature. Writing as a psychoanalyst with anthropological experience and an interest in the impact of historical contexts, he uses ego, self, and identity concepts as keys to social-psychological processes of development throughout the life-cycle.[13]

The concept Erikson terms "the sense of ego identity" (in ideally healthy individuals) is actually a kind of grand congruence of three personal meanings. This congruence is conceptualized as the achievement of a sense of *unity* among the person's own self-conceptions, plus the sense of *continuity* of the attributes over time, plus the sense of *mutuality* between that individual's conceptions of himself and those which significant others hold of him.[14]

Erikson's conceptualization certainly does capture the recurrent theme of interconnection between self and others. In its most complete form this interconnection seems to erase the borders of the self. Instances include the total joyful intimacy with another, the "peak experiences" and "oceanic mergings" of Maslow's self-actualizing people[15] and perhaps some forms of psychedelic experiences.

It is therefore not surprising that Erikson makes the developing sense of ego identity the basis of self-esteem, the most general evaluative dimension of self. Ideally, this will occur if the individual is able to overcome the adolescent identity crisis, with its common problem of identity diffusion. Resolution of the identity crisis often requires a "psychosocial moratorium" of relatively free and unthreatening role experimentation before the individual can learn to experience intimacy and achieve a meaningful connection between self and a small, unitary set of occupational, professional, ideological, membership, family, and interpersonal roles. Identity diffusion is epitomized by Biff's words in *Death of a Salesman*, "I just can't take hold, Mom, I can't take hold of some kind of a life."[16]

Parson's treatment of the intricacies of system integration at the personality level is far more complex than the simple version that heads this section. Further, he is not explicitly dealing with the kinds of self-representations formulated by Erikson. Yet I believe that the first of the three elements drawn from Erikson can be proposed as the individual's interpretation of his standing with regard to the problem of personality level system integration: *the sense of internal unity*.

24. The Sense of Unity: in harmony, mixed up, ambivalent, a whole person, straightened out now, etc. (predominantly attributive). 5%

The Sense of Competence: Adaptation at the Person Level The last of the system problems concerns development of general coping facilities, resources, and capacities. Parsons conceptualizes adaptation in this way:

> *As distinguished from goal attainment, adaptation is the degree to which a system has developed a generalized capacity to meet the exigencies imposed by an unstable and varying situation, without reference to any one particular goal interest.*[17]

This theme of generalized capacity has a direct equivalent in the recent work of Robert White.[18] White has proposed that both the Freudian libidinal model and the neo-Freudian interpersonal model need to be supplemented by a *competence* model before the stages of human development can be successfully interpreted in a way that squares with the realities of normal functioning. As White presents the major concepts:

> *I therefore introduce competence to describe a person's existing capacity to interact effectively with his environment. . . .* Sense of competence *describes the subjective side of*

one's actual competence. . . . We can reserve the term feeling of efficacy *for what is experienced in each individual transaction, using* sense of competence *for the accumulated and organized consequences in later stages of ego development.*[19]

White[20] argues that the sense of competence is the basis for the more general dimension, self-esteem. This view contrasts with that of Erikson, who sees the basis of overall evaluation in what I have called congruence of personal meanings: harmonious, stable, and consensually supported self-conceptions.

Let us select Robert White's concept of the *sense of competence* as the individual's reflexive interpretation regarding the system problem of adaptation, since it refers to just the generalized capacity put forward by Parsons as adaptation's core meaning.

25. Sense of Competence: intelligent, talented, creative, skillful, low in ability, good at many things, always making mistakes, etc. (primarily attributive). 36%

Summary This section has presented a proposal for conceptualizing four systemic senses of self, intermediate in degree of generality between the concrete descriptive contents of the first 21 categories and the most general dimensions of self-esteem or autonomy. Under one name or another, each of these four senses has had a long and substantial history in the literature of self theory. Further reports will describe efforts to move beyond Who Am I coding to treatment of the senses as problems in self-attitude scale construction. These studies use other aspects of general action theory to provide direct indexing of the four senses as continuous variables.

For the present, this portion of the coding scheme can be summarized as the formulation of a subjective sense of self to match each of the four functions held in action theory to be essential features of every system.

System Function	*Corresponding Personal Sense of Self*
Adaptation	The sense of competence
Goal-attainment	The sense of self-determination
Integration	The sense of unity
Pattern-maintenance	The sense of moral worth

G. Personal Characteristics

As we move from the categories and roles of social identity through the interests, activities, material references and the senses of self, there is a large and interesting set of more general self-descriptions which refer to the individual's typical manner of *acting* and his typical style of *psychic functioning.*

26. Interpersonal Style (how I typically act): friendly, fair, nice, shy, introverted, hard to get along with, affable, quiet, demanding, good with children, affectionate, cool, etc. (almost exclusively attributes). 59%

27. Psychic Style, Personality (how I typically think and feel): happy, sad, moody, a daydreamer, in love, depressed, confident, "crazy," lonely, curious, calm, searching for love, mature, objective, optimistic, etc. (predominantly adjectival attributes). 52%

H. External Meanings

Two remaining categories of relatively infrequent Who Am I elements refer not to the individual himself in any typical or continuing manner, but rather to the impression he feels that he makes on others, or to the immediate testing situation itself. References to the impressions or attitudes of others toward the respondent are actually representations of *them,* not him. This is the imputed generalized *Social Me* of James and Cooley.

28. Judgments Imputed to Others: popular, respected, well-liked, well-thought of, loved, etc. (preponderantly attributive). 18%

We use the term *situational reference* to denote the other major escape from self-description in terms of enduring, typical categories and attributes: fleeting reference to the person's immediate situation and activities at the moment of filling out the questionnaire.

29. Situational References: tired, hungry, bored, filling out this questionnaire, going on a date tonight, late for dinner, finished, etc. (usually attributive). 9%

These "situational" elements should not be confused with the valuable new concept of *situational self-image* introduced by Ralph Turner to capture the individual's sense of how well or how badly he is portraying his attributes over the moment-to-moment course of a particular interaction episode.[21] Turner's development of this sensed outcome of the processes of presentation of self that Goffman had analyzed from the perspective of the omniscient observer[22] was a precursor of the present attempt to provide the senses of self as the phenomenal or subjective side of the objective system problems. . . .

EDITOR'S NOTE

In classifying responses to the "Who Am I?" question, the author distinguishes between responses that refer to *categories* and those that refer to *attributes.* The categories, which are usually expressed in the language of nouns, refer to the classification of individuals according to the logic of membership. Thus, the person who classifies herself as female, lawyer, white, American, sister, is describing the self in terms of categories. The attributes are more likely to be expressed in the language of adjectives, reflected in such self-descriptions as intelligent, interesting, and well-organized.

NOTES

1 J. F. T. Bugental and S. L. Zelen, "Investigations into the self-concept," Journal of Personality 18 (1950), pp. 483–98.

2 Manford H. Kuhn and Thomas S. McPartland, "An empirical investigation of self-attitudes," American Sociological Review 19 (1954), pp. 68–76; Manford H. Kuhn, "Self-attitudes by age, sex, and professional training," Sociological Quarterly 9 (January 1960), pp. 39–55.

3 Kuhn, "Self-attitudes," pp. 39–55.

4 Thomas S. McPartland, John H. Cumming, and Wynona S. Garretson, "Self-conception and ward behavior in two psychiatric hospitals," Sociometry 24 (June 1961), pp. 111–24.

5 Barry S. McLaughlin, "Identity and Personality," unpublished doctoral dissertation, Harvard University, 1965, esp. pp. 93–100, 276–93. The present conceptual categories have been built into the McLaughlin dictionary, which has been expanded by Robert Aylmer, Jr. and Lane K. Conn, and thoroughly revised by Barry Wellman, the new dictionary containing about 5,000 words and idioms in 99 concept categories, is presently in use at Harvard with the General Inquirer content analysis system developed by Philip Stone: P. J. Stone, D. C. Dunphy, and D. M. Ogilvie, The General Inquirer: A Computer Approach to Content Analysis, Cambridge, Mass.: M.I.T. Press, 1967, esp. Chapter 18: "The Who Am I dictionary and self-perceived identity in college students."

6 A clear and concise formulation for the social system level appears as Chapter 2, "Outline of the social system," in Talcott Parsons, Edward Shils, Kaspar D. Naegele, and Jesse R. Pitts (eds.), Theories of Society, Vol. I, Glencoe, Ill.: Free Press, 1961; and, for the psychological level, see Talcott Parsons, "An approach to psychological theory in terms of the theory of action," in Sigmund Koch, Psychology: The Study of a Science, New York: McGraw-Hill, 1959, Vol. III, pp. 612–711.

7 The conceptualization on which this section is based was largely worked out in the spring of 1965, in connection with guiding the honors thesis, "Mental health, occupational choice, self-concept," of Linwood Laughy, then a senior in Harvard College. I am indebted to Mr. Laughy for many valuable suggestions.

8 William James, The Principles of Psychology, New York: Henry Holt and Company, 1890, esp. p. 106; James M. Baldwin, Social and Ethical Interpretations in Mental Development, New York: Macmillan 1897, esp. Chapter 1; Charles H. Cooley, Human Nature and the Social Order, New York: Charles Scribner's Sons, 1902, esp. Chapter 6; and, for example, Helen Merrell Lynd, On Shame and the Search for Identity (1958), New York: Science Editions, 1961.

9 Parsons, "An approach to psychological theory," esp. p. 657.

10 Parsons, "An approach to psychological theory," esp. pp. 632, 652.

11 Abraham H. Maslow, "Deficiency and growth motivation" (1955). reprinted in Maslow's Toward a Psychology of Being, Princeton, N.J.: D. Van Nostrand, 1962, p. 23. See also Chapter 12, "Self-actualizing people: a study of psychological health," in his Motivation and Personality, New York: Harper and Brothers, 1954.

12 Parsons, "An approach to psychological theory," p. 636. An interesting attempt at partial reconciliation of the psychoanalytic and symbolic interactionist perspective by means of the mechanisms of defense may be found in Tamotsu Shibutani, Society and Personality, Englewood Cliffs, N.J.: Prentice-Hall, 1961, esp. p. 438 ff.

13 See, for example, Erik H. Erikson, Childhood and Society, New York: W. W. Norton, 1950, and the papers "Growth and crises of the healthy personality" (1950) and "The problem of ego identity" (1956), in Identity and the Life Cycle [Psychological Issues 1 (1), 1959]. A valuable addition to the literature in this field is a recent interpretive work largely devoted to consideration of Erikson's theory of identity: David J. deLevita, The Concept of Identity, Paris: Mouton and Co., 1965.

14 Erikson, "Growth and crises of the healthy personality," p. 89.

15 Abraham H. Maslow, "Cognition of being in the peak-experiences," and "Peak experiences as identity experiences," in his Toward a Psychology of Being, pp. 67–96 and 97–108.

16 Clear analyses of identity diffusion and the example of Biff's plea may be found in "Healthy personality," pp. 91–94, and "The problem of ego identity," pp. 122–46. Another problem which would also cripple the individual's self-esteem but is not explicitly dealt with by Erikson points up the "integration bias" built into his concept of the sense of ego identity. What happens when the highly congruent match between

individual and significant others concerns mutual agreement on *negatively* valued attributes (unattractiveness, low intelligence, limited competence, immorality or traitorous activity, etc.)? Here there would likely be high agreement, but low self-satisfaction.

17 Parsons, "An approach to psychological theory," p. 633 (emphasis in original).

18 Robert W. White, "Motivation reconsidered: the concept of competence," Psychological Review 66 (1959), pp. 297–333; "Competence and the psychosexual stages of development," in M. Jones (ed.), Nebraska Symposium on Motivation, Lincoln, Neb.: University of Nebraska Press, 1960, pp. 97–141; and Ego and Reality in Psycholanalytic Theory (Psychological Issues, Monograph 11, 1963), especially the papers, "A way of conceiving of independent ego energies: efficacy and competence," pp. 24–43, and "Self-esteem, sense of competence, and ego strength," pp. 125–50.

19 White, "Efficacy and competence," p. 39 (emphases in original).

20 White, "Self-esteem," esp. pp. 129–136; and "Competence and the psychosexual stages of development," pp. 126–27.

21 Ralph H. Turner, "The self-conception in social interaction," in C. Gordon and K. Gergen (eds.). 'The Self in Social Interaction.' New York: Wiley, 1968.

22 Erving Goffman, Presentation of Self in Everyday Life, Garden City, N. Y.: Doubleday Anchor Books, 1959; and Behavior in Public Places, New York: Free Press, 1963.

Trait Salience in the Spontaneous Self-Concept

William J. McGuire
Alice Padawer-Singer

2

The self-concept has hardly been neglected in psychological research. Fifteen years ago Wylie (1961) described the results of a good thousand (if not a thousand good) studies on the topic. Her more recent edition (Wylie, 1974) analyzes over a thousand studies in only the first of two volumes. This continuing fascination with the self-concept is easy to understand: What we think about ourselves is probably the central concept in our conscious lives. Yet this vast input of research effort contrasts unfavorably with the low yield of interesting findings regarding the phenomenal self. We fear it may be said of the self-concept, as it has been said of sex (by the young, at least), that only psychological research could make so inherently interesting a topic seem dull.

This low yield we attribute primarily to researchers' having measured the self-concept almost exclusively by information-losing "reactive" methods, that is, by studying subjects' reactions to a dimension chosen a priori by the researcher. Subjects are thus reduced to saying how they would think of themselves with respect to the given dimension if they happened to think of it at all, without furnishing any information on the more important question of how salient the dimension is to them.

Source: William J. McGuire and Alice Padawer-Singer, "Trait Salience in the Spontaneous Self-Concept," Journal of Personality and Social Psychology 33 (1976): 743–54.

A second limitation explaining the somewhat disappointing yield of past self-concept research is that this researcher-chosen dimension is almost always self-evaluation or self-esteem, as if our thoughts about ourselves are concerned almost entirely with how good we are. Indeed, the landmark volumes of Wylie (1961, 1974), which necessarily reflect the content of the field they analyzed, might just as appropriately have been entitled *Self-Esteem as Self-Concept.* In contrast to the past preoccupation with self-esteem, the study we report here suggests that when people are allowed more freedom in describing themselves, fewer than 10 percent of their thoughts deal with self-evaluation (see Table 2).

We have been urging for some years (McGuire, Note 1, Note 2) that the researcher forgo this reactive approach and take a somewhat lower profile toward the participants by studying the "spontaneous" self-concept. Instead of presenting the participants with the dimension on which they must describe themselves, they can be allowed to choose the dimensions that are salient and significant to them. We feel that there is more interesting information about the self-concept in the dimensions one chooses for describing oneself than in the positions to which one assigns oneself on dimensions presented by the experimenter.

The spontaneous self-concept has not been entirely neglected. Two instruments, the Who Are You (WAY) Test introduced by Bugental and Zelen (1950) and the Twenty Statements Test (TST) used by Kuhn and McPartland (1954), are eminently suited for getting at the issue of what characteristics people use for thinking about themselves, although they have typically been employed for determining where the person stands on some dimension selected a priori by the investigator (Spitzer, Couch, & Stratton, 1971). Loevinger and her colleagues (Loevinger & Wessler, 1970; Loevinger, Wessler, & Redmore, 1970) employ a similarly open format primarily to assess a specific dimension of ego development, whereas Jourard's (1971) self-disclosure and Altman and Taylor's (1973) social penetration research use similar instruments to determine specifically the intimacy dimension. These open-ended descriptions of persons have occasionally been used to study our perceptions of other persons, as in the work of Kelly (1955), Rosenberg and Sedlak (1972), and Livesley and Bromley (1973).

Determinants of Spontaneous Salience

The determinant of spontaneous salience on which we particularly focus here is the distinctiveness of the personal characteristic in question. For several years we have been working (McGuire, Note 1, Note 2) on the problem of how people cope with informational overload. Although we pointed out that various coping strategies are available (e.g., chunking, temporary storage, parallel processing, and selectivity), our own empirical work has focused exclusively on perceptual selectivity as a means of handling informational overload. And while we have mentioned many determinants of which aspects of our perceptual field are singled out for noticing, we have concentrated on distinctiveness as a determinant of perceptual selectivity. Our guiding theoretical notion is that the person in a complex stimulus field focuses on points of maximum information, so that one selectively notices the aspects of the object that are most peculiar. Further discussion of the theoretical and empirical bases for this postulate and other applications of it can be found in McGuire (Note 1).

The spontaneous self-concept is a particularly appropriate domain in which to test this postulate. Each person is his or her own most complex stimulus object, both because the human being is intrinsically complex and because each of us is so familiar with our own complexities. Hence, when an internal need or external demand requires that we consider our identity (i.e., who we are, what kind of person we are), any of a vast variety of personal characteristics could occur to us. The distinctiveness theory of selective perception, when applied to this spontaneous self-concept, predicts that we notice any aspect (or dimension) of ourselves to the extent that our characteristic on that dimension is peculiar in our social milieu. For example, because the majority of our associates are right-handed, it is more likely for sinister people to notice their left-handedness than for dexterous people to think of themselves as right-handed. Again, given that a person is a black woman, she is more likely to be aware of her womanhood when she is associating with black men and of her blackness when she is associating with white women. The research reported here is designed to test this kind of prediction.

Our stress on personal distinctiveness as a determinant of what is noticed in one's spontaneous self-concept might overshadow other determinants of trait salience. To avoid complete neglect of these other factors, we shall mention briefly six other determinants of what is spontaneously salient in the self-concept. First, situational demand probably has a considerable effect. If someone says, "Tell me about yourself," the self-perceptions evoked are likely to be quite different depending on whether the question has been put by a prospective employer or by a smiling new acquaintance at a singles party. Second, stimulus intensity is probably operative because an individual is more likely to think of a more gross characteristic, such as hair color, than a more subtle one, such as shape of eyebrows, and of a broken leg rather than an ingrown toenail. Third, availability (in the sense of recency, familiarity, and expectation) will affect what is spontaneously salient to the self-concept: We are more likely, for example, to think of a current rather than an earlier activity; and a person is more likely to think of health status in response to the question "Tell me about yourself" if he or she has just visited a physician.

The three variables just mentioned are situational determinants of salience in the self-concept. To observe the equal-time provision, we must now mention three determinants which have to do with the individual's internal motivational state. A fourth determinant of salience in the self-concept is the individual's momentary need: If asked to "tell us about yourself" by the admissions officer of one's prospective college, one would probably think of one's assets and past achievements with a social desirability bias. However, asked the same question by a psychoanalyst to whom one has gone for help, one might think of one's anxieties and past difficulties, thus showing a rarer social-undesirability biased scanning. A fifth determinant is one's enduring values: Given a deeply religious Methodist and a Methodist who is rather casual about religion, the former is more likely than the latter to think of denominational membership when asked for a self-description. Past reinforcement is a sixth determinant of salience: Whether one thinks of oneself in terms of race or religion would be affected by which characteristic has been most influential in determining one's rewards and punishments in the past.

This list of determinants of what is salient in the spontaneous self-concept could be extended indefinitely or revised completely if one chose alternate bases for analysis and experiments could be devised to evaluate the effect of each. In the present study, however, we confine ourselves mainly to testing the hypothesis that the distinctiveness of one's own characteristic on a given dimension is a major determinant of whether that dimension is spontaneously salient in one's self-concept.

METHOD

Procedure and Measures

First session The participants were sixth graders who took part in two sessions, scheduled a week apart, during their regular classroom work. The first session was devoted to obtaining the children's spontaneous self-concepts. At a time prearranged with the teacher, the experimenters entered the classroom and announced that they were conducting the "Tell us about yourself" test. Copies of the mimeographed test booklet were distributed to each member of the class. The children were told not to put their names on the booklet and assured that no one would know who had filled out any given book. They were asked to open the booklet to the first page, which was headed "Tell us about yourself," beneath which there was a series of numbered lines. They were then told that they would have 7 minutes to write down on the lines all of the things about themselves that they thought of, writing each new thing on a new line as they thought of it. They were told that they could use a single word, a couple of words, or a whole sentence (whichever they preferred) to report each thing as they thought of it. The instruction to start was then given.

After 7 minutes, the children were asked to stop writing on that part of the test and turn to the next page, headed "Describe what you look like," beneath which was again a series of numbered lines. They were given similar instructions to write on these lines each of the things that came to mind in answer to the question about what they looked like. It was mentioned that they would have 4 minutes to answer this item. They were then told to start and allowed 4 minutes to respond. The 7-minute response to the first, "Tell us about yourself," item is hereafter called the *general self-concept*, and the response to the second, "Describe what you look like," item will be called the *physical self-concept*. The responses to these two items provide the dependent variable measures to test the hypotheses that the more distinctive the characteristic, the greater the likelihood that it will be salient in one's spontaneous self-concept.

Second session The researchers returned the following week with a more structured questionnaire entitled the "Describe yourself list" on which the participants were asked for specific information about their physical appearance (e.g., height, weight, hair color, eye color), demographic characteristics (e.g., birthdate, birthplace), and household composition. The children were given as much time as they needed to fill out this structured questionnaire about themselves. The responses to each of these specific questions provided information both on each child's own characteristic on the given dimension and about the child's classmates' distribution over the characteristics on that dimension. This information allowed scoring the independent variable to which characteristics on the dimension were common and which were distinctive in the social milieu constituted by the child's classmates. For example, each child was classified with respect to weight into either the middle half or upper or lower quarters of the class in weight; with respect to hair, into the modal color or some rarer color; with respect to sex, into the majority or the minority sex in the classroom, and so on. The distinctiveness theory was then tested by predicting, for example, that people who were found in the second session questionnaire to be unusually low or high in weight would have been more likely spontaneouly to have mentioned their weight.

At the end of each of the two sessions, the children were asked to draw some design of their choice on the cover sheet of that session's booklet, and they were asked to use the same design in each session so that we could match the first and second session booklets from a given child without endangering anonymity. Matching handwriting also helped.

Sample

We wanted to test whether people think of themselves in terms of their peculiarities with respect to their significant reference groups. We chose to study sixth-grade children several months into the school year in their intact classroom on the assumption that classmates constitute a meaningful reference group for 12-year-old students.

Our sample was drawn within a major east coast U.S. city from a school district bounded on two parallel sides by extensive nonresidential areas and on the other two sides by "round number" streets (50th and 100th). (We were initially drawn to this district by its extremely heterogeneous demographic composition. One of the implications of distinctiveness theory which first attracted our attention is that the salience of one's ethnicity in one's self-concept increases with the racial heterogeneity of one's classroom. However, the school administrators, as a condition for our being allowed to conduct the study, required that we not collect information on ethnicity or religion, so we could not test this derivation.) Prolonged negotiations with the Board of Education and the individual school principals secured permission for us to carry out the study in five of the six elementary schools in the district.

We chose to study elementary school children because only at this level do the classroom groupings tend to be intact throughout the school day, thus providing a more meaningful reference group in terms of which to define characteristic peculiarity for each respondent. We collected the data while the children were in their intact classroom setting to enhance the class's status as a meaningful reference group. Because of this group administration, it was necessary that the spontaneous self-concept probes be answered in writing to avoid interference. Young children have difficulty on written tasks, so we chose to use sixth graders because they are the oldest students still within elementary schools.

All five schools to which we were admitted were tracked: One "advanced" sixth-grade class comprised students who were judged able and willing to move rapidly in their studies; two or more "standard" classes included students who did adequately in their studies but were thought less inclined to move rapidly than those who were assigned to the advanced track; and an "exceptional" class was composed of sixth graders who had difficulties with their studies, were considered behavioral problems, or preferred a language other than English for instruction. In each of the five schools, we chose the one advanced class and randomly selected one of the standard classes to participate in the study, for a total of 10 classes. Hence, our sampling procedure eliminated the approximately 20 percent of the students who receive instruction in a language other than English, are considered behavioral problems, or are believed to have ability or motivational difficulties in keeping up with the usual pace of studies. Aside from these latter groups, our sampling procedures probably covered the range of sixth graders in this very heterogeneous urban setting. That all of our schools were tracked prevented our testing still another hypothesis drawn from our distinctiveness theory—that students in tracked classes are less likely than those in classrooms more heterogeneous in performance level to mention their ability level as part of their self-concept, because there would be more variance or information with respect to ability in the heterogeneously grouped classes and, hence, it would be more perceptually salient.

All students in each of the 10 classes (the advanced and a standard class from each of the five schools) were included in our sample if they attended school on both the days of our two sessions. A total of 252 students participated (class size ranged from 19 to 31), with 6 of the 10 classes having 23, 24, or 25 students present at both sessions. There were 132 students in the advanced and 120 in the standard track; the group included 127 girls and 125 boys.

RESULTS AND DISCUSSION

Number of Characteristics Mentioned

Permissive measures like our open-ended spontaneous self-concept instrument are attractive in that they allow respondents a great deal of freedom in expressing themselves and thus provide a large amount of information and unanticipated insights to the researcher. The disadvantage of such measures is that scoring the free responses is difficult and requires more subjective judgment on the part of the scorer than do instruments that enforce the participant's choosing responses from among a small set of predetermined alternatives.

Our procedure for scoring the two types of spontaneous self-concept protocols (the general and the physical) was to unitize each protocol and then classify each unit by a content-analysis procedure. Unitizing was achieved by dividing each protocol into individual thought elements, each of which expressed essentially one thing about the self. For example, a typical unitization is shown by the slash marks in the following paragraph:

I am twelve years old/ I was born in South Carolina/ I have two sisters/ and a dog/ I have a babysitting job every day after school/ I am a good roller skater/ I hate arithmetic/ but I like our teacher/ My father works in a bank/ I wish I could lose some weight.

By this unitizing procedure, it was determined that the 252 students produced 2,659 units in their 7-minute response protocols to the general "Tell us about yourself" probe, or an average of 10.98 units per student. On the 4-minute responses to the "Describe what you look like" physical self-concept probe, they produced 1,411 units, or an average of 5.62 units per student.

From a (perhaps overly) plausible postulate that more verbally skilled people generate more thoughts on a task like this, we derived two predictions. First, it was predicted that sixth graders who had been assigned to the advanced track would generate more characteristics as part of their spontaneous self-concepts than those in the standard track, on the assumption that the teachers were operating above chance in making the assignments to tracks and that the assignments reflect the child's verbal skills. The second prediction was that the girls would generate more characteristics as part of their spontaneous self-concepts than would the boys because it has been found that girls, from age 10 or 11, outperform boys at verbal tasks (Maccoby & Jacklin, 1974, pp. 84-85). Each prediction can be tested with data from both the general and the physical self-concepts. Table 1 shows that both predictions were confirmed for both response tasks. For both the general self-concept and the physical self-concept, students in the advanced track mentioned about 25 percent more characteristics than those in the standard track, a difference that was significant at the 0.01 level in each case. Likewise, with both the general self-concept and the physical self-concept, girls produced more items than boys. Girls mentioned 17 percent more characteristics than boys with the general self-concept and 20 percent more with the physical self-concept, both differences being significant at the 0.01 level. No interaction effect was anticipated, and with the general self-concept there was no appreciable interaction tendency; with the physical self-concept there was a borderline-significant interaction such that the superiority of the girls over the boys was slightly greater in the standard track classes than in the advanced track.

TABLE 1

Number of Items Generated by Sixth Graders in Response to Two Questions

	TYPE OF CLASS		
SEX	*ADVANCED*	*STANDARD*	*COMBINED*
*NO. GENERAL SELF-CONCEPT RESPONSES**			
Female	13.19	10.52	11.84
Male	11.28	8.64	10.10
Overall	12.19	9.65	10.98
NO. PHYSICAL SELF-CONCEPT RESPONSES†			
Female	6.54	5.73	6.13
Male	5.87	4.13	5.10
Overall	6.19	4.99	5.62

*Number of responses in 7 minutes to "Tell us about yourself."
†Number of responses in 4 minutes to "Describe what you look like."

Types of Characteristics Mentioned

After each self-concept protocol was divided into units, each item was copied on a separate slip and sorted among eight major categories (developed in a prestudy) which included significant other people, physical characteristics, demographic characteristics, self-evaluations, school, own activities, own attitudes and miscellaneous. Each of the eight categories was divided into subcategories (see Table 2). This classification system for the spontaneous self-concepts was devised without regard to the hypotheses and without knowledge of the respondents' scores on the independent variables that were obtained via the second session questionnaire.

TABLE 2

Categorization of Sixth Graders' Responses to "Tell Us About Yourself"

CATEGORY	PROPORTION OF TOTAL RESPONSES	PERCENT OF CHILDREN	CATEGORY	PROPORTION OF TOTAL RESPONSES	PERCENT OF CHILDREN
Own activities	(.24)		School (excluding teachers)	.15	71
Hobbies, amusements	.08	48	Miscellaneous	.01	5
Sports	.07	43	Demographic	(.12)	
Daily schedule	.03	43	Age, birthdate	.04	25
Places lived	.01	5	Name	.02	19
Skills	.01	8	Residence	.02	16
TV	.01	10	Birthplace	.01	11
Books	.01	6	Health	.01	11
Jobs	.00	3	Sex	.01	10
Miscellaneous experiences	.01	6	Race, ethnic	.00	5
			Religion	.00	3
Significant others	(.20)		Self-evaluation	(.07)	
Family	.07	38	Moral	.03	20
Friends	.07	43	Physical	.03	15
Pets	.03	22	Intellectual	.01	10
Teachers	.02	16	Emotional	.00	2
Public figures	.00	0	Physical characteristics	(.05)	
Attitudes	(.17)				
Likes and dislikes	.13	52	Hair color	.02	13
Vocational	.02	18	Weight	.01	11
Hopes and desires	.02	12	Height	.01	10
			Eye color	.01	11

Note. Proportion column indicates the proportion of all 2,659 responses that fell within the category: percentage column indicates percentage of the 252 children who gave at least one response in that category. (Numbers in parentheses represent category totals.)

Table 2 shows the distribution over the content-analysis categories of the 2,659 items generated by the 252 sixth graders in response to the request "Tell us about yourself." Almost a quarter of all of the responses fell in the habitual activities categories (recreations, daily routine, etc.). Another fifth of the items was composed of mentions of significant other people—mostly the children's parents, siblings, and friends, though pets were mentioned rather frequently. There were about half as many mentions of pets as of family members or friends, even though fewer than half of the students had pets. Hence, it might be said that given that a child has a pet, she or he is more likely to mention that pet than to mention all other family members combined. Teachers (almost always one's current teacher) were the only other category of significant others to receive frequent mention, though less frequent than one's dog, despite the fact that everyone had a teacher and only a minority had dogs. Aside from these four categories of significant others (family, friends, pets, and teachers) there were practically no other mentions of people in the life space represented by these children's spontaneous self-concepts.

The third most frequent category of mentions was one's attitudes, with particularly frequent mentions of likes and dislkes, which constituted the most popular of all 35 subcategories. There were numerous mentions also of hopes and desires (though far fewer than of likes and dislikes), especially regarding future jobs. Even though these children were only 12-years old, 18 percent of them did mention career aspirations in response to the request "Tell us about yourself."

Mentions of school constituted another 15 percent of all items (or 17 percent if we group mention of teachers here instead of with significant others). Demographic characteristics constituted 12 percent of the mentions, with age, residence, and name being the most frequent. It is interesting that in responding to the request "Tell us about yourself" 19 percent of the children mentioned their names, even though the preexperimental instructions stressed that the study was an anonymous one and that they should not write their names on top of the page. On the other hand, the specific instructions said that they should write down whatever came to mind, and for 19 percent of the children their names apparently occurred spontaneously to them and were written down, despite the inhibiting earlier instructions. Probably an even larger proportion think of their names as a salient part of their self-concept, but their giving names here was depressed due to the explicit instruction regarding anonymity. The somewhat "touchy" demographic characteristics of sex, ethnicity, and religion were relatively rare, spontaneous mention of one's sex accounting for only about 1 percent of the total items and mentions of race and especially religion rarer still.

The self-evaluation category accounted for only 7 percent of all the responses. We complained in the introduction that about 90 percent of all self-concept studies focus on that one dimension of self-evaluation or self-esteem. When asked to talk about themselves, sixth graders think about things other than self-evaluation about 93 percent of the time; therefore, it seems a disproportionate emphasis that researchers on the self confine almost all of their studies to the other 7 percent. When the children do mention self-evaluation, it tends to be in terms of morality ("I fight too much" or "I think I behave better than most people my age") and physical ("I'm not very well coordinated" or "I'm very strong"). Considerably less frequent are intellectual self-evaluations ("I'm terrible at arithmetic" or "I'm pretty smart"), and emotional self-evaluations appear very rarely ("I cry too easily").

Mentions of physical characteristics account for about 5 percent of the total spontaneous response units, these being confined almost entirely to the four categories of hair (usually hair color), weight, height, and eyes (almost invariably eye color). A final 1 percent of the items do not fall in any of the preceding seven categories and hence are classified as miscellaneous in Table 2.

Distinctiveness and Spontaneous Salience

Each of the 25 subcategories of our content analysis that were used by at least 10 percent of the participants in giving their general self-concepts (see Table 2) was examined for possible use in testing our distinctiveness hypothesis. Seven dimensions seemed to provide a suitable test. Three were demographic characteristics, of which two (age and birthplace) were testable only with the general self-concept because they were not reported as part of the physical self-concept; and the third characteristic (sex) could be tested with both the general and the physical self-concept since it was mentioned by at least 10 percent of the participants on each instrument. The other four usable dimensions were physical characteristics (hair color, eye color, weight, and height), each of which was testable with both general and physical self-concept data because it met the 10 percent occurrence criterion on each instrument. These seven categories of spontaneously salient characteristics supplied 9 percent of all mentions of the general self-concept and 41 percent of all physical self-concept mentions.

The other categories shown in Table 2 did not lend themselves to a clear test of the distinctiveness hypothesis either because their usage was rare or was very scattered and showed different bases of analysis from child to child. (For example, the "likes and dislikes" category is well used, but not only are they idiosyncratically scattered but also the fineness of category differs greatly from child to child with entries varying from "I like to eat" to "I like desserts" to "I like danish," making it unclear how to score meaningfully what are more common versus less common likes and dislikes.) Hence, our tests of the distinctiveness postulate are made in terms of hypotheses regarding the above-mentioned seven dimensions.

Spontaneous Mention of Age Age was mentioned by 25 percent of the children in response to the general "Tell us about yourself" self-concept probe. The distinctiveness theory prediction is that students close to the modal age of the class are less likely to mention their age spontaneously than are younger and older children who deviate more from the modal age. On the basis of the birthdate information they provided on their second-session questionnaire, the 252 children were partitioned into those who were within 6 months of the modal class age versus those more than 6 months younger or more than 6 months older than the class mode. Only 19 percent of children within 6 months of the class modal age spontaneously mentioned their ages, while 30 percent of those who were atypically young or atypically old spontaneously mentioned their ages, a difference significant at the 0.05 level.

Spontaneous Mention of Birthplace Regarding birthplace, the distinctiveness hypothesis predicts that people born at places different from that of most of their associates are more likely to think of themselves in terms of their origin than are those who share their birthplace with most of their associates. The sixth graders who participated in this study were typically born, as might be expected, in the city where the study was done, 70 percent of them having been born in this metropolis. Only 6 percent of these natives spontaneously mentioned their birthplace, whereas 22 percent of those who had been born elsewhere spontaneously mentioned their birthplaces, a difference which is significant at the 0.001 level. When we partition the respondents' birthplace distribution at a still more extreme point, namely, into those born in the U.S. and the foreign born, the difference is still more pronounced. Only 7 percent of the children born in the U.S. spontaneously mention their birthplaces while 44 percent of the foreign born do, a difference which again reaches the 0.001 level of significance despite the very asymmetrical cut.

This birthplace confirmation shows the distinctiveness hypothesis to be rather robust since several other determinants of perceptual selectivity are pitted against it. For example, both "social desirability" and "availability" factors would tend to push the relationship in the opposite direction. Coming from somewhere else and especially being foreign born would seem to be at least slightly undesirable and a social handicap in this sixth-grade milieu. Such a disadvantage would normally motivate repression of birthplace among the outsiders rather than the heightened salience which was found. Likewise, birthplace should be more "available" for the locally born because talking about the local city is probably much more frequent and recent in everyday conversation among these children than is talking about the more distant birthplaces. Yet the data indicate that the hypothesized peculiarity effect on these latter places apparently overcame their social undesirability and their lesser recency and frequency so that they were more salient in the spontaneous self-concept.

Spontaneous Mention of Physical Characteristics The remaining five dimensions about which predictions can be made on the basis of the distinctiveness hypothesis can be tested with both the general and the physical self-concept data because each dimension was spontaneously mentioned by at least 10 percent of the participants in response to both "Tell us about yourself" and "Describe what you look like." The results with respect to three of these dimensions (hair color, eye color, and weight) are very similar: For each dimension about 1½ times as many people having unusual characteristics on the dimension spontaneously mentioned it than did those with the more typical characteristics, on both the general self-concept and the physical self-concept. However, the split between mentioners and nonmentioners was near the more sensitive 50 : 50 ratio with the physical self-concept, whereas the split was very asymmetrical on the general self-concept where there was a 10 : 90 ratio in favor of the nonmentioners. Hence, with all three dimensions the relationship reached the conventional 0.05 level of significance on the physical self-concept but fell short of it on the general self-concept.

On the second-session questionnaire item, which specifically requested hair color information, most of the respondents (88 percent) reported that they had brown or black hair, and the remaining 12 percent answered that their hair color was either red or blond; hence, the former two colors were defined as typical and the latter two as distinctive. Table 2 illustrates that only 13 percent of the respondents spontaneously mentioned their hair color as part of their general self-concepts. The dark-haired participants mentioned hair color at only two-thirds the rate of the red- and blond-haired participants, but the difference did not attain the 0.05 significance level. More than half of the children spontaneously mentioned hair color as part of their physical self-concept; this mention was made by only 54 percent of those with brown or black hair, whereas 79 percent with red or blond hair mentioned it, yielding a difference significant beyond the 0.05 level.

To the second-session questionnaire item on eye color, 70 percent of the respondents reported brown eyes and only 21 percent reported blue or green eyes. The remaining 9 percent mentioned gradations of eye colors that we found difficult to classify, such as brownish-blue, green-brown, and the like, and so are not included in our analysis of the spontaneous mention data. On the general self-concept, the atypical blue or green eyes were mentioned half again more often than the usual brown eyes. On the physical self-concept, likewise, only 56 percent of those with the typical brown eyes spontaneously mentioned the fact, while 77 percent of those with the atypical blue or green eyes spontaneously mentioned it. This difference is significant at the 0.01 level for the physical self-concept but does not reach the 0.05 level with the general self-concept.

A similar picture emerges regarding the results on spontaneous mention of weight. The group of students could most nearly be partitioned into lower and upper quarters versus the intermediate 50 percent by cutting the distributions at 80 and at 102 pounds (36.29 and 46.27 kg). That is, students weighing from 80 through 102 pounds were defined as the typical intermediate 50 percent, those weighing 79 pounds (35.83 kg) or less were defined as the underweight quarter, and those weighing 103 pounds (46.72 kg) or more were placed in the overweight quarter. Of the 11 percent of the children who mentioned their weight as part of their general self-concept, the ratio of those in the upper and lower quarters who spontaneously mentioned their weight was 1½ times that of those in the middle half of the weight distribution. Likewise, with the physical self-concept, only 37 percent of the middle half spontaneously mentioned their weight, whereas 52 percent of those in the upper and lower quarters spontaneously mentioned weight. The difference is significant at the 0.05 level for the physical self-concept but falls short of the conventional level for the general self-concept. (This excessive mention was exhibited about equally by over- and underweight children, with both general and physical self-concepts.) Again as regards weight, the distinctiveness hypothesis is shown to be robust because it is once again pitted against the social desirability hypothesis which predicts that being overweight or underweight would be a social detriment and, thus, suppressed in thought and underreported. Any such suppression tendency seems to have been overridden by the increased salience produced by the distinctiveness effect.

The distinctiveness postulate received no support on the sixth dimension, height. Again, by dividing the distribution into those in the upper quarter and the lower quarter regarding height and pitting them against those in the middle half, we compared the means versus the extreme halves according to spontaneous mention of height in both general and specific self-concept responses. In neither case was there any appreciable difference between those of typical and atypical height. Our post factum conjecture is that perhaps 12-year olds have been undergoing considerable irregular growth spurts at this time of their lives, so that their momentary relative height is not as critical a determinant of the salience of height in their self-concept as is their momentary status on the more stable dimensions.

Spontaneous Mention of Sex Before turning to the question of distinctiveness in one's group as a determinant of spontaneous mention of sex, it is interesting to consider the relative salience of sex for boys as compared with girls. Sex was mentioned about equally often as part of the general self-concept and of the physical self-concept: about one fifth of the children spontaneously mentioned their sex in response to "Tell us about yourself" and in response to "Describe what you look like," as shown in Table 3. On the general self-concept, girls were slightly more likely than boys to mention their sex spontaneously, but this difference falls far short of the conventionally accepted 0.05 level of confidence. On the physical self-concept, boys were much more likely than girls to mention their sex, with 26 percent mention by boys versus 10 percent by girls, a difference significant beyond the 0.01 level. Viewed differently, girls are more likely to mention their

TABLE 3
Sixth Graders' Spontaneous Mention of Their Sex

OWN SEX	*SPONTANEOUS MENTION OF SEX*			
	YES	*NO*	*TOTAL*	*PERCENT*
GENERAL SELF-CONCEPT				
Female	29	98	127	23
Male	23	102	125	18
Total	52	200	252	21
PHYSICAL SELF-CONCEPT				
Female	13	114	127	10
Male	32	93	125	26
Total	45	207	252	18

sex as part of what they are (23 percent) rather than what they look like (10 percent); conversely, boys are somewhat more likely to mention their sex as part of what they look like (26 percent) rather than what they are (18 percent).

Various interpretations could be projected on this outcome. Perhaps society impresses upon women that their sex is part of their being while on men that it is only part of their external appearance. Or perhaps boys regard one's sex as a more circumscribed physical attribute and girls regard it as a more pervasive characteristic. Or it may bc that among 12-year olds, girls are more shy than boys about thinking about their sex as part of their physical appearance. These interesting sex differences were not anticipated, so we do not propose to explain them definitively here. However, they are provocative enough to invite further empirical research, for example, as regards whether comparable outcomes occur at younger and older ages and in conjunction with interaction variables that would test various hypotheses about the factors underlying these relationships.

Our main theoretical focus is on distinctiveness as a determinant of the spontaneous salience of one's sex in one's self-concept. When we lump all 10 classes together, there are almost exactly as many girls as boys among our 252 participants, 127 versus 125. But when we look at sex composition on a class-by-class basis, we find that in five of the classes, boys are in the majority, whereas girls represent the majority in the other five classes. The discrepancy is not great: The majority sex exceeds the minority by an average of 3 persons in these classes of over 25 students, with the within-class excess ranging from 1 to 5 persons. However, even though the excess of the majority over the minority sex in any one class is not great, it does allow us to test the hypothesis, with both general and physical self-concept data, that members of the minority sex will more often spontaneously mention their sex than will the majority sex in that class. There was one insignificant tendency in this direction with the general self-concept. With the physical self-concept, there was a much more sizable and significant difference in the direction predicted. Over the 10 classes, 26 percent of members of the minority sex in any given class spontaneously mentioned their sex, whereas only 11 percent of those in the majority sex mentioned their sex, yielding a difference significant beyond the 0.01 level. This sizable difference in the predicted direction is especially encouraging considering that the discrepancy in numbers between the two sexes in any classroom was not great. We have no conjecture regarding why the effect appeared so much more strongly in the physical self-concept than in the general self-concept, except perhaps that in the broader general self-concept, one's sex was evoked by a wider variety of yoked concepts, which tended to obscure this majority-minority factor. It fits the general picture that the distinctiveness hypothesis is supported more strongly by the physical self-concept than the general self-concept data, a difference that we had not anticipated.

NOTES

1 McGuire, W. J. Attitude change and social perception. Grant proposal GS-1108x to National Science Foundation from Columbia University, January 14, 1966.

2 McGuire, W. J. Perceptual selectivity and the self-concept. Division 8 presidential address at the meeting of the American Psychological Association, Montreal, August 1973.

REFERENCES

Altman, I. and D. A. Taylor
1973 Social Penetration. New York; Holt, Rinehart & Winston.
Bugental, J. F. T. and S. L. Zelen
1950 "Investigations into the self-concept—the W-A-Y technique." Journal of Personality 18: 438–98.
Jourard, S. M.
1971 Self-Disclosure. New York: Wiley.
Kelly, G.
1955 The Psychology of Personal Constructs. New York: Norton.
Kuhn, M. H. and T. S. McPartland
1954 "An empirical investigation of self attitudes." American Sociological Review 19: 68–76.
Livesley, W. J. and D. B. Bromley
1973 Person Perception in Childhood and Adolescence. London: Wiley.
Loevinger, J. and R. Wessler
1970 Measuring Ego Development 1: Construction and Use of a Sentence Completion Test. San Francisco: Jossey-Bass.
Loevinger, J., R. Wessler, and C. Redmore
1970 Measuring Ego Development 2: Scoring Manual for Women and Girls. San Francisco: Jossey-Bass.
Maccoby, E. E. and C. N. Jacklin
1974 The Psychology of Sex Differences. Stanford, Calif.: Stanford University Press.
Rosenberg, S. and A. Sedlak
1972 "Structural representation of implicit personality theory." In L. Berkowitz (ed.), Advances in Experimental Social Psychology, Vol. 6. New York: Academic Press.
Spitzer, S., C. Couch, and J. Stratton
1971 The Assessment of Self. Iowa City: Escort-Sernole.
Wylie, R. C.
1961 The Self-Concept: A Critical Survey of Pertinent Research Literature. Lincoln: University of Nebraska Press.
Wylie, R. C.
1974 The Self-Concept: A Review of Methodological Considerations and Measuring Instruments, Vol. 1. Lincoln: University of Nebraska Press.

Self-Efficacy: Toward a Unifying Theory of Behavioral Change

ALBERT BANDURA

3

The present article outlines a theoretical framework, in which the concept of *self-efficacy* is assigned a central role, for analyzing changes achieved in fearful and avoidant behavior. The explanatory value of this conceptual system is then evaluated by its ability to predict behavioral changes produced through different methods of treatment.

EFFICACY EXPECTATIONS AS A MECHANISM OF OPERATION

The present theory is based on the principal assumption that psychological procedures, whatever their form, serve as means of creating and strengthening expectations of personal efficacy. Within this analysis, efficacy expectations are distinguished from response-outcome expectancies. The difference is presented schematically in Figure 1.

Source: Albert Bandura, "Self-Efficacy: Toward a Unifying Theory of Behavioral Change," Psychological Review 84 (1977): 191–215.

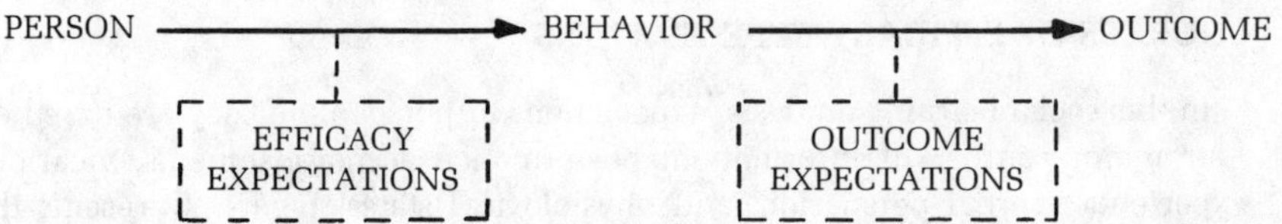

FIGURE 1 Diagrammatic representation of the difference between efficacy expectations and outcome expectations.

An outcome expectancy is defined as a person's estimate that a given behavior will lead to certain outcomes. An efficacy expectation is the conviction that one can successfully execute the behavior required to produce the outcomes. Outcome and efficacy expectations are differentiated, because individuals can believe that a particular course of action will produce certain outcomes, but if they entertain serious doubts about whether they can perform the necessary activities such information does not influence their behavior.

In this conceptual system, expectations of personal mastery affect both initiation and persistence of coping behavior. The strength of people's convictions in their own effectiveness is likely to affect whether they will even try to cope with given situations. At this initial level, perceived self-efficacy influences choice of behavioral settings. People fear and tend to avoid threatening situations they believe exceed their coping skills, whereas they get involved in activities and behave assuredly when they judge themselves capable of handling situations that would otherwise be intimidating.

Not only can perceived self-efficacy have directive influence on choice of activities and settings, but, through expectations of eventual success, it can affect coping efforts once they are initiated. Efficacy expectations determine how much effort people will expend and how long they will persist in the face of obstacles and aversive experiences. The stronger the perceived self-efficacy, the more active the efforts. Those who persist in subjectively threatening activities that are in fact relatively safe will gain corrective experiences that reinforce their sense of efficacy, thereby eventually eliminating their defensive behavior. Those who cease their coping efforts prematurely will retain their self-debilitating expectations and fears for a long time.

The preceding analysis of how perceived self-efficacy influences performance is not meant to imply that expectation is the sole determinant of behavior. Expectation alone will not produce desired performance if the component capabilities are lacking. Moreover, there are many things that people can do with certainty of success that they do not perform because they have no incentives to do so. Given appropriate skills and adequate incentives, however, efficacy expectations are a major determinant of people's choice of activities, how much effort they will expend, and of how long they will sustain effort in dealing with stressful situations.

SOURCES OF EFFICACY EXPECTATIONS

In this social learning analysis, expectations of personal efficacy are based on four major sources of information: performance accomplishments, vicarious experience, verbal persuasion, and physiological states. Figure 2 presents the diverse influence procedures commonly used to reduce defensive behavior and presents the principal source through which each treatment operates to create expectations of mastery. Any given method, depending on how it is applied, may of course draw to a lesser extent on one or more other sources of efficacy information. For example, as we shall see shortly, performance-based treatments not only promote behavioral accomplishments but also extinguish fear arousal, thus authenticating self-efficacy through enactive and arousal sources of information. Other methods, however, provide fewer ways of acquiring information about one's capability for coping with threatening situations. By postulating a common mechanism of operation, this analysis provides a conceptual framework within which to study behavioral changes achieved by different modes of treatment.

EFFICACY EXPECTATIONS

SOURCE	*MODE OF INDUCTION*
PERFORMANCE ACCOMPLISHMENTS	PARTICIPANT MODELING PERFORMANCE DESENSITIZATION PERFORMANCE EXPOSURE SELF-INSTRUCTED PERFORMANCE
VICARIOUS EXPERIENCE	LIVE MODELING SYMBOLIC MODELING
VERBAL PERSUASION	SUGGESTION EXHORTATION SELF-INSTRUCTION INTERPRETIVE TREATMENTS
EMOTIONAL AROUSAL	ATTRIBUTION RELAXATION, BIOFEEDBACK SYMBOLIC DESENSITIZATION SYMBOLIC EXPOSURE

FIGURE 2 Major sources of efficacy information and the principal sources through which different modes of treatment operate

Performance Accomplishments

This source of efficacy information is especially influential because it is based on personal mastery experiences. Successes raise mastery expectations; repeated failures lower them, particularly if the mishaps occur early in the course of events. After strong efficacy expectations are developed through repeated success, the negative impact of occasional failures is likely to be reduced. Indeed, occasional failures that are later overcome by determined effort can strengthen self-motivated persistence if one finds through experience that even the most difficult obstacles can be mastered by sustained effort. The effects of failure on personal efficacy therefore partly depend on the timing and the total pattern of experiences in which the failures occur.

Once established, enhanced self-efficacy tends to generalize to other situations in which performance was self-debilitated by preoccupation with personal inadequacies (Bandura, Adams, & Beyer, in press; Bandura, Jeffery, & Gajdos, 1975). As a result, improvements in behavioral functioning transfer not only to similar situations but to activities that are substantially different from those on which the treatment was focused. Thus, for example, increased self-efficacy gained through rapid mastery of a specific animal phobia can increase coping efforts in social situations as well as reduce fears of other animals. However, the generalization effects occur most predictably to the activities that are most similar to those in which self-efficacy was restored by treatment (Bandura, Blanchard, & Ritter, 1969).

Methods of change that operate on the basis of performance accomplishments convey efficacy information in more ways than simply through the evidence of performance improvements. In the course of treatments employing modeling with guided performance, participants acquire a generalizable skill for dealing successfully with stressful situations, a skill that they use to overcome a variety of dysfunctional fears and inhibitions in their everyday life (Bandura et al., in press; Bandura et al., 1975). Having a serviceable coping skill at one's disposal undoubtedly contributes to one's sense of personal efficacy. Behavioral capabilities can also be enhanced through modeling alone (Bandura, 1971; Flanders, 1968). However, participant modeling provides additional opportunities for translating behavioral conceptions to appropriate actions and for making corrective refinements toward the perfection of skills.

Most of the treatment procedures developed in recent years to eliminate fearful and defensive behavior have been implemented either through performance or by symbolic procedures. Regardless of the methods involved, results of comparative studies attest to the superiority of performance-based treatments. In the desensitization approach devised by Wolpe (1974), clients receive graduated exposure to aversive events in conjunction with anxiety reducing activities, usually in the form of muscular relaxation. A number of experiments have been reported in which relaxation is paired with scenes in which phobics visualize themselves engaging in progressively more threatening activities or with enactment of the same hierarchy of activities with the actual threats. Findings based on different types of phobias consistently reveal that performance desensitization produces substantially greater behavioral change than does symbolic desensitization (LoPicollo, 1970; Sherman, 1972; Strahley, 1966). Physiological measures yield similar results. Symbolic desensitization reduces autonomic responses to imagined but not to actual threats, whereas performance desensitization eliminates autonomic responses to both imagined and actual threats (Barlow, Leitenberg, Agras, & Wincze, 1969). The substantial benefits of successful performance are typically achieved in less time than is required to extinguish arousal to symbolic representations of threats.

More recently, avoidance behavior has been treated by procedures involving massive exposure to aversive events. In this approach, intense anxiety is elicited by prolonged exposure to the most threatening situations and sustained at high levels, without relief, until emotional reactions are extinguished. Several investigators have compared the relative success of prolonged exposure to aversive situations in imagery and actual encounters with them in ameliorating chronic agoraphobias. Real encounters with threats produce results decidedly superior to imagined exposure, which has weak, variable effects (Emmelkamp & Wessels, 1975; Stern & Marks, 1973; Watson, Mullett, & Pillay, 1973). Prolonged encounters that ensure behavioral improvements are more effective than distributed brief encounters that are likely to end before successful performance of the activity is achieved (Rabavilas, Boulougouris, & Stefanis, 1976).

The participant modeling approach to the elimination of defensive behavior utilizes successful performance as the primary vehicle of psychological change. People displaying intractable fears and inhibitions are not about to do what they dread. In implementing participant modeling, therapists therefore structure the environment so that clients can perform successfully despite their incapacities. This is achieved by enlisting a variety of response induction aids, including preliminary modeling of threatening activities, graduated tasks, enactment over graduated temporal intervals, joint performance with the therapist, protective aids to reduce the likelihood of feared consequences, and variation in the severity of the threat itself (Bandura, Jeffery, & Wright, 1974). As treatment progresses, the supplementary aids are withdrawn so that clients cope effectively unassisted. Self-directed mastery experiences are then arranged to reinforce a sense of personal efficacy. Through this form of treatment incapacitated people rapidly lose their fears, they are able to engage in activities they formerly inhibited, and they display generalized reductions of fears toward threats beyond the specifically treated conditions (Bandura, 1976a).

Participant modeling has been compared with various symbolically based treatments. These studies corroborate the superiority of successful performance facilitated by modeling as compared to vicarious experience alone (Bandura et al., 1969; Blanchard, 1970b; Lewis, 1974; Ritter, 1969; Roper, Rachman, & Marks, 1975), to symbolic desensitization (Bandura et al., 1969; Litvak, 1969), and to imaginal modeling in which clients visualize themselves or others coping successfully with threats (Thase & Moss, 1976). When participant modeling is subsequently administered to those who benefit only partially from the symbolic procedures, avoidance behavior is thoroughly eliminated within a brief period.

The findings summarized above are consistent with self-efficacy theory, but they do not shed much light on the mechanism by which specific mastery experiences produce generalized and enduring changes in behavior. Verification of the operative mechanism requires experimental evidence that experienced mastery does in fact alter the level and strength of self-efficacy and that self-efficacy is, in turn, linked to behavior. . . .

Vicarious Experience

People do not rely on experienced mastery as the sole source of information concerning their level of self-efficacy. Many expectations are derived from vicarious experience. Seeing others perform threatening activities without adverse consequences can generate expectations in observers that they too will improve if they intensify and persist in their efforts. They persuade themselves that if others can do it, they should be able to achieve at least some improvement in performance (Bandura & Barab, 1973). Vicarious experience, relying as it does on inferences from social comparison, is a less dependable source of information about one's capabilities than is direct evidence of personal accomplishments. Consequently, the efficacy expectations induced by modeling alone are likely to be weaker and more vulnerable to change.

A number of modeling variables that are apt to affect expectations of personal efficacy have been shown to enhance the disinhibiting influence of modeling procedures. Phobics benefit more from seeing models overcome their difficulties by determined effort than from observing facile performances by adept models (Kazdin, 1973; Meichenbaum, 1971). Showing the gains achieved by effortful coping behavior not only minimizes for observers the negative impact of temporary distress but demonstrates that even the most anxious can eventually succeed through perseverance. Similarity to the model in other characteristics, which increases the personal relevance of vicariously derived information, can likewise enhance the effectiveness of symbolic modeling (Kazdin, 1974b).

Modeled behavior with clear outcomes conveys more efficacy information than if the effects of the modeled actions remain ambiguous. In investigations of vicarious processes, observing one perform activities that meet with success does, indeed, produce greater behavioral improvements than witnessing the same performances modeled without any evident consequences (Kazdin, 1974c, 1975). Diversified modeling, in which the activities observers regard as hazardous are repeatedly shown to be safe by a variety of models, is superior to exposure to the same performances by a single model (Bandura & Menlove, 1968; Kazdin, 1974a, 1975, 1976). If people of widely differing characteristics can succeed, then observers have a reasonable basis for increasing their own sense of self-efficacy.

The pattern of results reported above offers at least suggestive support for the view that exemplifications of success through sustained effort with substantiating comparative information can enhance observers' perceptions of their own performance capabilities. . . .

Verbal Persuasion

In attempts to influence human behavior, verbal persuasion is widely used because of its ease and ready availability. People are led, through suggestion, into believing they can cope successfully with what has overwhelmed them in the past. Efficacy expectations induced in this manner are also likely to be weaker than those arising from one's own accomplishments because they do not provide an authentic experiential base for them. In the face of distressing threats and a long history of failure in coping with them, whatever mastery expectations are induced by suggestion can be readily extinguished by disconfirming experiences.

Results of several lines of research attest to the limitation of procedures that attempt to instill outcome expectations in people simply by telling them what to expect. In laboratory studies, "placebo" conditions designed suggestively to raise expectations of improvement produce little change in refractory behavior (Lick & Bootzin, 1975; Moore, 1965; Paul, 1966). Whether this is due to the low credibility of the suggestions or to the weakness of the induced expectations cannot be determined from these studies, because the expectations were not measured.

Numerous experiments have been conducted in which phobics receive desensitization treatment without any expectancy information or with suggestions that it is either highly efficacious or ineffective. The differential outcome expectations are verbally induced prior to, during, or immediately after treatment in the various studies. The findings generally show that desensitization reduces phobic behavior, but the outcome expectancy manipulations have either no effect or weak, inconsistent ones (Howlett & Nawas, 1971; McGlynn & Mapp, 1970; McGlynn, Mealiea, & Nawas, 1969; McGlynn, Reynolds, & Linder, 1971). As in the "placebo" studies, it is difficult to make conclusive interpretations because the outcome expectations induced suggestively are not measured prior to the assessment of behavior changes, if at all. Simply informing participants that they will or will not benefit from treatment does not mean that they necessarily believe what they are told, especially when it contradicts their other personal experiences. Moreover, in the studies just cited the verbal influence is aimed mainly at raising outcome expectations rather than at enhancing self-efficacy. It is changes on the latter dimension that are most relevant to the theory under discussion.

Although social persuasion alone may have definite limitations as a means of creating an enduring sense of personal efficacy, it can contribute to the successes achieved through corrective performance. That is, people who are socially persuaded that they possess the capabilities to master difficult situations and are provided with provisional aids for effective action are likely to mobilize greater effort than those who receive only the performance aids. However, to raise by persuasion expectations of personal competence without arranging conditions to facilitate effective performance will most likely lead to failures that discredit the persuaders and further undermine the recipients' perceived self-efficacy. It is therefore the interactive, as well as the independent, effects of social persuasion on self-efficacy that merit experimental consideration.

Emotional Arousal

Stressful and taxing situations generally elicit emotional arousal that, depending on the circumstances, might have informative value concerning personal competency. Therefore, emotional arousal is another constituent source of information that can affect perceived self-efficacy in coping with threatening situations. People rely partly on their state of physiological arousal in judging their anxiety and vulnerability to stress. Because high arousal usually debilitates performance, individuals are more likely to expect success when they are not beset by aversive arousal than if they are tense and viscerally agitated. Fear reactions generate further fear of impending stressful situations through anticipatory self-arousal. By conjuring up fear-provoking thoughts about their ineptitude, individuals can rouse themselves to elevated levels of anxiety that far exceed the fear experienced during the actual threatening situation.

As will be recalled from the earlier discussion, desensitization and massive exposure treatments aimed at extinguishing anxiety arousal produce some reductions in avoidance behavior. Anxiety arousal to threats is likewise diminished by modeling and is even more thoroughly eliminated by experienced mastery achieved through participant modeling (Bandura & Barab, 1973; Bandura et al., 1969; Blanchard, 1970a). Modeling approaches have other advantages for enhancing self-efficacy and thereby removing dysfunctional fears. In addition to diminishing proneness to aversive arousal, such approaches also teach effective coping skills by demonstrating proficient ways of handling threatening situations. The latter contribution is especially important when fear arousal partly results from behavioral deficits. It is often the case that fears and deficits are interdependent. Avoidance of stressful activities impedes development of coping skills, and the resulting lack of competency provides a realistic basis for fear. Acquiring behavioral means for controlling potential threats attenuates or eliminates fear arousal (Averill, 1973; Notterman, Schoenfeld, & Bersh, 1952; Szpiler & Epstein, 1976). Behavioral control not only allows one to manage the aversive aspects of an environment. It also affects how the environment is likely to be perceived. Potentially stressful situations that can be controlled are construed as less threatening, and such cognitive appraisals further reduce anticipatory emotional arousal (Averill, 1973).

Diminishing emotional arousal can reduce avoidance behavior, but different theories posit different explanatory mechanisms for the observed effects. In the theory from which the emotive treatments are derived, emotional arousal is conceived of as a drive that activates avoidance behavior. This view stresses the energizing function of arousal and the reinforcing function of arousal reduction. Social learning theory, on the other hand, emphasizes the informative function of physiological arousal. Simply acknowledging that arousal is both informative and motivating by no means resolves the issue in dispute, because these are not necessarily two separate effects that somehow jointly produce behavior. Rather, the cognitive appraisal of arousal to a large extent determines the level and direction of motivational inducements to action. Certain cognitive appraisals of one's physiological state might be energizing, whereas other appraisals of the same state might not (Weiner, 1972). Moreover, many forms of physiological arousal are generated cognitively by arousing trains of thought. When motivation is conceptualized in terms of cognitive processes (Bandura, 1977; Weiner, 1972), the informational and motivational effects of arousal are treated as interdependent rather than as separate events. . . .

Researchers working within the attributional framework have attempted to modify avoidance behavior by directly manipulating the cognitive labeling of emotional arousal (Valins & Nisbett, 1971). The presumption is that if phobics are led to *believe* that the things they have previously feared no longer affect them internally, the cognitive reevaluation alone will reduce avoidance behavior. In treatment analogues of this approach, phobics receive false physiological feedback suggesting that they are no longer emotionally upset by threatening events. Results of this procedure are essentially negative. Early claims that erroneous arousal feedback reduces avoidance behavior (Valins & Ray, 1967) are disputed by methodologically superior studies showing that false feedback of physiological tranquility in the presence of threats has either no appreciable effect on subsequent fearful behavior (Gaupp, Stern, & Galbraith, 1972; Howlett & Nawas, 1971; Kent, Wilson, & Nelson, 1972; Rosen, Rosen, & Reid, 1972; Sushinsky & Bootzin, 1970), or produces minor changes under such limited conditions as to be of little practical consequence (Borkovec, 1973).

Misattribution of emotional arousal is another variant of the attributional approach to modification of fearful behavior. The strategy here is to lead fearful people into believing that their emotional arousal is caused by a nonemotional source. To the extent that they no longer label their agitated state as anxiety, they will behave more boldly. It may be possible to reduce mild fears by this means (Ross, Rodin, & Zimbardo, 1969), but the highly anxious are not easily led into misattributing their anxiety to irrelevant sources (Nisbett & Schachter, 1966). When evaluated systematically, misattribution treatments do not produce significant changes in chronic anxiety conditions (Singerman, Borkovec, & Baron, 1976), and some of the benefits reported with other dysfunctions cannot be replicated (Bootzin, Herman, & Nicassio, 1976; Kellogg & Baron, 1975). There is also some suggestive evidence that in laboratory studies the attenuation of fear may be due more to the veridicality of arousal information than to the misattribution of fear arousal to an innocuous source (Calvert-Boyanowsky & Leventhal, 1975).

Any reduction in fear resulting from deceptive feedback is apt to be short-lived because illusory assurances are not an especially reliable way of creating durable self-expectations. However, more veritable experiences that reduce the level of emotional arousal can set in motion a reciprocal process of change. In the social learning view, potential threats activate fear largely through cognitive self-arousal (Bandura, 1969, 1977). Perceived self-competence can therefore affect susceptibility to self-arousal. Individuals who come to believe that they are less vulnerable than they previously assumed are less prone to generate frightening thoughts in threatening situations. Those whose fears are relatively weak may reduce their self-doubts and debilitating self-arousal to the point where they perform successfully. Performance successes, in turn, strengthen self-efficacy. Such changes can, of course, be reliably achieved without resort to ruses. Moreover, mislabeling arousal or attributing it to erroneous sources is unlikely to be of much help to the highly anxious. Severe acrophobics, for example, may be temporarily misled into believing that they no longer fear high elevations, but they will reexperience unnerving internal feedback when confronted with dreaded heights. It should also be noted that in attributional explanations of the success of behavioral treatments the heavy emphasis on physiological arousal derives more from speculations about the nature of emotion (Schachter, 1964) than from evidence that arousal is a major determinant of defensive behavior.

REFERENCES

Averill, J. R.

1973 "Personal control over aversive stimuli and its relationship to stress." Psychological Bulletin 80: 286–303.

Bandura, A.

1969 Principles of Behavior Modification. New York: Holt, Rinehart & Winston.

1976 "Effecting change through participant modeling." In J. D. Krumboltz & C. E. Thoresen (eds.), Counseling Methods. New York: Holt, Rinehart & Winston.

1977 Social Learning Theory. Englewood Cliffs, N.J.: Prentice-Hall.

Bandura, A. (ed.)

1971 Psychological Modeling: Conflicting Theories. Chicago: Aldine Atherton.

Bandura, A., N. E. Adams, and J. Beyer

In press. "Cognitive processes mediating behavioral changes." Journal of Personality and Social Psychology.

Bandura, A. and P. G. Barab

1973 "Processes governing disinhibitory effects through symbolic modeling." Journal of Abnormal Psychology 82: 1–9.

Bandura, A., E. B. Blanchard, and B. Ritter

1969 "The relative efficacy of desensitization and modeling approaches for inducing behavioral, affective, and attitudinal changes." Journal of Personality and Social Psychology 13: 173–99.

Bandura, A., R. W. Jeffery, and E. Gajdos

1975 "Generalizing change through participant modeling with self-directed mastery." Behavior Research and Therapy 13: 141–52.

Bandura, A., R. W. Jeffery, and C. L. Wright

1974 "Efficacy of participant modeling as a function of response induction aids." Journal of Abnormal Psychology 83: 56–64.

Bandura, A. and F. L. Menlove

1968 "Factors determining vicarious extinction of avoidance behavior through symbolic modeling." Journal of Personality and Social Psychology 8: 99–108.

Barlow, D. H., H. Leitenberg, W. S. Agras, and J. P. Wincze

1969 "The transfer gap in systematic desensitization: an analogue study." Behavior Research and Therapy 7: 191–96.

Blanchard, E. B.

1970a "The generalization of vicarious extinction effects." Behaviour Research and Therapy 7: 323–30.

1970b "Relative contributions of modeling, informational influences, and physical contact in extinction of phobic behavior." Journal of Abnormal Psychology 76: 55–61.

Borkovec, T. D.

1973 "The role of expectancy and physiological feedback in fear research: A review with special reference to subject characteristics." Behavior Therapy 4: 491–505.

Bootzin, R. R., C. P. Herman, and P. Nicassio

1976 "The power of suggestion: Another examination of misattribution and insomnia." Journal of Personality and Social Psychology 34: 673–79.

Calvert-Boyanowsky, J., and H. Leventhal

1975 "The role of information in attenuating behavioral responses to stress: a reinterpretation of the misattribution phenomenon." Journal of Personality and Social Psychology 32: 214–21.

Emmelkamp, P. N. G. and H. Wessels

1975 "Flooding in imagination vs. flooding *in vivo:* a comparison with agoraphobics." Behaviour Research and Therapy 13: 7–15.

Flanders, J. P.

1968 "A review of research on imitative behavior." Psychological Bulletin 69: 316–37.

Gaupp, L. A., R. M. Stern, and G. G. Galbraith

1972 "False heart-rate feedback and reciprocal inhibition by aversion relief in the treatment of snake avoidance behavior." Behavior Therapy 3: 7–20.

Howlett, S. C. and M. M. Nawas

1971 "Exposure to aversive imagery and suggestion in systematic desensitization." In R. D. Rubin, A. A. Lazarus, H. Fensterheim, and C. M. Franks (eds.), Advances in Behavior Therapy. New York: Academic Press.

Kazdin, A. E.

1973 "Covert modeling and reduction of avoidance behavior." Journal of Abnormal Psychology 81: 87–95.

1974a "Comparative effects of some variations of covert modeling." Journal of Behavior Therapy and Experimental Psychiatry 5: 225–32.

1974b "Covert modeling, model similarity, and reduction of avoidance behavior." Behavior Therapy 5: 325–40.

1974c "Effects of covert modeling and reinforcement on assertive behavior." Journal of Abnormal Psychology 83: 240–52.

1975 "Covert modeling, imagery assessment, and assertive behavior." Journal of Consulting and Clinical Psychology 43: 761–24.

1976 "Effects of covert modeling, multiple models, and model reinforcement on assertive behavior." Behavior Therapy 7: 211–22.

Kellogg, R. and R. S. Baron

1975 "Attribution theory, insomnia, and the reverse placebo effect: a reversal of Storms and Nisbett's findings." Journal of Personality and Social Psychology 32: 231–36.

Kent, R. N., G. T. Wilson, and R. Nelson

1972 "Effects of false heart-rate feedback on avoidance behavior: an investigation of 'cognitive desensitization'." Behavior Therapy 3: 1–6.

Lewis, S.

1974 "A comparison of behavior therapy techniques in the reduction of fearful avoidance behavior." Behavior Therapy 5: 648–55.

Lick, J. and R. Bootzin.

1975 "Expectancy factors in the treatment of fear: methodological and theoretical issues." Psychological Bulletin 82: 917–31.

Litvak, S. B.

1969 "A comparison of two brief group behavior therapy techniques on the reduction of avoidance behavior." The Psychological Record 19: 329–34.

LoPiccolo, J.

1970 "Effective components of systematic desensitization." (Doctoral dissertation, Yale University, 1969). Dissertation Abstracts International 31: 1543B (University Microfilms No. 70-16300).

McGlynn, F. D. and R. H. Mapp

1970 "Systematic desensitization of snake-avoidance following three types of suggestion." Behavior Research and Therapy 8: 197–201.

McGlynn, F. D., W. L. Mealiea, and M. M. Nawas

1969 "Systematic desensitization of snake-avoidance under two conditons of suggestion." Psychological Reports 25: 220-22.

McGlynn, F. D., E. J. Reynolds, and L. H. Linder

1971 "Systematic desensitization with pre-treatment and intra-treatment therapeutic instructions." Behavior Research and Therapy 9: 57–63.

Meichenbaum, D. H.

1971 "Examination of model characteristics in reducing avoidance behavior." Journal of Personality and Social Psychology 17: 298–307.

Moore, N.

1965 "Behaviour therapy in bronchial asthma: a controlled study." Journal of Psychosomatic Research 9: 257–76.

Nisbett, R. E. and S. Schachter

1966 "Cognitive manipulation of pain." Journal of Experimental Social Psychology 2: 227–36.

Notterman, J. M., W. N. Schoenfeld, and P. J. Bersh

1952 "A comparison of three extinction procedures following heart rate conditioning." Journal of Abnormal and Social Psychology 47: 674–77.

Paul, G. L.

1966 Insight vs. Desensitization in Psychotherapy. Stanford, Calif.: Stanford University Press.

Rabavilas, A. D., J. C. Boulougouris, and C. Stefanis

1976 "Duration of flooding sessions in the treatment of obsessive-compulsive patients." Behaviour Research and Therapy 14: 349–55.

Ritter, B.
1969 "The use of contact desensitization, demonstration-plus-participation, and demonstration alone in the treatment of acrophobia." Behaviour Research and Therapy 7: 157–64.
Roper, G., S. Rachman, and I. Marks
1975 "Passive and participant modelling in exposure treatment of obsessive-compulsive neurotics." Behaviour Research and Therapy 13: 271–79.
Rosen, G. M., E. Rosen, and J. B. Reid
1972 "Cognitive desensitization and avoidance behavior: a reevaluation." Journal of Abnormal Psychology 80: 176–82.
Ross, L., J. Rodin, and P. T. Zimbardo
1969 "Toward an attribution therapy: the reduction of fear through induced cognitive-emotional misattribution." Journal of Personality and Social Psychology 12: 279–88.
Schachter, S.
1964 "The interaction of cognitive and physiological determinants of emotional state." In L. Berkowitz (ed.), Advances in Experimental Social Psychology. New York: Academic Press.
Sherman, A. R.
1972 "Real-life exposure as a primary therapeutic factor in the desensitization treatment of fear." Journal of Abnormal Psychology 79: 19–28.
Singerman, K. J., T. D. Borkovec, and R. S. Baron
1976 "Failure of a 'misattribution therapy' manipulation with a clinically relevant target behavior." Behavior Therapy 7: 306–13.
Stern, R. and I. Marks
1973 "Brief and prolonged flooding: a comparison in agoraphobic patients." Archives of General Psychiatry 28: 270–76.
Strahley, D. F.
1966 "Systematic desensitization and counterphobic treatment of an irrational fear of snakes." (Doctoral dissertation, University of Tennessee, 1965). Dissertation abstracts 27: 973B (University Microfilms No.66-5366).
Sushinsky, L. W. and R. R. Bootzin
1970 "Cognitive desensitization as a model of systematic desensitization." Behaviour Research and Therapy 8: 29–33.
Szpiler, J. A. and S. Epstein
1976 "Availability of an avoidance response as related to autonomic arousal." Journal of Abnormal Psychology 85: 73–82.
Thase, M. E. and M. K. Moss
1976 "The relative efficacy of covert modeling procedures and guided participant modeling in the reduction of avoidance behavior." Journal of Behavior Therapy and Experimental Psychiatry 7: 7–12.
Valins, S. and R. E. Nisbett
1971 Attribution Processes in the Development and Treatment of Emotional Disorders. Morristown, N. J.: General Learning Press.
Valins, S. and A. Ray
1967 "Effects of cognitive desensitization on avoidance behaviour." Journal of Personality and Social Psychology 7: 345–50.
Watson, J. P., G. E. Mullett, and H. Pillay
1973 "The effects of prolonged exposure to phobic situations upon agoraphobic patients treated in groups." Behaviour Research and Therapy 11: 531–45.
Weiner, B.
1972 Theories of Motivation. Chicago: Markham.
Wolpe, J.
1974 The Practice of Behavior Therapy. New York: Pergamon Press.

Self-Schemata and Processing Information About the Self

HAZEL MARKUS

4

The quantity and variety of social stimulation available at any time is vastly greater than a person can process or even attend to. Therefore, individuals are necessarily selective in what they notice, learn, remember, or infer in any situation. These elective tendencies, of course, are not random but depend on some internal cognitive structures which allow the individual to process the incoming information with some degree of efficiency. Recently, these structures for encoding and representing information have been called *frames* (Minsky, 1975), *scripts* (Abelson, 1975), and *schemata* (Bobrow & Norman, 1975; Stotland & Canon, 1972; Tesser & Conlee, 1975).

The influence of cognitive structures on the selection and organization of information is probably most apparent when we process information about ourselves. A substantial amount of information processed by an individual (some might even argue a majority of information) is information about the self, and a variety of cognitive structures are necessarily involved in processing this information. Yet in research on the self, in the personality area for example, there has been a notable lack of attention to the structures used in encoding one's own behavior and in the processing of information about one's own behavior. Research on self-perception (Bem, 1967, 1972) and research on self-monitoring (Snyder, 1974; Snyder & Monson, 1975) clearly suggest that the individual is an active,

Source: Hazel Markus, "Self-Schemata and Processing Information About the Self," Journal of Personality and Social Psychology 35 (1977): 63–78.

constructive information processor, but no specific cognitive structures have yet been implicated in this theorizing and research.

It is proposed here that attempts to organize, summarize, or explain one's own behavior in a particular domain will result in the formation of cognitive structures about the self or what might be called self-schemata. *Self-schemata are cognitive generalizations about the self, derived from past experience, that organize and guide the processing of self-related information contained in the individual's social experiences.* The main purpose of the present studies is to examine some functions of self-schemata in the processing of information about the self.

Self-schemata include cognitive representations derived from *specific* events and situations involving the individual (e.g., "I hesitated before speaking in yesterday's discussion because I wasn't sure I was right, only to hear someone else make the same point") as well as more *general* representations derived from the repeated categorization and subsequent evaluation of the person's behavior by himself and by others around him (e.g., "I am very talkative in groups of three or four, but shy in large gatherings," "I am generous," "I am creative," or "I am independent").

Self-schemata are constructed from information processed by the individual in the past and influence both input and output of information related to the self. They represent the way the self has been differentiated and articulated in memory. Once established, these schemata function as selective mechanisms which determine whether information is attended to, how it is structured, how much importance is attached to it, and what happens to it subsequently. As individuals accumulate repeated experiences of a certain type, their self-schemata become increasingly resistant to inconsistent or contradictory information, although they are never totally invulnerable to it.

Self-schemata can be viewed as a reflection of the invariances people have discovered in their own social behavior. They represent patterns of behavior that have been observed repeatedly, to the point where a framework is generated that allows one to make inferences from scant information or to quickly streamline and interpret complex sequences of events. To the extent that our own behavior exhibits some regularity or redundancy, self-schemata will be generated because they are useful in understanding intentions and feelings and in identifying likely or appropriate patterns of behavior. While a self-schemata is an organization of the representations of past behavior, it is more than a "depository." It serves an important processing function and allows an individual to go beyond the information currently available. The concept of self-schema implies that information about the self in some area has been categorized or organized and that the result of this organization is a discernible pattern which may be used as a basis for future judgments, decisions, inferences, or predictions about the self.

There is substantial historical precedent for the schema term and for schemalike concepts, and it would entail a very lengthy discussion to trace the history of the term (cf. Bartlett, 1932; Kelley, 1972; Kelly, 1955; Piaget, 1951). In social psychology, schemalike concepts (e.g., causal schemata, scripts, implicit personality theories) have generally been vaguely defined heuristics with no real empirical moorings. Despite their assumed cognitive consequences, they have been viewed primarily as epiphenomena, inferred on the basis of behavior or invoked in various post hoc explanations. The investigation of self-schemata requires examining the hypothesized functions of schemata for their particular empirical implications. To date this has not been done.

Recent work in the general area of cognition suggests a number of ways of investigating self-schemata. This work provides models of information processing (e.g., Anderson & Bower, 1973; Atkinson & Shiffrin, 1968; Erdelyi, 1974), indicates the possible functions of cognitive structures, and makes use of a variety of measures (recognition, recall, response latency, etc.) and techniques (signal detection, chronometric descriptions of information flow, etc.) capable of empirically identifying these functions. The experimental work in this area, however, has concentrated largely on the processing of neutral or nonsense material. With the exception of some recent works (Mischel, Ebbesen, & Zeiss, 1976), there has been little empirical work on the influence of cognitive structures on the selective processing of significant *social* information (e.g., information about important aspects of one's self).

The idea of self-schemata as cognitive generalizations about the self has a number of implications for the empirical work on personality and cross-situational consistency. For example, an endorsement of a trait adjective as self-descriptive or an endorsement of an item on a self-rating scale *may* reflect an underlying, well-articulated self-schema. It is equally possible, however, that the mark on the self-rating scale is not the product of a well-specified schema, but is instead the result of the favorability of the trait term, the context of the situation, the necessity for a response, or other experimental demands. *Only when a self-description derives from a well-articulated generalization about the self can it be expected to converge and form a consistent pattern with the individual's other judgments, decisions, and actions.* Thus, a person who does not really think about herself as conscientious, yet would not object to labeling herself as such, cannot be expected to react to being late for an appointment in the same way as one who actively conceives of herself as conscientious, who can readily describe numerous displays of conscientiousness in the past, and who can enumerate the way she insures future conscientious behavior on her part.

To demonstrate the construct validity of the concept of self-schemata, a number of empirical referents can be specified. If self-schemata are built up from cognitive representations of past experiences, individual differences in self-schemata should be readily discovered because individuals clearly differ in their past experiences. If a person has a developed self-schema, he should be readily able to (a) process information about the self in the given domain (e.g., make judgments or decisions) with relative ease, (b) retrieve behavioral evidence from the domain, (c) predict his own future behavior in the domain, and (d) resist counterschematic information about himself. If a person has had relatively little experience in a given domain of social behavior or has not attended to behavior in this domain, then it is unlikely that he will have developed an articulated self-schema.

Consistency in patterns of response on a number of self-description tasks, as well as convergence in results from a number of diverse cognitive tasks involving self-judgments, should provide evidence for the existence of an organization of knowledge about the self on a particular dimension of behavior, or a self-schema. To the extent that individuals do not possess an articulated self-schema on a particular dimension of behavior, they will not exhibit consistency in response. Nor will they display the discrimination necessary for the efficient processing of information and the prediction of future behavior along this dimension.

The procedure of the first study is to select a dimension of behavior, to identify individuals with schemata and those without schemata on this dimension, and then to compare their performance on a variety of cognitive tasks. Several tasks utilizing self-rating, self-description, and prediction of behavior are combined to determine whether the processing of information about one's self varies systematically as a function of self-schemata. . . .

STUDY 1

This study is concerned with the impact of self-schemata on the selection and processing of information about the self. Individuals with self-schemata along a particular dimension of behavior are compared with individuals without such self-schemata. Also compared are individuals with different self-schemata along the same dimension of behavior. Specifically, it is hypothesized that a self-schema will determine the type of self-judgments that are made and that these judgments will vary in latency depending on the presence and content of self-schemata. Also, individuals with self-schemata should find it easier to describe specific behavior that is related to their schema and should be relatively more certain about prediction of their behavior along this dimension than individuals without schemata.

Method

To gain a preliminary idea of each subject's self-schema on various dimensions, a number of self-rating scales were administered in introductory psychology classes. The most appropriate pattern of variation in self-ratings was found on the independence-dependence dimension and thus it was selected as the dimension for further study. From among the individuals completing this questionnaire, 48 were selected to participate individually in the laboratory sessions.

The first laboratory session consisted of three separate cognitive tasks designed to assess the influence of self-schemata about independence on the processing of information about the self. These included:

1. Content and Latency of Self-Description Subjects were given a number of trait adjectives associated with independence and dependence and were asked to indicate for each whether it was self-descriptive or not. Response latency was recorded for each judgment.

2. Supplying Behavioral Evidence for Self-Description Subjects were asked to select trait adjectives that were self-descriptive and then to cite instances from their own past behavior to support their endorsement of a particular adjective as self-descriptive.

3. Predicting the Likelihood of Behavior Subjects were given a series of descriptions of independent and dependent behavior and were asked to judge how likely it was they would behave in these ways.

Subjects For the questionnaire phase of the experiment, subjects were 101 female students in introductory psychology classes at a large university. Subjects for the first laboratory sessions were 48 students selected from this group. Only female students were used in this study because the distribution of self-ratings on various dimensions appears to differ with sex. Using male and female students would have required selecting more dimensions.

Materials and Procedures Initial Questionnaire Individuals in introductory psychology classes were asked to rate themselves on the Gough-Heilbrun Adjective Check List (Gough & Heilbrun, 1965) and on several semantic differential scales describing a variety of behavioral domains. On the latter measure, subjects were also asked to rate the importance of each semantic dimension to their self-description. From these respondents, three groups of 16 subjects each were selected to participate in the experimental sessions.

1. Independents Individuals who rated themselves at the extreme end (points 8–11 on an 11-point scale) on at least two of the following semantic differential scales: Independent-Dependent, Individualist-Conformist, or Leader-Follower, and who rated these dimensions as important (points 8–11 on an 11-point scale), and who checked themselves as "independent" on the adjective checklist were termed *Independents.*[2]

2. Dependents Individuals who rated themselves at the opposite end (points 1–4) on at least two of these scales, and who rated these dimensions as important (points 8–11 on an 11-point scale), and who checked themselves as "dependent" on the adjective checklist were termed *Dependents.*

3. Aschematics Individuals who rated themselves in the middle range (points 5–7) on at least two of these three scales, and fell in the lower portion of the distribution on the importance scale, and did not check themselves as either "independent" or "dependent" on the adjective checklist were termed *Aschematics.* The term aschematic is used here to mean without schema on this particular dimension.[3]

Invoking the importance criterion conjointly with the extremity criterion made it possible to avoid confusing Aschematics with persons who act (and think of themselves) as independent in some classes of situations and as dependent in other classes of situations, and do so consistently. Making such fine discriminations would lead these individuals to develop a fairly well-articulated conception of the independence domain of social behavior, and thus it would be incorrect to classify them as Aschematics. However, if these people had a well-articulated conception of themselves as both dependent and independent, they would no doubt be quite sensitive to social behavior in the domain of independence and would consider it to be a significant and important area. Hence, they would not be classified as Aschematics according to our criteria. Among the Aschematics the average importance rating on the three semantic differential scales was 6.4, while among the Schematics it was 9.5.

Three to four weeks after the questionnaire was administered, the 48 subjects were called individually to the laboratory and received identical treatment. They were not informed of a connection between this session and the questionnaire, and it is unlikely that they could have inferred such a connection since different experimenters were used.

Task 1: Content and Latency of Self-Description Sixty-nine trait adjectives were prepared on 2 x 2 inch (5 x 5 cm) slides; 15 had been previously judged (by another group of 50 subjects) to be related to independence and nonconformity (independent words) and 15 were judged to be related to dependence and conformity (dependent words). These 30 words were the critical schema-related stimuli.[4] Thirty other words, included for comparison with the schema-related adjectives, clustered around the notions of creativity and noncreativity and were used as control words. In each group of 30 words, 10 were negatively rated, 10 were positively rated, and 10 neutral, according to Anderson's (1968) list of the likableness of 555 trait adjectives. The words were either of high frequency or moderate frequency (according to the norms of Carroll, Davies, & Richman, 1971). The remaining 9 words were 3 practice adjectives, 3 adjectives which nearly all subjects had indicated were self-descriptive on the initial questionnaire (honest, intelligent, friendly), and 3 adjectives which nearly all subjects had indicated were not self-descriptive (rude, obnoxious, unscrupulous).

Each of these 69 adjectives was presented on the screen for 2 seconds by a slide projector activated by the experimenter. Following the presentation of a word, the subject was required to respond by pushing a *me* button if the word was self-descriptive, or a *not me* button if the word was not self-descriptive. The response stopped an electronic clock which began with the presentation of the stimulus. The subject had to respond with one of the two buttons before the next stimulus would appear. For each word the experimenter recorded both response latency and the choice of *me* or *not me*. Subjects were not aware that response latency was being measured. Four different randomly determined orders of presentations were used for the slides, with 12 subjects in each order. In addition, for half of the subjects the *me* button was on the right side of the panel and for the remaining half on the left side. To insure that individuals were associating similar types of behaviors to the trait adjectives, a particular context was specified for the self-judgments. The instructions were:

When you are making these decisions about yourself, try to imagine yourself in a typical group situation, one that might occur for example, in a classroom, in the dorm lounge, or at a meeting in a friend's home. You are together to discuss an important and controversial issue and to make some decisions about it. Many of the people in the group you know or are familiar to you, while others are not.

Task 2: Supplying Behavioral Evidence for Self-Descriptions After the categorization task, each subject received a booklet containing 16 words (1 on each page) from the set described in Task 1. Seven of these words were from the set of independent words and 7 were from the set of dependent words. Two additional words were from the creative/noncreative set. Of the 16 words, 4 were positively rated for likeableness, 4 were negatively rated, and 8 were neutral. The order of the adjectives in each booklet was randomly determined. Subjects were given written instructions to circle each adjective they considered to be self-descriptive and were also asked the following:

Immediately after you circle an adjective, list the reasons you feel this adjective is self-descriptive. Give specific evidence from your own past behavior to indicate why you feel a particular trait is self-descriptive. . . . List the first kinds of behaviors that come to your mind. Do not worry about how other people might interpret a particular behavior; use your own frame of reference. (Several examples were given.)

Task 3: Predicting the Likelihood of Behavior The third task utilized a series of specific behavioral descriptions taken from a large number of descriptions that had been rated by a separate group of 40 introductory psychology students as characterizing either independence and nonconformity or dependence and conformity. This outside group of subjects was asked to decide how they would label or categorize each act if they saw it or if they heard someone describe themselves in these terms. The final list included 10 pairs of behavioral descriptions matched in content but differing in the way the behavior would be categorized, for example, "You hesitate before commenting, only to hear someone else make the point you had in mind" (rated dependent) and "You speak up as soon as you have some comments on the issue being discussed" (rated independent). Several filler items also were included. A context for the behavioral descriptions similar to the one in Task 1 was provided and then the subjects were given written instructions which read:

Listed below are a number of behaviors and reactions that might be true of you in a gathering like this. For each one, indicate how likely or how probable it is that you would behave or react in this way. You may assign each item any number from 0 to 100. A 0 means that this could not be true of you, that it is extremely unlikely that you would act or feel this way. A 100 means that this could very well be true of you, that it is likely that you would act or feel this way.

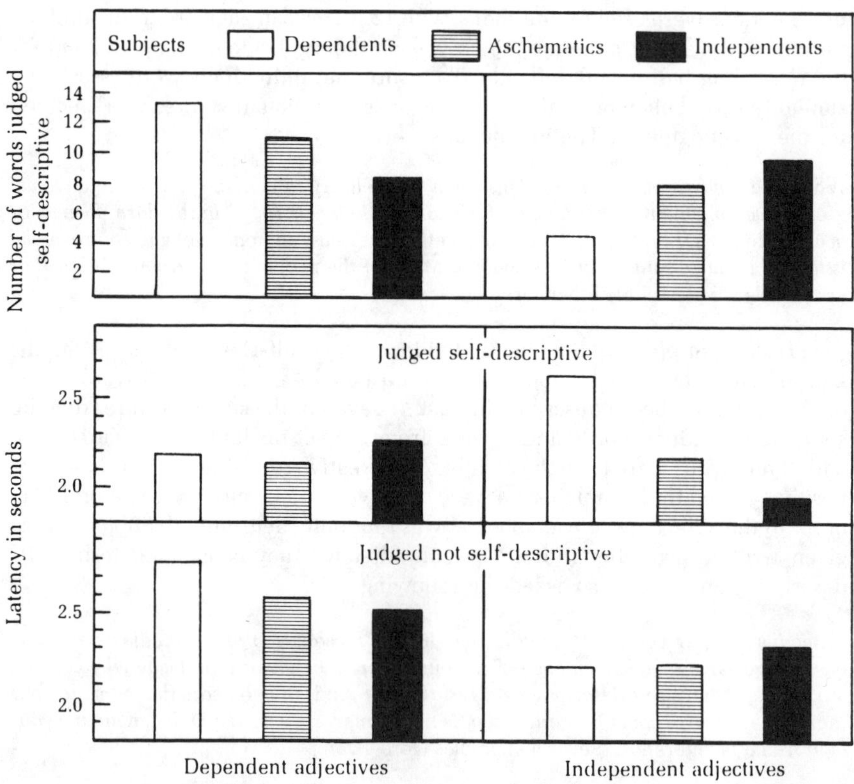

FIGURE 1 Top panel: Mean number of independent and dependent adjectives judged as self-descriptive. Bottom panel: Mean response latency for independent and dependent adjectives judged as self-descriptive and as not self-descriptive

Results

For the purpose of analysis, subjects were divided into three groups labeled Independents, Dependents, and Aschematics, as described in the Procedure section.

Task 1: Content and Latency of Self-Description As shown in the top panel of Figure 1, the three groups of subjects clearly differed in the average number of the 15 dependent words judged as self-descriptive, $F\,(2,45) = 14.89$, $p < .001$. The three groups also differed in the average number of the 15 independent adjectives judged as self-descriptive, $F\,(2,45) = 9.27$, $p < .001$. Using $p < .05$ as a criterion, Newman-Keuls comparisons showed that Dependents judged significantly more dependent words as self-descriptive than did Independents, and conversely, Independents judged significantly more independent words as self-descriptive than did Dependents.

The bottom panel of Figure 1 presents the average response latencies for self-descriptive judgments (*me*) and for not self-descriptive judgments (*not me*) for the independent and dependent adjectives. Dependent subjects were reliably faster at making *me* judgments for dependent words than for independent words, $t\,(15) = 2.63$, $p < .01$.[5] Congruently, Independent subjects were reliably faster at making *me* judgments for independent adjectives than for dependent adjectives, $t\,(15) = 2.72$, $p < .01$. The Aschematics, however, did not differ in response latency for independent and dependent words.

When the top and bottom panels in Figure 1 are considered together, a number of other points about the self-categorization of these three groups of subjects can be made. A *me* response to a particular adjective may be the result of an individual labeling her behavior or reactions in this way or thinking about herself in these terms. But it may also be the result of several other considerations, such as the positivity or social desirability of a particular adjective. Looking within groups, it can be seen from the top panel that Dependent subjects responded *me* to significantly more dependent words than independent words; there is a clear differentiation here, $t\,(15) = 10.55$, $p < .001$. Independent subjects however, although responding *me* to more independent words than either of the other two groups of subjects, found nearly as many dependent adjectives to be self-descriptive, $t\,(15) < 1$. On the basis of these findings alone, one might conclude that this group does not use independent or dependent words differentially or that independence is not a meaningful dimension for these subjects. The bottom panel indicates that this is not the case, however. Independent subjects respond much faster to the independent words than they do the dependent words. The faster processing times for the independent words suggest that it is indeed easier for Independent subjects to think about themselves in these terms or that they are used to thinking about themselves in these terms.

The latency measure is also useful in interpreting the results of the Aschematic group. From the top panel it can be seen that Aschematics respond *me* to more dependent words than independent words, $t\,(15) = 2.42$, $p < .05$. If the response latencies for these judgments are ignored, one might take this to mean that these subjects are similar to the Dependents. It is evident, however, that Aschematic subjects do not really use these two sets of words differentially in describing themselves in the same way Dependent subjects do. There is no difference among Aschematic subjects in processing time for the two sets of words. Even though they were constrained to think of a specific social situation, Aschematics appear to be equally at ease labeling their behavior with independent or dependent adjectives.[6]

Response latency for self-categorization appears to be a sensitive measure which reveals variations in judgments that rating scales and checklists cannot. Endorsements which result from the positivity or desirability of a stimulus can potentially be separated from responses which reflect more valid self-characterizations. This is clearly demonstrated in Figure 2. The top panel shows the responses of three groups of subjects to the three control words that were included in the list of presented adjectives. The number of subjects out of the total

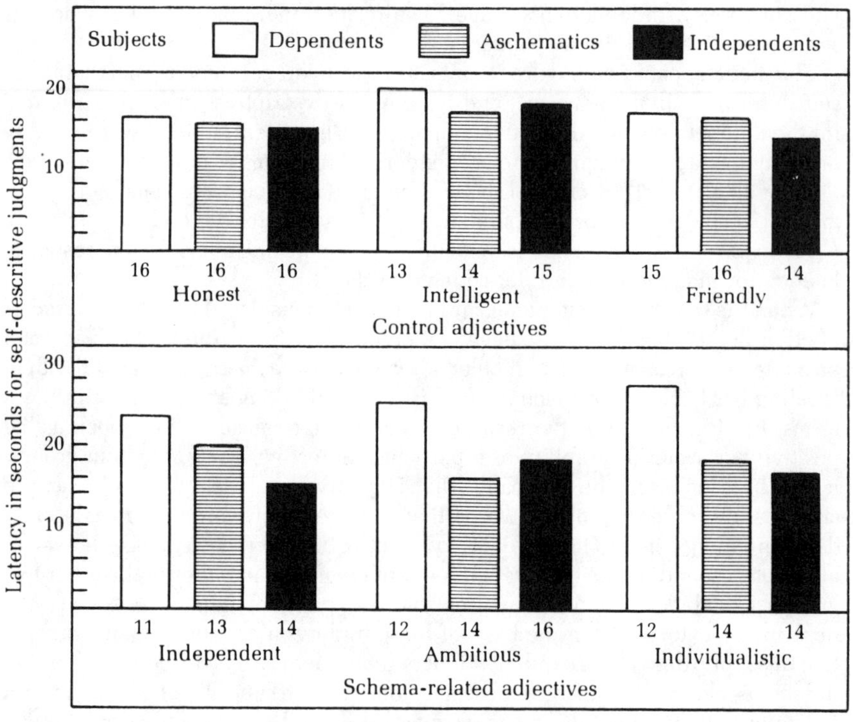

FIGURE 2 Mean response latency for schema-related and control adjectives

16 that responded *me* to each word is shown beneath the bar. Not surprisingly, nearly all subjects viewed themselves as honest, intelligent, and friendly. And there are no differences among the three groups in the processing time for these adjectives. The overall average latency for these three words was much shorter (1.67 sec) than the overall average latency for all words (2.23 sec). These adjectives appear to be synonymous with general "goodness" and do not convey unique information about an individual. The three groups of subjects also did not differ in processing time for *not me* judgments to the negatively rated adjectives rude, obnoxious, and unscrupulous.

This was not true, however, for other adjectives which presumably are tied to more specifically defined behaviors. The bottom panel of Figure 2 shows the responses of the three groups of subjects to three schema-related words, that is, three words from the set of independent words shown to subjects. Here again, just on the basis of their overt responses, it would appear that these subjects did not differ in their characterization of themselves, as the clear majority of subjects also responded *me* to these three schema-related words. The latency measures exhibited a much different pattern, however. Dependent subjects, for the most part, indicated that they were independent, ambitious, and individualistic, but it took them significantly longer to make this judgment than it did for Independent subjects. Separate analyses of variance performed on the response latencies for these three words yielded significant differences among the three groups of subjects: ambitious, $F(2,35) = 6.59$, $p < .01$; *independent*, $F(2,35) = 6.59$, $p < .01$; *individualistic*, $F(2,37) = 4.56$, $p < .01$. It is probable that Dependent subjects would like to label themselves with these words and subsequently do, but they experience some difficulty endorsing the words, a difficulty they do not experience with the dependent words. This result cannot be explained by assuming that Dependent subjects just take longer to make self-judgments, for on the control adjectives the latencies of the Dependents did not differ from those of the other groups of subjects. The faster processing times of the Independent subjects on schema-related words may be indicative of schemata which contain information about independence and individualism. Dependent subjects do not have information about themselves which might be reasonably labeled in this way, and their hesitation in making unsubstantiated judgments about themselves is reflected in relatively longer latencies.

The lack of differentiation in response latency to the schema-related adjectives shown by the Aschematics relative to the other two groups of subjects has been interpreted as evidence for the absence of a schema on this dimension. There is an alternative explanation, however. It may be that a clear self-definition in terms of one set of adjectives or another is not a result of past behavior which has been categorized or labeled in this way, but rather a function of general cognitive differentiation or articulation. Independents and Dependents might be individuals who generally prefer to have things compartmentalized along a number of different dimensions. Aschematics, in contrast, may have global or undifferentiated cognitive styles. A direct test of this possibility cannot be made given the present data. However, as an indirect test, an index which reflected the articulation of the schema for each subject was calculated on the basis of the number of independent and dependent words judged *me* and *not me*. The measure was the Kendall τ_b and it reflected a subject's departure from the standard of responding *me* to all 15 independent words and *not me* to all 15 dependent words. The closer the value to 1 or −1, the more clearly the subject defines herself on this dimension. This measure was also calculated for each subject on the basis of her *me* responses to the 30 creative/noncreative adjectives which were included in the list presented to subjects. A cognitive style explanation would predict that subjects with high τ_b values (either positive or negative) on the independent/dependent adjectives would also be the subjects with high absolute values of τ_b on the creative/noncreative words, reflecting a general tendency toward differentiation or articulation. In fact, there was no association between the sets of τ_b absolute values for Independents ($r = .00$), Dependents ($r = -.07$), or Aschematics ($r = -.14$).

The fact that subjects with schemata on independence-dependence do not necessarily have schemata on creativity-noncreativity and vice versa indicates that differences in self-categorizations may be the result of an individual's behavior and its subsequent cognitive interpretation rather than a reflection of differences in the general complexity of cognitive structure. It is also consistent with the idea that individuals develop schemata on dimensions they choose to attend to and do not develop schemata on others.

Task 2: Supplying Behavioral Evidence for Self-Description In this task, it was hypothesized that if one has a schema which is a reflection of past behavior, then one should be readily able to provide specific behavioral evidence related to it; that is, to generate specific instances of behavior which were labeled or categorized by oneself or others in a particular way.

This task appeared to be generally meaningful to subjects and they performed it with little difficulty. For example, the dependent adjective *conforming* elicited responses such as "I didn't go to any of the rallies about the teaching-fellow strike because my friends didn't" or "I watched a television show I couldn't stand last night just to save a hassle with my roommates" or "I pierced my ears because all my friends did."

Independent subjects wrote more behavioral descriptions for independent words than did either of the other two groups of subjects. The differences in the mean number of behavioral examples written for each independent adjective for the three groups were significant, $F\ (2,45) = 4.91$, $p < .005$. Across all of the seven independent adjectives, the Independent subjects supplied almost one specific example of behavior for each word (0.93 behavioral descriptions per adjective) compared to 0.56 for the Aschematics and 0.36 for the Dependent subjects. A significant opposite pattern occurred for the dependent words, $F\ (2,45) = 3.59$, $p < .05$.

Across all the adjectives, the subjects with schemata (the Dependents and the Independents) and the Aschematics did not differ in the average number of words that were judged as self-descriptive, but they did differ in the average number of behavioral descriptions that were written for each word, $t\,(46) = 1.78$, $p < .05$,[7] with the Aschematics supplying somewhat fewer examples of behavior than subjects with schemata. This result is consistent with the expectation that individuals without schemata on this dimension probably have not used many independent or dependent adjectives to label their behavior, and thus it should be more difficult for them to supply specific behavioral descriptions.

A more detailed analysis of the individual words revealed that the smaller number of behavioral examples supplied by the Aschematics was primarily the result of these subjects producing fewer examples for the four negatively rated adjectives. It is interesting in this respect that for the Aschematics there was a substantial relationship between the percentage of individuals judging a word as self-descriptive and the positivity of the word ($r = .53$, $p < .05$). This relationship was not evident for the other two groups of subjects (Dependents, $r = .11$; Independents, $r = .21$). As a group, then, the Aschematics appear to be relatively more affected by the positivity of the adjective and may use this attribute to decide whether a particular word is self-descriptive. Independent and Dependent subjects are relatively more willing to use negative labels for their behavior. It may be that an individual with a schema about her behavior on a particular dimension is aware of both the positive and negative aspects of it and has evidence for both.

This task employed 14 of the same adjectives used in Task 1 and thus it is possible to evaluate the consistency of self-descriptive responses for the three groups of subjects. For the Independents, the correlation between *me* responses on the two tasks was 0.64 ($p < .01$), for Dependents 0.56 ($p < .05$), and for the Aschematics it was 0.20. Of the 14 adjectives employed in this task, independent subjects exhibited the shortest processing time for the words *independent, self-confident,* and *cooperative* in Task 1. In the present task, these were the 3 words that were most likely to be judged self-descriptive by Independent subjects, and in addition, these were the 3 words that elicited the largest number of behavioral descriptions. Dependent subjects responded fastest to the adjectives *cooperative, cautious,* and *moderate* in Task 1. Again, in this task these were the words that were the most likely to be judged self-descriptive by the Dependent subjects and also the words for which they gave the greatest number of behavioral descriptions. This pattern, however, was not found for the Aschematic subjects; the adjectives requiring the least processing times were not those most likely to be judged self-descriptive. The lack of congruence between these two judgments suggests either that Aschematics were fluctuating from Task 1 to Task 2 on which adjectives they considered to be self-descriptive or that different types of considerations were mediating the two judgments. For the Independents and the Dependents, the two judgments appear to be mediated by a similar type of consideration, presumably whether or not they have previously characterized or labeled their own behavior in this way.

Task 3: Predicting the Likelihood of Behavior In this task, it was expected that people with self-schemata on the independence-dependence dimension would assign either relatively higher or lower probabilities to independent and dependent behaviors than individuals who do not have a self-schema on this dimension of behavior. It was assumed that subjects with self-schemata would be relatively more aware or more certain of what behaviors would be elicited from them in these situations and could make more confident predictions of their behavior.

Dependent subjects assigned a significantly higher likelihood to dependent behaviors than to independent behaviors, $t\ (15) = 3.30$, $p < .01$. In contrast, Independent subjects assigned a reliably higher likelihood to independent behaviors than they did to dependent behaviors, $t\ (15) = 3.31$, $p < .01$. For the Aschematics, however, there was no difference between the likelihood assigned to independent behaviors and the likelihood assigned dependent behaviors, $t\ (15) < 1$.

It was evident that the Independent and the Dependent subjects differ in the actions they think likely of themselves, although some items were better than others in differentiating among the groups. The average subjective likelihood assigned to the dependent behavior was 35.7 for Independent subjects, 45.9 for the Aschematic subjects, and 54.4 for Dependent subjects, $F\ (2, 45) = 5.57$, $p < .01$. The average likelihood assigned to the independent behaviors was 53.8 for Independent subjects, 45.7 for Aschematic subjects, and 37.1 for Dependent subjects, $F\ (2, 45) = 7.40$, $p < .001$.

Overall, the Independent and the Dependent subjects differ markedly from the Aschematic subjects. The former two groups are relatively polarized in their estimations of the probabilities of these behaviors occurring, indicating that they are more certain about what types of behavior might be characteristic of them in particular settings. For the independent behaviors, the average deviation from the mean likelihood rating was 7.60 for Independents, and –9.12 for Dependents. For the dependent behaviors the average deviation from the mean likelihood was –9.63 for the Independents and 8.99 for the Dependents. Aschematics, however, do not show this polarization in their judgments. For the independent behaviors their average deviation was 0.45, for dependent behaviors it was -.05. For these individuals there appears to be little difference in the subject likelihood of independent and dependent behaviors; they are equally likely to occur or not to occur. Recall again in this respect that the subjects were constrained to think of a fairly specific context. These data suggest, therefore, that the Aschematics have no articulated cognitive generalizations or self-schemata along the dimension of independence-dependence.

One possible alternative explanation for the lack of difference in the mean ratings of independent and dependent behaviors for Aschematics is that Aschematics are really a heterogeneous collection composed of approximately equal numbers of subjects responding like Independents and Dependents. However, inspection of the distributions of likelihood ratings yielded no evidence to support this possibility. The distributions of likelihood ratings for all three groups of subjects with respect to both independent and dependent behaviors are unimodal and fairly symmetric about the mean.

The consistent pattern of responses observed for the Independents and Dependents across these diverse tasks argues for the existence of prevailing self-schema which facilitates the processing of social information. Individuals assumed to have schemata clearly performed differently on these tasks than did individuals assumed not to have schemata.

Aschematics did not discriminate among the independent and dependent stimuli on any of the tasks. It seems that for these individuals, independence-dependence was not a meaningful dimension of behavior; that is, they did not categorize or make distinctions on the basis of the independence or dependence of their actions.

The pattern of findings describing the Aschematics clearly indicates why self-characterizations such as adjective self-descriptions may often be misleading as indicators of future behavior. For those individuals who had a self-schema about their independence or dependence, the responses to the self-categorization task were highly consistent with their responses to the other two tasks and would most likely be consistent with behavior along this dimension. The responses of the Aschematics to the self-categorization task, however, could not be generalized even to the other self-description tasks. It would be surprising, therefore, if these responses were consistent with observable behavior. . . .

The results of these studies have a number of implications for research on personality and the search for cross-situational consistency in behavior. It seems likely that those individuals who have schemata about themselves on a particular behavioral dimension are those most likely to display a correspondence between self-description and behavior and to exhibit cross-situational consistency on that dimension. In contrast, those individuals who have no clear schema about themselves are unlikely to exhibit such consistency in behavior. For example, Bem and Allen (1974) were able to identify a group of individuals who displayed substantial cross-situational consistency in behavior. Individuals who identified themselves as consistent on a particular trait dimension (claiming that they did not vary on this dimension across situations) exhibited substantial correspondence between self-description and behavior and were also cross-situationally consistent in their behavior. The subjects in Bem and Allen's studies who claimed they were consistent on a particular dimension may have been acknowledging a self-schema on this dimension. And the cross-situational consistency that was subsequently noted for these consistent individuals may have resulted from those individuals engaging in behavior that was motivated from a desire to be consistent with their self-schemata. Differences in the ways individuals generalize and interpret their own behavior may thus be a significant source of individual differences, and such differences may actually predict differential behavior.

These studies give empirical substance to the idea that not all people have a subjective position on every dimension of behavior. It is entirely possible that systematic effects in social behavior depend less on people having some amount of a particular substantive attribute, such as independence or dependence, and more on the readiness or ability to categorize behavior along certain dimensions. This, of course, was the notion behind Kelly's (1955) methodology of allowing the individual to generate his own constructs for categorizing himself and the social environment and is pertinent to Bem and Allen's (1974) call for an idiographic approach to personality. If the dimensions under study are not the ones an individual characteristically attends to, he cannot be expected to make corresponding conceptual and behavioral discriminations along that dimension.

The concept of self-schemata that function as selective mechanisms resulting in differential attention and processing of information about the self also has implications for self-perception and attribution theory. In the study of social attribution, there are a number of well-known studies (e.g., Davison & Valins, 1969; Schachter & Wheeler, 1962; Valins & Ray, 1967; Weick, 1967; Zimbardo, 1969) that reveal behavior changes in the absence of subsequent change in self-categorizations (how one says he thinks, feels, or is). These studies are discrepant with the model of self-attribution that assumes that inferences about internal states, dispositons, or attitudes follow from behavior and thus have been something of a puzzle for attribution theorists. Valins and Ray (1967), for example, gave snake phobic subjects false feedback about their fear of snakes.These subjects were able to approach a snake more closely than controls without false feedback. They did not, however, report themselves as any less fearful as a result of their experience. In view of the present results, this finding is perhaps not surprising. A correspondence between self-categorization and overt behavior depends on the mediating self-schemata. For example, snake phobic individuals probably have a fairly well-articulated self-schema about how they feel toward snakes. The elements of this generalization include cognitive representations of specific encounters with snakes and the subsequent evaluation of these encounters. If such an individual is induced to handle snakes, it does not follow that he will immediately perceive himself as no longer afraid of snakes. This type of dispositional attributions would be (a) based on only one isolated experience and (b) contradict a well-established schema. However, individuals with no particular generalizations about their attitudes towards snakes may readily interpret their positive experience with a snake as unambiguously self-diagnostic—as indicative that they don't mind snakes and are not afraid of them. If this argument is correct, it implies that individuals will use information about their own behavior to make an inference about their own internal state, disposition, or attitude only when the behavior appears to the individual to be related to the self-characterization to be made and when it does not run counter to a prevailing generalization about the self. Within an attribution theory framework, self-schemata can be viewed as implicit theories used by individuals to make sense of their own past behavior and to direct the course of future behavior. And a given chunk of behavioral information has decidedly different self-attribution consequences for an individual with an implicit theory or self-schema than it does for one without such a schema.

NOTES

1 Abelson, R. P. Script processing in attitude formation and decision making. Paper presented at the Eleventh Carnegie-Mellon Symposium on Cognition, April 24–26, 1975.

2 Although subjects were selected on the basis of their "extreme" scores on these self-rating scales, only 2 subjects of the 48 actually used the endpoints 11 or 1 in their self-ratings on the semantic differential scales.

3 Another indicator of a subject's self-schema about independence was her score on the Autonomy scale of the Gough-Heilbrun Adjective Check List (ACL). The Autonomy scale is one of the ACL's 24 empirically derived scales designed to correspond to dimensions of the California Psychological Inventory and Murray's need-press system. Autonomy is defined as the tendency to act independently of others or of social values and expectations. Subjects selected as Independents in this study were among the 25 with highest scores on this measure, and those selected as Dependents were among the 25 with lowest scores. Aschematics scored in the middle range on this measure. It is important to note that all of the subjects who would be labeled autonomous on the basis of this measure (that is, they were among the 25 highest scorers) also rated themselves extremely (points 8–11) on at least two of the semantic differential scales. Those who would be labeled nonautonomous or dependent on the basis of this measure also rated themselves extremely (points 1–5) on the three semantic differential scales.

4 The *independent* adjectives were individualistic, independent, ambitious, adventurous, self-confident, dominating, argumentative, aloof, arrogant, egotistical, unconventional, outspoken, aggressive, assertive, uninhibited. The *dependent* adjectives were dependable, cooperative, tactful, tolerant, unselfish, impressionable, conforming, dependent, timid, submissive, conventional, moderate, obliging, self-denying, cautious.

5 Except where specified, all t tests are two-tailed.

6 Overall, subjects find more dependent words than independent words to be self-descriptive, despite the fact that the two sets of words were initially matched for positivity and frequency. In fact, across all subjects an average of 7.4 independent words were judged to be self-descriptive compared to an average of 10.9 dependent words. This may also explain the relatively longer response times for *not me* judgments of dependent words obtained in all three groups of subjects. Across all subjects the average latency for a *not me* response to dependent words was 2.63 seconds compared with 2.22 seconds for independent words. It is possible that within the set of our 69 words (Anderson's subjects rated a set of 555 adjectives), the dependent words appeared as more positive or desirable, and thus it was difficult for subjects to respond *not me* to them.

7 One-tailed test of the hypothesis that individuals with schemata are able to provide more specific behavioral evidence for their self-judgments than Aschematics.

REFERENCES

Anderson, J. R. and G. H. Bower
1973 Human Associative Memory. Washington: V. H. Winston.
Anderson, N. H.
1968 "Likeableness ratings of 555 personality-trait words." Journal of Personality and Social Psychology 9: 272–79.
Atkinson, R. C. and R. M. Shiffrin
1968 "Human memory: a proposed system and its control processes." In K. W. Spence and J. T. Spence (eds.), Advances in the Psychology of Learning and Motivation Research and Theory, Vol. 2. New York: Academic Press.
Bartlett, F. C.
1932 Remembering. London: Cambridge University Press.
Bem, D. J.
1967 "Self-perception: an alternative interpretation of cognitive dissonance phenomena." Psychological Review 74: 183–200.
1972 "Self-perception theory." In L. Berkowitz (ed.), Advances in Experimental Social Psychology, Vol. 6. New York: Academic Press.
Bem, D. J. and A. Allen
1974 "On predicting some of the people some of the time: the search for cross-situational consistencies in behavior." Psychological Review 81: 506–20.
Bobrow, D. G. and D. A. Norman
1975 "Some principles of memory schemata." In D. G. Bobrow and A. Collins (eds.), Representation and Understanding: Studies in Cognitive Science. New York: Academic Press.
Carroll, J. B., P. Davies, and B. Richman
1971 Word Frequency Book. New York: American Heritage.
Davison, G. C. and S. Valins
1969 "Maintenance of self-attributed and drug-attributed behavior change." Journal of Personality and Social Psychology 11: 25–33.
Erdelyi, M. H.
1974 "A new look at the New Look: perceptual defense and vigilance." Psychological Review 81: 1–25.
Gough, H. G. and Heilbrun, A. B.
1965 The Adjective Check List Manual. Palo Alto, Calif.: Consulting Psychologists Press.
Kelley, H. H.
1972 "Causal schemata and the attribution process." In E. E. Jones, D. E. Kanouse, H. H. Kelley, R. E. Nisbett, S. Valins, and B. Weiner (eds.), Attribution: Perceiving the Causes of Behavior. New York: General Learning Press.
Kelly, G. A.
1955 The Psychology of Personal Constructs. New York: Norton.
Minsky, M.
1975 "A framework for representing knowledge." In P. Winston (ed.), The Psychology of Computer Vision. New York: McGraw-Hill.
Mischel, W., E. B. Ebbesen, and A. M. Zeiss
1976 "Determinants of selective memory about the self." Journal of Consulting and Clinical Psychology 44: 92–103.
Piaget, J.
1951 The Child's Conception of the World. New York: Humanities Press.

Schachter, S. and L. Wheeler
1962 "Epinephrine, chlorpromazine, and amusement." Journal of Abnormal and Social Psychology 65: 212–18.
Snyder, M.
1974 "Self-monitoring of expressive behavior." Journal of Personality and Social Psychology 30: 526–37.
Snyder, M. and T. C. Monson
1975 "Persons, situations, and the control of social behavior." Journal of Personality and Social Psychology 32: 637–44.
Stotland, E. and L. K. Canon
1972 Social Psychology: A Cognitive Approach. Philadelphia: Saunders.
Tesser, A. and M. C. Conlee
1975 "Some effects of time and thought on attitude polarization." Journal of Personality and Social Psychology 31: 262–70.
Valins, S. and A. A. Ray
1967 "Effects of cognitive desensitization of avoidance behavior." Journal of Personality and Social Psychology 7: 345–50.
Weick, K. E.
1967 "Dissonance and task enhancement: A problem for compensation theory?" Organizational Behavior and Human Performance 2: 175–216.
Zimbardo, P. G. (ed.)
1969 The Cognitive Control of Motivation. Glenview, Ill.: Scott, Foresman.

Effects of Objective Self-Awareness on Attribution of Causality

Shelley Duval
Robert A. Wicklund

5

Heider (1944, 1958) suggested that man attempts to bring order and meaning to his world by determining the causal antecedents of events. Since Heider's initial statement of what has come to be called attribution theory, several theorists have contributed important clarifications to the basic idea. Most notable among these contributors have been Jones and Davis (1965) and Kelley (1967).

In an analysis of the effects of environmental and personal factors on the attribution process, Jones and Davis have formulated a theory of correspondent inferences. They assume that any change in a preexisting state of affairs constitutes an event that will engage the attribution process, which is to say that the observer will attempt to attribute a cause for that event. In arriving at a sufficient explanation for someone's behavior, an observer uses various cues about the person and the relevant environment in attributing responsibility to the person for his actions. To the extent that the environment cannot be seen as a sufficient explanation for the

Source: Shelley Duval and Robert A. Wicklund, "Effects of Objective Self-Awareness on Attribution of Causality," Journal of Experimental Social Psychology 9 (1973): 17–31.

behavior, the observer will attribute the behavior to personal characteristics, motives, or dispositions of the actor.

Kelley has spelled out a model of attribution that parallels the Jones and Davis formulation. He has raised the idea of causal attribution to a motivational system in suggesting that attribution theory ". . . describes processes that operate *as if* the individual were motivated to attain a cognitive mastery of the causal structure of his environment" (p. 193). Kelley has proceeded to postulate some guidelines, or rules, that the individual employs in making attributions, and similar to Jones and Davis, the attribution process is viewed as an attempt by the observer to locate the unique causes for behavior, whether such causes reside in the environment or within the person.

The present status of attribution theory can be summed up as follows: Given that man desires to control his environment by understanding the causes of events (changes in his environment), any event that does not already have an adequate explanation will engage the attribution process. This process is essentially a search for the cause of the event, and the search is terminated only when the person infers or perceives dispositional properties of entities in the environment or person that serve as sufficient explanations. Given that the person is searching for the cause of an event, what rules or mechanisms determine where in the total environment he will locate the cause? One approach has been the Heider, Jones and Davis, and Kelley formulations, discussed above. Such an approach assumes that the observer operates as a scientist, in that he eliminates possible causal factors except for those that are uniquely associated with the event to be explained. That is, the person searches for a condition that is present when the effect is present and which is absent when the effect is absent.

Recently a second and third approach have been taken toward understanding the mechanisms of attribution. These formulations can be found in the theoretical ideas of Jones and Nisbett (1971) and Duval and Wicklund (1972). The Jones and Nisbett approach can be characterized by its concern with actor-observer differences in attribution and the role of salience of information. They indicate that a person who is actively engaged with his environment has a tendency to attribute the causes of the outcome of his activity to characteristics of the environment. By comparison, the person who passively observes the actor tends to attribute causality to dispositions of the actor. One reason for this actor-observer difference in attribution is that the two individuals seldom possess identical information. Since the actor is more likely than the observer to know about the extenuating circumstances surrounding his behavior, he is more likely to locate causality away from himself, and not within his personal dispositions. A second reason is that different aspects of the available information are salient for the actor and observer. Since environmental information is more salient for the actor, his attention is drawn to the environment and he attributes causality to the environment. Just the opposite holds for the observer, since for him the actor is the most salient part of the environment. There are at least three reasons for this differential salience: (1) Both the actor's and observer's sensory receptors are generally directed outward. For the actor, this outward direction means that he focuses on his environment rather than upon his own behavior. For the observer, the external focus of attention includes the actor's behavior. (2) Many of the actor's responses are habitual and do not require the self-examination involved in conscious control, but the observer is confronted by the actor's changing behavior pattern, which is "figured" against a relatively stable environment. (3) The actor is grappling with a changing environment that demands his attention for success while the role of the observer dictates that he should focus on the actor.

Objective self-awareness theory (Duval & Wicklund) approaches the question of attribution in a manner similar to Jones and Nisbett in that the area of the environment to which the individual is paying attention is central. But instead of emphasizing stable differences between actors and observers in their attribution tendencies, the theory provides a general model relating focus of attention to attribution. Given any event (change in the preexisting state of the environment), the theory proposes that the locus of causal attribution will be determined by the focus of attention. To the extent that a person focuses attention upon one object or area of the environment to the exclusion of other areas, he will tend to attribute causality for any event to that object or area. Of course, it is important that the element focused upon could reasonably cause the event as far as the individual is concerned. Given that there are two or more objects in the environment which could reasonably cause the event, the theory indicates that the focus of the person's attention will determine the locus of attribution.

A test of the objective self-awareness notion calls for the manipulation of a person's focus of attention toward one or another object. Such a manipulation can be drawn from the main body of objective self-awareness theory. When a situation consists of a person in an environment, objective self-awareness theory postulates that any element in the environment that reminds the person of his status as an object in the world will cause attention to focus upon the self to the exclusion of other parts of the environment. In previous research (Wicklund & Duval, 1971), it has been found that the person's image in a mirror, the sound of his tape-recorded voice, and the presence of a television camera all serve to bring his attention inward, toward himself. In the absence of such reminders, and especially when flux in the environment diverts the person's attention from himself, the focus of attention and consequent attribution should be outward and not toward the self.

In the first experiment to be reported the Ss were asked to imagine themselves in a hypothetical situation involving a negative outcome, where either the S or another person might be responsible for that outcome. It was assumed that a S who performs a motor activity will be relatively unable to focus upon himself, for the process of acting on the environment will draw his attention outward onto the environment. Once attention is limited to an area external to the self, the individual should scan the environment until he finds a reasonable or appropriate cause for the event in question, and in the present context, it is expected that he will locate causality in the other person in the hypothetical situation. In contrast, someone who is less active will be more likely to focus attention inward, and his objective self-awareness should result in attribution of responsibility to himself for the event in question.

In summary, the hypothesis for Experiment 1 is as follows: Given that the causality for an event is in question, activity involving the self acting on the environment will reduce the tendency to attribute causality for that event to the self.

EXPERIMENT 1

Method

Overview and Design Subjects were led to believe that a two-part experiment would require them to reply to some hypothetical attribution-of-responsibility items and then to perform a manual dexterity task. Some of the *Ss* were told to rotate a turntable while the questions were asked (Turntable condition), while the Control *Ss* did not expect to rotate the turntable until the questions had been completed. A total of 10 questions was asked, each of them asking the *S* to place himself in a hypothetical situation in which a negative consequence could be attributed to himself or to another.

Subjects The subjects were 12 female and 21 male undergraduates, recruited from an introductory psychology course at the University of Texas. Three of the males were deleted from the data analysis: two knew the hypothesis, and one refused to follow instructions.

Procedure When the *S* entered the cubicle, he was seated across the table from the *E* and was told that the experiment would consist of two different activities. The *E* said that the first half of the experiment would consist of answering some questions from a questionnaire that was being developed by several psychologists in the department, and the second part was described as a project in manual dexterity.

Control Condition The *S* was then shown the turntable of a pursuit rotor, and the *E* said that later in the session he would be asked to place a finger on the edge of it and rotate it slowly. At that point the *E* excused herself from the cubicle and said that she would return in a minute, which she did. Upon her return she asked the subject to reply to each of 10 hypothetical situations which are listed below. He was told to imagine himself in the situation and then to assess responsibility for the unfortunate event depicted by ascribing a "percentage at fault" to himself and to the other person or institution in the situation. It was required that the two percentages sum to 100. After the questions had been read and answered, the *S* was debriefed.

Turntable Condition The *S* was shown the turntable as in the control condition, but he was requested to place a finger on its edge and proceed to "warm up for the manual dexterity task." The *E* told him that it was important that the turning response be fairly automatic by the time the manual dexterity task begins. This provided a rationale for his rotating the device several minutes prior to the task. She instructed him to continue to rotate, then she left the room for a minute, returned, and asked him the 10 questions while he continued to move the turntable. The *S* was then debriefed.

Attribution of Responsibility Question

1. You're diving off a diving board and just as you dive off, someone swims up from under water and you land on top of him.
2. You're driving down the expressway when suddenly the woman in front of you slams on her brakes and you run right into the back of her.
3. You're taking a test and you notice that the guy sitting next to you is copying

every one of your answers. You don't say anything to him or cover your paper. Pretty soon the teacher takes up both papers and gives you both an F.

4. You have to have a serious operation and the doctor you've hired is reputable, but he's never performed this type of operation before. You decide to let him proceed with the operation, but afterwards, you have severe internal bleeding and you're in much worse shape than you were to begin with.
5. You have to get to campus one night, and you could walk in about 20 min. but you've been walking all day and you're pretty tired, so you decide to hitchhike. Instead of taking you to campus, the guy who picks you up takes all your money and drops you on the other side of town.
6. You pull up behind a bus that's stopped at a stop sign and you want to turn right at this intersection. After waiting for 1½ or 2 min., the bus hasn't moved. Finally, not knowing what he's going to do, you decide to pull out around him and have to cut back in front to turn right at the corner. Just as you do, he pulls out and runs right into you.
7. You bought a new shirt about a week ago. You've worn it a few times so it needs washing. There are no directions on the material from the manufacturer telling how to launder it so you go ahead and wash it like you usually do. Afterwards when you put it on, it's three sizes too small and the colors have faded.
8. You have an 8:30 class and you're there every morning. You have a report due the last Monday of classes, and you've known about it. One day you cannot possibly drag yourself out of bed so you stay home. On the same day the teacher changes the date of the assignment to the Friday before that Monday. When you return to class that Friday, you don't have your assignment and your grade is lowered.
9. You have a book checked out of the library and it's due in about 2 days. A friend of yours wants to borrow it, so instead of returning it, you let him use it. About 3 months later, you receive a note that the book has never been seen and you owe a huge fine.
10. You're driving down the street about 5 miles over the speed limit when a little kid suddenly runs out chasing a ball and you hit him.

Results

The hypothesis implied that the percentage of self-blame would be less in the Turntable condition, where Ss were active, than in the Control condition. Table 1 indicates that the data for almost all of the 10 questions were in the predicted direction, the only exceptions being Items 1 and 4. Although these items show a difference in a direction opposite the hypothesis, neither one shows a significant difference between conditions ($p > .20$); therefore, it is reasonable to combine all 10 items for a test of the hypothesis. As shown in Table 1, the combined mean of percentage of self-blame for the Turntable condition is 49.65, the mean for the Control condition is 57.63, and the difference is reliable ($F(1,28) = 5.06$, $p < .05$). In the interest of testing for possible sex differences each condition was divided into males and females, and it was found that there were no significant effects for any comparison involving the sex variable ($p > .20$ in every case.)

TABLE 1

Mean Attribution to Self (Experiment 1)

	ITEM NUMBER										
	1	*2*	*3*	*4*	*5*	*6*	*7*	*8*	*9*	*10*	*COMBINED*
Turntable ($N = 14$)	55.36*	45.43	35.71	56.79	63.21	38.21	26.43	75.36	38.57	61.43	49.65
Control ($N = 16$)	50.00	55.31	40.00	42.81	77.50	52.50	51.88	85.62	46.62	74.06	57.63

*Mean percentage blame attributed by the *S* to himself.

EXPERIMENT 2

The present approach to causal attribution postulates that attribution of causality for an event follows the focus of attention, given the presence of at least two objects that could reasonably cause the event. The first experiment employed a situation involving an event that could reasonably be caused either by the *S* himself or by the other person in the hypothetical situation. By imposing a task on the *S* while he estimated the causality of an event, the experiment demonstrated that activity can result in decreased attribution of causality to the self. Theoretically, this decrease occurred because activity decreases a person's ability to focus attention upon himself as an object. The primary assumption of the present approach to attribution is that the person's location of causality is solely determined by the direction and focus of his attention. If this assumption is correct, the favorability of the consequences of an event should not affect the attribution process. If a person is focused upon himself, he should tend to attribute the causes for both good and bad events to himself equally. The second experiment was designed to test this derivation.

In the present experiment both negative and positive hypothetical situations were employed in order to determine whether the focus of attention affects attribution differently for the two kinds of situations. A second difference from the first experiment is in the method of varying *Ss'* attention between themselves and the environment. Rather than a manipulation to reduce the focus of attention on the self, the present experiment introduces a factor for approximately half of the *Ss* that is expected to increase objective self-awareness. The following hypothesis was tested: An increase in objective self-awareness will bolster the tendency for *Ss* to attribute causality to themselves, and this effect should operate for both negative and positive consequences.

Method

Experimental Design The experimental design consisted of two manipulations. First, in order to vary objective self-awareness, approximately half of the *Ss* were exposed to a mirror image of themselves throughout the procedure (Mirror condition) while the other half were not confronted with a mirror image (No Mirror condition). Second, each *S* responded to five hypothetical attribution-of-responsibility questions. These either had positive consequences (Positive condition) or negative consequences (Negative condition). In summary, the 2 x 2 factorial design had two levels of objective self-awareness and two levels of favorability of outcome.

Subjects The *Ss* were 45 female undergraduates from the University of Texas at Austin who participated in the experiment as partial fulfillment of a course requirement. Two of these *Ss* were dropped from the data analysis because they were familiar with the ideas basic to the experiment and guessed the hypothesis.

Procedure The *S* was ushered into the experimental cubicle and was asked to be seated.

The *S*'s chair and the *E*'s chair were on opposite sides of a desk and were separated by a wooden screen placed on the desk. When the *E* sat down, the wooden screen prevented the *S* from being able to see the *E*. The purpose of the screen was to reduce the self-awareness that might result from the gaze of the *E*.

After the *S* was seated in the appropriate chair, the *E* stood at the end of the desk and proceeded to explain the nature of the experiment. He indicated that there was to be no experiment *per se* but that he was asking *Ss* to help test a questionnaire that a professor in the psychology department had recently developed. The *E* went on to explain that whenever a psychologist created a questionnaire, it was necessary to ask a large number of people to respond to the various items included. He noted that from these responses various statistics are computed which indicate whether or not all the questions are internally consistent.

Without further elaboration, the *E* went on to explain that the questions were actually hypothetical situations and that the *S* would be asked to imagine herself in each of the situations presented. The *S* was also told that each hypothetical situation would consist of two people, plus an outcome or event that would occur during the course of the situation. She was instructed to respond to each of the questions (situations) by indicating the extent to which she or the other person in the situation would be responsible for the event in question. The *E* elaborated on these instructions in the following way:

For example, when I ask you to estimate the extent to which your behavior caused the event to occur and the extent to which the other's behavior caused the event to occur, you might say 20% for yourself and 80% for the other; or 80% for yourself and 20% for the other, or it might be 60% to 40% or 40% to 60%. You can use any combination of percentages as long as they add up to 100%. Do you have any questions about what we are going to be doing?

When the *S* understood what she was being asked to do, the *E* told her that he would be seated behind the wooden screen and would ask the questions orally. He indicated that this procedure was necessary to try to eliminate any effects his facial expression and body movements might have upon her responses.

Before each *S* entered the experimental cubicle, a large mirror had been placed against the wall directly in front of the *S*'s chair. For half of the *Ss*, the mirror was turned such that its reflecting surface faced the *S* (Mirror condition). For the other half of the *Ss*, the mirror was turned such that the person faced the nonreflecting wooden back of the mirror (No Mirror condition). Thus, from the beginning of the experiment half of the *Ss* were seated so that they could see their full images reflected in the mirror, while the remainder of the *Ss* could not see themselves.

The presence of the mirror was rationalized in the following way for both the Mirror and No Mirror conditions. After explaining the nature of the questions and how they would be asked, the *E* indicated that there was one other matter that had to be settled. As he pointed to the various objects in the room (pursuit rotor, disconnected television camera, and mirror) he explained that these items, including the mirror, were not supposed to be in the cubicle and apparently had been left over from another experiment. The *E* said that his supervising professor was very strict about having extraneous material in the environment while the *S* was responding to the questions, but that he had indicated that it would be all right to leave those materials in the room as long as the *S* felt the objects would not interfere with her responses. The *S* was then asked to indicate whether or not she thought the materials would interfere.

At this point, the *E* seated himself behind the wooden screen and began the presentation of the hypothetical situations. Approximately half of the *Ss* were given five hypothetical situations which had negative outcomes (Negative condition) and the other *Ss* were given five hypothetical situations with positive outcomes (Positive condition). Consistent with previous instructions, *Ss* replied to the five hypothetical situations by ascribing a percentage of causality to themselves and to the other person in the situation. After the responses had been recorded, the *S* was questioned about various aspects of the procedure, and finally the purpose and nature of the experiment were explained.

Negative Items The five negative items were similar in content to negative items 6 through 10 on Experiment 1. However, the attribution of causality question asked at the end of each hypothetical situation was phrased in a slightly different manner. Instead of asking the *S* to estimate the extent of her fault, the *S* was asked to determine the degree to which her behavior in the hypothetical situation caused the event in question to occur.

Positive Items

1. Imagine that you have selected and purchased a race horse. You enter the horse in a major race and hire a good jockey to ride him. The horse wins first place. To what degree did your actions cause the victory and to what degree did the actions of the jockey cause the victory.

2. Imagine that a person you know is a stockbroker. One day he gives you a tip about two stocks that are supposed to rise in value. After looking at the records of both companies, you decide to buy only one of the two stocks that were recommended. The stock does go up and you make a good profit. To what degree did your actions cause the profit and to what degree did the actions of the stockbroker cause the profit?

3. Imagine that you have written a term paper. However, you have to leave town suddenly so you ask a friend to take the paper to the professor. When she delivers the paper to the professor, he glances at it and asks for clarification of several points in your essay. Your friend is familiar with the topic of the paper and successfully explains what the professor wants to know. You receive an A for the paper. To what degree did your actions cause the A and to what degree did the actions of the friend cause the A?

4. Imagine that a friend of yours wants to get you a date. You tell her what characteristics you like in a date and she selects one of her friends. You go out with him and have a very good time. To what degree did your actions cause the successful date and to what degree did the actions of your friend cause the successful date?

5. Imagine that you have an examination in a foreign language. Since you have done poorly in the past, you ask a friend of yours to help you. You study with her for about a week. However, you have also spent a great deal of your own time preparing for the examination. You get a B-plus on the test. To what degree did your actions cause the good grade and to what degree did the actions of your friend cause the good grade?

RESULTS

The dependent measure in the second experiment was percentage of attribution of causality to the self. Both within the Positive and Negative conditions the data were in the same direction for almost every item in that there was more self-attribution with the mirror than without the mirror (see Table 2). The only exceptions

TABLE 2

Mean Attribution to Self (Experiment 2)

	ITEM NUMBER					
	1	*2*	*3*	*4*	*5*	*COMBINED*
Mirror—Positive ($N = 11$)	44.09*	48.64	72.27	66.82	68.18	60.00
Mirror—Negative ($N = 10$)	53.50	49.50	85.00	47.50	65.50	60.20
No Mirror—Positive ($N = 11$)	30.00	51.36	70.45	48.64	59.09	49.91
No Mirror—Negative ($N = 11$)	44.09	20.91	87.27	39.54	63.64	51.09

*Mean percentage responsibility attributed by the *S* to herself.

to this finding were on Item 2 within the Positive condition and Item 3 within the Negative condition, where the means for the No Mirror condition were slightly higher than the means for the Mirror condition. These differences, however, are slight and nonsignificant, thus we can proceed to the combined data and disregard the individual items.

As predicted, the main effect for Mirror-No Mirror was reliable (F (1,39) = 14.43, $p < .001$). There was no effect for the Positive-Negative variable ($p < .20$) nor an interaction ($p < .20$). In addition, there was a significant difference between the Mirror and No Mirror means within the Positive condition ($t(20) = 2.88$, $p < .01$) as well as within the Negative condition ($t(19) = 2.54$, $p < .02$).

DISCUSSION

The two studies taken together appear to support the contention that the individual's focus of attention is a central determinant of attribution of causality in that the locus of causality is seen either in the self or in someone else, depending on the extent of the person's objective self-awareness. In the first experiment, objective self-awareness was decreased by placing the *S* in activity, and in the second experiment, objective self-awareness was increased by forcing the *S* to examine her mirror image. In both cases attribution to the self was a positive function of objective self-awareness.

If the focus of attention does, in fact, determine where causality will be located, the favorability of the consequences should have no effect on a person's attribution of causality. Whether the event is negative or positive, a person who focuses attention upon himself should attribute causality to himself; a person who focuses attention on the other should attribute causality to the other. This hypothesis is strongly confirmed by the results of the second experiment reported. Feather (1969) lends additional credibility to this finding. He reported no differential attribution of causality to self as a function of success or failure on a task, even when prior level of self-esteem is taken into account.

The hypothetical situations in the present experiments always involved two individuals who reasonably could have been targets for the *S*'s attribution: one of these was the *S*, and the other was the other person or institution in the situation, such as the driver, doctor, or race horse jockey. The theoretical idea assumes that attribution will follow the focus of attention, but it is necessary to qualify this statement with respect to the object of attribution. It seems doubtful that attribution will be in the direction of any object whatsoever simply because attention is directed toward that object. In the hypothetical situation involving an automobile wreck, it is not likely that the *S* would see the position of the stars or his grandmother as responsible simply because his attention happened to be directed at the stars or grandmother at the time of the event. Instead the object which is seen as having caused the event must fall roughly within the *S*'s category of objects that might reasonably be causal in the particular situation. Presumably a person learns what such objects are through experience. As he gains knowledge about the probable causes of effects to be explained, his scope of objects to which to attribute causality will narrow. In this regard, it is interesting to note that young children, who do not have a great deal of experience with the causal potential of different factors, manage to locate causality virtually everywhere, in inanimate as well as animate objects, and often in factors that adults would never consider to be first causes (Piaget, 1966).

The adult person will attribute causality for an event only to those objects which he believes possess the potential to have caused the event. Thus, the present formulation is limited in its application to situations containing at least two objects that could cause the event in question. However, we do not see this as a serious impairment of the range of applicability of the objective self-awareness notion. Virtually any situation has at least two potentially causal objects. This contention is supported by the effort experimental science has invested in designing controlled situations that possess only one possible cause. Normally there are too many reasonable accounts of phenomena, and only on occasion is there a total absence of a credible interpretation. It should be noted that the objective self-awareness notion is suited for understanding the usual situation that attribution theory has dealt with, i.e., an event produced by the interaction of a person and his environment. Since the person and environment actually interact to produce events, either of the two elements can reasonably be seen as having caused a particular event. Thus, the focus of attention will operate as an antecedent to attribution in any situation of this type.

REFERENCES

Duval, S. and R. A. Wicklund
1972 A Theory of Objective Self Awareness. New York: Academic Press.

Feather, N. T.
1969 "Attribution of responsibility and valence of success and failure in relation to initial confidence and task performance." Journal of Personality and Social Psychology 13: 129–44.
Heider, F.
1944 "Social perception and phenomenal causality." Psychological Review 51: 358–74.
1958 The Psychology of Interpersonal Relations. New York: Wiley.
Jones, E. E. and K. E. Davis
1965 "From acts to dispositions." In L. Berkowitz (ed.), Advances in Experimental Social Psychology. New York: Academic Press, pp. 219–66.
Jones, E. E. and R. E. Nisbett
1971 The Actor and the Observer: Divergent Perceptions of the Causes of Behavior. New York: General Learning Press.
Kelley, H. H.
1967 "Attribution theory in social psychology." Pp. 192–238 in D. Levine (ed.), Nebraska Symposium on Motivation. Lincoln, Nebraska: University of Nebraska Press.
Piaget, J.
1969 The Child's Conception of Physical Causality. (1st ed., 1927) Totowa, N.J.: Littlefield, Adams & Co.
Wicklund, R. A. and S. Duval
1971 "Opinion change and performance facilitation as a result of objective self-awareness." Journal of Experimental Social Psychology 7: 319–42.

The Real Self: From Institution to Impulse

Ralph H. Turner

6

Except at the most macroscopic and demographic levels, there is no way to study dynamics and change in social systems without attending to the attitudes and conceptions held by their members. Subjective data are essential because people are not just miniature reproductions of their societies (Bendix 1952; Wrong 1961; Etzioni 1968).

One important sociological tradition for bringing personal dynamics into the analysis of social structure began with Thomas and Znaniecki's (1918) concept of *life organization*, which Park (1931) translated into *conceptions of self* and Kuhn and McPartland (1954) converted into an easily applied set of empirical operations. The *self-conception* as an object arises in connection with self-process (Mead 1934). From early experience with the distinction between *mine* and *yours*, I learn to distinguish between *myself* and others (Cooley 1902).

The present discussion emphasizes a related point, that the idea of a self-as-object permits me to distinguish among the various feelings and actions that emanate from my person. Some emanations I recognize as expressions of my real self; others seem foreign to the real me. I take little credit and assume little blame for the sensations and actions that are peripheral to my real self (Turner 1968). Others are of great significance, because they embody my true self, good or bad. The articulation of *real selves* with social structure should be a major link in the functioning and change of societies. This approach to linking person and social structure is especially compatible with symbolic interactionist and phe-

Source: Ralph H. Turner, "The Real Self: From Institution to Impulse," American Journal of Sociology 81 (1976): 989–1016 by permission of the author and publisher.

nomenological perspectives which stress the ongoing creation of reality by each member of society.

The aim of this paper is to elaborate a dimension of self-conception that may have important implications for sociological theories of social control and other aspects of societal functioning. To varying degrees, people accept as evidence of their real selves either feelings and actions with an *institutional* focus or ones they identify as strictly *impulse*. There are suggestive signs that recent decades have witnessed a shift in the locus of self away from the institutional pole toward that of impulse. This shift may have altered substantially the world of experience in which people orient themselves, setting it apart from the one that much established sociological theory describes. I describe these types, examine the hypothesized shift, suggest some theories that might explain it, and explore the implications for sociological thought.

In another publication I shall describe a modification of the "Who am I?" technique that I have developed specifically to gather data for analysis in these terms.

Self as Object

Before presenting the thesis, I must briefly outline my assumptions concerning self-conception. Out of the distinctively human reflexive process emerges a sense or conception of self as an object, which, however, has no existence apart from the conceptions and attitudes by which one constitutes it (Blumer 1966, pp. 539–40). Identifying the self is not the same as identifying one's values, and self-conception is not to be confused with ideal self or ego ideal (Kuhn and McPartland 1954, p. 69). The self-conception identifies a person in qualitative and locational terms, not merely in evaluative ones such as self-esteem. The self is an object in relation to other objects, all of which are constantly modified in dynamic interrelationship (Berger 1966). Self-conception refers to the continuity—however imperfect—of an individual's experience of himself in a variety of situations. It is most usefully viewed as an intervening variable between some aspect of social structure and the working of the same or another aspect.

How the self can be so constituted as not to be coterminous with all the feelings and actions that emanate from a person has been a constant source of puzzlement. I suggest tentatively that the demarcation has three components. First, it relies on a more generalized discrimination between the real and the unreal in experience. We identify some experiences as fantasies, hallucinations, dreams, or other forms of the unreal. Under crisis conditions we sometimes go so far as to deceive ourselves concerning the reality of behavior and feelings that are not in accord with self (Spiegel 1969). More often we merely borrow the language of reality and unreality and employ its connotations. Second, bounding the self incorporates the general distinction between *attributions* to person and those to situation (Jones et al. 1971). Behaviors thought to reveal the true self are also ones whose causes are perceived as residing in the person rather than the situation. This distinction relies on a commonsense psychology held by the persons making attributions. The bases for bounding the self necessarily change whenever folk understandings of psychology change. The distinction also inextricably mixes normative conceptions of responsibility with naturalistic ones of cause. The emergence of self cannot be separated from the essentially moral process of establishing human accountability

(Kilpatrick 1941). Third, the idea of self incorporates a further sense of a realm that is distinctly personal or *propriative* (Allport 1955). This realm has not been effectively defined; yet awareness of it is a crucial and almost irreducible intuition. Attribution theorist's evidence that self-attribution does not follow entirely the same rules as person attribution gives some clues to the proprium. But beyond the attribution of causation for behavior, the realm of self is characterized by possessiveness, privacy, and sacredness.

INSTITUTION AND IMPULSE AS LOCI OF SELF

The self-conception is most frequently described sociologically by naming the roles that are preeminent in it. In a good example of this approach, Wellman (1971) finds that the self-conceptions of both black and white adolescents can be characterized on the basis of the same set of identities—namely, their age, gender, family, religion, race, and ethnic heritage, and their roles as students, athletes, and friends. Studies comparing the place of occupation and work in the life organizations of various groups of workers (Dubin 1956; Wilensky 1964) likewise relate the self-conception to particular roles in society.

Self-conceptions can also be compared on the basis of distinctions at a more abstract level. The relationship between self and social order is put in more comprehensive terms when we distinguish between self as anchored in *institutions* and self as anchored in *impulse*.

To one person, an angry outburst or the excitement of extramarital desire comes as an alien impetus that superficially beclouds or even dangerously threatens the true self. The experience is real enough and may even be persistent and gratifying, but it is still not felt as signifying the real self. The true self is recognized in acts of volition, in the pursuit of institutionalized goals, and not in the satisfaction of impulses outside institutional frameworks. To another person, the outburst or desire is recognized—fearfully or enthusiastically—as an indication that the real self is breaking through a deceptive crust of institutional behavior. Institutional motivations are external, artificial constraints and superimpositions that bridle manifestations of the real self. One plays the institutional game when he must, but only at the expense of the true self. The true self consists of deep, unsocialized, inner impulses. Mad desire and errant fancy are exquisite expressions of the self.

Again, conscientious acceptance of group obligations and unswerving loyalty can mean that the real self has assumed firm control and overcome the alien forces. But for those who find out who they really are by listening to the voice of impulse, the same behavior is a meaningless submission to institutional regimens and authoritarianism. A mother's self-sacrifice for her child is the measure of her real self when seen through institutional eyes, and it is a senseless betrayal of the parent's true being to those who find personal reality in the world of impulse.

It is no accident that this polarity parallels Freud's classic distinction between id and superego. To Freud, the id was more truly the person and the superego merely an external imposition. As he turned to examinations of society, he expressed the same conviction when he wrote, "Our civilization is entirely based upon the suppression of instincts" (1931, p. 13), and when he proposed a relaxation of social norms and standards as a solution to the discontents of modern civilization (1930). This position sharply contrasts with a view shared by many writers and exemplified in Park's assertion that "the role we are striving to live up to—this mask is our truer self" (1927, p. 739). Although in other writings Park sometimes expressed a different conviction, his statement epitomized the institutional locus of self, while Freud located the self chiefly in the world of impulse—until his belated concessions to ego.

The Key Differences

Several crucial differences between the two contrasting loci of self can be briefly stated.

1. Under the institution locus, the real self is revealed when an individual adheres to a high standard, especially in the face of serious temptation to fall away. A person shows his true mettle under fire. Under the impulse locus, the real self is revealed when a person does something solely because he wants to—not because it is good or bad or noble or courageous or self-sacrificing, but because he spontaneously wishes to do so.

2. To *impulsives*, the true self is something to be discovered. A young person drops out of school or out of the labor force in order to reflect upon and discover who he really is. To the *institutional*, waiting around for self-discovery to occur is ridiculous. The self is something attained, created, achieved, not something discovered. If vocational counseling to help the individual find his peculiar niche has elements of the impulse conception of self, the idea that a person can make of himself what he will, that one chooses a task and then works at it, is the view of institutionals. The contrast is well stated in a contemporary prescription for effective living, written from the institutional perspective:

> *So if we reach a point of insight at which we become disgustedly aware of how we stage ourselves, play games, and ingratiate others, to say nothing of using defense mechanisms and strategies, and if at this point we want to enrich life by finding honest, deeply felt, loving interactions with others, it is tempting to believe that we can change simply by opening a door and letting out our "true" unsullied impulses. Change is never so simple. What is really involved is not the releasing of a true self but the making of a new self, one that gradually transcends the limitations and pettiness of the old [White 1972, p. 387].*

3. Under the institution locus, the real self is revealed only when the individual is in full control of his faculties and behaviors. Allport (1955) locates the self in planning and volition, in contrast to impulse. "When the individual is dominated by segmental drives, by compulsions, or by the winds of circumstances, he has lost the integrity that comes only from maintaining major directions of striving" (pp. 50–51). When control is impaired by fatigue, stress, alcohol, or drugs, an alien self displaces the true self. The danger of any of these conditions is that after repeated experiences the individual may lose the capacity to distinguish between the true self and the counterfeit and become progressively less able to resume control and reinstate the true self. If use of alcohol is viewed with favor, it is only on condition that the user is able to practice moderation or "hold his liquor," maintaining control in spite of alcohol.

But under the impulse locus, the true self is revealed only when inhibitions are lowered or abandoned. In a magnificent statement of an institutional perspective, Wordsworth (1807) called upon Duty, "stern daughter of the voice of God," for relief from the "weight of chance-desires" and for "a repose that ever is the same." But let the barest suspicion arise that a good deed has been motivated by a sense of duty, and it loses all value as a clue to self in the eyes of the impulsive. For some impulsives drugs and alcohol are aids—often indispensable—to the discovery of self, for without them socially instilled inhibitions irresistibly overpower the true self. A participant in a Los Angeles "love-in" in 1971 said: "It's a place where people can get out, get smashed, get stoned, or whatever. A love-in is a place to get away from the apartment. It's like being out and touching people for a change, rather than working with paper and working with inanimate objects. It's like being out in the real world for a change."

4. Hypocrisy is a concern of both types, but the word means different things to each. For the institutionals, hypocrisy consists of failing to live up to one's standards. The remedy is not to lower standards but to make amends and adhere to the standards the next time. If one's failings persist, he ceases to represent himself as what he cannot be, so that he at least escapes the charge of hypocrisy by presenting himself only as what he is. For the impulsives, hypocrisy consists of asserting standards and adhering to them even if the behavior in question is not what the individual wants to do and enjoys doing. One who sets exacting standards for himself and by dint of dedicated effort succeeds in living up to them is still a hypocrite if he must suppress a desire to escape from these strict demands. Altruism, in the traditional sense of responding to duty and setting one's own interests aside, is a penultimate hypocrisy, compounded by the probability that it is a dissimulated self-seeking and manipulation. The institutional goal is correspondence between *prescription and behavior;* the goal of impulsives is correspondence between *impulse and behavior;* hypocrisy in either instance is a lack of the appropriate correspondence.

5. In the light of the foregoing differences, the qualities that make a performance admirable differ. The polished, error-free performance, in which the audience forgets the actor and sees only the role being played, is the most admired by institutionals. Whatever the task, perfection is both the goal and the means by which the real self finds expression. But impulsives find technical perfection repelling and admire instead a performance that reveals the actor's human frailties. They are in harmony with the motion picture star system, in which Gregory Peck, John Wayne, and Gina Lollobrigida, rather than the characters they play in a given picture, are the centers of attention. Ed Sullivan's popular appeal, generally attributed to his very awkwardness and ineptitude, is incomprehensible to the institutionals. Of course, the specific cues for spontaneity have changed, so a younger generation of impulsives no longer responds to these stars as did an older generation.

6. The difference between discovery and achievement also suggests a difference in time perspective. The self as impulse means a present time perspective, while the self as institution means a future time perspective. Institutionals, who build themselves a real world by making commitments, have difficulty retaining a vital sense of self when the future perspective is no longer tenable. The *malaise* of retirement is a common indication of this pattern. In contrast, freedom from past commitments is heralded poetically in the popular song "Gentle on My Mind," by John Hartford.

7. Just as hypocrisy takes on different meanings within the two patterns, individualism is found in both settings with different implications. The individualist is one who rejects some kind of social pressure that threatens his true identity. But there are different kinds of pressure. In one view, social pressures can divert a person from achievement, from adherence to ethical standards, and from other institutional goals. The rugged individualists of 19th-century America thought in these terms. Children were imbued with an individualistic ethic in order to protect them from peer group pressures toward mediocrity or compromise of principle, either of which meant failure to realize the potential that was the true self. But individualism can also be a repudiation of the institutional and inter-individual claims that compete with impulse. The individualist may be protecting himself against a conspiracy to force him into institutional molds, to make him do his duty, or to aspire. Both types would agree that one must resist the blandishments of friends and the threats of enemies in order to be true to himself. But the institutional individualist is most attentive to pernicious pressures on the side of mediocrity and abandonment of principle; the impulsive individualist sees clearly the social pressures in league with a system of arbitrary rules and false goals.

Both institution and impulse loci allow for individualistic and non-individualistic orientations. We have found it useful to employ a cross-cutting distinction between *individual* and *social* anchorages for the self. Institutionals stress either achievement, a relatively individual goal, or altruism, a social aim, as the road to self-discovery. Somewhere between the two lies adherence to an ethical code which will vary according to whether ethics is viewed as applied altruism or a forum for individual achievement. Impulsives may stress the simple disregard of duties and inhibitions in order to gratify spontaneous impulses; this is essentially an individual route to self-discovery. Or they may seek self-discovery through expressing potentially tabooed feelings to other persons and thereby attain a state of interpersonal intimacy that transcends the normal barriers between people.

Related and Unrelated Distinctions

It is essential not to confuse these alternative anchorages with the question of whether people are preoccupied with maintaining appearances or conforming instead of "being themselves." Describing a mass gathering of youths, a student wrote, "People tend to forget how they would hope to come across, and instead act as their true selves." This is a terse statement of how participants felt in the situation and expresses the point of view of an impulse self-anchorage. But from an institutional persepctive, the same youths appear to be tumbling over one another in their anxiety to comply with the latest youthful fad and to avoid any appearance of being square. The institutional hopes that after passing through this stage the youths will "find themselves," discovering their special niches in the institutional system. The self-anchorage determines which kinds of behavior seem genuine and which are concessions to appearances.

The polarity bears resemblances to several distinctions already advanced by others. McPartland's "Category B" responses and Kuhn and McPartland's consensual responses (Spitzer, Couch, and Stratton 1973) to the Twenty Statements

Test (TST) would all be institutional responses, but so would many responses in other categories. Institutionals have much in common with Riesman, Glazer, and Denney's (1950) inner-directed persons, but other-directed persons cannot be equated with impulsives. Sorokin's (1937–41) sensate types resemble the impulsives in their assignment of ultimate reality to the world of the senses. But Sorokin identifies striving for success with the sensate mind and altruism with the ideational, whereas I see these as alternative expressions of an institutional anchorage. Benedict's (1934) interpretation of Nietzsche's Dionysians suggests impulsives, who are unrestrained in acting on impulse and dream, while the Apollonians are more comfortable in an institutionally articulated system. But the dominating Apollonian theme of moderation certainly does not apply to heroic altruism or unrestrained striving for success.

Compared with the well-known dichotomies employed by Benedict, Sorokin, and Riesman et al., the institution-impulse distinction introduces a somewhat different dimension. It allows for the discovery of reality in either excess or moderation within both self-anchorages, and it allows in each orientation for both mystical and naturalistic realities and both individualizing and unifying realities. Goals of achievement, self-control, morality, and altruism lodge the self-conception more and more firmly in some institutional structure. The impulse release attained in encounter groups, expressive movements, and dropping out may in some forms promote a bond of intimacy with other individuals but always distinguishes the true self specifically from institutional values, norms, and goals.

This polarity has much in common with the widely discussed dimension of alienation. However, three important differences of approach make the concepts complementary rather than redundant. First, alienation is an intrinsically evaluative concept, incorporating a negative view of social trends and requiring that the search for explanation be directed toward disorganization in the social structure. Granted that each investigator's own self-locus will lead him to prefer one pole to the other, there are no a priori judgments that one locus is healthier than the other and no reasons to seek explanations for the shift in the pathologies of society. Second, while alienation implies a single continuum, self-locus implies two continua that may be loosely correlated but not identical. One is the continuum I have described. The other ranges from high to low *self-resolution*, according to whether the individual has a clear and stable self-conception or a vague and uncertain identity. Some scholars think of alienation as loss of self-resolution. But alienation from one's work can signify either an impulse locus or low self-resolution. And for some scholars in the Freudian tradition, self-estrangement *means* institutional anchorage. . . . [See EDITOR'S NOTE].

Concerning this initial statement of the two loci of self, the reader should bear in mind that specifying polar types such as these is merely a way to start thinking about variation in the sense of self. Except on the fringes of society, we are unlikely to find the extremes. Elements of both anchorages probably coexist comfortably in the average person. Yet differences among groups of people in key facets of self may be of sufficient importance that their experience of each other is noncongruent, and little true communication can occur.

EDITOR'S NOTE

The selection included here has been chosen to highlight the difference between the institutional and impulse orientations. In the remainder of the article from which this selection is drawn, Turner directs attention to the historical shift in the direction of impulse, to the variation in institutional and impulse orientations among different population segments, and to the various implications for social structure that a shift from institution to impulse would have. Readers interested in these elaborations are encouraged to consult the article from which this selection is drawn.

REFERENCES

Allport, Gordon W.
1955 Becoming: Basic Considerations for a Psychology of Personality. New Haven, Conn.: Yale University Press.
Bendix, Reinhard
1952 "Compliant behavior and individual personality." American Journal of Sociology 58 (November): 292–303.
Benedict, Ruth
1934 Patterns of Culture. Boston: Houghton Mifflin.
Berger, Peter L.
1966 "Identity as a problem in the sociology of knowledge." European Journal of Sociology 7: 105–15.
Blumer, Herbert
1966 "Sociological implications of the thought of George Herbert Mead." American Journal of Sociology 71 (March): 535–48.
Cooley, Charles H.
1902 Human Nature and the Social Order. New York: Scribner.
Dubin, Robert
1956 "Industrial workers' world." Social Problems 3 (January): 131–42.
Etzioni, Amitai
1968 "Basic human needs, alienation and inauthenticity." American Sociological Review 33 (December): 870–85.
Freud, Sigmund
1930 Civilization and Its Discontents. London: Hogarth.
1931 Modern Sexual Morality and Modern Nervousness. New York: Eugenics.
Jones, Edward E., David E. Kanouse, Harold H. Kelley, Richard E. Nisbett, Stuart Valins, and Bernard Weiner
1971 Attribution: Perceiving the Causes of Behavior. Morristown, N.J.: General Learning.
Kilpatrick, William H.
1941 Selfhood and Civilization: A Study of the Self-Other Process. New York: Macmillan.
Kuhn, Manford H. and Thomas S. McPartland
1954 "An empirical investigation of self-attitudes." American Sociological Review 19 (February): 68–76.
Mead, George H.
1934 Mind, Self, and Society. Chicago: University of Chicago Press.
Park, Robert E.
1927 "Human nature and collective behavior." American Journal of Sociology 32 (March): 733–41.

1928 "Human migration and the marginal man." American Journal of Sociology 33 (May): 881–93.
1931 "Human nature, attitudes, and the mores." Pp. 17–45 in Kimball Young (ed.), Social Attitudes. New York: Holt.

Riesman, David, Nathan Glazer, and Reuel Denney
1950 The Lonely Crowd. New Haven, Conn.: Yale University Press.

Seeman, Melvin
1967 "On the personal consequences of alienation in work." American Sociological Review 32 (April): 273–85.

Shils, Edward
1962 "The theory of mass society." Diogenes 39 (Fall): 45–66.

Sorokin, Pitirim A.
1937–41 Social and Cultural Dynamics. Englewood Cliffs, N.J.: Bedminster.

Spiegel, John P.
1969 "Campus conflict and professorial egos." Transaction 6 (October): 41–50.

Spitzer, Stephan, Carl Couch, and John Stratton
1973 The Assessment of the Self. Iowa City, Ia.: Sernoll.

Thomas, William I. and Florian Znaniecki
1918 The Polish Peasant in Europe and America. New York: Dover.

Turner, Ralph H.
1968 "The self in social interaction." Pp. 93–106 in Chad Gordon and Kenneth Gergen (eds.), The Self in Social Interaction. Vol. 1. New York: Wiley.
1975 "Is there a quest for identity?" Sociological Quarterly 16 (Spring): 148–61.

Wellman, Barry
1971 "Social identities in black and white." Sociological Inquiry 41 (Winter): 57–66.

White, Robert W.
1972 The Enterprise of Living: Growth and Organization in Personality, New York: Holt, Rinehart & Winston.

Wilensky, Harold L.
1964 "Varieties of work experiences." Pp. 125–54 in Henry Borow (ed.), Man in a World at Work. Boston: Houghton Mifflin.

Wordsworth, William
1807 "Ode to Duty."

Wrong, Dennis H.
1961 "The oversocialized conception of man in modern sociology." American Sociological Review 26 (April): 183–93.

Basking in Reflected Glory: Three (Football) Field Studies

Robert B. Cialdini

Richard J. Borden

Avril Thorne

Marcus Randall Walker

Stephen Freeman

Lloyd Reynolds Sloan

7

It is a common and understandable tendency for people who have been successful in some positive way to make others aware of their connection with that accomplishment. However, there also appears to be a seemingly less rational but perhaps more interesting tendency for people to publicize a connection with *another person* who has been successful. This latter inclination might be called the tendency to bask in reflected glory (BIRG). That is, people appear to feel that they can share in the glory of a successful other with whom they are in some way

Source: Robert B. Cialdini, Richard J. Borden, Avril Thorne, Markus Randall Walker, Stephen Freeman, and Lloyd Reynolds Sloan, "Basking in Reflected Glory: Three (Football) Field Studies." Journal of Personality and Social Psychology 34 (1976): 366–75.

associated; one manifestation of this feeling is the public trumpeting of the association. Such a phenomenon is not hard to understand when the one wishing to share in another's success has been instrumental to that success. However, the more intriguing form of the phenomenon occurs when the one who basks in the glory of another has done nothing to bring about the other's success. Here, a simple case of affiliation or membership is sufficient to stimulate a public announcement of the critical connection.

There does seem to be abundant anecdotal evidence that people try to make us cognizant of their connections with highly positive or successful others. The forms of these connections are varied. For example, they may imply similarity of residence, past or present: States and cities like to list the names of famous entertainers, statesmen, beauty contest winners, etc., who live or were born within their boundaries; the state of Indiana has even gone so far as to brag that more vice-presidents of the United States have come from Indiana than any other state. Other such connections involve ethnic or religious affiliation: Italians speak proudly of the ethnic background of Marconi, and Jews refer to Einstein's heritage. Still other connections reflect physical similarities: "Napoleon was short, too." Sexual identity may also give rise to the BIRG phenomenon: At a women's movement forum attended by one of the authors, there was a round of feminine applause when it was announced that Madame Curie was a woman and Lee Harvey Oswald was not. Finally, connections suitable for BIRGing may be as tenuous as in incidental contact: We all know people who delight in recounting the time they were in the same theater, airplane, or restroom with a famous movie star.

While there appears to be rich informal support of the sort described above for the existence of a BIRG phenomenon, there seem to be no experimental investigations of the effect. Thus, it was the purpose of this series of studies to examine this tendency to bask in the reflected glory of another or group of others. In so doing, it was hoped to (a) reliably demonstrate the existence of the phenomenon, (b) establish its generality over experimental contexts and measures, (c) determine a mediating process for its occurrence, and (d) discover some of its limiting conditions and thereby gain further information as to its nature.

One of the most obvious arenas for the working of BIRG effects in our society is the athletic arena. Fans of championship teams gloat over their team's accomplishments and proclaim their affiliation with buttons on their clothes, bumper stickers on their cars, and banners on their public buildings. Despite the fact that they have never caught a ball or thrown a block in support of their team's success, the tendency of such fans is to claim for themselves part of the team's glory; it is perhaps informative that the chant is always "*We're* number one," never "They're number one."

It was our view that a sports context would be ideal for a test of some of our notions concerning BIRG effects. Our expectation was that an individual would attempt to bask in the glory of an associated, successful source by publicly announcing his or her affiliation with the source and that this effect would obtain even when the affiliation was clearly irrelevant (i.e., noninstrumental) to the success of the source. In order to gather data relevant to the above hypothesis, an experiment was simultaneously conducted at seven universities with powerful intercollegiate football teams during part of the 1973 football season. It was predicted that students at these schools would be more likely to announce publicly their connection with their universities after the varsity football teams had been successful than after the teams had not been successful. We decided to measure students' tendency to announce their university affiliation by means of an examination of wearing apparel. The frequency with which students wore apparel that clearly identified the university that they attended was hoped to be a subtle yet sensitive measure of the willingness to declare publicly a university affiliation.

EXPERIMENT 1

Method

Procedure From the third week of the 1973 collegiate football season through the last week of regular play, the apparel of students enrolled in sections of introductory psychology courses at seven large universities was covertly monitored. At each school, three types of data were recorded in the same classes every Monday during the season: (a) the number of students present in the class, (b) the number of students with apparel identifying the school of attendance, and (c) the number of students with apparel identifying a school other than the school of attendance. Data recorders at each place received the following definitions prior to data collection:

Apparel identifying the school of attendance is identified as apparel which unambiguously identifies your school through names, insignia, or emblems. Examples would be buttons, jackets, sweatshirts, tee shirts, etc., which display the school name, team nickname or mascot, or university insignia. Apparel which appears school-related solely through the use of colors would not qualify. Also excluded are utilitarian objects such as briefcases, notebooks, or bookcovers. Apparel identifying a school other than the school of attendance are those which meet the same criteria for inclusion as above but which identify a school other than your own.

The data recorders were not members of the classes they monitored.

Results

Over all schools and across all weeks, an average of 176.8 students were present in the monitored classes; an average of 8.4 percent of these students wore apparel identifying the university of attendance, while 2 percent of them wore apparel identifying a school other than the university of attendance. Because of huge differences among the schools in absolute amount of these two kinds of apparel wearing and in order to make comparisons between the universities as well as between the types of apparel wearing, standardized indexes of relevant apparel wearing were considered necessary. The standard we decided on was the highest percentage of relevant apparel wearing that occurred on any Monday during the season; this standard was simply computed as the number of students wearing relevant apparel that day divided by the number of students in class that day. The percentages of apparel wearing on all other Mondays of the season were scored as proportions of the highest percentage. So, the Monday with the largest percentage of relevant apparel wearing was scored as 1.00, and any other Monday percentage was scored as a fraction (proportion) of that standard. This procedure was performed on the data from each school for the two relevant categories of apparel wearing: school-of-attendance apparel wearing and school-of-nonattendance apparel wearing. A mean proportion for each category was obtained for Mondays following a team's wins and nonwins; these are the mean proportions presented in Table 1. As can be seen from Table 1, these indexes showed a generally consistent tendency for students to wear school-of-attendance apparel more after victories than nonvictories; but this was not the case for school-of-nonattendance apparel.

TABLE 1

Indexes of Relevant Apparel Wearing at the Seven Monitored Universities

	SCHOOL-OF-ATTENDANCE APPAREL WEARING		*SCHOOL-OF-NONATTENDANCE APPAREL WEARING*	
SCHOOL	*WINS*	*NONWINS*	*WINS*	*NONWINS*
Arizona State	.63 (5)	.61 (1)	.58 (5)	.68 (1)
Louisiana State	.80 (5)	.33 (3)	.58 (5)	.51 (3)
Ohio State	.69 (4)	.30 (1)	.56 (4)	.94 (1)
Notre Dame	.67 (7)	.49 (1)	.62 (7)	.52 (1)
Michigan	.52 (5)	.83 (1)	.20 (5)	.00 (1)
Pittsburgh	.76 (4)	.27 (2)	.31 (4)	.50 (2)
Southern California	.36 (6)	.26 (1)	.17 (6)	.00 (1)
M	.63	.44	.43	.45

Note. Numbers in parentheses represent the number of games that fell into wins and nonwins categories for each school.

Because of the nonnormality of the proportion data, the scores were converted to ranks, and Wilcoxon matched-pairs signed-ranks tests were performed using school as the unit of analysis.[1] Despite the conservativeness of such an approach (for this mode of analysis, n is only 7), the Wilcoxon T reflected a conventionally significant difference on the school-of-attendance measure ($T = 2$, $p < .05$, two-tailed). This result indicated, as predicted, that Mondays following football victories ranked significantly higher in school-of-attendance apparel wearing than Mondays following nonvictories.[2] The mean rank for victories was 3.2, while that for nonvictories was 4.9. A similar test for school-of-nonattendance apparel did not show any effect; the victory and nonvictory mean ranks for this measure were 3.4 and 3.7, respectively. This latter result suggests that the obtained effect on the school-of-attendance measure is not attributable to a simple tendency to wear clothing of a certain type (e.g., athletic team jackets, sweat shirts, tee shirts, etc.) after an athletic team victory.

Discussion

In all, we found support for our expectations concerning the BIRG phenomenon. Students chose to display more apparel indicators of their academic affiliation after their university's varsity football team had recently been successful. It appears, then, from these data and from numerous anecdotal reports that people desire to make others aware of what seem to be their causally meaningless associations with positive sources.[3] Why? What do they intend to get from it? Perhaps, the answer has to do with Heider's balance formulation (1958). Heider discussed two types of perceived relations between things: sentiment relations, which imply a feeling state between stimuli, and unit relations, which merely imply that things are connected in some manner. It is the unit relationship that seems akin to the noninstrumental connection that people tend to publicize between themselves and a successful or otherwise positive source. The results of the present experiment could well be seen as consistent with balance theory. For example, if observers perceive a positive unit relationship (e.g., university affiliation) between a student and a successful football team and if observers generally evaluate successful teams positively, then in order to keep their cognitive systems in balance, the observers would have to evaluate the student positively as well. Hence, we might expect the student to want to make the unit connection evident to as many observers as possible, in this case, through the wearing of university-identifying clothing. The process whereby one publicly seeks to associate himself or herself with a successful other, then, may be reinforced by the tendency of observers to respond in a similar fashion to associated stimuli.

Indirect evidence that tends to support this hypothesis comes from research concerning the transmission of positive and negative information. Manis, Cornell, and Moore (1974) have shown that one who transmits information that the recipient favors is liked more by the recipient than one who transmits information that the recipient disfavors and that this liking occurred even though it was understood that the transmitters did not necessarily endorse the communicated information. Like the royal messengers of old Persia who were feted when they brought news of military victory but killed when they brought news of defeat, the transmitters in the Manis et al. (1974) study acquired the valence of the message with which they were simply paired. Moreover, there is evidence that people recognize this generalization effect and tend to take actions that connect them in the eyes of observers, with positive rather than negative news. For example, Rosen and Tesser have repeatedly shown (e.g., Rosen & Tesser, 1970; Tesser, Rosen, & Batchelor, 1972; Tesser, Rosen, & Tesser, 1971) that people prefer to be connected with the communication of good news to another than with the communication of bad news. Investigating the basic effect, Johnson, Conlee, and Tesser (1974) found their subjects reluctant to communicate negative information not because they felt guilty about transmitting bad news but because they feared that they would be negatively evaluated by the recipient of such news; again, this was true even though all concerned knew that the communicators had in no way caused the bad news. Thus, it appears from these data that: first, individuals who are merely associated with a positive or negative stimulus (in this case, favorable or unfavorable information) will tend to share, in an observer's eyes, the affective quality of the stimulus; and second, at some level individuals seem to understand the workings of this phenomenon and make use of it in the ways they present themselves to others. We wish to interpret the results of Experiment 1 in terms of this formulation. Students at our seven monitored universities chose to wear school-of-attendance apparel after football team victories in order to *display* their connection with the successful team and thereby to enhance their esteem in the eyes of observers to the connection. However, another explanation of our findings exist as well. Perhaps the tendency to wear university-related clothing following team wins had nothing to do with an attempt to proclaim the favorable connection to others but only reflected an increased positivity toward the university as a consequence of team success. That is, it is possible that a football victory caused students to like their school more, and this heightened attraction manifested itself in the tendency to wear school-identified apparel. To test these alternative explanations and to establish the generality of the tendency to BIRG in a different experimental situation than that of Experiment 1, a second experiment was conducted.

EXPERIMENT 2

The major distinction between the competing interpretations described above is the contention of the BIRG model that students wore school-of-attendance clothing after victories in order to publicize their university affiliations and hence increase their prestige in the view of *others*. The "heightened attraction" formulation makes no such claim: One is simply seen to like the school more following victories, and this, rather than the possibility of increased interpersonal prestige, is said to stimulate the wearing of relevant apparel. We decided to test these explanations by way of an examination of the pronoun usage of university students describing the outcome of one of their school's football contests. Earlier in this article we alluded to the tendency of athletic fans to crowd in front of television cameras, wave their index fingers high, and shout, "*We*'re number one!" The choice of this pronoun seemed to us a very good measure of the tendency to BIRG. By employing the pronoun *we*, one is publicly able to associate oneself with another person or group of persons. Through the use of some other designation, for example, *they*, one is able to distance oneself from (i.e., to weaken the perceived association with) another person or persons. It was our feeling that in order to BIRG a successful football team, students would be more likely to describe the outcome of a team victory using the pronoun *we* than they would a team nonvictory. Thus, it was our expectation that this tendency to connect oneself with a positive source but distance oneself from a negative source would influence subjects to use the term, "We won," to describe a team win but use the third person (e.g., "They lost") to describe a team loss.[4] Further, in line with our BIRG model, it was expected that this differential use of language would be most pronounced when the subject's esteem in the eyes of an observer had been recently lowered. That is, if we are correct in proposing that one proclaims a connection with a positive source in an attempt to raise one's esteem in the view of others, then one should be most likely to declare such a connection when that esteem has recently been jeopardized. Thus, if we were to create experimentally in subjects a need to bolster esteem in the eyes of an observer, subjects should be most likely to announce publicly (through use of the pronoun *we*) a connection with a successful team and be least likely to publicize a connection with an unsuccessful team. On the other hand, subjects who have less need to elevate an observer's evaluation of themselves should show a lesser effect. The simple "heightened attraction" model would not make such a prediction, since one's prestige in the eyes of others is not a critical variable in that formulation.

Method

Subjects The subjects were 173 undergraduates at a large state university with a nationally ranked football team. Subjects were randomly selected from student listings in the university phone directory. The sample included approximately equal distributions of males and females.

Procedure During a 3-day period midway through the 1974 football season, subjects were contacted on the phone by one of 16 experimenters (8 males and 8 females) identified as an employee of a "Regional Survey Center" with headquarters in an out-of-state city. The caller explained that he (she) was conducting a survey of college students' knowledge of campus issues and was in town that day calling students at the subject's university. Subjects agreeing to participate (93 percent) were then asked a series of six factually oriented forced-choice questions about aspects of campus life (e.g., "What percent of students at your school are married? Would you say it's closer to 20 percent or 35 percent?"). Following the subject's sixth response, the caller administered the first manipulation. Half of the subjects were told that they had done well on the test, and half were told they they had done poorly. Specifically, subjects were told:

That completes the first part of the questions. The average student gets three out of six correct. You got [five; one] out of six correct. That means you [did really well; didn't do so well] compared to the average student.

Subjects were then told that there were a few more questions and that the first concerned students' knowledge of campus athletic events. At this point the second experimental manipulation occurred. Half of the subjects were asked to describe the outcome of a specific football game; their school's football team had won this game. The other half were asked to describe the outcome of a different game; this was a game that their team had lost. The question was phrased as follows:

In the [first; third] game of the season, your school's football team played the University of [Houston, Missouri]. Can you tell me the outcome of that game?

If a subject did not know the results of the game, a new subject was called. Otherwise the subject's verbatim description of the game outcome was recorded. At the end of the interview, all subjects were fully debriefed.

Independent Variables Two factors were manipulated; a subject's personal outcome on the survey task (success or failure) and the affiliated football team's outcome in the game described (win or non-win). These factors combined to produce a 2 x 2 factorial design.

Dependent Variables Subjects' tendency to use a *we* or *non-we* response in describing a team outcome constituted our dependent measure. Descriptions such as "We won," "We got beat," etc., were considered *we* responses. All other descriptions (e.g., "The score was 14–6, Missouri," "They lost.") were classified as *non-we* responses.

Predictions Two predictions were made. First, it was hypothesized that subjects would emit more *we* responses in describing a team victory than a team defeat. Second, it was expected that the effect of Hypothesis 1 would be greatest for subjects who had "failed" the survey test. The latter hypothesis was based on the assumption that subjects in the personal failure conditions would attempt to associate themselves publicly with a positive event or distance themselves from a negative event through language usage in order to bolster or salvage their damaged images in the eyes of the caller. Subjects in the personal success conditions were not expected to show a similar-sized effect, as their prestige had already been ensured via their successful task performance. Evidence that public success and failure on an experimental task leads to differential tendencies for social approval has been offered by Schneider (1969). He manipulated success and failure and found failure subjects to present themselves more favorably to an observer who could provide an evaluation. Thus, if the BIRG phenomenon is indeed an attempt to gain social approval, we should see our failure subjects BIRG more than our success subjects.

Results

Of the 173 subjects, the data of 5 were discarded because they clearly reported the game results incorrectly. For example, the description "We won" was not counted if in fact the subject's team had lost the game in question. The percentages of *we* responses emitted in the four experimental conditions are presented in Table 2. The first prediction, that *we* usage would be greater in the descriptions

TABLE 2

Percentage of Subjects Using "We," Experiment 2

	PERCENT PERSONAL OUTCOME		
TEAM OUTCOME	*SUCCESS*	*FAILURE*	*MEAN PERCENT*
Win	24 (11/45)	40 (16/40)	32 (27/85)
Nonwin	22 (9/41)	14 (6/42)	18 (15/83)

of team victories than team defeats, was tested by comparing the team win conditions against the team nonwin conditions. A significant effect was obtained, $x^2(1) = 4.20$, $p < .05$, confirming Hypothesis 1. The second prediction, that the tendency for *we* responses to attend victory rather than defeat descriptions would be strongest after a personal failure, was tested as an interaction of the two major independent variables. The resultant statistic, suggested by Langer and Abelson (1972) for testing interactions within a 2 x 2 contingency table, just missed conventional significance levels, $Z = 1.75$, $p < .08$, two-tailed. Tests of the simple main effects of the interaction strongly supported Hypothesis 2. The difference in *we* responding between the team success and team failure cells of the personal failure condition was highly significant, $x^2(1) = 6.90, p < .01$. The comparable test within the personal success condition did not approach significance, $x^2(1) = .07$, *ns*. There were no significant sex effects in the data.

DISCUSSION

The data of Experiment 2 seem clearly to support the general BIRG formulation. Subjects used the pronoun *we* to associate themselves more with a positive than a negative source, and this effect was most pronounced when their public prestige was in jeopardy. We interpret these results as evidence for our contention that people display even the most noninstrumental connections between themselves and the success of others so as to receive positive evaluations from the observers of those connections.

It should be evident that the observer's tendency to assign positivity to one who is associated with positive things is crucial to our hypothesizing about the BIRG phenomenon. It follows from our previously stated assumption that if a person understood that a given observer did not value the success of a specific source, that person would be less likely to try to BIRG that source to the observer. So, if one of our subjects knew that an observer abhorred successful college athletic programs, we would predict that there would be little likelihood of the subject attempting to make visible a connection with a winning football team. But this is a fairly obvious example; few people would predict otherwise. A more subtle and perhaps more informative demonstration might be obtained through a somewhat different manipulation of the observer's relationship to the connection. When an observer to a highly positive association can also lay claim to the association, the prestige of the connection is diffused and, consequently, reduced for anyone attempting to bask in its glory. It is when one's bond to a positive source is not shared by an audience that its prestige value is optimal.Thus, when everyone has a similar positive characteristic, there is no special prestige involved in possessing it, and the likelihood that any one person will boast about that quality should be reduced. For example, a resident of California is less likely to brag to fellow Californians about the favorable climate than to geographically distant others, especially those who cannot claim similarly pleasant weather. It is our hypothesis, then, that the tendency to BIRG a positive source should occur most often when one's connection with the source is stronger than the observer's.[5] A third study was conducted to test this contention.

EXPERIMENT 3

In Experiment 2, it was shown that a personal failure experience increased our subjects' tendency to associate themselves with a positive source and decreased their tendency to associate themselves with a negative source. We have argued that this result occurred because the failure experience lowered perceived prestige and motivated subjects to try to either bolster their images in the eyes of others or prevent them from being further degraded. Central to this argument is the assumption that one's simple, noninstrumental connections are seen to influence observers' personal evaluations. If so, it should be the case that in addition to their use as dependent measures, such connections could be used as effective independent variables. That is, it should be possible to influence subjects' behavior by publicly connecting them with either positive or negative events. In fact, if we are correct in our assumption, manipulating one's public connections with good or bad things should have the same effect as manipulating one's personal success or failure experiences. For example, just as Experiment 2 showed that subjects who failed a task increased the tendency to affiliate themselves with a winner and decreased the tendency to affiliate themselves with a loser in the eyes of an observer to their failure, it follows from our formulation that subjects who are merely publicly connected with a negative event should emit comparable BIRG responses in the presence of an observer to that connection. Experiment 3 was designed to test this possibility and represented a conceptual replication and extension of Experiment 2.

Method

Subjects The subjects were 170 undergraduates at a large state univesity with a powerful football team. The university was not the same as that of Experiment 2; however, subjects were selected for participation in a fashion identical to that of Experiment 2.

Procedure Following the completion of play for the university's football team, subjects were called on the phone by 1 of 18 experimenters (11 males and 7 females) identified as an employee of either the "university's Survey Center" located on campus or the "Regional Survey Center" located in an out-of-state city. Subjects were told that a survey was being conducted of "undergraduates' knowledge of university athletic events." Those agreeing to participate (96 percent) were asked to describe the outcome of first one, then another of their football team's last games of the year. One of the games constituted an important victory, and the other an important nonvictory in the team's season. Half of the subjects were first requested to describe the nonvictory game and, having responded, to describe the victory game. The other subjects had the requests put to them in reverse order. The subjects' verbatim descriptions of the game results were recorded.

Independent Variables Two factors were orthogonally varied: the strength of the subject's affiliation to the university team compared with that of the observer (same as observer's or stronger than observer's) and order of presentation of the games to be described (victory game description requested first or nonvictory game description requested first).

Dependent Variables The dependent measure was the pattern of *we* and *non-we* usage employed by subjects to describe the combination of the victory and nonvictory games. Three combinations were possible. A subject could have used the same *we* or *non-we* term to describe both the victory and the nonvictory, could have used *we* to describe the nonvictory, and *non-we* to describe the victory, or finally, could have used *we* for a victory and *non-we* for a nonvictory.

Predictions It was predicted, first, that there would be an overall tendency for subjects to use *we* in their descriptions of a team victory and *non-we* in their descriptions of a team nonvictory. Such a finding would replicate the basic BIRG effect obtained in Studies 1 and 2. A second hypothesis was that the tendency to use *we* for victory and *non-we* for nonvictory descriptions would be greater in the nonvictory-description-requested-first conditions. Such a result would constitute a conceptual replication of the second finding of Experiment 2. On the basis of the BIRG model, we expected that the effect of publicly describing a negative event with which one is connected would be equivalent in nature to publicly failing on a task. Both operations were thought to reduce subjects' perceptions of their prestige as seen by an observer and, hence, to increase the likelihood of subjects' attempts to ensure the positivity of subsequent evaluations. The third prediction was that Hypothesis 2 would hold most strongly when the observer was identified with an off-campus organization. This expectation was based on the belief that felt prestige to be gained from one's connections to a source is greater and, thus more sought after, when one's connections to that source are stronger than an observer's. Confirmation of this prediction would appear as an interaction of the independent variables of the study.[6]

Results

As expected and consistent with the results of Experiments 1 and 2, the basic BIRG effect occurred in Experiment 3 to support our first hypothesis. That is, subjects used the term *we* nearly twice as often to describe a victory than a nonvictory (26 percent vs. 13.5 percent). This effect is further confirmed when the data are examined in terms of individual subjects' *we/non-we* usage patterns. The majority of subjects were constant in their pattern of responding to the two requests for descriptions; they consistently used either *we* or *non-we* to describe both game outcomes. Thus, there was a strong tendency for our subjects to be consistent in their verbal usage patterns for the two descriptions. However, in 23 instances subjects provided an inconsistent *we/non-we* pattern. In 22 of those instances, the pattern supported the BIRG model; the pronoun *we* was used for the victory description and a *non-we* term was used for the nonvictory description. Using McNemar's test for the significance of changes (Siegel, 1956, pp. 63–67) and

TABLE 3

Percentage of Subjects Using both "We" for Victory Descriptions and "Non-We" for Nonvictory Descriptions, Experiment 3

	*ORDER OF REQUEST**	
STRENGTH OF SUBJECT'S CONNECTION TO TEAM RELATIVE TO OBSERVER'S	*VICTORY DESCRIPTION REQUESTED FIRST*	*NONVICTORY DESCRIPTION REQUESTED FIRST*
Stronger than observer's	3 (1/39)	21 (10/47)
Same as observer's	11 (4/36)	14 (7/48)
Mean percent	7 (5/75)	18 (17/95)

*Numbers given are percentages.

correcting for continuity, the data are highly significant, $x^2(1) = 17.39$, $p < .001$. The tests of Hypothesis 2 and 3 were conducted by considering the distribution (across the cells of our design) of the instances of *we/non-we* usage fitting the pattern predicted by the BIRG model. Table 3 presents these data.

Hypothesis 2 stated that more subjects would use *we* to describe the victory and *non-we* to describe the nonvictory when they were asked to describe the nonvictory first. As expected, subjects were significantly more likely to so respond in the nonvictory-description-requested-first conditions, $x^2(1) = 4.69$, $p < .05$. Hypothesis 3 stated that Hypothesis 2 would hold most clearly when the subjects were more strongly connected with the university team than was the observer. As predicted, Hypothesis 2 was supported to a greater extent when the observer was affiliated with an off-campus rather than a campus agency. However, this tendency did not quite reach conventional levels of significance, $Z = 1.72$. $p < .085$. As in Experiment 2, there were no significant effects for sex of subject.

GENERAL DISCUSSION

Overall, Experiments 1, 2, and 3 provided strong support for the BIRG formulation. All three experiments showed a significant tendency for students to strive to associate themselves publicly with their university's football team more after the team had been successful. A striking aspect of the phenomenon is that subjects sought to proclaim their affiliation with a successful source even when they in no way caused the source's success. This component of the effect suggests a mediator consistent with balance theory. It is our contention that people make known their noninstrumental connections with positive sources because they understand that observers to these connections tend to evaluate connected objects similarly. It appears that the tendency to BIRG is an attempt to secure esteem from those who can perceive the connection. Studies 2 and 3 provided support for such an interpretation. Both showed that experimental operations designed to threaten a subject's esteem in the eyes of an observer caused subjects to be more likely to try publicly to associate themselves with positive sources. Intriguingly, it was possible to increase the tendency to BIRG in these experiments either by initially causing the subject to experience personal failure in an observer's eyes or by initially causing the subject to be noninstrumentally connected with a negative event in an observer's eyes. These manipulations proved functionally equivalent in modifying subject pronoun usage. Thus, in support of our basic argument, being merely associated with someone else's success and failure had much the same effect as personal success and failure. Experiment 3 provided evidence in a different way as well that the desire for prestige is the mediator of the BIRG response. It demonstrated that when subjects' affiliation with a positive source was stronger than an observer's (and therefore carried a greater amount of prestige), they were most likely to BIRG that source in the presence of the observer.

The studies suggest a way to understand how the fortunes of affiliated sports teams can cause lavish displays of civic gratitude and pride in American cities, or "sports riots" in Europe, or murders in South America of players and referees whose actions had caused a home-team defeat. Through their simple connections with sports teams, the personal images of fans are at stake when their teams take the field. The team's victories and defeats are reacted to as personal successes and failures.

Throughout this article we have stressed an interpersonal mediator of the BIRG phenomenon—the perceived esteem of others. We do not wish, however, to preclude the possibility of the tendency to BIRG privately. That is, for wholly intrapersonal reasons, people may draw connections between themselves and positive sources. For example, one may well feel an enhancement of self-esteem that is unrelated to the assessments of others when one is associated with success or positivity. Such an effect could also be interpreted in terms of a tendency to respond similarly to associated objects. It might be that the result of our experiments are, in some degree at least, due to a desire to bolster or maintain one's self-concept. The tendency to employ appropriate apparel or language in a way that connects oneself to something good may involve an attempt to remind oneself of such connections and, thereby, positively affect self-esteem. The fact that in Experiment 2 we are able to influence the BIRG response simply by manipulating the characteristics of the observer suggests that the BIRG phenomenon is not mediated solely by intrapersonal phenomena. Nonetheless, it remains possible that the tendency to BIRG has its basis in a desire to affect self-image as well as social image. In fact, since there is evidence that how we regard ourselves is influenced by how we perceive that others regard us (e.g., Harvey, Kelley, & Shapiro, 1957), these two mediators are not mutually exclusive.

NOTES

1 In any conversion of parametric data to ranks, the possibility exists that the ranked scores will not fully reflect the character of the parametric data. In order to examine such a possibility with respect to our results, a correlational analysis was performed on the standardized index scores and their derived rank scores. A highly similar relationship ($r = -.83$) between the two forms of scores was found; the negativity of this correlation is simply due to the fact that the better ranks of those of lower numerical value.

2 It may be instructive to note that the single exception from this pattern in Table 1 occurred at the University of Michigan as a direct result of a 10–10 tie with Ohio State University in a game for the Big Ten Conference Championship. Most observers, especially the Michigan supporters, felt that the Michigan team had outplayed Ohio State that day and that the game demonstrated Michigan's superiority. However, that tie game constituted Michigan's only entry in our nonwin category, resulting in the only reversal in our data.

3 It might be argued that some subjects felt that their presence in the stands on the day of a game *directly* contributed to their team's success. This seems an unlikely explanation for the obtained results, as an analysis of the data of Experiment 1 showed an equally strong BIRG effect for home and away games.

4 It should be evident to the reader that the general statement of the BIRG formulation includes not only the tendency to bask in reflected glory but also the tendency to distance unnattractive sources.

5 We do not wish to suggest that the tendency to BIRG a positive source never takes place when the observer's association to a successful other is as strong as one's own

but only that the prestige to be derived from a unique (vis-à-vis the observer) connection is relatively more desirable.

6 The experimenters, undergraduate students in a laboratory social psychology course, were not fully aware of these predictions. In order to test the influence of conscious or unconscious experimenter bias on the results of this study, the experimenters were informed of the nature of Hypothesis 1. However, they were blind to the more subtle Hypotheses 2 and 3. If only Hypothesis 1 were confirmed, the data would likely have to be interpreted as potentially influenced by the experiment bias artifact.

The investigation of such a possibility was deemed an important one, since in the prior experiments, experimenters had knowledge of the experimental hypothesis. In Experiment 1, some data recorders were unintentionally informed of the major hypothesis, while others were not. An analysis of the data from these two groups found only a minimal difference in the data patterns, with the uninformed group's data actually more favorable to prediction than the informed group. However, in Experiment 2, all experimenters had knowledge of the prediction.

REFERENCES

Harvey, O. J., H. H. Kelley, and M. M. Shapiro

1957 "Reactions to unfavorable evaluations of self made by other persons." Journal of Personality 25: 393-411.

Heider, F.

1958 The Psychology of Interpersonal Relations. New York: Wiley.

Johnson, R., M. Conlee, and A. Tesser

1974 "Effects of similarity of fate on bad news transmission: a reexamination." Journal of Personality and Social Psychology 29: 644–48.

Langer, E. J. and R. P. Abelson

1972 "The semantics of asking a favor: how to succeed in getting help without really dying." Journal of Personality and Social Psychology 24: 26–32.

Manis, M., S. D. Cornell, and J. C. Moore

1974 "Transmission of attitude-relevant information through a communication chain." Journal of Personality and Social Psychology 30: 81–94.

Rosen, S. and A. Tesser

1970 "On the reluctance to communicate undesirable information. The MUM effect." Sociometry 33: 253–63.

Schneider, D. J.

1969 "Tactical self-presentation after success and failure." Journal of Personality and Social Psychology 13: 262–68.

Siegel, S.

1956 Nonparametric statistics for the behavioral sciences. New York: McGraw-Hill.

Tesser, A., S. Rosen, and T. Batchelor

1972 "On the reluctance to communicate bad news (the MUM effect): a role play extension." Journal of Personality 40: 88–103.

Tesser, A., S. Rosen and M. Tesser

1971 "On the reluctance to communicate undesirable messages (the MUM effect): a field study." Psychological Reports 29: 651–54.

The Search for Glory

Karen Horney

8

Self-idealization always entails a general self-glorification, and thereby gives the individual the much-needed feeling of significance and of superiority over others. But it is by no means a blind self-aggrandizement. Each person builds up his personal idealized image from the materials of his own special experiences, his earlier fantasies, his particular needs, and also his given faculties. If it were not for the personal character of the image, he would not attain a feeling of identity and unity. He idealizes, to begin with, his particular "solution" of his basic conflict: compliance becomes goodness; love, saintliness; aggressiveness becomes strength, leadership, heroism, omnipotence; aloofness becomes wisdom, self-sufficiency, independence. What—according to his particular solution—appear as shortcomings or flaws are always dimmed out or retouched.

He may deal with his contradictory trends in one of three different ways. They may be glorified, too, but remain in the background. It may, for instance, appear only in the course of analysis that an aggressive person, to whom love seems unpermissible softness, is in his idealized image not only a knight in shining armor but also a great lover.

Secondly, contradictory trends, besides being glorified, may be so isolated in the person's mind that they no longer constitute disturbing conflicts. One patient was, in his image, a benefactor of mankind, a wise man who had achieved a self-contained serenity, and a person who could without qualms kill his enemies. These aspects—all of them conscious—were to him not only uncontradictory but also even unconflicting. In literature this way of removing conflicts by isolating them has been presented by Stevenson in *Doctor Jekyll and Mr. Hyde*.

Source: Karen Horney. "The Search for Glory." Selection is reprinted from Neurosis and Human Growth by Karen Horney, M.D., with permission of W. W. Norton and Company, Inc.

Lastly, the contradictory trends may be exalted as positive faculties or accomplishments so that they become compatible aspects of a rich personality. I have cited elsewhere [1] an example in which a gifted person turned his compliant trends into Christlike virtues, his aggressive trends into a unique faculty for political leadership, and his detachment into the wisdom of a philosopher. Thus the three aspects of his basic conflict were at once glorified and reconciled each with the others. He became, in his own mind, a sort of modern equivalent to *l'uomo universale* of the Renaissance.

Eventually the individual may come to identify himself with his idealized, integrated image. Then it does not remain a visionary image which he secretly cherishes; imperceptibly he becomes this image: the idealized image becomes an *idealized self*. And this idealized self becomes more real to him than his real self, not primarily because it is more appealing but because it answers all his stringent needs. This transfer of his center of gravity is an entirely inward process; there is no observable or conspicuous outward change in him. The change is in the core of his being, in his feeling about himself. It is a curious and exclusively human process. It would hardly occur to a cocker spaniel that he "really" is an Irish setter. And the transition can occur in a person only because his real self has previously become indistinct. While the healthy course at this phase of development—and at *any* phase—would be a move toward his real self, he now starts to abandon it definitely for the idealized self. The latter begins to represent to him what he "really" is, or potentially is—what he could be, and should be. It becomes the perspective from which he looks at himself, the measuring rod with which he measures himself.

Self-idealization, in its various aspects, is what I suggest calling a *comprehensive* neurotic solution—i.e., a solution not only for a particular conflict but one that implicitly promises to satisfy all the inner needs that have arisen in an individual at a given time. Moreover, it promises not only a riddance from his painful and unbearable feelings (feeling lost, anxious, inferior, and divided), but in addition an ultimately mysterious fulfillment of himself and his life. No wonder, then, that when he believes he has found such a solution, he clings to it for dear life. No wonder that, to use a good psychiatric term, it becomes *compulsive*.[2] The regular occurrence of self-idealization in neurosis is the result of the regular occurrence of the compulsive needs bred in a neurosis-prone environment.

We can look at self-idealization from two major vantage points: it is the logical outcome of an early development and it is also the beginning of a new one. It is bound to have far-reaching influence upon the further development because there simply is no more consequential step to be taken than the abandoning of the real self. But the main reason for its revolutionary effect lies in another implication of this step. *The energies driving toward self-realization are shifted to the aim of actualizing the idealized self.* This shift means no more and no less than a change in the course of the individual's whole life and development.

We shall see throughout this book the manifold ways in which this shift in direction exerts a molding influence upon the whole personality. Its more immediate effect is to prevent self-idealization from remaining a purely inward process, and to force it into the total circuit of the individual's life. The individual wants to—or, rather, is driven to—express himself. And this now means that he wants to express his idealized self, to prove it in action. It infiltrates his aspirations, his goals, his conduct of life, and his relations to others. For this reason, self-idealization inevitably grows into a more comprehensive drive which I suggest calling by a name appropriate to its nature and its dimensions: *the search for glory*. Self-idealization remains its nuclear part. The other elements in it, all of them always present, though in varying degrees of strength and awareness in each individual case, are the need for perfection, neurotic ambition, and the need for a vindictive triumph.

Among the drives toward actualizing the idealized self *the need for perfection* is the most radical one. It aims at nothing less than molding the whole personality into the idealized self. Like Pygmalion in Bernard Shaw's version, the neurotic aims not only at retouching but at remodeling himself into his special kind of perfection prescribed by the specific features of his idealized image. He tries to achieve this goal by a complicated system of shoulds and taboos. . . .

The most obvious and the most extrovert among the elements of the search for glory is *neurotic ambition*, the drive toward external success. While this drive toward excelling in actuality is pervasive and tends toward excelling in everything, it is usually most strongly applied to those matters in which excelling is most feasible for the given individual at a given time. Hence the content of ambition may well change several times during a lifetime. At school a person may feel it an intolerable disgrace not to have the very best marks in class. Later on, he may be just as compulsively driven to have the most dates with the most desirable girls. And again, still later, he may be obsessed with making the most money, or being the most prominent in politics. Such changes easily give rise to certain self-deceptions. A person who has at one period been fanatically determined to be the greatest athletic hero, or war hero, may at another period become equally bent on being the greatest saint. He may believe, then, that he has "lost" his ambition. Or he may decide that excelling in athletics or in war was not what he "really" wanted. Thus he may fail to realize that he still sails on the boat of ambition but has merely changed the course. Of course, one must also analyze in detail what made him change his course at that particular time. I emphasize these changes because they point to the fact that people in the clutches of ambition are but little related to the *content* of what they are doing. What counts is the excelling itself. If one did not recognize this unrelatedness, many changes would be incomprehensible.

For the purposes of this discussion, the particular area of activity which the specific ambition covets is of little interest. The characteristics remain the same whether it is a question of being a leader in the community, of being the most brilliant conversationalist, of having the greatest reputation as a musician or as an explorer, of playing a role in "society," of writing the best book, or of being the best-dressed person. The picture varies, however, in many ways, according to the nature of the desired success. Roughly, it may belong more in the category of power (direct power, power behind the throne, influence, manipulating), or more in the category of prestige (reputation, acclaim, popularity, admiration, special attention).

These ambitious drives are, comparatively speaking, the most realistic of the expansive drives. At least, this is true in the sense that the people involved put in actual efforts to the end of excelling. These drives also seem more realistic because, with sufficient luck, their possessors may actually acquire the coveted glamor, honors, influence. But, on the other hand, when they do attain more money, more distinction, more power, they also come to feel the whole impact of the futility of their chase. They do not secure any more peace of mind, inner security, or joy of living. The inner distress, to remedy which they started out on the chase for the phantom of glory, is still as great as ever. Since these are not accidental results, happening to this or that individual, but are inexorably bound to occur, one may rightly say that the whole pursuit of success is intrinsically unrealistic.

Since we live in a competitive culture, these remarks may sound strange or unworldly. It is so deeply ingrained in all of us that everybody wants to get ahead of the next fellow, and be better than he is, that we feel these tendencies to be "natural." But the fact that compulsive drives for success will arise only in a competitive culture does not make them any less neurotic. Even in a competitive culture there are many people for whom other values—such as, in particular, that of growth as a human being—are more important than competitive excelling over others.

The last element in the search for glory, more destructive than the others, is the drive *toward a vindictive triumph.* It may be closely linked up with the drive for actual achievement and success but, if so, its chief aim is to put others to shame or defeat them through one's very success; or to attain the power, by rising to prominence, to inflict suffering upon them—mostly of a humiliating kind. On the other hand, the drive for excelling may be relegated to fantasy, and the need for a vindictive triumph then manifests itself mainly in often irresistible, mostly unconscious impulses to frustrate, outwit, or defeat others in personal relations. I call this drive "vindictive" because the motivating force stems from impulses to take revenge for humiliations suffered in childhood—impulses which are reinforced during the later neurotic development. These later accretions probably are responsible for the way in which the need for a vindictive triumph eventually becomes a regular ingredient in the search for glory. Both the degree of its strength and the person's awareness of it vary to a remarkable extent. Most people are either entirely unaware of such a need or cognizant of it only in fleeting moments. Yet it is sometimes out in the open, and then it becomes the barely disguised mainspring of life. Among recent historical figures Hitler is a good illustration of a person who went through humiliating experiences and gave his whole life to a fanatic desire to triumph over an ever-increasing mass of people. In his case vicious circles, constantly increasing the need, are clearly discernible. One of these develops from the fact that he could think only in categories of triumph and defeat. Hence the fear of defeat made further triumphs always necessary. Moreover, the feeling of grandeur, increasing with every triumph, rendered it increasingly intolerable that anybody, or even any nation, should not recognize his grandeur.

Many case histories are similar on a smaller scale. To mention only one example from recent literature, there is *The Man Who Watched the Train Go By.*[3] Here we have a conscientious clerk, subdued in his home life and in his office, apparently never thinking of anything but doing his duty. Through the discovery of the fraudulent maneuvers of his boss, with the resultant bankruptcy of the firm, his scale of values crashes. The artificial distinction between superior beings, to whom everything is allowed, and inferior ones like himself, to whom only the narrow path of correct behavior is permitted, crumbles. He too, he realizes, could be "great" and "free." He could have a mistress, even the very glamorous mistress of his boss. And his pride is by now so inflated that when he actually approaches her, and is rejected, he strangles her. Sought by the police, he is at times afraid, but his main incentive is to defeat the police triumphantly. Even in his attempted suicide, this is the chief motivating force.

Much more frequently the drive toward a vindictive triumph is hidden. Indeed, because of its destructive nature, it is the most hidden element in the search for glory. It may be that only a rather frantic ambition will be apparent. In analysis alone are we able to see that the driving power behind it is the need to defeat and humiliate others by rising above them. The less harmful need for superiority can, as it were, absorb the more destructive compulsion. This allows a person to act out his need and yet feel righteous about it.

It is, of course, important to recognize the specific features of the individual trends involved in the search for glory, because it is always the specific constellation that must be analyzed. But we can understand neither the nature nor the impact of these trends unless we see them as parts of a coherent entity. Alfred Adler was the first psychoanalyst to see it as a comprehensive phenomenon and to point out its crucial significance in neurosis.

There are various solid proofs that the search for glory is a comprehensive and coherent entity. In the first place, all the individual trends described above regularly occur together in one person. Of course, one or another element may so predominate as to make us speak loosely of, say, an ambitious person, or of a dreamer. But that does not mean that the dominance of one element indicates the absence of the others. The ambitious person will have his grandiose image of himself too; the dreamer will want realistic supremacy, even though the latter factor may be apparent only in the way in which his pride is offended by the success of others.[4]

Furthermore, all the individual trends involved are so closely related that the prevailing trend may change during the lifetime of a given person. He may turn from glamorous daydreams to being the perfect father and employer, and again to being the greatest lover of all time.

Lastly, they all have in common *two general characteristics,* both understandable from the genesis and the functions of the whole phenomenon: their compulsive nature and their imaginative character. Both have been mentioned, but it is desirable to have a more complete and succinct picture of their meaning.

Their *compulsive nature* stems from the fact that the self-idealization (and the whole search for glory developing as its sequel) is a neurotic solution. When we call a drive compulsive, we mean the opposite of spontaneous wishes or striving. The latter are an expression of the real self; the former are determined by the inner necessities of the neurotic structure. The individual must abide by them regardless of his real wishes, feelings, or interests lest he incur anxiety, feel torn by conflicts, be overwhelmed by guilt feelings, feel rejected by others, etc. In other words, the difference between spontaneous and compulsive is one between "I want" and "I must have in order to avoid some danger." Although the individual may consciously feel his ambition or his standards of perfection to be what he *wants* to attain, he is actually *driven* to attain it. The need for glory has him in its clutches. Since he himself is unaware of the difference between wanting and being driven, we must establish criteria for a distinction between the two. The most decisive one is the fact that he is driven on the road to glory with an utter *disregard for himself, for his best interests.* (I remember, for example, an ambitious girl, aged ten, who thought she would rather be blind than not become the first in her class.) We have reason to wonder whether more human lives—literally and figuratively—are not sacrificed on the altar of glory than for any other reason. John Gabriel Borkman died when he started to doubt the validity and the possibility of realizing his grandiose mission. Here a truly tragic element enters into the picture. If we sacrifice ourselves for a cause which we, and most healthy people, can realistically find constructive in terms of its value to human beings, that is certainly tragic, but also meaningful. If we fritter away our lives enslaved to the phantom of glory for reasons unknown to ourselves, that assumes the unrelieved proportion of tragic waste—the more so, the more valuable these lives potentially are.

Another criterion of the compulsive nature of the drive for glory—as of any other compulsive drive—is its *indiscriminateness.* Since the person's real interest in a pursuit does not matter, he *must* be the center of attention, *must* be the most attractive, the most intelligent, the most original—whether or not the situation calls for it; whether or not, with his given attributes, he *can* be the first. He *must* come out victorious in any argument, regardless of where the truth lies. His thoughts in this matter are the exact opposite of those of Socrates: ". . .for surely we are not now simply contending in order that my view or that of yours may prevail, but I presume that we ought both of us to be fighting for the truth."[5] The compulsiveness of the neurotic person's need for indiscriminate supremacy makes him indifferent to truth, whether concerning himself, others, or facts.

Furthermore, like any other compulsive drive, the search for glory has the quality of *insatiability*. It must operate as long as the unknown (to himself) forces are driving him. There may be a glow of elation over the favorable reception of some work done, over a victory won, over any sign of recognition or admiration—but it does not last. A success may hardly be experienced as such in the first place, or, at the least, must make room for despondency or fear soon after. In any case, the relentless chase after more prestige, more money, more women, more victories and conquests keeps going, with hardly any satisfaction or respite.

Finally, the compulsive nature of a drive shows in the *reactions to its frustration.* The greater its subjective importance, the more impelling is the need to attain its goal, and hence the more intense the reactions to frustration. These constitute one of the ways in which we can measure the intensity of a drive. Although this is not always plainly visible, the search for glory is a most powerful drive. It can be like a demoniacal obsession, almost like a monster swallowing up the individual who has created it. And so the reactions to frustration must be severe. They are indicated by the terror of doom and disgrace that for many people is spelled in the idea of failure. Reactions of panic, depression, despair, rage at self and others to what is conceived as "failure" are frequent, and entirely out of porportion to the actual importance of the occasion. The phobia of falling from heights is a frequent expression of the dread of falling from the heights of illusory grandeur.

Consider the dream of a patient who had a phobia about heights. It occurred at a time when he had begun to doubt his established belief of unquestioned superiority. In the dream he was at the top of a mountain, but in danger of falling, and was clinging desparately to the ridge of the peak. "I cannot get any higher than I am," he said, "so all I have to do in life is to hold on to it." Consciously, he referred to his social status, but in a deeper sense this "I cannot get any higher" also held true for his illusions about himself. He could not get any higher than having (in his mind) a godlike omnipotence and cosmic significance!

NOTES

1 Our Inner Conflicts
2 We shall discuss the exact meaning of *compulsiveness* when we have a more complete view of some further steps involved in this solution.
3 By Georges Simenon, Reynal and Hitchcock, New York.
4 Because personalities often look different in accordance with the trend which is prevailing, the temptation to regard these trends as separate entities is great. Freud regarded phenomena which are roughly similar to these as separate instinctual drives with separate origins and properties. When I made a first attempt to enumerate compulsive drives in neurosis, they appeared to me too as separate "neurotic trends."
5 From Philebus, The Dialogues of Plato, translated into English by B. Jowett, M.A., Random House, New York.

On Face-Work: An Analysis of Ritual Elements in Social Interaction

Erving Goffman

9

Every person lives in a world of social encounters, involving him either in face-to-face or mediated contact with other participants. In each of these contacts, he tends to act out what is sometimes called a *line*—that is, a pattern of verbal and nonverbal acts by which he expresses his view of the situation and through this his evaluation of the participants, especially himself. Regardless of whether a person intends to take a line, he will find that he has done so in effect. The other participants will assume that he has more or less willfully taken a stand, so that if he is to deal with their response to him he must take into consideration the impression they have possibly formed of him.

The term *face* may be defined as the positive social value a person effectively claims for himself by the line others assume he has taken during a particular contact.[1] Face is an image of self delineated in terms of approved social attributes—albeit an image that others may share, as when a person makes a good showing for his profession or religion by making a good showing for himself.

A person tends to experience an immediate emotional response to the face which a contact with others allows him; he cathects his face; his "feelings" become attached to it. If the encounter sustains an image of him that he has long taken for granted, he probably will have few feelings about the matter. If events

Source: Erving Goffman, "On Face-Work: An Analysis of Ritual Elements in Social Interaction," Psychiatry (1955) 18: 213-31.

establish a face for him that is better than he might have expected, he is likely to "feel good"; if his ordinary expectations are not fulfilled, one expects that he will "feel bad" or "feel hurt." In general, a person's attachment to a particular face, coupled with the ease with which disconfirming information can be conveyed by himself and others, provides one reason why he finds that participation in any contact with others is a commitment. A person will also have feelings about the face sustained for the other participants, and while these feelings may differ in quantity and direction from those he has for his own face, they constitute an involvement in the face of others that is as immediate and spontaneous as the involvement he has in his own face. One's own face and the face of others are constructs of the same order; it is the rules of the group and the definition of the situation which determine how much feeling one is to have for face and how this feeling is to be distributed among the faces involved.

A person may be said to *have*, or *be in*, or *maintain* face when the line he effectively takes presents an image of him that is internally consistent, that is supported by judgments and evidence conveyed by other participants, and that is confirmed by evidence conveyed through impersonal agencies in the situation. At such times the person's face clearly is something that is not lodged in or on his body, but rather something that is diffusely located in the flow of events in the encounter and becomes manifest only when these events are read and interpreted for the appraisals expressed in them.

The line maintained by and for a person during contact with others tends to be of a legitimate institutionalized kind. During a contact of a particular type, an interactant of known or visible attributes can expect to be sustained in a particular face and can feel that it is morally proper that this should be so. Given his attributes and the conventionalized nature of the encounter, he will find a small choice of lines will be open to him and a small choice of faces will be waiting for him. Further, on the basis of a few known attributes, he is given the responsiblity of possessing a vast number of others. His coparticipants are not likely to be conscious of the character of many of these attributes until he acts perceptibly in such a way as to discredit his possession of them; then everyone becomes conscious of these attributes and assumes that he willfully gave a false impression of possessing them.

Thus while concern for face focuses the attention of the person on the current activity, he must, to maintain face in this activity, take into consideration his place in the social world beyond it. A person who can maintain face in the current situation is someone who abstained from certain actions in the past that would have been difficult to face up to later. In addition, he fears loss of face now partly because the others may take this as a sign that consideration for his feelings need not be shown in the future. There is nevertheless a limitation to this interdependence between the current situation and the wider social world: an encounter with people whom he will not have dealings with again leaves him free to take a high line that the future will discredit, or free to suffer humiliations that would make future dealings with them an embarrassing thing to have to face.

A person may be said to *be in wrong face* when information is brought forth in some way about his social worth which cannot be integrated, even with effort, into the line that is being sustained for him. A person may be said to *be out of face* when he participates in a contact with others without having ready a line of the kind participants in such situations are expected to take. The intent of many pranks is to lead a person into showing a wrong face or no face, but there will also be serious occasions, of course, when he will find himself expressively out of touch with the situation.

When a person senses that he is in face, he typically responds with feelings of confidence and assurance. Firm in the line he is taking, he feels that he can hold his head up and openly present himself to others. He feels some security and some relief—as he also can when the others feel he is in wrong face but successfully hide these feelings from him.

When a person is in wrong face or out of face, expressive events are being contributed to the encounter which cannot be readily woven into the expressive fabric of the occasion. Should he sense that he is in wrong face or out of face, he is likely to feel ashamed and inferior because of what has happened to the activity on his account and because of what may happen to his reputation as a participant. Further, he may feel bad because he had relied upon the encounter to support an image of self to which he has become emotionally attached and which he now finds threatened. Felt lack of judgmental support from the encounter may take him aback, confuse him, and momentarily incapacitate him as an interactant. His manner and bearing may falter, collapse, and crumble. He may become embarrassed and chagrined; he may become shamefaced. The feeling, whether warranted or not, that he is perceived in a flustered state by others, and that he is presenting no usable line, may add further injuries to his feeling, just as his change from being in wrong face or out of face to being shamefaced can add further disorder to the expressive organization of the situation. Following common usage, I shall employ the term *poise* to refer to the capacity to suppress and conceal any tendency to become shamefaced during encounters with others.

In our Anglo-American society, as in some others, the phrase "to lose face" seems to mean to be in wrong face, to be out of face, or to be shamefaced. The phrase "to save one's face" appears to refer to the process by which the person sustains an impression for others that he has not lost face. Following Chinese usage, one can say that "to give face" is to arrange for another to take a better line than he might otherwise have been able to take,[2] the other thereby gets face given him, this being one way in which he can gain face.

As an aspect of the social code of any social circle, one may expect to find an understanding as to how far a person should go to save his face. Once he takes on a self-image expressed through face he will be expected to live up to it. In different ways in different societies he will be required to show self-respect, abjuring certain actions because they are above or beneath him, while forcing himself to perform others even though they cost him dearly. By entering a situation in which he is given a face to maintain, a person takes on the responsibility of standing guard over the flow of events as they pass before him. He must ensure that a particular *expressive order* is sustained—an order which regulates the flow of events, large or small, so that anything that appears to be expressed by them will be consistent with his face. When a person manifests these compunctions primarily from duty to himself, one speaks in our society of pride; when he does so because of duty to wider social units and receives support from these units in doing so, one speaks of honor. When these compunctions have to do with postural things, with expressive events derived from the way in which the person handles his body, his emotions, and the things with which he has physical contact, one speaks of dignity, this being an aspect of expressive control that is always praised and never studied. In any case, while his social face can be his most personal possession and the center of his security and pleasure, it is only on loan to him from society; it will be withdrawn unless he conducts himself in a way that is worthy of it. Approved attributes and their relation to face make of every man his own jailer; this is a fundamental social constraint even though each man may like his cell.

Just as the member of any group is expected to have self-respect, so also he is expected to sustain a standard of considerateness; he is expected to go to certain lengths to save the feelings and the face of others present, and he is expected to do this willingly and spontaneously because of emotional identification with the others and with their feelings.[3] In consequence, he is disinclined to witness the defacement of others.[4] The person who can witness another's humiliation and unfeelingly retain a cool countenance himself is said in our society to be "heartless," just as he who can unfeelingly participate in his own defacement is thought to be "shameless."

The combined effect of the rule of self-respect and the rule of considerateness is that the person tends to conduct himself during an encounter so as to maintain both his own face and the face of the other participants. This means that the line taken by each participant is usually allowed to prevail, and each participant is allowed to carry off the role he appears to have chosen for himself. A state where everyone temporarily accepts everyone else's line is established.[5] This kind of mutual acceptance seems to be a basic structural feature of interaction, expecially the interaction of face-to-face talk. It is typically a "working" acceptance, not a "real" one, since it tends to be based not on agreement of candidly expressed heartfelt evaluations, but upon a willingness to give temporary lip service to judgments with which the participants do not really agree.

The mutual acceptance of lines has an important conservative effect upon encounters. Once the person initially presents a line, he and the others tend to build their later responses upon it, and in a sense become stuck with it. Should the person radically alter his line, or should it become discredited, then confusion results, for the participants will have prepared and committed themselves for actions that are now unsuitable.

Ordinarily, maintenance of face is a condition of interaction, not its objective. Usual objectives, such as gaining face for oneself, giving free expression to one's true beliefs, introducing depreciating information about the others, or solving problems and performing tasks, are typically pursued in such a way as to be consistent with the maintenance of face. To study face-saving is to study the traffic rules of social interaction; one learns about the code the person adheres to in his movement across the paths and designs of others, but not where he is going, or why he wants to get there. One does not even learn why he is ready to follow the code, for a large number of different motives can equally lead him to do so. He may want to save his own face because of his emotional attachment to the image of self which it expresses, because of his pride or honor, because of the power his presumed status allows him to exert over the other participants, and so on. He may want to save the others' face because of his emotional attachment to an image of them, or because he feels that his coparticipants have a moral right to this protection, or because he wants to avoid the hostility that may be directed toward him if they lose their face. He may feel that an assumption has been made that he is the sort of person who shows compassion and sympathy toward others, so that to retain his own face, he may feel obliged to be considerate of the line taken by the other participants.

By *face-work* I mean to designate the actions taken by a person to make whatever he is doing consistent with face. Face-work serves to counteract "incidents"—that is, events whose effective symbolic implications threaten face. Thus poise is one important type of face-work, for through poise the person controls his embarrassment and hence the embarrassment that he and others might have over his embarrassment. Whether or not the full consequences of face-saving actions are known to the person who employs them, they often become habitual and standardized practices; they are like traditional plays in a game or traditional steps in a dance. Each person, subculture, and society seems to have its own characteristic repertoire of face-saving practices. It is to this repertoire that people partly refer when they ask what a person or culture is "really" like. And yet the particular set of practices stressed by particular persons or groups seems to be drawn from a single logically coherent framework of possible practices. It is as if face, by its very nature, can be saved only in a certain number of ways, and as if each social grouping must make its selections from this single matrix of possibilities.

The members of every social circle may be expected to have some knowledge of face-work and some experience in its use. In our society, this kind of capacity is sometimes called tact, *savoir-faire*, diplomacy, or social skill. Variation in social skill pertains more to the efficacy of face-work than to the frequency of its application, for almost all acts involving others are modified, prescriptively or proscriptively, by considerations of face.

If a person is to employ his repertoire of face-saving practices, obviously he must first become aware of the interpretations that others may have placed upon his acts and the interpretations that he ought perhaps to place upon theirs. In other words, he must exercise perceptiveness.[6] But even if he is properly alive to symbolically conveyed judgments and is socially skilled, he must yet be willing to exercise his perceptiveness and his skill; he must, in short, be prideful and considerate. Admittedly, of course, the possession of perceptiveness and social skill so often leads to their application that in our society terms such as politeness or tact fail to distinguish between the inclination to exercise such capacities and the capacities themselves.

I have already said that the person will have two points of view—a defensive orientation toward saving his own face and a protective orientation toward saving the others' face. Some practices will be primarily defensive and others primarily protective, although in general one may expect these two perspectives to be taken at the same time. In trying to save the face of others, the person must choose a tack that will not lead to loss of his own; in trying to save his own face, he must consider the loss of face that his action may entail for others.

In many societies there is a tendency to distinguish three levels of responsibility which a person may have for a threat to face that his actions have created. First, he may appear to have acted innocently; his offense seems to be unintended and unwitting, and those who perceive his act can feel that he would have attempted to avoid it had he foreseen its offensive consequences. In our society one calls such threats to face *faux pas, gaffes*, boners, or bricks. Second, the offending person may appear to have acted maliciously and spitefully, with the intention of causing open insult. Third, there are incidental offenses; these arise as an unplanned but sometimes anticipated by-product of action—action which the offender performs in spite of its offensive consequences, although not out of spite. From the point of view of a particular participant, these three types of threat can be introduced by the participant himself against his own face, or by the others against himself. Thus the person may find himself in many different relations to a threat to face. If he is to handle himself and others well in all contingencies, he will have to have a repertoire of face-saving practices for each of these possible relations to threat.

THE BASIC KINDS OF FACE-WORK

The Avoidance Process

The surest way for a person to prevent threats to his face is to avoid contacts in which these threats are likely to occur. In all societies one can observe this in the avoidance relationship[7] and in the tendency for certain delicate transactions to be conducted by go-betweens.[8] Similarly, in many societies, members know the value of voluntarily making a gracious withdrawal before an anticipated threat to face has had a chance to occur.[9]

Once the person does chance an encounter, other kinds of avoidance practices come into play. As defensive measures, he keeps off topics and away from activities which would lead to the expression of information that is inconsistent with the line he is maintaining. At opportune moments he will change the topic of conversation or the direction of activity. He will often present initially a front of diffidence and composure, suppressing any show of feeling until he has found out what kind of line the others will be ready to support for him. Any claims regarding self may be made with belittling modesty, with strong qualifications, or with a note of unseriousness; by hedging in these ways he will have prepared a self for himself that will not be discredited by exposure, personal failure, or the unannounced acts of others. And if he does not hedge his claims about self, he will at least attempt to be realistic about them, knowing that otherwise events may discredit him and make him lose face.

Certain protective maneuvers are as common as these defensive ones. The person shows respect and politeness, making sure to extend to others any ceremonial treatment which might be their due. He employs discretion; he leaves unstated facts which might implicitly or explicitly contradict and embarrass the positive claims made by others.[10] He employs circumlocutions and deceptions, phrasing his replies with careful ambiguity so that the others' face is preserved even if their welfare is not.[11] He employs courtesies, making slight modifications of his demands on or appraisals of the others so that they will be able to define the situation as one in which their self-respect is not threatened. In making a belittling demand upon the others, or in imputing uncomplimentary attributes to them, he may employ a joking manner, allowing them to take the line that they are good sports, able to relax from their ordinary standards of pride and honor. And before engaging in a potentially offensive act, he may provide explanations as to why the others ought not to be affronted by it. For example, if he knows that it will be necessary to withdraw from the encounter before it has terminated, he may tell the others in advance that it is necessary for him to leave, so that they will have faces that are prepared for it. But neutralizing the potentially offensive act need not be done verbally; he may wait for a propitious moment or natural break—for example, in conversation, a momentary lull when no one speaker can be affronted—and then leave, in this way using the context instead of his words as a guarantee of inoffensiveness.

When a person fails to prevent an incident, he can still attempt to maintain the fiction that no threat to face has occurred. The most blatant example of this is found where the person acts as if an event which contains a threatening expression has not occurred at all. He may apply this studied nonobservance to his own acts—as when he does not by any outward sign admit that his stomach is rumbling—or to the acts of others, as when he does not "see" that the other has stumbled.[12] Social life in mental hospitals owes much to this process; patients employ it in regard to their own peculiarities, and visitors employ it, often with tenuous desperation, in regard to patients. In general, tactful blindness of this kind is applied only to events which, if perceived at all, could be perceived and interpreted only as threats to face.

A more important, less spectacular kind of tactful overlooking is practiced when a person openly acknowledges an incident as an event that has occurred, but not as an event that contains a threatening expression. If he is not the one who is responsible for the incident, then his blindness will have to be supported by his forbearance; if he is the doer of the threatening deed, then his blindness will have to be supported by his willingness to seek a way of dealing with the matter which leaves him dangerously dependent upon the cooperative forbearance of the others.

Another kind of avoidance occurs when a person loses control of his expressions during an encounter. At such times he may try not so much to overlook the incident as to hide or conceal his activity in some way, thus making it possible for the others to avoid some of the difficulties created by a participant who has not maintained face. Correspondingly, when a person is caught out of face because he had not expected to be thrust into interaction, or because strong feelings have disrupted his expressive mask, the others may protectively turn away from him or his activity for a moment, to give him time to assemble himself.

The Corrective Process

When the participants in an undertaking or encounter fail to prevent the occurrence of an event that is expressively incompatible with the judgments of social worth that are being maintained, and when the event is of the kind that is difficult to overlook, then the participants are likely to give it accredited status as an incident—to ratify it as a threat that deserves direct official attention—and to proceed to try to correct for its effects. At this point one or more participants find themselves in an established state of ritual disequilibrium or disgrace, and an attempt must be made to reestablish a satisfactory ritual state for them. I use the term *ritual* because I am dealing with acts through whose symbolic component the actor shows how worthy he is of respect or how worthy he feels others are of it. The imagery of equilibrium is apt here because the length and intensity of the corrective effort is nicely adapted to the persistence and intensity of the threat.[13] One's face, then, is a sacred thing, and the expressive order required to sustain it is therefore a ritual one.

The sequence of acts set in motion by an acknowledged threat to face, and terminating in the reestablishment of ritual equilibrium, I shall call an *interchange.*[14] Defining a message or move as everything conveyed by an actor during a turn at taking action, one can say that an interchange will involve two or more moves and two or more participants. Obvious examples in our society may be found in the sequence of "Excuse me" and "Certainly," and in the exchange of presents or visits. The interchange seems to be a basic concrete unit of social activity and provides one natural empirical way to study interaction of all kinds. Face-saving practices can be usefully classified according to their position in the natural sequence of moves which comprise this unit. Aside from the event which introduces the need for a corrective interchange, four classic moves seem to be involved.

There is, first, the challenge, by which participants take on the responsibility of calling attention to the misconduct; by implication they suggest that the threatened claims are to stand firm and that the threatening event itself will have to be brought back into line.

The second move consists of the offering, whereby a participant, typically the offender, is given a chance to correct for the offense and reestablish the expressive order. Some classic ways of making this move are available. On the one hand, an attempt can be made to show that what admittedly appeared to be a threatening expression is really a meaningless event, or an unintentional act, or a joke not meant to be taken seriously, or an unavoidable, "understandable" product of extenuating circumstances. On the other hand, the meaning of the event may be granted and effort concentrated on the creator of it. Information may be provided to show that the creator was under the influence of something and not himself, or that he was under the command of somebody else and not acting for himself. When a person claims that an act was meant in jest, he may go on and claim that the self that seemed to lie behind the act was also projected as a joke. When a person suddenly finds that he has demonstrably failed in capacities that the others assumed him to have and to claim for himself—such as the capacity to spell, to perform minor tasks, to talk without malapropisms, and so on—he may quickly add, in a serious or unserious way, that he claims these incapacities as part of his self. The meaning of the threatening incident thus stands, but it can now be incorporated smoothly into the flow of expressive events.

As a supplement to or substitute for the strategy of redefining the offensive act or himself, the offender can follow two other procedures: he can provide compensations to the injured—when it is not his own face that he has threatened; or he can provide punishment, penance, and expiation for himself. These are important moves or phases in the ritual interchange. Even though the offender may fail to prove his innocence, he can suggest through these means that he is now a renewed person, a person who has paid for his sin against the expressive order and is once more to be trusted in the judgmental scene. Further, he can show that he does not treat the feelings of others lightly, and that if their feelings have been injured by him, however innocently, he is prepared to pay a price for his action. Thus he assures the others that they can accept his explanations without this acceptance constituting a sign of weakness and a lack of pride on their part. Also, by his treatment of himself, by his self-castigation, he shows that he is clearly aware of the kind of crime he would have committed had the incident been what it first appeared to be, and that he knows the kind of punishment that ought to be accorded to one who would commit such a crime. The suspected person thus shows that he is thoroughly capable of taking the role of the others toward his own activity, that he can still be used as a responsible participant in the ritual process, and that the rules of conduct which he appears to have broken are still sacred, real, and unweakened. An offensive act may arouse anxiety about the ritual code; the offender allays this anxiety by showing that both the code and he as an upholder of it are still in working order.

After the challenge and the offering have been made, the third move can occur: the persons to whom the offering is made can accept it as a satisfactory means of reestablishing the expressive order and the faces supported by this order. Only then can the offender cease the major part of his ritual offering.

In the terminal move of the interchange, the forgiven person conveys a sign of gratitude to those who have given him the indulgence of forgiveness.

The phases of the corrective process—challenge, offering, acceptance, and thanks—provide a model for interpersonal ritual behavior, but a model that may be departed from in significant ways. For example, the offended parties may give the offender a chance to initiate the offering on his own before a challenge is made and before they ratify the offense as an incident. This is a common courtesy, extended on the assumption that the recipient will introduce a self-challenge. Further, when the offended persons accept the corrective offering, the offender may suspect that this has been grudgingly done from tact, and so he may volunteer additional corrective offerings, not allowing the matter to rest until he has received a second or third acceptance of his repeated apology. Or the offended persons may tactfully take over the role of the offender and volunteer excuses for him that will, perforce, be acceptable to the offended persons.

An important departure from the standard corrective cycle occurs when a challenged offender patently refuses to heed the warning and continues with his offending behavior, instead of setting the activity to rights. This move shifts the play back to the challengers. If they countenance the refusal to meet their demands, then it will be plain that their challenge was a bluff and that the bluff has been called. This is an untenable position; a face for themselves cannot be derived from it, and they are left to bluster. To avoid this fate, some classic moves are open to them. For instance, they can resort to tactless, violent retaliation; destroying either themselves or the person who had refused to heed their warning. Or they can withdraw from the undertaking in a visible huff—righteously indignant, outraged, but confident of ultimate vindication. Both tacks provide a way of denying the offender his status as an interactant, and hence denying the reality of the offensive judgment he has made. Both strategies are ways of salvaging face, but for all concerned the costs are usually high. It is partly to forestall such scenes that an offender is usually quick to offer apologies; he does not want the affronted persons to trap themselves into the obligation to resort to desperate measures.

It is plain that emotions play a part in these cycles of response, as when anguish is expressed because of what one has done to another's face, or anger because of what has been done to one's own. I want to stress that these emotions function as moves, and fit so precisely into the logic of the ritual game that it would seem difficult to understand them without it. In fact, spontaneously expressed feelings are likely to fit into the formal pattern of the ritual interchange more elegantly than consciously designed ones.

COOPERATION IN FACE-WORK

When a face has been threatened, face-work must be done, but whether this is initiated and primarily carried through by the person whose face is threatened, or by the offender, or by a mere witness, is often of secondary importance. Lack of effort on the part of one person induces compensative effort from others; a contribution by one person relieves the others of the task. In fact, there are many minor incidents in which the offender and the offended simultaneously attempt to initiate an apology. Resolution of the situation to everyone's apparent satisfaction is the first requirement; correct apportionment of blame is typically a secondary consideration. Hence terms such as tact and *savoir faire* fail to distinguish whether it is the person's own face that his diplomacy saves or the face of the others. Similarly, terms such as *gaffe* and *faux pas* fail to specify whether it is the actor's own face he has threatened or the face of other participants. And it is understandable that if one person finds he is powerless to save his own face, the others seem especially bound to protect him. For example, in polite society, a handshake that perhaps should not have been extended becomes one that cannot be declined. Thus one accounts for the *noblesse oblige* through which those of high status are expected to curb their power of embarrassing their lessers, as well as the fact that the handicapped often accept courtesies that they can manage better without.

Since each participant in an undertaking is concerned, albeit for differing reasons, with saving his own face and the face of the others, then tacit cooperation will naturally arise so that the participants together can attain their real shared but differently motivated objectives.

One common type of tacit cooperation in face-saving is the tact exerted in regard to face-work. The person not only defends his own face and protects the face of the others, but also acts so as to make it possible and even easy for the others to employ face-work for themselves and him. He helps them to help themselves and him. Social etiquette, for example, warns men against asking for New Year's Eve dates too early in the season, lest the girl find it difficult to provide a gentle excuse for refusing. This second-order tact can be further illustrated by the widespread practice of negative-attribute etiquette. The person who has an unapparent negatively valued attribute often finds it expedient to begin an encounter with an unobtrusive admission of his failing, especially with persons who are uninformed about him. The others are thus warned in advance against making disparaging remarks about his kind of person and are saved from the contradiction of acting in a friendly fashion to a person toward whom they are unwittingly being hostile. This strategy also prevents the others from automatically making assumptions about him which place him in a false position and saves him from painful forbearance or embarrassing remonstrances.

Tact in regard to face-work often relies for its operation on a tacit agreement to do business through the language of hint—the language of innuendo, ambiguities, well-placed pauses, carefully worded jokes, and so on.[15] The rule regarding this unofficial kind of communication is that the sender ought not to act as if he had officially conveyed the message he has hinted at, while the recipients have the right and the obligation to act as if they have not officially received the message contained in the hint. Hinted communication, then, is deniable communication; it need not be faced up to. It provides a means by which the person can be warned that his current line or the current situation is leading to loss of face, without this warning itself becoming an incident.

Another form of tacit cooperation, and one that seems to be much used in many societies, is reciprocal self-denial. Often the person does not have a clear idea of what would be a just or acceptable apportionment of judgments during the occasion, and so he voluntarily deprives or depreciates himself while indulging and complimenting the others, in both cases carrying the judgments safely past what is likely to be just. The favorable judgments about himself he allows to come from the others; the unfavorable judgments of himself are his own contributions. This "after you, Alphonse" technique works, of course, because in depriving himself he can reliably anticipate that the others will compliment or indulge him. Whatever allocation of favors is eventually established, all participants are first given a chance to show that they are not bound or constrained by their own desires and expectations, that they have a properly modest view of themselves, and that they can be counted upon to support the ritual code. Negative bargaining, through which each participant tries to make the terms of trade more favorable to the other side, is another instance; as a form of exchange perhaps it is more widespread than the economist's kind.

A person's performance of face-work, extended by his tacit agreement to help others perform theirs, represents his willingness to abide by the ground rules of social interaction. Here is the hallmark of his socialization as an interactant. If he and the others were not socialized in this way, interaction in most societies and most situations would be a much more hazardous thing for feelings and faces. The person would find it impractical to be oriented to symbolically conveyed appraisals of social worth, or to be possessed of feeling—that is, it would be impractical for him to be a ritually delicate object. And as I shall suggest, if the person were not a ritually delicate object, occasions of talk could not be organized in the way they usually are. It is no wonder that trouble is caused by a person who cannot be relied upon to play the face-saving game.

NOTES

1 For discussions of the Chinese conception of face, see the following: Hsien Chin Hu, "The Chinese concept of 'face,'" American Anthropologist n.s. 46 (1944): 45–64. Martin C. Yang, A Chinese Village (New York, Columbia University Press, 1945), pp. 167–72. J. Macgowan, Men and Manners of Modern China; London, Unwin, 1912, pp. 301–12. Arthur H. Smith, Chinese Characteristics (New York, Fleming H. Revell Co., 1894), pp. 16-18. For a comment on the American Indian conception of face, see Marcel Mauss, The Gift (Ian Cunnison, tr.) (London, Cohen & West, 1954), p. 38.

2 See, for example, Smith, Chinese Characteristics, p. 17.

3 Of course, the more power and prestige the others have, the more a person is likely to show consideration for their feelings, as H. E. Dale suggests in The Higher Civil Service of Great Britain (Oxford, Oxford University Press, 1941), p. 126*n*. "The doctrine of 'feelings' was expounded to me many years ago by a very eminent civil servant with a pretty taste in cynicism. He explained that the importance of feelings varies in close correspondence with the importance of the person who feels. If the public interest requires that a junior clerk should be removed from his post, no regard need be paid to his feelings; if it is a case of an Assistant Secretary, they must be carefully considered, within reason; if it is a Permanent Secretary, his feelings are a principal element in the situation, and only imperative public interest can override their requirements."

4 Salesmen, especially street "stemmers," know that if they take a line that will be discredited unless the reluctant customer buys, the customer may be trapped by considerateness and buy in order to save the face of the salesman and prevent what would ordinarily result in a scene.

5 Surface agreement in the assessment of social worth does not, of course, imply equality; the evaluation consensually sustained of one participant may be quite different from the one consensually sustained of another. Such agreement is also compatible with expression of differences of opinion between two participants, provided each of the disputants shows "respect" for the other, guiding the expression of disagreement so that it will convey an evaluation of the other that the other will be willing to convey about himself. Extreme cases are provided by wars, duels, and barroom fights, when these are of a gentlemanly kind, for they can be conducted under consensual auspices, with each protagonist guiding his action according to the rules of the game, thereby making it possible for his action to be interpreted as an expression of a fair player openly in combat with a fair opponent. In fact, the rules and etiquette of any game can be analyzed as a means by which the image of a fair player can be expressed, just as the image of a fair player can be analyzed as a means by which the rules and etiquette of a game are sustained.

6 Presumably social skill and perceptiveness will be high in groups whose members frequently act as representatives of wider social units such as lineages or nations, for the player here is gambling with a face to which the feelings of many persons are attached. Similarly, one might expect social skill to be well developed among those of high station and those with whom they have dealings, for the more face an interactant has, the greater the number of events that may be inconsistent with it, and hence the greater the need for social skill to forestall or counteract these inconsistencies.

7 In our own society an illustration of avoidance is found in the middle- and upper-class Negro who avoids certain face-to-face contacts with whites in order to protect the self-evaluation projected by his clothes and manner. See, for example, Charles Johnson, Patterns of Negro Segregation (New York, Harper, 1943), ch. 13. The function of avoidance in maintaining the kinship system in small preliterate societies might be taken as a particular illustration of the same general theme.

8 An illustration is given by K. S. Latourette, The Chinese: Their History and Culture (New York, Macmillan, 1942): "A neighbor or a group of neighbors may tender their good offices in adjusting a quarrel in which each antagonist would be sacrificing his face by taking the first step in approaching the other. The wise intermediary can effect the reconciliation while preserving the dignity of both" (vol. 2: p. 211).

9 In an unpublished paper, Harold Garfinkel has suggested that when the person finds that he has lost face in a conversational encounter, he may feel a desire to disappear or "drop through the floor," and that this may involve a wish not only to conceal loss of face but also to return magically to a point in time when it would have been possible to save face by avoiding the encounter.

10 When the person knows the others well, he will know what issues ought not to be raised and what situations the others ought not to be placed in, and he will be free to introduce matters at will in all other areas. When the others are strangers to him, he will often reverse the formula, restricting himself to specific areas he knows are safe. On these occasions, as Simmel suggests, "...discretion consists by no means only in the respect for the secret of the other, for his specific will to conceal this or that from us, but in staying away from the knowledge of all that the other does not expressly reveal to us." See The Sociology of Georg Simmel, Kurt H. Wolff, tr. and ed. (Glencoe, Ill, Free Press, 1950), pp.320–21.

11 The Western traveler used to complain that the Chinese could never be trusted to say what they meant but always said what they felt their Western listener wanted to hear. The Chinese used to complain that the Westerner was brusque, boorish and unmannered. In terms of Chinese standards, presumably, the conduct of a Westerner

is so gauche that he creates an emergency, forcing the Asian to forgo any kind of direct reply in order to rush in with a remark that might rescue the Westerner from the compromising position in which he had placed himself. (See Smith, Chinese Characteristics, ch. 8, "The Talent of Indiscretion.") This is an instance of the important group of misunderstandings which arise during interaction between persons who come from groups with different ritual standards.

12 A pretty example of this is found in parade-ground etiquette which may oblige those in a parade to treat anyone who faints as if he were not present at all.

13 This kind of imagery is one that social anthropologists seem to find naturally fitting. Note, for example, the implications of the following statement by Margaret Mead in her "Kinship in the Admiralty Islands" (Anthropological Papers of the American Museum of Natural History, 34: 183-358); "If a husband beats his wife, custom demands that she leave him and go to her brother, real or officiating, and remain a length of time commensurate with the degree of her offended dignity" (p. 274).

14 The notion of interchange is drawn in part from Eliot D. Chapple, "Measuring human relations," Genetic Psychology Monographs 22 (1940): 3–147, especially pp. 26–30, and from A. B. Horsfall and C. A. Arensberg, "Teamwork and productivity in a shoe factory," Human Organization 8 (1949): 13–25, especially p. 19. For further material on the interchange as a unit see E. Goffman, "Communication conduct in an island community," unpublished Ph.D. dissertation, Department of Sociology, University of Chicago, 1953, especially chs. 12 and 13, pp. 165–95.

15 Useful comments on some of the structural roles played by unofficial communication can be found in a discussion of irony and banter in Tom Burns, "Friends, enemies, and the polite fiction," American Sociological Review 18 (1943): 654–62.

Self-Monitoring of Expressive Behavior

Mark Snyder

10

A common observation in literature and cultural folklore has been that certain nonlanguage behaviors, such as voice quality, body motion, touch, and the use of personal space appear to play a prominent role in communication. Furthermore, laboratory and field research clearly indicates that much information about a person's affective states, status and attitude, cooperative and competitive nature of social interaction, and interpersonal intimacy is expressed and accurately communicated to others in noverbal expressive behavior (e.g., Ekman, 1971; Hall, 1966; Mehrabian, 1969; Sommer, 1969).

Much interest in nonverbal expressive behavior stems from a belief that it may not be under voluntary control and might function as a pipeline or radarscope to one's true inner "self" (e.g., Freud, 1959). Although nonverbal behavior may often escape voluntary attempts at censorship (Ekman & Friesen, 1969), there have been numerous demonstrations that individuals can voluntarily express various emotions with their vocal and/or facial expressive behavior in such a way that their expressive behavior can be accurately interpreted by observers (e.g., Davitz, 1964). In fact, some social observers have proposed that the ability to manage and control expressive presentation is a prerequisite to effective social and interpersonal functioning. Thus Goffman (1955) has likened social interaction to a theatrical performance or "line" of verbal and nonverbal self-expressive acts which are managed to keep one's line appropriate to the current situation. Such self-management requires a repertoire of face-saving devices, an awareness of the interpretations which others place on one's acts, a desire to maintain social

Source: Mark Snyder, "Self-Monitoring of Expressive Behavior," Journal of Personality and Social Psychology 30 (1974): 526–37.

approval, and the willingness to use this repertoire of impression management tactics. Within the more restricted domain of facial expressions of emotional affect, Ekman (1971) has suggested that individuals typically exercise control over their facial expressions to intensify, neutralize, or mask the expression of a felt affect, according to various norms of social performance.

There are, however, striking and important individual differences in the extent to which individuals can and do monitor their self-presentation, expressive behavior, and nonverbal affective display. Clearly, professional stage actors can do what I cannot. Politicians have long known how important it is to wear the right face for the right constituency. La Guardia learned the expressive repertoires of several different cultures in New York and became "chameleon-like" the son of whatever people he was facing. Yet little research has directly concerned such individual differences in the self-control of expressive behavior. At best, some dispositional correlates of spontaneous and natural expression of emotion have been reported (e.g., Buck, Savin, Miller & Caul, 1972; Davitz, 1964).

A Concept of Self-Monitoring of Expressive Behavior How might individual differences in the self-control of expressive behavior arise? What might be the developmental, historical, and current motivational origins of self-control ability and performance? Perhaps some individuals have learned that their affective experience and expression are either socially inappropriate or lacking. Such people may *monitor* (observe and control) their self-presentation and expressive behavior. The goals of self-monitoring may be (*a*) to communicate accurately one's true emotional state by means of an intensified expressive presentation; (*b*) to communicate accurately an arbitrary emotional state which need not be congruent with actual emotional experience; (*c*) to conceal adaptively an inappropriate emotional state and appear unresponsive and unexpressive; (*d*) to conceal adaptively an inappropriate emotional state and appear to be experiencing an appropriate one: (*e*) to appear to be experiencing some emotion when one experiences nothing and a nonresponse is inappropriate.

An acute sensitivity to the cues in a situation which indicate what expression of self-presentation is appropriate and what is not is a corollary ability to self-monitoring. One such set of cues for guiding self-monitoring is the emotional expressive behavior of other similar comparison persons in the same situation.

There is some evidence of an acute version of this process. When persons are made uncertain of their emotional reactions, they look to the behavior of others for cues to define their emotional states and model the emotional expressive behavior of others in the same situation who appear to be behaving appropriately (Schachter & Singer, 1962).

On the other hand, persons who have not learned a concern for appropriateness of their self-presentation would not have such well-developed self-monitoring skills and would not be so vigilant to social comparison information about appropriate patterns of expression and experience. This is not to say that they are not emotionally expressive or even that they are less so than those who monitor their presentation. Rather, their self-presentation and expressive behavior seem, in a functional sense, to be controlled from within by their affective states (they express it as they feel it) rather than monitored, controlled, and molded to fit the situation.

Self-Monitoring and Consistency in Expression: Between Modalities and Across Situations Do people, as Freud (1959) believed, say one thing with their lips and another with their fingertips? More specifically, what governs the consistency between expression in different channels of expression, such as vocal and facial, and the consistency between nonverbal and verbal expression? The self-monitoring approach provides one perspective on differences and consistencies across channels of expression, including verbal self-presentation.

It is likely that when one is monitoring, various channels are monitored differently, and perhaps some forgotten. Thus, what may be communicated by one channel may differ from what is communicated by another. For example, I may cover my sadness by putting on a happy face but forget to use a happy voice.

Ekman and Friesen (1969, 1972) have demonstrated with psychiatric patients and student nurses that in deception situations people are more likely to monitor their facial than body presentation, with the result that the deception is more likely to be detected from an examination of body cues than facial cues. Thus, the information encoded in monitored channels should differ from that encoded in nonmonitored channels. However, it is likely that great consistency characterizes that set of channels of expressive (verbal or nonverbal) behaviors which are simultaneously monitored according to the same criteria. Furthermore, self-monitored expressive behavior should vary more from situation to situation than nonmonitored expressive behavior. Self-monitoring individuals should be most likely to monitor and control their expression in situations which contain reliable cues to social appropriateness. Thus, such a person would be more likely to laugh at a comedy when watching it with amused peers than when watching it alone. The laughing behavior of the nonself-monitoring person should be more invariant across those two situations and more related to how affectively amused he himself actually is. The expressive behavior of self-monitoring individuals should be more reflective of an internal affect state when it is generated in a situation with minimal incentives for, and cues to, self-monitoring.

The cross-situational variability of the self-monitoring versus the consistency of the nonself-monitoring individuals is similar to the "traits versus situations" issue: Is behavior controlled by situational factors and hence predictable from characteristics of the surrounding situation, or is it controlled by internal states and dispositions which produce cross-situational consistency and facilitate prediction from characteristics of the person, measures of internal states, or dispositions (Mischel, 1968; Moos, 1968, 1969)? Bem (1972) has proposed that the issue be redirected from an "either traits or situations for all behavior of all people" debate to a search for moderating variables which would allow the specification for an individual of equivalence classes of situations and responses across which he monitors his behavior with respect to a particularly central self-concept. In these areas he would show trait-like cross-situational and interresponse mode consistency: in others he would not. In the domain of expressive behavior, individual differences in self-monitoring are a moderating variable which identifies individuals who demonstrate or fail to demonstrate consistency across channels of expression and between situations differing in monitoring properties.

In Search of a Measure of Individual Differences in Self-Monitoring How can we capture individual differences in self-monitoring? A review of the literature suggests as least one currently available measure which might serve to identify individuals who differ in self-monitoring.

The self-monitoring individual is one who, out of a concern for social appropriateness, is particularly sensitive to the expression and self-presentation of others in social situations and uses these cues as guidelines for monitoring his own self-presentation. Is there then any difference between this person and the individual with a high "need for approval" as measured by the Marlowe-Crowne Social Desirability Scale (Crowne & Marlowe, 1964)? In a wide variety of situations, individuals who have a high need for approval give socially desirable responses. They conform more than low-need-for-approval individuals in an Asch situation; they verbally condition better; they do not show overt hostility toward one who has insulted and double-crossed them; and they are less likely to report dirty words in a perceptual defense task (Crowne & Marlowe, 1964). All of this would suggest that the high-need-for-approval person is one who modifies his behavior from situation to situation. However, other evidence suggests that this ability to alter behavior may be severely limited to contingencies of social approval (Bem, 1972).

In addition, it may be only the social approval of adult experimenters which is reinforcing and sought after. In a sociometric study, fraternity members with a high need for approval were described by their peers as individuals who spend most of their time alone rather than with other people, do not go out of their way to make friends, are not very conversational, and do not act friendly toward other fraternity members (study by Stephen C. Bank, reported in Crowne & Marlowe, 1964, pp. 162–63).

In another study on verbal conditioning, high and low-need-for-approval subjects did not differ in the extent to which they modeled the behavior of a peer (actually a confederate) they had previously observed perform the experimental task appropriately (Crowne & Marlowe, 1964, pp. 61-72). Furthermore, and particularly relevant to the self-monitoring of expressive behavior, this self-control ability may not extend into the domain of expressive behavior. Zaidel and Mehrabian (1969) reported that individuals who scored high on the Need for Approval Scale were actually less able to communicate either positive or negative affect facially or vocally than were low-need-for-approval subjects. In this experimental situation, the socially desirable response and the one which would gain the approval of the experimenter would clearly be the accurate expression and communication of affect. Thus, although high-need-for-approval individuals may be motivated to modify their expressive self-presentation in order to gain approval, they may lack the necessary self-control abilities and skills.

Self-monitoring would probably best be measured by an instrument specifically designed to discriminate individual differences in concern for social appropriateness, sensitivity to the expression and self-presentation of others in social situations as cues to social appropriateness of self-expression, and use of these cues as guidelines for monitoring and managing self-presentation and expressive behavior. Accordingly, an attempt was made to transpose the self-monitoring concept into a self-report scale which reliably and validly measures it.

The convergence between diverse methods of measuring self-monitoring was examined according to the strategy of construct validation (Cronbach & Meehl, 1955). To demonstrate discriminant validity (Campbell & Fiske, 1959), comparisons were made between self-monitoring and need for approval in the prediction of each external criterion in the validation strategy. Need for approval was chosen for these critical comparisons for two reasons. Its conceptual relationship to self-monitoring has already been discussed. Naturally, this procedure also further individuates the type of person identified by the Need for Approval Scale. In addition, Campbell (1960) has recommended that in view of the general response tendency of some individuals to describe themselves in a favorable manner, and the close relationship between probability of endorsement of personality statements and their social desirability, all tests of the voluntary self-descriptive sort should be demonstrated to predict their criterion measures better than a measure of the general social desirability factor.

CONSTRUCTION OF THE SELF-MONITORING SCALE

Forty-one true-false self-descriptive statements were administered to 192 Stanford University undergraduates. The set included items which describe (*a*) concern with the social appropriateness of one's self-presentation (e.g., "At parties and social gatherings, I do not attempt to do or say things that others will like"); (*b*) attention to social comparison information as cues to appropriate self-expression (e.g., "When I am uncertain how to act in social situation, I look to the behavior of others for cues"); (*c*) the ability to control and modify one's self-presentation and expressive behavior (e.g., "I can look anyone in the eye and tell a lie with a straight face (if for a right end)"); (*d*) the use of this ability in particular situations (e.g., "I may deceive people by being friendly when I really dislike them"); and (*e*) the extent to which the respondent's expressive behavior and self-presentation is cross-situationally consistent or variable (e.g., "In different situations and with different people, I often act like very different persons").

The individual items were scored in the direction of high self-monitoring. For approximately half the items, agreement was keyed as high SM; for the remainder, disagreement was keyed as high SM.

An item analysis was performed to select items to maximize internal consistency. In this procedure, the top and bottom thirds in total test scores of persons were found. Then the percentages of persons in each group who responded in the manner keyed as high SM were determined. Finally, the percentage in the bottom group was subtracted from the percentage in the top group. This difference (*D*) served as an index of item validity to discriminate total test scores (Anastasi, 1968). *D* is directly proportional to the difference between the number of "correct" and "incorrect" total score discriminations made by an item. *D* values are not independent of item difficulty and are biased in favor of items of intermediate difficulty level. *D* is, then, an appropriate criterion for selecting items according to both discriminative power and intermediate difficulty level (Nunnally, 1967).

Items were discarded on the basis of low *D* scores until a set of 25 items remained which maximized the internal consistency of the scale (Nunnally, 1967, pp. 263–65). The Self-Monitoring Scale has a Kuder-Richardson 20 reliability of 0.70, and a test-retest reliability of 0.83 $(d) = 51$, $p < .001$, one-month time interval).

Cross-validation on an independent sample of 146 University of Minnesota undergraduates yielded a Kuder-Richardson 20 reliability coefficient of 0.63.

The 25 items of the SM, proportions of respondents answering the item in the low-SM-scored direction, their *D* values, and item-total point-biserial correlations calculated for the University of Minnesota sample are presented in Table 1.

Correlations with Other Scales Correlations between the SM and related but conceptually distinct individual differences measures provide some evidence for its discriminant validity. There is a slight negative relationship ($r = -.1874$, $df = 190$, $p < .01$) between the SM and the Marlowe-Crowne Social Desirability Scale (M-C SDS, Crowne & Marlowe, 1964). Individuals who report that they observe, monitor, and manage their self-presentation are unlikely to report that they engage in rare but socially desirable behaviors.

There is a similarly low negative relationship ($r=-.2002$, $df=190$, $p < .01$) between the SM and the Minnesota Multiphasic Personality Inventory Psychopathic Deviate scale. High-SM subjects are unlikely to report deviant psychopathological behaviors or histories of maladjustment.

There is a small and nonsignificant negative relationship ($r=-.25$, $df=24$, *ns*) between the SM and the *c* scale of the Performance Style Test, (e.g., Ring & Wallston, 1968). The *c* scale was designed to identify a person who is knowledgeable about the kind of social performance required in a wide range of situations and who seeks social approval by becoming whatever kind of person the situation requires. He is literally a chameleon. Clearly the SM and *c* do not identify the same individuals.

The SM was also found to be unrelated to Christie and Geis's (1970) Machiavellianism ($r=-.0931$, $df=51$, *ns*), Alpert-Haber (1960) Achievement Anxiety Test ($r=+.1437$, $df=51$, *ns*), and Kassarjian's (1962) inner-other directedness ($r=-.1944$, $df=54$, *ns*).

It thus appears that SM is relatively independent of the other variables measured.

VALIDATION: SELF-MONITORING AND PEER RATINGS

As a first source of validity evidence for the SM, a sociometric study of peer ratings was conducted. In choosing this method, it was assumed that a person who has good control of his self-presentation and expressive behavior and who is sensitive to social appropriateness cues should be seen as such a person by others who have had the opportunity for repeated observation of his self-presentation in a wide variety of social situations.

Method

Subjects The subjects in this study were 16 members of a male fraternity living group at Stanford University who agreed to participate in an investigation of person perception.

Procedures Each subject completed the SM and the M-C SDS and then participated in a sociometric person perception task.

Each subject indicated for each of six other members of the fraternity specified

TABLE 1

Instructions, Items, Scoring Key, Difficulty, and Discrimination Indexes for the Self-Monitoring Scale*

ITEM AND SCORING KEY†		*DISCRIMINATION*			
	DIFFICULTY‡	*D*§	x^2**	*p*	b_p††
1. I find it hard to imitate the behavior of other people. (F)	.63	.50	32.07	.0005	.33
2. My behavior is usually an expression of my true inner feelings, attitudes, and beliefs. (F)	.67	.23	7.26	.01	.13
3. At parties and social gatherings, I do not attempt to do or say things that others will like. (F)	.17	.21	8.29	.005	.34
4. I can only argue for ideas which I already believe. (F)	.43	.29	8.91	.005	.22
5. I can make impromptu speeches even on topics about which I have almost no information. (T)	.69	.21	6.41	.025	.32
6. I guess I put on a show to impress or entertain people. (T)	.65	.44	26.5	.0005	.45
7. When I am uncertain how to act in a social situation, I look to the behavior of others for cues. (T)	.20	.19	6.55	.025	.24
8. I would probably make a good actor. (T)	.69	.36	17.8	.0005	.43
9. I rarely need the advice of my friends to choose movies, books, or music. (F)	.64	.24	6.78	.01	.15
10. I sometimes appear to others to be experiencing deeper emotions than I actually am. (T)	.57	.20	4.78	.05	.39
11. I laugh more when I watch a comedy with others than when alone. (T)	.33	.23	6.51	.025	.29
12. In a group of people I am rarely the center of attention. (F)	.64	.32	13.09	.0005	.40
13. In different situations and with different people, I often act like very different persons. (T)	.40	.22	5.54	.025	.40
14. I am not particularly good at making other people like me. (F)	.30	.27	10.12	.005	.22
15. Even if I am not enjoying myself, I often pretend to be having a good time. (T)	.61	.21	5.67	.025	.24

ITEM AND SCORING KEY†		DISCRIMINATION			
	DIFFICULTY‡	D§	x^2**	p	b_p††
16. I'm not always the person I appear to be. (T)	.26	.23	7.17	.01	.33
17. I would not change my opinions (or the way I do things) in order to please someone else or win their favor. (F)	.61	.34	15.5	.0005	.34
18. I have considered being an entertainer. (T)	.79	.28	12.64	.0005	.46
19. In order to get along and be liked, I tend to be what people expect me to be rather than anything else. (T)	.79	.25	9.96	.005	.29
20. I have never been good at games like charades or improvisational acting. (F)	.52	.45	25.96	.0005	.31
21. I have trouble changing my behavior to suit different people and different situations. (F)	.36	.38	19.35	.0005	.45
22. At a party I let others keep the jokes and stories going. (F)	.65	.24	6.80	.01	.36
23. I feel a bit awkward in company and do not show up quite so well as I should. (F)	.54	.21	11.05	.001	.32
24. I can look anyone in the eye and tell a lie with a straight face (if for a right end). (T)	.58	.38	19.25	.0005	.33
25. I may deceive people by being friendly when I really dislike them. (T)	.46	.35	15.07	.0005	.32

Note. T = true; F = false; SM = Self-Monitoring Scale.

*Directions for Personal Reaction Inventory were: The statements on the following pages concern your personal reactions to a number of different situations. No two statements are exactly alike, so consider each statement carefully before answering. If a statement is *TRUE* or *MOSTLY TRUE* as applied to you, blacken the space marked *T* on the answer sheet. If a statement is *FALSE* or *NOT USUALLY TRUE* as applied to you, blacken the space marked *F*. Do not put your answers on this test booklet itself.

It is important that you answer as frankly and as honestly as you can. Your answers will be kept in the strictest confidence.

†Items keyed in the direction of high SM.

‡Difficulty = proportion of individuals not responding in SM-keyed direction.

§Discrimination = difference between proportions of individuals in upper and lower thirds of total scores responding in high-SM direction.

**x^2 calculated from the contingency table relating frequencies of T, F for each item and upper third, lower third for *total* SM score (including that item).

††Point-biserial correlations between individual items and total scores with that item excluded.

for him by the experimenter whether the following self-monitoring attributes were very true, mostly true, somewhat true, or not at all true.

(1) Concerned about acting appropriately in social situations;

(2) Openly expresses his true inner feelings, attitudes, and beliefs;

(3) Has good self-control of his behavior. Can play many roles;

(4) Is good at learning what is socially appropriate in new situations;

(5) Often appears to lack deep emotions; and

(6) Has good self-control of his emotional expression. Can use it to create the impression he wants.

In addition, two other judgments were required: "Is ingratiating. Attempts to do or say things designed to make others like him more" (same 4-point scale as above) and "How much do you like this person?" (very much, moderately, somewhat, not at all).

Results and Discussion

Each subject in the experiment served as a judge of six others and was in turn judged by six other members of his living group. For each person as a stimulus, ratings of him were summed across his six judges to form a single score on each dimension which could range from 0 (six ratings of not at all true) to 18 (six ratings of very true). For each person, a single "peer rating of self-monitoring" score was computed by summing across the six self-monitoring dimensions.

The group of 16 subjects was then dichotomized at the median to form a high-SM group ($n=8$) and a low-SM group ($n=8$).

Self-monitoring characteristics were seen as more true of high-SM ($M=50.5$) than of low-SM ($M=40.2$) individuals ($t=2.69$, $df=14$, $p < .02$, two-tailed test). No differences were observed between high-SM and low-SM individuals on ingratiation or liking ($t=0.49$ and 0.20, respectively, $df=14$, *ns*).

Mean peer rating of self-monitoring, ingratiation, and liking for high M-C SDS (above the median, $n=8$) and low M-C SDS (below the median, $n=8$) were also calculated. In contrast to SM scores, M-C SDS scores were unrelated to peer rating of self-monitoring (high M-C SDS $M=54.0$, low M-C SDS $M=56.7$, $t=.59$, $df=14$, *ns*).

The relationship between the SM, M-C SDS, and peer rating of self-monitoring may be examined in terms of product-moment correlations. There is a significant relationship between the SM and peer rating of self-monitoring ($r=.45$, $df=14$, $p < .05$). The higher an individual's score on the SM, the more frequently self-monitoring characteristics were attributed to him. The M-C SDS and peer rating of self-monitoring are not related ($r=-.14$, $df=14$ *ns*).

An image emerges of the high-SM individual as perceived by his peers. He is a person who, out of a concern for acting appropriately in social situations, has become particularly skilled at controlling and modifying his social behavior and emotional expression to suit his surroundings on the basis of cues in the situation which indicate what attitudes and emotions are appropriate. The low-SM individual, as perceived by his peers, is less able and/or less likely to control and modify his self-presentation and expressive behavior to keep it in line with situational specification of appropriateness. He is also less vigilant to such cues.

High and low scorers on the M-C SDS, by contrast, do not differ in these characteristics. In fact, the evidence suggests that if in fact the M-C SDS is a measure of need for approval, this need is not related to the ability (as perceived by one's peers) to control and monitor one's self-presentation and emotional expressive behavior on the basis of situation-to-situation variation in contingencies of social appropriateness.

VALIDATION: SELF-MONITORING, STAGE ACTORS, AND PSYCHIATRIC WARD PATIENTS

Another means of establishing the validity of an instrument is by predicting how predetermined groups of individuals would score when the instrument is administered to them. According to this strategy, SM scores of criterion groups chosen to represent extremes in self-monitoring were compared with the unselected sample of Stanford University undergraduates.

Professional Stage Actors Groups of individuals known to be particularly skilled at controlling their expressive behavior (e.g., actors, mime artists, and politicians) should score higher on the SM than an unselected sample. The SM was administered to a group of 24 male and female dramatic actors who were appearing in professional productions at Stanford and in San Francisco.

Their average score on the SM was 18.41 with a standard deviation of 3.38. This is significantly higher than the mean SM score for the Stanford sample ($t=8.27$, $df=555$, $p < .001$).

Thus, stage actors do score higher than nonactors on the SM. Actors probably do have particularly good self-control of their expressive behavior and self-presentation while on stage. It is not clear that actors are any more concerned about monitoring their expressive presentation in other situations.

Hospitalized Psychiatric Ward Patients The behavior of hospitalized psychiatric patients is less variable across situation than that of "normals." Moos (1968) investigated the reactions of patients and staff in a representative sample of daily settings in a psychiatric inpatient ward in order to assess the relative amount of variance accounted for by settings and individual differences. The results indicated that for patients, individual differences accounted for more variance than setting differences; whereas for staff, individual differences generally accounted for less variance than setting differences. One interpretation of this finding is that psychiatric ward patients are unable or unwilling to monitor their social behavior and self-presentation to conform to variations in contingencies of social appropriateness between situations. In fact, diagnoses of "normal" and "psychopathological" may be closely related to cross-situational plasticity or rigidity (Cameron, 1950). Moos (1969) has reported that situational factors play an increasingly potent role in the behavior of institutionalized individuals as therapy progresses.

Accordingly, it was expected that a sample of hospitalized psychiatric ward patients should score lower on the SM than nonhospitalized normals.

The SM was administered to 31 male hospitalized psychiatric patients at the Menlo Park Veterans Administration Hospital. Their psychiatric diagnoses varied, and most had been previously institutionalized. Each patient's cumulative length of hospitalization varied from several months to several years.

The average SM score for this group was 10.19 with a standard deviation of 3.63. This is significantly lower than the mean SM score for the Stanford sample ($t=3.44$, $df=562$, $p < .001$).

VALIDATION: SELF-MONITORING AND THE EXPRESSION OF EMOTION

If the SM discriminates individual differences in the self-control of expressive behavior, this should be reflected behaviorally. In a situation in which individuals are given the opportunity to communicate an arbitrary affective state by means of nonverbal expressive behavior, a high-SM individual should be able to perform this task more accurately, easily, and fluently than a low SM.

Method

Subjects: Expression of Emotion Male and female students whose SM scores were above the 75th percentile (SM > 15) or below the 25th percentile (SM < 9) were recruited by telephone from the pool of pretested introductory psychology students. In all, 30 high-SM and 23 low-SM subjects participated in the study and received either course credit or $1.50.

Procedure: Expression of Emotion Each subject was instructed to read aloud an emotionally neutral three-sentence paragraph (e.g., "I am going out now. I won't be back all afternoon. If anyone calls, just tell him I'm not here.") in such a way as to express each of the seven emotions—anger, happiness, sadness, surprise, disgust, fear, and guilt or remorse using their vocal and facial expressive behavior. The order of expression was determined randomly for each subject. The subject's facial and upper-body expressive behavior was filmed and his voice tape-recorded. It was suggested that he imagine he was trying out for a part in a play and wanted to give an accurate, convincing, natural, and sincere expression of each emotion—one that someone listening to the tape or watching the film would be able to understand as the emotion the subject had been instructed to express. The procedure is similar to one used by Levitt (1964).

These filmed and taped samples of expressive behavior were scored by judges who indicated which of the seven emotions the stimulus person was expressing. Accuracy of the judges was used as a measure of the expressive self-control ability of the stimulus subjects.

Judgments of Expressive Behavior: Subjects The films and tapes of expressive behavior were scored by a group of 20 high-SM (SM > 15, or top 25 percent) and 13 low-SM (SM < 9, or bottom 25 percent) naive judges who were paid $2.00 an hour.

Judgments of Emotional Expressive Behavior: Procedure Judges participated in small groups of both high- and low-SM judges who watched films for approximately one fourth of the subjects in the expression experiment and listened to the tapes of approximately another one fourth of the subjects. For each stimulus segment, judges indicated which of the seven emotions had been expressed.

Results and Discussion

Accuracy of Expression and SM Scores Accuracy of the judges in decoding the filmed and taped expressive behavior for each stimulus person was used as a measure of his self-control of expressive behavior ability. For each of the 53 subjects in the expression task, the average accuracy of his judges was computed separately for films and tapes and high- and low-SM judges. Table 2 represents these accuracy scores as a function of stimulus (expresser) SM scores, facial or vocal channel of expression, and judge SM score for naive judges. Each stimulus person expressed seven emotions. Therefore, mean accuracy scores can range from 0 to 7.

TABLE 2

SM and Accuracy of Expression of Emotion: Naive Judges

STIMULUS	*HIGH-SM JUDGE*		*LOW-SM JUDGE*	
	FACE	*VOICE*	*FACE*	*VOICE*
High SM				
(n = 30)				
M*	3.353	4.047	3.196	3.564
Variance	.718	.636	1.117	1.769
Low SM				
(n = 23)				
M	2.518	2.957	2.493	3.094
Variance	1.348	.982	1.479	2.102

Note. SM = Self-Monitoring Scale.

*Average accuracy computed for each stimulus across all judges who rated him and then averaged across n stimulus persons; range = 0–7.

The average accuracy scores for each stimulus person's facial and vocal expressive behavior, as judged by high-SM and low-SM judges, were entered into an analysis of variance. Expresser SM score (high SM or low SM) was a between-stimulus-persons factor; channel of expression (face or voice) and judge SM score (high SM or low SM) were within-stimulus-persons factors.

The following pattern of results emerges. Individuals who scored high on the SM were better able to communicate accurately an arbitrarily chosen emotion to naive judges than were individuals who scored low on the SM. That is, judges were more often accurate in judging both the facial and vocal expressive behavior generated in this emotion communication task by high-SM stimuli than by low-SM stimuli ($F = 11.72$, $df = 1/51$, $p < .01$). For both high- and low-SM stimuli, accuracy was greater in the vocal than the facial channel ($F = 19.12$, $df = 1/153$, $p < .001$). Finally, there was a tendency for high-SM judges to be better judges of emotion than low-SM judges ($F = 1.69$, $df = 1/153$, $p < .25$). In addition, high-SM judges may have been more differentially sensitive to the expressive behavior of high- and low-SM stimuli. That is, the difference in accuracy for judging high-SM and low-SM stimuli for high-SM judges was greater than the corresponding difference for low-SM judges. However, once again the differences are not significant ($F = 2.41$, $df = 1/153$, $p < .25$).

Discriminant Validation: SM versus M-C SDS In the sample of 192 from which the subjects for the expression task were selected, scores on the SM and M-C SDS were very slightly correlated ($r = -.1874$). However, in the sample of 53 subjects chosen for this experiment, the correlation was $-.3876$ ($df = 51$, $p < .01$). Furthermore, individuals who scored below the median on the M-C SDS were better able than those who scored above the median to voluntarily communicate emotion in this experimental task ($F = 4.426$, $df = 1/51$, $p < .05$). These differences present a rival explanation of the differences observed in self-control of expressive behavior between high-SM and low-SM groups.

To discriminate between the SM and M-C SDS as predictors of self-control of expression ability, two analyses of covariance were performed. In the first, accuracy scores for naive judges collapsed across judge SM score and channel were examined as a function of stimulus SM scores as the independent variable and stimulus M-C SDS scores as the covariate. After removing the effects of the covariate (M-C SDS), there is still a highly significant treatment (SM) effect ($F = 7.13$, $df = 1/50$, $p < .01$). That is, individuals who scored high on the SM were better able than low-SM scorers to accurately express and communicate arbitrary emotions independent of their M-C SDS scores.

In the second analysis of covariance, accuracy scores for naive judges collapsed across judge SM score and channel were examined as a function of stimulus M-C SDS as the independent variable and stimulus SM scores as the covariate. The results of this analysis are quite conclusive. After removing the effects of the covariate (SM), there is no remaining relationship between the independent variable (M-C SDS) and expression accuracy ($F = .75$, $df = 1/50$, *ns*). That is, whatever relationship exists between M-C SDS scores and self-control by expression ability is entirely accounted for by the slight negative correlation between the M-C SDS and SM.

Thus, the results of this experiment clearly indicate that scores on the SM are related to the self-control of expressive behavior. High-SM individuals were better able than low-SM individuals to express arbitrary emotional states in facial and vocal behavior.

VALIDATION: SELF-MONITORING AND ATTENTION TO SOCIAL COMPARISON INFORMATION

It has been proposed that out of a concern for social appropriateness of his behavior, a high-SM individual is particularly attentive to social comparison information and uses this information as guidelines to monitor and manage his self-presentation and expressive behavior.

Consistent with this formulation, high-SM individuals are seen by their peers as better able to learn what is socially appropriate in new situations than are low-SM. Two SM items which best predict performance in the emotion expression task are: "When I am uncertain how to act in a social situation, I look to the behavior of others for cues," and "I laugh more when I watch a comedy with others than when alone."

All of this suggests that, given the opportunity in a self-presentation situation, a high-SM individual should be more likely to seek out relevant social comparison information.

Method

Subjects Subjects were recruited from the pretested introductory psychology subject pool on the basis of high-SM scores (SM $>$ 15) or low-SM scores (SM $<$ 9). A total of 14 high-SM and 13 low-SM subjects participated in the experiment and were paid $1.00.

Procedure Each subject performed a self-presentation task in a situation designed to facilitate self-monitoring. He was asked to respond to a series of true-false self-descriptive personality test items in preparation for a discussion of how test-takers decide how to respond to ambiguously worded questionnaire items. During the task he was given the opportunity to consult a "majority response sheet" which listed the modal response of his introductory psychology class for each item in order to consider possible alternative interpretations of the items in preparation for the discussion.

Pretesting had indicated that the task was interpreted as neither social pressure to consult the information nor a test of resistance to temptation to cheat. Rather it appears that a situation was created in which the subjects knew that normative social comparison information was available to them and they could consult it or not as they wished in preparation for a later discussion of their self-descriptions on the questionnaire items.

Unknown to the subject who performed this task alone, an observer in the next room recorded the frequency with which the subject consulted the majority response sheet and timed each look. The sheet had been left by the experimenter at the far corner of the subject's table so that consulting it required observable but not effortful behavior by the subject. It was expected that a high-SM subject would look more often, as measured by frequency and duration of looking, at this social comparison information than would a low-SM subject.

Results and Discussion

Results on the dependent measures of seeking out of social comparison information were analyzed as a function of both SM and M-C SDS scores (r SM.M-C SDS = –.067, df = 25, ns) in a 2 x 2 (High SM, Low SM x High M-C SDS, Low M-C SDS) unweighted means analysis of variance.

There were three measures of seeking out social comparison information during the self-presentation task: (a) frequency of looking at the majority response sheet as recorded by the observer; (*b*) frequency of looking at the majority response sheet as measured by the subject's retrospective self-report; and (*c*) total duration of looking at the majority response sheet as timed by the observer. These three measures are highly intercorrelated ($r^{12} = .92$, $r^{13} = .90$, $r^{23} = .83$, $df = 25$, $p < .001$). The means for each of these measures are presented in Table 3.

TABLE 3

Three Measures of Looking at Social Comparison Information

MEASURE	*n*	*FREQUENCY OF LOOKING**	*FREQUENCY OF LOOKING†*	*TOTAL DURATION OF LOOKING (IN SECONDS)*
High SM, low M-C SDS	6	14.67	15.83	20.83
High SM, high M-C SDS	8	12.25	12.25	19.38
Low SM, low M-C SDS	7	5.14	5.83	5.43
Low SM, high M-C SDS	6	4.83	4.13	4.83

Note. SM = Self-Monitoring Scale; M-C SDS = Marlowe-Crowne Social Desirability Scale.
*Recorded by observer.
†Subject's self-report.

For frequency of looking as recorded by an observer, a high-SM subject looked more frequently than a low-SM at the majority response sheet ($F = 4.70$, $df = 1/23$, $p < .05$). Given the opportunity to consult social comparison information in a self-presentation situation in which they expected to justify their self-descriptions, high self-monitors did so more frequently than did low self-monitors. There was no systematic relationship between M-C SDS and looking behavior ($F = .122$, $df = 1/23$, *ns*), nor was there any interaction between SM and M-C SDS scores ($F = .011$, $df = 1/23$, *ns*). Thus, there was no relationship between the tendency to describe oneself in socially desirable fashion and consulting social comparison information in this self-presentation situation.

Analyses of subjects' self-report of looking behavior and total time looking measured by the observer result in identical conclusions. For either measure, high-SM subjects were more likely than low-SM to seek out social comparison information.

CONCLUSIONS

Individuals differ in the extent to which they monitor (observe and control) their expressive behavior and self-presentation. Out of a concern for social appropriateness, the self-monitoring individual is particularly sensitive to the expression and self-presentation of others in social situations and uses these cues as guidelines for monitoring and managing his own self-presentation and expressive behavior. In contrast, the nonself-monitoring person has little concern for the appropriateness of his presentation and expression, pays less attention to the expression of others, and monitors and controls his presentation to a lesser extent. His presentation and expression appear to be controlled from within by his experience rather than by situational and interpersonal specifications of appropriateness.

A self-report measure of individual differences in self-monitoring was constructed. The Self-Monitoring Scale is internally consistent, temporally stable, and uncorrelated with self-report measure of related concepts.

Four studies were conducted to validate the Self-Monitoring Scale. According to their peers, individuals with high SM scores are good at learning what is socially appropriate in new situations, have good self-control of their emotional expression, and can effectively use this ability to create the impressions they want. Theater actors scored higher and hospitalized psychiatric ward patients scored lower than university students. Individuals with high SM scores were better able than those with low SM scores to intentionally express and communicate emotion in both the vocal and facial channels of expressive behavior. In a self-presentation task, individuals with high SM scores were more likely than those with low scores to seek out and consult social comparison information about their peers. Self-monitoring and need for approval were compared as predictors of each external criterion to demonstrate the discriminant validity of the SM.

REFERENCES

Alpert R. and R. Haber

1960 "Anxiety in academic achievement situations." Journal of Abnormal and Social Psychology 61: 207–15.

Anastasi, A.

1968 Psychological Testing. New York: Macmillan.

Bem, D. J.

1972 "Constructing cross-situational consistencies in behavior: some thoughts on Alker's critique of Mischel." Journal of Personality 40: 17–26.

Buck, R., V. J. Savin, R. Miller, and W. F. Caul

1972 "Nonverbal communication of affect in humans." Journal of Personality and Social Psychology 23: 362–71.

Cameron, N. W.

1950 "Role concepts in behavior pathology." American Journal of Sociology 55: 464–67.

Campbell, D. J.

1960 "Recommendations for APA test standards regarding construct, trait, and discriminant validity." American Psychologist 15: 546–53.

Campbell, D. J. and D. W. Fiske

1959 "Convergent and discriminant validation by the multitrait-multimethod matrix." Psychological Bulletin 56: 81–105.

Christie, R. and F. L. Geis
1970 Studies in Machiavellianism. New York: Academic Press.
Cronbach, L. J. and P. E. Meehl
1955 "Construct validity in psychological tests." Psychological Bulletin 52: 281–302.
Crowne, D. P. and D. Marlowe
1964 The Approval Motive. New York: Wiley.
Davitz, J. R. (ed.)
1964 The Communication of Emotional Meaning. New York: McGraw-Hill.
Ekman, P.
1971 "Universals and Cultural Differences in Facial Expressions of Emotion." In J. Cole (ed.), Nebraska Symposium on Motivation: 1971. Lincoln: University of Nebraska Press.
Ekman, P. and W. V. Friesen
1969 "Nonverbal leakage and clues to deception." Psychiatry 32: 88–105.
1972 "Judging deception from the face or body." Paper presented at the meeting of the Western Psychological Association, Portland, Oregon.
Freud, S.
1959 "Fragment of an analysis of a case of hysteria (1905)." In Collected Papers. Vol. 3. New York: Basic Books.
Goffman, E.
1955 "On face work: an analysis of ritual elements in social interaction." Psychiatry 18: 213–21.
Hall, E. T.
1966 The Hidden Dimension. Garden City, N.Y.: Doubleday.
Kassarjian, W. M.
1962 "A study of Riesman's theory of social character." Sociometry 25: 213–30.
Levitt, E. A.
1964 "The relationship between abilities to express emotional meanings vocally and facially." In J. R. Davitz (ed.), The Communication of Emotional Meaning. New York: McGraw-Hill.
Mehrabian, A.
1969 "Significance of posture and position in the communication of attitude and status relationship." Psychological Bulletin 71: 359–72.
Mischel, W.
1968 Personality and Assessment. New York: Wiley.
Moos, R. H.
1968 "Situational analysis of a therapeutic community milieu." Journal of Abnormal Psychology 73: 49–61.
1969 "Sources of variance in responses to questionnaires and in behavior." Journal of Abnormal Psychology 74: 403–12.
Nunnally, J. C.
1967 Psychometric Theory. New York: McGraw-Hill.
Ring, K. and K. Wallston
1968 "A test to measure performance styles in interpersonal relations." Psychological Reports 22: 147–54.
Schachter, S. and J. Singer
1962 "Cognitive, social, and physiological determinants of emotional state." Psychological Review 69: 379–99.
Sommer, R.
1969 Personal Space. Englewood Cliffs, N.J.: Prentice-Hall.
Zaidel, S. and A. Mehrabian
1969 "The ability to communicate and infer positive and negative attitudes facially and vocally." Journal of Experimental Research in Personality 3: 233–41.

Prevalence of the Self-Esteem Motive

Howard B. Kaplan

11

The self-esteem motive is universally and characteristically a dominant motive; in all past and contemporary cultures it characteristically develops as a result of processes set in motion by the child's initial dependence upon others for satisfaction of basic physical needs present at birth. However, this is not to say that the development of the self-esteem motive is inevitable. Indeed, a number of circumstances might arise that could disrupt the processes such as those described above as ordinarily eventuating in an acquired self-esteem motive. For example, if the adults in the child's early experiences were either invariable (that is, uniformly positive or negative regardless of the nature of the child's behavior) or inconsistent (that is, the same behavior would sometimes evoke positive responses and at other times negative responses), the child might not learn to associate particular behaviors on his part with particular adult attitudes toward him and thus might not develop the need for positive attitudinal responses from others or the need for positive self-attitudes (which is based, presumably, on the need for positive attitudinal responses by others). However, such circumstances are regarded as rare, and the development of the self-esteem motive is viewed as a normal outcome in the psychosocial development of the human being.

If indeed the acquisition of the self-esteem motive is normal, then existing empirical data should be compatible with the inference of the prevalence of this motive. Even a brief examination of the relevant literature suggests that such an inference is warranted. The prevalence in a specified population of a motive to

Source: Howard B. Kaplan, "Prevalence of the Self-Esteem Motive," from Howard B. Kaplan, (ed.), Self-Attitudes and Deviant Behavior (Pacific Palisades, Calif.: Goodyear Publishing Co., Inc., 1975), pp. 16–27.

behave so as to maintain positive self-attitudes may be inferred from four kinds of observations: the relative frequency of positive/negative self-descriptions; the characteristic responses to self-devaluing situations and histories; the association between self-devaluing experiences and subjective distress; and the relative stability of positive/negative self-attitudes over time.

FREQUENCY OF POSITIVE/NEGATIVE SELF-DESCRIPTIONS

The prevalence of the self-esteem motive could be inferred from observations that at any given time self-descriptions couched in negative terms are relatively rare, and self-descriptions in terms of qualities that are personally and/or socially desirable are relatively frequent in a specified population. This inference could be drawn whether the self-descriptions truly reflected the objective prevalence of admirable qualities, the subjects' misperceptions of their (in fact) nonadmirable qualities as if they were admirable, or the subjects' desire to avoid describing themselves in terms of their realistically perceived nonadmirable qualities. All three outcomes could be outcomes of behavior in the service of the self-esteem motive. In the first instance the subjects would have behaved to achieve admirable qualities and thus justify positive self-evaluation and consequent positive self-attitudes. In the second instance the subjects would have distorted their perceptions of reality in ways that again would permit positive self-evaluations and consequent positive self-feelings. In the third instance the subjects would have behaved to cloak their nonadmirable qualities thereby avoiding negative evaluations by others, which would have presumably influenced negative self-evaluation and consequent negative self-attitudes.

The following studies will serve to illustrate the range of investigations that provide observations of the relative frequency of favorable self-descriptions in given populations.

Chamblis (1964) presented data derived from the responses of undergraduates to adjective checklists that suggested that positive self-images are prevalent and negative self-images are relatively rare. The responses of 375 undergraduate freshmen to a 137-item adjective checklist revealed that the items most frequently used by respondents to describe themselves had highly favorable connotations while the adjectives least frequently checked were unflattering. Moreover, the responses of 140 subjects to a 30-item checklist revealed that respondents were more likely to see the positive than the negative traits as typical of them and were much more likely to see the negative traits as "never typical" of them (37 percent) than they were to thus characterize the positive traits (less than 1 percent).

Wylie (1965) hypothesized and observed among 387 Air Force male subjects a tendency toward a "self-favorability bias" in ratings of evaluative traits. That is, the subjects generally rated themselves more favorably than the reality of the situation demanded. This observation was based on the results of two analyses. In the first analysis the subjects' estimates of how others in their living group would most likely rate them on five evaluative traits (friendliness, likability, generosity, intelligence, and sense of humor) were compared with the ratings actually received by the subject from his peers. The subjects significantly overestimated the ratings they would receive from their peers on the last four traits. In the second analysis a self-favorability bias was indicated by the proportion of subjects whose estimates of where their peers would rate them on the evaluative scales fell in the top half of the ratings they assigned to their group "as compared to a fifty-fifty proportion one would expect if all subjects' social self-concept ratings were accurate, or if chance alone determined their ratings" (Wylie, 1965:137). The observed proportions of subjects who placed their self-ratings on the top half were significantly higher than 50 percent once again on the last four of the five evaluative traits.

In a similar vein a self-favorability bias was apparent from the results of a study (French, 1968:114) in which 92 members of management offered self-evaluations of their performance relative to other men on the same unit doing the same job. Presumably if the subjects were evaluating themselves in a totally objective manner, they would have been equally distributed above and below the fiftieth percentile of the scale. However, it was reported in fact that only two of the subjects evaluated their performance as falling below the fiftieth percentile. In addition it was observed that "eighty-two percent of the men reported that their self-evaluation was higher than the evaluation given them by their employer."

The tendency of subjects to rate themselves positively and/or to avoid rating themselves negatively is suggested by results from a number of other studies cited by Crowne and Stephens (1961:113-117) in the course of their discussion of the possible relationship between self-evaluating responses on the one hand and phenomena variously referred to by such terms as "defensive behavior," "self-protective responses," and "social desirability" on the other hand. For example, in one investigation Cowan and Tongas (1959) reported a high (0.91) correlation between ratings of social desirability and the self-concept score of the Index of Adjustment and Values. In another study Kogan and his associates (1957) found a correlation of 0.85 between self-description and social desirability values among a grouping of male college students.

French (1968:148) also reviewed a number of studies and tentatively concluded that these studies tended to agree in their observation of a high degree of association ($r=0.85$ to 0.90) between social desirability values of self-descriptive items and the mean endorsement rate of the item. He interprets these results as indicating "that there are common values in our culture and that these common values are related to the proportion of people endorsing self-descriptive statements embodying these values."

The studies cited up to this point refer to the tendency of subjects to consciously describe themselves in favorable terms. However, reports exist that suggest that a tendency toward *unconscious* favorable self-evaluating may also exist in the population. Fisher and Mirin (1966:1097) cite earlier observations by another investigator to the effect that "when persons were asked to judge representations of themselves (e.g., shadow profile) in a context where they had no reason to expect to encounter such self-representations, they showed a surprising inability to recognize them and simultaneously gave evidence of responding in an exaggeratedly favorable fashion" and presented other data compatible with these observations. Thirty-one male college students were asked to rate tachistoscopically presented shadow profiles and full-face pictures of themselves and four other people for degree of friendliness and intelligence. The pictures were obtained without the subjects' knowledge. With the exceptions of three instances of partial recognition of the full-face pictures, the subjects did not appear to recognize their pictures. Although significant differences were not observed for the full-face pictures, the subjects did tend to ascribe significantly more favorable intelligence and friendliness ratings to their own shadow profiles than to the profiles of others.

It has been argued that the several studies cited above that offer evidence of the tendency of subjects to describe themselves in overly favorable terms may be interpreted as support for the assertion that the self-esteem motive is "universal" and "characteristic" among human beings. Nevertheless, occasionally data describe a tendency among subjects in certain cultural groupings to underrate themselves on desirable traits. Such data could be interpreted as supporting the hypothesis that the self-esteem motive, rather than being universal, is variably prevalent from culture to culture. A case in point is the observation reported by Trow and Pu (1927) of the tendency, among a grouping of 18 Chinese college students, for the subjects to underrate themselves on desirable traits, a conclusion that contradicts the results of specified self-rating studies among American subjects. However, it is argued here that such data could be accounted for by the values of the culture in question: as the authors assert, the tendency to underrate the self may be an expression of a highly valued character trait in traditional Chinese culture—the trait of humility. Thus, rather than contraindicating the existence of the self-esteem motive, the behavior of the Chinese subjects (in underrating themselves) suggests that they are being guided by just such a motive. Self-underestimating behavior is interpretable as approximating a culturally (and presumably personally) prized value and therefore as a partial justification for self-enhancing attitudes among the Chinese student subjects. Through apparent self-depreciation the subject in fact gains self-acceptance.

CHARACTERISTIC RESPONSES TO SELF-DEVALUATION

The second kind of observation from which the prevalence of the self-esteem motive could be inferred is that relating to the ways in which the population characteristically responds to self-devaluating experiences. The prevalence could be inferred if the subjects' responses were apparently calculated to increase positive (and defend against negative) self-evaluation and, consequently, increase positive (and decrease negative) self-attitudes, whether through readjustment of their response patterns to more closely approximate positively valued goals; misperception of their attributes, behaviors, or circumstances; or a reordering of their values, and so on.

Investigations of such responses to self-devaluation may be distributed conveniently among four categories: responses to current self-devaluation; responses associated with relatively low self-esteem; responses to both current self-devaluation and to relatively low self-esteem; and self-devaluation in the service of self-esteem.

Responses to Current Self-Devaluation

The first category includes observations of the ways people respond to current self-devaluing experiences with behaviors that have self-enhancing implications. These observations generally make no assumptions regarding the subject's characteristic level of self-esteem. Among the potentially self-enhancing responses illustrated by the following studies are physical avoidance, reordering of values, devaluation of the source, and perceptual distortion.

Defensive avoidance in response to potentially devaluing circumstances was suggested by data reported by Dosey and Meisels (1969). In three experimental situations, university student subjects who were subjected to the presumed personal stress of having their physical attractiveness called into question were compared with subjects in nonstress conditions with regard to their use of personal space. The three situations in which personal space was determined called for the subjects to physically approach each other, take seats close to or far from the experimenter, and trace one silhouette in relation to another. In two of the three situations (the first and third), the subjects in the stress condition were observed to employ significantly greater spatial distances than the subjects in the nonstress condition. The results were thus interpretable as indicating that the increase of spatial distance is used by individuals to protect themselves in response to situations in which their self-esteem is threatened.

Another possible mode of response to self-devaluating circumstances would be a reordering of one's values. Such a pattern of response would decrease a subject's degree of self-rejection to the extent that he was able to decrease his valuation of qualities that he lacked and to increase his valuation of attributes that he possessed. Data reported by Ludwig and Maehr (1967) suggest that a reordering of values does take place following self-devaluing circumstances. These data concerned the relationship between the experience of approval/disapproval and changes in behavioral preference. The experimental situation called for a physical development expert to indicate either approval or disapproval of the junior high school student subjects' performance on various physical tasks. Changes in behavioral preference were determined with reference to responses to a 20-item "Behavioral Choice Questionnaire" through which the subjects rated their preference for physical or nonphysical activity along a 9-point scale. Ten of the items were directly pertinent to the experimental evaluation situation while the other 10 items referred to physical activities that were relatively unrelated to the experimental evaluation situation. The behavioral preference ratings were obtained one week before the experimental evaluation treatment, immediately following the evaluation, one week later, and three weeks later. Among the findings was the observation that the approval treatment tended to be followed by an increased preference for activities directly related to the treatment while the disapproval treatment tended to be followed by a decreased preference for such activities. Thus the results are compatible with the expectations that people would defensively respond to self-devaluing experiences by lowering the value they previously attached to associated aspects of the experimental situation.

The influence of self-devaluing circumstances in evoking self-enhancing responses is suggested by a study (Harvey, 1962) in which 188 undergraduate university student subjects were exposed to ratings of themselves that were more unfavorable than their initial self-ratings by one of five gradations. The negative ratings were apparently made by either a friend or a comparative stranger. In general, increasingly negative ratings by others tended to result in increasingly negative evaluations of the source; increasing error in recall (in a positive direction) of the ratings received up to the most extreme discrepancy; increasing judgments that the source used the scale differently from them (the subjects), was not serious in his ratings, and did not follow instructions in making the evaluations; increasing ratings of the source as careless and socially insensitive; decreasing belief that the source knew the subject well; and increasing disbelief that the source had actually made the negative ratings they saw.

Responses Associated with Low Self-Esteem

The studies in the first category were characterized by the introduction of self-devaluing experiences into the situation and the observation of subsequent responses to these experiences. Unlike these studies the second grouping of investigations contains studies in which subjects with different preexisting levels of self-esteem are compared with regard to the presence of behaviors interpretable as serving self-defensive or self-enhancing functions. In these studies a given level of self-esteem is viewed as the end product of a history of experiences that are appropriate to that level. That is, low self-esteem is said to imply a history of self-devaluing experiences. An association between low self-esteem and a potentially self-enhancing pattern thus would be congruent with the assertion that self-devaluing experiences tend to evoke self-enhancing responses, an observation from which the prevalence of the self-esteem motive is inferred. The following investigations were selected to illustrate this category of studies.

In support of the postulate that individuals tend to behave in ways that reduce the adverse impact of self-devaluing circumstances are those observations relating to the tendency of people who more frequently have such experiences (that is, people with characteristically low self-evaluation) to assume self-defensive postures. Such observations were reported in the course of a study (Washburn, 1962: 85–86), . . . which offered support for the hypotheses that subjects with low self-evaluations, in comparison with subjects with high self-evaluations, were more likely to develop hostile defenses ("to be critical, suspicious, and lack identification with others") and retreating defenses ("to avoid coming to grips with problems and to deny reality").

The tendency of people to (perceptually and physically) avoid potentially self-devaluing situations is suggested by certain of Rosenberg's (1965: 219, 226–227, 231) observations among a sample of high school students. He reports that subjects with lower self-esteem scores (and, therefore, those that may be presumed to be sensitive to the self-devaluation potential of certain situations) were more likely to manifest a tendency to daydream; express preferences for occupations that leave them free of supervision and involve little or no competition; and to indicate that it is relatively less important to them to get ahead in life than to subjects with higher self-esteem scores. These behaviors are all interpretable as patterns that facilitate the avoidance of situations in which they are likely to fail or the disappointment accompanying the failure.

Based on a study of some male Air Force trainees and women from an Eastern college, referred to earlier in another connection, Wylie (1965) reported that subjects with low self-regard were more likely to display the relatively specific defensive behaviors of rationalizing and protecting than subjects with high self-regard. The measures of rationalizing and projecting were based on the subject's tendency to systematically underestimate others when rating them (projection) and/or scores on a Rationalization-Projection Inventory. Self-regard was indexed by discrepancies between subject ratings of social self-concept on the one hand and the culturally stereotyped ideal self and/or personally stated self-ideal ratings on the other hand. It was expected that subjects with smaller self-ideal discrepancies would manifest less defensive behavior since they would have less need to so behave on the assumption that the smaller discrepancies indicated either realistically favorable self-concepts or the effective use of denial to alleviate anxiety.

Responses to Self-Devaluation and Low Self-Esteem

A third category of studies includes those investigations of self-enhancing responses to both current self-devaluing experiences and characteristic level of self-esteem rather than to either of these phenomena alone. The following study will serve to illustrate this category.

The presence of the self-esteem motive might be indicated if people who frequently encounter self-devaluing circumstances (compared to people who infrequently encounter such circumstances) or people who find themselves in a particular self-devaluing situation (compared to people who are not currently experiencing self-devaluation) tended to respond with a behavior pattern that in the past has been subjectively associated with the production of self-enhancing experiences but that does not necessarily have any relevance to changing the current self-devaluing circumstances. Such a response pattern is suggested by data reported by Dittes (1959) concerning the relationship between self-esteem and a general response tendency to achieve closure defined as "the structuring of otherwise ambiguous stimuli so as to provide meaning and to end deliberation" (p. 355). The author assumed that in circumstances that threatened self-esteem the subject would become more motivated to increase his self-esteem through any of a number of means. One such method of increasing self-esteem would be through the achievement of closure on the further assumption that "such closure commonly acquires reward value as a source of self-esteem through learning experiences in which it has been associated with achievements, praise by other persons, and other fundamental sources of self-esteem . . ." (p. 355).

Based on these assumptions it was hypothesized that situationally induced threats to self-esteem would be associated with greater impulsiveness of closure. This hypothesis was supported in an experimental situation in which self-esteem was manipulated through the communication to the subjects of fictitious ratings of the subject by other group members. The data indicated that indeed the presumed threat to self-esteem of being poorly accepted was associated with significantly greater impulsiveness in closure. This relationship between situationally induced threats to self-esteem and closure was stronger for subjects with generally low self-esteem than among subjects with high self-esteem. The findings then are compatible with the general postulate of a self-esteem motive in that people (particularly those with generally low self-esteem) in specific self-devaluing circumstances tend to behave in ways which will increase self-esteem. In the present case, the tendency toward impulsive closure observed among such people was interpreted as just such "a compensating source of self-esteem" (p. 354).

Self-Devaluation in the Service of the Self-Esteem Motive

All of the studies discussed above involve various methodological problems. For example, the investigations described in the second category above involve collecting data regarding self-devaluation and presumably self-enhancing responses at the same point in time, thus rendering it difficult to establish cause-effect relationships. However, studies involving one type of hypothetical self-enhancing or defensive responses pose a very special problem. The responses in question involve the expression of self-derogation as a way of reducing the degree of, or forestalling further, self-rejection. The demonstration of defensive responses involves the observation of presumably self-enhancing behaviors by self-derogating people in response to self-derogating circumstances. However, to say that self-derogating responses may also serve defensive, self-enhancing functions is to place the observer in the awkward position of hypothesizing that self-rejecting attitudes may eventuate in either self-enhancing (in the instance of effective defensive responses) or self-derogating (in instances where self-devaluation is said to serve a defensive function) attitudes. Thus whatever the actual result the findings may be said to support the hypothesis. In instances where negative self-attitudes are observed to be the consequence of self-devaluating experiences, the resultant self-derogation may be interpreted in terms of either the absence of effective defensive responses or the use of self-derogation as a defense against the even more intense self-derogation which would occur in the absence of this response. Yet in spite of the methodological difficulties in distinguishing between self-derogation as a response to self-devaluating experiences and self-derogation as a defensive response, self-rejecting attitudes may be said to serve as an attempt to reduce the degree of, or prevent even more intense, self-derogating attitudes. Certainly the serving of such functions is consistent with a number of findings in the literature relating to self-attitudes.

Self-rejection may be thought of as an attempt to serve self-enhancing functions in either or both of two ways. First, the adoption of self-derogating attitudes may be a more or less effective attempt by the subjects to evoke positive attitudes toward themselves by significant others who in the past had held negative attitudes toward them. This would appear to be a particular instance of earning another person's approval by adopting his attitudes. Thus, paradoxically a person adopts another person's negative attitudes toward himself as a way of gaining approval from significant others and, through this approval, enhancing his self-attitudes. Congruent with this reasoning are the findings of certain studies reviewed by Wylie (1961:153). These findings tended to support the hypothesis, based on the assumption that compliance was a defensive attempt to avoid displeasing others, that self-esteem would be inversely related to persuasibility.

The adoption of negative self-attitudes might function to prevent subsequent self-devaluation in a second way, by forestalling circumstances in which the individual would be likely to experience self-devaluation. For example, a person who defined himself as a person of low ability (a negative self-attitude) would not expect himself to perform well in a situation in which the ability in question was required. Nor, to the extent that his negative attitudes toward himself were shared by others, would others expect him to perform well. Consequently when he actually failed to perform well in future situations, he would not become the object of negative attitudes from others and negative self-attitudes. Such reasoning is compatible with the interpretation of their findings offered by Jones and Ratner (1967). Through the experimental communication of false test scores the subjects were induced to adopt low ability appraisals. The subjects then met either of two conditions. They were either given or not given the opportunity to commit themselves to the low ability appraisals by choosing a more or less difficult task to perform. The subjects then participated in a three-person social exchange situation in which they were positively evaluated by one peer and negatively evaluated by another. The results indicated that the subjects who were given the opportunity for commitment to self-appraisal more positively evaluated the peer sending positive evaluations than the peer sending negative evaluations. However, subjects who were not given the opportunity for commitment more positively evaluated the peer sending negative evaluations than the peer sending positive evaluations. The authors argued that ordinarily the acceptance of praise from others implies that the subject will participate effectively in difficult activities. However, the commitment to a low self-appraisal permits the individual to accept praise without the expectation of a high level of performance and the concomitant risk of failure. The experimental results thus were interpreted as providing support for the assertion that

commitment to a low self-appraisal may protect a person from the undesirable implications of accepting social praise and rejecting social censure. People appear to like praise, and they will respond favorably to it, providing that in so doing they are not also accepting its contingent responsibilities. Commitment to a low self-appraisal can effectively eliminate these responsibilities, and under such conditions praise can be accepted with impunity [Jones and Ratner, 1967: 445].

SELF-DEVALUATION AND SUBJECTIVE DISTRESS

If the self-esteem motive was indeed prevalent in a specified population, then by definition individuals would display negative affect, that is subjective distress, in response to negative self-perceptions and self-evaluations. Such subjective distress would be appreciably less in evidence in the absence of negative self-perceptions and self-evaluations. Thus, a third type of observation from which the prevalence of the self-esteem motive could be inferred is that relating to the affective responses of the subject to self-devaluating circumstances. The prevalence of the self-esteem motive could be inferred if subjects were observed to more characteristically respond to negative self-evaluating experiences with negative affect and to more characteristically respond to positive self-evaluation with positive affect.

Empirical studies in fact have consistently observed significant associations between chronically self-devaluating circumstances (as reflected in scores on self-esteem measures) on the one hand and such indices of subjective distress as anxiety and depressive affect on the other hand. The associations have been observed among subjects with variable characteristics (preadult as well as adult, and hospitalized as well as nonhospitalized) and over a period of time as well as at a single point in time.

Among studies of preadult populations is an investigation (Horowitz, 1962) of the relationship between anxiety and self-concept among a sample of upper elementary school children in Oregon. The investigator reported consistent negative correlations between the two variables such that high anxiety tended to be associated with a low self-concept. Rosenberg and Simmons (1972) in a study of third-to-twelfth grade pupils in Baltimore City public schools observed a tendency for pupils with low self-esteem scores to manifest high scores on a Guttman scale of depression as well as on a measure of anxiety.

In a study of subjects drawn from among New York State high school juniors and seniors, Rosenberg (1965) reported data indicating a strong association between self-esteem and measures of subjective distress including depressive affect and anxiety. Thus, on the basis of scores on a "depressive affect" scale, only 4 percent of the highest self-esteem grouping were classified as highly depressed while 80 percent of the subjects in the lowest self-esteem category were so classified. Similar results were obtained with regard to symptoms described as secondary physiological manifestations of anxiety, such as hands sweating, sick headaches, nightmares, and trouble in getting to sleep and staying asleep. Considering ten such symptoms, only 19 percent of the subjects in the highest self-esteem category reported experiencing four or more of the symptoms "often" or "sometimes" while 69 percent of the lowest self-esteem subjects reported experiencing four or more of the symptoms often or sometimes.

In addition to the observations of relationships between self-esteem and self-reports of anxiety and depression, Rosenberg (1965) reported on the relationships between self-esteem and subject depression as observed by others. Among 50 young adult volunteers at the Clinical Center of the National Institutes of Health, it was observed that nurses at the center were appreciably more likely to deny that subjects with high self-esteem scores, compared with subjects with low self-esteem scores, were "often gloomy" or "frequently disappointed."

Among the studies of adult populations were those reported by Kaplan and Pokorny (1969) and French (1968). Paralleling the findings of Rosenberg, Kaplan and Pokorny reported significant relationships between low self-esteem on the one hand and relatively high depressive affect and relatively frequent experiences of psychophysiological symptoms on the other hand among a sample of 500 adults. They also cited a number of other studies making similar observations. French (1968:143) referred to a study of 81 blue-collar workers in which a measure of self-esteem was inversely correlated at moderate levels (0.50 to 0.73) with a number of variables interpretable as indices of emotional distress, including depression, anxiety and tension, irritation, feeling burdened, and sadness.

The relationship between self-rejecting attitudes and manifestations of subjective distress were observed among psychiatric patients as well as normal subjects. For example, Harrow and his associates (1968) studying the self-perceptions of 34 recently hospitalized psychiatric patients, reported that depressed patients tended to have significantly lower self-images than nondepressed patients.

The studies reviewed above concerned the relationship between low self-esteem and indices of subjective distress at a single point in time. However, similar findings are apparent in investigations of changes in self-esteem over time. Thus Engel (1959), studying eighth- and tenth-grade pupils over a two-year period, observed that subjects who decreased in self-regard (as measured by Q sort) over the two-year period also manifested significantly higher scores on the D (depression) scale of the MMPI.

The consistent observation of significant associations between low self-evaluation and subjective distress then is congruent with the assumption of the prevalence of the self-esteem motive.

STABILITY OF POSITIVE/NEGATIVE SELF-ATTITUDES

On the assumption that the avoidance of negative self-attitudes and the attainment of positive self-attitudes are indeed motives of human behavior it is to be expected that persons with initially negative self-attitudes would tend to change their attitudes in a more positive direction over time and those with initially positive self-attitudes would tend to be stable in their self-attitudes, that is, would maintain their positive self-attitudes. Observations consistent with these expectations constitute a fourth category of observations in support of the postulated prevalence of the self-esteem motive.

With regard to this fourth category of observations, individuals do appear to be more likely to change their self-attitudes over time in a positive direction than in a negative direction. Engel (1959:214), reporting on the results of a study of the stability of the self-concept over a two-year period among public school student subjects, reported that indeed most of the change in the positive/negative quality of the self-concept occurred in the initially negative self-concept grouping:

Ss who were classified as having negative self-concepts in 1954 more closely approached the mean by 1956. Such shift could be attributed to regression, except that no such shifting toward the mean took place in the case of Ss originally giving evidence of a positive self-concept.

The tendency of individuals to maintain this positive quality of their self-attitudes is suggested by certain of Rosenberg's (1965:152–154) data. Adolescents with high self-esteem were observed to be appreciably more stable in their self-picture (that is, to be constant rather than changeable in the opinions or ideas they have of themselves) than adolescents with low self-esteem.

French (1968:149) also reports that stability of self-esteem, using the same measure of stability of self-esteem employed by Rosenberg, was positively correlated with measures of self-esteem among a sample of 188 tenth-grade boys.

Thus, this fourth grouping of studies along with those previously considered appear to be compatible with the inference of the prevalence of the self-esteem motive.

SUMMARY

The emerging theoretical outline, intended to explain the adoption of deviant behavior patterns, is based upon the premise that the self-esteem motive, defined in terms of the person's need to achieve positive self-attitudes and to avoid negative self-attitudes, is universally characteristic of human beings. Self-attitudes in turn refer to the individual's emotional responses to self-perception and self-evaluation.

The self-esteem motive is said to be the normal outcome of the human infant's early dependency upon adult human needs for satisfaction of his basic biological needs. On the basis of this initial dependency the human being successively develops needs for the presence of other human beings, the expression of positive (and the avoidance of negative) attitudes toward himself by other human beings, and the experience of positive (and the avoidance of negative) self-attitudes.

In support of the assertion of the prevalence of the self-esteem motive, four categories of empirical observations are discussed: the tendency of individuals to describe themselves in positive terms and to avoid negative self-descriptions; the tendency of people with low self-esteem and people in self-threatening circumstances to respond with behaviors serving self-defensive or self-enhancing functions; the tendency for people with low self-esteem to manifest subjective distress; and the tendency for subjects with positive self-attitudes to maintain this quality of their self-attitudes while people with negative self-attitudes tend to change their attitudes toward themselves in a more positive direction. These observations were interpreted as compatible with the postulate of the prevalence of the self-esteem motive in the sense that the assertion of the motive provides a parsimonious explanation of these various observations.

REFERENCES

Chamblis, William

1964 "The negative self: an empirical assessment of a theoretical assumption." Sociological Inquiry 34: 108–12.

Cowen, E. L. and P. N. Tongas

1959 "The social desirability of trait-descriptive terms: applications to a self-concept inventory." Journal of Consulting Psychology 23: 361–65.

Crowne, Douglas P. and Mark W. Stephens

1961 "Self-acceptance and self-evaluative behavior: a critique of methodology." Psychological Bulletin 58: 104–21.

Dittes, J. E.

1959 "Effects of changes in self-esteem upon impulsiveness and deliberation in making judgments." Journal of Abnormal and Social Psychology 58: 348–56.

Dosey, Michael A. and Murray Meisels

1969 "Personal space and self-protection." Journal of Personality and Social Psychology 21: 171–77.

Engel, Mary

1959 "The stability of the self-concept in adolescence." Journal of Abnormal and Social Psychology 58: 211–15.

Fisher, S. and S. Mirin
1966 "Further validation of the special favorable responses occurring during unconscious self-evaluation." Perceptual and Motor Skills 23: 1097–98.
French, John R. P.
1968 "The conceptualization and measurement of mental health in terms of self-identity theory." In S. B. Sells (ed.), The Definition and Measurement of Mental Health. Washington, D.C.: U.S. Department of Health, Education, and Welfare.
Harrow, Martin, David A. Fox, Kathryn I. Markhus, Richard Stillman, and Carolyn B. Hallowell
1968 "Changes in adolescents' self-concepts and their parents' perceptions during psychiatric hospitalization." Journal of Nervous and Mental Disease 147: 252–59.
Harvey, O. J.
1962 "Personality factors in resolution of conceptual incongruities." Sociometry 25: 336–52.
Horowitz, Frances D.
1962 "The relationship of anxiety, self-concept and sociometric status among fourth, fifth, and sixth grade children." Journal of Abnormal and Social Psychology 65: 212–14.
Jones, Stephen C. and Carl Ratner
1967 "Commitment to self-appraisal and interpersonal evaluations." Journal of Personality and Social Psychology 6: 442–47.
Kaplan, Howard B. and Alex D. Pokorny
1969 "Self-derogation and psychosocial adjustment." Journal of Nervous and Mental Disease 149: 421–34.
Kogan, W. S., R. Quinn, A. F. Ax, and H. S. Ripley
1957 "Some methodological problems in the quantification of clinical assessment by Q Array." Journal of Consulting Psychology 21: 57–62.
Ludwig, D. J. and M. L. Maehr
1967 "Changes in self-concept and stated behavioral preferences." Child Development 38: 453–67.
Rosenberg, Morris
1965 Society and the Adolescent Self-Image. Princeton: Princeton University Press.
Rosenberg, Morris and Roberta G. Simmons
1972 Black and White Self-Esteem: The Urban School Child. Washington, D.C.: American Sociological Association.
Trow, William Clark and Alfred S. T. Pu
1927 "Self-ratings of the Chinese," School and Society 26: 213–16.
Washburn, Wilbur C.
1962 "Patterns of protective attitudes in relation to differences in self-evaluation and anxiety level among high school students." California Journal of Educational Research 13: 84–94.
Wylie, Ruth C.
1961 The Self Concept. Lincoln: University of Nebraska Press.
1965 "Self-ratings, level of ideal-self ratings, and defensiveness." Psychological Reports 16: 135–50.

Self and Interpersonal Evaluations: Esteem Theories Versus Consistency Theories

Stephen C. Jones

12

Although the interpersonal events involving the evaluations an individual receives from other people occur experimentally and in the "real world" with some regularity, confusions arise in attempting to explain these regularities. We observe that people typically talk more (e.g., Bavelas, Hastorf, Gross, & Kite, 1965; Jones, 1968b) appraise themselves more highly (e.g., Videbeck, 1960), and like others better (e.g., Aronson & Worchell, 1966; Backman & Secord, 1959; Jones & Panitch, 1971) when they receive approval from others than when they receive disapproval, but we know surprisingly little about why these things happen. There are wide differences of opinion about what underlying motivational processes affect a person's reactions to the knowledge that he is liked or disliked, that his opinions are valued or worthless, that he is accepted as a co-worker or rejected as a roommate, or in other ways praised or derogated by others.

Source: Stephen C. Jones, "Self and Interpersonal Evaluations: Esteem Theories Versus Consistency Theories," Psychological Bulletin 79 (1973): 185–99

The bulk of the investigations relating to this motivational issue unfortunately have been couched in terms of "mini theories" (Aronson, 1969), and attempts at more integrated approaches which go beyond a few intuitively appealing variables, or attempts to force a confrontation among various approaches have been all too few and far between. The purpose of this paper is to focus attention on two broad traditions in social psychology which relate to problems of interpersonal evaluations—self-esteem theories and cognitive consistency theories. Using as a focal point the question of how an individual reacts to evaluations received from others as a function of his self-evaluation, this paper discusses the distinctions between these theoretical positions, evaluates the evidence bearing on these distinctions, and suggests possible directions for resolving the differences.

THEORIES

"I am good/You love me/therefore you are good. . . . /I am bad/You love me/therefore you are bad." Does Laing's (1970, p. 10) poem of a schizophrenic relation represent a typical, self-consistent pattern of interpersonal evaluations? Or, if I think I am bad and discover that you love me, am I pleased as punch to get a little affection along the way? This "knot" of Laing's strikes at the heart of the controversy between esteem and consistency approaches to the relation between self and interpersonal evaluations.

TABLE 1

Predicted Favorability of Ratings of Others as a Function of Self-Evaluation and Appraisals Received from Others

SELF-EVALUATION	*APPRAISALS FROM OTHERS*			
	SELF-CONSISTENCY THEORY		*SELF-ESTEEM THEORY*	
	POSITIVE	*NEGATIVE*	*POSITIVE*	*NEGATIVE*
High	+	–	+	–
Low	–	+	++	––

Self-Consistency Theories

The central notion of self-consistency theorists is that an individual's actions, attitudes, and his receptivity to information from other people are strongly affected by a tendency to create and maintain a consistent cognitive state with respect to his evaluations of himself. Various reasons are given for this cognitive tendency including economy in the organization of one's perceptions (Heider, 1958), the reduction of dissonance (Festinger, 1957), predictability in relationships with others (Newcomb, 1961; Secord & Backman, 1965), or avoiding cognitions with conflicting implications for action (Jones & Gerard, 1967).

As elaborated by Secord and Backman (1961, 1964, 1965), a state of self-consistency or congruency is said to exist "when [his own and others'] behaviors imply definitions of self congruent with relevant aspects of the self-concept (1961, p. 23)." Given a state of inconsistency or incongruency involving relationships with another person, the individual may change his conception of himself, change or misperceive his own actions, or in a variety of ways transform his relationship with the other person. Concerning the latter, he may interact only with those whose behavior validates his self-concept or misperceive an attempt to change those actions of the other person which produce the inconsistency. Finally, Secord and Backman (1961) propose that inconsistencies may be eliminated by selective evaluation of other people, and they predict that the individual "tends to increase his liking for [others] who behave toward him in a congruent fashion, and to decrease his liking for those who behave in an incongruent manner (p. 25)."

The self-consistency notion has played a role in other theoretical approaches to interpersonal relationships such as Heider's (1958) balance theory, Newcomb's (1961) symmetry model, and Baron's (1966) social reinforcement theory. It also has been central to the thinking of humanistically oriented self-concept theorists such as Lecky (1945) and Rogers (1951, 1959). Although these positions contain many differences in their foci and in their implications for action involving self and others, the common characteristic which concerns us is the proposal that relations between evaluations of the self and others are mediated by a tendency toward self-consistency.

To clarify this point and anticipate its distinction from the self-esteem theories, consider an experimental paradigm in which subjects have either high self-evaluations or low self-evaluations and receive either positive evaluations or negative evaluations from other members of their group. The question is to what extent the subjects accept or reject their peers. For individuals with high evaluations of themselves or some aspect of self, positive evaluations from others are consistent and negative evaluations are inconsistent, whereas for individuals with low self-evaluations, positive evaluations are inconsistent and negative evaluations are consistent. Therefore, the prediction from the self-consistency theories is that high self-evaluators will react more favorably to approval than to disapproval and that low self-evaluators will react more favorably to disapproval than to approval. This prediction is described in Table 1.

Self-Esteem Theories

The self-esteem position assumes that the individual has a need to enhance his self-evaluation and to increase, maintain, or confirm his feelings of personal satisfaction, worth, and effectiveness. Although this need is assumed to be general, at any given point in time it may manifest itself with respect to a particular aspect of one's self-evaluation rather than to more global feelings about the self. Furthermore, the state of the need varies with the degree of personal satisfaction or frustration the individual experiences in a particular situation or period of time. The self-esteem need also varies across individuals. It is assumed that this individual difference variation is reflected in attitudinal measures of self-esteem and that persons with high self-esteem are relatively more satisfied with respect to this need than persons with low self-esteem.

As was the case with the self-consistency theories, the self-esteem need is responsive to evaluative information the individual gains from his own behavior and comparative or reflected appraisals from other people. Coping effectively with the tasks and problems one encounters in his physical and social environment as well as gaining information from others that he is liked and respected or that his actions or characteristics are highly evaluated produce satisfactions for his self-esteem need. Data from a variety of social psychological studies, including, for example, studies of social influence (Hovland & Janis, 1959), self-presentation (Jones, 1964) and social comparison (Morse & Gergen, 1970), have been interpreted in terms of this direct relation between self-esteem needs and social acceptance or rejection.

The critical question for purposes of comparison with self-consistency theories is what predictions self-esteem theories make regarding the individual's reactions to positive or negative evaluations received from other people. In concert with the self-consistency theories, the major sources of change in thought or action involve the individual's evaluation of himself, his choice of activities or social roles, and his relationships with others. The difference is that these changes are designed to enhance self-esteem rather than to achieve self-consistency.

In general, one would expect people to respond favorably (i.e, like, benefit, agree with, etc.) to positive evaluations of themselves which are assumed to satisfy esteem needs and to respond unfavorably (i.e., dislike, aggress against, disagree with, etc.) to negative evaluations of themselves which are assumed to frustrate esteem needs. This prediction follows from the social exchange notions of Homans (1961) and Thibaut and Kelley (1959), the notion that attraction to a group is directly proportional to the needs satisfied by the group (Cartwright & Zander, 1960; Dittes, 1959), as well as the frustration-aggression hypothesis (Dollard, Doob, Miller, Mowrer, & Sears, 1939). Furthermore, this tendency should interact with the magnitude of the esteem needs as experimentally manipulated or measured. Specifically, low self-esteem individuals are predicted to respond more favorably to positive evaluations from others and more unfavorably to negative evaluations from others as compared to high self-esteem individuals. This prediction, first articulated by Dittes (1959), follows from the assumption that low self-esteem people have greater needs for esteem enhancement and are therefore more satisfied by the approval of others and more frustrated by the disapproval of others than are high self-esteem people. The prediction is described in Table 1.

EMPIRICAL EVIDENCE

The critical test between the self-esteem and self-consistency theories involves manipulating or measuring the individual's evaluation of himself and the evaluations he receives from other people, then measuring the feelings he expresses to or about his associates, their characteristics or actions. At the present time there are a substantial number of studies which meet in whole or in part the conditions necessary for this critical test.

Self-Consistency Findings

Consider, first, the research which generally is viewed as supporting the self-consistency position. Three of the six studies are correlational in design, and they differ from other investigations described in that all the evaluative components measured are reports made by the subject. In particular, the evaluations purportedly received by the subject from others are *estimates* as to how he thinks others are evaluating him.

In a study of fourth-, fifth-, and sixth-grade school children of both sexes, Wiest (1965) measured global self-esteem and correlated these measures with indices of the degree of congruency existing between a student's attraction for each other member of his group and his perception of others' feeling toward himself. Wiest obtained a significant positive correlation (0.23) which he had predicted from Heider's balance theory. As self-esteem increased, interpersonal congruency also increased. Backman and Secord (1962) asked each member of a college sorority to select from a list of 16 adjective pairs the 5 adjectives most characteristic of herself, to indicate which 5 adjectives each other sorority member would attribute to her, and to rank order the other members according to their attractiveness. Interpersonal congruency was measured by the degree of overlap between the adjectives a subject selected for herself and those she estimated would be attributed to herself by others. In support of the Secord and Backman (1961) model, more congruency was obtained for the subject's ratings of the sorority members most liked by the subject than for the members least liked by the subject. From results obtained in a longer range investigation, Newcomb (1956) reported that interpersonal attraction was closely related to the perceived agreement between a person's self-description and his estimate of how other members of the dormitory would describe him.

In experimental studies as contrasted with correlational studies of the self-consistency theory, evaluations from others (which were manipulated) actually were received rather than estimated by the subject. In one of the three studies which partially fulfill the design conditions described above, Wilson (1965) led subjects to believe that they had failed on a task. Then either by having subjects make their own decisions (personal decision condition) or by having these decisons made for them by a "chance" procedure (chance decision condition), he brought about the decision that subjects would not proceed with a second task. After this decision, subjects received a bogus comment supposedly written by their partners, which in half of the conditions described a subject as competent and implied that he should accept the second task, and in half of the conditions described him as incompetent and implied that he should not accept the task. Wilson found that of the subjects in the personal decision conditions, those receiving a negative note rated their partners as more accurate and slightly more attractive than those receiving a positive note. For subjects in the chance decision condition, those receiving a positive note rated their partners as more emotionally supportive, more attractive, and slightly more accurate than those receiving the negative note.

Although this study is often cited as support for the self-consistency position (e.g., Aronson & Mettee, 1968; Secord & Backman, 1965), there is the question of why chance decision subjects who had also failed the first task and presumably held negative evaluations of their own abilities actually preferred partners who evaluated them positively but inconsistently. What most clearly distinguishes the chance from personal decision conditions is not a difference in level of self-evaluation but whether or not the subject made a *personal* decision not to continue. Therefore, although self-evaluative processes may be involved in the study, the results can be interpreted quite easily by assuming that individuals tend to like better and view as more accurate others who agree with their decisions as compared with those who disagree (cf. Festinger, 1954, 1957).

The most widely cited study of self-consistency and interpersonal evaluations is Deutsch and Solomon's (1959) test of derivations from Heider's (1958) balance theory. In their 2 x 2 design, self-evaluation was manipulated by informing subjects that they had either succeeded or failed on each of two tasks, and evaluations from others were manipulated by having each subject receive a note from one of her teammates stating either (e.g.) "You are the person I most prefer to have on my team again" or (e.g.) "You are the person I least prefer to have on the same team with me again." Analyses of evaluative ratings each subject made of her note-sending teammate showed, first, a "positivity" effect, that is, a tendency for subjects to rate more favorably the positive note sender than the negative note sender, and second, a self-consistency effect, that is, an interaction between self-evaluation and evaluations received from others in which the tendency for such a positivity effect was obtained only for subjects in the high-self-evaluation treatment. Low-self-evaluators tended to rate the negative note sender slightly, though not significantly, more favorably.

This experiment has not gone uncriticized. Pepitone (1966) reinterpreted their data by arguing that subjects may have been attempting to fulfill the announced purpose of the experiment by demonstrating their skill at evaluating their teammates. An inconsistent evaluator would be perceived as inaccurate and, in this context, be less attractive than consistent evaluators. A more serious problem for the Deutsch and Solomon study is Skolnick's (1971) failure to replicate their results even though he used an almost identical procedure. In fact, Skolnick found support for the prediction from self-esteem theory; low self-evaluators rated the positive note sender more favorably and the negative note sender less favorably than did high self-evaluators.

A third experiment tending to support the self-consistency prediction was reported by Dutton and Arrowood (1971). Subjects were led to believe that they had performed either well or poorly in presenting arguments about draft resistance to a panel of peers who, independently of, and crosscutting the performance manipulation, ostensibly judged the subjects' performances as either a "good job" or a "poor job." The results showed that subjects who thought they had done well were more attracted to the peers who made positive evaluations than to those who made negative evaluations. Subjects who thought they had done poorly were more attracted to peers who made negative evaluations.

Although this study appears to support consistency theory, there is reason to question whether or not the good and poor performance conditions represent a self-evaluation manipulation. The task that subjects performed consisted of reading arguments prepared by the experimenter, not the subject. In the poor-performance condition, the subject was given an objectively confusing task, then informed by a physiological measure that she felt "extremely anxious" a condition which presumably arose from the "cognition that she was performing poorly." In the good performance condition, the task was objectively clear and the physiological measure indicated no anxiety. Thus, the subject merely read an argument, which was either clear or confusing and which the *experimenter* created, and subsequently her peers either agreed or disagreed with what her body presumably was telling her. Under these circumstances, it is hard to see how the subject felt any personal responsibility for either her performance or the consequences of her performance.

Self-Esteem Findings

Both correlational and experimental data have supported self-esteem theory.

In an extensive field investigation of the correlates of self-esteem, Rosenberg (1965) asked his sample of high school juniors and seniors, "How much does it bother you to find that someone has a poor opinion of you?" Since Rosenberg correlated answers to this question with a range of self-esteem scores, this aspect of his study partially fulfills the design criteria for this review. In effect, high and low self-evaluators react to imagined negative evaluations from others. In support of the prediction from self-esteem theory, Rosenberg found that the lower a person's self-esteem, the more he was bothered by the poor opinion of another person.

The earliest experimental study of the relationship between self-esteem and interpersonal attraction based on the self-esteem formulation was conducted by Dittes (1959). Self-esteem was measured by various self-reports made by the subjects and by the actual evaluations made by other members of their groups. At the end of a group discussion, the members were permitted to see experimentally manipulated peer ratings of their acceptability to the group. Dittes found that acceptance by the group interacted significantly with self-esteem. For subjects who learned that they were not acceptable to the group, the lower their self-esteem, the less attracted they were to the group. However, for subjects learning that they were acceptable to the group, there was a slight tendency for those with lower self-esteem to be attracted more to the group. A similar interaction effect was obtained by Jones, Knurek, and Regan (in press). In their experiment self-esteem was measured with the Janis-Field scale (Hovland & Janis, 1959). Following a half-hour period for becoming acquainted with another person, subjects learned that their partners either liked them or disliked them. On both a "desire to change partner" measure and a "general emotional reaction" measure, low self-esteem subjects indicated more attraction to their partners in the like condition and slightly less attraction to their partners in the dislike condition than did high-self-esteem subjects.

Walster and her colleagues have obtained similar results from experiments in which self-esteem was manipulated rather than measured. They provided subjects with false feedback from personality tests indicating either that they were mature, strong, competent, socially responsible, etc. (high-self-esteem conditions) or immature, inflexible, and possessing other negative characteristics (low-self-esteem conditions). In the first study, Walster (1965) found that female subjects in the low-self-esteem condition were more attracted to a male suitor than were subjects in the high-self-esteem condition. In the second study (Jacobs, Berscheid, & Walster, 1971), the dating skills of a male subject were either praised and he was accepted as a potential date by a same-aged female, or his dating skills were derogated and he was rejected as a potential date. Once again, males in the low-self-esteem condition liked the female evaluator more in the accepting condition but also disliked her more in the rejecting condition than did males in the high-self-esteem condition.

Results supporting the self-esteem theory have been obtained not only for measures and manipulations of global self-esteem but also for more specific aspects of the self. In addition to Skolnick's study (1971) already cited, Jones (1966) manipulated subjects' evaluations of their design judgment ability and subsequently had groups of subjects exchange evaluations of performances relating to this ability. Half of the subjects received mostly positive evaluations from the group, and the remainder received mostly negative evaluations. The evaluations subjects made of their own and other members' performances constituted the main dependent variables. Although the pattern of data indicating subjects' ratings of their peers' performances were in the direction predicted by self-esteem theory, the interaction between manipulated self-evaluation and evaluations received from others was not statistically significant. However, Jones correlated the subject's evaluations of their own performance with those made of other members' performances and found results supporting the self-esteem theory. Specifically, in the positive evaluation condition, the more positively subjects rated their own performances, the more negatively they rated the responses of others, but in the negative evaluation condition, the correlation between ratings of self and others were positive. Although this latter correlation was not significant, it differed significantly from the corresponding correlation in the positive evaluation condition.

Regarding these correlational findings, it is interesting to note that Harvey (1962) obtained comparable results in a study which generally is viewed as support for the self-consistency theory. His main finding was that the more negative the evaluations a subject received from another person, the less favorable were his attitudes toward the other person. These results can be explained by either self-consistency or self-esteem theory. However, in an internal correlational analysis, Harvey found that the more a subject changed his evaluation of himself in a negative direction, the more he also changed his evaluation of the other person in a negative direction. Since the experimentally controlled evaluations subjects received from the other person were in four out of five conditions negatively discrepant from his self-ratings, this positive correlation contradicts the self-consistency theory. This theory would predict that as the self-evaluation changes in the negative direction advocated by the other person, the attraction to this other person will increase.

Secord and Backman's (1961) version of self-consistency theory views the self-evaluation as more flexible and subject to change than most other versions of the theory. Consequently, studies apparently supporting self-esteem theory but measuring only the evaluations a subject makes of others and not changes in his self-evaluation must be interpreted with some caution. In this light the findings of Jones, and of Harvey, which had evaluations of both self and others as dependent variables, become particularly important in a comparative evaluation of self-esteem and self-consistency theories.

One further study relevant in this issue of the correlations between evaluations of self and others was conducted by Jones, Hester, Farina, and Davis (1959). Self-evaluation was measured indirectly by asking subjects to indicate how they expected to be rated by two observers on such dimensions as self-centeredness, popularity, tolerance, generosity, and self-confidence. The data reported by Jones and his colleagues concerned subjects' evaluations of the likability of an observer who evaluated them in a highly derogatory fashion on the same dimensions for which subjects had predicted the observers' reactions. The characteristics of the derogator were manipulated. In one condition the derogator was portrayed as unstable and maladjusted and in the other condition as well adjusted and insightful.

Before viewing the data, consider the predictions deriving from the two theories. As noted above, when the evaluations received from the other person are negative, as they were in the present study, the self-consistency theory prediction is that the lower the self-evaluation (in this case the expected ratings of others), the more positive the evaluation of others (i.e., a negative correlation). The self-esteem prediction is that the lower the self-evaluation, the more negative the evaluation of others (i.e., a positive correlation). Furthermore, assuming that the appraisals received from the well-adjusted derogator are more important than those received from the maladjusted derogator, then, on the one hand, from self-consistency theory one would expect a more negative correlation in the adjusted other condition than the maladjusted other condition. The evaluations of the adjusted other presumably are more accurate, and consistency with regard to self-ratings is corresponding more important. On the other hand, from self-esteem theory one would expect a more positive correlation in the adjusted other condition than the maladjusted other condition. The derogation of the well-adjusted peer is more damaging to self-esteem needs and should have more negative impact on the person with low expectancies about his value for others.

The correlational data support the self-esteem analysis. First, in the adjusted derogator condition, the relation between ratings of self and other is highly positive (0.84) and corresponds in direction to the results obtained by Jones (1966) and Harvey (1962). Second, this correlation is significantly more positive than in the maladjusted derogator condition where, in fact, the correlation is strongly negative (-0.62).

One final piece of supporting evidence for the self-esteem position comes from a study by Potter[1] who manipulated subjects' appraisals of their own social sensitivity as well as whether or not they were liked by their partners. Although subjects were more attracted to their partners when their partners liked them as compared to when their partners disliked them, this tendency was significantly greater for low-self-evaluators than for high-self-evaluators.

Summary of Evidence

The implications of these studies, which may be viewed as "critical tests" between the two theories, are summarized in Table 2. The table also summarizes the status of the evaluations subjects experienced from others—that is, whether these evaluations were estimated by the subject or experimentally controlled. Two aspects of the table are worth noting. First, the evidence, in general, tends to favor self-esteem theory over self-consistency theory. Of the 16 investigations reviewed, 10 support self-esteem theory, and the author has suggested that there are serious problems of interpretation or replication with the experimental studies often cited as support for self-consistency theory. Furthermore, the self-esteem evidence becomes more impressive when one considers the variety of different procedures and measures used in these studies. However, at this point, to draw any firm conclusions about the relative value of self-esteem theory would be premature. Some data do seem to support self-consistency theory, and the question is whether these data can be accounted for within an expanded self-esteem theory framework.

TABLE 2

Summary of Studies

AUTHOR(S)	STATUS OF EVALUATIONS FROM OTHERS	THEORY SUPPORTED
Backman & Secord (1962)	Estimated by subject	Consistency
Deutsch & Solomon (1959)	Controlled by experimenter	Consistency
Dittes (1959)	Controlled by experimenter	Esteem
Dutton & Arrowood (1971)	Controlled by experimenter	Consistency
Harvey (1962)	Controlled by experimenter	Esteem
Jacobs, Berscheid, & Walster (1971)	Controlled by experimenter	Esteem
Jones, Hester, Farina, & Davis (1959)	Controlled by experimenter	Esteem
Jones (1966)	Controlled by experimenter	Esteem
Jones, Knurek, & Regan (*in press*)	Controlled by experimenter	Esteem
Newcomb (1956)	Estimated by subject	Consistency
Potter (1970)	Controlled by experimenter	Esteem
Rosenberg (1965)	Controlled by experimenter	Esteem
Skolnick (1971)	Controlled by experimenter	Esteem
Walster (1965)	Controlled by experimenter	Esteem
Wiest (1965)	Estimated by subject	Consistency
Wilson (1965)	Controlled by experimenter	Consistency

A second feature of Table 2 is that all three studies in which peer evaluations were estimated by the subject support self-consistency theory, whereas 10 of the 13 studies in which these evaluations were in some way controlled by the experimenter support self-esteem theory. This pattern of results suggests that a subject may be confronted with quite different problems depending upon whether he must estimate another person's feelings or is actually informed of those feelings as they relate to some aspect of himself. This difference is discussed later on in the paper.

TOWARD A RESOLUTION

People often comment on the "counter-intuitive" quality of many predictions from cognitive consistency theories, and some of the implications of self-consistency theory are subject to this general bafflement. Many authors working primarily within a cognitive consistency framework have acknowledged the discrepancies between cognitive consistency motivations and self-esteem, self-enhancement, or even achievement motivations, and have expressed such reservations. Rosenberg (1968), for example, observed that one of the most important failings of the consistency approach

seems to be experimental affirmation of this hard, intractable fact: the need for (or trend toward) the maintenance of internally consistent affective cognitive structures is often subordinated to man's penchant for trying to think well of himself and optimistically of his prospects [p. 384]."

In response to this dilemma, some authors have viewed esteem motivations as "in addition to" forces affecting behavior in experiments designed to demonstrate self-consistent responses (e.g., Aronson and Carlsmith, 1962; Pepitone, 1964) whereas others have tried to expand theories of consistency to account for self-esteem tendencies (e.g., Secord & Backman, 1965).

The author's own orientation to this problem was to ask whether apparently self-consistent actions and attitudes might not be explicable solely in terms of self-esteem theory. In particular, two variables which may be viewed as extensions of this latter theory—the anticipation of future consequences from accepting or rejecting the evaluations of others, and the degree of personalistic focus attributable to these evaluations—proved to be useful in accounting for a variety of results in this area of self- and interpersonal evaluations.

Consequences of Accepting or Rejecting Evaluations

As one alternative interpretation of self-consistent responses, consider the possibility that they reflect a tendency for people to react to evaluative information in terms not only of its present but also its future implications for esteem enhancement. In general, people prefer to accept approval from others and to reject disapproval. However, there are numerous occasions on which a person's accepting inconsistent and inaccurate evaluations for himself has important and potentially hazardous consequences for his future decisions, responsibilities, and performances, and these consequences can be as frightening for the low-self-evaluator who is overrated as they are humiliating for the high-self-evaluator who is underrated. In addition to the failures and limited successes of his actual performances, the individual also may suffer social embarrassment from misrepresenting himself or from the exposed discrepancy between others' expectancies and his actual effectiveness.

These anticipated successes or failures and expressions of approval or disapproval which are contingent on the individual's accepting evaluations of himself can be satisfying or frustrating to his need for self-esteem enhancement. Hence, this position assumes that some apparently self-consistent responses can be viewed in terms of people forfeiting immediate gratifications of esteem needs in anticipation of more self-enhancing or less self-derogating experiences in the future.

Two classes of conditions have been identified which are assumed to increase the salience of the future consequences of interpersonal evaluations: *predecisional conditions* in which a person anticipates making choices for himself which involve his self-evaluation, and *self-exposure conditions* in which a person anticipates the public revelation of his actual successes or failures. The general hypothesis guiding the research described below is that the anticipation of making a personal decision or of self-exposure will increase the tendency of the individual to make apparently self-consistent responses in his relations with others.

In a study of the effects on interpersonal evaluations of anticipating personal decisions, Jones and Ratner (1967) induced all subjects to adopt negative evaluations of their "personality inference" ability by giving them false low scores on each of a series of four personality tests. In a second part of the experiment, three subjects at a time participated in a group session in which they evaluated each other's responses to items like those appearing on the personality tests. The evaluations from peers were experimentally controlled so that each subject received mostly positive evaluations from one peer and mostly negative evaluations from the other. Before actually beginning this second phase of the experiment, subjects were told that there would be a third part of the study in which they would be required to use this "personality inference" ability in a case analysis which would be evaluated by a clinical psychologist. Half the subjects immediately chose how difficult a clinical case they wished to work on (postdecision condition), and, as expected, their choices were from among the easier cases. The remainder of the subjects anticipated making their choices after the group session (predecision condition).

The argument made by Jones and Ratner was that prior to making a decision for himself, a subject would prefer accurate, self-consistent information from others, but that after making the decision as to clinical task he would, in effect, be protected from the hazardous consequences of accepting erroneous evaluations and would prefer information providing more esteem gratifications, that is, positive evaluations. The results showed that in the postdecision condition subjects evaluated the responses of the positive evaluator more favorably than the negative evaluator but that in the predecision condition subjects more favorably evaluated the responses of the negative evaluator.

Three experimental investigations have been conducted which relate to the anticipation of self-exposure. A study by Jones and Pines (1968) used a procedure very similar to the study just described. Once again, subjects were given negative feedback on the "personality inference" tests and, subsequently, during a group session received mostly positive evaluations from one peer and mostly negative evaluations from the other. One further manipulation involved self-exposure. Half the subjects were led to believe that following the group session they would once again give their answers aloud but the correctness of their answer would be indicated publicly by the experimenter. Thus, in this condition subjects expected to have their level of skill (which they thought was low) revealed to their peers. The other half of the subjects were not led to expect such self-exposure.

As predicted and in support of the theoretical analysis presented above, subjects expecting self-exposure increased the favorability of their appraisals of the negative evaluator relative to the positive evaluator as the time of the experimenter's public evaluation approached, and those not expecting self-exposure became increasingly more favorable to the positive evaluator. Furthermore, subjects in the self-exposure condition reported that the negative test evaluation from experts was a more meaningful indication of their abilities, whereas those in the no self-exposure condition found the relatively more positive evaluations of the peers (in combination) were the better indicators of their ability).

An unpublished dissertation by Haraguchi[2] was a conceptual replication of the Jones-Pines study but employed a quite different procedure suggested by Jones' (1964) analysis of self-presentation. Subjects were led to believe from a highly qualified source that they would do relatively poorly on an achievement test. However, the subsequent estimate of an inexperienced clinical interviewer was that they would do very well on the test. The prediction was that subjects would present themselves in a more modest fashion to the interviewer under self-exposure conditions in which they expected to discuss their test scores with the interviewer as compared to the no-self-exposure conditions.

Although the main analysis of the self-presentation data revealed no significant effect of the self-exposure variable, Haraguchi found in an internal analysis that the results were very much affected by the perceived attractiveness of the interviewer. She reasoned that subjects would be more likely to avoid embarrassment and disapproval to the extent that they favorably evaluated their interviewers. The results of this internal analysis showed that for the half of the subjects who were most attracted to their interviewers the results were in accordance with her initial prediction; that is, those subjects in the self-exposure condition evaluated themselves less favorably (and more consistently with respect to their self-evaluations) than those in the no-self-exposure conditions. These results were significantly reversed for the remainder of the subjects who were least attracted to their interviewers.

Finally, Eagly and Acksen (1971) conducted a study which may be viewed within the present framework. In their experiment, subjects received notes from trained graduate students indicating that they were either more creative or less creative than they had evaluated themselves. Subsequently, changes in self-appraisals were measured either under two conditions in which subjects expected to take a creativity test in which their degree of success would be obvious to themselves and the graduate student administering the test, or under a condition in which no tests were expected. The authors obtained an interaction between expectancy of testing and favorability or unfavorability of the student's note. Only when subjects received a favorable note and expected no test did they change their self-evaluation in the direction of being more creative . . . . Furthermore, in the favorable note conditions subjects changed their self-evaluations more in the direction of the message when they anticipated no test as compared to when they did expect the test; the corresponding comparison for the unfavorable note conditions revealed no significant differences.

In general, the results reported in this section support the notion that apparently self-consistent behavior may result from the future implication of evaluations for esteem-enhancement. Whether people enhance self-esteem by accepting positive evaluations of themselves or by being more realistic about themselves has been shown to be affected by their expectancies regarding events which could reveal their true worth.[3]

Implications of "Personalism" for Self-Esteem Enhancement

There is a second analysis which suggests that self-consistent interpersonal evaluations may be interpreted with the assumptions of self-esteem theory. Given that an individual is liked, approved of, or agreed with by another person, he probably finds this information more rewarding to the extent that its cause is attributable to characteristics of himself rather than to some cause which is unrelated to himself. For example, thinking "He likes me because of the kind of person I am." is undoubtedly more rewarding than thinking "He likes me because he's the kind of person who likes everybody." By the same token various sorts of negative evaluations may well be increasingly more damaging to self-esteem needs when the individual sees himself as the cause of the evaluations as compared to when the cause is externally attributed.

This analysis draws heavily upon Jones and Davis' (1965) concept of personalism.

In line with their thinking, I assume that to the extent that actions (such as interpersonal evaluations) are attributable to, or "uniquely focused" on the self, those actions have more impact on the self-esteem needs of the individual. Thus, to the degree that positive evaluations are perceived as focusing on the self, esteem needs are satisfied; and to the degree that negative evaluations are focused in this manner, esteem needs are frustrated.

An important variable affecting personalistic attributions may well be the similarity or consistency existing between the individual's evaluation of himself and the evaluations he receives from the actor. When the individual and another party have similar opinions about an entity, there is at least the possibility that the other person is focusing on, and being directly affected by the same events as the subject in question (cf. Kelley, 1967).

If self-consistency produces the attribution of personal cause, then this analysis, once again, leads to the conclusion that self-consistency per se is not a general motivational state. Rather, personalism via self-consistency interacts with the esteem enhancing or derogating value of the actions directed toward the individual. Thus, the hypothesis to be considered is that when an individual is accepted or liked by others, the more self-consistent their evaluations of his characteristics, the more he is attracted to them, but when an individual is rejected or disliked by others, the more self-consistent their evaluations, the less he is attracted to them.

Two studies were designed to test this general notion. In the first study, Jones, Knurek, and Regan (in press) assumed (and self-report data confirmed this assumption) that subjects would have generally favorable ratings of their own characteristics and manipulated self-consistency by providing the subjects with positive (and consistent) trait ratings by their partners or with negative (and inconsistent) ratings. Subsequently, whether a partner liked or disliked a subject was varied, and measures of the subject's attraction to his partner revealed a significant interaction between self-consistency and liking which partially supported the above hypothesis. When subjects were liked by their partners, their attraction was greater when they received positive trait ratings rather than negative ratings from their partners; when subjects were disliked they were slightly less attracted when they received positive ratings. Although alternative interpretations of these findings were implausible in the light of other data obtained in this study, a more substantial test of the personalism hypothesis requires a direct manipulation of self-consistency.

An unpublished dissertation by Potter (see Footnote 1) permits such a test. Subjects were first given two written tests of their social sensitivity and received test feedback indicating that they had either a high level of skill or a low level of skill. Then they participated in a structured "social sensitivity interview" in the presence of a partner who subsequently evaluated them as being either well above average or well below average in social sensitivity. Since there was evidence that the test feedback affected self-evaluations, the test and interpersonal evaluations of social sensitivity, which constituted a 2 x 2 design may be considered in conjunction as a manipulation of self-consistency. Evaluations which are similarly high or low are consistent, but evaluations which were dissimilar are inconsistent. Finally, on an additional evaluation form subjects were informed that their partners either liked or disliked them.

TABLE 3

Attraction to Partners as a Function of Self-Consistency and Liking

SELF-CONSISTENCY	*LIKE**	*DISLIKE*
Consistent	2.34	4.65
Inconsistent	3.06	3.44

*The lower the number, the greater the subject's liking for his partner.

The major dependent variable of this study was a question designed to assess how much a subject liked his partner. If self-consistency is a general motivational tendency, then one would expect that regardless of whether they were liked or disliked by their partners, subjects would be more attracted to them in the consistent conditions than the inconsistent conditions. If, on the other hand, the analysis of personalism is correct, subjects in the like condition would be attracted to partners in the consistent condition more than partners in the inconsistent condition, but subjects in the dislike condition would like consistent partners less than inconsistent partners. As shown in Table 3, the pattern of results is precisely as predicted by the personalism analysis, and the interaction between self-consistency and liking is highly significant ($p < .001$).

The results of these studies provide support for the assumption that personalism via self-consistency increases the impact of others' feelings on the individual's self-esteem needs. People do prefer self-consistent evaluations from others when they feel that they are accepted or liked by others. However, the fact that inconsistent evaluations are preferred when the individual finds himself disliked strongly indicates that esteem enhancement and not maintenance of stable cognitions is the motivational force operating in these social relations.

This analysis of self-consistency has implications for two of the correlational studies reported earlier in the paper. Backman and Secord (1962) and Newcomb (1956) showed that an individual's liking for others is a direct function of the similarity between his evaluations of himself and those he attributes to others. Although these findings seem to support self-consistency theory, a self-esteem interpretation now becomes possible. To make this interpretation meaningful it is necessary to consider how much the individual felt he was liked by each of his peers. In these survey studies of ongoing relations, it is probably safe to assume that the individual's liking for others is highly correlated with how much others like him or at least with his perception of their liking for him (see, e.g., Tagiuri, Bruner, & Blake, 1958, for evidence supporting this assumption). From this assumption follows the possibility that Backman and Secord's and Newcomb's findings indicate that the more the individual likes and thinks he is liked by another person, the more he attributes similarity with regard to opinions about himself. This tendency falls into line with the pattern of results found by Potter. It suggests that self-consistent opinions are attributed to friends to enhance the value of their affection whereas dissimilar opinions tend to be attributed to enemies to defend against the sting of their rejection.

"Warm" and "Cool" Studies of Social Evaluation

The analyses of future consequences and personalism suggest the conclusion that a variety of self-consistent results may be explained within the framework of self-esteem theory and that cognitive consistency motivations play at best a minor role in interpersonal evaluations of the sort discussed here. However, there may be limitations to the generalizability of this conclusion to some kinds of investigations of social perception and evaluation. There are a number of studies (e.g., Aronson & Cope, 1968; Jordan, 1953) showing that people tend to hold consistent or balanced cognitions with respect to their evaluations of others. Indeed the correlational studies reviewed earlier (Backman & Secord, 1962; Newcomb, 1956; and Wiest, 1965), although open to alternative interpretations, show similar consistency effects. A major distinction which may be useful in those studies which obtain results supporting cognitive consistency theory from those supporting self-esteem theory involves whether or not the experimental subjects are themselves targets of evaluative action from the stimulus person being evaluated. Experiments in which the subject is liked or disliked, agreed or disagreed with, benefited or harmed, or in other ways directly affected by the stimulus person may be considered "warm" studies. Since these subjects are to some extent the focus of actions having evaluative implications, such studies should be interpretable within the self-esteem theory framework. However, experiments in which the subject is in no way personally affected by the stimulus person may be viewed as "cool" studies. In the literature on person perception, there are many such investigations in which the subject observes but does not interact with some staged slice of life involving other people, then is asked to form impressions of these others based on his observations. Since there is no direct personal involvement and the orientation of the subject is essentially clinical or diagnostic, these studies may well be more explicable in terms of cognitive consistency theory.

This distinction is helpful in accounting for the pattern of results reported previously in Table 2. Those studies in which the subject estimates the reactions of others are relatively cool because the subject is neither interacting with, nor receiving evaluative information from others. Hence, his esteem needs are of less concern to him than the cognitive task of making sense of the social world he watches, and, indeed, his attitudes in these situations do tend to be self-consistent. Those studies in which the subject receives evaluations from others are warm studies. The subject learns what others actually think of him, he worries about his own esteem and worth, and, as the data indicate in most cases, he is differentially satisfied or frustrated depending upon others' evaluations and his self-evaluation.

The variable differentiating warm and cool studies—whether or not the subject is the focus of evaluative actions from the target person—is easily manipulable, and the idea that warm situations will lead to esteem theory results whereas cool situations will lead to consistency theory results should be experimentally tested. In addition, systematically applying this distinction to other studies in person perception should be undertaken before drawing any firm conclusions. If the difference proposed turns out to be meaningful, there is an interesting implication for the person perception literature in general; namely, the popularity of consistency theories in this area may be in part at least a function of the many studies conducted in which the subject is required to comment upon or evaluate a social game that he observes from the sidelines but in which he rarely participates. Furthermore, if living with others is a matter of playing the game rather than watching it, then the generality of consistency models to real life situations may be quite limited.

SUMMARY AND CONCLUSIONS

The purpose of this paper was to compare two rather broad theoretical traditions in social psychology as they related to the determinants of interpersonal evaluations. evaluations. On the one hand, proponents of self-consistency theory argue that the individual adjusts his cognitions and orients his relations with others so as to maintain similarity between his evaluations of himself and those he receives from others. On the other hand, the assumptions of self-esteem theory are that the individual has a need for self-esteem which is satisfied primarily by the approval he receives from others and is frustrated by their disapproval, and that to the extent that his esteem need is satisfied by others' evaluations, the individual will respond favorably to them.

In spite of the fact that the cognitive consistency approach has been widely accepted as a theoretical framework for these problems as well as many other problems in social psychology, I suggest that a stronger case can be made for the value of the self-esteem theory outlined in this paper. The evidence from experiments which permit a test between these positions provides more substantial support for the self-esteem predictions. Time and again, the unhappy self-derogator seems to glow when praised and glare when censured even more than his self-confident counterpart. Futhermore, two rather straightforward extensions of self-esteem theory are capable of explaining apparently self-consistent interpersonal evaluations. First, the anticipated exposure of his qualities tends to make the individual more "honest" about himself (and, therefore, more self-consistent) so as to avoid the eventual disapproval of others. Second, people respond more favorably to negative evaluations to the extent that those evaluations are perceived as uniquely focused on themselves. Not only can these propositions account for some of the data often cited as support for a self-consistency motivation, but they also point in the direction of sorting out self-consistent responses from other strategies designed to gain esteem enhancement.

Whether or not these conclusions have implications for other social psychological problems involving cognitive consistency models remains to be seen. Bramel (1968) has recently suggested that certain cognitive dissonance phenomena may reflect underlying needs for self-esteem enhancement through social approval. He argues that "dissonance is a feeling of personal unworthiness (a type of anxiety) traceable to rejection of oneself by other people either in the present or in the past" and that the "consequences of anxiety about one's worth are likely to be such things as self-justification and the search for information that will reflect favorably upon the self [p. 365]." Deutsch, Krauss, and Rosenau (1962) have made a similar argument. Exploring the similarities and differences among these various lines of analysis could lead to a more clearly articulated self-esteem theory as well as sharpen the distinction between it and cognitive consistency theories.

EPILOGUE

I am good
You love me
therefore you are good.
I am bad
You love me
therefore you are truly beautiful!

NOTES

1 D. A. Potter. "Accuracy and interpersonal attraction." Unpublished doctoral dissertation, Cornell University, 1970.

2 R. S. Haraguchi. "Interpersonal conditions affecting self-presentation." Unpublished doctoral dissertation, State University of New York at Buffalo, 1967.

3 Jones (1968a) and Mettee (1971) have made a similar argument in an attempt to explain apparently self-consistent responses in a nonsocial testing situation designed by Aronson and Carlsmith (1962).

REFERENCES

Aronson, E.
1969 "Some antecedents of interpersonal attraction." In W. J. Arnold & D. Levine (eds.), Nebraska Symposium on Motivation. Lincoln, Nebraska: University of Nebraska Press.

Aronson, E. and J. M. Carlsmith
1962 "Performance expectancy as a determinant of actual performance." Journal of Abnormal and Social Psychology 65: 178–82.

Aronson E. and V. Cope
1968 "My enemy's enemy is my friend." Journal of Personality and Social Psychology 8: 8–12.

Aronson, E. and D. R. Mettee
1968 "Dishonest behavior as a function of differential levels of induced self-esteem." Journal of Personality and Social Psychology 9: 121–27.

Aronson, E. and P. Worchel
1966 "Similarity vs. liking as determinants of interpersonal attractiveness." Psychonomic Science 5: 157–58.

Backman, C. W. and P. F. Secord
1959 "The effect of perceived liking on interpersonal attraction." Human Relations 12: 379–84.
1962 "Liking, selective interaction, and misperception in congruent interpersonal relations." Sociometry 25: 321–35.

Baron, R. M.
1966 "Social reinforcement effects as a function of social reinforcement history." Psychological Review 73: 527–39.

Bavelas, A., A. H. Hastorf, A. E. Gross, and W. R. Kite
1965 "Experiments on the alteration of group structure." Journal of Experimental Social Psychology 1: 55–70.

Bramel, D.
1968 "Dissonance, expectation, and the self." In Abelson et al. (eds.), Theories of Cognitive Consistency: A Sourcebook. Chicago: Rand McNally.
Cartwright, D. and A. Zander
1960 Group Dynamics. 2d ed. Evanston, Ill.: Row, Peterson.
Deutsch, M., R. M. Krauss and N. Rosenau
1962 "Dissonance or defensiveness?" Journal of Personality 30: 16–28.
Deutsch, M and L. Solomon
1959 "Reactions to evaluations by others as influenced by self-evaluation." Sociometry 22: 92–113.
Dittes, J. E.
1959 "Attractiveness of group as a function of self esteem and acceptance by group." Journal of Abnormal and Social Psychology 59: 77–82.
Dollard, J., L. Doob, N. E. Miller, O. H. Mowrer, and R. R. Sears
1939 Frustration and Aggression. New Haven: Yale University Press.
Dutton, D. G. and A. J. Arrowood
1971 "Situational factors in evaluation congruency and interpersonal attraction." Journal of Personality and Social Psychology 18: 222–29.
Eagly, A. H. and B. A. Acksen
1971 "The effect of expecting to be evaluated on change toward favorable and unfavorable information about oneself." Sociometry 34: 411–22.
Festinger, L.
1954 "A theory of social comparison processes." Human Relations 7: 117–50.
1957 A Theory of Cognitive Dissonance. Evanston, Ill.: Row, Peterson.
Harvey, O. J.
1962 "Personality factors in resolution of conceptual incongruities." Sociometry 25: 336–52.
Heider, F.
1958 The Psychology of Interpersonal Relations. New York: Wiley.
Homans, G. C.
1961 Social Behavior: Its Elementary Forms. New York: Harcourt, Brace & World.
Hovland, C. I. and I. L. Janis (ed.)
1959 Personality and Persuasibility. New Haven: Yale University Press.
Jacobs, L., E. Berscheid, and E. Walster
1971 "Self-esteem and attraction." Journal of Personality and Social Psychology 17: 84–91.
Jones, E. E.
1964 Ingratiation: A Social Psychological Analysis. New York: Appleton-Century-Crofts.
Jones, E. E. and K. E. Davis
1965 "From acts to dispositions: The attribution process in person perception." In L. Berkowitz (ed.), Advances in Experimental Social Psychology. Vol. 2. New York: Academic Press.
Jones, E. E. and H. B. Gerard
1967 Foundations of Social Psychology. New York: Wiley.
Jones E. E., S. L. Hester, A. Farina, and K. E. Davis
1959 "Reactions to unfavorable personal evaluations as a function of the evaluator's perceived adjustment." Journal of Abnormal and Social Psychology 59: 363–70.
Jones, S. C.
1966 "Some determinants of interpersonal evaluating behavior." Journal of Personality and Social Psychology 3: 397–403.
1968a "Expectation, performance and anticipation of self-revealing events." Journal of Social Psychology 74: 189–97.
1968b "Some effects of interpersonal evaluations on group process and social perception. Sociometry 31: 150–61.

Jones, S. C., D. A. Knurek and D. J. Regan
In press "Variables affecting reactions to social acceptance and rejections." Journal of Social Psychology.
Jones, S. C. and D. Panitch
1971 "The self-fulfilling prophecy and interpersonal attraction." Journal of Experimental Social Psychology 7: 356–66.
Jones, S. C. and H. A. Pines
1968 "Self-revealing events and interpersonal evaluations." Journal of Personality and Social Psychology 8: 277–81.
Jones, S. C. and C. Ratner
1967 "Commitment to self-appraisal and interpersonal evaluations." Journal of Personality and Social Psychology 6: 442–47.
Jordan, H.
1953 "Behavioral forces that are a function of attitudes and of cognitive organization." Human Relations 6: 273–87.
Kelley, H. H.
1967 "Attribution theory in social psychology." In D. Levine (ed.), Nebraska Symposium on Motivation, 1967. Lincoln, Nebraska: University of Nebraska Press.
Laing, R. D.
1970 Knots. New York: Pantheon.
Lecky, P.
1945 Self-Consistency: A Theory of Personality. New York: Island Press.
Mettee, D. R.
1971 "Rejection of unexpected success as a function of the negative consequences of accepting success." Journal of Personality and Social Psychology 17: 332–42.
Morse, S. and K. J. Gergen
1970 "Social comparison, self-consistency, and the concept of self." Journal of Personality and Social Psychology 16: 148–56.
Newcomb, T. M.
1956 "The prediction of interpersonal attraction." American Psychologist 11: 575–86.
1961 The Acquaintance Process. New York: Holt, Rinehart & Winston.
Pepitone, A.
1964 Attraction and Hostility. New York: Atherton Press.
1966 "Some conceptual and empirical problems of consistency models." In Feldman (ed.), Cognitive Consistency. New York: Academic Press.
Rogers, C. R.
1951 Client-Centered Therapy. Boston: Houghton.
1959 "A theory of therapy, personality, and interpersonal relationships as developed in the client-centered framework." In S. Koch (ed.), Psychology: A Study of Science. Vol. 3. New York: McGraw-Hill.
Rosenberg, M.
1965 Society and the Adolescent Self-Image. Princeton, N. J.: Princeton University Press.
Rosenberg, M. J.
1968 "Discussion: the concepts of self." In Abelson et al. (eds.), Theories of Cognitive Consistency: A Sourcebook. Chicago: Rand McNally.
Secord, P. F. and C. W. Backman
1961 "Personality theory and the problem of stability and change in individual behavior: An interpersonal approach." Psychological Review 68: 21–32.
1964 Social Psychology. New York: McGraw-Hill.
1965 "An interpersonal approach to personality." In B. A. Maher (ed.), Progress in Experimental Personality Research. Vol. 2. New York: Academic Press.
Skolnick, P.
1971 "Reactions to personal evaluations: a failure to replicate." Journal of Personality and Social Psychology 18: 62–67.

Tagiuri, R., J. S. Bruner, and R. R. Blake
1958 "On the relation between feelings and perception of feelings among members of small groups." In E. E. Maccoby, T. M. Newcomb, and E. L. Hartley (eds.), Readings in Social Psychology. New York: Holt, Rinehart & Winston.

Thibaut, J. W. and H. H. Kelley
1959 The Social Psychology of Groups. New York: Wiley.

Videbeck, R.
1960 "Self-conception and the reactions of others." Sociometry 23: 351–59.

Walster, E.
1965 "The effect of self-esteem on romantic liking." Journal of Experimental and Social Psychology 1: 184–97.

Wiest, W. M.
1965 "A quantitative extension of Heider's theory of cognitive balance applied to interpersonal perception and self-esteem." Psychological Monograph 79 (14, Whole No. 607).

Wilson, D. T.
1965 "Ability evaluation, postdecision dissonance, and coworker attractiveness." Journal of Personality and Social Psychology 1: 486–89.

TWO

PRINCIPLES OF SELF-CONCEPT FORMATION

That social influences bear on self-concept formation will be made abundantly evident in the course of this work. But one cannot understand how such factors exercise their effects unless one takes account of certain general principles of self-concept formation. Four principles deserve special attention: reflected appraisals, social comparison, self-attribution, and psychological centrality.

REFLECTED APPRAISALS

The social psychological nature of the self-concept is best illustrated by the principle of reflected appraisals. *This principle was most fully elaborated in the work of George Herbert Mead (1934). In Mead's view, the self-concept was unequivocally a social product, arising out of the process of communication. In order to communicate, Mead stressed, people employ certain gestures, primarily vocal, which become significant symbols. Symbols become significant "when they implicitly arouse in the individual making them the same responses which they explicitly arouse, or are supposed to arouse, in other individuals, the individuals to whom they are addressed. . . the flow of meaning involved depends on [the individual's] taking the attitude of the other toward his own gestures"(p. 47). Such role-taking makes possible adjustment and response among those engaged in the interaction.*

Several aspects of these processes merit special attention. The first is that, in order for a gesture to have meaning, we must take the attitude of others toward our own gesture; we must put ourselves in the other's shoes, see and respond to ourselves from the other's viewpoint. The second point is that, in taking the attitudes of others toward ourselves, we see ourselves as objects external to ourselves; hence, we not only emit vocal gestures but we respond to them as well. We may hear ourselves talking, realize that the words or tone we are using are not those we intended, and change our speech accordingly; we thus respond to ourselves just as others respond to us.

In terms of this sharply condensed and oversimplified version of Mead's ideas, two inferences seem clear: (1) we become objects to ourselves, thereby developing a self-concept; and (2) as a consequence of taking the role of the other, we tend to see ourselves from the viewpoint of particular others or the generalized other.

In subsequent years, Mead's contention that we come to see ourselves as others see us has been empirically supported in numerous studies (for example, Miyamoto and Dornbusch, 1956; Reeder, Donohue, and Biblarz, 1960; Sherwood, 1965, 1967). Simple and straightforward as this statement seems, however, it is a generalization in need of refinement. At best, we can only say that we tend to see ourselves as we think others see us since, after all, no one can ever see into the mind of another with unerring accuracy. Charles Horton Cooley's (1912) concept of the looking-glass self stressed that this was an imputed sentiment, our imagination of what the other thinks of us. The reflected appraisals principle must thus distinguish between what others actually think of us and what we believe they think of us.

Furthermore, the statement that we see ourselves as others see us cannot literally be true since different people see us differently. Hence, the degree to which others agree—or to which we impute agreement—may have a bearing on our self-concepts. What, then, is the effect of such inferred consensus or dissensus among others on our self-attitudes? An ingenious experiment reported by Backman, Secord, and Pierce (Selection 13) demonstrates that it is much more difficult to change one's self-attitude if one believes that one's significant others agree in their judgments of what one is like than if they do not. The impact of reflected appraisals on the self-concept thus hinges in part on the assumed consensus among significant others.

SOCIAL COMPARISON

Evaluations of the self as smart or stupid, attractive or homely, interesting or dull do not take place in a vacuum; they almost invariably require reference points which serve as bases of comparison. The question of how good we are can only be answered with the question: compared to whom or what? Self-evaluations are thus based heavily on social comparison processes (Festinger, 1954).

Pettigrew (1967) has described some of the standards or reference points employed in the literature. For one thing, people's self-satisfaction depends on their comparison level. One such comparison level is the past self: one is not as good as one used to be, or one is getting better all the time. Another reference point is the "ego-level" or level of aspiration. Nowhere is the self-concept relevance of such aspirations better expressed than in James' famous formula: He notes:

$$\text{self-esteem} = \frac{\text{success}}{\text{pretensions}}.$$

"So we have the paradox of a man shamed to death because he is only the second pugilist or the second oarsman in the world. That he is able to beat the whole population of the globe minus one is nothing; he has 'pitted" himself to beat that one; and as long as he doesn't do that nothing else counts. He is to his own regard as if he were not, indeed he is not" (James, 1890: 310).

The idea that we can only judge our worth with reference to some standard is well entrenched in the self-concept literature, which frequently measures global self-esteem as the discrepancy between the individual's self-concept and his or her ideal self.

The social comparison principle has usually been applied to comparisons with other people. As Pettigrew observes, one may judge oneself by comparing oneself to those in one's peer groups (classroom, gang, factory or neighborhood), to others in the same social categories (to most ten-year olds, to most professors, or to most women), to remote reference groups (the upper class, the Christian martyrs, or the early revolutionary Bolsheviks), or to a single person. Furthermore, such comparisons may be situational (for example, comparing ourselves with competitors in a foot race) or general (comparing ourselves with most Americans, most students, or most lawyers).

Morse and Gergen (Selection 14) afford a striking illustration of how implicit comparisons with a single other person in a specific situation may affect self-esteem (at least temporarily). If such a marked effect can be demonstrated with regard to a single other person, it probably applies even more strongly to comparisons with most other people in one's environment.

SELF-ATTRIBUTION

The third principle of self-concept formation is self-attribution. *Essentially this principle rests on the radical behaviorist position of B. F. Skinner which, according to Bem (1967:184), "eschews any reference to hypothetical internal processes and seeks, rather, to account for observed functional relations between current stimuli and responses in terms of the individual's past training history." According to this argument, when we attribute traits or other internal states to other people, what we are actually doing is applying terms to certain behavior occurring under certain circumstances on the basis of our past learning.*

Bem advances the bold idea that people draw conclusions about themselves on the same bases. "Individuals come to 'know' their own attitudes, emotions, and other internal states partially by inferring them from observations of their own overt behavior and/or the circumstances in which this behavior occurs" (Bem, 1972: 5). Thus, the man who, after consuming a huge meal, concludes that "I guess I was hungrier than I thought" is drawing conclusions about his state of hunger not on the basis of the internal physiological experience but on the basis of his observed behavior. Similarly, the woman who listens to the swelling volume of her voice may conclude that she must be angrier than she realized.

In focusing on such subtle and elusive phenomena as the explanation of one's own internal states on the basis of one's overt behavior, it is easy to neglect the more gross and obvious cases of self-attribution. Certainly, in the realm of competence—a realm of importance for self-esteem—people generally judge their abilities on the basis of the same overt evidence used to judge the abilities of others. We conclude that we are intelligent by observing that we characteristically get the right answers or do well on tests; that we are good tennis players when we emerge victorious over talented opponents; that we have manual skill when our efforts at repair or construction are crowned with success. Our own actions teach us new things about ourselves, modifying our self-concepts (Bandura, 1977). After engaging in these activities for the first time, we discover, to our surprise, that we actually have hidden talent for chess or painting. The self-concept influences behavior; however, behavior (or its consequences) also influences the self-concept. The importance of the observation of one's own behavior for self-concept formation is clearly described in Bandura's discussion of self-efficacy in Section One, Selection 3.

PSYCHOLOGICAL CENTRALITY

The principle of psychological centrality rests on the proposition that the self-concept is a structure whose diverse components have unequal salience and importance. Some dispositions are central to the individual's feeling of worth, whereas others are peripheral. Some people pride themselves on their attractiveness and care little about their literary skill; for others, the reverse is the case. It thus follows that if we are to understand what difference a particular self-concept component makes for one's global feeling of worth, we must know not simply how one evaluates oneself in that regard but also how much importance one attaches to it. This point has received empirical support (Rosenberg, 1965).

What is true of dispositions is equally true of social identity elements (such as gender, race, age, occupation, and family status). Stryker (Selection 15) argues that the relevance of each status for behavior depends on its identity salience. For example, one may see oneself as a homosexual, embezzler, or convict, and one may also see oneself as a county resident or a state citizen, but the former identity elements will almost certainly be more salient to the individual than the latter. When labeling theorists (such as Schur, 1971) speak of role engulfment, they are suggesting that some social identity element becomes so prominent in the individual's mind that all others are cast into shadow by comparison. According to Stryker (1968: 560), "the discrete identities which comprise the self exist in a hierarchy of salience, such that other things equal one can expect behavioral products to the degree that a given identity ranks high in the hierarchy. The concept of identity salience may be defined as the probablility, for a given person, of a given identity being invoked in a variety of situations. . . . A rank order of probabilities defines the hierarchy of salience." Stryker then specifies certain conditions under which differential salience will explain differential behavior. As we shall see in Section Three, one reason studies of the relationships between minority group status and self-esteem have so often produced puzzling results is that investigators have neglected to take account of the centrality or peripherality of this status in the individual's phenomenal field.

REFERENCES

Bandura, A.

1977 "Self-efficacy: toward a unifying theory of behavioral change." Psychological Review 84: 191–215.

Bem, D. J.

1967 "Self-perception: an alternative interpretation of cognitive dissonance phenomena." Psychological Review 74: 183–200.

1972 Beliefs, Attitudes and Human Affairs. Belmont, Calif: Brooks Cole.

Cooley, C. H.

1912 Human Nature and the Social Order. New York: Scribners.

Festinger, L.

1954 "A theory of social comparison processes." Human Relations 7: 117–40.

James, W.

1890 The Principles of Psychology. New York: Henry Holt. Reprint: Dover, 1950.

Mead, G. H.

1934 Mind, Self and Society. Chicago: University of Chicago Press.

Miyamoto, S. F. and S. Dornbusch

1956 "A test of the symbolic interactionist hypothesis of self-conception." American Journal of Sociology 61: 399–403.

Pettigrew, T. F.
1967 "Social evaluation theory: convergences and applications." Pp. 241–311 in D. Levine (ed.), Nebraska Symposium on Motivation, 1967. Lincoln, Nebr.: University of Nebraska Press.
Reeder, L. G., G. A. Donohue, and A. Biblarz.
1960 "Conceptions of self and others." American Journal of Sociology 66: 153–59.
Rosenberg, M.
1965 Society and the Adolescent Self-Image. Princeton, N. J.: Princeton University Press.
Schur, E. M.
1971 Labeling Deviant Behavior: Its Sociological Implications. New York: Harper & Row.
Sherwood, J. J.
1965 "Self identity and referent others." Sociometry 28: 66–81.
1967 "Increased self-evaluation as a function of ambiguous evaluations by referent others." Sociometry 30: 404–9.
Stryker, S.
1968 "Identity salience and role performance: the relevance of symbolic interaction theory for family research." Journal of Marriage and the Family 30: 558–64.

Resistance to Change in the Self-Concept as a Function of Consensus Among Significant Others

Carl W. Backman
Paul F. Secord
Jerry R. Pierce

13

The self-concept has been the focus of considerable research and theorizing since the early work of James,[1] Cooley,[2] and Mead.[3] All too often, however, research has not been guided except in a loose fashion by theory. Consequently the total accumulation of substantive findings has been disappointing.[4] At the same time, self-theory has remained vague and rudimentary. More recently the development of a number of cognitive theories[5] closely integrated with programs of systematic research has given promise of a greater articulation between research and theory in this area. While these theories in general have been concerned with the broader problem of stability and change of attitudes, their work has implications for attitudes pertaining to the self. One of these approaches, in particular, interpersonal congruency theory, while not focusing exclusively on the self, affords

Source: Carl W. Backman, Paul F. Secord, and Jerry R. Pierce. "Resistance to Change in the Self-Concept as a Function of Consensus Among Significant Others," Sociometry 26 (1963): 102–11.

it a central place and outlines the conditions under which the self remains stable or changes.

Basic to interpersonal congruency theory is the assumption that there exists within the cognitive organization of the individual a tendency to achieve a state of congruency between three components of what has been termed the interpersonal matrix. These components include an aspect of self of an individual (S), S's interpretation of his behavior relevant to that aspect, and S's perception of the related aspects of the other person (O) with whom he is interacting. Thus an interpersonal matrix is a recurring functional relation among these three components. S strives to achieve congruency among the components of the matrix. Congruency is a cognitive phenomenon; i.e., each component enters into a state of congruency only as a perceptual-cognitive experience on the part of S. All three components of the matrix are in a *state of congruency when S perceives his behavior and that of O as implying definitions of self congruent with relevant aspects of his self-concept.*

Forces that stabilize or bring about changes in either of the other two components of the matrix will, by virtue of this principle, affect the stability of the self. Sources of stability in S's behavior as well as that of O include the residues of previous experience—learned responses—as well as constancies in the stimulus environment. These constancies in turn result not only from the expectations that constitute the social system and guide the behavior of S and O, but also from the operation of a number of interpersonal processes that stem ultimately from the tendency to achieve congruency. While the role of the social system is recognized by most theories that regard the self as a reflection of the views of other persons toward S, these interpersonal processes require further comment. Interpersonal congruency theory, while recognizing the importance of the social structure in fashioning the self, does not view S as passive in the process. Rather S is seen as actively structuring his relations with others so as to achieve and maintain congruency. He does this in the following ways.

In the first place, he selectively interacts with other persons, preferring those who treat him in a manner congruent with his self-concept, and avoiding those who do not. Similarly, he selectively evaluates others, depending upon their attitudes toward him. He does this by liking those who treat him in a congruent fashion, and disliking those who do not. Thus he maximizes the effect of congruent actions and minimizes the effect of incongruent actions on the self-concept. He may also misperceive the actions of others toward him in the belief that they see him as he sees himself, when in actuality, their views of him are somewhat discrepant with his own. Finally, he develops certain behavior patterns that elicit from others reactions that are congruent with his self-definitions. These include not only manipulative behavior, calculated to evoke certain congruent responses, but also less self-conscious, more enduring actions that lead others to treat S in a manner congruent with his self-concept.

A final source of stability and change stems from the manner in which matrices are related to each other. A given matrix may be considered *relevant* to those matrices that contain one or more of the same or similar components as the given matrix. For example, an S who considers himself intelligent may exhibit behaviors in a variety of situations that are interpreted by him as congruent or incongruent with his belief concerning his intelligence. Thus he may obtain high grades in school, play expert chess, but may be a poor bridge player. With respect to the matrix component involving other persons people may ask him for help in solving problems, he may generally win debates, but his father may criticize his intellectual accomplishments. Matrices having no components in common are considered irrelevant, and as having no effect upon each other.

Matrices vary with respect to *centricality*. The centricality of a matrix is a function of the number of relevant other matrices that stand in a supportive relation to it, and the value of the O-components in these matrices. The term *centricality* is chosen in preference to salience or centrality, since the latter terms already have several other established meanings in this field. The greater the centricality of a matrix, the more resistant it is to change, and should it change, the greater the resultant shifts in other matrices. The present study is concerned with one aspect of centricality, namely, the relative number of *O-components* having congruent relations with a given aspect of self. The contribution of S's *behavior-components* to centricality is ignored for the purposes of the present paper. Put simply, the thesis of the present paper is as follows: If a variety of significant other persons are perceived by S to agree in defining an aspect of S's self-concept congruently, their views support each other and his self-concept. If this condition were to prevail, the particular aspect of self involved would be expected to be more resistant to change than if S were to perceive less consensus among significant others. Thus, the main hypothesis of the present study may be stated as follows: *The greater the number of significant other persons who are perceived to define an aspect of an individual's self-concept congruently, the more resistant to change is that aspect of self.*

The hypothesis was tested by choosing for comparison, for each S, a self-ascribed trait on which S perceived high consensus to exist among five significant other persons, and a self-ascribed trait on which perceived consensus was low. Individuals were then subjected to strong pressure to change their perception of these traits, created by means of a highly credible, but false personality assessment. The degree of change in the high consensus trait was compared with change in the low consensus trait.

METHOD

To create strong pressure toward changing certain self-cognitions, it was necessary to have an assessment of S's personality that would be highly credible. This was accomplished by using only subjects willing to volunteer two Saturday mornings for a project in personality assessment. Subjects were offered a personality assessment as a reward for serving in the experiment. In this manner, only those Ss likely to believe in the validity of personality tests would be included. In addition, high credibility was obtained by presenting a rationale emphasizing prestigious sources and serious purpose: the investigation was presented as part of a cooperative research project sponsored by the National Institute of Mental Health, of the U.S. Public Health Service, with the University of Nevada as a cooperating institution. Mention was made of the fact that several sociologists and psychologists from the University of Nevada were participating in the project. The purported purpose of the project was to discover how much insight individuals had into their own personalities.

Subjects were undergraduate students from introductory classes in several fields of study. A total of 40 students attended two sessions held one week apart.

Assessment Devices

The various ranking forms and checklists used were based upon the 15 needs measured by the Edwards Personal Preference Schedule (EPPS).[6] These forms contained 15 brief statements each describing one need, adapted from the need descriptions appearing in the EPPS manual. For example, the need for *nurturance* was represented by the statement, "This person enjoys helping others," and the need for *exhibition* by, "This person likes to receive a lot of attention from others; to be the center of attention."

In the first session, the following instruments were administered.

1. Reflected-self checklist S was asked to write down the names of five close friends or relatives whose opinion he valued. He was given one checklist form for each of these five persons. For each person, he was asked to select the five need-statements that he believed would be most likely to be assigned to him by that person. A 20-minute break followed the completion of these forms.

2. Self-ranking form S ranked himself from 1 to 15 on the 15 abbreviated need statements, from those he believed to be most characteristic to those he considered least characteristic.

3. Edwards Personal Preference Schedule and Gordon Personality Profile[7] These standard tests were administered to lend credence to the assessment process. In addition, the EPPS was scored and profiles were distributed after the experiment had been completed and its real purpose explained to S.

In the second session, S was given a profile sheet indicating the rank order of the 15 needs supposedly characterizing him. Although he was told that professional psychologists had prepared the profile from a careful analysis of the personality tests and the other forms he had taken, actually the order of the needs was the same as S's initial self-ranking, except that two needs from among the highest-ranking five had been moved eight rank-steps downward. The needs on the profile were described in some detail by a psychologist while S was given time to study the profile. Finally these profiles were placed under the chairs in which the Ss were seated, and S was asked to rank himself again on the 15 needs.

The two needs were selected for each S for manipulation by the following means. For each of the five need statements ranking highest on the initial self-ranking form, a measure of consensus was obtained from the reflected-self checklist. This consensus score ranged from 0 to 5 depending upon the number of significant other persons that S perceived as likely to assign the need to him. The following criteria were used to determine what two needs should be manipulated: (a) they had to be included in the five highest-ranking statements on the initial self-form, (b) one had to have relatively high consensus and the other low consensus, (c) they had to have adjacent ranks on the self-form, and (d) the needs had to be balanced for *saliency*.

The higher the ranking of the need-statement on the self-form, the more *salient* it is, and thus probably more resistant to change. But needs that rank high are also likely to be high on consensus, compared with lower-ranking needs. To control for saliency, the subjects were divided into two groups, and the needs to be manipulated selected in a counterbalanced design, as follows:

TYPE OF NEED	*GROUP 1*	*GROUP 2*
High consensus need	high saliency	low saliency
Low consensus need	low saliency	high saliency

In addition, the magnitude of the difference in consensus for each need pair selected for persons in Group 1 was matched with the magnitude of the difference in consensus of the need pair selected for Group 2. Thus any difference obtained between high and low consensus needs in susceptibility to manipulation can legitimately be attributed to the effects of consensus alone, and not saliency.

RESULTS

Several factors point to successful manipulation of the two chosen traits. The great majority of subjects (30 on the high consensus trait; 26 on the low consensus trait) ranked the two manipulated traits lower after receiving the false assessment. Moreover, on the post-experimental questionnaire most subjects indicated that they had been surprised upon reading the assessment profile, particularly stressing the point that the position of certain traits surprised them. On the other hand, only a few subjects stated that they believed any profile traits in the assessment were invalid: they found the assessment credible even though a few traits were unexpected. Somewhat inconsistently, however, subjects in general were not conscious of making deliberate changes in their self-rankings subsequent to the manipulation. The success of the experimental manipulation was also apparent from the loud sighs of relief that arose when the subjects learned that they had been deceived with respect to the assessment.

The main hypothesis of the study, as stated previously, is that an aspect of self will be more resistant to change when S believes that there is consensus among significant other persons concerning that aspect. A need high in consensus and one low in consensus for each individual were manipulated downward in an attempt to secure movement of these needs on a second self-ranking form. In general, several forces could be expected to be generated by this manipulation. One is a tendency to lower one's self-ratings on these two traits. Another is the arousal of resistance to change, and some individuals in whom resistance is aroused might even rank themselves higher than they did initially on the need. Resistance of this sort would be expected because the acceptance of an incongruent self-definition not only requires a change in the matrix containing that aspect but in all related matrices in which that aspect is imbedded. Thus the threat of widespread incongruence could easily create resistance to acceptance. More frequently, of course, this resistance effect might be expected for the high consensus trait. While these two forces are represented by downward and upward movement in self-ranks, respectively, a certain amount of random movement in both directions due to error of measurement will be superimposed upon these other movements. In order to examine the movement due to acceptance or resistance to manipulation uncontaminated by random movement, the best test of the hypothesis is a comparison of the movement of the high consensus trait with the movement for the low consensus trait.

Table 1 lists in the first two columns the number of steps that the high and low consensus need was moved by each individual. Downward movements are positively labeled; upward movements are given a negative sign. Relative movement, shown in the last column of Table 1, was determined by subtracting the movement of the high consensus trait from the low. If the relative movement

TABLE 1
Changes in High and Low Consensus Manipulated Traits for Each Subject

		MOVEMENT OF		
SUBJECT	*TRAITS MANIPULATED LOW, HIGH*	*LOW CONSENSUS TRAIT*	*HIGH CONSENSUS TRAIT*	*DIFFERENCE*
1	Def,Aut	8	−2	10
2	Aut,Aff	8	0	8
3	Def,Aba	8	1	7
4	Chg,Nur	7	0	7
5	Aba,Nur	7	0	7
6	Def,Nur	6	−1	7
7	Agg,End	8	1	7
8	Int,Nur	5	0	5
9	Suc,Aff	5	0	5
10	Exh,Chg	5	0	5
11	Def,Chg	4	−1	5
12	Def,Aba	9	5	4
13	Chg,Suc	4	1	3
14	Aff,Int	3	0	3
15	Ord, Ach	5	2	3
16	Chg,Ach	6	3	3
17	Aba,Int	2	−1	3
18	Het,Def	5	2	3
19	Int,Chg	3	1	2
20	Het,End	5	3	2
21	Chg,Aba	5	3	2
22	Het,Chg	4	2	2
23	Het,Int	−1	−3	2
24	Exh,Ach	3	1	2
25	Ord,Ach	5	4	1
26	Aba,Het	1	0	1
27	Chg,Int	0	0	0
28	Chg,Aut	3	3	0
29	Int,Aut	0	1	−1
30	Aff,End	1	2	−1
31	Ach,Nur	0	1	−1
32	Het,Chg	0	2	−2
33	Exh,Ach	7	9	−2
34	Ach,Aba	−2	0	−2
35	Suc,Ach	−2	1	−3
36	Aba,Suc	1	5	−4
37	Dom,Ord	4	8	−4
38	Het,Dom	−3	4	−7
39	End,Nur	0	7	−7
40	Int,Aff	−2	6	−8

represented by the difference score is positive, the hypothesis is supported for that subject. This analysis allows for random effects operating to move a need upward and still permits a test of the relative effects of the degree of consensus. For example, as indicated in the first row on Table 1, deference was chosen as the low consensus need for subject 1 and autonomy as the high consensus need. From the initial self-ranking to the post-manipulation self-ranking he moved deference 8 rank steps downward and autonomy 2 rank steps upward. This yields a net change of 10 steps in the direction of the hypothesis. As may be seen by inspection of the difference column, 26 individuals produced a net difference in the direction of the hypothesis, 2 showed no change, and 12 changed in an opposite direction. Table 2 offers a more precise comparison taking into account the magnitude of the change. The low consensus need moved an average of 3.43 rank steps, and the high consensus need only 1.75 rank steps. The magnitude of the differences between the two needs is significant at the 0.008 level as tested by the Wilcoxon signed-ranks test[8] (T=229.0, N=40, z=2.43). Thus it appears that the reaction to information incongruent with self-definition is a function of the perceived consensus of opinion among significant others.

TABLE 2

Net Mean Movement of Manipulated Trait

LOW CONSENSUS	*HIGH CONSENSUS*	*DIFFERENCE*	*P*
3.43	1.75	1.68	<.008*

*Wilcoxon signed-ranks test: T = 229.0; N = 40; z = 2.43, one-tailed.

As a final check on whether the movement of the manipulated traits was in fact due to the false personality appraisal, for each individual two nonmanipulated traits, differing in consensus by the same amount as the previously chosen manipulated traits, were selected for analysis. These traits were compared to determine whether the low consensus trait moved to a greater extent than the high. The mean difference between them was only 0.21, and the differences were not significant (T=342.5, N=37, Z=135, P=.44).

DISCUSSION

The relatively greater movement in the manipulated direction of the low consensus trait supports the theoretical position that the degree of resistance to the acceptance of an incongruent self-definition is a function of the number of interpersonal matrices supporting that self-definition. In this instance, the element of each matrix supporting or weakening resistance was represented by the perceived attitude of a different significant other person toward a given aspect of an individual's self-concept. The possibility that the differing resistance of the high and low consensus needs resulted from a difference in salience (importance of the trait to S, as indicated by its self-rank position) was ruled out by equating on salience the two kinds of needs manipulated. Social desirability was presumed to be similarly controlled by the same matching process.

Encountering information contrary to self-definitions will result in a threat to congruency that must be resolved in some manner. In many instances, congruency is retained without a change in self or behavior. This is much more likely to occur when perceived consensus is high than when it is low. As described in more detail elsewhere,[9] in his attempts to restore congruency an individual may employ one or more of the following modes of resolution. He may reduce his interaction with those whose definition of his behavior threaten congruence and increase interaction with others whose definitions he perceives as congruent. A second mode involves evaluating selected other persons positively or negatively depending upon whether they are behaving congruently with certain aspects of self: he increases his liking for those who behave in a congruent fashion and decreases his liking for those behaving incongruently. A third means of resolution is the misperception of the other person's behavior in a manner allowing congruency to be achieved. Finally, he may employ techniques permitting him to elicit congruent responses from the other person that confirm aspects of self.

For the most part, the experimental situation was designed so as to minimize the occurrence of these various forms of resolving incongruency while maintaining self unchanged. Some of these modes require situations outside the laboratory where the individual has freedom of interaction. Nevertheless, the minority of subjects who failed to change appreciably either manipulated trait may have questioned the validity of the assessment devices, the intentions, or the competence of the experimenters in order to support nonchange.

NOTES

1 William James, Principles of Psychology, New York: Holt, 1890. 2 volumes.

2 Charles H. Cooley, Human Nature and the Social Order, New York: Charles Scribners Sons, 1902.

3 George H. Mead, Mind, Self and Society from the Standpoint of a Social Behaviorist, Chicago: University of Chicago Press, 1934.

4 Ruth C. Wylie, The Self Concept, Lincoln, Nebraska: University of Nebraska Press, 1961.

5 Charles E. Osgood and Percy H. Tannenbaum, "The principle of congruity in the prediction of attitude change," Psychological Review 62 (January, 1955): 42–55; Dorwin Cartwright and Frank Harary, "Structural balance: a generalization of Heider's theory," Psychological Review 63 (September, 1956): 277–93; Leon Festinger, A Theory of Cognitive Dissonance. Evanston, Ill.: Row, Peterson, 1957; Milton J. Rosenberg and Robert P. Abelson, "An analysis of cognitive balancing," Carl I. Hovland and Milton J. Rosenberg, (eds.). Attitude Organization and Change, New Haven: Yale University Press, 1960, pp. 112–63; Fritz Heider, The Psychology of Interpersonal Relations, New York: Wiley, 1958.

6 Allen Edwards, Edwards Personal Preference Schedule, New York: Psychological Corporation, 1954.

7 Leonard V. Gordon, Gordon Personal Profile, New York: World Book Company, 1953.

8 James V. Bradley, Distribution-free Statistical Tests. Washington, D.C.: United States Department of Commerce, Office of Technical Services, August 1960.

9 Paul F. Secord and Carl W. Backman, "Personality theory and the problem of stability and change in individual behavior: an interpersonal approach," Psychological Review 68 (January 1961): 21–32.

Social Comparison, Self-Consistency, and the Concept of Self

Stanley J. Morse
Kenneth J. Gergen

14

One assumption which underlies much work on the self-concept is that the individual's picture of himself crystallizes in early childhood and remains relatively stable thereafter. According to the symbolic interactionist position (cf. Cooley, 1902; Mead, 1934), the child learns to see himself as "significant others" in his environment see him, and over time these views become incorporated into a stable view of self. This assumption of stability in self-concept is also supported by clinical observation. Rogers (1961) and Kelly (1955), for example, felt that massive therapeutic efforts are required to produce even slight shifts in how the individual views himself. Armed with such evidence, students of individual differences have felt relatively safe in using variations in self-esteem to predict behavior in a wide range of situations.

In contrast to this view, there is good reason to believe that the categories the individual applies to himself are in a constant state of flux. First, as the person goes through life, the significant others in his environment may change. Indeed, several studies (cf. Gergen, 1965; Videbeck, 1960) have demonstrated that a person's concept of self at any given moment is dependent on the views others have of him in the situation. It would also seem that self-conception is vitally affected by social comparison. As Festinger (1954) has pointed out, people have a constant need to

Source: Stanley J. Morse and Kenneth J. Gergen. "Social Comparison, Self-Consistency, and the Concept of Self," Journal of Personality and Social Psychology 16 (1970): 148–56.

evaluate their abilities and test the validity of their opinions. Since there are few uniform yardsticks to aid in such evaluation, the person will compare himself with others in order to reach conclusions about himself.

While social comparison theory has generated a considerable amount of research (cf. Latané, 1966), most of it has dealt with the effects of comparison in the evaluation of particular skills and opinions. It also seems clear that people are often concerned with their personal attractiveness and general value as human beings. They may frequently compare themselves with others in their immediate environment (and in the mass media) to judge their own personal worth. Thus, for example, to find oneself disheveled when those around are tastefully dressed may be humiliating. Or, for the typical student to discover that he has obtained the highest score in his class may boost his self-esteem. Rosenberg (1965) reports that high school students from minority ethnic groups have lower self-esteem when living in ethnically mixed neighborhoods than when living in homogeneous ones. Likewise Clark and Clark (1939) found that black children attending integrated, northern schools show more self-hatred than those in segregated southern classrooms. In both cases, respondents in the ethnically and racially mixed environments may have had more opportunity to compare themselves with their more affluent and better established neighbors.

Half the subjects in the present study casually encountered an individual whose personal characteristics could be described as socially desirable, while the remaining subjects encountered another whose characteristics were quite the opposite. Based on social comparison theory, it was predicted that the former group would suffer a decrement in generalized self-esteem, while the latter group would experience an increment.

In addition to the personal characteristics of the target, other factors may enhance or mitigate the impact of the comparison process on self-conception. Earlier research has dealt with such factors as the similarity between the person and the target of comparison, the amount of threat in the comparison situation, and subjects' motivation (cf. Latané, 1966). In the present study, attention was directed toward two variables heretofore unexamined. The first resides in the nature of the comparison situation and the second in the personality of the individual.

An individual encounters a large number of others during an average day, and yet it is safe to say that not all of these serve as targets for comparison. One major factor influencing the impact which any one target might have may be called the *utility of comparison*. As Jones and Gerard (1967) have reasoned, the individual engages in social comparison primarily because it is useful for him to do so. The information obtained in some comparison situations is more valuable to a person in assessing his position and planning his behavior than that obtained in other situations. In short, situations vary in the utility of the comparison opportunities they present. A junior executive may be little concerned when he sees a person on a street corner who has all the earmarks of success, but should the same person attend the office party, he may pay close attention to him and suffer accordingly.

Half the subjects in this study encountered an individual (with either positive or negative characteristics) in a situation where comparison had high utility—one in which they were competing with the other for the same employment opening. The remaining subjects were exposed to the same person in a noncompetitive, low-utility setting. Greater self-esteem change was predicted in the former case than in the latter.

In addition to the characteristics of the target of comparison and the utility of comparison, the personality of the individual may also affect the extent to which his self-esteem is altered in such situations. Personality theorists have long recognized that an important determinant of an individual's behavior and psychological adjustment is the extent to which he sees the various components of his self-concept as forming a coherent whole, as being consistent with one another (cf. Erikson, 1946; Lecky, 1945; Rogers, 1961). Gergen and Morse (1967) constructed a scale to assess individual differences along this dimension. They found, for example, that those who showed a high level of perceived inconsistency on this test perceived more disagreement in others' evaluations of them, had more frequently changed their residence, and showed greater maladjustment on subscales of the California Psychological Inventory. The inconsistency scale also predicted extent of dissonance reduction in a replication of the Aronson and Carlsmith (1962) study of performance expectancy. Consistent subjects showed significantly more dissonance reduction (Winer, 1966). This latter finding suggested that persons whose conceptions of self are highly consistent should be *least* susceptible to the effects of social comparison. They should experience greater difficulty in incorporating new and potentially inconsistent information about themselves into their relatively well-ordered and coherent systems of self-conception.

The discussion thus far can be summarized with three hypotheses:

1. The presence of a person perceived to have highly desirable characteristics produces a decrease in self-esteem. If the other's characteristics are undesirable, self-esteem increases.

2. Both the increment in self-esteem in the former case and the decrement in the latter are greater when the utility of comparison is high rather than low.

3. Both the increment in self-esteem in the former case and the decrement in the latter are greater when the person has an inconsistent self-concept than when he has a consistent one.

Attention was also paid in this study to the degree of difference between the subject's characteristics and those of the target. Festinger (1954) suggested that greater comparison occurs the more similar the two individuals. On the other hand, the greater the difference between the two, the sharper the contrast and the more one's positive (or negative) characteristics are thrown into relief. From this viewpoint, greater self-esteem change seem likely when the subject and target were dissimilar.

METHOD

The 78 subjects used in this study were male undergraduates at the University of Michigan, assigned randomly to the different experimental conditions. None had actually volunteered to be subjects in an experiment, but had answered an advertisement placed in the campus newspaper and at the student employment office offering two part-time jobs in "personality research." The job paid $3 an hour. When an applicant arrived for his job interview at the University's Institute for Social Research, he was met by a secretary. She seated him at one side of a long table and gave him the job application and a set of self-rating forms to complete. A letter from the project director explained that these forms contained various questionnaires being developed as part of a study of "new ways of selecting people for jobs" and that responses to them would in no way be used to screen current job applicants. These initial forms included the Gergen and Morse (1967) self-consistency scale and half the items from a slightly revised version of the Coopersmith (1959) self-esteem inventory.

Stimulus Persons—Mr. Clean and Mr. Dirty

The secretary could observe the subject through the glass wall of the room in which he was seated. When she saw that he had completed the questionnaires, she entered the office to collect them. She also brought with her "another job applicant" whom she seated opposite the subject, mentioning that she would return shortly with additional forms for the subject to complete.

Half of the subjects found themselves confronted with a person whose personal appearance was highly desirable. He wore a dark suit and appeared well-groomed and self-confident. After he had been seated, he immediately opened an attache case, pulled out several sharpened pencils, and began to work on his forms diligently. The subject could see that he also had a statistics book, a slide rule, and a copy of a college philosophy text in his case. For descriptive purposes, this stimulus person will be called *Mr. Clean.*

The other half of the subjects were exposed to *Mr. Dirty*, an individual whose appearance was in sharp contrast to Mr. Clean's. He wore a smelly sweatshirt, ripped trousers, no socks, and seemed somewhat dazed by the whole procedure. He placed his worn paperback edition of *The Carpetbaggers* on the table in front of him, and after staring aimlessly around the office for a few seconds, began searching for a pencil, which he finally found on the table. Once he began filling out the application, he would periodically stop, scratch his head, and glance around the office as if looking for guidance. There was absolutely no verbal interaction between the subject and the stimulus person.

Utility of Comparison

The experiment had been designed to create a high-incentive situation for all subjects . It was conducted during the summer when job applicants were much more plentiful than the supply of jobs. The work was relatively attractive, and the pay offered exceeded the going campus rate. It seemed reasonable, then, that if the subject were to encounter another applicant for the same job, face-to-face, he would be inclined to evaluate his prospects by comparing himself with this competitor. Were the other not applying for the same position, the utility of comparison for the subject would be far less. Thus, when the subject appeared for his interview, the secretary off-handedly asked him whether he was applying for the job in personality research or computer programming. This impressed upon the subject that two different types of jobs were open at the same time. All subjects, of course, replied that they were applying for the position in personality research, the only job for which they had requisite skills. To clarify this distinction between jobs, the personality application had a blue cover containing a sociometric diagram and the computer programming application had a yellow cover with a flow chart on it. Both of these covers were conspicuously taped to the wall next to the table at which the subject sat. When the stimulus person entered with the secretary, half of the subjects in each of the above conditions could clearly see from his application that he was applying for the same position as they (high-utility condition). The remaining subjects could immediately notice that he was applying for an entirely different job (low-utility condition). Subjects could also easily observe that his questionnaire resembled theirs in the first situation, or contained mathematical problems which did not appear on their forms at all in the second.

After 1½ minutes, during which the subject had nothing to do but observe the stimulus person, the secretary returned with the remaining forms. These contained, among other things, the second half of the Coopersmith self-esteem measure. When the subject completed these questionnaires, he left the room, as instructed and handed them to the secretary. She gave him a final questionnaire to complete, on which appeared a series of rating scales and questions concerning the procedure he had just completed. Among the rating scales were a series of items in semantic differential format which reflected various personal attributes (e.g., confident-anxious, neat-sloppy). The secretary casually asked the subject to use the scales to rate anyone who was present during the assessment procedure. The subject was paid $1.50 for helping with the job selection and was told that he would be notified shortly by mail whether or not he had been chosen for the job. At the completion of the study, two applicants were actually hired—to help analyze the data for the study.

Consistency and Esteem Measures

The Gergen-Morse self-consistency scale was administered prior to the completion of the pretest self-esteem measure. The scale presents the respondent with a list of 17 positive and 17 negative traits and asks him to select those 5 traits from each list which "best describe" him. He next lists these 10 traits down the side and across the bottom of a 10 x 10 matrix, so that all traits intersect one another. Finally, he rates the degree of "conflict or incompatibility" he perceives between each pair on a 0-5 scale, with 0 indicating that the two traits "don't contradict each other, but tend to go hand in hand or cohere," and a 5 indicating the opposite. The sum of these matrix entries yields a total perceived self-inconsistency score; the higher the score, the greater the level of perceived self-inconsistency. Reliability and validity data for this scale appear in an earlier report (Gergen & Morse, 1967). A median split across all conditions was used to divide the subjects into low- and high-consistency groups.

The Coopersmith inventory has commonly been used to assess what is assumed to be one's basic level of self-esteem. The modified version employed here contained 58 items covering a wide variety of characteristics. Items appear in the form of self-descriptive sentences, such as, "I can make up my mind without too much trouble" and "I'm proud of my work at college so far." Half were administered before the arrival of the stimulus person and half after. On one of these sets of 29 randomly selected items, the respondent checked his agreement or disagreement with each statement of a 6-point Likert scale, ranging from "strongly agree" to "strongly disagree." On the other, he checked one of six boxes going from "almost always true" to "almost never true." The order in which the two sets were used was reversed for half of the subjects in each condition.

In summary, the study has a 2 x 2 x 2 factorial design, with two different types of stimulus persons (Mr. Clean and Mr. Dirty), high and low utility of comparison, and high and low subject self-consistency. Approximately 10 subjects appeared within each of the 8 conditions.

RESULTS

Validation Measures

As will be recalled, the subjects were asked to rate the person who had been present during the testing procedure on a series of semantic differential scales. These ratings showed that Mr. Clean was seen as significantly more handsome, more intellectual, more qualified for the job, stronger, less irresponsible, and less "sloppy" in appearance than Mr. Dirty ($p < .001$, in all cases). In addition, subjects did not see themselves as being more similar to one of the stimulus persons than to the other, as indicated by their ratings of the stimulus person on the "like me—unlike me" dimension. Given the extreme differences in perceived desirability of the stimulus persons, and the fact that each stimulus person was seen by the subjects to differ from them in roughly equal amounts, it is reasonable to conclude that subjects perceived Mr. Clean to be superior to them in certain respects and Mr. Dirty as inferior in these respects.

The utility of comparison manipulation was much less successful. All subjects correctly reported whether the stimulus person had been applying for the same job as they or a different one. However, the variation of his personal appearance was apparently so powerful that it overshadowed the impact of this piece of information. None of the semantic differential ratings reflected significant differences between the competitive (high utility) and noncompetitive (low utility) stimulus persons. In fact, on the dimension "competitor-noncompetitor," the only significant difference was produced by variations in the character of the stimulus person. Mr. Clean was seen as significantly more of a competitor than Mr. Dirty ($p < .05$).

High- and low-consistency subjects were not found to differ in their ratings of the stimulus person or to the situation. Thus, differences in self-esteem change found for these two groups cannot be attributed to obvious variations in how they interpreted their environment and others within it.

Experimental Results

The primary interest of the study was in the effects of the varying conditions on subjects' self-esteem ratings. Mean self-esteem change for each condition is featured in Table 1, and the summary of a four-way analysis of variance comparing prescores versus postscores in self-esteem, in Table 2. As can be seen, the variation in the characteristics of the stimulus person had a pronounced effect on self-esteem ratings. For subjects exposed to Mr. Clean, self-esteem ratings were diminished across varying conditions of utility and consistency. Mr. Dirty produced exactly the opposite effect. Mean change in self-esteem was positive in each of the relevant cells. The analysis of variance[1] in Table 2 indicated that the difference in prepost change between the Mr. Clean and Mr. Dirty conditions was significant beyond the 0.03 level. Within-conditions comparisons showed that the decrease in self-esteem ratings for subjects encountering Mr. Clean was significant beyond the 0.05 level, while the increase for those facing Mr. Dirty reached the 0.07 level. These findings provide sound support for the first of the three hypotheses.

TABLE 1

Mean Change in Self-Esteem

Ss	MEAN SELF-ESTEEM CHANGE	
	MR. CLEAN	*MR. DIRTY*
Inconsistent		
High utility	−3.88	2.44
n	8	9
Low utility	−8.20	9.90
n	10	10
Consistent		
High utility	−3.80	2.22
n	10	9
Low utility	−1.89	1.40
n	9	13

TABLE 2

Four-Way Analysis of Variance

SOURCE OF VARIATION	*df*	*MS*	*F*
Between *Ss*	71		
Consistent vs. inconsistent (B)	1	877.77	
High vs. low comparison utility (C)	1	306.24	
Mr. Clean vs. Mr. Dirty (D)	1	34.02	
B × C	1	300.46	
C × D	1	26.71	
B × D	1	64.01	
B × C × D	1	160.43	
Error (b)	63	293.82	
Within *Ss*	72		
Pre vs. post self-esteem (A)	1	2.24	
A × B	1	4.01	
A × C	1	14.71	
A × D	1	616.56	5.02†
A × B × C	1	14.67	
A × B × D	1	365.09	2.98*
A × C × D	1	111.09	
A × B × C × D	1	53.80	
Error (w)	63	122.82	

* $p < .10$.
† $p < .03$.

It is also clear from the results that self-esteem change is not uniform across levels of comparison utility and subject self-consistency. In the former case, low utility of comparison appears to contribute heavily to self-esteem change for inconsistent subjects. However, this tendency was reversed for consistent subjects, and neither the main effect for utility of comparison nor its interaction with self-consistency was significant ($F < 1$). Considering that the manipulation of utility of comparison does not seem to have been effective, it is not surprising that this variable failed to account for a significant amount of variance. More is said about this issue in the Discussion section.

However, we cannot rule out the effects of the third variable, self-consistency, in such summary fashion. Self-esteem change for high- versus low-consistency subjects in the Mr. Clean and Mr. Dirty conditions is shown in Figure 1. As can be seen, when exposed to Mr. Clean, high-consistency subjects were less likely than low-consistency subjects to experience a decrement in self-esteem; in the Mr. Dirty condition, they were also less likely to experience an increment. Although the relevant F ratio did not reach customery standards of statistical significance ($F = 2.98$), the results were in the predicted direction, and the variable did account for a moderate amount of the variance.

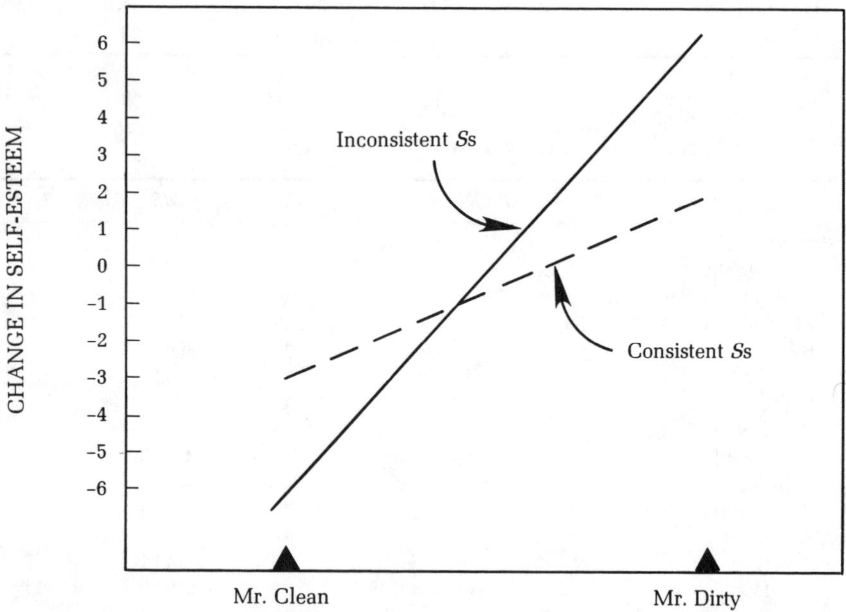

Fig. 1 **Changes in self-esteem as a function of characteristics of the other and level of self-consistency.**

Internal analyses of the data support these observations. Inconsistent subjects underwent a significant ($p < .05$) decrease when confronting Mr. Clean and a significant ($p < .05$) increase when exposed to Mr. Dirty. In neither situation did consistent subjects show a significant change in self-esteem. The results thus lend reasonable support to the hypothesized relationship between self-consistency and self-esteem change. Inconsistent subjects were significantly affected by the character of the stimulus person, while consistent subjects were not. Lacking was a significant difference between the two groups.

Similarity of Subject and Stimulus Person

It will be recalled that an additional interest of the study was in the relationship between the similarity of subject and stimulus person and the extent of self-esteem change. Two measures of similarity were employed. First, the post-experimental questionnaire contained a 7-point rating scale, on which subjects rated the degree of difference they perceived between themselves and the stimulus person. This single rating, however, yielded very low variability in ratings. A more differentiating measure of subject-stimulus person similarity was provided by ratings made of each subject by the secretary. This unbiased and unsophisticated observer independently rated each subject's posture, dress, grooming, manners, overall appearance, speech, and general attitude on a series of a 10-point scale ranging from "very much like Mr. Clean" to "very much like Mr. Dirty." These ratings could then be summed and a mean subject-appearance score derived. Scores did not differ significantly by experimental condition, by level of consistency, or by initial level of self-esteem.[2] Subjects could be divided at the midpoint on this scale into two groups, one evaluated as being more like Mr. Clean, the other more like Mr. Dirty. Approximately half of the subjects in each of these groups had encountered the former stimulus person and half of the latter.

Mean self-esteem change for subjects in each similarity group, encountering each stimulus person, appears in Table 3. As can be seen, Mr. Clean elicited the greatest negative change in self-esteem among subjects rated most like Mr. Dirty. Subjects rated as similar to Mr. Clean actually underwent a slight increase in self-esteem. These findings are generally consistent with the notion that a larger self-other discrepancy provides a sharper contrast and thus has greater impact on self-esteem. In the case of Mr. Dirty, however, this reasoning proved unsatisfactory. The results were in the opposite direction. Those subjects rated most like Mr. Dirty experienced an increase in self-esteem, while those dissimilar to him demonstrated a slight decrement. A two-way analysis of variance comparing self-esteem change in the four groups yielded an interaction significant beyond the 0.001 level ($F=6.32$).

TABLE 3

Mean Self-Esteem Change as a Function of Rated Similarity to Stimulus Person

S's CHARACTERISTICS	*STIMULUS PERSON*	
	MR. CLEAN	*MR. DIRTY*
Resembles Mr. Clean		
$\bar{X}$	3.78	−1.39
n	20	17
Resembles Mr. Dirty		
$\bar{X}$	−10.69	5.13
n	19	22

Rather than speculate about separate processes that might be at stake in affecting reactions to Mr. Clean as opposed to Mr. Dirty, it seems more parsimonious to examine possible similarities between the two cases. Specifically, in both situations those subjects rated most like the stimulus person in question underwent an increase in self-esteem; those who were unlike him experienced a decrease. Viewed in this light, the finding is an intriguing one. It suggests that the mere presence of another person who is like oneself may be sufficient to boost one's self-esteem, while a person who is dissimilar may tend to reduce one's self-estimate. When another is seem to be similar to self, he places a stamp of legitimacy on one's conduct or appearance. Interpersonal support of this sort may be particularly important in circumstances, such as those involved here, in which public appraisal is highly salient. Encountering an individual whose characteristics differ from one's own may initiate a process of self-questioning and doubt. We return to this issue shortly.

DISCUSSION

This study indicates that casual exposure to another person is sufficient to produce a marked impact on a person's momentary concept of self. The presence of someone with highly desirable characteristics appears to produce a generalized decrease in level of self-esteem. Exposure to a socially undesirable person produces the opposite effect. These findings are not only consistent with the proposition that a person may use others to gauge his own self-worth, but extend the range of phenomena to which social comparison theory has been applied. As a result of others' characteristics appearing more desirable or less desirable than his own, a person's generalized self-estimate is displaced downward or upward.

The results raise further questions concerning the long-standing assumption of stability in self-conception. They suggest that rather than possessing a crystallized and enduring identity, a person is subject to momentary fluctuations in self-definition. This view is futher supported in studies showing that changes in an individual's presentation of self are often accompanied by subtle shifts in his underlying feelings of who he is within the situation (cf. Gergen, 1965; Gergen & Wishnov, 1965). And yet, it seems unreasonable to abandon completely the assumption of self-concept stability in favor of a view of man as chameleon. An individual probably receives fairly consistent evaluations from others about certain aspects of himself (e.g., sex role), and heterogeneous evaluations concerning others (e.g., his appealingness to others). When such learning experiences are consistent and continuous, a certain degree of stability in self-conception may result. With variability in what is learned about self comes flexibility in feelings of identity from moment to moment. This study demonstrates the ease with which momentary shifts in certain self-conceptions may be brought about for persons at a particular stage in life.

There is much less to be said about the results concerning utility of comparison. Although subjects did discern whether the stimulus person was or was not competing with them for the same job, there is no indication that they felt comparison would be more useful in the competitive as opposed to the noncompetitive situation. One possibility is that their framework for judging competition and, thus, comparison utility, included more than the immediate situation. Subjects may have felt that the noncompetitive stimulus person *could* also apply for the position in personality research, a possibility not specifically ruled out by the procedure. And they may have seen him as a potential competitor for academic marks and other rewards within the university. Finally, as suggested, the personal characteristics of the stimulus person may have been sufficiently demanding that the more subtle effects of utility were obscured. In any case, given the potential importance of this variable, future research might well attempt to test its effects more directly.

The findings concerning self-consistency were not powerful, but they are compatible with the results of previous work in the area and lend further construct validity to the measure. Persons characterized as inconsistent, by virtue of their scale scores, underwent a significant decrease in self-esteem when faced with Mr. Clean, while self-esteem increased significantly in the presence of Mr. Dirty. Consistent subjects were not affected significantly in either condition. It seems quite likely that inconsistent persons, having been subjected to a less homogeneous set of learning experiences related to self (Gergen & Morse, 1967), are more susceptible to situational shifts in feelings of identity. Future work might fruitfully concentrate on fluctuations in, and adaptability of, overt behavior. If the person whose psychological life is dominated by inconsistency is more flexible with respect to self-definition, he might also be more prone to change in outward behavior from one situation to the next.

But nowhere is the need for future research more apparent than in the case of the relationship between interpersonal similarity and self-esteem change. Subjects were subdivided into two groups on the basis of rated similarity between themselves and the two stimulus persons. When subjects were rated as having socially desirable characteristics, their self-esteem was boosted when in the presence of another who shared these characteristics, and was diminished in the presence of one who did not. On the other hand, if the subjects were judged to have undesirable characteristics, they experienced an enhanced state of self-esteem when the undesirable other was present, and a reduced state if not.

One major implication stemming from these findings is that self-esteem may be a unique member of the family of self-assessments to which the comparison process is relevant. In the case of opinions and abilities, comparison effects may be enhanced the more similar the person to the target of comparison. However, in the case of self-esteem, there may be effects over and above those produced by comparison. Superimposed on the comparison effect may be an esteem increment produced by increasing the similarity between the person and the target of comparison.

The findings also have important implications for social attraction. A large number of studies demonstrate a positive relationship between interpersonal similarity and attraction (see Secord & Backman's 1964 review). And it has also been found that people prefer to interact with those whom they perceive to be similar to themselves in attitudes (Newcomb, 1961) and personality (Freedman & Doob, 1968). While balance theory has often been used to explain such findings, the present research suggests an alternative way in which they may be viewed. As indicated, one major reason for an increase in self-esteem in the presence of someone who is similar is that he validates or lends social support to one's manner of being. This increment in self-esteem may be a major intervening mechanism prompting social attraction. Because another is similar. he increases one's esteem for self, and inasmuch as enhanced self-esteem is positively valued, the other may become a target of attraction.

NOTES

1 In order to assess the significance of change within single conditions, pre-post analysis was necessitated. However, because this analysis calls for equal cell frequencies, and the sample sizes for the various cells differed slightly (range 9–13), it was necessary to equalize cell frequencies. A preliminary analysis of prescores across the conditions indicated significant discrepancies between conditions. Thus, in equalizing cell frequencies, subjects were deleted whose prescores most contributed to these discrepancies—regardless of the direction of subsequent change in self-esteem. Mean change by condition remained relatively unaffected by this procedure, and prescore differences were reduced to nonsignificance.

2 Correlations were carried out within the Mr. Clean and Mr. Dirty conditions between this measure and subjects' single rating of similarity to the stimulus person. Tendencies were found within both conditions for subjects who rated themselves as similar to the stimulus person to have been rated similarly by the observer. However, due to the constructed range of responses in subjects' perceptions, these tendencies were not significant.

REFERENCES

Aronson, E. and J. M. Carlsmith
1962 "Performance expectancy as a determinant of actual performance." Journal of Abnormal and Social Psychology 65: 178–83.
Clark, K. B. and M. P. Clark
1939 "The development of consciousness of self and the emergence of racial identification in Negro preschool children." Journal of Social Psychology 10: 591–99.
Cooley, C. H.
1902 Human Nature and the Social Order. New York: Scribner's.
Coopersmith, S.
1959 "A method for determining self-esteem." Journal of Abnormal and Social Psychology 59: 87–94.
Erikson, E. H.
1946 "Ego development and historical change." The Psychoanalytic Study of the Child. New York: International University Press.
Festinger, L.
1954 "A theory of social comparison processes." Human Relations 7: 117–40.
Freedman, J. L. and A. N. Doob
1968 Deviancy: The Psychology of Being Different. New York: Academic Press.
Gergen, K. J.
1965 "Interaction goals and personalistic feedback as factors affecting the presentation of self." Journal of Personality and Social Psychology 1: 413–24.
Gergen, K. J. and S. J. Morse
1967 "Self-consistency: measurement and validation." Proceedings of the 75th Annual Convention of the American Psychological Association 2: 207–08 (Summary).

Gergen, K. J. and B. Wishnov
1965 "Others' self-evaluations and interaction anticipation as determinants of self-presentation." Journal of Personality and Social Psychology 2: 348–58.
Jones, E. E. and H. B. Gerard
1967 Foundations of Social Psychology. New York: Wiley.
Kelly, G. A.
1955 The Psychology of Personal Constructs. New York: Norton.
Latané, B.
1966 "Studies in social comparison." Journal of Experimental Social Psychology, Supplement 1.
Lecky, P.
1945 Self-Consistency. New York: Island Press.
Mead, G. H.
1934 Mind, Self and Society. Chicago: University of Chicago Press.
Newcomb, T. M.
1961 The Acquaintance Process. New York: Holt, Rinehart & Winston.
Rogers, C. R.
1961 On Becoming a Person. Boston: Houghton Mifflin.
Rosenberg, M.
1965 Society and the Adolescent Self-Image. Princeton, N.J.: Princeton University Press.
Secord, P. F. and C. W. Backman
1964 "Interpersonal congruency, perceived similarity, and friendship." Sociometry 27: 115–27.
Videbeck, R.
1960 "Self-conception and the reaction of others." Sociometry 23: 351–59.
Winer, C. H.
1966 "Self-perceived consistency and the reduction of dissonance." Unpublished honor's thesis, Harvard University.

Identity Salience and Role Performance: The Relevance of Symbolic Interaction Theory for Family Research

Sheldon Stryker

15

This paper explicates a general research problem and a set of hypotheses to deal with that research problem. Its starting point is a paragraph from the writer's chapter on symbolic interaction as theory and as theoretical framework in the *Handbook of Marriage and the Family*.[1] Set in the context of a discussion of the possibilities for exploiting the symbolic interaction framework in family-related research, that paragraph raised a set of questions around the concept of identity:

The question of self-conception or identity in relation to the family remains virtually virgin in many respects. What accounts for the differentials which obviously exist in the salience of family identities? What are the consequences of . . . differentials in degree of commitment to a family identity for parent-child relations, for husband-wife relations, for the family

Source: Sheldon Stryker. "Identity Salience and Role Performance: The Relevance of Symbolic Interaction Theory for Family Research," from Sheldon Stryker, "Relevance of symbolic interaction theory for family research," Journal of Marriage and the Family 30 (1968): 558–64. Copyrighted 1968 by the National Council on Family Relations. Reprinted by permission.

as a functioning unit? . . . What determines whether or not a family-related identity is invoked in a given situation?[2]

These questions can be supplemented by others which are closely related. What accounts for the varying degrees of ease or difficulty with which persons adopt novel familial identities? Why is it that some experience little difficulty in modifying the salience of a family identity they hold, while for some such modification occurs—if at all—only with considerable stress?

To answer questions of the sort posed requires that one have a theory. The latter implies the specification of the premises and assumptions entering into the theory; the development of the conceptual apparatus in terms of which the theory is stated; and the articulation of a set of hypotheses, deriving from the premises and assumptions, stating expected relationships among the phenomena pointed to by the concepts. It is to these tasks that the writer now turns.

UNDERLYING PREMISES

1. The ultimate objective of students of the sociology of the family is the explanation of variability in family *behavior*. From the standpoint of a sociological theory of the family, this premise asserts, investigations of familial role expectations as dependent variable, or studies which relate familial role expectations as independent variable to the structure of the self as dependent variable, are incomplete. While such concerns are certainly legitimate from the standpoint of numerous theoretical concerns, and while research on such problems as the impact of family on self is patently important, sociological students of the family must require their theories to specify the consequences of familial role expectations or of self for familial role performance.

These assertions should not be misread. It is not necessary, to make them, to assume that any discrete set of variables can account for all the variability in family behavior. Nor is it necessary, having recognized that any discrete set of variables will always leave a residue of unexplained variance, for the sociological student of the family to invoke theoretically extraneous variables—genetic, biological, psychological, economic, etc.—in a search for "complete" explanations of family behavior.

2. The generalized symbolic interactionist model (to use a word that may not be technically appropriate) has it that:

a. Behavior is premised on a "named" or classified world, and "names" or class terms carry meaning consisting of shared behavioral expectations emergent from the process of social interaction.[3] One learns, in interaction with others, both how to classify objects with which he comes into contact and how he is expected to behave towards these objects. The meaning of the classifications one constructs resides in the shared expectations for behavior the classifications invoke;

b. Among these class terms are symbols used to designate the stable, morphological components of social structure usually termed "positions," and it is these positions which carry the shared behavioral expectations conventionally labeled "roles".

c. Actors within this social structure name one another, in the sense that they recognize each other as occupants of positions, and in naming one another invoke expectations with respect to one another's behavior;

d. Actors within this social structure name themselves as well—it is to these reflexively applied positional designations that the concept of self is typically intended to refer—and in so doing they create internalized expectations with respect to their own behavior;

e. Social behavior is not, however, given by these expectations (either reflected or internalized). That behavior is the product of a role-making process,[4] initiated by expectations but developing through a subtle, tentative, probing interchange among actors in given situations that continually reshapes both the form and the content of the interaction.

3. Empirical work which has sought to make use of the model generalized above has suffered from a failure to go beyond Mead's formulation of the self as "that which is an object to itself." It is essential to treat the self as a complex, differentiated unit rather than as an undifferentiated unity.[5]

4. Empirical work has also suffered from the failure to take sufficiently seriously the idea that the self is an organized structure.

NECESSARY REFINEMENTS IN CONCEPTUAL FRAMEWORK

It has been asserted that the self must be seen as complex and differentiated if one is to advance the understanding of familial role performance, i.e., that the self must be conceptualized as constructed from diverse "parts." The parts which can be taken to comprise the self are discrete identities. One can speak meaningfully of familial identities (e.g., father, husband, in-law), political identities (e.g., senator, candidate, ward captain), occupational identities (e.g., doctor, salesman, employee), and so on, all of which are incorporated into the self as that which is an object to itself.

The meaning, and in degree the implications, of the concept of identity are well stated by Gregory Stone, whose writing presages in part the argument of this paper:

> *When one has an identity, he is situated—that is, cast in the shape of a social object by the acknowledgment of his participation or membership in social relations. One's identity is established when others place him as a social object by assigning him the same words of identity that he appropriates for himself or announces. . . .*
>
> *Such a conception of identity is, indeed, close to Mead's conception of the 'me,' the self as object related to and differentiated from others. . . . Identity is intrinsically associated with all the joinings and departures of social life. To have an identity is to join with some and depart from others, to enter and leave social relations at once.*[6]

Identities, in this usage, exist insofar as persons are participants in structured social relationships. They require that positional designations be attributed to and accepted by participants in the relationships.

It has also been asserted that the self must be viewed as an organized structure.

The self may be said to be organized in at least two relevant senses. One may postulate that the discrete identities which comprise the self exist in a hierarchy of salience, such that other things equal one can expect behavioral products to the degree that a given identity ranks high in this hierarchy. The concept of identity salience may be defined as the probability, for a given person, of a given identity being invoked in a variety of situations. Alternatively, this concept may be defined as the differential probability among persons of a given identity being invoked in a given situation. With either formulation, a rank order of probabilities defines the hierarchy of salience.

A caveat must be added at this point. The invocation of an identity—i.e., the perception of an identity as relevant to a particular interaction—may be purely situational: a baby crying in the middle of the night does not ordinarily invoke a political identity in a parent. To the degree that situations are structurally isolated, the hierarchy of salience in which identities exist within the self is irrelevant to the prediction of behavior. It may be, however, that saliency interacts with situations to affect the threshold of invocation of an identity: it is not inconceivable that for some a political identity is so salient that it is indeed invoked in the "baby crying in the middle of the night" situation. In fact, it is implicit in the definition of salience previously given that this concept is best operationalized in precisely these terms.

In general, the hierarchy of salience becomes important in the prediction of behavior in the event of what may be called structural overlap, that is, when analytically distinct sets of relationships are mutually contingent at some point in time and so do invoke concurrently different identities. More often than not, perhaps, one faces situations in which more than one of his identities is pertinent: the interaction of one man with another who is both his employee and his brother-in-law can serve as an example. Concurrently invoked, different identities do not necessarily call for incompatible behavior. But sometimes they do, and it is under this circumstance that the hierarchy of salience becomes potentially an important predictor of behavior. Thus, to follow through with the foregoing example, there is presumably a much higher probability that the familial identity will be invoked in a "typical" representative of a strong kinship society such as Italy than in a "typical" representative of American society, and, therefore, there is presumably a much higher probability that conflicting behavioral expectations will be resolved in the direction of meeting kinship-linked expectations in the Italian case.

The self may be said to be an organized structure in a second sense. The self is, by definition, a set of responses of an organism to itself. These responses are differentiated, as well as in the manner noted above, along cognitive—conative—cathectic lines. Although the meaning of any of these may be said to reside in interpersonal behavior, the assumption here is that it will make a difference with respect to behavior whether the organism responds to itself by, in effect, beginning an assertion with the stem "I am," "I want," or "I feel." Presumably, these modalities of response to oneself are not randomly related to one another; it is a reasonable assumption that the "I want" and "I feel" modalities of reflexive response to oneself are, for a given person, linked in a systematic way to the variety of "I ams" of the self. Thus, some identities can be expected to be linked with strong feelings, and some can be expected to be perceived as closely connected with the achievement of wants.[7]

One more concept, namely, that of commitment, needs to be introduced, for it will play a central part in the development of the theory that follows. Commitment, here, is used in the sense Kornhauser[8] used this term in analyzing the retention and loss of membership in political groups; it refers to the relations to others formed as a function of acting on choices, such that changing the pattern of choice requires changing the pattern of relationships to others. To the degree that one's relationships to specific others depend on one's being a particular kind of person, one is committed to being that kind of person. In this sense, commitment is measured by the "costs" of giving up meaningful relations to others should alternative courses of action be pursued.

Three points concerning the concept of commitment need to be noted. First, while the writer will be concerned in what follows to hypothesize relationships among identity salience, the modalities of response to oneself outlined above, and commitment, the latter concept is analytically independent of the former. That is, relations formed with others as a function of choices are not the same thing as the probability that a given identity will be invoked in a situation, nor as cognitive, cathectic, or conative responses to self.[9]

Second, commitments are premised on identities insofar as entering into relationships requires the attribution and acceptance of positional designations. A man's relationships to his wife, her relatives, her friends, the member of the couples' bridge club, etc., presuppose his identity as husband.

Third, there appear to be two dimensions of commitment: the sheer number of relationships entered by virtue of an identity, or extensivity of commitment; and the depth of the relationships entered by virtue of an identity, or intensivity of commitment. In what follows, commitment will be used to refer to both dimensions indifferently. Proceeding in this manner obviously ignores a number of significant theoretical and empirical problems. Are there systematic individual or group differences in preference for and importance attached to extensive versus intensive relationships? Is there a functional equation relating these two dimensions of commitment? Are these two dimensions functionally equivalent in their impact on identity salience and role performance? Such questions deserve answers which cannot at this time be forthcoming.

A RESEARCH PROBLEM AND A SET OF HYPOTHESES

What has been said to this point can serve as the basis on which to sketch a general research problem that seems to be strategic to advances in knowledge in the sociology of the family.

The empirical problem is set by the kind of commonplace observations that lay behind the abstractly stated questions with which this paper began. One man takes into consideration the probable impact of a new physical and social environment on his family in the process of arriving at a job-relocation decision. Another does not. A Mayor Wagner decides not to pursue another term of office in New York, apparently on the grounds that to do so would impair his relationships with his sons. That some reacted to his announcement with incredulity indicates that, for some, a family identity does not have the salience which would make that rationale a sufficient motivator of behavior rather than a convenient rationalization. For some, a trip to the library with the children takes precedence over a trip to the golf course; for others, the priorities are reversed. For some, parenthood is the occasion for a restructuring of activities which make the home the center of life; for others, change on the occasion of parenthood is minimal. The research problem, obviously, is to account for such variability in behavior as is exhibited in these observations.

A set of hypotheses giving promise of doing this job can be proposed. The most general hypothesis is the familiar one to the effect that the self mediates the relationship between role expectations and role performance. This general hypothesis, apart from being almost an article of faith of symbolic interaction theory, is (a) true and (b) not very powerful. That is, the evidence supports the validity of this proposition, but also leaves much to be desired by way of accounting for the variability of role performance. If the foregoing conceptual analysis is reasonable, this state of affairs is a function of widespread failure to see the self as composed of differentiated identities and to recognize that these differentiated identities exist in a hierarchy of salience. Given this specification of the concept of self, what is required in order to improve the predictive power of self theory are (1) hypotheses which can account for the position of given identities in the salience hierarchy and (2) hypotheses which tie identity salience to role performance.

The previous discussion suggests the following hypotheses with regard to, first, the position of an identity in the salience hierarchy and secondly, the relationship between identity salience and role performance. These are not intended to be exhaustive; undoubtedly other major as well as derivative hypotheses could be formulated. While it may be too much to say that these hypotheses issue deductively from the previously sketched theoretical model, together with the suggested modifications of it, they do in fact relate strongly to these.

Hypothesis 1 The greater the commitment premised on an identity, i.e., the more extensive and/or intensive the network of relationships into which one enters by virtue of a given identity, the higher will be that identity in the salience hierarchy.

Hypothesis 1a The greater the commitment premised on an identity, the more that identity will be invested with a positive cathectic response; and the more a given identity is invested with a positive cathectic response, the higher will be that identity in the salience hierarchy.[10]

Hypothesis 1b The greater the commitment premised on identity, the more that identity will be perceived as instrumental to "wants" of the person; and the more a given identity is perceived as instrumental to "wants," the higher will be that identity in the salience hierarchy.

Hypothesis 2 The more a given network of commitment is premised on a particular identity as against other identities which may enter into that network of commitment, the higher will be that identity in the salience hierarchy.

Hypothesis 3 The more congruent the role expectations of those to whom one is committed by virtue of a given identity, the higher will be that identity in the salience hierarchy.

Hypothesis 4 The larger the number of persons included in the network of commitment premised on a given identity for whom that identity is high in their own salience hierarchies, the higher will be that identity in the salience hierarchy.

These hypotheses, relating salience to commitment, elaborate a fundamental theme of symbolic interaction theory, namely, that it is out of social relationships that the self emerges. Each develops from the assumption that the investment one has in his network of social relationships reinforces the significance to the person of the identity on which this network is based.[11]

The first hypothesis above is a straightforward consequent of this assumption. Hypotheses 1a and 1b suggest the bases of the linkage between commitment and the position of an identity in the salience hierarchy. The evidence is quite clear that man's behavior is vitally affected by affect and by wants. Theoretical ideas deriving from George Herbert Mead have been properly criticized for their almost total emphasis on the cognitive components of man's experience. These two hypotheses seek to take into account these other ways in which men characteristically respond to themselves, but to do so in a manner retaining the basic insights of Mead.

Cathectic and conative responses can be expected to have a cumulative impact on the position of an identity in the salience hierarchy. That is to say, the combination of a strongly positive cathectic and a highly valued "want" response presumably would be especially potent in fixing an identity at a high salience level. There appears to be no basis at the present time on which to estimate the differential impact on identity salience of the strong cathectic-low want versus the weak cathectic-high want combinations, and it is therefore preferable not to present any hypothesis with respect to this differential impact.

Hypothesis 2 refers to the situation in which multiple identities are involved in a given network of commitment. For example, one may relate to members of a couples' bridge club not only through one's identity as husband but also through one's identity as friend. The hypothesis asserts that the more these relationships require the husband rather than the friend identity, the higher will be the husband identity in the salience hierarchy. The operational test of such a ranking is whether or not the specified relationships are more likely to continue given the disappearance of the former versus the latter identity.

When others to whom an actor relates by virtue of an identity hold role expectations which are congruent, their behaviors vis-a-vis that actor are likely to be consistent. Consistent behaviors are likely to be cumulatively reinforcing to an identity through providing the actor opportunity to respond consistently in terms of that identity.[12] Conversely, when such role expectations are incongruent, the actor's behavior in terms of an identity is likely to be confused. Such confusion is likely to result in a lowering of the identity in the salience hierarchy. While it may be that people can live with more dissonance than is implied by cognitive dissonance theory, the reasoning incorporated into hypothesis 3 assumes that dissonant expectations from within the same commitment network will motivate a reduced investment in a given identity.

If an identity as husband is important to all other members of the couples' bridge club, rather than being important to only a few others, that identity as husband is likely to be important to a given member. Hypothesis 4 generalizes this example and assumes the operation of the mechanisms suggested above in support of the preceding hypothesis.

The writer turns now to the relationship between identity salience and role performance.

Hypothesis 5 The higher an identity in the salience hierarchy, the higher the probability of role performance consistent with the role expectations attached to that identity.

This hypothesis makes the important assumption that identities are themselves motivators of human action,[13] an assumption built into the assertion that class terms carry meaning consisting of shared behavioral expectations. But, clearly, motivation to perform in keeping with an identity is insufficient to produce that performance: the structure of opportunities is relevant as well. As stated, hypothesis 5 also assumes the equivalence among persons, or for a given person over situations, of opportunity. In this light, the next two hypotheses are perhaps especially interesting. They are interesting, as well, because they translate into researchable terms the assumption of symbolic interaction theory that human beings are actors as well as reactors.[14]

Hypothesis 6 The higher an identity in the salience hierarchy, the higher the probability that a person will perceive a given situation as an opportunity to perform in terms of that identity.

Hypothesis 7 The higher an identity in the salience hierarchy, the higher the probability that a person will seek out opportunities to perform in terms of that identity.

The hypotheses thus far stated are in static form, but each can be converted into a statement relating changes in component parts (e.g., increases in the commitment premised on an identity will result in the movement upward in the salience hierarchy of that identity). They then can be used in the attempt to account for shifts in the position of an identity in the salience hierarchy or to account for shifts in role performance variables. Rather than running through the exercise of altering the form of hypotheses already reviewed, two having specifically to do with identity change can be stated.

Hypothesis 8 External events which cut existing commitments ease the adoption of a novel identity.

Hypothesis 9 The more the perceived consequences of a projected identity change are in the direction of reinforcing valued commitments, the less the resistance to that change. Conversely, the more the perceived consequences of a projected identity change are in the direction of impairing valued commitments, the greater the resistance to that change.

NOTES

1 Sheldon Stryker. "The interactional and situational approaches," in Handbook on Marriage and the Family, ed. by Harold T. Christensen, Chicago: Rand McNally, 1964, pp. 125–70.

2 Stryker, "Interactional and situational approaches," p. 163.

3 This view of class terms, which emphasizes the function of symbols in arousing expectancies, has received support in recent years in the work of psychologists interested in psycholinguistics and in the process of thinking. See, for example, Roger W. Brown, Words and Things, Glencoe, Ill.: Free Press, 1958; and J. S. Bruner, J. J. Goodnow, and G. A. Austin, A Study of Thinking, New York: Wiley, 1956.

4 Ralph H. Turner, "Role-taking: process versus conformity," in Human Behavior and Social Processes, ed. by Arnold M. Rose, Boston: Houghton Mifflin, 1962, pp. 20–40.

5 This point of view is taken in a recent work, appearing after this paper was initially prepared, which in many respects parallels the development contained herein. See George J. McCall and J. L. Simmons, Identities and Interaction, New York: Free Press, 1966.

6 Gregory P. Stone, "Appearance and the self," in Human Behavior and Social Processes, ed. by Arnold M. Rose, Boston: Houghton Mifflin, 1962, pp. 93–94. For a closely related formulation of the concept of identity, see McCall and Simmons, Identities and Interaction. See also Anselm Strauss, Mirror and Masks, Glencoe, Ill.: Free Press, 1959.

7 Just as identity is related to the "me" aspect of Mead's concept of the self, the conative and cathectic modalities of response are related to the "I" aspect. See George Herbert Mead, Mind, Self and Society, Chicago: University of Chicago Press, 1934.

8 William Kornhauser, "Social bases of political commitment: a study of liberals and radicals," in Human Behavior and Social Processes, ed. by Arnold M. Rose, Boston: Houghton Mifflin, 1962, pp. 321–29. For somewhat different, but nevertheless related, usages of the concept of commitment, see McCall and Simmons, Identities and Interaction; Howard Becker, "Notes on the concept of commitment," American Journal of Sociology 66 (July 1960): 32–40.

9 Identities are, of course, cognitive categories in terms of which individuals respond to themselves. But not all cognitive categories are identities. There is, that is, a difference between responding to oneself by saying, "I am a sociologist," and by saying, "I am honest." The former announces an identity; the latter does not.

10 The writer is aware that one may hate his strongest attachments, i.e., that negative affect may be linked to commitments. Empirically, one supposes, this linkage is comparatively rare: the probability of commitments generating positive rather than negative affect is high. Hypothesis 1a assumes this high probability. This hypothesis may be seen as a variant of Homan's hypothesis to the effect that high rates of interaction lead to high rates of liking. See George C. Homans, The Human Group, New York: Harcourt, Brace, 1950. For those cases in which commitment generates negative affect, the writer would argue that hypothesis 1a remains as stated. However, the link between salience and role performance, as expressed in hypothesis 5, would have to be altered.

11 Each of these hypotheses, it should be noted, is in effect a double hypothesis insofar as the concept of commitment has the double referent of extensivity and intensivity.

12 Alexander and Simpson explicitly note a convergence among a variety of theories which is implicit throughout this paper, but nowhere more pointed than in conection with this discussion of hypothesis 3. In their words, "Theories of balance, congruity, dissonance, equity, expectation, and justice are based on the same general postulates and are headed in the same direction.... [T]here is sufficient similarity of these approaches to justify reference to them all as balance theories.... The basic postulate of the balance theories is that there exists a need for the socialized human being to establish and maintain stable and consistent orientations toward the self, other persons, and the non-person environment.... In an unorderly flux the consequences of action would be indeterminate; it can be assumed that such lack of predictability is psychologically stressful and that the individual will engage in behaviors oriented toward maintaining a state of stability and consistency." C. Norman Alexander, Jr. and Richard L. Simpson, "Balance theory and distributive justice," Sociological Inquiry 34 (Spring 1964): 183.

13 Nelson N. Foote, "Identification as the basis for a theory of motivation," American Sociological Review 16 (February 1951): 14–21.

14 For a more detailed statement of this assumption, as well as of other assumptions of the theory, see Stryker, "Interactional and situational approaches," pp. 134–35.

THREE

SOCIAL IDENTITY AND SOCIAL CONTEXT

Along with dispositions (such as intelligent, cheerful, honest), social identity elements constitute the chief components of the self-concept. These social identity elements consist of the groups, statuses, or social categories to which the individual is socially recognized as belonging. The capsule terms sociodemographic characteristics or background characteristics are frequently used to subsume these categories. An individual's statuses include the various social positions he or she holds in diverse institutional structures (lawyer, brother, wife, PTA president, parent). The individual also belongs to certain groups or collectivities (including such formal groups as debating team members, hiking club members, Baptists). Finally, people may be classified in terms of certain social categories (bachelors, veterans, adolescents, unemployed, first-borns).

These social identity elements bear on individual self-concepts in two distinct ways. The first is that they serve as determinants of the self-concept, the second as components. Social identity elements serve as self-concept determinants by structuring the individual's life experiences. Certain things happen to us as a consequence of falling into one category rather than another. The most important things that happen to us are how we are treated by other people. If we are black, we are more likely to be treated in terms of negative stereotypes than if we are white; if male, we are treated differently than if female; if we are doctors, we are accorded greater respect and deference than if we are farm laborers. The interpersonal experiences to which we are subjected as a consequence of these social identity elements may profoundly influence our self-concepts.

The social identity element expresses not only how we are treated by others but how we live and what we do. A doctor and a hod carrier differ not only in the amount of social respect that they command but also in what they actually do at work. The person who exercises occupational self-direction (Kohn, 1969, 1977) at work will confront the kinds of challenges and make the kinds of decisions conducive to the development of feelings of efficacy and competence. On the other hand, the person whose work renders him or her subject to the power of external rules and authorities is less likely to develop what Franks and Marolla (1976) have called inner self-esteem. The self-concept components and self-values of the social worker and the master sergeant differ at least in part because of the role demands of the work involved.

Social identity elements are thus more than simply an arbitrary set of tags or labels affixed by society to individuals for classificatory convenience. People so labeled are treated differently by others, are subjected to different social expectations, are socialized in different ways, and have different opportunities—in short, undergo different life experiences. These experiences help to shape the constituents of the self-concept.

In addition, these social identity elements themselves constitute components of the self-concept. Not only are individuals socially defined as parents, engineers, Americans, and so on, but they also define themselves accordingly. For example, Kuhn and McPartland (1954) showed that when people were asked to answer the question "Who Am I?" in 20 statements, the first answers on the list tended to be these social identity elements. (Although there is some evidence—Zurcher, 1977; Turner, 1976—that this priority may be changing, social identity elements persist as self-concept components.) Several points are worth noting about these components.

The first is that (as noted in the earlier discussion of self-schemata), certain self-concept components are clear, definite, and crystallized whereas others are not. Although the illustrations offered by Markus refer to personality dispositions (independent-dependent), the same holds true for social identity elements. Some of the hardest and most stubborn self-schemata are social identity elements. There may be some question in one's mind as to how moral, interesting, or affectionate one is, but one has no doubts whatever about whether one is a black, a veteran, and an anthropologist. But the self-concept also contains ambiguous or uncertain social identity elements. For example, it may be unclear, both to society and to ourselves, whether we are an adolescent or an adult; a member of the middle or the working class; a music student or a musician; "really" a Jew or just a nominal Jew; and so on. Uncrystallized social identity elements can generate tension, interpersonal difficulty, and problems of self-definition.

The second point is that these social identity elements are accompanied by culturally defined expectations of behavior and attitudes called roles. These role standards are used by individuals as models to guide their behavior and as criteria to evaluate their worth. The boy assesses himself in terms of how masculine he is; the nurse in terms of how competent and sympathetic he or she is; the mother in terms of how nurturant she is; the soldier in terms of how courageous he is; the judge in terms of how impartial he or she is. The identity elements thus serve as standards for self-evaluation.

A third issue relates to the accuracy of the self-concept component. Centers (1949) demonstrated empirically that people frequently failed to identify with the social class to which they objectively belonged. Since social class is a relatively ambiguous position in American society, and since people are motivated to enhance self-esteem, it is understandable that they should show a stronger tendency to identify with a higher social class than the reverse. Individuals do not always define themselves as they are defined by the social scientist or even by the society at large.

Finally, since everyone's self-concept includes numerous elements, the relationship among these elements must be considered. One question relates to the consistency or inconsistency of the components. To be a judge and a cocktail lounge pianist, or a priest and bookie, though physically possible, is socially difficult. In addition, since our self-concepts contain numerous social identity elements, the effects of some may counteract the effects of others. As Hispanic-Americans, we are subject to social derogation, but as doctors or lawyers we command respect. How do these multiple social identity elements, then, bear upon our self-concepts? Are stresses associated with a situation of status inconsistency?

Finally, our self-concepts are influenced by the social contexts in which we are immersed. These refer primarily to the qualities or characteristics of other people in our environment. Although social contexts impinge on the individual in many ways, their impact on individual self-concepts are particularly likely to be strong if these contexts are dissonant, that is, if the qualities of the individual diverge from those prevailing in his or her environment.

This section considers the relationship of four social identity elements—minority group status, gender, social class, and age—to the self-concept and then examines the influence of social contexts.

MINORITY GROUP MEMBERSHIP

Few topics have commanded greater attention in self-concept research than racial, religious, and ethnic group membership (Wylie, 1979: chap. 4). Most researchers have expected lower self-esteem among minority group members, for reasons described in Section Two. The most obvious is the principle of reflected appraisals. If Mead is correct in asserting that we tend to see ourselves from the other's point of view, then group members derogated by society would be expected to develop negative self-attitudes. Furthermore, the damage would probably be worst at precisely the time of life when the individual is most vulnerable—childhood—because taunts, name calling, and other attacks are so common at this time.

The second basis for expecting lower self-esteem among minority group members is the social comparison principle, which holds that we judge ourselves by comparing ourselves to others. In a number of socially valued respects, many minority groups compare unfavorably with the majority. These unfavorable comparisons, though stemming from discrimination, may in themselves damage self-esteem. Consider the situation of blacks in American society. Because of discrimination, black socioeconomic status is considerably lower than that of white; black children's school achievement scores are, on the average, lower than whites'; and black children are more likely to come from stigmatized family structures. Thus, not only are the black children subjected to direct prejudice but also to certain secondary or derivative consequences of prejudice and discrimination which issue in unfavorable comparisons with the white majority.

The third theoretical basis for expecting lower self-esteem among minority group members is the self-attribution principle. This principle holds that individuals judge and evaluate themselves as they would judge and evaluate anyone else, on the basis of their overt behavior or its outcomes. For example, both black and white children generally judge how smart they are by observing their report card grades, test scores, and so on. Insofar as minority achievement is lower, the minority child would be expected to judge the self, as others do, less favorably.

Guided by these or related theories, most writers have taken it for granted that minority group members would have lower self-esteem. This assumption has also been subjected to a great deal of empirical research, with rather remarkable results. As one reviews the available evidence (Rosenberg and Simmons, 1972, Gordon, 1977; Wylie, 1979), it is difficult to see how any reasonably dispassionate analysis supports the view that minority group members have lower self-esteem. Such negative findings, flying squarely in the face of common sense, sound social psychological theory, and previous experimental evidence, demand explanation. Somewhat different explanations, of course, apply to each minority group. Because the literature on blacks is the most abundant, we shall focus on this group, recognizing that the factors responsible for black self-esteem do not necessarily apply in the same way to other minority groups.

Porter and Washington's examination of the evidence (Selection 16) leads them to conclude that there is no clear difference in global self-esteem between blacks and whites. Porter and Washington attribute the healthy global self-esteem of blacks to social comparison processes, to the supportive black community, and to attribution processes (system-blame interpretation).

Such discussions clarify considerably the otherwise puzzling findings on the relationship of minority group status to self-esteem. They do not, of course, *necessarily apply identically to all minority groups, nor do they exhaust the reasons for the results. What they do make plain, however, is that even the most compelling theory and most self-evident conclusion—the "obvious" fact of low self-esteem among minorities—cannot be taken for granted. A number of erroneous theoretical conclusions, we believe, may stem from the social scientists' tendency to view the situation of the minority group member from the perspective of the broader society rather than from the viewpoint of the minority group member.*

But how can one reconcile such data and theory with the influential body of psychological and psychoanalytic literature published in the '40s and '50s which concluded that minority group members had substantially lower self-esteem? (For a description of the contrasting findings at different time periods, see Gordon, 1977.) Far and away the most significant of the early experimental studies in this area, both in terms of research and policy, was that of Kenneth and Mamie Clark (1947). These investigators presented a sample of four-, five-, and six-year old black children with two dolls—one dark brown, one white—and asked them a number of questions about these dolls: Which doll looks like you? Which is the nice doll? Which is the prettiest doll? Which doll would you like to play with? and so on. The investigators found that many of these black children not only expressed preference for the white doll—prettiest doll, nice to play with—but actually said that they looked more like the white doll. Such misidentification was interpreted as racial disidentification and, by implication, low self-esteem. Over the years, numerous studies representing variants on this basic theme have appeared, using dolls, pictures, or puppets (Goodman, 1952; Morland, 1958; Brody, 1963), and have consistently supported the Clarks' findings. One point overlooked in many of these studies, however, was that the young children might be responding to these dolls in terms of literal skin color rather than in terms of symbolic meanings. Black children might have been taught that lighter skin color was more aesthetic and that the light doll was thus prettier and nicer to play with. Two items of evidence lend some support to this interpretation. The first comes, paradoxically, from an overlooked finding in the original Clark and Clark study noting that those black children saying that they looked like the white doll actually did look more like the white doll, that is, they tended to have lighter skin. The second item comes from a study by Greenwald and Oppenheim, included as Selection 17, which involved the use of three dolls—dark, mulatto, and white—and questioning children of both races. Some of the black children, to be sure, said that they looked like the white doll, but many of the white children also said they looked like the mulatto doll. In terms of doll choice, as a matter of fact, racial misidentification proved to be more common among the white than among the black children.

GENDER

One familiar theme in the sex role literature is the argument that women are accorded lower social status in the society, that they have internalized this widespread cultural assumption about their inferiority, and that they consequently have damaged self-concepts (Bardwick, 1971; Freeman, 1970). In this view, both boys and girls are socialized to think of women as less competent, able, and praiseworthy. As a consequence of reflected appraisals, girls come to see themselves as inferior—to have lower self-esteem.

The data bearing on this issue, however, are inconsistent. Some studies (Bush et al., 1977–78) do show evidence of lower self-esteem among girls (in the sixth and seventh grades) and find essentially no change in this pattern between 1968 and 1975. On the other hand, Maccoby and Jacklin's (1974) and Wylie's (1979) research review show no consistent evidence of lower self-esteem among girls or women. O'Malley and Bachman's study (Selection 29), based on a carefully selected sample of adolescent boys and girls across America, offers some evidence of lower self-esteem among girls but shows that the difference is very small—only 8 percent of a standard deviation.

This is not the place to attempt to explain why boys' and girls' self-esteem levels are similar, but certain observations are relevant. First, it should be noted that most of the data are inappropriate to most of the theory. The great bulk of the research has been conducted with school populations whereas much of the theory has relevance to adults. For example, it is argued that higher status enhances self-esteem. But even if men have higher status than women, this does not mean that boys have higher status than girls. Within the school system, girls tend to be better students and they are less likely to be school problems. If, as we believe, people are influenced by their particular life situations, then the statuses of women and men should have different self-esteem consequences than the statuses of boys and girls.

But even among adults the argument that male prestige and success must necessarily be converted into global self-esteem runs counter to certain theoretical principles enunciated in Section Two. One of these is the social comparison principle—the principle that one judges one's worth by comparing oneself to others. But which others? The fact is that there is an enormous amount of occupational sex stereotyping in American society, that is, male occupations and female occupations (Oppenheimer, 1970; Lyle and Ross, 1973; Ritzer, 1977; Rosenberg and Rosenberg, 1981). Most women, then, may compare their achievements with those of other women in their own occupations. A female nurse may compare her level of success with that of other nurses (or women in other occupations), not with the success of male doctors. To the extent that within-sex comparisons are made, the average feeling of success and achievement of men and women will be the same.

Furthermore, self-esteem is dependent not only on achievement but on aspirations. This principle applies both to traits and to statuses. Maccoby and Jacklin (1974) observe that the fact that girls are less likely than boys to stake themselves on competence and more on interpersonal success does not reflect lower self-esteem on their part. If they succeed in those areas to which they aspire, then their self-esteem should not suffer.

We thus see that here, as in so much research on the relationship of social identity elements to self-esteem, the simple and straightforward idea that a group with lesser social prestige will have lower global self-esteem receives little support from the available facts. But if male and female self-esteem differs little, this does not mean that male and female self-concepts are the same. A comparison of certain other self-concept constituents does reveal distinct differences between males and females.

One of these refers to the focus of attention—specifically, to the dimension of self-consciousness. Treating self-consciousness as a general disposition rather than as a situational response, F. Rosenberg and Simmons (Selection 18) show that girls are characterized by decidedly higher levels of objective self-awareness and a greater tendency to engage in self-monitoring (Snyder, 1974, Selection 10). Rosenberg and Simmons attempt to trace this self-consciousness to the other-directedness of adolescent girls—to their greater concern with other's thoughts and feelings about them (in contrast to boys, who are more concerned with competence and success) and to their greater awareness of the self in interpersonal situations. Other self-concept differences between males and females include differences in self-confidence (Maccoby and Jacklin, 1974), self-values (Rosenberg, 1965), self-components (McKee and Sherriffs, 1959), salience of components (Mulford and Salisbury, 1964), and self-concept stability (Simmons, Rosenberg, and Rosenberg, 1973).

Such self-concept differences represent consequences of being male or female in American society. But gender is itself an important self-concept component—indeed, probably the most stable and fundamental of all social identity elements (Kohlberg, 1966). In Selection 19, Kagan provides a description of how sex roles are learned in childhood. In the course of cognitive development, children learn to classify the objects of the world (including people) into certain categories. As the self-concept—the self as an object of observation—develops, children place themselves in the appropriate category—as boys or girls, Catholics or Protestants, children or adults, and so on. These constitute fundamental components of self-definition. Children also learn that certain kinds of characteristics (looks, attitudes, traits) and behavior are socially appropriate to members of these categories. Kagan argues that the individual is motivated to live up to these standards. The male who behaves in a feminine way or the adult who acts childishly is derogated by others. The self-concept, then, includes both the culturally prescribed definitions of behavior, attributes, and attitudes appropriate to the role as well as a personal definition of the self in terms of these standards. One's feeling of worth will hinge in part on the degree to which one's personal definition matches the culturally defined standard. But over and above global self-esteem, the failure to meet the culturally prescribed standards is an affront to one's gender identity—to one's sense of masculinity and femininity. It is thus no accident that boys and girls devote so much effort and interest to creating a self that matches the culturally defined gender standards.

SOCIAL CLASS

That people are unequal in terms of power, prestige, and possessions is a universal characteristic of human societies. Prestige—the respect accorded individuals by virtue of their location in the stratification system—is especially relevant for self-esteem. Thus one's self-respect may be expected to correspond to the respect one commands in society. As Veblen (1899: 30) observed: "In order to stand well in the eyes of the community, it is necessary to come up to a certain, somewhat indefinite, conventional standard of wealth. . . . Those members of the community who fall short of this, somewhat indefinite, normal degree of prowess or of property suffer in the esteem of their fellow-men; and consequently they suffer also in their own esteem, since the usual basis of self-respect is the respect accorded by one's neighbors."

The social comparison principle would also lead one to expect a strong association between social class and self-esteem. The stratification system is inherently comparative; high or low status has meaning only in relation to other people. People who have high status would thus be expected to have high self-esteem because they compare favorably with others; the converse would be expected of lower status members of society.

One question is: With whom does the individual actually compare himself or herself? Luck and Heiss (1972) examined the relationship between social class and self-esteem among a sample of retired men in New England. These men were in a position to look back over their long careers and to see how well they had done in life. At first glance, it would seem that such achievement left little mark on the individual's feelings of self-worth; overall, the self-esteem of the more successful men was not higher than that of the less successful men. But this finding concealed a surprising fact. Among men with a high school education, those of higher income had higher self-esteem than those with lower income; and among those with college education, those of higher occupational prestige had higher self-esteem than those with lower prestige. But the self-esteem of the average high school man was not lower than that of the average college man. In other words, success was related to self-esteem only among those of equivalent educational levels; apparently, people are more likely to compare themselves with those in the same general category than with those in other categories.

Another question is: Whose self-esteem is social class assumed to affect? Although the theory on which the assumed social class-self-esteem relationship is built refers essentially to adults, the research has been conducted primarily with children. One obvious difference is that, among adults, social class is achieved, whereas, among children, it is ascribed. Furthermore, the entire experience of social class has a different meaning for children and adults. This difference is considered in Selection 20 by Rosenberg and Pearlin.

AGE

Although self-concept formation goes on in childhood, it is still a matter of dispute how much subsequent change occurs. The self-concept formed in childhood is sometimes thought to become fixed and to remain essentially ossified. That there is an important element of continuity in the self-concept is undeniable; between middle adolescence and early adulthood, global self-esteem is reasonably stable (Engel, 1959; Carlson, 1965; Bachman, O'Malley, and Johnston, 1978). But the idea of a completely unchanging self-concept is quite inaccurate. Many of the other aspects or components of the self-concept undergo radical change in the course of development.

Both social experience and biological maturation contribute to these changes. The importance of maturation lies in the fact that the conceptualization of the self is bounded and structured by the modes of conceptualization current at a given stage of development. Otherwise expressed, a major reason why children, as they grow older, think about themselves differently is that they think differently.

First, as the child grows older, the level of abstraction of the self-concept changes. With increasing age, Gardner Murphy (1947) once pointed out, the self becomes less and less a perceptual object and more and more a conceptual trait system. The individual comes to see himself or herself in terms of a system of abstractions. So long as young children are incapable of grasping certain subtle concepts, they cannot recognize in themselves the response tendencies reflected by these concepts. The content of the self-concept thus depends on the level of cognitive development of the child.

This point is well illustrated in Selection 21, by Montemayor and Eisen. These investigators administered the Twenty Statements Test to children in grades four, six, eight, ten, and twelve. The answers were classified according to Gordon's 30 categories (presented in Section One of this book). The younger children, it turns out, were much more likely to conceptualize the self (as they conceptualize other objects of the world) in such concrete terms as territoriality (American), possessions (own a bike), or physical characteristics (blonde hair), whereas older children were more likely to conceptualize the self in terms of abstract traits or dispositions.

A second change that occurs with increasing age is the shift from an exterior to an interior mode of conceptualization. The young child generally attends to the overt, exterior, public aspects of persons rather than to their underlying qualities or feelings (Livesley and Bromley, 1973; Flavell, 1974; Secord and Peevers, 1974; Rosenberg and Rosenberg, 1981; Rosenberg, 1979). In the realm of person perception, according to Flavell (1974), the young child likes a person because of external actions ("He gives me things"), whereas the older child describes a person in terms of some abstract, universal property ("She is kind"). "The young child is less prone than his elders to automatically conceptualize others in terms of inner, dispositional properties" (p. 77). But the same is true of the child's self-concept; the young child tends to conceptualize the self in terms of external qualities, the older in terms of internal motives, intentions, or dispositions. As Selection 21 demonstrates, the older children are more likely than the younger to answer the Twenty Statements Test in terms of existential, individuating references and with regard to self-determination, whereas the younger are more likely to conceptualize the self in terms of physical characteristics or other exterior components.

A third change relates to interpersonal concepts. As Piaget (1948) teaches, young children are egocentric; seeing the world from private viewpoints, they are less able to enter the minds of others and to see themselves from others' perspectives. Hence, young children are disinclined to see themselves as interpersonal actors—as people who make a certain impression on the minds of others. Whereas adolescents are nearly obsessed with what others think of them, this matter rarely enters the younger child's mind. The younger children are thus much less likely than the older to conceptualize the self in terms of interpersonal traits (Secord and Peevers, 1974; Rosenberg, 1979).

A fourth developmental change in the self-concept occurs on the plane of fantasy or desire. Selection 22, by Havighurst and MacDonald, demonstrates that the desired self-concept also changes with age. As noted in Section One, one remarkable feature of the human mind, which firmly distinguishes it from other *forms of consciousness, is its ability to think of itself as other than it is. Since childhood largely involves the molding and preparation of the self for the future, the child creates in his or her mind a picture of a future desired self. But from what materials is the cloth woven? These change with the individual's stage of development. In Selection 22—one of the very rare systematic investigations of the idealized image—the investigators show how their subjects proceed to incorporate into their desired self-concepts different elements or components as they advance in age. In the early years, the children envision the self as similar to the parent; in early adolescence, as some glamorous figure in public view; somewhat later, as similar to some admired other adult; and still later, as an original creation based on elements drawn from diverse sources. These results, according to Havighurst and MacDonald, are remarkably similar in New Zealand and the United States.*

MULTIPLE SOCIAL IDENTITY ELEMENTS

In examining the relationship of race or social class or gender to self-esteem, what is frequently overlooked is the fact that everyone belongs to a race and a class and a sex, and so on. When investigators direct attention to a specific social identity element, it is easy for them to disregard the other elements. For example, to many research workers—particularly white ones—the only important thing about a black appears to be that he or she is black. For the black, of course, race is important, but so are many other dispositions and social identity elements. The fact that race may be of sole interest to the investigator does not mean that it is of sole interest to the research subject.

Since numerous social identity elements are incorporated in the self-concept, it becomes an empirical question to learn which of these is more salient, important, or central, and, furthermore, whether they are experienced as consistent or contradictory. This issue is examined by Herman in Selection 23. The subjects of Herman's study are Israeli Jewish adolescents and their parents. Some of the questions examined in this selection are the following: Are the Jewish identity and the Israeli identity experienced as independent or as overlapping? How central is Jewishness or Israeliness in the individual's system of self-values? How strongly do the respondents identify with these social identities, and which identity is most salient (see Stryker, Section Two)? In the book from which this selection is drawn, Herman provides evidence that age, national origin, and religious ideology are all associated with these aspects of self-concept structure, and that differing importance, salience, and centrality of these identity elements are associated with a wide range of attitudes, values, and beliefs.

DISSONANT SOCIAL CONTEXTS

Although there are several different types of contexts (Lazarsfeld and Menzel, 1972), the one most relevant to the self-concept appears to be the dissonant context. In speaking of dissonance, we are primarily concerned with the relationship or interaction between an individual characteristic and an environmental characteristic. Neither is primary; it is the agreement between the two that is decisive. For a black, for example, it is likely to be a different experience to grow up in a white than in a black neighborhood. The question is: Does the individual's similarity to, or difference from, those around him affect his self-concept?

But this question is more complicated than it appears. First, what is meant by similarity to, or difference from? We can be similar to or different from those around us in a thousand ways. Contextual analysis thus requires us to specify the contextual component, that is, the characteristic of the individual and group that is being compared. Second, what is meant by those around him? Each of us is at the center of numerous social concentric circles having different radii. Who are the people around us—Those in our school class? In our whole school? In our city? In our nation? Contextual analysis thus requires us to specify the relevant contextual unit. Third, what is meant by self-concept? Different contexts may affect different constituents of the self-concept in the same way or the same context may affect various self-concept constituents in different ways. For example, a particular context may affect our global self-esteem in one way but our academic self-concept in another.

Consider, first, the contextual components, that is, the specific ways in which individuals are seen as similar to, or different from, those around them. The best known of these are the social identity contexts. Is the individual's race, religion, age, nationality, or socioeconomic status similar to or different from that predominant in his or her environment? Second, there are physical characteristic contexts. Do the people around us look like we do, that is, is our weight, height, hair color, or eye color similar to or different from other people's in our environment? Third, there are competence contexts. Are we smart or dull, attractive or unattractive, fast or slow? To make a judgment, we require some point of reference, and this will usually be those people in our environment. An IQ of 100 results in radically different social experiences depending on whether the surrounding mean IQ is 85 or 115. How many premier high school seniors suffer rude blows to their sense of worth when they enter highly selective colleges? Fourth, it is necessary to take account of values contexts. The effect of athletic skill on our self-esteem may depend on whether athletic skill is or is not prized and praised in our environment. Piano skill in a musical family has a different value than in a musically indifferent family.

Consider now the issue of the contextual unit. Such units vary widely in scope, ranging from a single other individual in a room for ten minutes to an entire historical epoch (symbolized by the expression that an individual is out of tune with the times). The contextual unit may be a person, a small group, a family, a platoon, an army company, a hospital ward, a neighborhood, a city, a nation, and so on. The selection of the appropriate contextual unit is, therefore, of utmost importance. McPartland (1969) has shown that the beneficial academic effects of racial integration have been concealed by selecting the entire school as the contextual unit rather than the specific classroom. A school may be desegregated but the classroom segregated. Furthermore, the meanings of familiar concepts change depending upon the contextual unit under consideration. It is meaningful to refer to American Jews as a minority group if the total society is the contextual unit, since they represent about 3 percent of the population. But in a neighborhood that is 90 percent Jewish and 10 percent Gentile, who is the minority group member? Both the psychological effects and the conceptual definition of a given characteristic will vary depending on the contextual unit selected.

Finally, many diverse self-concept constituents are affected by the contexts. Dissonance has been shown to be related to academic self-concept, global self-esteem, self-concept stability, and salience of components (for example, Rosenberg, 1979; McGuire and Padawer-Singer, Section One; McGuire et al., 1978). In addition, the individual's aspirations (components of the future-desired self) have also been shown to be affected by the competence context. An outstanding example is Davis' frog-pond effect (1966) showing that college students' postgraduate aspirations are influenced by their achievements in the specific college context rather than the broader system of higher education.

In Selection 24, by Rosenberg, the religious context is the contextual component; the neighborhood is the contextual unit; and self-esteem is the self-concept constituent. This selection suggests that global self-esteem suffers some damage in a dissonant religious context. Rosenberg's study empirically tests the hypothesis that this effect is attributable to direct exposure to discrimination and to the psychic consequences of cultural dissimilarity.

An example of physical characteristics contexts is found in Selection 2. Using the classroom as the contextual unit, McGuire and Padawer-Singer found that those physical characteristics that were distinctive in these contexts were highly salient self-concept components. Subsequent research has demonstrated that ethnic and racial distinctiveness (McGuire et al., 1978) tend to be associated with greater salience of self-concept components (although there are exceptions). Similarly, Herman's study of American Jewish adolescents in Israel (Selection 23) showed that the identity American was much more salient when in Israel than in America.

Rogers, Smith, and Coleman (Selection 25) consider the impact of competence contexts on the child's self-concept. The sample in this study consists of academic underachievers in special classrooms—children all chosen because of severe learning difficulties. Despite their common academic deficiencies, the self-esteem of these children, like that of normal children, is also influenced by academic achievement. But the impact of academic achievement depends on the contextual unit under consideration. If the entire school is used as the contextual unit, then there is little relationship between academic achievement and self-esteem. But if the analysis is confined to individual classrooms, then clear relationships appear. Children apparently compare themselves with others within their classrooms rather than with the general run of schoolmates. This article also demonstrates the importance of specifying the particular self-concept component at issue. The authors show that the contextual effect is most powerful when the more relevant component—academic self-concept—is considered than when the less relevant components are considered. However, the context does appear to have a spillover effect on such self-concept variables as physical attractiveness and popularity. This suggests the possibility of a generalization effect.

What these several studies are intended to illustrate is that research investigations that undertake to explain certain aspects of the self-concept in terms of some individual characteristic—whether a social identity element such as race or sex *or an ability such as academic achievement—are incomplete insofar as they overlook the meaning, interpretation, and response to that individual characteristic in different environments. In order to understand the individual, it is also necessary to know about the people around him or her.*

REFERENCES

Bachman, J., P. O'Malley, and J. Johnston
1978 Adolescence to Adulthood: Change and Stability in the Lives of Young Men. Ann Arbor, Mich.: Institute for Social Research.
Bardwick, J.
1971 Psychology of Women. New York: Harper & Row.
Brody, E. B.
1963 "Color and identity conflict in young boys: observations on Negro mothers and sons in urban Baltimore." Psychiatry 26: 188–201.
Bush, D., R. Simmons, B. Hutchinson, and D. Blyth.
1977–78 "Adolescent perception of sex roles in 1968 and 1975." Public Opinion Quarterly 41: 459–74.
Carlson, R.
1965 "Stability and change in the adolescent's self-image." Child Psychology 36: 659–66.
Centers, R.
1949 The Psychology of Social Classes. Princeton, N.J.: Princeton University Press.
Clark, K. B. and M. P. Clark.
1947 "Racial identification and preference in Negro children." Pp. 169–78 in T. M. Newcomb and E. L. Hartley (eds.), Readings in Social Psychology. New York: Holt.
Davis, J. A.
1966 "The campus as a frog-pond." American Journal of Sociology 72: 17-31.
Davis, K.
1949 Human Society. New York: Macmillan.
Engel, M.
1959 "The stability of the self-concept in adolescence." Journal of Abnormal and Social Psychology 58: 211–15.
Flavell, J.
1974 "The development of inferences about others." In T. Mischel (ed.), Understanding Other Persons. Oxford: Blackwell.
Franks, D. D. and J. Marolla.
1976 "Efficacious action and social approval as interacting dimensions of self-esteem: formulation through construct validation." Sociometry 39: 324–41.
Freeman, J.
1970 "Growing up girlish." Transaction 8: 36–43.
Goodman, M. E.
1952 Race Awareness in Young Children. Cambridge, Mass.: Addison-Wesley.
Gordon, V.
1977 The Self-Concept of Black Americans. Washington, D.C.: University Press of America.
Kohlberg, L.
1966 "A cognitive developmental analysis of children's sex-role concepts and attitudes." In E. E. Maccoby (ed.), The Development of Sex Differences. Stanford, Calif.: Stanford University Press.
1969 "Stage and sequence: the cognitive-developmental approach to socialization." In D. Goslin (ed.), Handbook of Socialization Theory and Research. Chicago: Rand McNally.

Kohn, M. L.

1969 Class and Conformity: A Study in Values. Homewood, Ill.: Dorsey Press.

1977 "Reassessment, 1977." Pp. xxv-lx in Class and Conformity: A Study in Values. 2d Edition. Chicago: University of Chicago Press.

Kuhn, M. H. and T. McPartland

1954 "An empirical investigation of self-attitudes." American Sociological Review 19: 68–76.

Lazarsfeld, P. F. and H. Menzel

1972 "On the relation between individual and collective properties." Pp. 225–37 in P. F. Lazarsfeld, A. Pasanella, and M. Rosenberg (eds.), Continuities in the Language of Social Research. New York: Free Press.

Livesley, W. J. and D. B. Bromley

1973 Person Perception in Childhood and Adolescence. London: Wiley.

Luck, P. W. and J. Heiss

1972 "Social determinants of self-esteem in adults." Sociology and Social Research 57: 69–84.

Lyle, J. R. and J. L. Ross

1973 Women in Industry. Lexington, Mass.: D. C. Heath.

Maccoby, E. E. and C. N. Jacklin

1974 The Psychology of Sex Differences. Stanford, Calif.: Stanford University Press.

McGuire, W. J., et al.

1978 "Salience of ethnicity in the spontaneous self-concept as a function of one's ethnic distinctiveness in the social environment." Journal of Personality and Social Psychology 36: 511–20.

McGuire, W. J. and A. Padawer-Singer

1976 "Trait salience in the spontaneous self-concept." Journal of Personality and Social Psychology 33: 743–54.

McKee, J. P. and A. C. Sherriffs

1959 "Men's and women's beliefs, ideals, and self-concepts." American Journal of Sociology 64: 356–63.

McPartland, J.

1969 "The relative influence of school and of classroom desegregation on the academic achievement of ninth-grade Negro students." Journal of Social Issues 25: 93–102.

Morland, J. K.

1958 "Racial recognition by nursery school children in Lynchburg, Virginia." Social Forces 37: 132–37.

Mulford, H. W. and W. S. Salisbury

1964 "Self-conceptions in a general population." Sociological Quarterly 5: 35–46.

Murphy, G.

1947 Personality. New York: Harper.

Oppenheimer, V. K.

1970 The Female Labor Force in the United States. Berkeley, Calif.: Institute of International Studies.

Piaget, J.

1948 The Moral Judgment of the Child. Glencoe, Ill.: Free Press.

Ritzer, G.

1977 Working: Conflict and Change. Englewood Cliffs, N.J.: Prentice-Hall.

Rosenberg, M.

1965 Society and the Adolescent Self-Image. Princeton, N.J.: Princeton University Press.

1979 Conceiving the Self. New York: Basic Books.

Rosenberg, M. and F. Rosenberg

1981 "The occupational self: a developmental study." In M. D. Lynch, A. Norem-Hebeissen, and K. J. Gergen (eds.), Self-Concept: Advances in Theory and Research. Cambridge, Mass.: Ballinger.

Rosenberg, M. and R. G. Simmons
1972 Black and White Self-Esteem: The Urban School Child. Rose Monograph Series. Washington, D.C.: American Sociological Association.
Secord, P. F. and B. H. Peevers
1974 "The development and attribution of person concepts." In T. Mischel (ed.), Understanding Other Persons. Oxford: Blackwell.
Simmons, R. G., F. Rosenberg, and M. Rosenberg
1973 "Disturbance in the self-image at adolescence." American Sociological Review 38: 533–68.
Snyder, Mark
1974 "Self-monitoring of expressive behavior." Journal of Personality and Social Psychology 4: 526-37.
Turner, R.
1976 "The real self: from institution to impulse." American Journal of Sociology 81: 989–1016.
Veblen, T.
1899 The Theory of the Leisure Class. New York: Mentor Books.
Wylie, R.
1979 The Self-Concept: Revised Edition. Volume 2. Theory and Research on Selected Topics. Lincoln, Neb.: University of Nebraska Press.
Zurcher, L. A., Jr.
1977 The Mutable Self: A Self-Concept for Social Change. Beverly Hills, Calif.: Sage Publications.

Black Identity and Self-Esteem: A Review of Studies of Black Self-Concept 1968-1978

Judith R. Porter

Robert E. Washington

16

INTRODUCTION

Self-concept is in large part a social product, determined by the attitudes and behavior of others toward the individual. Since many American ethnic groups have been the victims of prejudice, it has been assumed that low self-esteem may result from minority status. The research tradition on black self-image has continuity with literature on the personality patterns of other ethnic groups. Within the past decade, however, many of the standard theoretical assumptions in this body of research have been questioned. We review the past decade's major social and psychological studies of black self-esteem and conclude by evaluating the sources of problems in this literature.

Social science literature of the 1920s–1940s, which dealt with the effects of marginal status on feelings of personal insecurity (Stonequist 1937; Lewin 1948), linked minority status and low self-esteem. Notions of personal disorganization and in-group rejection were developed in discussions of European immigrant populations and were also applied to analysis of personality patterns of blacks (Dollard 1937; C. Johnson 1967).

By the late 1940s, public policy needs had created increasing demand for social

Source: Judith R. Porter and Robert E. Washington, "Black Identity and Self-Esteem: A Review of Studies of Black Self-Concept, 1968–1978." Reproduced, with permission, from the Annual Review of Sociology, Volume 5.

research on racial integration. Study of black self-image was given impetus by the social science brief appended to the *Brown* v. *Board of Education* decision in 1954, which emphasized that racial segregation had the potential to damage the self-esteem of black children. Research on ethnic identity thus began to shift from European immigrants to blacks, utilizing both quantitative and psychoanalytic techniques rather than participant observation.

One major focus of the 1950s and early 1960s can be characterized as the "mark of oppression" approach. Blacks were assumed to internalize negative racial images of themselves with a devastating effect on comprehensive self-esteem. The best-known elaboration of this thesis is the psychoanalytic study by Kardiner & Ovesey, *The Mark of Oppression* (1962). They proposed that racial discrimination led to idealization of whites and to an introjected white ideal, which in turn resulted in inner-directed rage and self-hatred among blacks. This orientation is still present in recent work (Grier & Cobbs 1968; Pouissant 1970).

Social-psychological role theorists reached similar conclusions. The necessity of enacting the role of accommodating, subordinate Negro could not easily be separated from the core self, and lowered self-esteem was the concomitant of this process (Pettigrew 1964). Role theorists cautioned that all blacks did not respond in the same manner. Response to the "Negro role" was contingent upon socioeconomic factors and personality patterns (Pettigrew 1964; Clark 1965). Several typologies of response to the minority situation were suggested (Allport 1958; R. Johnson 1958; Pettigrew 1964). Yet in both the social-psychological and psychoanalytic perspectives, the assumption was made that most blacks suffered from poor self-image.

By the mid-1960s, as black militancy increased, a new theoretical trend emerged. The possibilities of nondefensive orientations to racial status and of positive coping strategies were explored (Erikson 1964; Coles 1967). Recent research has continued this trend. . . .

PERSONAL SELF-ESTEEM

Distinct from his feelings about being black, an individual acquires a general evaluative view of the self. We call this personal self-esteem, which, if high, comprises feelings of intrinsic worth, competence, and self-approval rather than self-rejection and self-contempt (Proshansky & Newton 1968; Hulbary 1975). Prior to the past decade researchers assumed that since race is a highly salient dimension of identity to blacks and since racial self-esteem was presumably poor, personal self-esteem should also be low among blacks. Studies during the past ten years, however, have increasingly disputed this contention.

Differences in Personal Self-Esteem by Race

The literature on personal self-esteem is contradictory. One group of studies finds lower personal self-esteem among blacks than among whites. These findings have been reported among both preschoolers (Long & Henderson 1968, 1970; Porter 1971; Samuels 1973; Ratusnik & Koenigsknecht 1975) and adolescents (McClain 1967; Peterson & Ramirez 1971; Hauser 1971; Lefebre 1973). A much larger body of literature, however, finds personal self-esteem among black populations either equal to or greater than that among whites. Findings of equal self-esteem have been reported among preschoolers (Davids 1973), elementary school children (Carpenter & Busse 1969; Henderson, Goffeney & Butler 1969; White & Richmond 1970; Brand, Ruiz & Padilla 1974), adolescents (Rosenberg 1965; Hodgkins & Stakenas 1969; Kuhlman & Bieliauskas 1976), and adults (Flanagan & Lewis 1969). Greater self-esteem among blacks than among whites has been reported among elementary school children (Baughman & Dahlstrom 1968; Rosenberg & Simmons 1971; Trowbridge, Trowbridge & Trowbridge 1972; Cicirelli 1977) and adolescents (Hartnagel 1970; Baughman 1971; Rosenberg & Simmons 1971; Dales & Keller 1972; Greenberg 1972; Hurtsfeld 1978). High levels of personal self-esteem have also been found among some subgroups of black adults (Crain & Weissman 1972; Jacques 1976).

Estimates of personal self-esteem, and reports of racial differences in its level, obviously depend on the dimension being measured. Higher levels of self-regard but lower feelings of personal efficacy are reported among blacks than among whites (Hunt & Hunt 1975, 1977; Hulbary 1975). Other investigators find little difference in estimate of one's own academic ability between blacks and whites but note that blacks felt they had considerably less control over the environment than did whites (Coleman et al. 1966; Gordon 1969). When asked to compare themselves with whites, black adults rated themselves equal on some traits (e.g., performance of family roles) and lower on others (e.g., work-related traits) (Heiss & Owens 1972; Turner & Turner 1974).

On the MMPI, blacks score lower than whites on scales measuring self-satisfaction and feelings of adequacy (Baughman & Dahlstrom 1968). Other studies utilizing the MMPI have indicated that blacks score more negatively on scales of self-worth, isolation, and cynicism than whites but score more positively on scales of personal warmth and energy (Guterman 1972). Hauser (1971) and Goldman & Mercer (1976) report equal self-esteem but deeper emotional or identity problems among blacks.

It is difficult to reconcile these discrepancies. Many of the studies reporting poor personal self-esteem among blacks are characterized by small samples, preschool-age subjects, and/or projective techniques. Most of the research demonstrating high personal self-esteem utilizes direct self-report techniques. Although studies disagree on whether the personal self-esteem of blacks is equal to or greater than that of whites, the bulk of studies do not report lower personal self-esteem among blacks.

Among blacks personal self-esteem varies with sex and region, but the findings are not consistent. Several studies of children find that black males have lower personal self-esteem than black females (Baughman & Dahlstrom 1968; Greenberg 1972); others report either the opposite finding (Carpenter & Busse 1969; Brand, Ruiz & Padilla 1974) or no difference between the sexes (Trowbridge, Trowbridge & Trowbridge 1972). Some studies find higher personal self-esteem among Northern than among Southern blacks (Crain & Weissman 1972); other evidence shows high self-esteem in Southern blacks (Baughman & Dahlstrom 1968). Differences in sample age and in methodology explain some of these discrepancies. Social class and degree of interracial contact (variables discussed in the following sections) also cause variations in personal self-esteem. A number of investigators have found that social class is a more powerful predictor of personal self-esteem than race is (Gordon 1969; Yancey, Rigsby & McCarthy 1972; Samuels 1973).

Theoretical Approaches to Personal Self-Esteem

Several paradigms, often with conflicting predictions about personal self-esteem and social context, have been proposed.

Social Evaluation Theory The basic tenet of social evaluation theory is that human beings learn about themselves by comparing themselves to others. The process of social evaluation leads to positive, neutral, or negative self-ratings relative to the standard employed for comparison (Pettigrew 1967). Although hopes among blacks for improvement in *group* economic and social status employ white America as a referent, Pettigrew (1971) suggests that egoist or personal comparisons use black referents.

Utilization of blacks as a reference group for personal comparison has been stressed by a number of recent theorists who introduce the notion of consonant context in promoting high personal self-esteem. The child compares himself to those with whom he is in actual association in sustained social relations. The typical black child spends his formative years in essentially a black world. The black community provides him with his frame of reference, and he compares himself on a personal level with other black children, not with white children. The critical factor is how the black child perceives he is treated by significant others in his world compared to how his peers are treated by these same individuals. In this consonant context, black children are exposed to norms and practices that insulate them from low societal ranking. The confrontation with the white world occurs for most black children after the foundation of their self-esteem has been established by their experience within the black setting (Rosenberg 1965; Rosenberg & Simmons 1971; Baughman 1971; McCarthy & Yancey 1971). This theoretical approach has been used to explain the findings (cited above) that blacks do not feel lower personal self-esteem than whites.

In addition, this orientation predicts that blacks who are in a consonant, protective context—i.e., lower SES or segregated blacks—should exhibit especially high self-esteem. Although several studies find no difference in personal self-esteem among black children of different SES (Rosenberg & Simmons 1971; Larkin 1972; Healey & DeBlassie 1974; Dillard 1976), others find higher self-esteem among lower-class than among middle-class blacks (McDonald 1968; Soares & Soares 1970–1971; Bruch, Kunce & Eggeman 1972; Trowbridge, Trowbridge & Trowbridge 1972; Hulbary 1975). Personal self-esteem among black children from father-absent homes is not lower than that among other blacks in their SES group (Rosenberg & Simmons 1971; Rubin 1974); in fact, the absence of the father is more damaging to the self-esteem of white than of black children (Hartnagel 1970; Hunt & Hunt 1975).

Research on the effects of school segregation on self-esteem also supports the paradigm of the protective effect of a consonant context. In a comprehensive review of literature on the effects of school integration, St. John (1975) notes either no significant relationship between degree of school integration and general self-esteem or a negative relationship; low-income children are particularly vulnerable to the stress of desegregation. On the other hand, feelings of control over the environment are found to be positively related to degree of school integration in a number of studies. (The relationship between control and self-esteem is discussed in the next section.) Research on adults suggests that integration may be related in the long run to higher self-esteem (Pettigrew 1967; St. John 1975).

The positive effect of a consonant context on personal self-esteem thus seems to have much empirical support. Yet there are theoretical problems. Rosenberg & Simmons (1971), for example, usually treat positive self-reports as evidence of authentic positive self-evaluations resulting from consonant social context. Sometimes, however, they imply that these responses may instead be defensive reactions. If this is the case, then either the context is less consonant than they assume or the effects of consonant context are not genuinely positive. In addition, Rosenberg & Simmons do not fully explore the interpenetration of dominant and ghetto institutions and the effect of this interaction on the process of social evaluation. The consonant context is assumed rather than clearly specified.

The situational specificity of behavior has been well established in social psychology. Pettigrew (1971, 1978) has suggested that an individual may compare himself to members of different groups in different situations; social comparison is a multidimensional process. Working-class blacks, for instance, may use whites for fraternal comparisons, middle-class blacks for personal economic comparisons, and their peers for comparison on other dimensions, such as personal appearance. St. John's (1975) work further indicates that different subcomponents of self-esteem may be differentially affected by the same context. Situational variations in comparison group and the effects of these multiple comparisons on subcomponents of self-esteem have not been carefully investigated for various socioeconomic groups of blacks.

Locus of Control and Personal Self-Esteem Psychologists like Atkinson and Rotter have defined the sense of internal control as a perception that reward is contingent on individual behavior; the sense of external control is the notion that rewards are controlled by external forces, like chance. The feeling of internal control has been considered by some psychologists to be a normal or healthy response (see Gurin et al. 1969 for a review of this literature).

A number of studies utilizing versions of Rotter's locus of control scale have found that blacks more than whites feel that control is external (Coleman et al. 1966; Gruen, Korte & Baum 1974; Valecha & Ostrum 1974; Jacobson 1975). However, the relationship between locus of control and self-esteem for blacks is complex. Crain & Weissman (1972) found that feelings of external control in conjunction with reports of high self-esteem characterized their working-class sample. They interpreted this constellation as a defensive reaction to cover a basic sense of insecurity. But Gurin and associates have disputed this interpretation, suggesting that for blacks the relationship between high self-esteem and highly developed sense of external control may be normative and healthy (Gurin et al. 1969; Gurin 1970; Gurin & Epps 1975).

Locus of control is a complex concept composed of three dimensions: control ideology, sense of personal control, and extent to which the individual blames either himself or the system. Black scores are like those of whites on the first scale; they are lower on the second. But it is the third dimension, blame of self vs. blame of system, that is crucial for self-esteem. Certain obstacles experienced by blacks, e.g., racial discrimination, operate systematically and reliably. Feelings of external control may thus represent not a passive belief in chance or fate but instead system-blame, which indicates a healthy sensitivity to the real world. A combined feeling of high system-blame and high personal control may represent the healthiest adjustment (Gurin & Epps 1975).

Others have also suggested the positive implications of feelings of external control (blaming the system) for high personal self-esteem among blacks (Pettigrew 1967; Hulbary 1975; Williams 1977). This paradigm may explain why most studies do not find blacks lower than whites on personal self-esteem. System-blame is more intense among the young (Gurin & Epps 1975) and thus should be especially likely to affect personal self-esteem in this age group. It is difficult to interpret the relationship between self-esteem and feelings of external control by social class on the one hand, and degree of integration on the other, because most studies in this area use the entire Rotter scale and do not separate locus of control into subdimensions.

The Tangle of Pathology The tangle-of-pathology approach has been the framework most often used to analyze the self-esteem of the black lower class. Racial discrimination blocks economic opportunity for lower-class blacks. Poverty, in turn, leads to deterioration of family structure and function. These economic and family problems result in ambivalence toward the child and thus to both inadequate socialization (Schulz 1969; Wyne, White & Coop 1974; Silverstein & Krate 1975) and unattractiveness of parental role models (Liebow 1967; Hauser 1971). Poor self image, premature identity foreclosure, and deviant behavior result from these problems (Schulz 1969; Rainwater 1970; Hauser 1971; Wyne, White & Coop 1974). In the tradition of the Moynihan Report, the contribution of father-absence to the poor self-esteem of the black lower-class male has been a focus of particular interest (Proshansky & Newton 1968; Wyne, White & Coop 1974). These personality problems in turn make it more difficult for the lower-income black to handle the direct effects of prejudice and discrimination. A stable and secure family environment creates high self-esteem (Coopersmith 1967). Individuals with a strong ego, raised in such a secure environment, handle prejudice most successfully (Pettigrew 1964). Thus the lower-income subculture, which develops as an adaptation to economic and family problems and low self-esteem, cannot successfully bolster the self-image of lower-income blacks; they are aware of their failure by mainstream standards (Liebow 1967; Hannerz 1969; Rainwater 1970). This orientation is summed up by Kenneth Clark's statement that "the dark ghetto is institutionalized pathology" (Clark 1965, p. 81).

An offshot of this approach, popular in the late 1960s, substituted a model of cultural for economic determinism and placed the blame for failure and poor self-image not on the system but on the individual's involvement in a subcultural tradition that stressed personal disorganization and fatalism. The cultural-deprivation and culture-of-poverty theses are examples of this "blaming-the-victim" approach (see Adam 1978).

Some studies do in fact report higher personal self-esteem among middle-class than among impoverished blacks (Gordon 1969; Porter 1971; Samuels 1973). Yet the tangle-of-pathology data are contradicted by the data of the social-evaluation theorists (see above), which suggest that high self-esteem exists among lower-class blacks as a result of a consonant context. The source of this discrepancy is in part methodological. The social-evaluation approach relies on objective self-report of personal esteem, while the tangle-of-pathology orientation relies on either participant observation or more projective techniques based on small samples.

The latter paradigm also focuses on the very bottom of the socioeconomic spectrum, rather than on mixed working- and lower-class populations. Evidence supporting social-evaluation theory comes for the most part from child populations, while much of the tangle-of-pathology evidence is based on adults who have already met economic failure.

Implicit in the tangle-of-pathology paradigm is the notion that the lower-class black environment is characterized by disorganized, unsupportive institutions and culture. The next model we consider questions this interpretation.

The Supportive Black Subcommunity During the late 1960s, some social scientists of both races began to challenge the focus on pathology in the lower-income black community. Black subculture must be viewed, it was suggested, as an organized, ongoing entity different from white culture but not deficient or pathological. Patterns such as kinship-based networks and mutual exchange offset the supposed negative effects of female-headed households on the self-image of the child (Stack 1975). Positive male role models are present in the environment, even though they may deviate from middle-class standards (Taylor 1976). The existence of a distinctive black subculture has been increasingly emphasized (Keil 1966; Ladner 1973; Nobles 1973). The notion of socialization into a highly positive tradition, rather than simply isolation from mainstream culture and comparison with peers, is involved in the explanation of good self-image among the black lower class. The subcommunity paradigm, however, fails to delineate explicitly the effects of variations in the political climate of the black community on black subculture. . . .

REFERENCES

Adam, B.
1978 "Inferiorization and self-esteem." Social Psychology 41: 47–53.
Allport, G.
1958 The Nature of Prejudice. New York: Doubleday.
Baughman, E.
1971 Black Americans. New York: Academic Press.
Baughman, E. and G. Dahlstrom
1968 Negro and White Children in the Rural South. New York: Academic Press.
Brand, E., R. Ruiz, and A. Padilla
1974 "Ethnic identification and preference: a review." Psychological Bulletin 81: 860–90.
Bruch, M., J. Kunce and D. Eggeman
1972 "Parental devaluation: a protection of self-esteem." Journal of Counseling Psychology 19: 555–58.
Carpenter, T. and T. Busse
1969 "Development of self-concept in Negro and white welfare children." Child Development 40: 935–39.
Cicirelli, V.
1977 "Relationship of SES and ethnicity to primary grade children's self-concept." Psychology in Schools 14: 213–15.

Clark, K.
1965 Dark Ghetto. New York: Harper & Row.
Coleman, J., E. Campbell, J. McPartland, A. Mood, F. Weinfeld, and R. York
1966 Equality of Educational Opportunity. Washington D.C.: U.S. Government Printing Office.
Coles, R.
1967 Children of Crisis. New York: Little, Brown.
Coopersmith, S.
1967 The Antecedents of Self-Esteem. San Francisco: W. Freeman.
Crain, R. and C. Weissman
1972 Discrimination, Personality, and Achievement. New York: Seminar Press.
Dales, R. and J. Keller
1972 "Self-concept scores among black and white culturally deprived adolescent males." Journal of Negro Education 4: 31–34.
Davids, A.
1973 "Self-concept and mother-concept in black and white preschool children." Child Psychiatry and Human Development 4: 30–43.
Dillard, J.
1976 "Relationship between career maturity, and self-concepts of suburban and urban middle and lower-class black males." Journal of Vocational Behavior 9: 311–20.
Dollard, J.
1937 Caste and Class in a Southern Town. New York: Doubleday.
Erikson, E.
1964 "Memorandum on identity and Negro youth." Journal of Social Issues 20: 29–42.
Flanagan, J. and G. Lewis
1969 "Comparison of Negro and white lower-class men on the general aptitude test battery and MMPI." Journal of Social Psychology 78:289–91.
Goldman, R. and B. Mercer
1976 "Self-esteem and self-differentiation: a comparison between black and white children in Follow-Through and non-Follow Through programs." Educational Research Quarterly 1: 43–49.
Gordon, C.
1972 Looking Ahead. Washington D.C.: American Sociological Association.
Greenberg, E.
1972 "Black children, self-esteem and the liberation movement." Politics in Society 2, 3: 293–307.
Grier, W. and P. Cobbs
1968 Black Rage. New York: Basic Books.
Gruen, G., J. Korte, and J. Baum
1974 "Group measure of locus of control." Developmental Psychology 10:683–86.
Gurin, G.
1970 "An expectancy approach to job-training programs." Pp. 277–99 in V. Allen (ed.), Psychological Factors in Poverty. Chicago: Markham.
Gurin, P. and E. Epps
1975 Black Consciousness, Identity and Achievement. New York: Wiley.
Gurin, P., G. Gurin, R. Lao, and M. Beattie
1969 "Internal/external control and the motivational dynamics of Negro youth." Journal of Social Issues 25: 29–53.
Guterman, S.
1972 Black Psyche: The Modal Personality Patterns of Black Americans. Berkeley: Glendessary Press.
Hannerz, U.
1969 Soulside. New York: Columbia Univ. Press.

Hartnagel, T.
1970 "Father absence and self-conception among lower class white and Negro boys." Social Problems 18: 152–63.
Hauser, S.
1971 Black and White Identity Formation. New York: Wiley.
Healey, G. and R. DeBlassie
1974 "A comparison of Negro, Anglo, and Spanish-American adolescents' self-concept." Adolescence 9: 15–24.
Henderson, N., B. Goffeney, and B. Butler
1969 "Do Negro children project a self-image of helplessness and inadequacy in drawing a person?" Proceedings of the American Psychological Association, 77th, 4: 437–38.
Heiss, J. and S. Owens
1972 "Self-evaluation of blacks and whites." American Journal of Sociology 78: 360–70.
Hodgkins, B. and R. Stakenas
1969 "A study of self-concepts of Negro and white youth in segregated environments." Journal of Negro Education 38: 370–77.
Hulbary, W.
1975 "Race, deprivation, and adolescent self-image." Social Science Quarterly 56: 105–14.
Hunt, J. and L., Hunt
1977 "Racial inequality and self-image: identity maintenance and identity diffusion." Sociology and Social Research 61: 539–59.
Hunt, L. and J. Hunt
1975 "Race and the father-son connection: the conditional relevance of father absence for the orientations and identities of adolescent boys." Social Problems 23: 35–52.
Hurstfeld, J.
1978 "Internal colonialism: white, black, and Chicano self-concept." Ethnic and Racial Studies 1: 60–79.
Jacobson, C.
1975 "The saliency of personal control and racial separatism for black and white southern students." Psychological Record 25: 243–53.
Jacques, J.
1976 "Self-esteem among southern black American couples." Journal of Black Studies 7: 11–280.
Johnson, C.
1967 Growing Up in the Black Belt. 2d ed. New York: Schocken Books.
Johnson, R.
1958 "Negro reactions to minority group status." Pp. 192–214 in M. Barron (ed.), American Minorities. N.Y.: Alfred Knopf.
Kardiner, A. and L. Ovesey
1962 Mark of Oppression. 2d ed. New York: Meridian Books.
Keil, C.
1966 Urban Blues. Chicago: University of Chicago Press.
Kuhlman T. and V. Bieliauskas
1976 "A comparison of black and white adolescents on the HTP." Journal of Clinical Psychology 32: 728–31.
Ladner, J.
1973 "The urban poor." Pp. 3–24 in W. Wilson (ed.), Through Different Eyes. New York: Oxford Press.
Larkin, R.
1972 "Class, race, sex, and preadolescent attitudes." California Journal of Educational Research 23: 213–23.
Lewin, K.
1948 Resolving Social Conflicts. New York: Harper and Brothers.

Liebow, E.
1967 Tally's Corner. Boston: Little, Brown.
Long, B. and E. Henderson
1968 "Self-social concepts of disadvantaged school beginners." Journal of General Psychology 113: 41–51.
1970 "Social schemata of school beginners: some demographic correlates." Merrill-Palmer Quarterly 16: 305–24.
McCarthy, J. and W. Yancey
1971 "Uncle Tom and Mr. Charlie: metaphysical pathos in the study of racism and personal disorganization." American Journal of Sociology 76: 648–72.
McClain, E.
1967 "Personality characteristics of Negro college students in the South: a recent reappraisal." Journal of Negro Education 36: 320–25.
McDonald, R.
1968 "Effects of sex, race, and class on self, ideal-self, and parental ratings in southern adolescents." Perception and Motor Skills 27: 15–25.
Nobles, W.
1973 "Psychological research and the black self-concept: a critical review." Journal of Social Issues 29: 11–31.
Peterson, B. and M. Ramirez
1971 "Real-ideal self-disparity in Negro and Mexican-American children." Psychology 8: 22–26.
Pettigrew, T.
1964 Profile of the Negro American. New York: Van Nostrand.
1967 "Social evaluation theory: convergences and applications." In Nebraska Symposium on Motivation 15: 241–311.
1971 Racially Separate or Together? New York: McGraw-Hill.
1978 "Placing Adam's argument in a broader perspective." Social Psychology 41: 58–61.
Porter, J.
1971 Black Child, White Child: The Development of Racial Attitudes. Cambridge, Mass: Harvard University Press.
Pouissant, A.
1970 "A Negro psychiatrist explains the Negro psyche." Pp. 129–38 in A. Meier and E. Rudwick (eds.), Black Protest in the Sixties, Chicago: Quadrangle Books.
Proshansky, H. and P. Newton
1968 "The nature and meaning of Negro self-identity." Pp. 178–218 in M. Deutsch, B. Katz, and A. Jensen (eds.), Social Class, Race, and Psychological Development. New York: Holt, Rinehart, & Winston.
Rainwater, L.
1970 Behind Ghetto Walls. Chicago: Aldine.
Ransford, J. E.
1968 "Isolation, powerlessness, and violence: a study of attitudes and participation in the Watts riots." American Journal of Sociology 73: 581–91.
Ratusnik, D. and R. Koenigsknecht
1975 "Normative study of the Goodenough drawing test and the Columbia Mental Maturity Scale in an urban setting." Perception and Motor Skills 40: 835–38.
Rosenberg, M.
1965 Society and the Adolescent Self-Image. Princeton: Princeton University Press.
Rosenberg, M. and R. Simmons
1971 Black and White Self-Esteem: The Urban School Child. Washington D.C.: American Sociological Association.
Rubin, R.
1974 "Adult male absence and the self-attitudes of black children." Child Studies Journal 4: 33–46.

St. John, N.
1975 School Desegregation: Outcomes for Children. New York: Wiley.
Samuels, S.
1973 "An investigation into the self-concepts of lower and middle-class black and white kindergarten children." Journal of Negro Education 42: 467–72.
Schulz, D.
1969 Coming Up Black. Englewood Cliffs, N.J.: Prentice Hall.
Silverstein, B. and R. Krate
1975 Children of the Dark Ghetto. New York: Praeger.
Soares, L. and T. Soares
1970–71 "Self-concepts of disadvantaged and advantaged students." Child Studies Journal 1: 69–73.
Stack, C.
1975 All Our Kin. New York: Harper & Row.
Stonequist, E.
1937 The Marginal Man: A Study in Personality and Culture Conflict. New York: Scribner's.
Taylor, R.
1976 "Psychosocial development among black children and youth: a reexamination." American Journal of Orthopsychiatry 46: 4–19.
Trowbridge, N., L. Trowbridge, and L. Trowbridge
1972 "Self-concept and socioeconomic status." Child Studies Journal 2: 123–43.
Turner, B. and C. Turner
1974 "Evaluations of women and men among black college students." Sociological Quarterly 15: 442–56.
Valecha, G. and T. Ostrum
1974 "An abbreviated measure of internal/external locus of control." Journal of Personality Assessment 38: 369–76.
White, W. and B. Richmond
1970 "Perception of self and of peers by economically deprived black and advantaged white fifth graders." Perception and Motor Skills 30: 533–34.
Williams, R.
1977 Mutual Accommodation: Ethnic Conflicts and Cooperation. Minneapolis, Minn: University of Minnesota Press.
Wyne, M., K. White, and R. Coop
1974 The Black Self. Englewood Cliffs, N.J.: Prentice-Hall.
Yancey, W., L. Rigsby, and J. McCarthy
1972 "Social position and self-evaluation: the relative importance of race." American Journal of Sociology 78: 338–59.

Reported Magnitude of Self-Misidentification Among Negro Children—Artifact?

Herbert J. Greenwald
Don B. Oppenheim[1]

17

Clark and Clark (1947), in a classic study of racial self-awareness, found that 33 percent of Negro children (39 percent of northern Negro children) said that a white rather than a brown doll looked like them. In Horowitz (1939), misidentifications were 42 percent (which dropped to 17 percent when a more reliable test was used). In Goodman (1946), misidentifications were 60 percent, in Morland (1958), 32 percent, and in Morland (1963), 54 percent. These studies, the Clarks' in particular, have had strong impact. For example, those prior to 1954 played a role in the United States Supreme Court desegregation ruling. The results might also lead psychologists to pursue such mediating factors as "denial of racial identity" and "confused self-image."

However, certain methodological aspects of these studies merit consideration. In the Clark and Clark, Horowitz, and Morland studies, the Negro children were given a choice of only two skin colors (e.g., white versus dark brown). But in the Clarks' study, 80 percent of the light-skinned Negro children misidentified themselves, compared to only 23 percent for medium- and dark-skinned children.

Source: Herbert J. Greenwald and Don B. Oppenheim. "Reported Magnitude of Self-Misidentification Among Negro Children—Artifact?" Journal of Personality and Social Psychology 8 (1968): 49–52.

Perhaps the lighter-skinned children were objectively correct: the white doll actually may have resembled their skin color more than the dark doll. And the Clarks' study, the only one which tabulated responses by Negro children's skin color, did not compare Negroes' responses with those of whites, although some of the later studies did make this comparison.

Perhaps the misidentification results are misleading. In studies employing only two alternatives, the responses of light-skinned Negro children may have been forced artifactually. Moreover, a certain percentage of children in any race may have an erroneous picture of themselves. The authors hoped to clarify these issues.

METHOD

The authors' study followed the Clarks', with six basic changes: (*a*) Three dolls were used, dark brown, mulatto, and white (instead of dark brown and white); (*b*) white children's responses were also obtained; (*c*) all subjects were from the north where misidentification has been found to be greatest; (*d*) the dolls were identical except for skin color (including the hair); (*e*) the questions were more open-ended (e.g., "Is there a doll that . . .?" instead of "Give me the doll that . . ."); (*f*) the investigators were white (the Clarks are Negro).

Subjects and Experimental Procedure

Subjects were 75 nursery school children, 39 Negro and 36 white. Most were 4 or 5 years old, a few were as young as 3. Of the Negro children, 21 were male. 18 were female, and among the white children, 21 were male and 15 were female. Subjects were interviewed in integrated and nonintegrated nursery schools in Manhattan and New Rochelle (a suburb of New York City).

After initial contact with each child at play, the child was brought into a separate play room by the nursery teacher and the friendly contact was continued after the teacher excused herself. The child was asked to point to a doll, clad in diapers, in answer to each question. The first question was, "Is there a doll that you like to play with best?" The other eight questions, which also began, "Is there a doll that . . ." were in sequence: ". . . you don't want to play with?" ". . . is a good doll? ". . . is a bad doll?" ". . . is a nice color?" ". . . is not a nice color?" ". . . looks like a white child?" ". . . looks like a colored child?" and the critical question, ". . . looks like you?" Responses were scored in one of five ways: one, two, all (three) dolls, none of the dolls, or no answer. The last three answers, because they were noncommittal, were tabulated as "evasive." Each experimenter rated the Negro children's skin color independently. Nine Negro children were classified as light-skinned, 16 as medium, and 14 as dark. The Negro children were judged to be from the lower and middle classes, while all the whites appeared to be middle class. Two subjects in different subgroups were reinterviewed to check the reliability of the interview.

RESULTS

Reliability of the Findings

The two experimenters' judgments of Negro children's skin color agreed completely, as did the reinterviews. Judgments about socioeconomic status matched with one exception. The conclusions were similar for boys and girls, and regardless of whether the nursery was or was not integrated. These categories were pooled to aid clarity of presentation.

Responses to the eight preliminary questions (e.g., "Is there a doll that is a good doll?") are given in Table 1. Both Negro and white children rejected the colored dolls. This pattern is perhaps most clearly seen when the eight questions are categorized into four groups as in Table 1: it was the white doll which was preferred for play (68 percent versus 21 percent for the Negro dolls), was thought to be good (69 percent versus 21 percent), and was believed to have a nice color (75 percent versus 20 percent).[2] (These percentages sum to 100 percent when the evasive responses are included.)

TABLE 1

Negro and White Children's Responses to Initial Questions About Racial Dolls, in Percentages*

QUESTION	*DOLL†*	*NEGRO CHILDREN* (*N* = 39)	*WHITE CHILDREN* (*N* = 36)	*CLARKS' RESULTS* (*N* = 253)
Play preference				
1. Doll want to play with best	D	28	22	32
	M	13	4	—
	W	56	63	67
2. Doll don't want to play with	D	14	31	
	M	56	51	
	W	12	4	
Goodness evaluation				
3. Doll that is good	D	35	20	38
	M	15	3	—
	W	50	69	59
4. Doll that is bad	D	21	26	59
	M	59	51	—
	W	10	3	17
Color preference				
5. Doll that is a nice color	D	31	18	38
	M	8	8	—
	W	56	71	60
6. Doll that is not a nice color	D	17	37	
	M	62	57	
	W	13	3	
Color accuracy				
7. Doll that looks like a white child	D	5	0	5
	M	3	17	—
	W	90	78	94
8. Doll that looks like a colored child	D	73	54	93
	M	19	33	—
	W	5	6	6

*To aid clarity of presentation evasive answers are not included.
†D = dark brown doll, M = Mulatto doll, W = white doll.

Moreover, just as the other researchers had found, the dolls' skin colors were accurately labeled by the children. Mean accuracy, for the two questions asking which doll was white and which colored, was 89 percent for the colored dolls and

84 percent for the white doll. (The Negro children were slightly more accurate.)[3]

These similarities to the previous researchers' results on the initial questions indicate high reliability over time, despite the intervening 20 years. (The Clarks' data had been gathered in 1939–1941, the present data in 1961.) And the similarity of the Negro and white children's answers suggests internal consistency. Apparently, then, different samples and sample sizes, the difference of an entire generation, the use of different dolls, and also white examiners did not bring about appreciably different answers to these basic questions.

Children's Misidentification of Themselves

However, changes occurred with regard to the critical question—which doll looked like them. As Table 2 shows, only 13 percent of the Negro children misidentified themselves in the present sample, compared to 39 percent among the Clarks' northern Negro children (33 percent in their total sample). As hypothesized, the mulatto doll did play a role in reducing the percentage of misidentifications. As Table 2 indicates, of the light-skinned Negro children only 11 percent misidentified themselves (i.e., reported that the white doll looked like them) in the present study—whereas 80 percent did in the Clarks' study. This reduction of incorrect responses was highly significant ($\chi^2 = 83.37$, $df = 2$, $p < .0001$).[4] The results are similar to Horowitz' (1939) report of only 17 percent misidentifications. Interestingly, the number of misidentifications among medium-colored Negroes remained about the same (25 percent in the present study, 26 percent in the Clarks' study), but dark-skinned Negroes no longer misidentified themselves (compared to 19 percent misidentification in the Clarks' results). Perhaps this was because 50 percent of the dark-skinned Negro children were now able to identify with the mulatto doll.

TABLE 2

Percentage of Negro and White Children's Selections of the Doll which Looked like Them*

RESULTS	*NEGRO CHILDREN BY SKIN COLOR*			*TOTAL NEGRO CHILDREN*	*WHITE CHILDREN*
	LIGHT	*MEDIUM*	*DARK*		
Present study†‡					
Doll color					
Dark brown	22	50	43	41	19
Mulatto	*56*	*19*	*50*	*38*	*25*
White	11	25	0	13	47
N	9	16	14	39	36
Clarks' study					
Doll color					
Dark brown	20	73	81	63	
White	*80*	*26*	*19*	*33*	
N	46	126	79	253	

*To aid clarity of presentation, evasive answers are not included.

†White children misidentified themselves more than Negro children in the present study ($X^2 = 16.29$, $df = 2$, $p < .0001$). But see text for possible artifact. It appears that whites and Negroes may have misidentified themselves to about the same extent.

‡To aid comparison with the Clarks' study, results for the mulatto doll and the white children are italicized.

On the other hand, misidentification among the white children was 44 percent. That is, it appeared whites were more likely than Negroes to make errors when matching themselves with a skin color (see Table 2, $\chi^2 = 16.29$, $df = 2$, $p < .0001$). However, the authors' procedure may have artifactually contributed to the whites' misidentifications. Perhaps the mulatto doll was also an appropriate choice for some white children—those who were darker skinned. Unfortunately, this problem was not anticipated and no measures of white children's skin color were obtained. If the whites' selections of a mulatto doll (25 percent) are viewed as appropriate choices, then the picture changes considerably. The white children's misidentification would drop to 19 percent, resembling Morland's (1963) finding of 14 percent misidentification among white children. While still sizable, a fifth of the sample, this 19 percent of whites' misidentification would not be significantly different from the Negroes' 13 percent misidentification ($\chi^2 = 0.05$, $df = 1$, p nonsignificant).

"Evasive" Responses

"Evasive" responses were tabulated when an answer was noncommittal. However, there wasn't much "evasiveness," 6 percent for Negro children and 8 percent for white children overall. Most evasiveness occurred in response to questions about which doll was preferred for play and which dolls were good or bad, especially when the questions had a negative implication (e.g., "Is there a doll that is bad?") Interestingly, the critical question in this study, subjects' identification of themselves with one of the dolls, did not elicit much evasiveness. Perhaps this question is not as disturbing to subjects as it might appear.

DISCUSSION

These results suggest that Negro children's misidentification in the previous studies, particularly the Clarks', may have been due to an artifact inadvertently introduced by having given Negro subjects a forced choice between two starkly contrasting skin colors, dark brown and white. By including an in-between (mulatto) color, the light-skinned Negro children had a more appropriate color with which to match themselves.[5] Also, white children misidentified themselves to about the same degree as did the Negro children (perhaps even more so). This suggests that a certain amount of misidentification may occur among children regardless of race. Since recent replications of the Clarks' approach (choice of only two skin colors) have continued to produce sizable misidentification among Negro children, it appears likely that the present study's finding of more appropriate self-identification was due to improvement in the experimental design rather than to changes in the phenomenon under investigation. The authors conclude that Negro children do not manifest an unusual tendency to misidentify themselves. However, the similarity of the evaluative responses in all the studies corroborates the unpopularity of Negro's skin color among children.

The mulatto doll received especially adverse evaluations. For example, only 13 percent of the Negro and 4 percent of the white children preferred to play with the mulatto doll, while the dark doll was chosen by 28 percent and 22 percent, respectively (see Table 1). Similar responses occurred for the "goodness" and color-preference questions. Perhaps the doll's color, light grayish-brown (see Footnote 2), was a factor. If so, the evaluative responses should be interpreted with caution, although both the color accuracy and self-identification responses for the mulatto doll seemed appropriate.

Two fundamental methodological issues were interestingly illustrated in this study: the striking misinterpretations which can arise when (*a*) subjects' response range is restricted, and (*b*) no base line is available with which to compare the results. In the first instance, providing a more continuous response range improved the precision of subjects' responses. And in the second instance, the Clarks' implicit independent variable (subjects' race) had a "missing level" (white children). With inclusion of the latter for comparison a clearer perspective emerged for viewing both the direction and the magnitude of the Negro children's responses.

NOTES

1 This study was conducted in 1961 when both authors were in Goodwin Watson's social psychology course at Columbia University. They wish to express their appreciation for the assistance given to them by the nurseries and to Abraham Blum, Ralph Rosnow, and Roberta Marmer for their comments on the manuscript. Writing was partially supported by Boston University Grant GRS Ps-145.

2 These figures combine both Negro and white children's responses. Negro children's preference for white dolls was further corroborated by the difficulty in locating Negro dolls in the highly populated Negro areas of New York City. And only a few doll manufacturers were found who made both Negro and white dolls. None manufactured a doll of mulatto color. Three all-plastic dolls from the same mold were purchased, two white and one dark brown. One white doll was painted a "mulatto color" by a doll hospital. Then each doll was painted to be identical to each other except for body skin color. The nonfactory-produced color of the mulatto doll, light grayish-brown, may have affected subjects' responses (see discussion).

3 Westie's (1964, p. 992) hypothesis that Negro children may have preferred the white doll because of greater familiarity with it could not be checked with the present data since Negro dolls were still relatively uncommon (see Footnote 2). Nor could a second hypothesis be checked, that preschool children may not be able to understand the term, "Negro," since the present study used the term "colored doll." However, the Clarks' (1947, p. 172) data indicated that the majority of Negro children as young as 3 years were able to correctly identify the "Negro doll."

4 If the single light-skinned Negro child who identified himself with the white doll was objectively correct, then the overall misidentification among Negroes would be only 10 percent. Some of the Negro and white children's misidentification was due to inaccurate labeling of the skin colors.

5 It seems reasonable to expect a larger number of light-skinned Negroes in the north, through intermarriage. This may explain why the Clarks found more identification with the white doll among Negro children in the north (39 percent overall) than in the south (29 percent overall).

REFERENCES

Clark, K. B. and M. P. Clark
1947 "Racial identification and preference in Negro children." Pp. 169–78 in T. M. Newcomb and E. L. Hartley (eds.), Readings in Social Psychology. New York: Holt.

Goodman, M. E.
1946 "Evidence concerning the genesis of interracial attitudes." American Anthropologist 48: 624–30.
Horowitz, R.
1939 "Racial aspects of self-identification in nursery school children." Journal of Psychology 7: 91–99.
Morland, J. K.
1958 "Racial recognition by nursery school children in Lynchburg, Virginia." Social Forces 37: 132–37.
1963 "Racial self-identification: a study of nursery school children." American Catholic Sociological Review 24: 231–42.
Westie, F. R.
1964 "Race and ethnic relations." Pp. 576–618 in R. E. L. Faris (ed)., Handbook of Modern Sociology. Chicago: Rand McNally.

Sex Differences in the Self-Concept in Adolescence

Florence R. Rosenberg
Roberta G. Simmons

18

At the present time, there is much discussion and controversy regarding the status and role of women in our society. It is acknowledged that men and women are expected to perform different functions in the society. Some believe physiological differences "naturally" adapt the sexes to these different roles. Many social scientists, however, assert that it is differential socialization patterns, existing from the earliest years, that guide males and females in different directions. Women's Liberation groups argue that women are educated to want to fulfill traditional women's roles—that society molds their attitudes, values, and self-concept toward family-oriented goals. . . .

The solutions recommended have been two-fold: One is to change society's attitudes toward women, the other to change women's attitudes toward themselves. It is a major objective of the consciousness-raising ideology to change women's self-concepts as an important step on the road to equality. Hence, the present report focuses on the development and change of certain selected aspects of the self-concept among boys and girls.

By and large, self-concept research has overwhelmingly focused on global self-esteem, investigating those factors contributing to a general positive or negative attitude toward the self. But there is another dimension of the self-concept which

Source: Florence R. Rosenberg and Roberta G. Simmons, "Sex Differences in the Self-Concept in Adolescence." Sex Roles: A Journal of Research 1 (1975): 147–59.

also merits attention but has been neglected. This is the dimension of the *salience* of the self, i.e., the degree to which the self as an object moves to the top of the mind, to the forefront of attention. In more familiar terminology, this is the dimension of *self-consciousness*.

It may reasonably be contended that the self is always in the forefront of consciousness, that it is a condition of communication and of action. As Mead (1934) observed, the process of communication requires us to take the role of the other, to see ourselves from his standpoint; we thereby become an object of perception and reflection to ourselves. Furthermore, any situation in which the individual is engaged requires him to assess himself as an actor in that situation before he is able to adopt any rational plan of action. Hence, while it is easy to recognize that at one time or another we may be more or less conscious of the President, or China, or the stock market, it may be difficult to imagine a time when, once a self-concept is formed and crystallized, we are not highly conscious of ourselves.

Yet differing degrees of self-consciousness are also matters of immediate experience. If called upon to address a group, we may be keenly conscious of how we look, whether our dress is suitable, or whether our words convey the impression or the personality we wish to project; in such a situation, we are intensely aware of ourselves as objects, for we see ourselves from the standpoints of others. On other occasions, however, we appear to forget about ourselves—in a play, in a game, in a task, in listening to music; the self is not in the forefront of attention. Thus, instead of solely considering whether boys and girls differ in their general positive or negative attitudes toward themselves, we shall focus in this paper on whether the self is more prominent in the mind of one or another sex.

Since the self-concept evolves through social interaction, it is largely the product of the socialization process (although there may be some innate factors involved). Our interest then will be developmental—to see whether changes occur among boys and girls as they grow older, and, if so, which and when.

METHOD

The data for this analysis were collected as part of a larger cross-sectional study of the development of self-image among children from grades 3 to 12 (Rosenberg & Simmons, 1972). Baltimore, Maryland, was chosen as a typical large metropolis for the site of the study. A random sample of 2,625 pupils distributed among 25 schools was drawn from the population of third- to twelfth-grade pupils in Baltimore.

How do boys and girls differ in the development of self-esteem and self-consciousness over time? This is the question to which we now turn.

RESULTS

Overall, the data show that, while girls in this sample are somewhat more likely than boys to have low self-esteem (a 5 percent difference), they are considerably more likely to have high self-consciousness (11 percent difference). Of special interest, however, is the pattern of change over time. While self-*esteem* differences of boys and girls show change over the years, there is a sharper divergence in self-*consciousness* among boys and girls. As Table 1 shows, in the 8–11 age group, the sex differences in self-consciousness are only 2 percent; but by the age of 15 or older, the differences have risen to 24 percent; at this point, nearly twice as many girls as boys are highly self-conscious.

TABLE 1

Self-Esteem and Self-Consciousness of Boys and Girls, by Age

	AGE					
	8–11		*12–14*		*15+*	
	BOYS	*GIRLS*	*BOYS*	*GIRLS*	*BOYS*	*GIRLS*
Percent low self-esteem	23	27	26	32	19	26
N =	(362)	(421)	(305)	(320)	(259)	(226)
Percent high self-consciousness	17	19	29	41*	21	45†
N =	(362)	(421)	(307)	(327)	(266)	(235)

* $p < .01$.
† $p < .001$.

The most striking finding thus appears to be the very sharp increase in self-consciousness in early adolescence among girls. Both sexes, to be sure, show an increase in self-consciousness at this age, and one might explain this finding as indicating that they have reached the Piagetian (1932/1948) stage of reciprocity and cooperation; obliged to take the viewpoint of others into account, they may become more self-aware. What Piaget never mentions, however, but what is clearly revealed here, is that the rise in self-consciousness in early adolescence is much sharper among girls than among boys. Furthermore, while self-consciousness declines among boys in later adolescence, it continues to rise modestly among girls.

As children, then, boys and girls show little difference in terms of taking the role of the other or showing concern for interpersonal response, but in early adolescence a sharp difference appears and is enhanced over time. This suggests that girls become much more "other-directed" (Riesman, Denney, & Glazer, 1950) or "people-oriented" (Rosenberg, 1957) than boys. Their self-consciousness may derive from the fact that they are much more concerned with others' attitudes toward them and thus tend to see themselves through the eyes of others. Is there any evidence to indicate a sharp divergence in social values in early adolescence? Do girls become more people-oriented, more concerned with others' attitudes toward them at this stage?

One obvious reflection of this orientation would be the desire to be well liked. This dimension was tapped by asking respondents how much they cared about what their classmates thought of them; what their friends thought of them; whether they preferred to be "able to do things for yourself, well liked, or the best in the things you do"; and how important their close groups of friends were to them. Table 2 shows that, among younger children, boys and girls are essentially equal on this "care about being well liked" score; in early adolescence, however, a sex gap develops. Fewer boys and more girls value being well liked, and this difference is maintained in later adolescence. The same general pattern obtains in answer to the question, "Do you ever worry about what other people think of you?" (See Table 2.) Adolescent girls thus appear to be relatively more concerned with others' reactions to them and more desirous of being well liked.

TABLE 2

Boys' and Girls' Concern with Opinions of Others, by Age

	AGE					
	8–11		*12–14*		*15+*	
CONCERN WITH OTHERS' OPINIONS	*BOYS*	*GIRLS*	*BOYS*	*GIRLS*	*BOYS*	*GIRLS*
Percent high on "care about being well liked" score	20	21	15	23*	18	25
$N =$	(326)	(385)	(286)	(298)	(236)	(210)
Percent "worry about what other people think of you"	41	43	58	69*	65	75
$N =$	(355)	(414)	(303)	(326)	(263)	(238)

*$p < .01$.

A second indicator of girls' other-directedness at this stage is their concern with avoiding negative reactions from others by acting in ways instrumental to minimizing social unpleasantness. This is reflected in responses to the following two questions:

A kid told me: "I smile even when I'm not happy." How often do you smile when you're not happy?

A kid told me: "I act nice even to people I don't like." How often do you act nice even to people you don't like?

Both these items reflect a desire to inhibit expression of negative feelings (i.e., unhappiness, hostility) in the interests of promoting interpersonal harmony. Table 3 indicates that in both cases a sex gap either originates or increases in adolescence.

TABLE 3

Boys' and Girls' Control of Negative Interpersonal Behavior, by Age

	AGE					
	8–11		*12–14*		*15+*	
CONTROL OF NEGATIVE INTERPERSONAL BEHAVIOR	*BOYS*	*GIRLS*	*BOYS*	*GIRLS*	*BOYS*	*GIRLS*
Percent smile (often) when not happy	16	16	13	13	13	20†
$N =$	(376)	(436)	(312)	(334)	(271)	(240)
Percent act nice (often) to people don't like	37	46*	29	37*	28	44†
$N =$	(377)	(438)	(312)	(334)	(273)	(239)

*$p < .01$.
†$p < .001$.

With regard to "smiling when not happy," there is no sex difference until later adolescence, when a greater proportion of girls answer "often." In the case of "acting nice to people you don't like," more girls claim to do so at every age, although the sex difference increases from 9 percent for the 8-11 age group to 16 percent in later adolescence.

Generally speaking, certain personal qualities are calculated to elicit warm or approving responses from others. Being a succorant person usually has this effect. We thus asked these respondents: "How much do you care about how helpful you are?" While the sex difference in this regard is modest in childhood and early adolescence, by late adolescence the sex gap has widened to 14 percent.

It may be asked whether the differences in interpersonal orientations appearing in adolescence are simply a matter of social norms lacking in affect—"That's the way girls are supposed to behave" or "That's what girls are supposed to worry about"—or whether they enter more deeply into the individual's motivational system. In the latter case, of course, such orientations would be much more difficult to change. According to our data, it turns out, the emotional involvement of girls in harmonious interpersonal relations is strong, for interpersonal attacks are experienced as unusually threatening and painful.

Consider the following questions in our study:

When someone blames you for something you have done wrong, does that bother you very much, some, or not much?

When someone gets angry at you, do you get very upset, pretty upset, or not upset?

When someone laughs at you, do your feelings get hurt very easily, pretty easily, or not very easily?

Do your feelings get hurt very easily, pretty easily, or not very easily?

The last three items turned out to form a Guttman scale of "Vulnerability to Interpersonal Threat," with a 96 percent coefficient of reproducibility and 88 percent coefficient of scalability. Table 4 compares boys and girls in each age group with regard to each item and the total scale. In almost every instance, girls appear more upset, hurt, or disturbed by negative behavior from others. This tendency, it may be noted, does appear initially in childhood, but it is either maintained or strengthened in adolescence.[1] This is especially the case when we look at the Vulnerability Scale. Table 4 shows that, among 8 to 11-year-olds, 17 percent more girls are highly sensitive and this sex difference increases to 22 percent in later adolescence. Whether or not this sex difference reflects life experience (i.e., girls, in fact, may experience more hurt), it is manifest in relatively higher vulnerability among girls.

But if adolescent girls are more eager to be liked, more desirous of making a favorable impression on others, the question remains: *Are* they more well liked, more popular, more interpersonally successful? While we lack data on the girls' actual interpersonal success, we do have information on their *perception* of others' attitudes toward them. This is reflected in several indicators:

How easy to get along with are you? . . . What if your best friend wanted to tell someone all about you. What type of person would your best friend say you were? [Coded positive, mixed, or negative.]

TABLE 4
Interpersonal Vulnerability of Boys and Girls, by Age

	AGE					
	8–11		12–14		15+	
	BOYS	GIRLS	BOYS	GIRLS	BOYS	GIRLS
Percent very upset if someone gets angry	28	34	17	28*	14	33*
N =	(373)	(435)	(307)	(333)	(267)	(236)
Percent bothered when someone blames you	36	30	37	44	38	46
N =	(378)	(436)	(311)	(333)	(272)	(240)
Percent feelings hurt when laughed at	15	25*	9	22*	6	17*
N =	(378)	(438)	(311)	(334)	(272)	(240)
Percent feelings hurt very easily	16	34*	15	37*	14	33*
N =	(375)	(436)	(311)	(334)	(270)	(238)
Percent high vulnerability score	20	37*	15	32*	12	34*
N =	(372)	(434)	(305)	(333)	(265)	(236)

*$p < .001$.

In addition, a score of "perceived attitudes of others," based on the respondent's perception of how much boys liked him, how much girls liked him, and what the kids in his class thought of him, was constructed.

With regard to these three indicators, Table 5 indicates very minor sex differences at any age. Boys and girls attribute equally favorable attitudes toward themselves by others.

In sum, our data suggest that the adolescent girl is considerably more sensitive than the boy to others' opinions. The adolescent girl appears to be more self-

TABLE 5
Perceived Interpersonal Success of Boys and Girls, by Age

	AGE					
	8–11		12–14		15+	
	BOYS	GIRLS	BOYS	GIRLS	BOYS	GIRLS
Percent "very easy to get along with	54	48	41	44	46	47
N =	(360)	(425)	(297)	(327)	(254)	(221)
Percent friends' attitude "very favorable"	80	78	82	75	83	83
N =	(292)	(351)	(258)	(274)	(232)	(216)
Percent well liked on estimate of popularity	80	86	88	90	93	92
N =	(307)	(345)	(276)	(280)	(251)	(217)

conscious (i.e., concerned with the self in social situations), more concerned with others' opinions of her, more eager to avoid behavior eliciting negative reactions, and more vulnerable to others' negative reactions. In every case, the difference between boys and girls either emerges or grows stronger during the adolescent period.

Why these motivations? There is little in the biological state of puberty to arouse them. Rather, they appear to be the products of the socialization process directed toward the filling of socially defined sex roles. In the occupational realm, research has shown that girls, even those of unusual education and ability, are strikingly more disposed toward what have been called "people-oriented" occupations (e.g., social work, teaching, or nursing) while men's attention is directed either toward self-expression and the use of abilities or toward extrinsic rewards, such as money, prestige, and security (Rosenberg, 1957). Similarly, girls expect family life but boys expect occupation to yield the major life satisfaction. The people-orientedness of girls is thus functional to the *current* social distribution of sex roles. If these social roles were to be redefined, presumably the social indoctrination regarding the importance of these interpersonal values would change.

But if society teaches girls to stake themselves on making an agreeable impression on others, on what do boys stake themselves? As one would expect, on achievement and success. Those respondents with occupational aspirations were asked: "How good do you *want* to be at your job? Do you want to be at the very top, better than most, about in the middle, or below the middle?" [The data show] that even at an early age the boys are somewhat more likely to "want to be at the very top," and this difference increases materially in early adolescence. Incidentally, even at an early age girls are more likely to expect to be no better than average occupationally, and this difference is again most striking in early adolescence. . . .

SUMMARY AND DISCUSSION

While many recent discussions have emphasized the importance of changing women's self-concepts, empirical research on this subject is rare. The brunt of the argument is that women are socialized to feel inferior and thus have lower self-esteem. While the present study does show girls to have somewhat lower self-esteem than boys, the differences are quite modest in comparison to sex differences in self-consciousness. In other words, the self-concept contains a multiplicity of components and can be characterized in terms of numerous dimensions.[2] One of these is the salience of the self, reflected in self-consciousness. Although younger boys and girls differ little in their sensitivity to the impression they are making on other people, a sharp difference in such self-awareness emerges in early adolescence and is maintained in later adolescence.

In general, our data suggest that early adolescence is accompanied by a sharp rise in "people-orientedness" among girls. Relative to boys, quite suddenly girls become very worried about what other people think of them, whether they are pleasing and helpful to people. Relative to boys, girls are much more fearful of displeasing people; they become more vulnerable than boys to criticism or disapproval. Our analysis indicates that this sharp increase in people-orientedness of female adolescents helps to account for their higher level of self-consciousness; they must see themselves through the eyes of others in order to achieve the desired goals. With regard to the data, even where adolescent sex differences are not statistically significant, they follow a consistent trend—it is this *pattern* which is sociologically significant.

Obviously, this is a consequence of sex role socialization. As children, boys and girls differ little in their self-consciousness and concern with the opinions of others. In early adolescence, however, the attention of girls seems to turn toward being pleasing to others while that of boys focuses on accomplishment and achievement. Among respondents who expect to have jobs, boys are more eager to be "at the very top," girls are more satisfied to be "in the middle." And when confronted squarely with a choice, there is a stronger tendency for girls to most want to be "well liked," for boys to be "best in things you do" or "successful."

Different dimensions of the self-concept are thus differently affected by the socialization process. Sex differences in self-esteem in adolescence are smaller than sex differences in self-consciousness. Our data offer some indication of why this should be so. It is generally assumed, for example, that women are socially defined as less competent, rational, and organized than men, and that as a consequence they have much lower self-esteem. But even if women did internalize this social definition, the conclusion that they have considerably lower self-esteem overlooks James's (1890/1950) seminal insight that self-esteem = success ÷ pretensions. This casts the matter in a very different light. If girls focus on interpersonal success, not occupational achievement, and if they then succeed in the former and fail in the latter, their self-esteem is protected to some extent. According to our data, the girl whose occupational achievement is mediocre will be quite contented with herself, whereas the boy will be more frustrated if he is not near the top. Hence, it is possible for girls' global self-esteem to be reasonably high—close to that of boys—but for her self-consciousness to be considerably greater; and this is what the data in this paper suggest.

NOTES

1 The one exception involves "sensitivity to blame" where 8 to 11-year-old boys are more sensitive; however, this reverses in adolescence and maintains the consistent pattern.

2 The dimensions considered in this paper, of course, do not exhaust the total range of elements or aspects of the self-concept. In current analyses, we are also examining boys' and girls' attitudes toward their sex roles and toward their looks. In addition, racial differences in boys' and girls' self-esteem are under investigation.

REFERENCES

Douvan, E., & J. Adelson
1966 The Adolescent Experience. New York: John Wiley & Sons.
Horney, K.
1945 Our Inner Conflicts. New York: Norton.
1950 Neurosis and Human Growth. New York: Dover.

James, W.
1950 The Principles of Psychology. New York: Dover. (Originally published, 1890.)
Mead, G. H.
1934 Mind, Self and Society. Chicago: University of Chicago Press.
Piaget, J.
1948 The Moral Judgment of the Child. Trans. by M. Gabain. Glencoe: Free Press. (Originally published, 1932.)
Riesman, D., R. Denney, and N. Glazer
1950 The Lonely Crowd. New Haven: Yale University Press.
Rosenberg, M.
1957 Occupations and Values. Glencoe: Free Press.
1965 Society and the Adolescent Self-Image. Princeton: Princeton University Press.
Rosenberg, M. and R. G. Simmons
1972 Black and White Self-Esteem: The Urban School Child. Rose Monograph Series. Washington, D.C.: American Sociological Association.

Acquisition and Significance of Sex Typing and Sex Role Identity

Jerome Kagan

19

The concept of sex role and its close relatives, sex typing and sex role identification, have achieved much prominence during the past decade. It is surprising, however, that this concept has been so tardy in acquiring theoretical popularity among psychologists. For the behavioral differences between the sexes are public and have an ancient and transcultural heritage. Sociology and anthropology have not been as neglectful of this concept, for over a quarter of a century ago Linton (1936) wrote: "The division and ascription of statuses with relation to sex seems to be basic in all social systems. All societies prescribe different attitudes and activities to men and women." One reason the concept of sex role has played a subordinate theoretical role rests with the history of theory development in psychology. The two major attempts to construct comprehensive schemes for understanding behavior—behavioral and psychoanalytic theory—placed needs at the center of their systems and made strivings for the goals of food, protection from pain, love, security, aggression, sex, and dependency the primary determinants of behavior. These needs are common to both sexes and neither theory directed attention to sex differences in the hierarchy of patterning of these needs. Moreover, an emphasis on needs or motives that require the attainment of external goals to

Source: Jerome Kagan. "Acquisition and Significance of Sex Typing and Sex Role Identity," in M. Hoffman and L. Hoffman (eds.), Review of Child Development Research. Volume 1, pp. 137–65.

satisfy them camouflaged a more fundamental human motive—the desire to make one's behavior conform to a previously acquired standard.

The motive to match one's behavior to an internal standard—to make one's behavior conform to a standard of masculinity, let us say—differs in two fundamental ways from the traditional description of the motivational process associated with aggression, dependency, or sexuality. The strength of the former set of motives does not wax or wane to the degree that is characteristic of sexual or aggressive motivation. The arousal of sexual or aggressive motives is dependent, in large measure, on external provocations. The desire to make one's behavior conform to a standard of masculinity, however, typically does not drift from negligible strength to intense values in different situations or over short periods of time. Further, receipt of whatever reward maintains the tendency to appear masculine does not weaken the motive underlying the response. The performance of masculine acts does not weaken or destroy temporarily the desire to continue such behavior. For sex and aggression, on the other hand, consummation often attenuates the strength of the motive for a period of time.

We shall use the word *standard* to refer to a correlated set of responses (that is, overt acts, attitudes, wishes, or feelings) and external attributes that the individual views as desirable to possess. It is assumed that the cluster of responses and attributes that defines the standard acquires its desirability through three processes: (a) identification with models who possess the cluster, (b) expectation of affection and acceptance for possession of the trait cluster, and (c) expectation that possession of the cluster will prevent social rejection. Once the standard has been acquired, it acts as an internal judge to whom decisions about the initiation of behavior or maintenance of an attitude are referred for evaluation. Thus the probability of a particular action depends, in part, upon the child's standards surrounding the action. It is obvious that children acquire standards for a variety of responses—cleanliness, obedience, honesty, mastery of academic subjects, coherence of speech, and maturity of judgment. Many of these standards are of approximately equal salience for boys and girls. However, a sex role standard dictates the adoption of different responses for boys and girls. The significance of a sex role standard rests with its governing influence on the initiation of a broad band of behaviors.

WHAT IS A SEX ROLE STANDARD?

A sex role standard refers to a learned association between selected attributes, behaviors, and attitudes, on the one hand, and the concepts male and female, on the other. In effect, a sex role standard summarizes the culturally approved characteristics for males and females. During the period three to seven years of age, the child gradually realizes that people fall into one of two related language categories—boys or girls, men or women, fathers or mothers. The early discrimination of social objects into these distinct classes is facilitated by the presence of a variety of clearly discriminable cues, including dress, bodily form and proportion, strength, distribution of hair, depth of voice, posture at the toilet, modal interactive behavior with a child, and characteristic behavior in the kitchen, the garage, or the backyard. Existing empirical evidence clearly indicates that the school-age child has acquired the concepts male and female (Hartup and Zook,

1960; Kagan, Hosken, and Watson, 1961) and this assumption is fundamental for the theoretical discussions that appear later in this essay.

Core Attributes of Masculinity and Femininity

The characteristics that define the concepts male and female can be divided into primary and secondary, depending on the communality of agreement among members of the culture. Both primary and secondary sex role characteristics fall into one of three classes: (a) physical attributes, (b) overt behaviors, (c) feelings, attitudes, motives, and beliefs (that is, covert attributes).

Although the characteristics that are differentially associated with maleness and femaleness among most adults in our culture are not clearly crystallized in the mind of a six-year-old, there is considerable overlap between the standards of the first grader and those of the adult. Let us consider these sex-type characteristics and note where there appear to be important developmental changes.

Physical Attributes

Analysis of the public media's representation of males and females and the result of studies of preadolescent and adolescent youngsters reveal that American girls regard an attractive face, hairless body, a small frame, and moderate-sized breasts as the most desirable characteristics for a girl; boys regard height, large muscle mass, and facial and bodily hair as the most desirable physical characteristics for boys. A girl should be pretty and small; boys, large and strong (Cobb, 1954; Frazier and Lisonbee, 1950; Harris, 1959; Jersild, 1952; Nash, 1958). For the child eight to ten years of age, it appears that an attractive face is a primary sex-typed attribute for girls; a tall, muscular physique primary for boys (Cobb, 1954).

Overt Behaviors

The culture's differential standards regarding the behavioral face to be exposed to the public are not as clearly delineated as the standards for physical attributes, but these rules are strongly felt none the less. One of the primary classes of sex-typed behavior involves aggression. The standard requires inhibition of verbal and physical aggression among girls and women; but gives boys and men license—and even encouragement—to express aggression when attacked, threatened, or dominated by another male. We would expect, therefore, more aggressive behavior from males and the data support this expectation. Indeed, it is difficult to find a sound study of preschool or school-age children in which aggressive behavior was not more frequent among boys than among girls (Bandura, 1962; Bandura, Ross, and Ross, 1961; Dawe, 1934; Hattwick, 1937; Maccoby and Wilson, 1957; Muste and Sharpe, 1947). This difference is also present in the make-believe themes children tell to dolls or to pictures (Bach, 1945; Pintler, Phillips, and Sears, 1946; P. S. Sears, 1951; Whitehouse, 1949), and in the child's differential perception of adult males and females. If children are asked which parent is more dangerous or more punitive (that is, aggressive), both boys and girls agree that the father is more aggressive than the mother (Emmerich, 1959; Kagan, 1956; Kagan and Lemkin, 1960; Kagan, Hosken, and Watson, 1961). The association between maleness and aggression has also been demonstrated in a study in which stimuli symbolic of aggression are used; for example, a tiger versus a rabbit, an alligator versus a bird (Kagan, Hosken, and Watson, 1961). Moreover, adults also regard men as more aggressive that women (Bennett and Cohen, 1959; Jenkins and Russell, 1958), and parents hold differential standards regarding aggression for their children, for they expect more overt aggression from boys than from girls (Kohn, 1959; Sears, Maccoby, and Levin,1957).

A second class of sex-typed behavior includes the correlated trio of dependency, passivity, and conformity. Girls are allowed greater license to express these behaviors; whereas boys and men are pressured to inhibit them. The data on sex differences in passivity and dependency are less consistent than those for aggression, but there are more studies reporting greater dependency, conformity, and social passivity for females than for males at all ages (Beller and Turner, unpublished; Crutchfield, 1955; Hovland and Janis,1959; Kagan and Moss, 1962; Lindzey and Goldberg, 1953; McCandless, Bilous, and Bennett, 1961; Sanford et al., 1943; Sears et al., 1953; Siegel et al., 1959). Moreover, affiliative and nurturant behaviors are generally regarded as more appropriate for females than for males, and a majority of investigations of overt behavior or story-telling responses reveal more frequent occurrence of affiliative and nurturant behavior among girls, and greater preoccupation with people and harmonious interpersonal relations among girls than among boys (Goodenough, 1957; Hildreth, 1945; Honzik, 1951; Lansky et al., 1961; Terman and Miles, 1936; Whitehouse, 1949; Winker, 1949).

Correspondingly, children view women as more nurturant than men, and adult women see themselves as more nurturant than their male counterparts (Bennett and Cohen, 1959). The circle is complete with both children and adults expecting and receiving more dependence, passivity, and nurturance from females, more aggression from males.

Additional sets of sex-typed responses include the development of skill and interest in gross motor and mechanical tasks for boys (Tyler, 1947; Kagan and Moss, 1962) and an interest in clothes, dolls, and babies for girls (Tyler, 1947; Honzik, 1951).

During the adolescent and early adult years, some refined derivatives of these sex-typed patterns are added to the sex role standard. For females, these include submissiveness with males, inhibition of overt signs of sexual desire, and cultivation of domestic skills (Douvan and Kaye, 1957; Harris, 1959). For males, independence, interpersonal dominance with men and women, initiation of sexual behavior, sexual conquests, and acquisition of money and power become critical sex-typed requirements (Bennett and Cohen, 1959; Child, Potter, and Levine, 1946; Douvan and Kaye, 1957; Harris, 1959; Jenkins and Russell, 1958; Kagan and Moss, 1962; Tuddenham, 1951; Walters, Pearce, and Dahms, 1957).

Game Choices as an Index of Sex-Typed Standards for Behavior

The games, toys, and fantasy heroes chosen by young children corroborate the behavioral standards outlined above. The large body of research on children's game and toy preferences indicates that boys choose objects related to sports, machines, aggression, speed, and power roles; whereas the girls select games and objects associated with the kitchen and home, babies, personal attractiveness, and fantasy roles in which they have a subordinate relation to a male (nurse, secretary). Thus knives, boats, planes, trucks and cement mixers are regarded by school children as masculine; dolls, cribs, dishes, and nurses' equipment are regarded as feminine (Foster, 1930; Honzik,1951; Rosenberg and Sutton-Smith, 1960; Vance and McCall, 1934).

Many investigators have made up their own tests to assess sex-typed game preferences, and several of these instruments have become popular. The "IT" test (Brown, 1957) presents the child with a figure (the IT), which is supposed to be ambiguous with respect to sex, and a variety of toys and objects. The child is usually asked to select the object or activity the IT figure prefers. It is assumed that the child's choices reflect his personal preferences.

The major results from studies using these kinds of instruments indicate that boys show an increasing preference for sex appropriate games with age. As early as three, boys are aware of some of the activities and objects that our culture regards as masculine. Among girls, however, preferences are more variable up to nine or ten years of age. Many girls between three and ten years of age show a strong preference for masculine games, activities, and objects; whereas, it is unusual to find many boys who prefer feminine activities during this period. Thus five-year-old boys show a clearer preference for masculine toys than girls show for feminine toys (Brown, 1957; Hartup and Zook, 1960). This difference in game preferences is matched by a relatively greater frequency of girls stating a desire to be a boy or wanting to be a daddy rather than a mommy when they grow up (Brown, 1957).

Since our culture assigns greater freedom, power, and value to the male role, it is understandable that the girl might wish for the more attractive male role. This devaluation of the female role is probably one reason that the typical woman regards herself as less adequate and more fearful than most men (Bennett and Cohen, 1959).

Rosenberg and Sutton-Smith (1960) tested children in Grades 4, 5, and 6 for game preferences. The results suggest that in the year 1960 girls were more masculine in their game choices than they had been 30 years earlier. It may be that the wall separating male and female recreational activities is cracking and some of the traditional differences in sex-typed game choices may be undergoing some change.

Finally, it should be noted that there are social class differences in the game choices of children. Rabban (1950) asked children (age three to eight) in two diverse social groups (middle- and working-class homes) to select the toys they liked the best. The choices of lower-class boys and girls conformed more closely to traditional sex-typed standards than the choices of middle-class children, suggesting that the differentiation of sex roles is sharper in lower-class families. This finding agrees with the fact that lower-class mothers encourage sex typing more consistently than middle-class mothers (Kohn, 1959). Moreover, the difference in sex typing between the classes is greatest for girls (Rabban, 1950). Apparently the middle-class girl, unlike the middle-class boy, is much freer to express an interest in toys and activities of the opposite sex. This finding agrees with the fact that, among girls, there is a positive correlation between the educational level of the family and involvement in masculine activities (Kagan and Moss, 1962).

Feelings, Attitudes, Motives, and Wishes

The cluster of covert attributes that are closely linked to the concept of female in our culture include the ability to gratify a love object and the ability to elicit sexual arousal in a male; the desire to be a wife and mother and the correlated desires to give nurturance to one's child and affection to a love object; and the capacity for emotion. For males, the primary covert attributes include a pragmatic attitude, ability to gratify a love object, suppression of fear, and a capacity to control expression of strong emotion in time of stress (Bennett and Cohen, 1959; Jenkins and Russell, 1958; Parsons, 1955). There are fewer systematic data in support of these covert attributes than there are for the overt behaviors listed earlier. However, clinical studies (Bieber et al., 1962) and self-ratings by adults (Bennett and Cohen, 1959) agree with these statements.

In sum, females are supposed to inhibit aggression and open display of sexual urges, to be passive with men, to be nurturant to others, to cultivate attractiveness, and to maintain an affective, socially poised, and friendly posture with others. Males are urged to be aggressive in face of attack, independent in problem situations, sexually aggressive, in control of regressive urges, and suppressive of strong emotion, especially anxiety. Parsons' (1955) dichotomy of masculine and feminine roles into instrumental versus expressive is consistent with the attributes we have assigned to the categories masculine and feminine.

This list may strike readers as old fashioned or unrealistically traditional, and not representative of contemporary values. Existing data on children indicate that despite a common adult assumption that sex role standards are changing at a rapid rate, children continue to believe that aggression, dominance, and independence are more appropriate for males; passivity, nurturance and affect more appropriate for females (Parsons, 1948; Hartley, 1960a). Hartley writes:

> *In response to those who are overly concerned about the effect of apparent recent sex role changes . . . from the child's point of view, there are no changes; he sees only the picture as it appears in his time and this picture . . . shows remarkably little change from traditional values (p. 91).*

Moreover, analysis of the areas in which female role changes have occurred reveals that increased license for sexual provocation and work outside the home are the standards that have undergone the most dramatic alteration. The decreased anxiety and inhibition associated with making one's self sexually attractive to males does not contradict—and, in fact, supports—the contention that the ability to attract and arouse a male sexually is a pivotal sex-typed attribute for the female. Parsons writes:

> *Emancipation . . . means primarily emancipation from traditional and conventional restrictions on the free expression of sexual attraction and impulses, but in a direction which tends to segregate the element of sexual interest . . . and in so doing tends to emphasize the segregation of the sex roles . . . the feminine glamour pattern has appeared as an offset to masculine occupational status (1948, p. 275).*

The increased frequency of working women is predominantly in positions subordinate to males. Moreover, a frequent motivation for this work is to increase the family income. In effect, the work is often viewed as a reflection of a nurturant attitude toward the family, for the increased income is regarded as a way of providing more material goods for the children (Hartley, 1960b).

The fact that the proportion of women in professional and technical occupations has decreased during the last quarter-century (Nye and Hoffman, 1963) suggests that the increasing number of working women does not necessarily reflect a growing tendency for females to assume the masculine role in our society. Moreover, it appears that many working mothers feel guilty about leaving their children to caretakers while they work. They feel they are not "being good mothers." The presence of this anxiety supports the notion that the typical woman believes that a nurturant attitude toward the children is a more essential component of her femininity than a career skill (Hartley, 1960b).

SEX ROLE IDENTITY

We have defined sex role standards as a publicly shared belief regarding the appropriate characteristics for males and females. But the abstracted concept of the ideal male or female, as viewed by the culture, is to be distinguished from a particular individual's conceptualization of his own degree of masculinity or femininity. Such a conceptualization is determined, in part, by the degree to which an individual believes he possesses sex-typed traits. *The degree to which an individual regards himself as masculine or feminine will be called his sex role identity*. This belief is but one component of a complex interlocking set of beliefs the individual holds about himself. The complete set of attitudes is generally regarded as a self-concept or self-identity. Although the individual's assessment of his masculinity or femininity comprises only one aspect of his identity, it is mandatory that the individual assign himself a value on this dimension. Unlike some specialized attributes (for example, knowledge of the habits of birds, ability to prune trees), most individuals cannot declare an indifference to their sex role identity.

The degree of match or mismatch between the sex role standards of the culture and an individual's assessment of his own overt and covert attributes provides him with a partial answer to the question, "How masculine (or feminine) am I?" The belief system we call a sex role identity is not completely conscious, and there is an imperfect correlation between possession of standard sex role attributes and the integrity of one's sex role identity. A man who possesses many masculine behaviors may not neccessarily regard himself as highly masculine. But it is probably impossible for a man to possess none of the culturally approved sex-typed attributes and regard himself as highly masculine. Thus possession of some sex-typed traits is necessary but not sufficient for a firm sex role identity.

Unfortunately, there is little empirical information that deals with the mode of establishment of a child's sex role identity. We are forced, therefore, to speculate on this issue and the following suggestions should be regarded as conjecture.

The major determinants of sex role identity for the young child include (*a*) perceptions of similarity to parents, and (*b*) degree to which the child adopts the games, and masters the skills that are traditionally encouraged for his sex. The child who perceives major elements of similarity to the parent of the same sex will initially regard himself as masculine (or feminine), for the parents are the original prototypes of masculinity and femininity for the young child. However, when the child enters school, he comes into direct contact with peers and the wider culture's definition of the sex roles. As a consequence of this confrontation, the child gradually is forced to accommodate his definition of maleness and femaleness to the values of this broader community.

A second basic assumption in this essay (the first was that the young child was clearly aware of the sex roles) is that the child wishes to believe that his actions, attitudes, and affects are congruent with the sex role standard. This standard is a condensation of characteristics perceived in the same-sexed parent together with the culture's prescriptive rules for males and females. There will be a core of communality in this concept for all persons in the culture, but there will be slight differences from child to child, depending on the particular family and subcultural milieu in which he is reared.

ACQUISITION OF SEX ROLE IDENTITY AND SEX ROLE STANDARDS

There are two distinct response classes whose acquisition must be explained; namely, a covert label applied to the self (sex role indentity), and a set of attributes that the culture has labeled as masculine or feminine (sex role standards). There is no need to dwell on the concept of sex role preference (Lynn, 1959) at this point in the discussion. It is acknowledged that some children either resent or experience anxiety over the behaviors that are assigned to their biological sex. But it is assumed that all children have a need to acquire a self-label that matches their biological sex. This assumption is not inconsistent with the fact some adolescents and adults strive to avoid adoption of sex-typed responses because of anxiety over the behaviors that are prescribed for their sex role. These individuals are typically in conflict and are likely to manifest a variety of psychopathological symptoms.

In the discussion that follows we shall not deal with the possible effect of constitutional variables on the adoption of sex-typed characteristics. There is, however, some evidence suggesting that constitutional variables may predispose the male toward activity and dominance; the female toward passivity (DeVore and Jay, in press; Harlow and Zimmerman, 1959; Hebb, 1946).

Acquisition of a Sex Role Identity

There are at least three kinds of experiences that determine the degree to which an individual regards himself as masculine or feminine: (*a*) differential identification with mother, father, parental surrogates, older siblings, and special peers; (*b*) acquisition of the attributes or skills that define masculine or feminine behavior; and (*c*) a perception that other people regard the individual as possessing appropriate sex-typed characteristics. Let us discuss each of these processes in some detail.

Identification as a Base for Sex Role Identity The concept of identification is, to some degree, controversial. There is disagreement as to its usefulness in explaining aspects of human development, and even among those who regard the concept as fruitful there is no unanimity as to definition. Since Freud's original discussion of identification (Freud, 1925) contemporary writers have presented searching analyses of this concept and suggested significant modifications (Bronfenbrenner, 1960; Kagan, 1958; Lynn, 1959; Maccoby, 1959; Mowrer, 1950; Parsons, 1955; Sanford, 1955; R. R. Sears, 1957; Whiting, 1960). A major point of disagreement revolves around the question: "To what events or processes does this term refer?" For the term *identification* has been applied to overt behavior, to a motive system (the need to identify with a model), to the process by which behaviors are acquired, and to a belief about the self. In an earlier paper (Kagan, 1958), the author presented a definition and analysis of identification. We shall summarize this position here with a special reference to sex role identification.

A Definition of Identification An identification is a belief that some of the attributes of a model (parents, siblings, relatives, peers, and so on) belong to the self (Kagan, 1958). If a six-year-old-boy is identified with his father, he necessarily regards himself as possessing some of his father's characteristics, one which is maleness or masculinity. Moreover, if a child is identified with a model, he will behave, to some extent, as it events that occur to the model are occurring to him. If a child is identified with his father, he shares vicariously in the latter's victories and defeats; in his happiness and in his sorrow; in his strengths and in his weaknesses. It has been argued elsewhere that the establishment of an optimally strong identification requires that three conditions be met: (*a*) the model must be perceived as nurturant to the child; (*b*) the model must be perceived as being in command of desired goals, especially power, love from others, and task competence in areas the child regards as important; and (*c*) the child must perceive—before the identification belief begins its growth—some objective bases of similarity in external attributes or psychological properties between himself and the model (Kagan, 1958).

The child's motivation to develop an identification with a model is based on his desire to command the attractive goals possessed by the model. At this point a critical assumption is introduced into the argument. The child assumes that if he possessed some of the external—and more objective—characteristics of the model, he might also possess his desirable psychological properties (for example, power, love from others). In effect, the child behaves as if he believed that objects that appear alike on the outside have similar properties on the inside, and that the greater the external similarity between himself and a model, the greater the possibility that he will possess the model's power, competence, and affection. One of the important consequences of the boy's desire for a strong identification with the father is his attempt to take on the father's characteristics. For each time he successfully imitates a behavior or adopts an attitude of the father he perceives an increased similarity to the latter. This perception of increased similarity strengthens his belief that he possesses some of the father's covert characteristics. One of these covert attributes is the self-label of masculinity. Thus a strong identification with the same-sexed parent at seven years of age facilitates the future establishment of an appropriate sex role identity.

Let us now consider some of the differential consequences attending those parent-child dyads in which one boy identifies with a father who practices traditional masculine behavior; whereas the second boy identifies with a father who does not display sex-typed behavior. We must assume that both fathers are equally nurturant and that each son perceives the same degree of similarity to his father.

The boy with the minimally masculine father will confront the societal standard for masculinity when he enters school. Since his overt behavior will be less sex typed than that of his peers, he will perceive a discrepancy between his actions and those of the "other boys." He will be tempted to conclude that he is not masculine because his behavior does not match that of the male peer group, and because he may be the target of accusatory communications implying that he is not masculine. As a result of these experiences,his sex role identity is likely to be weakened.

The child who has identified with a masculine father does not experience this dissonant discrepancy upon school entrance. This boy's sex role identity becomes based not only on the identification with the masculine father, but also on the perception of similarity between his own attributes and the societal standard for masculinity as displayed by his peers. The boy with a masculine father gains two products from an identification with him—the vicarious power and strength that facilitate future attempts to master sex-typed skills, and the continued exposure to sex-typed behavior. This exposure facilitates the acquisition of sex-typed responses.

The process may be similar for the girl. The girl who identifies with a mother who displays traditionally feminine behavior should display submissiveness with boys, inhibition of aggression, the cultivation of personal attractiveness, and an interest in domestic and nurturant activities. The girl who identifies with a mother who does not manifest traditional feminine attributes is not likely to have adopted sex role characteristics. She will begin to question her femininity when she confronts the values of the peer group, and her sex role identity will be weakened to some degree.

But what of those children who have minimal identifications with their same-sexed parent? If these children adopt the sex role behavior displayed by peers, siblings, or relatives of their own sex, they will possess some basis for an appropriate sex role identity. But it is possible that a weak identification with the same-sexed parent may prevent the child from developing the confidence to master many sex appropriate skills. The boy with a fragile identification with his father and a moderately strong one with his mother would be predisposed to adopt her traits. If she displays feminine attributes, the boy is likely to be passive, to feel inadequate in comparison to his peers, to be reluctant to defend himself against attack, and to have difficulty suppressing anxiety. Since a feeling of strength and a retaliatory posture to stress are masculine traits, this boy will have some difficulty establishing an appropriate sex role identity. The clinical literature, despite its methodological deficiencies, is in general accord in indicating that boys who have a stronger identification with mother than with father (owing to maternal dominance of the family, a perception of greater maternal than paternal competence, and paternal rejection with maternal acceptance) tend to be dependent and more prone to anxiety in threatening situations (Bieber et al., 1962). Moreover, the occurrence of maternal dominance over a passive father, together with maternal rejection of the child, is frequent in the histories of schizophrenic males (Kohn and Clausen, 1956).

Similarly, the girl with a minimal identification with her mother will probably begin to question her potential attractiveness to males and her ability to master feminine attributes. This girl will experience some strain in attaining a firm sex role identity. In sum, both the strength of the child's identification with the same-sexed parent as well as the parents' sex-typed behaviors must be assessed if we are to predict the strength of the child's sex role identity.

One of the implications of this discussion—albeit conjectural—involves the placement of young children in foster homes. If we assume that strong identification with the same-sexed parent is a desirable outcome, then one could argue that a boy should be placed in a home where the father is clearly dominant over the mother; whereas a girl should be placed in a home where the mother has some degree of power and competence. For the child is predisposed to identify with the parental model he perceives to possess power and competence. Unfortunately, there are no definitive empirical tests of these hypothetical ideas. The studies most pertinent to the relation between identification and sex role behavior are subject to multiple interpretations, but we shall consider some of them briefly.

Comparison of the doll play themes of boys whose fathers were absent from the home in contrast to those from intact families revealed less aggressive fantasy from the former than from the latter group (Bach, 1946; Sears, Pintler, and Sears, 1946). Though these results are predictable from several points of view, they are also consonant with the interpretation that absence of the father—who typically displays dominant and aggressive behavior—left the boy without a male model from whom he might imitate aggressive actions. This rehearsal of the model's behavior is one of the concomitants of the identification process. The results of other studies also suggest the relevance of father's presence for an adequate sex role identification.

In a study of Norwegian children with father absent or present (Lynn and Sawrey, 1958), boys with father absent had greater difficulty establishing peer relations than boys from intact families. Failure to develop the masculine skills valued by the peer culture often leads to peer rejection. Thus the relation between father-absence and poor peer relations could result from retardation in the acquisition of masculine interests as a consequent of a weak identification with the father.

A related pair of studies (Mussen and Distler, 1959: Payne and Mussen, 1956) suggest the importance of a nurturant relation between father and son in the formation of an identification. In the Payne and Mussen study, junior and senior high school boys and their parents filled out the California Psychological Inventory. The 20 boys with the highest father identification scores, defined in terms of similarity of father-son answers on the Inventory, were compared with 20 low father-identified boys. The 40 boys were then given an incomplete-stories test to assess perception of the father-son relation. The boys with a strong identification with father produced more frequent evidence of warm father-son relations and a perception of the father as nurturant, than did the low-identified subjects. Moreover, the boys who were identified with the father possessed more sex-typed masculine behavior and attitudes than the boys with minimal identification with their fathers.

In the Mussen and Distler study, kindergarten boys were given a test to assess degree of adoption of sex-typed masculine interests. The ten most masculine and ten least masculine boys were tested in a doll play situation. The doll play themes of the masculine boys contained more evidence of a perception of the father as nurturant and powerful than the themes of the nonmasculine boys. These results support the notion that identification is facilitated when the model is seen as nurturant to the child and powerful *vis-à-vis* the mother. Finally, a recent experimental investigation (Bandura, 1962) suggests that a child is more likely to imitate the behavior of a nurturant adult model than one who is not nurturant.

Changes in Sex Role Identity as a Function of Acquisition of Sex-Typed Attributes In addition to identification with an appropriate model, sex role labels may be altered as a result of the acquisition of desirable sex-typed attributes. The boy who learns to be dominant with peers, sexually agressive with girls, or competent on the athletic field often begins to regard himself as more masculine. The girl who becomes popular with boys, socially poised with adults, or capable of giving nurturance labels herself as more feminine. It has been suggested that the strength of a sex role identity is a function of the discrepancy between the inventory of actual sex-typed attributes and the ideal attributes prescribed by the culture. We are assuming that acquisition of appropriate attributes can reduce this discrepancy and lead to corresponding modifications in the self-label. The opposite effect is also possible. Loss of attributes or goal states that are essential parts of the self-label "I am (masculine) (feminine)" can widen the gap between actual attributes and the ideal and make a sex role identity more vulnerable.

A third set of events that influences a sex role identity is closely related to the acquisition of sex-typed skills discussed above. In this process, experiences with other people in ways that are congruent with sex-typed standards may alter self-labels. If men and women react toward Bill as though the latter were dominant and strong, the discrepancy between Bill's idealized model and existing self-concept will be attenuated. Correlatively, if a girl continually hears praises of her attractiveness, she may gradually alter her conception of herself and the self-ideal discrepancy will be reduced. Of course, these experiences comprise only one aspect of the process of sex role identity. The identification with each parent is presumed to form the basic foundation for a sex role identification. There is no guarantee, therefore, that the social experiences mentioned above will always lead to marked changes in the content of the self-labels that characterize sex role identity.

In sum, differential identification with parents and parent surrogate models, acquisition of sex-typed skills, and sex role congruent experiences are each influential in determining the degree to which an individual labels himself as masculine or feminine.

Overt Sex-Typed Behaviors: Establishment and Maintenance

The learning of sex role behaviors—like a sex role identity—is facilitated by the desire to identify with a model of the same sex. But there are other motives that influence this learning, especially desire for receipt of affection and acceptance from parents and peers, and anxiety over rejection by significant others. Most parents punish aggression and open sexuality more consistently in daughters than in sons; they punish passivity, dependency, and open display of fear more consistently in sons than daughters (Aberle and Naegele, 1952; Kohn, 1959; Sears, Maccoby, and Levin, 1957). Moreover, children feel that their parents want them to adopt sex role attributes (Fauls and Smith, 1956). Thus parental reward of sex appropriate behavior and punishment of inappropriate responses facilitate the adoption of sex-typed traits. The typical child desires the acceptance of parents and peers and wants to avoid their rejection. These motives predispose him to shun sex inappropriate activities and preferentially choose responses that are congruent with sex role standards. It is conceivable, of course, that a child might have a same-sexed parent who does not reward—and perhaps punishes—sex role attributes. This child should be ambivalent with respect to the display of sex role behavior. Thus in order to predict with maximal accuracy the occurrence of sex role behavior one must assess (*a*) the degree of identification with the same-sexed parent, (*b*) degree of sex-typed behavior displayed by each parent, and (*c*) the pattern of rewards issued by each parent.

It is of interest to note that most of the *overt sex-typed responses the girl must acquire require reactions from other people.* It is almost impossible for a girl to assess whether she is attractive, socially poised, or passive with others without continued interaction and feedback from the social environment. The girl is forced to be dependent upon people and to court their acceptance in order to obtain those experiences that help to establish sex-typed behaviors. The critical significance of adult and peer acceptance for girls probably contributes to the greater degree of conformity and concern with socially desirable behaviors typically found among females (Crutchfield, 1955; Hovland and Janis, 1959).

The boy, on the other hand, develops many important sex-typed behaviors while alone. Many sex-typed skills involve solitary practice for which the boy does not require the reactions of others in order to assess when he has reached an adequate level of mastery. Perfection of gross motor or mechanical skills are examples of such activities. Witness the ten-year-old boy shooting baskets in his backyard or fixing his bicycle. The boy receives from these solitary endeavors information that strengthens his conviction that he is acquiring masculine attributes. Moreover, independence of the attitudes and opinions of others—and this implies relative independence of the wishes of others—is in itself a sex-typed trait. The typical boy, therefore, tries to suppress anxiety over social rejection because these reactions are not regarded as masculine in this culture. . . .

REFERENCES

Aberle, D. F. and K. D. Naegele

1952 "Middle class fathers' occupational role and attitudes toward children." American Journal of Orthopsychiatry 22: 366–78.

Bach, G. R.

1945 "Young children's play fantasies." Psychological Monographs 59, no. 2.

1946 "Father fantasies and father typing and father separated children." Child Development 17: 63–79.

Bandura, A.

1962 "Social learning through imitation." In M. R. Jones (ed.), Nebraska symposium on motivation. Lincoln: University of Nebraska Press.

Bandura, A., D. Ross, and S. A. Ross

1961 "Transmission of aggression through imitation of aggressive models." Journal of Abnormal and Social Psychology 63: 575–82.

Beller, E. K. and J. LeB. Turner

n.d. "A study of dependency and aggression in early childhood." Unpublished report from progress report on NIMH Project M-849.

Bennett, E. M. and L. R. Cohen
1959 "Men and women: personality patterns and contrasts." Genetic Psychology Monographs 60: 101–53.
Bieber, I., H. J. Dain, P. R. Dince, M. G. Drellich, H. G. Grand, R. H. Gundlach, M. W. Kremer, A. H. Rifkin, C. B. Wilbur, and T. B. Bieber
1962 Homosexuality. New York: Basic Books.
Bronfenbrenner, U.
1960 "Freudian theories of identification and their derivatives." Child Development 31: 15–40.
Brown, D. G.
1957 "Masculinity-femininity development in children." Journal of Consulting Psychology 21: 197–202.
Child, I. L., E. H. Potter, and E. M. Levine
1946 "Children's textbooks and personality development: an exploration in the social psychology of education." Psychological Monographs 60, no. 3.
Cobb, H. V.
1954 "Role wishes and general wishes of children and adolescents." Child Development 25: 161–71.
Crutchfield, R. S.
1955 "Conformity and character." American Psychologist 10: 191–98.
Dawe, H. C.
1934 "An analysis of 200 quarrels of preschool children." Child Development 5: 139–57.
De Vore, I. and P. Jay
In press. "Mother-infant relations in baboons and langurs." In H. L. Rheingold (ed.), Maternal Behavior in Mammals, New York: Wiley.
Douvan, E. and C. Kaye
1957 Adolescent Girls. Ann Arbor: Survey Research Center, University of Michigan.
Emmerich, W.
1959 "Young children's discriminations of parent and child roles." Child Development 30: 403–19.
Fauls, L. B. and W. D. Smith
1956 "Sex role learning of five-year-olds." Journal of Genetic Psychology 89: 105–17.
Foster, J. D.
1930 "Play activities of children in the first six grades." Child Development 1: 248–54.
Frazier, A. and L. K. Lisonbee
1950 "Adolescent concerns with physique." School Review 58: 397–405.
Freud, S.
1925 "Mourning and melancholia." Pp. 30–59 in Collected Papers of . . . . Vol. IV. London: Hogarth Press.
Goodenough, F. W.
1957 "Interest in persons and aspects of sex differences in the early years." Psychological Monographs 55: 287–323.
Harlow, H. F. and R. R. Zimmerman
1959 "Affectional responses in the infant monkey." Science 130 (3373): 421–32.
Harris, D. B.
1959 "Sex differences in the life problems and interests of adolescents, 1935 and 1957." Child Development 30: 453–59.
Hartley, R. E.
1960a "Children's concepts of male and female roles." Merrill-Palmer Quarterly 6: 83–91.
1960b "Some implications of current changes in sex role patterns." Merrill-Palmer Quarterly 6: 153–64.
Hartup, W. W. and E. A. Zook
1960 "Sex role preferences in three- and four-year-old children." Journal of Consulting Psychology 24: 420–26.

Hattwick, B. A.
1937 "Sex differences in behavior of nursery school children." Child Development 8: 343–55.
Hebb, D. O.
1946 "Behavioral differences between male and female chimpanzees." Bulletin of the Canadian Psychological Association 6: 56–58.
Hildreth, G.
1945 "The social interests of young adolescents." Child Development 16: 119–21.
Honzik, M. P.
1951 "Sex differences in the occurrence of materials in the play constructions of preadolescents." Child Development 22: 15–35.
Hovland, C. I. et al.
1959 Personality and Persuasibility. New Haven, Conn.: Yale Univ. Press.
Jenkins, J. J. and W. A. Russell
1958 "An atlas of semantic profiles for 360 words." American Journal of Psychology 71: 688–99.
Jersild, A. T.
1952 In Search of Self. New York: Teacher's College, Columbia University.
Kagan, J.
1956 "The child's perception of the parent." Journal of Abnormal Psychology 53: 257–58.
1958 "The concept of identification." Psychological Review. 65: 296–305.
Kagan, J., B. Hosken and S. Watson
1961 "The child's symbolic conceptualization of the parents." Child Development 32: 625–36.
Kagan, J. and J. Lemkin
1960 "The child's differential perception of parental attributes." Journal of Abnormal Psychology 61: 446–47.
Kagan, J. and H. A. Moss
1962 Birth to Maturity. New York: Wiley.
Kohn, M. L.
1959 "Social class and parental values." American Journal of Sociology 64: 337–51.
Kohn, M. L. and J. A. Clausen
1956 "Parental authority behavior and schizophrenia." American Journal of Orthopsychiatry 26: 297–318.
Lansky, L. M., V. J. Crandall, J. Kagan, and C. T. Baker
1961 "Sex differences in aggression and its correlates in middle class adolescents." Child Development 32: 45–58.
Lindzey, G. and M. Goldberg
1953 "Motivational differences between male and females as measured by the TAT." Journal of Personality 22: 101–17.
Linton, R.
1936 "Status and role." Pp. 113–31 in The Study of Man. New York: Appleton-Century-Crofts.
Lynn, D. B.
1959 "A note on sex differences in the development of masculine and feminine identification." Psychological Review 66: 126–35.
Lynn, D. B. and W. L. Sawrey
1958 "The effects of father-absence on Norwegian boys and girls." Journal of Abnormal Psychology 59: 258–62.
Maccoby, E. E.
1959 "Role taking in childhood and its consequences for social learning." Child Development 30: 239–52.
Maccoby, E. E. and W. C. Wilson
1957 "Identification and observational learning from films." Journal of Abnormal Psychology 55: 76–87.

McCandless, B. R., C. B. Bilous, and H. L. Bennett
1961 "Peer popularity and dependence on adults in preschool age socialization." Child Development 32: 511–18.
Mowrer, O. H.
1950 "Identification: a link between learning theory and psychotherapy." Pp. 573–616 in Learning Theory and Personality Dynamics. New York: Ronald Press.
Mussen, P. H. and L. Distler
1959 "Masculinity, identification, and father-son relationships." Journal of Abnormal Psychology 59: 350–56.
Muste, M. J. and D. F. Sharpe
1947 "Some influential factors in the determination of aggressive behavior in preschool children." Child Development 18: 11–28.
Nash, H.
1958 "Assignment of gender to body regions." Journal of Genetic Psychology 92: 113–15.
Nye, F. J. and L. W. Hoffman
1963 The Employed Mother in America. Chicago: Rand McNally.
Parsons, T.
1948 "Age and sex in the social structure of the United States." Pp. 269–81 in C. Kluckhohn & H. A. Murray (eds.), Personality in Nature, Society and Culture. New York: Knopf.
1955 "Family structures and the socialization of the child." In T. Parsons and R. F. Bales (eds.), Family, Socialization and Interaction Process. Glencoe, Ill.: Free Press.
Payne, D. E. and P. H. Mussen
1956 "Parent-child relations and father identification among adolescent boys." Journal of Abnormal Psychology 52: 358–62.
Pintler, M. H., R. Phillips, and R. R. Sears
1946 "Sex differences in the projective doll play of preschool children." Journal of Psychology 21: 73–80.
Rabban, M.
1950 "Sex role identification in young children in two diverse social groups." Genetic Psychology Monographs 42: 81–158.
Rosenberg, B. G. and B. Sutton-Smith
1960 "A revised conception of masculine-feminine differences in play activities." Journal of Genetic Psychology 96: 165–70.
Sanford, R. N.
1955 "The dynamics of identification." Psychological Review 62: 106–17.
Sanford, R. N. et al.
1943 "Physique, personality and scholarship: a cooperative study of school children." Monographs of the Society for Research in Child Development 8, no. 1, serial no. 34.
Sears, P. S.
1951 "Doll play aggression in normal young children: influence of sex, age, sibling status, father's absence." Psychological Monographs, 65, no. 6.
Sears, R. R.
1957 "Identification as a form of behavior development." Pp. 149–61 in D. B. Harris (ed.), The Concept of Development. Minneapolis: University of Minnesota Press.
Sears, R. R., E. E. Maccoby, and H. Levin
1957 Patterns of Child Rearing. Evanston, Ill.: Row, Peterson.
Sears, R. R., M. H. Pintler, and P. S. Sears
1946 "Effect of father separation on preschool children's doll play aggression." Child Development 17: 219–43.
Sears, R. R., J. Whiting, V. Nowlis, and P. S. Sears
1953 "Some child-rearing antecedents of aggression and dependency in young children." Genetic Psychology Monographs 47: 135–234.
Siegel, A. E., S. M. Stolz, A. E. Hitchcock, and J. Adamson
1959 "Dependence and independence in children of working mothers." Child Development 30: 533–46.

Terman, L. M. and C. C. Miles
1936 Sex and Personality Studies in Masculinity and Femininity. New York: McGraw-Hill.
Tuddenham, R. D.
1951 "Studies in reputation: III. Correlates of popularity among elementary school children." Journal of Educational Psychology 42: 257–76.
Tyler, L. E.
1947 The Psychology of Human Differences. New York: Appleton-Century-Crofts.
Vance, T. F. and L. T. McCall
1934 "Children's preference among play materials as determined by the method of paired comparisons of pictures." Child Development 5: 267–77.
Walters, J., D. Pearce, and L. Dahms
1957 "Affectional and aggressive behavior of preschool children." Child Development 28: 15–26.
Whitehouse, E.
1949 "Norms for certain aspects of the Thematic Apperception Test on a group of nine- and ten-year-old children." Personality 1: 12–15.
Whiting, J. W. M.
1960 "Resource mediation and learning by identification." Pp. 112–26 in I. Iscoe and H. W. Stevenson (eds.), Personality Development in Children. Austin: University of Texas Press.
Winker, J. B.
1949 "Age trends and sex differences in the wishes, identifications, activities and fears of children." Child Development 20: 191–200.

Social Class and Self-Esteem Among Children and Adults

Morris Rosenberg
Leonard I. Pearlin[1]

20

After decades of research on both social class and self-esteem, it is somewhat surprising to find so little firm knowledge about their relationship. Perhaps this is because social class has commanded the attention of sociologists while self-esteem has primarily concerned psychologists; or it may be that investigators have considered it pointless to attempt to establish a conclusion too obvious to require confirmation. And, indeed, the argument that the individual's social status should be related to his personal feeling of worth seems so self-evident as to represent a virtual triviality. Although there certainly are successful people consumed with self-doubts and unsuccessful ones entirely satisfied with themselves, nevertheless, as William James ([1890] 1950, pp. 306–7) long ago noted:

> *One may say, however, that the normal provocative of self feeling is one's actual success or failure, and the good or bad actual position one holds in the world. . . . he who has made one blunder after another, and still lies in middle life among the failures at the foot of the hill, is liable to grow all sicklied o'er with self-distrust, and to shrink from trials with which his powers can really cope.*

Source: Morris Rosenberg and Leonard I. Pearlin, "Social Class and Self-Esteem Among Children and Adults." American Journal of Sociology 84 (1978): 53–77. Reprinted by permission of the authors and publisher.

James's impressions are entirely consistent with Mead's (1934) theory of reflected appraisals. If the essential characteristic of social class, in the Weberian sense of "status group" (Gerth and Mills 1946), is unequal prestige, then one would expect those looked up to by society to develop a high level of self-respect, and vice versa.

Obvious though these expectations are, the data are surprisingly inconsistent, at times showing no relationship (or even inverse relationships), at other times modest relationships, and at still other times moderate ones. The aim of this paper is to suggest that beneath this diversity is an underlying consistency which can be understood on theoretical grounds. The pattern of relationships, we believe, has been obscured by failing to take account of the factor of age and, hence, by overlooking the fact that a social structural variable, such as social class, may signify a radically different set of social experiences and may be endowed with entirely different psychological meanings for individuals of unequal maturity. The most obvious demonstration of this point is that, for the adult, social class is achieved (at least in principle), whereas for the child it is unequivocally ascribed. From a sociological perspective, then, the fundamental meaning of social class differs for children and adults. The bulk of this paper will be devoted to advancing certain theoretical reasons for expecting the relationship of social class to self-esteem to vary across the age span and to examining these theoretical ideas in the light of empirical data. But, first, it is necessary to consider the empirical basis for the assumption that this relationship is stronger among adults than among children.

SOCIAL CLASS AND SELF-ESTEEM: CHILDREN, ADOLESCENTS, ADULTS

The data for this paper are drawn primarily from two sources. The first is a sample of Baltimore City public school children. A random sample of 2,625 pupils distributed among 25 schools was drawn from the population of pupils in grades 3 through 12. Each school in Baltimore was initially stratified by two variables: (1) proportion of nonwhite and (2) median income of census tract. Twenty-five schools falling into the appropriate intervals were randomly selected, and 105 pupils chosen within each school by random procedures. Interviews were conducted with 1,917 pupils, that is, 79 percent of the sample still registered in school and 73 percent of those originally drawn from the central records. Sampling considerations obliged us to assign double weight to one combined elementary and junior high school; as a result, the basis of our analysis amounts to a sample of 1,988 pupils in 26 schools.

The study of adults is based on information gathered through scheduled interviews with a sample of 2,300 people, aged 18–65, representative of the census-defined urbanized area of Chicago (U.S. Bureau of the Census 1972), which includes sections of northwestern Indiana as well as some of the suburban areas of Chicago. The sample was draw in clusters of four households per block and used a total of 575 blocks, one-fourth the total sample of 2,300. The 1970 census reports that there are 2,137,185 households in the Chicago urbanized area (U.S. Bureau of the Census 1972); when this total is divided by the total number of blocks in which households were to be chosen (575), the result, 3,716, is the skip factor for the selection of households. That is, every 3,716th household was selected; the three additional households of the block cluster were then chosen by dividing the total number of households on each block by four and using the result as the factor for counting from the initially selected address. Among those contacted, 30 percent refused to be interviewed. In anticipation of refusals and to make allowance for households where contact could not be established within three callbacks, substitute addresses in each block were also prelisted. The targeting of households thus was entirely separated from the interviewing.

In the school pupil study, self-esteem is measured by a 6-item Guttman scale (coefficients of reproducibility and scalability are 90 percent and 68 percent, respectively). Issues of reliability and validity of measurement are dealt with in the Appendix. The adult study uses the 10 items of the Rosenberg Self-Esteem Scale (Rosenberg 1965), scoring them according to the Likert method. Because race operates as a suppressor variable (Rosenberg 1968, 1973a; Davis 1971) in the school pupil data,[2] its effect is statistically controlled for both children and adults in Table 1.

TABLE 1

Social Status and Self-Esteem Among Baltimore School Pupils and Chicago Adults (Controlled for Race)

	BALTIMORE SCHOOL PUPILS (SOCIAL CLASS AND SELF-ESTEEM, BY AGE)			CHICAGO ADULTS		
	8–11	12–14	15+	EDUCATION AND SELF-ESTEEM	OCCUPATION AND SELF-ESTEEM	INCOME AND SELF-ESTEEM
Partial gamma	+.029	+.072	+.102	+.197	+.160	+.233
N	(699)	(571)	(468)	(2,288)	(1,689)	(1,988)

Table 1 shows virtually no association between social class, measured by the Hollingshead Index of Social Position (Hollingshead and Redlich 1958, pp. 387–97), and self-esteem among the 8–11-year-olds (partial gamma = +.029) and a modest association for early adolescents (for 12–14-year-olds, partial gamma = +.072) and for later adolescents (for those 15 or older, partial gamma = +.102). In the adult data, on the other hand, the relationships are considerably stronger: controlling for race, the relationship (partial gamma) of education and self-esteem is +.197, that of occupation and self-esteem, +.160, and that of income and self-esteem, +.233. In order to determine whether the associations in these various groups are significantly different from one another, Pearson r's have been compared (Blalock 1972, pp. 405–7). For the 8–11 group, the correlation is significantly different from all three adult correlations at the 0.01 level; for the 12–14 group, the differences are all significant at the 0.08 level; and for the 15+ group, they are all significant at the 0.05 level. The three age groups, however, are not significantly different from one another.

Results of earlier research have been too inconsistent to permit simple comparisons with our findings. Among younger children, several studies show inverse relationships between social class and self-esteem (Clark and Trowbridge 1971; Trowridge 1970, 1972; Piers 1969; Soares and Soares 1969, 1970, 1972), and some show null or close to null relationships (Coleman et al. 1966; Long and

Henderson 1970; St. John 1971). Among adolescents, Bachman (1970), Rosenberg (1965), and Jensen (1972) show weak associations between social class and self-esteem, Epps (1969) shows null or close to null relationships, and Soares and Soares (1972) show an inverse relationship. Finally, among adults, Weidman, Phelan, and Sullivan (1972) and Yancey, Rigsby, and McCarthy (1972) report clear positive relationships, Luck and Heiss (1972) find positive associations within educational groups, and Kaplan (1971) finds no overall association (although relationships appear under certain conditions).

To these findings must be added the results of two unpublished studies of adults. One of these is Middleton's investigation of over 900 black and white adult men (Middleton 1977), which showed the following zero-order correlations of social class with self-esteem: education, $r = 0.359$; occupational status, $r = 0.366$; and income, $r = 0.378$. Although these relationships decline somewhat when controls are introduced, they remain reasonably strong—certainly stronger than in any of the data concerning children.

The second unpublished study is Kohn and Schooler's (Kohn 1969; Kohn and Schooler 1969) nationwide sample of 3,101 working men. Socioeconomic status was measured by the Hollingshead scale and self-esteem by a Guttman scale of global self-esteem. The correlation, which is highly significant, is $r = 0.1929$.[3]

Since studies of adults and children often use different measures of self-esteem, different measures of social class, different types of samples, different measures of association, and different statistical controls, one cannot compare the exact strengths of the relationships. Nevertheless, we believe the available evidence is reasonably consistent with the Baltimore and Chicago findings, which show virtually no association between social class and self-esteem among preadolescents, a modest relationship among adolescents, and a moderate relationship among adults.

The most compelling explanation of this relationship among adults is that advanced by Kohn (1969) and Kohn and Schooler (1969). In their nationwide study of 3,101 working men, they demonstrated that members of different social classes differ radically in the types of occupational activities in which they are actually engaged. The job imperatives are such that the work of those in higher status positions is characterized by a high level of occupational self-direction—an opportunity to make one's own decisions, to exercise independent judgment, to be exempt from close supervision—in large part because of the substantive complexity of the work. Kohn (1969, p. 184) showed that when occupational self-direction was controlled, the originally significant relationship of social class to two self-esteem factors vanished almost completely.[4] From these findings, we may deduce that one reason social class has little effect on the self-esteem of children is that children are not yet exposed to the class-related occupational conditions that help to shape self-esteem.

This paper seeks to add to our understanding by advancing additional theoretical reasons for expecting the observed variations across the age span, exemplified in Table 1, to occur. Two general explanations will be suggested: The first is that social class organizes the interpersonal experiences of children and adults in different ways; the second is that social class is interpreted within different frameworks of meaning by children and adults. These two factors, we believe, can help us to understand why the identical social structural variable (social class) can produce different psychological outcomes (self-esteem) for different social groups (children and adults).

This is not to suggest that different general principles of self-esteem formation operate among children and adults. On the contrary, we shall attempt to show that the principles are identical. Indeed, it is the operation of these identical principles which help us to understand why social class, on theoretical grounds, should have different effects on the self-esteem of children and adults. Four theoretical ideas relevant to self-esteem formation will be considered: social comparison processes, reflected appraisals, self-perception theory, and psychological centrality.

SOCIAL COMPARISON PROCESSES

In 1954 Leon Festinger set forth his theory of social comparison processes, holding that "there exists, in the human organism, a drive to evaluate his opinions and his abilities. . . . To the extent that objective, nonsocial means are not available, people evaluate their opinions and abilities by comparison respectively with the opinions and abilities of others" (pp. 117–18). One could add that it is not only opinions and abilities but also social identity elements—groups, statuses, and social categories—that are evaluated. The individual compares his own group or position with that of other people. Nowhere is this more apparent than with reference to social class. The very meaning of social class is founded on the idea of inequality—of superior and inferior, higher or lower, better or worse. Since social class involves the vertical ordering of members of society along a prestige continuum, it is inherently comparative and invidious. The special relevance of social class for self-esteem obviously rests in the comparison of one's prestige with that of other people.

But with whom does the individual compare his social status? Does he compare it with some general social average or with a narrower population subgroup? This must depend, we believe, on the homogeneity or heterogeneity of the socioeconomic environment in which the individual is ensconced. Under conditions of visible social class heterogeneity, the higher classes may pride themselves on their superior status, and the lower classes may be made painfully aware of their relative inferiority (Kaplan 1971, p. 46). In the company of peers, on the other hand, status neither enhances nor diminishes self-esteem. In other words, in a completely classless—or single class—environment, class will have no effect on self-esteem because no one is below or above anyone else.

One reason social class makes less difference for the self-esteem of the child, we suggest, is that the SES of his interpersonal environment is more homogeneous. In examining this proposition, two questions will be considered. First, is the younger child more likely than his seniors to perceive his environment as socioeconomically homogeneous? Second, is the socioeconomic environment of the young child actually more homogeneous?

The Baltimore data provide rather clear evidence that children tend to perceive their socioeconomic environments as homogeneous. When asked, "Would you say that most of the kids in your class at school are richer than you, the same as you, or poorer than you?" fully 93 percent of the subjects said "the same." Only a miniscule proportion of subjects of any class considered themselves either above or below most of those in their school environments.

Furthermore, subjects were asked, "Do you know any kids whose families are richer than your family?" and "Do you know any kids whose families are poorer than your family?" "Any" is a large umbrella, indeed. It turns out that the younger the child, the less likely is he to say that he knows either richer children or poorer children. Among the youngest, 24 percent said that they knew richer kids and 32 percent that they knew poorer ones. Among the oldest, 66 percent said that they knew richer kids, and 71 percent that they knew poorer ones (Simmons and Rosenberg 1971). In fact, the association between age and knowing "richer kids" is gamma = 0.5189 and between age and knowing "poorer kids" is gamma = 0.4933. As the child grows older, he apparently becomes increasingly conscious of economic inequality.

Although the relative obliviousness of younger children to economic inequality is due in part to limited social learning, the interesting point is that it also reflects reality. Children are more likely to perceive their environments as socioeconomically homogeneous because these environments are in reality more homogeneous. Two items of evidence point to this conclusion.

First, most children, of whatever SES level, attend schools whose average socioeconomic level is similar to their own. Irrespective of age, the great bulk of lower-class children attend schools whose average socioeconomic status is low, higher-class children, ones where it is high. Among the younger children, only 3 percent of the lower-class (Hollingshead Class V) children, compared with 50 percent of the higher-class children (Hollingshead Classes I and II), attend higher-class schools (school SES mean 3.0 or above); in the 12–14 age group, the corresponding figures are 5 percent and 53 percent; and among those 15 or older, the figures are 13 percent and 82 percent. Expressed another way, the relationships between the individual's class and the social class mean of his school for the various age groups are as follows: 8–11 years, gamma = 0.6173; 12–14 years, gamma = 0.6395; 15+ years, gamma = 0.5891.

When children of whatever age say their SES is pretty much "the same" as that of those in their environments, then, they are simply describing reality. But what about the fact that adolescents are more likely to be aware of some socioeconomic heterogeneity in their environments, to say that they know at least some children who are richer or poorer than themselves? Is greater socioeconomic heterogeneity more likely to be a part of their experience? If we look at the SES standard deviations of schools attended by younger and older children, we find a second item of evidence: The standard deviations tend to be larger for older subjects (Table 2). For example, while 47 percent of the youngest children attended schools

TABLE 2
Age by Standard Deviation of School SES (Percent)

	AGE		
SCHOOL SES (SDs)	*8–11*	*12–14*	*15+*
Less than .7	47	35	20
.7 to 1.09	46	61	51
1.1 or more	7	4	29
N = 100%	(821)	(649)	(514)

$x^2 = 324$; $df = 4$; $P < .001$; gamma = .2809

with a relatively small standard deviation (under 0.7), this was true for only 20 percent of the oldest subjects. Nor is this surprising. High schools are not only much larger than elementary schools but also, drawing from a much wider geographical area, tend to recruit children of more diverse socioeconomic backgrounds. Hence, it is understandable that the older child should be more likely to encounter a wider range of poor and well-to-do in his school.

The younger the child, then, the greater the perceived and actual homogeneity of his school (and probably neighborhood) environment. If children's interpersonal environments are such that most SES comparisons are with equals (or perceived equals), it is understandable that, feeling neither above nor below others, their social class should neither raise nor lower their self-esteem.

The adult experience, to be sure, is not entirely dissimilar: a good deal of adult interaction also goes on within socioeconomically homogeneous environments.[5] Yet it is clear that adults are more conscious of, and more exposed to, socioeconomic inequality.

It will be recalled that 93 percent of the children, asked whether they were richer, poorer, or the same as most schoolmates, replied "the same." In the Chicago adult study, subjects were asked, "Would you say your total family income is higher, lower, or about the same as the following groups: Most of your friends? Most of your relatives? Most of your neighbors?" As one might expect, many adult subjects also considered themselves average in terms of these comparable membership groups. Nevertheless, 43 percent saw themselves as either richer or poorer than most of their friends, 61 percent thought they were above or below most of their relatives, and 49 percent considered themselves economically superior or inferior to most of their neighbors.

Furthermore, it is this feeling of economic superiority or inferiority that partly accounts for the relationship between social class and self-esteem among adults. Table 3 shows that the zero-order gamma of income and self-esteem is 0.2485; controlling for whether they consider themselves richer or poorer than friends, the partial gamma = 0.1509. For relatives, the corresponding figures are 0.2594 and 0.1834; for neighbors, 0.2462 and 0.1598. In other words, among adults who consider their income unequal to that of their "peers," between 29 percent and 39 percent of the relationship between income and self-esteem is apparently

TABLE 3

Income and Self-Esteem, Controlling for Comparison with Peers, Among Adults Perceiving Their Income as Higher or Lower Than Others

CONTROLLING FOR WHETHER SUBJECT CONSIDERS SELF RICHER OR POOORER THAN ...		*INCOME AND SELF-ESTEEM*		
	N	*ZERO-ORDER GAMMA*	*PARTIAL GAMMA*	*REDUCTION PERCENT*
Friends	(421)	.2485	.1509	39
Relatives	(594)	.2594	.1834	29
Neighbors	(423)	.2462	.1598	35

attributable to social comparison processes. Invidious economic comparisons thus appear to play some part in accounting for the relationship between income and self-esteem among adults although other factors are also involved.

These data, however, do not adequately reflect the degree of socioeconomic heterogeneity that actually characterizes the adult environment. The reason is that it is not among friends, neighbors, and relatives, after all, that the individual experiences the greatest SES heterogeneity (by and large, these are his peers) but rather in the world of work. Within these institutional structures —the worlds of business, industry, and government—life is organized in hierarchical fashion. In such environments, there is virtually no way to evade the brute reality of differences in power, prestige, and possession. In these organizations, everyone knows who gives the orders and who takes them; who commands great respect and who little; who is paid well, who poorly. The adult certainly knows, at least in a gross way, where he stands along the continuum. It is thus the experience of an adult in the world of work which calls to his attention his place in a recognized stratification system. Although the environment and experience of the school child is such that he may be relatively oblivious to the system of social stratification, nothing is more omnipresent in the life of the adult. Is it any wonder that, comparing himself with others he encounters, the adult's social class should show a stronger relationship to his self-esteem than the child's?

The general principle of social comparison, of course, applies equally to children and adults. The self-esteem of both groups is influenced by comparing themselves with those around them. But, given their social roles, the interpersonal environments of children and adults differ radically. Schooling is, after all, the main business of the child's life; working, the main business of the adult's. In school, children (especially younger ones), whatever their own SES levels, tend to be more or less equal to most of those around them; there is nothing in this to raise or lower their self-esteem. In the world of work, on the other hand, the social comparisons adults make place them above or below others and may understandably affect their feelings of self-worth. Both children and adults make social comparisons, but the differing structures of interpersonal relations in school and work place make SES irrelevant to the child's self-esteem, relevant to the adult's.

REFLECTED APPRAISALS

Since the process of human communication obliges the individual to respond to himself from the standpoint of others (Mead 1934), it is generally assumed that people come to see themselves as they believe others—particularly significant others (Sullivan 1953)—see them. In this simplified form, the theory of reflected appraisals—the theory that we come to see ourselves as we perceive others as seeing us—has been clearly supported by empirical research (Miyamoto and Dornbusch 1956; Reeder, Donohue, and Biblarz 1960; Manis 1955; French 1968; Quarantelli and Cooper 1966; Sherwood 1965; Rosenberg 1965). The results are clear and unequivocal: There is a strong and definite relationship between the "perceived self" (Miyamoto and Dornbusch 1956) and the individual's own picture of what he is actually like. The Baltimore data showed that 62 percent of the children who believed their significant others thought well of them but only 20 percent of those who thought they did not had high global self-esteem. It is thus what we believe others think of us that usually counts.

Assuming that the attitudes of others toward us affect our self-esteem, the critical question is, Do those people with whom we predominantly interact and about whose opinions we most care judge us by our social class position? Do they respect us because we are in a higher class or lack respect for us because we are in a lower class?

In order to deal with this question in a nomothetic rather than an idiographic sense, we must ask which categories of people characteristically enter the individual's experience by virtue of his location in the social structure. Who has opinions of us and whose opinions we care about are not so much matters of accident as of our "role-sets," that is, "the complement of role relationships which persons have by virtue of occupying a particular social status" (Merton 1957, pp. 368–84). To use Merton's example, the status of the public school teacher involves patterned relationships with incumbents of a number of other statuses—with pupils, with colleagues, with the school principal, with the superintendent of schools, with the board of education, with parent-teacher associations, and so on. The child also has his characteristic role-set. The child has patterned relationships with his mother, father, siblings, other relatives, teachers, friends, and classmates; in fact, the overwhelming bulk of the child's interactions are with people with whom he has primary relations.

The relevance of these observations is this: Whereas the adult's role-set consists largely of status unequals, almost all of the individuals who constitute the child's role-set are of his own socioeconomic status. This is true of his mother, father, and siblings; probably true of his school and neighborhood peers; and possibly true of his teachers or more remote relatives. This is not to say that these others do not judge and evaluate the child. On the contrary, they may rank him high in looks, medium in intelligence, and low in cleanliness; they may admire his athletic ability, but have a poor opinion of his charm; they may approve of his friendliness, yet deplore his laziness. But one thing that parents, siblings, and probably peers neither admire nor deplore, approve nor disapprove, respect nor disrespect is his social class. No father looks up to his child as a member of the social elite; no brother looks down on him because of his working-class origins. Yet mothers, fathers, siblings, and peers are precisely those people whose opinions count most to him and who, as research (Rosenberg 1973*b*; Rosenberg and Simmons 1972) indicates, most powerfully affect his self-esteem. Among possible status unequals, teachers alone are likely to have comparable influence. In sum, if significant others neither look up to nor down on the child by virtue of his socioeconomic status, then, taking the role of these others, his objective SES should have little impact upon his feeling of self-worth.

Contrast this situation with the adult's status-set, particularly his occupational role-set. To return to Merton's example of the teacher, he or she may be treated deferentially by the illiterate parent, but imperiouly by the highly educated parent; may be condescended to by the school principal, yet addressed respectfully by the janitorial staff. Not all of these people, of course, are significant others, but neither are their views of the self irrelevant. Since work is such an important part of the adult's life, what those who enter his work experience think of him is likely to have a bearing on his self-attitudes.

Furthermore, consider the adult's family statuses. A father cannot consider his child an economic failure, but a child can consider his father an occupational or economic failure. A wife may express satisfaction with her husband's occupational success or dissatisfaction with his failure, and so, in fact, may the adult's own father, mother, brothers, sisters, and other relatives. Unlike the child, many of the individuals who enter the adult's life by virtue of his structural location in the society—his various role-sets—do view him in social status terms.

In addition, the adult's status-set is obviously much broader than that of the child. For the child, most interactions with others are exhausted by the categories of others who enter his role-set as child; for the adult, role-sets beyond occupation and family are involved. Hence, the adult's status-set brings him into contact with many more people who view him in status terms; to the extent that he sees himself from their viewpoints, his social status should affect his self-esteem.

Again, we see that an identical principle—reflected appraisals—helps explain why social class should have different effects on the self-esteem of children and adults. A child's self-attitudes are at least as influenced by others' attitudes toward him as an adult's; but if others do not judge him in status terms, then status will have little effect on self-esteem.

Thus far, in calling attention to social comparison processes and reflected appraisals, we have suggested that the significance of social class for self-esteem depends on the interpersonal context in which it is embedded. The immediate environments and role-sets of children and adults are such that social class enters the interpersonal experiences of children and adults in different ways, with corresponding effects on self-esteem.

But the differential impact of social class on self-esteem must also take into account how social class enters the phenomenal fields of children and adults. In other words, the significance of social class for the feeling of self-worth also depends on the subjective meaning assigned to the objective fact of social class and on the position of social class in the individual's structure of awareness and values. Two additional principles of self-esteem formation will therefore be invoked: self-perception theory and psychological centrality.

SELF-PERCEPTION THEORY

In advancing self-perception theory as an alternative explanation for cognitive dissonance phenomena, Bem (1965, 1967) set forth the radical behavioristic view that we come to know ourselves not by introspection but by observation of our overt behavior. In this view, we learn about ourselves in much the same way that others learn about us—by observing and interpreting our own behavior and its outcomes. If this is true of such inner states as attitudes, motives, and intentions, it is still more obviously true of more readily recognizable dispositions, such as abilities. Someone who tries skiing for the first time and does well at it may come away with a new view of himself as a skier. We thus draw conclusions about ourselves in part by observing our actions or their outcomes (e.g., successes or failures).

But our self-regard depends primarily on what we have done, secondarily on what our ego-extensions have done.[6] As noted earlier, for the adult, socioeconomic status is achieved; for the child, ascribed. For the former, this status (high or low) is earned—the outcome of his efforts and his actions; for the latter, it is conferred—the product of another's accomplishments. If people evaluate themselves largely in terms of their own behavior, it is certainly easy to understand why social class should be more closely tied to the self-esteem of adults than of children.

Children's self-esteem, it should be stressed, is probably just as dependent as adult self-esteem on achievement; but this achievement is their own, not their parents'. Several items of evidence support this assertion. First, many studies (summarized by Purkey 1970) show a consistent (though not always strong) relationship between school marks and self-esteem. Second, there is evidence that sociometric status and self-esteem are related (Rosenberg 1965). Third, the student's election as an officer of a high school club has been found to be related to his self-esteem (Rosenberg 1965; Rosenberg and Simmons 1972). What the child himself has wrought, then, appears to bear on his self-esteem; his father's achievements, on the other hand, are not his own.

But the identical principle applies to adults. What the adult has achieved may affect his feeling of self-worth, but what his father has achieved is largely irrelevant. For example, the Chicago study showed a relationship of gamma = 0.18 between the individual's own occupation and his own self-esteem and of gamma = 0.07 between his father's occupation and his own self-esteem. The point is that the partial gamma of the father's occupation and one's own self-esteem, controlling on own occupation, is only gamma = 0.01. Even if the father's status helped one to get ahead (or otherwise) in the first place, it is the proximal fact of one's own success or failure, not the distal fact of paternal prestige, that directly affects the adult's self-esteem.

Like the other principles of self-esteem formation, self-perception theory applies equally to children and adults. The reason social class affects the self-esteem of adults more than of children is that different interpretations are assigned the same structural facts by members of these age categories. The general implication is that the impact of a structural arrangement on a psychological disposition depends on the meaning of that objective fact to the individual involved.

PSYCHOLOGICAL CENTRALITY

Unlike self-esteem, which is a comparatively straightforward idea (a global positive or negative attitude toward the self), the self-concept is an extremely intricate, complex, multifaceted structure. The chief elements or components of the self-concept are dispositions (e.g., intelligence, kindness, morality, optimism) and social identity elements (e.g., race, sex, religion, age, social class). (For more elaborate and sometimes differing views, see Kuhn and McPartland 1954; Gordon 1968, 1976; Brissett 1972; Franks and Marolla 1976; Rosenberg 1976.)

But we cannot understand the self-concept without considering the relationship among its components. In the words of Combs and Snygg (1959, p. 126): "The phenomenal self is not a mere conglomeration or addition of isolated concepts of self, but a patterned interrelationship or Gestalt of all these." Some elements of the self-concept are at the center of attention, at the heart of the individual's major concerns, others at the periphery; some self-values are critically important, others are of the utmost triviality. Thus, the impact of any given component on global self-esteem will depend on its importance or unimportance, centrality or peripherality, in the individual's cognitive structure.

The relevance of this point has been demonstrated in several empirical investigations. A study of adolescents (Rosenberg 1965) showed that a high self-rating on a trait was most closely related to global self-esteem when the trait was one that the youngster considered very important to himself. The principle of psychological centrality applies not only to dispositions but to social identity elements as well. One study (Rosenberg 1976) showed a small relationship between the individual's pride in his race or religion and his self-esteem. But, again, the relationship proved to be stronger among those who felt their race or religion to be an integral part of the self than among those who did not.

The question we shall raise here is whether the same principle applies to social status, that is, Does social status have a particularly powerful bearing on the self-esteem of those who value status highly?

Take the matter of income. Those with higher income, we have seen above, are more likely to have high self-esteem than the economically less successful. But the strength of this relationship, it turns out, depends on how much importance the individual attaches to money, how prominent it is in his scale of values. For example, the Chicago adults were asked to agree or disagree with the statement, "One of the most important things about a person is the amount of money he has." Table 4 shows that the more strongly the individual agrees with this statement, the more powerful is the relationship between his income and his self-esteem. Among those who strongly agree, the relationship of income to self-esteem is gamma = 0.52; for those who agree somewhat or disagree somewhat, the gammas are 0.39 and 0.37; for those who strongly disagree, gamma = 0.21. As noted earlier, the Chicago study showed a clear, though moderate, association between adult occupational status and self-esteem. But this association, we find, depends also on the importance attached to status. Subjects were asked, "How important is it to you to move to a higher prestige class?" Among those who considered it very or somewhat important, the association is gamma = 0.25; but among those considering it unimportant, gamma = 0.11 (Table 5).

The impact of social class or status on global self-esteem, then, depends in large measure on its psychological centrality for the individual.[7] The importance of this point for our argument lies in the fact that social status is more psychologically central to the adult than to the child. Adults are more aware of, attuned to, concerned with social status than children; the adult is more likely to perceive his world in terms of stratification, to be alert and sensitive to his own and others' social rank. Let us consider some of the evidence bearing on this point.

One indication of whether class plays a major role in the individual's cognitive structure is simple familiarity with the vocabulary of stratification. Although it is possible to be class conscious without knowing the term, in general we would expect awareness of the term to be associated with awareness of the concept. In the Baltimore study, children were asked, "Have you ever heard about 'social class,' or haven't you ever heard this term?" The results (Simmons and Rosenberg 1971, p. 244) show that only 15 percent of the elementary school subjects had ever

TABLE 4

Self-Esteem, Level of Family Income (in Thousands) and Importance Attached to Money by Adults

	CONSIDER MONEY "ONE OF THE MOST IMPORTANT THINGS"											
	STRONGLY AGREE			SOMEWHAT AGREE			SOMEWHAT DISAGREE			STRONGLY DISAGREE		
SELF-ESTEEM	16+	8–16	8–	16+	8–16	8–	16+	8–16	8–	16+	8–16	8–
High	72	26	16	35	24	17	42	23	15	51	47	32
Medium	6	40	22	38	24	13	30	22	18	24	22	24
Low	22	35	62	27	51	70	28	55	67	25	31	43
N = 100%	(18)	(43)	(69)	(48)	(115)	(83)	(81)	(224)	(123)	(325)	(563)	(292)
	$x^2 = 30$; $df = 4$; P < .001; gamma = .5222			$x^2 = 23$; $df = 4$; P < .001; gamma = .3868			$x^2 = 31$; $df = 4$; P < .001; gamma = .3688			$x^2 = 31$; $df = 4$; P < .001; gamma = .2140		

TABLE 5

Self-Esteem, Occupational Status, and the Importance of Status Aggrandizement for Adults

	IMPORTANCE OF MOVING TO HIGHER PRESTIGE CLASS											
	GREAT OR SOME				LITTLE				NONE			
SELF-ESTEEM	LOW AND HIGH PRO-FESSIONALS	CLERKS, TECHNI-CIANS, AND SALES	SKILLED	UN- AND SEMI-SKILLED	LOW AND HIGH PRO-FESSIONALS	CLERKS, TECHNI-CIANS, AND SALES	SKILLED	UN- AND SEMI-SKILLED	LOW AND HIGH PRO-FESSIONALS	CLERKS, TECHNI-CIANS, AND SALES	SKILLED	UN- AND SEMI-SKILLED
High	43	34	24	21	45	38	36	29	53	42	49	38
Medium	25	26	32	19	24	25	23	26	22	29	21	20
Low	32	40	44	60	31	37	41	45	25	29	29	42
N = 100%	(47)	(129)	(82)	(99)	(97)	(191)	(152)	(144)	(108)	(197)	(160)	(123)
	$x^2 = 17$; $df = 6$; P < .01; gamma = .2498				$x^2 = 8$; $df = 6$; P < .21; gamma = .1413				$x^2 = 13$; $df = 6$; P < .04; gamma = .1074			

heard the term, compared with 39 percent of those in junior high school and 75 percent of those in senior high school.

The identical question was asked of a sample of younger and older English and American school subjects (Stern and Searing 1976). (The younger English children were 11–12, the older, 15–16; the younger American children were 12–13, the older, 17–18.) In both countries, the results were the same. The older subject were much more likely to have heard of the term "social class." Although we are aware of no comparable data among adult samples, it seems unlikely that the sharp rise in awareness demonstrated in adolescence should not continue into adulthood; probably few adults have never heard the term "social class."

There are other indications that the younger the child, the less aware he is of a social class system. In the Stern and Searing (1976) study, younger subjects were less likely to believe that "there are social classes in England (the United States)," to deny that "there are no such things as social classes nowadays," and to deny that "in England (the United States) we are all middle class really." Similarly, when respondents in the Baltimore study who said they had heard of social classes were asked which of four classes (upper, middle, working, or lower) they belonged to, 11 percent of the younger but only 3 percent of the older said "don't know."

Equally important from the self-esteem viewpoint is the accuracy of the individual's perception of his own location in the stratification system. If, for example, there was a random association between objective-class and subjective-class identification, then an objectively high position would not generate feelings of pride nor an objectively low position, feelings of shame.

We shall draw upon data from three studies to examine whether children are in fact less likely to be aware of their actual status in society.

Table 6 presents the following data: (1) the association of objective-class (Hollingshead scale) and subjective-class identification among those Baltimore children and adolescents who had heard the term "social class" and who identified with one of the social classes; (2) two measures of class association among Chicago adults: that between occupational status and prestige-class identification and that between income and income-class identification; and (3) the association between objective-class (Hollingshead scale) and subjective-class identification among Kohn and Schooler's (1969) national sample of adult working men.

The differences are striking. Among the youngest children, there is virtually no association (gamma = –0.0184) between their objective-class and their social class identification. In the 12–14 age group, gamma = 0.1972; in the 15 or older group, gamma = 0.4412.[8] Three measures of association appear for adults. In the Chicago study, the occupation–prestige-class identification association is gamma = 0.4912, and the income–income-class identification association is gamma = 0.6935. Finally, the Kohn and Schooler study of 3,101 working men shows an objective-class–subjective-class identification association of $r = 0.3954$. If the correlations of objective and subjective class among each of the three school age groups are compared with each of the three adult correlations, they all prove to be significantly different at the 0.01 level. The 8-11 and 12-14 age groups are also significantly different from the 15+ age group at the 0.02 level, but they are not significantly different from one another.

TABLE 6

Objective-and Subjective-Class Identification

ASSOCIATION OF OBJECTIVE AND SUBJECTIVE CLASS	BALTIMORE CHILDREN* (BY AGE)			CHICAGO ADULTS		NATIONWIDE MALE ADULTS§
	8–11	12–14	15+	PRESTIGE CLASS†	INCOME CLASS‡	
Gamma	–.0184	.1972	.4412	.4912	.6935	.3954
N	(88)	(163)	(304)	(1,234)	(1,935)	(3,074)
P <	.142	.193	.001	.001	.001	.001

*Among those who had heard of social class and who identified with a class.
†Occupational level and prestige-class identification.
‡Income and income-class identification.
§Kohn and Schooler nationwide sample of 3,101 men using the Hollingshead SES measure.

Thus, adults appear to be far more accurate than children about their relative status position in society. In particular, they are highly sensitive to income differences; the rich know they are richer, the poor, poorer. Although there is variation in results depending upon the samples and indicators used, in general among adults objective position does bear a strong and clear relationship to where one sees oneself in the stratification system.

Compared with their seniors, then, the data suggest that younger children are less likely to have heard of the term "social class"; if they have heard of it, they are less likely to have formed an opinion of where they belong; and if they have formed such an opinion, they are more likely to be mistaken. It does not seem rash to conclude that social status is less psychologically central to children than to adults. And, in the light of our earlier discussion, it is understandable that objective social status should have less impact on a child's self-esteem than on an adult's.

Like the other principles enunciated above, the principle of psychological centrality is just as significant for children as for adults. The objective fact of social class, however, has a different personal relevance for adults and children and, hence, different self-esteem consequences. To the child, the social stratification system and his place in it is relatively vague, blurred, inaccurate, and peripheral; hence, objective class has little bearing on his self-esteem. For the adult, the reverse is the case. The significance of the objective demographic fact thus depends on the place of that fact in the individual's psychological field.

DISCUSSION

If social science is to go beyond the level of description, it is imperative to understand how a demographic variable enters the individual's life, is converted into interpersonal experiences, is processed by a particular cognitive structure, and reflects the individual's relationship to his environment. Ultimately, all experience must be filtered through the sieve of the individual mind; what is essential is to distinguish which objective experiences constitute an actual part of the individual's life and how these are interpreted within his own phenomenal field. We have attempted to illustrate this point by comparing the impact of social class on the self-esteem of children and of adults.

It is important to stress that we are not speaking of differences in the cognitive processes of children and adults. On the contrary, the general principles governing self-esteem among children and adults are, we believe, identical. Two of these—social comparison processes and reflected appraisals—deal with interpersonal processes. Both children and adults learn their worth, in part, by comparing themselves with others; for social structural reasons, such comparisons are more likely to be socioeconomic among adults than among children. Again, both children's and adults' self-attitudes are influenced to a large degree by the attitudes of others toward themselves. Again, for social structural reasons, the others with whom the adult interacts are much more likely than those with whom the child interacts to judge him in social class terms.

The other two general principles—self-perception theory and psychological centrality—pertain to the psychological treatment of social structural facts. It is not simply the objective fact but what one makes of the fact that determines its impact on the individual. Both children and adults learn their worth by observing their behavior and its outcomes; by the adult, social class is interpreted as an outcome of one's own behavior, by the child, it is not. Again, for both children and adults the impact of a given self-concept component (disposition or social identity element) on global feeling of self-worth depends on the awareness and importance of that element to the individual. For structural reasons, adults are more aware of their actual location in the stratification system and probably attach more importance to it.

In sum, one cannot understand the significance of a social structural variable for the individual without learning how this variable enters his actual experience and is processed within his own phenomenal field. As both the phenomenologists and the symbolic interactionists remind us, facts must be interpreted within their "meaning contexts." In emphasizing the importance of an interactional or subjective interpretation of objective reality, we are not reducing sociological forces to psychological ones but specifying intervening variables which themselves may be shaped by objective forces.

Although the primary purpose of this paper has been to show why social class *should* affect the self-esteem of adults, we have found it equally important to attempt to demonstrate why social class should *not* have this effect on children. If we hope to appreciate the meaning of social class for the child, it is essential to see social class from his viewpoint, to adopt the child's eye view of stratification, to understand how it enters his experience and is processed internally. To the sociologist, social class means differential prestige, respect, possessions, and power, with obvious self-esteem implications. But from the viewpoint of the child, the matter appears entirely different. First, the child, as he looks around himself in the actual world of the school and neighborhood in which he lives, finds that most of the children he meets are socioeconomically much like himself—neither richer nor poorer. His effective interpersonal environment, which provides the primary social experiences which enter his phenomenal field, is largely a classless society, a world in which status plays little or no role. (This is not to say that it is unstratified—age and authority stratification is sharp and strong—but it is not socioeconomically stratified.) Second, the child sees himself through the eyes of others, and what he believes they think of him largely affects his self-esteem. And, indeed, significant others may think well or ill of him in many ways but rarely with reference to socioeconomic status. Third, even if the child knows where he stands, he is surely aware that this position has nothing to do with his own efforts or accomplishments.

It is certainly understandable that he should feel greater pride or shame in his school marks or athletic skill than in paternal accomplishments. Fourth, he is relatively oblivious to the social class system. Since his actual social class position has only a modest connection with the class with which he identifies, one can understand why the young child is unlikely to take pride in high status or experience shame in low status. The differential association of social class to self-esteem for children and adults stems from the different social experiences and psychological interpretations associated with this structural fact in these age groups.

APPENDIX

Since a weak association of social class and self-esteem among children might be due to measurement error, it is important to consider issues of reliability and validity. Guttman (1950, chap. 8) has shown that a high coefficient of reproducibility necessarily insures instrument reliability. Since age comparisons are involved, however, it is necessary to consider whether this reliability level is the same among children of different ages or in different groups. For the Baltimore self-esteem scale, the coefficients of reproducibility among black children of different ages are as follows: 8–11, 90 percent; 12–14, 90 percent; 15 and older, 91 percent. For white children, the corresponding figures are 91 percent, 90 percent, and 90 percent. There is also evidence of convergent validity of the Baltimore measure, although it is limited to pupils in the seventh grade or higher. These subjects were administered 7 of the 10 items on the Rosenberg Self-Esteem Scale (RSE). (A discussion of the validity of this measure appears in Rosenberg 1965, chap. 2; Wylie 1974; Robinson and Shaver 1973; Silber and Tippett 1965.) The relationship of the Baltimore and the truncated RSE measure was gamma = 0.6119. (The RSE items were not considered suitable for use with those in the lower grades.) Construct validity (Cronbach and Meehl 1955; American Psychological Association 1954) was assessed by examining the relationship between the self-esteem measure and other variables with which it should, on theoretical grounds, be associated. The relationship of the Baltimore self-esteem measure to the following variables was examined (figures in parentheses are gammas): depression scale (0.31); anxiety score (0.34); "perceived self" (Miyamoto and Dornbusch 1956), that is, how the child believes significant others see him (0.31); school marks (0.10); and, among secondary school club members, club presidency (0.17). These relationships are all in the expected direction and, with the exception of club presidency (due to the small number of club members), statistically significant. In addition, the relationships of the Baltimore measure and the RSE measure to these other variables are very similar. (Further details on the internal reliability, convergent validity, and construct validity of the Baltimore self-esteem scale appear in Rosenberg and Simmons 1972, chap. 2.)

As far as social class measurement error is concerned, the data from secondary school pupils were obtained from the pupils themselves, but the data for elementary school pupils were obtained from the parents (precisely because young children are often unaware of the objective facts relevant to social class). There is no particular reason to expect any difference in social class measurement error between the adult sample and the parents of children, although it is possible that adolescent reports are less accurate.

There is evidence to indicate that the sample is representative of the population from which it is drawn (the public school population of Baltimore from grades 3 through 12). A comparison of sample data with population data shows an impressive similarity in terms of race, grade level, size of school, racial context of school, and median family income of census tract of school. For example, the population is 64.1 percent black, the sample 63.6 percent black. The sole deviation is some overrepresentation of elementary and underrepresentation of senior high school pupils (for details, see Rosenberg and Simmons 1972, app.A).

NOTES

1 The authors would like to thank B. Claire McCullough and Clarice Radabaugh for their technical assistance in the preparation of this paper.

2 A suppressor variable is one which operates to conceal the true strength of the zero-order relationship. Whereas extraneous and intervening variables reduce the strength of the original zero-order relationship, suppressor variables increase it. In the pupil study, the black children were more likely to be in the lower class but also more likely to have higher self-esteem. The fact that this test factor was negatively related to the independent variable but positively related to the dependent variable obscured the true relationship between social class and self-esteem in this sample. Hence, we have partialed out the effects of race.

3 We wish to thank Melvin Kohn for preparing this and several other special tabulations for the purposes of this paper.

4 Kohn's (1969) and Kohn and Schooler's (1969) two factors of self-confidence and self-deprecation are based on 6 of the 10 Rosenberg self-esteem items. These items also satisfy the requirements of a Guttman scale and may, for present purposes, be treated as a single self-esteem measure. This has the advantage of making the data more comparable with most of the other studies of adults which have combined the Rosenberg items into a single scale. As noted earlier, the original association of social class and the Guttman scale of self-esteem is $r = 0.1929$. When this relationship is controlled on the index of occupational self-direction, however, the relationship reduces to partial $r = 0.0470$—a proportional reduction of 76 percent. One cannot, of course, be absolutely certain that this reduction in the social class–self-esteem relationship is due solely to occupational self-direction and not at all to some related variable; but there can be little doubt that the job imperatives play a major role.

5 Although Max Weber (Gerth and Mills 1946) stressed the contrast between classes and status groups, in the long run, he suggested, people in the same tax bracket end up dancing with one another.

6 Except insofar as the ego-extension's achievements are viewed as a product of one's own efforts. A mother may take pride if her child achieves professional success, an athletic coach if his pupil wins an Olympic victory, a professor if his former assistant writes a successful book, because the achievements of these ego-extensions are felt to represent the outcomes of one's own efforts and energies. In the present context, a parent may feel responsible for what the child accomplishes, but a child will scarcely feel responsible for what the parent accomplishes.

7 Such a valuation of self-concept components, of course, is no mere accident. People not only attempt to be successful at those things they value, but they also elect to value those things at which they are successful. The point is that whatever factors operate to make a disposition or social identity element psychologically central in the first place, once it acquires that location in the individual's phenomenal field, its impact on the individual's global feeling of self-worth is amplified.

8 The developmental trend observed in Baltimore is reproduced in other research. Stendler (1949) showed that younger children had less accurate perceptions of others' statuses than older ones. About two-thirds of the first graders' estimates of their peers were wrong, in contrast to only a fourth of the eighth graders'. And Stern and Searing (1976, p. 185)note: "By the end of secondary school, family social class correlates with self-selected social class labels at gamma = 0.46 . . . in England and gamma = 0.58 in the United States"—results consistent with gamma = 0.44 among Baltimore adolescents.

REFERENCES

American Psychological Association

1954 "Technical recommendations for psychological tests and diagnostic techniques." Psychological Bulletin Supplement 51, no. 2, pt. 2: 1–38.

Bachman, Jerald G.

1970 Youth in Transition. Vol 2: The Impact of Family Background and Intelligence on Tenth-Grade Boys. Ann Arbor, Mich.: Survey Research Center, Institute for Social Research.

Bem, Daryl J.

1965 "An experimental analysis of self-persuasion." Journal of Experimental Social Psychology 1 (3): 199–218.

1967 "Self-perception: an alternative interpretation of cognitive dissonance phenomena." Psychological Review 74 (3): 183–200.

Blalock, Hubert M.

1972 Social Statistics. 2d ed. New York: McGraw-Hill.

Brissett, Dennis

1972 "Toward a clarification of self-esteem." Psychiatry 35 (3): 255–62.

Clark, B. M. and N. T. Trowbridge

1971 "Encouraging creativity through inservice teacher education." Journal of Research and Development in Education 4 (3): 87–94.

Coleman, James, et al.

1966 Equality of Educational Opportunity. Washington, D.C.: Department of Health, Education and Welfare.

Combs, A. W. and D. Snygg

1959 Individual Behavior. Rev. ed. New York: Harper.

Cronbach, L. J. and P. E. Meehl

1955 "Construct validity in psychological tests." Psychological Bulletin 52 (May): 177–93.

Davis, James A.

1971 Elementary Survey Analysis. Englewood Cliffs, N.J.: Prentice-Hall.

Epps, Edgar G.

1969 "Correlates of academic achievement among northern and southern urban Negro students." Journal of Social Issues 25 (3): 55–70.

Festinger, L.

1954 "A theory of social comparison processes." Human Relations 7 (2): 117–40.

Franks, David D. and Joseph Marolla

1976 "Efficacious action and social approval as interacting dimensions of self-esteem: a tentative formulation through construct validation." Sociometry 39 (4): 324–41.

French, John R.P.

1968 "The conceptualization of mental health in terms of self-identity theory." Pp. 136–59 in S. B. Sells (ed.), The Definition and Measurement of Mental Health. Washington, D.C.: Department of Health, Education, and Welfare.

Gerth, Hans H. and C. Wright Mills

1946 From Max Weber: Essays in Sociology. New York: Oxford.

Gordon, Chad
1968 "Self-conceptions: configurations of content." Pp. 115–36 in C. Gordon and K. Gergen (eds.), The Self in Social Interaction. New York: Wiley.
1976 "Development of evaluated role identities." Annual Review of Sociology 2: 405–33.
Guttman, L.
1950 "The basis for scalogram analysis." Pp. 60–90 in S. A. Stouffer et al. (eds.), Measurement and Prediction. Princeton, N.J.: Princeton University Press.
Hollingshead, August B. and Frederick C. Redlich
1958 Social Class and Mental Illness. New York: Wiley.
James, William
1950 The Principles of Psychology. New York: Dover (Originally published 1890).
Jensen, Gary F.
1972 "Delinquency and adolescent self-conceptions: a study of the personal relevance of infraction." Social Problems 20 (1): 84–103.
Kaplan, Howard B.
1971 "Social class and self-derogation: a conditional relationship." Sociometry 34 (1): 41–64.
Kohn, Melvin L.
1969 Class and Conformity: A Study in Values. Homewood, Ill.: Dorsey.
Kohn, Melvin L. and Carmi Schooler
1969 "Class, occupation and orientation." American Sociological Review 34 (5): 659–78.
Kuhn, M. H. and T. McPartland
1954 "An empirical investigation of self-attitudes." American Sociological Review 19 (1): 68–76.
Long, B. H. and E. H. Henderson
1970 "Social schemata of school beginners: some demographic correlates." Merrill-Palmer Quarterly 16 (4): 305–24.
Luck, Patrick W. and Jerold Heiss
1972 "Social determinants of self-esteem in adult males." Sociology and Social Research 57 (1): 69–84.
Manis, Melvin.
1955 "Social interaction and the self-concept." Journal of Abnormal and Social Psychology 51 (3): 362–70.
Mead, George Herbert
1934 Mind, Self and Society. Chicago: University of Chicago Press.
Merton, Robert K.
1957 Social Theory and Social Structure. Rev. ed. New York: Free Press.
Middleton, Russell
1977 Personal communication to M. Rosenberg, March 28.
Miyamoto, S. F. and S. M. Dornbusch
1956 "A test of interactionist hypotheses of self-conception." American Journal of Sociology 61 (5): 399–403.
Piers, E. V.
1969 Manual for the Piers-Harris Children's Self-Concept Scale. Nashville, Tenn.: Counselor Recordings & Tests.
Purkey, W. W.
1970 Self-Concept and School Achievement. Englewood Cliffs, N.J.: Prentice-Hall.
Quarantelli, E. L. and J. Cooper
1966 "Self-conceptions and others: a further test of Meadian hypotheses." Sociological Quarterly 7 (Summer): 281–97.
Reeder, L. G., G. A. Donohue, and A. Biblarz
1960 "Conceptions of self and others." American Journal of Sociology 66 (2): 153–59.
Robinson, J. and P. Shaver
1973 Measures of Social Psychological Attitudes. Ann Arbor, Mich.: Institute for Social Research.

Rosenberg, Morris
1965 Society and the Adolescent Self-Image. Princeton, N.J.: Princeton University Press.
1968 The Logic of Survey Analysis. New York: Basic Books.
1973a "The logical status of suppressor variables." Public Opinion Quarterly 37 (3): 359–72.
1973b "Which significant others?" American Behavioral Scientist 16 (6): 829–60.
1976 "Beyond self-esteem: some neglected aspects of the self-concept." Paper presented at the annual meeting of the American Sociological Association, New York City, September 3.

Rosenberg, Morris and Roberta G. Simmons
1972 Black and White Self-Esteem: The Urban School Child. Rose Monograph Series. Washington, D.C.: American Sociological Association.

Sherwood, J. J.
1965 "Self-identity and referent others." Sociometry 28 (March): 66–81.

Silber, E. and J. S. Tippett
1965 "Self-esteem: clinical assessment and measurement validation." Psychological Reports 16 (4): 1017–71.

Simmons, Roberta G. and Morris Rosenberg
1971 "Functions of children's perceptions of the stratification system." American Sociological Review 36 (April): 235–49.

Soares, Anthony and Louise Soares
1969 "Self-perceptions of culturally disadvantaged children." American Education Research Journal 6 (1): 31–45.
1970 "Critique of Soares and Soares' self-perceptions of culturally disadvantaged children: a reply." American Educational Research Journal 7 (4): 631–35.
1970–71 "Self-concepts of disadvantaged and advantaged students." Child Study Journal 1 (1): 69–73.
1972 "The self-concept differential in disadvantaged and advantaged students." Pp. 195–96 in Proceedings of the Annual Convention of the American Psychological Association, vol. 6, pt. 1.

Stendler, Celia B.
1949 Children of Brasstown. Urbana: University of Illinois Press.

Stern, Alan J. and Donald D. Searing
1976 "The stratification beliefs of English and American adolescents." British Journal of Political Science 6, pt.2 (April): 177–201.

St. John, Nancy H.
1971 "The elementary classroom as a frog pond: self-concept, sense of control and social context." Social Forces 49 (4): 581–95

Sullivan, Harry Stack.
1953 The Interpersonal Theory of Psychiatry. New York: Norton.

Trowbridge, Norma T.
1970 "Self-concept and socio-economic class." Psychology in the Schools 7 (3): 304–6.
1972 "Self-concept and socio-economic status in elementary school children." American Educational Research Journal 9 (4): 525–37.

U.S. Bureau of the Census
1972 Census of Housing: 1970 Block Statistics. Chicago, Illinois-Northwestern Indiana Urbanized Area. Financial Report HC(3)-68. Washington, D.C.: Government Printing Office.

Weidman, John C., William T. Phelan, and Mary A. Sullivan
1972 "The influence of educational attainment on self-evaluations of competence." Sociology of Education 45 (3): 303–12.

Wylie, Ruth
1974 The Self-Concept. Rev. ed. Lincoln: University of Nebraska Press.

Yancey, William L., Leo Rigsby, and John D. McCarthy
1972 "Social position and self-evaluation: the relative importance of race." American Journal of Sociology 78 (2): 338–59.

The Development of Self-Conceptions from Childhood to Adolescence

Raymond Montemayor
Marvin Eisen

21

Traditional approaches to the study of self-concept development between childhood and adolescence have been primarily based on either role theory (Elder, 1968) or a psychodynamic perspective (Erikson, 1968; Freud, 1969). The focus of these theoretical orientations is on possible ontogenetic changes in traits, dispositions, or motivational states (Carlson, 1965; Engel, 1959; Monge, 1973) and on identifying age changes in the factor organization of traits applicable to the self (Kokenes, 1974).

One aspect of self-concept development previously neglected concerns possible structural changes in the types of constructs used to describe oneself. Both Piaget (Inhelder & Piaget, 1958) and Werner (1961) have argued that an individual's cognitions about the physical world undergo important qualitative changes between childhood and adolescence. In particular, Werner's "orthogenetic principle" states that "whenever development occurs, it proceeds from a state of relative globality and lack of differentiation to a state of increasing differentiation, articulation, and hierarchic integration" (Werner, 1957, p. 126). Werner's principle suggests that as

Source: Raymond Montemayor and Marvin Eisen, "The Development of Self-Conceptions from Childhood to Adolescence," Developmental Psychology 13 (1977): 314–19.

an individual matures, his cognitions about the physical world undergo a shift from a concrete to an abstract mode of representation.

The orthogenetic principle, although not specifically concerned with ontogenetic changes in social cognition, has been fruitfully extended by Crockett (1965) to the area of the development of person perception. According to Crockett, an individual's developing ability to think abstractly allows him to differentiate between another person's appearance or behavior and his underlying dispositional qualities. Scarlett, Press, and Crockett (1971) found that with increasing age, children use a greater number of constructs to describe their peers and that the proportion of egocentric and concrete descriptions declines while the proportion of nonegocentric and abstract descriptions increases. More recently, Bigner (1974) found similar developmental changes to occur between kindergarten and the eighth grade in children's descriptions of their siblings. In general, research on the development of person perception suggests that with increasing age, other people are viewed in a more interpersonal, complex and abstract manner (Peevers & Secord, 1973; Hill & Palmquist[1]).

The results of these studies demonstrate the utility of applying a cognitive-structural approach to the issue of the development of person perception and suggest that such an approach may be advantageously applied to the development of other aspects of social cognition, such as self-conceptions. As a general statement about development, the orthogenetic principle suggests that an individual's increasing ability to think abstractly not only results in the greater use of psychological and abstract constructs to describe others but also a correspondingly greater use of these types of constructs to describe the self. In addition, social psychologists consider the knowledge that an individual acquires about himself and about others to be the result of social interaction (Mead 1934). For these two reasons, self-concept development may show a sequence of development that parallels the sequence found for the development of person perception.

The purpose of this study is to extend the cognitive-structural perspective to the area of self-concept development. Based upon this orientation, it is hypothesized that young children primarily conceive of and describe themselves in terms of such concrete characteristics as their physical appearance and possessions, while adolescents conceive of themselves more abstractly and describe themselves in more psychological and interpersonal terms. In addition, data collected by Mullener and Laird (1971) suggest that between the ages of 12 and 29 years self-evaluations become increasingly more differentiated and less global. A similar trend may also occur for self-concept development between childhood and adolescence and may be reflected in the adolescent's use of a greater variety of constructs to describe himself.

METHOD

Subjects

Subjects were 136 males and 126 females drawn from four schools in a suburban, midwestern, university community. Approximately equal numbers of males and females from Grades 4, 6, 8, 10, and 12 completed the test instrument. The mean ages in years for students in each respective grade were 9.8, 11.8, 14.0, 15.9, and 17.9. The students were almost exclusively white and within an average and above average range of intelligence as indicated by academic performance and teacher evaluation. Almost all of the parents were in professional, entrepreneurial, or upper white-collar classes—Classes I and II according to Hollingshead's two-factor index of social position.[2]

Procedure

Students were administered the Twenty Statements Test (Bugental & Zelen, 1950; Kuhn & McPartland, 1954) in class groups. Students were given a test form with 20 spaces and were asked to write 20 different answers to the question "Who am I?"

Scoring System

A 30-category scoring system developed by Gordon (1968) was used to classify each answer. Each answer was assigned to the one category that was judged to most accurately reflect the meaning of the response. The system was designed to capture the major varieties of self-representations and the categories are mutually exclusive and exhaustive. The 30 categories are listed in Table 1.

Two undergraduates were trained in the use of the scoring system. Interjudge agreement was tested by having both coders independently score a random sample of 20 tests drawn from the original sample. These students' data were not part of the final analysis. Responses assigned to the same category by both coders were scored as agreed. Interjudge agreement was 85 percent (mean agreement per test, 17 out of 20 responses).

RESULTS

The data was summarized in terms of the percentage of students who used each category at least once. Since the sample size was large, and many chi-square tests were performed, only *p* values less than 0.001 were considered reliable. With the age factor collapsed, chi-square tests for sex differences were computed for each category. No reliable differences were observed and the data for both sexes were combined for all subsequent analyses ($N = 262$). Statistically reliable age changes in self-conceptions were found for 15 of the 30 categories. Table 1 shows the percentage of students at each age using a particular category at least once.

There were significant *increases* between childhood and adolescence in the percentage of subjects who used the following seven categories: occupational role (e.g., hoping to become a doctor, paper-boy), $\chi^2 (4) = 26.13$, existential, individuating (e.g., me, I, myself), $\chi^2 (4) = 38.24$; ideological and belief references (e.g., a liberal, a pacifist), $\chi^2 (4) = 19.10$; sense of self-determination (e.g., ambitious, a hardworker),

TABLE 1
Percentage of Subjects at Each Age Using Category at Least Once

CATEGORY	*AGE* 10	12	14	16	18
Sex	45	73	38	48	72‡
Age	18	35	30	25	41
Name	50	10	8	11	31‡
Racial or national heritage	5	4	2	13	15
Religion	7	0	4	5	10
Kinship role	37	28	18	25	57‡
Occupational role	4	12	29	28	44‡
Student role	67	59	37	54	72†
Political affiliation	0	0	4	3	5
Social status	4	0	0	2	3
Territoriality, citizenship	48	16	21	13	11‡
Membership in actual interacting group	57	39	34	38	57
Existential, individuating	0	34	19	26	54‡
Membership in an abstract category	2	80	31	45	52‡
Ideological and belief references	4	14	24	24	39‡
Judgments, tastes, likes	69	65	80	45	31‡
Intellectual concerns	36	28	40	24	23
Artistic activities	23	36	30	28	18
Other activities	63	62	82	75	60
Possessions, resources	53	22	24	14	8‡
Physical self, body image	87	57	46	49	16‡
Sense of moral worth	4	23	17	28	26*
Sense of self-determination	5	8	26	45	49‡
Sense of unity	0	0	15	17	21‡
Sense of competence	36	37	44	48	36
Interpersonal style	42	76	91	86	93‡
Psychic style	27	42	65	81	72‡
Judgments imputed to others	23	23	24	28	57†
Situational references	9	7	20	20	10
Uncodable responses	19	15	10	6	8
n	53	50	55	65	39

Note. df = 4 in all cases.
*Chi-square significant at .05 level.
†Chi-square significant at .01 level.
‡Chi-square significant at .001 level.

χ^2 (4) = 41.63; sense of unity (e.g., in harmony, mixed-up), χ^2 (4) = 20.38; interpersonal style (how I typically act, e.g., friendly, fair, shy), χ^2 (4) = 48.44; and psychic style (how I typically think and feel, e.g., happy, calm), χ^2 (4) = 45.30. Adolescents were more likely than children to refer to themselves with terms that were future oriented, abstract, interpersonal, and psychological.

There were significant *decreases* between childhood and adolescence in the percentage of subjects who used the following three categories: territoriality, citizenship (e.g., an American, living on Oak Street, χ^2 (4) = 27.95; possessions, resources (e.g., own a dog, have a bike), χ^2 (4) = 33.72; and physical self, body image (e.g., 5' 10", fat), χ^2 (4) = 48.13. These categories generally indicate a concrete description of physical self, such as height or weight.

Finally, there were significant *curvilinear* age changes in the percentage of subjects who used the following five categories: sex (e.g., a girl, a guy), χ^2 (4) = 19.62; name (e.g., Shirley), χ^2 (4) = 44.89; kinship role (e.g., a son, a sister), χ^2 (4) = 18.53; membership in an abstract category (e.g., a person, a human, a speck in the universe), χ^2 (4) = 69.41; and judgments, tastes, likes (e.g., hate school, like sports), χ^2 (4) = 30.53. One's sex, name, and kinship status are concrete, objective aspects of the self, and the use of terms referring to these characteristics produced U-shaped developmental functions. The abstract designation of oneself as "a person" or "a human" reached a surprising peak at age 12, declined at age 14, and steadily increased from age 14 onward. Evaluation of one's activities, such as "like to play baseball" and "hate to clean my room," were classified judgments, tastes, likes. These responses contain both concrete and abstract aspects, and their use increased until age 14 and declined thereafter.

The mean number of categories used at least once by students at each age was as follows: 8.6, 9.0, 9.1, 9.5, and 11.1; $F(4,257) = 3.86$, *ns*. Although adolescents used more categories than children in describing themselves, the difference was not significant.

DISCUSSION

The results of this study support the general hypothesis that with increasing age an individual's self-concept becomes more abstract and less concrete. The children in this study primarily describe themselves in terms of concrete, objective categories such as their address, physical appearance, possessions, and play activities, while adolescents used more abstract and subjective descriptions such as personal beliefs, motivational and interpersonal characteristics. These overall findings are in general agreement with data from studies of the development of social cognitions.[1] The date from the present investigation are also similar to data obtained by Livesley and Bromley (1973) who studied self-concept development among English school children and who used a different scoring system.

The concrete-abstract change is not a simple linear one, however, since additional findings suggest that curvilinear changes occur in the use of categories that could be considered either concrete or abstract. These changes primarily involve the use of concrete description by adolescents rather than the use of abstract descriptions by children. For example, many adolescents referred to concrete characteristics such as their sex and name when describing themselves, suggesting that this type of information has an important phenomenological meaning even to individuals who characteristically define themselves in more abstract terms. Alternatively, few young children described themselves in abstract terms with the exception of the many 12-year-olds who referred to themselves as "a person" or "a human," abstract ideas which may reflect the initial appearance of advanced cognitive skills.

The presentation of a few protocols may provide a more vivid picture of self-concept change in children and adolescents. The following examples were chosen to represent typical self-descriptions at different ages. The original spellings and emphases have been retained.

The first set of responses is from a 9-year-old boy in the fourth grade. Note the concrete flavor of his self-descriptions and the almost exclusive use of terms referring to his sex, age, name, territory, likes, and physical self:

My name is Bruce C. I have brown eyes. I have brown hair. I have brown eyebrows. I'm nine years old. I LOVE! Sports. I have seven people in my family. I have great! eye site. I have lots! of friends. I live on 1923 Pincrest Dr. I'm going on 10 in September. I'm a boy. I have a uncle that is almost 7 feet tall. My school is Pinecrest. My teacher is Mrs. V. I play Hockey! I'am almost the smartest boy in the class. I LOVE! food. I love freash air. I LOVE School.

The next protocol is from a girl aged 11½ in the sixth grade. Although she frequently refers to her likes, she also emphasizes her interpersonal and personality characteristics.

My name is A. I'm a human being. I'm a girl. I'm a truthful person. I'm not pretty. I do so-so in my studies. I'm a very good cellist. I'm a very good pianist. I'm a little bit tall for my age. I like several boys. I like several girls. I'm old-fashioned. I play tennis. I am a very good swimmer. I try to be helpful. I'm always ready to be friends with anybody. Mostly I'm good, but I lose my temper. I'm not well-liked by some girls and boys. I don't know if I'm liked by boys or not.

The final example is from a 17-year-old girl in the twelfth grade. Note the strong emphasis on interpersonal description, characteristic mood states, and the large number of ideological and belief references.

I am a human being. I am a girl. I am an individual. I don't know who I am. I am a Pisces. I am a moody person. I am an indecisive person. I am an ambitious person. I am a very curious person. I am not an individual. I am a loner. I am an American (God help me). I am a Democrat. I am a liberal person. I am a radical. I am a conservative. I am a pseudoliberal. I am an atheist. I am not a classifiable person (i.e, I don't want to be).

One notes in these examples and in the protocols from our other subjects a developmental increase in the depth and vividness of self-conceptions. Children describe where they live, what they look like, and what they do. Their self-concept seems somewhat shallow and undifferentiated, both from other people and from their environment. Adolescents, however, describe themselves in terms of their beliefs and personality characteristics, qualities which are more essential and intrinsic to the self and which produce a picture of the self that is sharp and unique.

Self-concept development is not an additive process. Adolescents do not simply add more complex and abstract ideas about themselves to their earlier, childish, concrete conceptions. In comparison to children, adolescents conceive of themselves quite differently; earlier notions either drop out or are integrated into a more complex picture.

Self-conceptions appear to undergo a developmental transformation, perhaps based on the developing ability of the individual to draw inferences and form hypotheses about underlying characteristics. It is not uncommon, for example, for a young child to say that he likes to play baseball, football, hockey, and so on. A much more common response would be for him to say, "I am an athlete" or "I like athletics." Adolescents seem to infer from their own behaviors the existence of underlying abilities, motives and a personality style. As Inhelder and Piaget (1958) point out, adolescent thinking is a "second order system" in that the adolescent does not solve problems in terms of concrete givens, but uses those concrete facts to form hypotheses about an underlying reality. What appears to be the self for the child is only the set of elements from which the adolescent infers a set of personal beliefs and psychic style that uniquely characterize himself.

NOTES

1 Hill, J. P., & Palmquist, W. J. "Social cognition and social relations in adolescence: a precursory view." Paper presented at the annual meeting of the Eastern Psychological Association, Philadelphia, April 1974.

2 Hollingshead, A. B. "Two-factor index of social position." Unpublished manuscript, 1957.

REFERENCES

Bigner, J. J.

1974 "A Wernerian developmental analysis of children's descriptions of siblings." Child Development 45: 317–23.

Bugental, J. F. T. and S. L. Zelen

1950 "Investigations into the 'self-concept.' I. The W-A-Y technique." Journal of Personality 18: 483–98.

Carlson, R.

1965 "Stability and change in the adolescent's self-image." Child Development 36: 659–66.

Crockett, W. H.

1965 "Cognitive complexity and impression formation." In B. A. Maher (ed.), Progress in Experimental Personality Research, Vol. 2. New York: Academic Press.

Elder, G. H.

1968 "Adolescent socialization and development." In E. F. Borgatta & W. W. Lambert (eds.), Handbook of Personality Theory and Research. Chicago: Rand McNally.

Engel, M.

1959 "The stability of the self-concept in adolescence." Journal of Abnormal and Social Psychology 58: 211–15.

Erikson, E. H.

1968 Identity: Youth and Crisis. New York: Norton.

Freud, A.

1969 "Adolescence as a developmental disturbance." In G. Caplan & S. Lebovici (eds.), Adolescence: Psychosocial Perspectives. New York: Basic Books.

Gordon, C.

1968 "Self-conceptions: configurations of content." In G. Gordon & K. J. Gergen (eds.), The Self in Social Interaction, Vol. 1. New York: Wiley.

Inhelder, B. and J. Piaget

1958 The Growth of Logical Thinking from Childhood to Adolescence. New York: Basic Books.

Kokenes, B.
1974 "Grade level differences in factors of self-esteem." Developmental Psychology 10: 954–58.
Kuhn, M. H. and T. S. McPartland
1954 "An empirical investigation of self-attitudes." American Sociological Review 19: 68–76.
Livesley, W. J. and D. B. Bromley
1973 Person Perception in Childhood and Adolescence. New York: Wiley.
Mead. G. H.
1934 Mind, Self, and Society. Chicago: University of Chicago Press.
Monge, R. H.
1973 "Developmental trends in factors of adolescent self-concept." Developmental Psychology 8: 382–93.
Mullener, N. and J. D. Laird
1971 "Some developmental changes in the organization of self-evaluations." Developmental Psychology 5: 233–36.
Peevers, B. H. and P. F. Secord
1973 "Developmental changes in attribution of descriptive concepts to persons." Journal of Personality and Social Psychology 27: 120–28.
Scarlett, H. H., A. N. Press, and W. H. Crockett
1971 "Children's descriptions of peers: a Wernerian developmental analysis." Child Development 42: 439–53.
Werner, H.
1957 "The concept of development from a comparative and organismic point of view." In D. B. Harris (ed.), The Concept of Development. Minneapolis: University of Minnesota Press.
1961 Comparative Psychology of Mental Development. New York: Science Editions.

Development of the Ideal Self in New Zealand and American Children

Robert J. Havighurst
Donald V. MacDonald

22

This paper is a sequel to one published by the senior author and colleagues in 1946, which described the development of the ideal self, or ego-ideal, as this is revealed during childhood and adolescence by self-reports of American youth.[1]

Using similar procedures, we have secured data from a sample of New Zealand children aged 9–16 with which we can compare the American data.

Securing from boys and girls a brief essay on the subject, "The Person I Would Like to Be Like," we found that the persons mentioned by the children could be placed in the same categories that had been used to classify the American data. These categories are:

P *Parents*
S *Parent-substitutes or surrogates: grandparents, teachers.*
G *Glamorous adults: people with a romantic or ephemeral fame, due to the more superficial qualities of appearance and behavior; e.g., movie stars, athletes, military figures, characters in radio serials or comic strips.*
H *Heroes, people with a substantial claim to fame, usually tested by time.*
St. *Saints or other religious figures.*

Source: Robert J. Havighurst and Donald V. MacDonald, "Development of the Ideal Self in New Zealand and American Children," Journal of Educational Research 49 (1955): 263–76.

A *Attractive adults known to the child: usually young people who are neighbors, older siblings or young aunts and uncles, scout or bible-class leaders.*

C *Composite or imaginary characters: These are abstractions of a number of people. Sometimes they appear to be wholly imaginary. Other times they are clearly a coalescence of qualities of two or three real persons.*

M *Age-mates; while the directions sought to prevent naming of persons the same age as the children, some were named.*

O *Occupatioon stated only: hence not classifiable in one of the other categories.*

NC *Responses not classifiable elsewhere.*

In the earlier study, it was found that there was a progression with age, from P to G to A to C, with the other categories seldom used. This is a progression out from the family circle, becoming more mature and more abstract as the child grows older.

The present study was made in a more systematic way and allows us to test the hypothesis of developmental sequence of the ideal self, as well as to compare this phenomenon in children of two different, though closely related societies.

PROCEDURE

The procedure used was very similar to that used in the American study. Children in school were asked to write a brief essay on the topic "The Person I Would Like to Be Like." Each child was given a mimeographed sheet with the following directions at the top.

Describe in a page or less the person you would most like to be like when you grow up. This may be a real person, or just someone you have made up, or he or she may be partly like several people. Tell something about how old this person is, what he or she is like in character, looks like, works at, and does for pleasure and in spare time. If he is a real person, say so. You need not give his real name if you do not want to.

The exercise was presented to the children in most cases by one or the other of the writers, who assured them that their essays would be treated as confidential, and would not be seen by people who knew them. In most cases, they were asked to write their names on their papers, together with their age, sex, and father's occupation. But experience with some of the secondary school students led to the suggestion that the names be omitted, in high schools M and N in Community C. This seemed to reassure them that their essays would be treated as confidential. This procedure was adopted after a few high school students objected to writing the essay in Community A, where the writing was supervised in the high school by the classroom teachers. The number who objected was very small, but the authors decided to have the names omitted in the work they did subsequently. The New Zealand data were collected in the months of August and September 1953, while the senior author was acting as Fulbright Professor at the University of New Zealand.[2] Data were secured from children in 14 New Zealand schools in three communities.

Community A is a borough with its surrounding rural territory on the North Island. The urban part of this district contains about 5,000 people, and there are another 10,000 people in the rural townships and on the farms which comprise one of the most fertile and prosperous dairy-farming and sheep-raising districts in New Zealand. Schools A, B, C, I and K are situated in this community. The primary schools constitute all schools which are situated in or contiguous to the borough and include children of urban people as well as children of the farms who live closest to the borough. School K is a comprehensive high school. Thus for community A we have a fairly good cross section of rural and town children in the secondary school, and a good cross section of town children together with some rural children in the primary schools.

Community B is a village of about 500 population and its surrounding rural territory of about 800 population on the South Island. The district comprises a fairly good farm area, with mixed farms and sheep farms, two or three small saw mills, and the usual businesses and services of a rural village. School J is a combined primary school and district high school, which serves both farm and town children, more from farms than from the village.

Community C is the city of Christchurch, a city of about 180,000 population, including its suburbs. This is the largest city on the South Island, and has a definitely urban character. Schools D, E, F, G, and H are primary and intermediate schools of Christchurch selected so as to provide a fair cross section of the socioeconomic groups in the city. School L is a coeducational high school with substantial numbers of pupils in the homecraft and engineering forms, and drawing largely from working-class homes. Schools M and N are boys' and girls' high schools which have an emphasis on preprofessional courses and draw from middle-class professional and business homes as well as from working-class homes.

While it would be inaccurate to say that the New Zealand children are representative of New Zealand as a whole, yet the three communities are typical of communities of their size, and the children are a fair cross section of the children of these communities.

Children were selected from alternate classes: Standard 3, and Forms 1, 3, and 5. Papers were grouped by age. The numbers writing the essay on "The Person I Would Like to Be Like" at each age level were as follows:

Age	9	10	11	12	13	14	15	16
Boys	79	67	127	88	179	141	111	74
Girls	86	72	100	81	177	127	142	76

In the larger secondary schools where there were several ability groups for each grade, classes were selected to give a cross section of ability levels. In certain of the smaller schools all children above Standard 3 were included.

The New Zealand children were approximately equivalent in age to American children of grades 4, 6, 8, and 10.

RESULTS

The New Zealand data are summarized in Table 1.

For comparison of the New Zealand data with American data, we have used the following procedure: Ten to twelve year old New Zealand boys and girls were compared with a group of American children consisting of three sub-groups as follows: 60 boys and 100 girls aged 10, 11, and 12 in a typical small midwestern community; 26 boys and 36 girls, 6th graders (age 11–12) in an industrial section of Chicago; and 89 boys and 105 girls, 5th and 6th graders (age 11–12) in a war industry community.

Thirteen- to sixteen-year old New Zealand boys and girls were compared with three other American groups in combination. These were: 94 boys and 114 girls, 7th and 8th graders (age 13–13) in a war industry community; 106 boys and 80 girls, 9th graders (age 14–15) in a lower-middle-class suburb of Chicago; and 48 boys and 86 girls, 16- and 17-year olds in a typical small midwestern community.

TABLE 1

Classification of Persons Described as the Ideal Self by New Zealand Youth

				BOYS				
Age group	9	10	11	12	13	14	15	16
Number of papers	79	67	127	88	179	141	111	74
CATEGORY			*PERCENTAGE OF RESPONSES*					
P	11	15	9	7	8	4	5	—
S	—	3	—	1	1	—	—	—
G	11	16	24	25	22	17	14	23
H	1	—	2	2	3	—	3	4
St	—	—	—	—	—	—	2	1
A	34	33	30	32	25	28	24	20
M	—	—	1	—	1	—	—	—
C	32	24	28	28	35	42	48	47
O	10	8	5	3	3	4	2	1
NC	—	2	1	—	3	4	4	3
				GIRLS				
Age Group	9	10	11	12	13	14	15	16
Number of papers	86	72	100	81	177	127	142	76
CATEGORY			*PERCENTAGE OF RESPONSES*					
P	11	8	3	5	1	2	2	4
S	—	—	—	—	—	1	—	1
G	13	10	13	14	17	13	9	11
H	2	6	1	4	3	5	5	7
St	—	1	1	—	—	—	1	—
A	34	36	44	49	38	38	26	21
M	4	4	1	1	1	1	1	—
C	34	25	34	26	39	35	52	54
O	2	7	1	1	1	4	1	—
NC	1	3	2	—	—	2	4	3

In computing averages, each age group of the New Zealand children was given equal weighting and each American group was treated as being of equal size and with equal numbers at each age level. In the absence of exact information on the composition of the groups, these assumptions seemed the best that could be made. Comparison, is then, between two groups only very roughly equivalent.

The comparison of New Zealand and American data is shown by Table 2. The differences which are reliable at least at the 2 percent level are the following: American boys aged 10 to 12 chose more Glamorous Persons and fewer Composites; American girls of the same age chose more Parents and Glamorous Persons and fewer Attractive Adults than did New Zealand girls. For the 13–16 age group, the American boys and girls chose significantly fewer Composite characters than did the New Zealand children and significantly more Parents.

TABLE 2

Comparison of New Zealand and American Youth

	PERCENTAGE FREQUENCIES			
	AGE: 10–12		*AGE: 13–16*	
	U.S.	*N.Z.*	*U.S.*	*N.Z.*
Category				
P	14	11	13	4
G	30	22	23	19
Boys				
A	35	32	23	24
C	13	27	30	43
Number of Subjects	175	282	248	505
Category				
P	14	5	11	2
G	20	12	14	13
Girls				
A	25	43	25	31
C	26	28	37	45
Number of Subjects	241	253	280	522

DISCUSSION OF RESULTS

In comparing New Zealand and American data, it is necessary to bear in mind the fact that the American data may not be fairly representative of American children. The American data came from three different communities, all located in the north central part of the country, though of rather different socioeconomic composition. We are comparing a set of American data obtained in relatively haphazard fashion with a set of New Zealand data gathered systematically to represent a fair cross section of New Zealand youth. With this in mind we draw certain tentative conclusions.

The Question of Age Progression

Both sets of data give clear evidence of a progression of the ideal self with increasing age toward a Composite, imaginary character and away from specific persons, whether they be Parents, Glamorous Persons, or Attractive Adults. The more mature stage is reached at age 16 by approximately half of the New Zealand youth and by a lesser proportion of American youth.

It is not clear whether the ideal self usually passes through the four stages represented by Parent, Glamorous Person, Attractive Adult, and Composite Character. Probably this type of progression occurs only in a minority of cases, with most children moving from a choice of a Parent either to a Glamorous Person or to an Attractive Adult, but not showing both stages. It is also not clear from these data whether a very high proportion of youth eventually reach the Composite stage. It is quite possible that a considerable group of people never achieve the ability to conceive and to put in words an ideal self who is composite or imaginary. There is some evidence both in the American and New Zealand data, that children of lower socioeconomic status are more likely to describe a Glamorous Person as the ideal self, and that fewer of them describe a Composite Character than do so among higher status children.

To settle the question of age progression in the individual, rather than in the group, it would be useful to study the ideal self phenomenon in a number of children as they moved from the age of 7 or 8 up to adulthood.

The Question of Relative Maturity

If we take the choice of a Composite Character as a sign of greater maturity on the part of children aged 10 to 16, while the choice of a Parent or of a Glamorous Person is a sign of immaturity, it is clear that the New Zealand youth display greater maturity than this sample of American youth. The disparity is more striking in boys than in girls. This conclusion should be held very tentatively. In fact, if we compare the New Zealand Community A with the small middle western American community which is very much like it, leaving out of consideration the other New Zealand and American communities, we find the two groups to be quite similar. Another reason for caution in drawing conclusions from the comparison of New Zealand and American data is that the American data were secured in 1942–45, while the New Zealand data were secured in 1953. There may be a shift in this phenomenon from one decade to another. That this has been true in America prior to 1940 is indicated by the summary of previous studies given in the earlier publication.[3]

CONCLUSIONS

This study shows that the same developmental trend in the ideal self occurs in New Zealand children that has been observed in American children. This trend goes from an identification in early childhood with a parental figure to a stage in late adolescence which may be symbolized by an attractive, visible young adult, or by an imaginary character who is a composite of desirable qualities. Intermediate in this trend is a stage of romanticism and glamor, when the ideal self is a glamorous, unreal character such as a movie star, a military figure, or a character in juvenile fiction who possesses superhuman abilities. Some children appear to omit this intermediate stage, while others pass through it quickly, and still others prolong it into late adolescence.

NOTES

1 Robert J. Havighurst, Myra Z. Robinson, and Mildred Dorr, "The development of the ideal self in childhood and adolescence." Journal of Educational Research (December 1946): 241–57.

2 For a fuller description of the New Zealand data, see Robert J. Havighurst et al. Children and Society in New Zealand, Chapter 3, by Donald V. MacDonald on "The development of the ideal self in New Zealand children" (Christchurch, N.Z.: Canterbury University College, Department of Education Publication, 1954).

3 Havighurst, Robinson, and Dorr, "Development of the ideal self."

Israelis and Jews: The Continuity of an Identity

Simon N. Herman

23

[This study "is based on the data obtained from a representative sample of all the eleventh graders—the sixteen- to seventeen-year old group—in schools within the framework of the Israel Ministry of Education in the 1964–65 school year. The sample comprised 3,679 students in 117 schools" (Herman, 1970:31). In addition to student data, questionnaires were completed by a subsample of 443 parents. On the basis of their responses, it was possible to classify both the adolescents and adults as either religious, traditionalist, or nonreligious. The following excerpt discusses certain criteria for group identification and raises the question of which of two overlapping subidentities—Israeli or Jewish—is more salient to the individuals. — Editors]

Nowhere in the world does a Jewish subidentity exist in isolation as an individual's exclusive ethnic identity. It is everywhere linked with another ethnic subidentity with which it interacts and by which it is influenced. And so the Jewishness of the Israeli can be adequately comprehended only if seen in the context of its association with his Israeliness—just as the Jewishness of an American Jew needs to be examined in the context of his Americanism.

JEWISHNESS AND ISRAELINESS AS OVERLAPPING AND CONSONANT

The great majority of our subjects regard their Jewishness and their Israeliness as interrelated. Less than a third of the students—and a much smaller minority of parents—fail to observe any overlap and declare there is no connection between feeling Israeli and feeling Jewish (see Tables 1 and 2).

TABLE 1

Overlap and Consonance When I feel more Jewish:

	ALL RESPONDENTS		RELIGIOUS		TRADITIONALIST		NON-RELIGIOUS	
	PARENTS	STUDENTS	PARENTS	STUDENTS	PARENTS	STUDENTS	PARENTS	STUDENTS
I also feel more Israeli	83	70	81	83	88	76	76	62
There is no relationship between my feeling Jewish and my feeling Israeli	17	27	19	15	12	22	24	36
I feel less Israeli	—	3	—	2	—	2	—	2
Total Percent	100	100	100	100	100	100	100	100
N	434	2980	147	680	165	942	122	1358

TABLE 2

Overlap and Consonance When I feel more Israeli:

	ALL RESPONDENTS		RELIGIOUS		TRADITIONALIST		NON-RELIGIOUS	
	PARENTS	STUDENTS	PARENTS	STUDENTS	PARENTS	STUDENTS	PARENTS	STUDENTS
I also feel more Jewish	84	67	84	87	85	72	79	54
There is no relationship between my feeling Israeli and my feeling Jewish	15	29	16	10	13	24	18	41
I feel less Jewish	1	4	—	3	2	4	3	5
Total Percent	100	100	100	100	100	100	100	100
N	434	2980	147	680	165	942	122	1358

The perception of overlap is widely shared by all categories of parents—whether religious, traditionalist, or nonreligious. While the perception of the religious students closely resembles that of the parents, a gap begins to appear between traditionalist students and traditionalist parents (the latter of whom are particularly high in the perception of overlap). The difference between parents and students widens still further when we examine the responses of the nonreligious students, as many as 41 percent of whom declare there is no connection.

There is thus a not inconsiderable minority of students who view their being Israeli and being Jewish as separate compartments in their lifespace. This points to a basic difference between the structure of their ethnic identity and that of the other students, in particular the religious students, with whom the Jewish and Israeli identities are closely interwoven. We shall later examine the implication of this difference.

Not only do the majority perceive an overlap between the Israeli and Jewish subidentities. If we take a further look at the responses in Tables 1 and 2, we note the large degree of perceived consonance or compatibility. "Feeling more Israeli" is seen as implying "feeling more Jewish," and vice versa. Here again the parents (84 percent) recognize more than do the students (67 percent) the consonance between the subidentities; similarly, the religious students (87 percent) do so more than the traditionalists (72 percent), and the traditionalists much more than the nonreligious (54 percent) (see Table 2). In the interviews the religious students are the most frequent proponents of the view that their Israeli subidentity is a reinforcement of the Jewish subidentity and that the Israeli Jew is the more complete type of Jew. What is most striking, however, is the almost total absence on the part of all students, nonreligious as well as religious, of any experience of dissonance between the two elements. For only few of them (no more than 4 percent) does feeling more Israeli mean feeling less Jewish, or feeling more Jewish imply feeling less Israeli.

Typical remarks in the interviews:

As a religious person, I see Jew and Israeli as one and the same thing. Therefore the more Jewish the more Israeli and vice versa. It is easier to be a good Jew in Israel and there is a connection.

As a Jew I was taught to love Israel. "Israeliness" is one of the duties imposed on a Jew.

Not only are Israeliness and Jewishness seen as entering into identical regions but there is no clear demarcation between them. Insofar as lines of demarcation can be observed they are clearer to overseas-born parents and to the religious students. In the case of the parents (unlike their children who were Israelis from birth), the Israeli subidentity was superimposed at a later stage of their lives on the preexisting Jewish subidentity. In the case of the religious students, clearly defined regions of religious observance are seen as pertaining primarily to the Jewish subidentity. At the same time these students see their Israeliness as an extension of their Jewishness and the line between the two is blurred. In the nonreligious sector those students who feel that their Jewishness and Israeliness overlap have difficulty in defining in what ways their "being Jewish" specifically expresses itself.

It would seem that nowhere else is the Jewish subidentity interwoven so closely with another subidentity as it is with the Israeli subidentity. The Jewishness of a Jew in the Diaspora is generally limited to specific spheres of his life and there are relatively clear boundaries between his Jewishness and his other subidentity.

When questions parallel to those asked of the Israeli students were addressed to a group of American Jewish students spending a year in Israel more than 60 percent of the group maintained there was no connection between their feeling Jewish and feeling American. . . . A group of visiting students is, of course, not representative—neither of American Jewry nor necessarily even of American Jewish students. But other studies too suggest that American Jews, located within a prestigious majority culture dominating many areas of their lives, regard their Jewishness as pertinent only in certain settings and on particular occasions, and it would seem a reasonable hypothesis that an American Jew would find less of a connection between his Americanism and his Jewishness than would an Israeli between his Israeli and Jewish subidentities. As an American psychologist (Isidor Chein) has observed: "... A competitive situation thus develops and one can do (or think, or feel) something Jewish only by giving up or withdrawing from something in the stream of general activities."

The lack of specificity about the Jewishness of the Israelis does not necessarily mean that it plays a less important role in their lives. Indeed, while the Jewishness of the Jew in the Diaspora relates only to specific, delimited regions, the Jewishness of many Israelis is more pervasive, i.e., it enters—along with their Israeliness—into a large number of regions.

CENTRALITY: THE IMPORTANCE OF BEING JEWISH OR ISRAELI

From an exploration of the perceived interrelatedness of the two subidentities we now proceed to examine their centrality (which we shall in this context equate with "importance"). To what extent is being Jewish and being Israeli important in the lives of the students and their parents?

As was to be expected, the parents are much more emphatic (62 percent "very important" and another 29 percent "important") than are their sons and daughters (23 percent "very important" and 45 percent "important") about the part being Jewish plays in their lives (see Table 3). Not only have the parents experienced the deprivations to which members of a Jewish minority have been subject in the Diaspora, but it is precisely because of the fact of their Jewishness that they either chose, or were obliged, to transplant their lives to Israel.

TABLE 3

Centrality of Jewishness

"Does the fact that you are Jewish play an important part in your life?"

	ALL RESPONDENTS		*RELIGIOUS*		*TRADITIONALIST*		*NON-RELIGIOUS*	
	PARENTS	*STUDENTS*	*PARENTS*	*STUDENTS*	*PARENTS*	*STUDENTS*	*PARENTS*	*STUDENTS*
It plays a very important part	62	23	79	62	58	18	52	7
It plays an important part	29	45	15	36	33	60	33	39
It is of little importance	8	25	6	1	9	18	9	44
It plays no part	1	7	—	1	—	4	6	10
Total Percent	100	100	100	100	100	100	100	100
N	434	2980	147	680	165	942	122	1358

When the students amplify their responses their comments are often typical of the feelings of members of a majority in their own land whose day-to-day life is not characterized by a special awareness of problems of ethnic identity. This is so as long as their thoughts focus on their position inside Israel, but when they look beyond their own country a different note is sometimes sounded.

I am like everybody else over here. Perhaps if I am outside the country, it will be different.

As long as I am in the country it doesn't matter much. But the moment I leave (and I know because I was overseas) it will matter a good deal.

The afterthoughts some of them express indicate that they indeed share the historical time perspective of a people which for centuries has been (and a large part of which still is) in a minority situation.

In Israel, no, because the majority are Jews. Outside of Israel possibly yes, because there may be some prejudice against me. Here all are like me and there the majority are different.
I think yes. Because overseas if there was anti-Semitism I would be amongst those suffering from it.

The religious students attribute much greater importance to being Jewish in their lives than do the traditionalists or nonreligious; considerable areas of their daily conduct are governed by Jewish codes of observance and they see their Jewishness as an all-encompassing way of life.

My whole way of life is determined by Judaism.
I am all the time a Jew and cannot conceive of myself thinking otherwise.
It expresses itself in every detail of my life . . . to what school I go, what sort of education I receive . . . whom I visit, who are my friends, everything!

For the traditionalists it means less than this. While they are on the whole positively oriented towards Jewish tradition, they do not see their daily practice as guided by a comprehensive religious code. Such religious proclivities as they possess find expression mainly at the time of the festivals and other ceremonial occasions.

The nonreligious students differ sharply from the religious students on the question of the part played by being Jewish. They also differ sharply from their nonreligious parents. As many as 44 percent feel that being Jewish "is of little importance" in their lives and another 10 percent say "no part at all" (see Table 3). For some of them, indeed, "being Jewish"—in the context of this question—carries a strong, though not an exclusively, religious connotation.

I am nonreligious and Judaism appears to me to be mainly a religion. Therefore the fact that I am Israeli matters more to me [than the fact of being Jewish].

The parallel question on the importance of "being Israeli" elicits a far higher endorsement by traditionalist and nonreligious students than does the question about being Jewish. While the religious students are more emphatic about the role of their Jewishness than about that of their Israeliness, they at the same time do not fall below the other categories of students in the importance they attach to the part played in their lives by "being Israeli." (see Table 4).

TABLE 4

Centrality of Israeliness
"Does the fact that you are Israeli play an important part in your life?"

	ALL RESPONDENTS		RELIGIOUS		TRADITIONALIST		NON-RELIGIOUS	
	PARENTS	STUDENTS	PARENTS	STUDENTS	PARENTS	STUDENTS	PARENTS	STUDENTS
It plays a very important part	70	43	73	44	73	43	64	42
It plays an important part	22	47	15	48	23	49	30	48
It is of little importance	6	7	9	5	2	5	6	8
It plays no part	2	3	3	3	2	3	—	2
Total Percent	100	100	100	100	100	100	100	100
N	434	2980	147	680	165	942	122	1358

Differing views about the relative importance of "being Jewish" and "being Israeli" are reflected in the following remarks by students in the interviews:

I always have to think about the fact that I am a Jew and as such have to carry out mitzvot *[religious obligations]. I don't have to think so much about being an Israeli.*

Being Israeli obliges me to be loyal to the State. Being Jewish obligates me to much more.

Both are important. They are linked together. As Jews we have been yearning two thousand years for our country.

I attribute more importance to being Israeli, more love for the country. I live in a country surrounded by enemies and do not intend to leave. By contrast, a Jew can live in any country.

Noteworthy is the high percentage of parents (70 percent) who see being Israeli as playing "a very important" part in their lives—considerably higher than the corresponding percentage of students (see Table 4). The parents who have come to Israel from the Diaspora have had to acquire the Israeli identity which the students obtained by birth. It would seem that the importance of being Israeli is highlighted for them as a result of the comparison they make with the period of their lives in which they were not Israelis.

VALENCE: THE ATTRACTIVENESS OF BEING JEWISH OR ISRAELI

A renunciation of identity is regarded by Israeli students as an act of cowardice—irrespective of whether such identity is attractive to them or not. In order to obtain some measure of the valence, or attractiveness, of their Jewishness for the students we accordingly placed them in a hypothetical situation in which they were called upon to choose their ethnic identity anew. The question was worded as follows: "If you were to be born all over again, would you wish to be born a Jew?" This was followed by the further question: "If you were to live abroad, would you wish to be born a Jew?"

TABLE 5

Valence of Jewishness
"If you were to be born all over again, would you wish to be born a Jew?"

	ALL RESPONDENTS		RELIGIOUS		TRADITIONALIST		NON-RELIGIOUS	
	PARENTS	STUDENTS	PARENTS	STUDENTS	PARENTS	STUDENTS	PARENTS	STUDENTS
Yes	80	70	97	94	82	76	61	54
It makes no difference to me	16	28	—	6	18	23	27	43
No	4	2	3	—	—	1	12	3
Total Percent	100	100	100	100	100	100	100	100
N	434	2980	147	680	165	942	122	1358

Seventy percent of the students would wish to be born again as Jews; for 28 percent it is a matter of indifference (see Table 5). When it becomes a question of living outside of Israel, only 54 percent would wish to be born again as Jews, for 25 percent it is a matter of indifference, and 21 percent answer "no" (see Table 6).

TABLE 6

Valence of Jewishness in Life Abroad
"If you were to live abroad, would you wish to be born a Jew?"

	ALL RESPONDENTS		RELIGIOUS		TRADITIONALIST		NON-RELIGIOUS	
	PARENTS	STUDENTS	PARENTS	STUDENTS	PARENTS	STUDENTS	PARENTS	STUDENTS
Yes	73	54	86	84	71	57	58	37
It makes no difference to me	9	25	4	8	12	23	12	34
No	18	21	10	8	17	20	30	29
Total Percent	100	100	100	100	100	100	100	100
N	434	2980	147	680	165	942	122	1358

A breakdown on the basis of the religious factor shows significant differences between the three categories of students. The religious students are staunch in their desire to be born Jews—whether they would be living in Israel (94 percent) or outside of it (84 percent). The great majority of traditionalist students (76 percent) would wish to be born Jews, but only 57 percent give a positive answer when it means life outside of Israel. Among the nonreligious students a slight majority (54 percent) would wish to born as Jews. When it comes to life outside of Israel, however, only a minority (37 percent) of the nonreligious students give an affirmative response while the others either declare it would not matter to them (34 percent) or would prefer not to be born Jews (29 percent).

It would seem that the responses to this question—whether they would wish to be born Jewish if they had to live abroad—provide an index to fundamental differences among students in feelings about Jewishness. There are those for whom the attractiveness of their Jewishness is sufficiently high for them to wish to be Jewish wherever they reside, even if being Jewish in another setting may subject them to discrimination or other disadvantage. By contrast with these students, the attachment of a considerable minority to their Jewishness is predicated on their living in Israel; their Jewishness loses its attraction for them when removed from the context of life in Israel.

Students in this latter category give a variety of explanations for not wishing to be born Jews in the Diaspora. Thus, some recoil at the thought of living as members of a minority:

In Israel I prefer to be a Jew but in the Diaspora I would prefer to be a non-Jew so as not to be a member of a minority.

Others feel that the expression of Jewishness in the Diaspora is mainly religious and as such has no meaning for them if they themselves are nonreligious.

Jewish religion has no meaning for me. In Israel where all are Jews I don't mind also being a Jew. But outside of Israel—why be a Jew?

A few others in the interviews express distaste or shame at the picture of the Jew of the Diaspora as it is conjured up in their minds:

The image of the Jew in the Diaspora arouses negative feelings in me. In Israel the Hebrew is proud and prepared to fight for the State. (Note how the student differentiates in this context between "Jew" and "Hebrew.")

The parents show a greater readiness to be born Jews than do the students. While the parents—like the students—are less ready to be born Jews abroad than in Israel, the percentage (73 percent) who prefer to be Jews even in such circumstances remains high. The attitudes of religious parents and students are close to one another in their highly positive response to both questions. In the question of life outside of Israel the gap widens between traditionalist parents (71 percent) and students (57 percent) and even more sharply between nonreligious parents (58 percent) and students (37 percent).

A third question was added in order to ascertain the attractiveness of the Israeli subidentity. Would they wish to be born again as Israelis?

The great majority of both parents (89 percent) and students (81 percent) express a desire to be born Israelis (see Table 7). This is somewhat higher than the percentages (80 percent of parents and 70 percent of students) desiring to be born Jewish. While the percentage of religious students wishing to be born Jews (94 percent) is higher than the percentage expressing a desire to be born Israelis (79 percent) and while the percentage of traditionalist students is approximately equal for the two questions (76 and 78 percent respectively), there is a marked difference in the position of the nonreligious students. Eighty-three percent would wish to be born Israelis as against 54 percent who would wish to be born Jews.

TABLE 7

Valence of Israeliness
"If you were to be born again, would you wish to be born an Israeli?"

	ALL RESPONDENTS		RELIGIOUS		TRADITIONALIST		NON-RELIGIOUS	
	PARENTS	STUDENTS	PARENTS	STUDENTS	PARENTS	STUDENTS	PARENTS	STUDENTS
Yes	89	81	86	79	93	78	82	83
It makes no difference to me	10	17	10	17	7	18	18	17
No	1	2	4	4	—	4	—	—
Total Percent	100	100	100	100	100	100	100	100
N	434	2980	147	680	165	942	122	1358

RELATIVE SALIENCE: WHICH SUBIDENTITY IS IN THE FOREFRONT OF CONSCIOUSNESS?

In order to ascertain which of the two subidentities will actually determine behavior or attitudes in a given situation, it does not suffice to know their relative valence. There are situations which will bring the one rather than the other subidentity to the fore of consciousness, i.e., heighten its salience. Thus, the students in the interviews indicate that they are particularly conscious of being Israeli on Yom Ha'atzmaut (Independence Day), or when border incidents are reported, or when they are thinking about their enlistment in the Israel Defense Forces after matriculation. The salience of their Jewishness rises on the Jewish festivals, or when they study the Bible or Jewish history, or when they hear about the Holocaust, or when they read about attacks on Jews in any part of the world. (There are students for whom the attacks on Jews also heighten the salience of their Israeliness. As one of them remarked: "I then realize how good it is to be an Israeli.")

RELATIVE POTENCY: WHICH SUBIDENTITY DETERMINES ATTITUDES AND BEHAVIOR?

We proceeded to juxtapose the two component elements in the ethnic identity of the Israeli in order to determine their relative potency or strength. Strictly speaking, relative potency is a function of the relative valence of the two elements and of their relative salience in a particular situation. But, straining the use of the term somewhat, we sought to obtain a rough general measure—over and above situations—of relative potency by asking the students to locate their position on a seven-point Israeli-Jewish rating scale. The instructions read as follows:

Below is a rating scale, at one end of which appears the world "Jewish" and at the other end the word "Israeli." Indicate your position on this scale by placing a checkmark X within the appropriate compartment on this scale. To the extent that the mark is nearer to "Israeli" it means that you feel yourself so much more Israeli than Jewish. To the extent that the mark X is nearer to "Jewish" it means that you feel yourself so much more Jewish.

Please note that the mark X should be placed inside the space between the points on the scale.

Israeli : ___ : ___ : ___ : ___ : ___ : ___ : ___ Jewish
1 2 3 4 5 6 7

Table 8 indicates the distribution of responses. When forced into a choice, a third of the students and 40 percent of the parents locate themselves at the midpoint 4. The rest choose the one or the other side of the scale.

TABLE 8
The Israeli—Jewish Continuum

	ALL RESPONDENTS		*RELIGIOUS*		*TRADITIONALIST*		*NON-RELIGIOUS*	
	PARENTS	*STUDENTS*	*PARENTS*	*STUDENTS*	*PARENTS*	*STUDENTS*	*PARENTS*	*STUDENTS*
Israeli (1-3)	32	44	3	7	38	40	45	69
Midpoint (4)	40	32	42	33	42	38	39	27
Jewish (5-7)	28	24	55	60	20	22	16	4
Total Percent	100	100	100	100	100	100	100	100
N	434	2980	147	680	165	942	122	1358

A glance at a table of the mean scores (see Table 9) facilitates a comparison between the various categories of students and parents. The mean position (3.5) of the entire sample of students is to the Israeli side of the scale, but not extremely so. The religious students are on the Jewish side (mean 5.1), the traditionalist students slightly to the Israeli side (mean 3.6), and the nonreligious students more pronouncedly to the Israeli side (mean 2.6). The parents are near the center, inclining slightly to the Jewish side (mean 4.2). Religious parents and students and traditionalist parents and students are close to one another; the gap is wider between nonreligious parents and students.

TABLE 9
The Israeli—Jewish Continuum (mean scores)

	ALL RESPONDENTS	*RELIGIOUS*	*TRADITIONALIST*	*NON-RELIGIOUS*
Parents	4.2	5.5	3.4	3.3
Students	3.5	5.1	3.6	2.6

The scale was then broken up into two separate scales and the respondent was asked to rate himself according to the extent he felt Jewish or just "a private individual" and similarly to locate himself on an Israeli-"private individual" continuum. The parents reveal both the stronger Jewish and the stronger Israeli orientation as opposed to a "private individual" orientation. The religious students, as would be expected, have a stronger Jewish orientation than the other students; at the same time, their Israeli orientation is not weaker than that of the others—indeed it is slightly stronger than that of the nonreligious students. . . .

The Dissonant Religious Context and Emotional Disturbance

Morris Rosenberg

24

INTRODUCTION

The influence of the individual's social context upon his attitudes and behavior has been pointed up in a number of recent sociological studies.[1] Several of these studies have highlighted the importance of the discrepancy between, or concordance of, the individual's social characteristics and those of the population by which he is surrounded. For example, it may be a very different experience for a white child to be raised in a Negro neighborhood than for a Negro child to be raised in the same neighborhood; for a Catholic child to be raised in a Protestant neighborhood than for a Protestant child to be raised in the same neighborhood; for a middle-class child to raised in a working-class neighborhood than for a working-class child to be reared in this social context. In other words, it is not simply the individual's social characteristics nor the social characteristics of those in the neighborhood in which he lives which are crucial, but the *relationship* between the two—their concordance or discordance—which is of central significance.

In this paper, we wish to examine the relationship between one such dissonant context—the religious context—and certain signs of psychic or emotional disturbance. Does a Catholic child raised in a Protestant neighborhood, for example, show more symptoms of anxiety and depression than one reared in an environment inhabited mostly by his coreligionists? Does such an experience affect his self-

Source: Morris Rosenberg, "The Dissonant Religious Context and Emotional Disturbance," American Journal of Sociology 68 (1962): 1–10. Reprinted by permission of the author and publisher.

esteem? Does a dissonant context have the same effect upon the other religious groups? Does it make a difference *what* the nature of the dissonant context is, for example, is it a different experience for a Catholic child to be raised in a Protestant neighborhood than it is for him to be raised in a Jewish neighborhood? These are some of the questions to which the present research is addressed.

Our data are drawn from questionnaires administered to high-school juniors and seniors in ten high schools in New York State. The population of New York State public high schools was stratified by size of community, and the sample of schools was selected from this population through use of a table of random numbers. Three separate but overlapping questionnaires were administered alternately to the respondents; each student completed one questionnaire. Some of the data to be presented, then, come from different questionnaire forms.

RELIGIOUS DISSONANCE AND EMOTIONAL DISTURBANCE

In the course of completing questionnaires dealing with the values, goals, and self-conceptions of youth, these high-school upperclassmen were told:

This section deals with the neighborhood in which you grew up. If you lived in more than one neighborhood, think of the neighborhood in which you lived longest.

Think back to the time when you were in grammar school. Generally speaking, what was the religious affiliation of most of the people in the neighborhood in which you lived?

Respondents were then asked to fill in the approximate proportions of each religious group in these neighborhoods. It was thus possible to compare those who were predominantly surrounded by coreligionists in childhood, those whose neighborhoods were about evenly divided between members of their own and another religion, and those who were in a distinct religious minority.

Table 1 suggests that the experience of living in a dissonant religious context has certain psychic consequences for the individual exposed to it. In every case, we see, students who have been raised in a dissonant social context are more likely than those who have been reared in a consonant or mixed[2] religious environment to manifest symptioms of psychic or emotional disturbance. For example, Catholics raised in non-Catholic neighborhoods are more likely than Catholics raised in predominantly Catholic or half-Catholic neighborhoods to have low self-esteem, to feel depressed, and to report many psychosomatic symptoms.[3] Similarly, Protestants or Jews raised in dissonant social contexts are more likely than those reared in neighborhoods inhabited chiefly or equally by their coreligionists to manifest these signs of emotional disturbance. These three measures are, of course, highly related to one another, but they are neither conceptually nor empirically identical. Whatever measure is used, the results are essentially similar.

The effect of the dissonant context does not appear to be a large and powerful one; many of the differences are quite small. While some of these differences are not statistically significant and some others are barely so, note that the results are all perfectly consistent. For all nine comparisons made, those in the dissonant

TABLE 1

Contextual Dissonance and Self-Esteem, Psychosomatic Symptoms, and Depression, by Religious Affiliation

	CATHOLICS		*PROTESTANTS*		*JEWS*	
MEASURE	*IN NON-CATHOLIC NEIGHBOR-HOODS (PERCENT)*	*IN CATHOLIC OR MIXED NEIGHBOR-HOODS (PERCENT)*	*IN NON-PROTESTANT NEIGHBOR-HOODS (PERCENT)*	*IN PROTEST-ANT OR MIXED NEIGHBOR-HOODS (PERCENT)*	*IN NON-JEWISH NEIGHBOR-HOODS (PERCENT)*	*IN JEWISH OR MIXED NEIGHBOR-HOODS (PERCENT)*
Self-esteem:						
Low	41	29	31	25	29	18
Medium	30	25	27	30	10	23
High	30	46	42	45	61	60
Number of respondents*	(37)	(458)	(164)	(241)	(41)	(80)
Psychosomatic symptoms:						
Many	65	55	54	48	55	51
Few	35	45	46	52	45	49
Number of respondents	(37)	(467)	(164)	(245)	(42)	(77)
Depressive affect:						
Depressed	20	18	22	11	28	16
Not depressed	80	82	78	89	72	84
Number of respondents	(35)	(429)	(148)	(221)	(39)	(70)

*The difference in number of cases in the tables is due to the fact that "no answers" have been omitted from the calculations. Most of the "no answers" have been so classified because they did not complete all the items in each scale or score because of lack of time. Since several of the "depression" items appeared near the end of the questionnaire, the largest proportion of "no answers" appears on this scale.

context are without exception more likely than others to manifest these symptoms of psychological disturbance. For this reason, these results may merit attention.

It is important to note that there is no clear difference in emotional distress between those raised in neighborhoods inhabited *almost exclusively* by coreligionists and those reared in areas in which only *about half* the members are coreligionists. This result would suggest that whether everyone in the neighborhood is of one's group is less important than whether there are *enough* of them to give one social support, a feeling of belongingness, a sense of acceptance. Thus, two groups may well look down upon one another, but each group may take pride in itself. Even though members of each group may challenge and attack the other, every individual still has a group with which he can identify. It is only when the individual is in the distinct minority, when it is impossible for him to restrict his associations to members of his own group, that the deleterious psychological consequences of the dissonant religious context become evident.

THE EFFECT OF DISCRIMINATION

The child who is isolated from his religious group thus tends to face his immediate environment without the sustenance of group support. It is not difficult to envision the experiences he might undergo. The nature of ethnocentrism is such that the majority group tends to define the minority out-group member as different and inferior. Specifically, this may take the form of excluding the minority-group member from participation in activities, taunting him, hurling derogatory epithets at him, or using the abundant variety of instruments of cruelty of which children are capable.

To examine this question we asked our respondents: "When you were a child, were you ever teased, left out of things, or called names by other children because of . . . your religion?" Table 2 shows that within every religious group students reared in the dissonant context are much more likely than those raised in a consonant or mixed context to have experienced such taunting or exclusion on the basis of religious affiliation.

TABLE 2
Dissonant Context and Subjection to Religious Discrimination by Religious Affiliation

	CATHOLICS		*PROTESTANTS*		*JEWS*	
QUESTION	*IN NON-CATHOLIC NEIGHBOR-HOODS (PERCENT)*	*IN CATHOLIC OR MIXED NEIGHBOR-HOODS (PERCENT)*	*IN NON-PROTESTANT NEIGHBOR-HOODS (PERCENT)*	*IN PROTEST-ANT OR MIXED NEIGHBOR-HOODS (PERCENT)*	*IN NON-JEWISH NEIGHBOR-HOODS (PERCENT)*	*IN JEWISH OR MIXED NEIGHBOR-HOODS (PERCENT)*
"When you were a child, were you ever teased, left out of things, or called names by other children because of your religion?"						
Ever*	22	5	22	6	48	26
Never	78	95	78	94	52	74
Number of respondents	(37)	(454)	(162)	(238)	(42)	(78)

*"Ever" refers to those who answered "often," "sometimes," or "rarely."

Such discrimination, we would expect, can hardly fail to have some effect upon the psychic state of the individual. And Table 3 shows that this is so. Within each religious group, those who have experienced discrimination are more likely to have low self-esteem, more likely to have many psychosomatic symptoms, and more likely to be depressed. This is true for all nine comparisons made. The most conspicuous relationship is found between the experience of prejudice and the report of psychosomatic symptoms. Such psychosomatic symptoms represent physiological indicators of anxiety, and there is reason to believe that they are closely associated with neuroticism.[4] This would suggest that the child who experiences prejudice is more likely to develop feelings of fear, anxiety, insecurity, and tension—a striking testimony to the penalty in human happiness and psychic well-being paid by the innocent and unwitting victims of prejudice.

We have seen that students raised in dissonant social contexts experience greater psychic disturbance than others, that such students are more likely to have

TABLE 3

Experience of Prejudice and Self-Esteem, Depression, and Psychosomatic Symptoms, by Religious Affiliation

	PERCENT EXPERIENCED PREJUDICE IN CHILDHOOD					
	CATHOLICS		*PROTESTANTS*		*JEWS*	
MEASURE	*EVER*	*NEVER*	*EVER*	*NEVER*	*EVER*	*NEVER*
Self-esteem:						
Low	36	30	37	29	24	23
Medium	40	26	26	27	20	18
High	25	44	37	45	55	59
Number of respondents	(40)	(601)	(62)	(494)	(61)	(112)
Psychosomatic symptoms:						
Many	74	54	64	48	55	44
Few	26	46	36	52	45	56
Number of respondents	(40)	(613)	(61)	(496)	(59)	(112)
Depressive affect:						
Depressed	56	40	53	34	39	36
Not depressed	44	60	47	66	61	64
Number of respondents	(36)	(561)	(51)	(452)	(51)	(102)

experienced prejudice, and that those who have experienced prejudice are more likely to manifest such disturbance. This would suggest that one reason students in the dissonant context are more disturbed is that they have experienced such prejudice. In order to see whether this is so, we have examined the relationship of contextual dissonance to psychic disturbance, controlling experiences of prejudice; the method of control employed is "test factor standardization."[5] The results show that in eight out of nine cases the relationship between contextual dissonance and emotional disturbance is reduced when prejudice experiences are controlled. The relationships do not, however, completely disappear.

These data would suggest, then, that the experience of discrimination does contribute to the psychological consequences of contextual dissonance but that it does not account for them completely. To be reared in a dissonant context thus reflects more than the experience of being taunted, ridiculed, attacked, or excluded on the basis of one's group affiliation. What is also probably involved is the insecurity which stems from lack of integration in a group, issuing from a feeling of social isolation, a sense of being "different," an absence of "belongingness." It is apparent why such experiences may be associated with an individual's level of self-acceptance as well as his feelings of anxiety and depression.

DIFFERENTIAL RESPONSIVENESS TO DISCRIMINATION

While the data in Table 3 suggests that all the religious groups are emotionally responsive to the effects of prejudice, attention is drawn to the fact that they are not *equally* responsive to it. Specifically, it appears that Catholics and Protestants are more affected by the experience than Jews. Why the Jewish children, who have experienced by far the most prejudice, should be least affected by it is not certain. Perhaps the prejudice against Jews in the society is so pervasive that its expression is taken for granted; perhaps Jewish children are taught early to expect such slights and to harden themselves against them; perhaps, since discrimination plays such a relatively large role in the lives of Jewish children, they may tend to react to it by attributing the fault to the discriminator rather than to themselves. Whatever the reason, our results suggest that the group which experiences the most prejudice is, in terms of our indicators of emotional disturbance, least affected by it, whereas the group which, in our sample, experiences the least prejudice is most affected by it. Many of the most serious victims of prejudice, then, are those in the majority group.

CONTEXTUAL SPECIFICATION

Given the fact that children reared in a dissonant religious context are more likely to suffer the pangs of self-contempt, to feel depressed, and to experience various psychosomatic manifestations of anxiety, the question arises: Are certain dissonant contexts more prejudicial to the individual's psychic well-being than others? Perhaps Catholics living in Protestant neighborhoods are less affected by their minority group position than Catholics in Jewish neighborhoods. Perhaps Jews in Protestant neighborhoods are less affected than Jews in Catholic neighborhoods. In other words, while we have seen that the dissonant religious context appears to have a bearing upon one's psychic and emotional state, it may be that certain contexts are "more dissonant" than others.

Considering only those students who have been reared in a dissonant religious context, we have compared the levels of self-esteem, depression, and anxiety of members of each religious group reared in neighborhoods occupied chiefly by members of the other two religious groups. Table 4 suggests the following: (1) that

TABLE 4

Psychic States of Students in Different Religious Contexts

	CATHOLICS IN PREDOMINANTLY		*PROTESTANTS IN PREDOMINANTLY*		*JEWS IN PREDOMINANTLY*	
MEASURE	*PROTESTANT AREAS (PERCENT)*	*JEWISH AREAS (PERCENT)*	*CATHOLIC AREAS (PERCENT)*	*JEWISH AREAS (PERCENT)*	*PROTESTANT AREAS (PERCENT)*	*CATHOLIC AREAS (PERCENT)*
Self-esteem:						
Low or medium	68	75	58	78	20	45
High	32	25	42	22	80	55
Number of respondents	(28)	(8)	(149)	(9)	(10)	(20)
Psychosomatic symptoms:						
Many	68	62	56	62	55	60
Few	32	38	44	38	45	40
Number of respondents	(28)	(8)	(150)	(8)	(11)	(20)
Depressive affect:						
Depressed	19	25	23	25	11	29
Not depressed	81	75	77	75	89	71
Number of respondents	(26)	(8)	(138)	(4)	(9)	(21)

Catholics in Protestant areas experience less emotional disturbance than Catholics in Jewish areas; (2) that Protestants in Catholic areas experience less disturbance than Protestants in Jewish areas: and (3) that Jews in Protestant areas experience less disturbance than Jews in Catholic areas. Since we are dealing only with those in dissonant contexts, the number of cases is small and results therefore cannot be considered reliable.[6] Further studies utilizing a larger number of cases would be required to strengthen these conclusions. Nevertheless, it is relevant to note that in eight out of nine comparisons made, the results are in agreement with the conclusions cited above. Since such a high level of consistency obtains, these results appear to warrant further analysis.

Though we lack a sufficient number of cases for statistical adequacy, there is another way of approaching the problem. If some principle can be enunciated which is consistent with these findings, it would increase our confidence that the observed differences are real and meaningful. The principle we propose to account for these findings is the concept of *cultural similarity or dissimilarity*. We will suggest that, if an individual lives in a culturally dissimilar neighborhood, then this context is "more dissonant" than if he lives in a culturally similar neighborhood.

To recapitulate, our data suggest that Catholics in Protestant neighborhoods are less disturbed than Catholics in Jewish neighborhoods; that Protestants in Catholic neighborhoods are less disturbed than Protestants in Jewish neighborhoods; and that Jews in Protestant neighborhoods are less disturbed than Jews in Catholic neighborhoods. If these results are due to the fact that more dissonant contexts are associated with more emotional disturbance, then it would have to be shown (1) that Catholics are culturally more similar to Protestants than they are to Jews; (2) that Protestants are culturally more similar to Catholics than they are to Jews; and (3) that Jews are culturally more similar to Protestants than they are to Catholics. Before we can determine whether this is so, it is first necessary to discuss the nature of "cultural similarity."

Cultural Similarity

The question of cultural similarity is a complex one. In gross terms, of course, it is obvious that American and British societies have more cultural elements in common than, say, American and Chinese societies. If one were to make a more detailed comparison of two cultures, however, one would have to compare their traditions, customs, mores, values, perspectives, philosophies, art, technology, goals, ideals, and so on. Given our limited data, such comparisons are manifestly impossible. We have, however, selected one area which would generally be considered culturally relevant—the area of values.

If we consider a value to be "a conception of the desirable which influences the selection from available modes, means, and ends of action,"[7] then there are four areas in our study which appear to fit this description: (1) self-values—which traits, qualities, or characteristics does the individual consider important in judging himself? (2) maternal values—for what types of behavior was the individual most likely to gain the approval of his mother? (3) paternal values—for what types of behavior was the individual most likely to gain the approval of his father? and (4) occupational values—what satisfactions, gratifications, or rewards is the individual most concerned with obtaining from his life's work?[8]

A simple procedure for comparing the similarity of religious groups was employed. With regard to each item, we asked whether the proportion of Catholics choosing the item was closer to the proportion of Protestants choosing it or to the proportion of Jews; whether the proportion of Protestants choosing it was more similar to the proportion of Catholics or of Jews; and whether the proportion of Jews choosing it was more similar to the proportion of Protestants or of Catholics. This involved 44 comparisons of self-values, 5 comparisons of maternal values, 6 comparisons of paternal values, and 6 comparisons of occupational values.

Table 5 indicates that, in each of the four value areas under consideration, Catholics were more often similar to Protestants than they were to Jews; Protestants were more often similar to Catholics than they were to Jews; and Jews were more often similar to Protestants than they were to Catholics.

TABLE 5

Comparisons of Cultural Similarity or Dissimilarity

	NUMBER OF COMPARISONS			
GROUP COMPARED	*SELF-VALUES*	*MATERNAL VALUES*	*PATERNAL VALUES*	*OCCUPATIONAL VALUES*
Catholics more similar to Protestants	27	5	6	4
Catholics more similar to Jews	11	..	..	2
Equal	6	..	..	..
Number of comparisons	44	5	6	6
Protestants more similar to Catholics	29	3	4	4
Protestants more similar to Jews	12	1	1	2
Equal	3	1	1	..
Number of comparisons	44	5	6	6
Jews more similar to Protestants	22	4	2	4
Jews more similar to Catholics	15	1	1	2
Equal	7	..	3	..
Number of comparisons	44	5	6	6

Of course, we cannot be certain that similar results would appear if other areas of culture were considered. Assuming, however, that these are reasonable indicators of cultural similarity, this would mean that some contexts are "more dissonant" than others in the manner specified.

With these results, we can now return to our earlier discussion of varying dissonant contexts. As we noted in Table 4, Catholics in Protestant areas generally showed less disturbance than Catholics in Jewish areas; Protestants in Catholic areas showed less disturbance than Protestants in Jewish areas; and Jews in Protestant areas showed less disturbance than Jews in Catholic areas. In each of these three comparisons, those who were reared in a "more dissonant" religious context appeared to experience greater disturbance than those reared in a "less dissonant" context. These results would suggest that it may not only be a question of *whether* the context is dissonant, but *how* dissonant it is, which has implications for mental health.

It is obvious, of course, that given the small number of cases in this section of the report and the breadth of the concepts involved, one can only advance such a generalization with the utmost tentativeness. It can only be stated that the results are consistent with such a conclusion. Further studies utilizing more adequate samples and broader indicators of cultural similarity would be required to support or falsify this conclusion.

DISCUSSION

We have seen that children raised in dissonant religious contexts are in subsequent years more likely to manifest disturbances in self-esteem, depressive affect, and psychosomatic symptoms. Our data do not suggest that the dissonant social context is a powerful factor in producing these signs of emotional disturbance, but the consistency of the results suggests that it may be a real factor. We doubt whether the dissonant context often produces these psychological consequences independently of other factors. Rather, we would be inclined to assume that its main influence is exercised upon those already predisposed to psychological disturbance; those standing near the cliff are pushed ever closer to it or actually over it. The child who is uncertain about his worth becomes all the more doubtful when others define him as different and inferior; the child who is tense becomes all the more tense when threatened by others; the child who is moderately depressed becomes more so when he is rejected by his age mates. But if these predispositions did not exist, it is doubtful whether the dissonant religious context per se would be powerful enough to generate such consequences.

Let us, however, attempt to spell out in greater detail how the dissonant social context might exercise its influence on one of the psychological consequences discussed, namely, self-esteem. Our data have suggested that children raised in a dissonant religious context have lower self-esteem than those raised in a consonant context, and that the more dissonant the context, the smaller the proportion who accept themselves. One factor which undoubtedly plays a role is prejudice in its direct and unabashed form. Thus, children who have been raised in a dissonant context are far more likely than others to report that they have been teased, called names, or left out of things because of their religion, and those who have had such experiences are less likely to accept themselves. It may be that this effect is intensified the more dissimilar the individual's group affiliation and that of his neighborhood. To be taunted, jeered at, or rejected by one's peers might well be expected to leave its imprint upon the individual's picture of himself.

But it is probably more than simple prejudice, narrowly conceived as hostility to members of a group, which is responsible for these results. Beyond this, actual cultural dissimilarity may produce rejection. It is characteristic of cultural groups that they tend to feel united on the basis of shared norms, values, interests, attitudes, perspectives, goals, etc. Ease of communication and a sense of solidarity spring directly from such similarity of thought and feelings. The likelihood that an individual will be accepted into the group is thus not only a question of whether he is socially defined as different by virtue of his group membership, but also by whether he *actually is* different—in interests, values, "personality" traits—

by virtue of the fact that he has, perhaps through his parents and relatives, absorbed the values of his own membership group. For example, a Jewish child may learn from his parents, relatives, etc., that it is extremely important to be a good student in school. If he is raised in a Catholic neighborhood, where, according to our data, less stress is placed upon this quality, then he may be scorned by his peers as a "grind," an "eager beaver," an "apple polisher," etc. At the same time he may place little value on being "tough," a "good fighter," etc.; these qualities, more highly valued in the group by which he is surrounded, may give him the reputation of being a "sissy." If cultural dissimilarity does have such an effect, then it is likely that the greater the cultural dissimilarity, the greater the effect.

The point, then, is that qualities which may be accepted or admired in one's own group may be rejected by members of another group. Hence, there is a real likelihood that one will feel different when in a dissonant social context, and this sense of difference may lead the individual to question himself, doubt himself, wonder whether he is unworthy.

The same factors may operate to generate depression and anxiety. While it is not possible to enter into detail at this point, there is theoretical and empirical reason for expecting disturbances in self-esteem to be associated with depression and anxiety. It is thus possible that the relationship between the dissonant context and depression and anxiety may in part be mediated through its influence on the self-picture. In addition, the tension generated by prejudice, the threat of attack, the lack of social support, the feeling of isolation, the possible feeling of helplessness, could all be expected to contribute to depression and anxiety among those predisposed in that direction.

It is also possible that the effect of contextual dissonance may be heightened by living in a neighborhood chiefly inhabited by people who are, in the broader society, defined as a minority group. To be an "outsider" in a predominantly Catholic or Jewish neighborhood appears to be associated with greater emotional disturbance than to be an "outsider" in a Protestant neighborhood. It is thus possible that Catholics and Jews, defined as "minority groups" in the broader society, develop stronger religious group solidarity within their own neighborhoods. Hence, the youngster who lives in a neighborhood chiefly inhabited by members of such solidary religious groups, but who is himself not a member of the group, may experience particularly strong feelings of isolation.

We noted earlier that contextual consonance or dissonance can only be defined by the *relationship* between the individual's social characteristics and the social characteristics of those by whom he is surrounded. Thus, we have spoken of a context as dissonant if the individual is immersed in an environment whose predominant social characteristics are different from his own. In principle, the social characteristics under consideration might be race, religion, social class, nationality, etc., or it might be a social quality defined by a narrower environment. In this sense, then, a white child in a Negro neighborhood, a Negro child in a white neighborhood, a working-class child in a middle-class neighborhood, a Catholic child in a Protestant neighborhood, an Irish child in a Polish neighborhood would all be imbedded in dissonant social contexts. But this does not mean that all dissonant contexts would be expected to have the same effect. First, to be a middle-class child in a working-class neighborhood may be quite different from being a working-class child in a middle-class neighborhood. In other words, *relative status* ranks may have an influence, even though both contexts are equally dissonant. Second, to be of Spanish origin in an Italian neighborhood may have little effect if nationality is not a highly *salient* group characteristic. Third, the effect of contextual dissonance might vary with the *clarity of social definition*. Thus, social classes are not sharply and unequivocally defined, and the awareness of class difference may be vague if contiguous classes are involved. For these reasons, conclusions concerning the effect of religious dissonance cannot simply and readily be transferred to other kinds of dissonant contexts.

The quality of religious affiliation thus has certain properties which are not necessarily characteristic of other social qualities. Membership in the group is quite clear and unequivocal; it is a socially salient characteristic; and it tends to be subject to differential social evaluation in the broader society. Whether other group characteristics lacking certain of these qualities, or possessing others, would produce similar results under conditions of contextual dissonance can only be determined by further research.

NOTES

1 Alan B. Wilson, "Residential segregation of social classes and aspirations of high school boys," American Sociological Review 24 (1959): 836–45; Robert K. Merton and Alice S. Kitt, "Reference group behavior," in R. K. Merton and P. F. Lazarsfeld (eds.), Continuities in Social Research: Studies in the Scope and Method of "The American Soldier" (Glencoe, Ill.: Free Press, 1950), pp. 71ff.; Paul F. Lazarsfeld and Wagner Thielens, The Academic Mind (Glencoe, Ill.: Free Press, 1958), *passim*; Leonard Pearlin and Morris Rosenberg, "Nurse-patient social distance and the structural context of a mental hospital." American Sociological Review 27, no. 1 (1962): 56–65. A methodological discussion of contextual analysis appears in Paul F. Lazarsfeld, "Problems in methodology," in R. K. Merton, L. Broom, and L. S. Cottrell, Jr. (eds.), Sociology Today (New York: Basic Books, 1959), pp. 69–73.

2 "Consonant" means that almost all or about three-quarters of the people in the neighborhood were of the same religion as the respondent; "mixed" means that about one-half were of the same religion; and "dissonant" means that one-quarter or almost none were of the same religion.

3 The measure of self-esteem is a ten-item Guttman scale which, through the use of "contrived" items (see S. A. Stouffer *et al.*, "A technique for improving cumulative scales." Public Opinion Quarterly 16 [1953]: 273–91) yields a seven-point scale. The reproducibility is 93 percent and the scalability is 72 percent. The items in this scale, with which respondents were asked to strongly agree, agree, disagree, or strongly disagree, are the following: (1) On the whole, I am satisifed with myself. (2) At times I think I am no good at all. (3) I feel that I have a number of good qualities. (4) I am able to do things as well as most other people. (5) I feel I do not have much to be proud of. (6) I certainly feel useless at times. (7) I feel that I'm a person of worth, at least on an equal plane with others. (8) I wish I could have more respect for myself. (9) All in all, I am inclined to feel that I am a failure. (10) I take a positive attitude toward myself.

Depressive affect is measured by a six-item Guttman scale with a reproducibility of 95 percent and a scalability of 75 percent. The items in this scale, which were randomly distributed throughout the questionnaire, are the following: (1) On the whole, how happy would you say you are? (2) On the whole, I think I am quite a happy person. (3) In general, how would you say you feel most of the time—in good spirits or in low spirits? (4) I get a lot of fun out of life. (5) I wish I could be as happy as others seem to be. (6) How often do you feel downcast and dejected?

The psychosomatic symptoms score is based upon 10 of the 15 symptoms which appeared in the Neuropsychiatric Screening Adjunct used by the Research Branch of the United States Army in World War II. The development and validation of these psychosomatic items are presented in Shirley A. Star, "The screening of psychoneurotics in the army: technical development of tests," in S. A. Stouffer *et al.*, Measurement and Prediction (Princeton, N.J.: Princeton University Press, 1950). The items utilized were: (1) Do you ever have trouble getting to sleep or staying asleep? (2) Do your hands ever tremble enough to bother you? (3) Are you bothered by nervousness: (4) Have you ever been bothered by your heart beating hard? (5) Have you ever been bothered by pressures or pains in the head? (6) Do you ever bite your fingernails now? (7) Have you ever been bothered by shortness of breath when you were not exercising or working hard? (8) Are you ever troubled by your hands sweating so that they feel damp and clammy? (9) Are you ever troubled with sick headaches? (10) Are you ever bothered by having nightmares (dreams that frighten or upset you very much)?

3 See Star, "Screening of Psychoneurotics," chaps. xiii-xiv.

4 This procedure is described in Morris Rosenberg, "Test factor standardization as a method of interpretation," Social Forces 41 (1962): 53–61.

5 It may be noted that there are discrepancies in the total number of cases classified as "dissonant" in Tables 1 and 4, particularly among Jewish respondents. One reason is that a number of respondents reported that they grew up in "Christian" neighborhoods. Jewish students who gave this reply were classified in Table 1 as growing up in non-Jewish neighborhoods, but it was not possible to determine whether these neighborhoods were Catholic or Protestant. Hence, these cases have been omitted from Table 4. Another reason is that in Table 4 we are dealing with those who grew up in *predominantly* (all or three-quarters) Catholic, Protestant, or Jewish neighborhoods. We have thus omitted, for example, Catholics reared in approximately half-Protestant, half-Jewish neighborhoods; Protestants reared in half-Catholic, half-Jewish neighborhoods; and Jews reared in half-Catholic-half-Protestant neighborhoods.

7 Clyde Kluckhohn *et al.*, "Values and value-orientations in the theory of action," in T. Parsons and E.A. Shils (eds.), Toward a General Theory of Action (Cambridge, Mass.: Harvard University Press, 1954), p. 395.

8 Self-values included such items as ambitious; clear-thinking or clever; hard-working or conscientious; dependable and reliable; etc. Parental values were measured by asking whether mothers and fathers were most likely to approve of the child for being strong and aggressive; for doing well in school; for getting along with other children; etc. Occupational values dealt with whether the individual was most concerned with using his abilities at this work, gaining status and prestige, having the opportunity to be creative and original, etc. The list of occupational values is drawn from Morris Rosenberg, Occupations and Values (Glencoe, Ill.: Free Press, 1957), pp. 141–42.

Social Comparison in the Classroom: The Relationship Between Academic Achievement and Self-Concept

Carl M. Rogers
Monte D. Smith
J. Michael Coleman

25

Numerous studies have examined the relationship between children's academic achievement and self-concept (Purkey, 1970). Although many studies have reported a significant relationship between these two variables (e.g., Black, 1974; Bledsoe, 1967; Coopersmith, 1959; Fink, 1962; Lamy 1965; R. Williams & Cole, 1968; Kohr, Note 1), others have failed to find any substantial relationship between academic achievement and self-concept (e.g., Lewis, 1972; Wattenberg & Clifford, 1964; J. Williams, 1973). Even studies that reported significant academic achievement/

Source: Carl M. Rogers, Monte D. Smith, and J. Michael Coleman, "Social Comparison in the Classroom: The Relationship Between Academic Achievement and Self-Concept," Journal of Educational Psychology 70 (1978): 50–57.

self-concept relationships typically reported low correlations between the two variables which, although statistically significant, had low predictive utility in terms of accounting for much of the observed variability of scores. This difficulty was summarized by Kohr[1] who stated, "Although the relationship between self-concept and academic achievement was statistically significant, it would appear to be neither substantial in degree nor simple in direction."

A pervasive problem in self-concept/academic achievement investigations, has been a relative lack of concern with theoretical models, often resulting in technically adequate but conceptually weak investigations potentially masking rather than clarifying any existing relationship. Researchers examining the relationship between academic achievement and self-concept typically have seemed to assume that this relationship is invariant and is manifest independently of other environmental or psychological factors. Hence, research in this area has paid little attention to other factors, such as the academic or social environment from which samples were drawn and how such factors might have influenced the hypothesized relationship.

Several theoretical statements on the developement and maintenance of the self-concept, however, emphasize the importance of the social environment. For example, Gecas, Calonico, and Thomas[2] discussed two prominent theoretical orientations, model theory and mirror theory, both of which emphasize the interplay between the environment and the individual. Model theory suggests that a child develops a sense of self-regard through the process of imitating others in the immediate environment; mirror theory proposes that the self-concept is a product of the reflected appraisals of others significant to the child. Closely related to mirror theory is Festinger's (1954) theory of social comparison. Festinger suggested that in the absence of objective standards of comparison, people use significant others in their environment as the bases for forming estimates of self-worth. The theory of social comparison processes, as it articulates with self-theory, has been explicated most clearly by Hyman and Singer (1967), who concluded that the self-concept is constructed on an edifice of social comparisons. Despite their differences, each of these theories would maintain that the process by which the individual develops and maintains self-regard is critically dependent on the social group in which the individual resides.

These orientations suggest that the self-concept/academic achievement relationship can best be understood within the context of the person's immediate social environment. Specifically, in terms of social comparison theory, we would expect that the importance of academic achievement for self-concept lies not in the absolute level of achievement but in the child's perceptions of how his/her level of achievement compares with the achievement of those in his/her social comparison group, in this case other classmates. Two children having identical achievement test results but residing in different classrooms would be expected to have differing self-concepts to the extent that their relative academic standing in each class differed.

The implications of this theoretical derivation for research on the self-concept/academic achievement relationship are far from trivial. Most studies in this area have sought large samples in order to augment generalizability and statistical power. This has led many researchers to gather data from different classrooms, schools, or even communities and then pool the data together for purposes of analysis. This could potentially lead, in its extreme form, to a total masking of the relationship between academic achievement and self-concept. For example, consider two third-grade classrooms in each of which there is a perfect positive relationship between academic achievement and self-concept but in which the general level of academic achievement differs substantially, with the highest achiever in the first classroom achieving at the same level as the lowest achiever in the second classroom. If the self-concept and achievement data for these two classrooms were pooled and then a correlation between the two variables was computed, the analysis might reveal a limited or even inverse relationship between the two variables even though within each classroom a perfect correlation existed.

In this view, the maintenance of self-concept is a phenomenological process related to the attributes of the social comparison group within which the individual resides. This study tested the hypothesis that the relationship between academic achievement and self-concept is manifest most clearly within the context of specific social comparison groups, or classrooms. Specifically, two predictions were made. First, it was predicted that academic achievement and self-concept would be positively related, even among academic underachievers in special education classrooms. Second, it was predicted that the self-concept/academic achievement relationship would be manifest most strongly when academic standing within immediate peer-reference groups (i.e., classrooms) was incorporated into the analyses.

METHOD

Participants

Participants in this study were 159 academic underachievers in 17 classrooms in 7 elementary schools of a major metropolitan school system. Participants ranged in age from 6 years 1 month to 12 years 1 month ($M = 9$ years 6 months); 22 percent were black and 25 percent were female. Classroom enrollment ranged from 6 to 14 children.

Children had been placed in the classrooms on the basis of severe academic deficits. Metropolitan Achievement Test scores indicated that the children were functioning approximately 2 years below age-appropriate grade levels. The children had been enrolled in the special education classrooms an average of 14 academic months. Prerequisites for referral were severe academic deficiencies, normal or low-normal intellectual capability, parental consent, and freedom from visual, hearing, or neurological handicaps. The objective of placement in the special classrooms was academic remediation. The 17 special education teachers employed a variety of teaching techniques, focusing on the attainment of sufficient remediation to warrant returning the children to regular classrooms.

Family socioeconomic (SES) information was available from school records on 134 children. A composite family SES score was calculated for each child (Smith, Zingale, & Coleman, in press), based on parental education and occupation, with the utilization of a scale adapted from Warner, Meeker, and Eels (1949). The scale values ranged from 1 (highest SES) to 5 (lowest SES). Mean SES scores for the seven schools ranged from 3.54 to 4.24, which indicated lower-middle-class and working-class student composition. An analysis of variance (ANOVA) indicated no significant SES differences across schools, $F(6,127) = 1.98$, *ns*.

Procedure

Participants were tested within their classrooms. Two testing instruments were group administered, the Metropolitan Achievement Test (MAT) and the Piers-Harris Children's Self-Concept Scale. Given the age and ability differences across the entire sample, two different versions of the MAT were used: The MAT Primary 1 and the MAT Primary II. For children taking the MAT Primary I, Total Reading and Total Mathematics achievement grade equivalents were obtained for each child. For children taking the MAT Primary II, the Word Knowledge, Reading, Math Computation and Math Concepts subtests were administered, yielding a Total Reading grade equivalent and two different mathematics grade equivalents (Computation and Concepts). For the purposes of this study, we treated the average of these two math achievement grade equivalents as roughly comparable with the Total Mathematics achievement grade equivalent yielded by the Primary I.

The second instrument, the Piers-Harris Children's Self-Concept Scale (Piers, 1969), consists of 80 statements of a declarative nature (e.g., "My friends think that I have good ideas") to each of which the respondent marks yes or no. Approximately one half of the statements are positively worded, and the remainder are negatively worded to attenuate potential acquiescent response sets. Items were orally administered, a procedure that has been suggested for administration of the Piers-Harris to children functioning at or below the fifth-grade level (Piers, 1969). The Piers-Harris yields a composite self-concept score that may range from 0 to 80. In addition, the scale may be scored for six cluster scores, each purporting to measure one of these subdimensions of self-concept: (a) Behavior, (b) Intellectual and School Status, (c) Physical Appearance and Attributes, (d) Anxiety, (e) Popularity, and (f) Happiness and Satisfaction. The Piers-Harris manual (Piers, 1969) reported Kuder-Richardson Formula 21 homogeneity coefficients of stability ranging from 0.78 to 0.93. Four-month test-retest coefficients of stability ranged from 0.71 to 0.77. Two recent comparative reviews of the Piers-Harris scale were by Robinson and Shaver (1973) and Wylie (1974).

Analyses

Two series of analyses were computed. First, all 159 subjects[3] were pooled together and rank ordered on the basis of their achievement scores (once for math achievement and once for reading achievement) and on the basis of these rank orderings were assigned to either a high-, medium-, or low-achieving group for mathematics and for reading. On the basis of these two trichotomizations of achievement data, 14 one-factor between-groups ANOVAS were computed (7 for reading achievement and 7 for math achievement), with composite self-concept scores and individual cluster scores as the dependent measures.

Second, participants were rank ordered within each classroom according to their performance on the measure of mathematics achievement and then according to their performance on the measure of reading achievement. Within each class, for each of the two rank orderings, the participants were assigned to one of three groups: high, medium, or low within-classroom academic achievement. To avoid any systematic placement bias, we decided that when class size was not divisible by three, the number of participants assigned to the high and low groups for a given class would be equal. Hence, if the classroom contained 11 children, 3 were assigned to the high-achieving group, 3 to the low-achieving group, and 5 to the medium-achieving group. Finally, for both mathematics and reading achievement, high within-class achievers were pooled together across classrooms, as were medium and low within-class achievers, and 14 one-factor between-groups ANOVAS were computed, 7 for mathematics achievement and 7 for reading achievement, with composite self-concept scores and individual cluster scores as the dependent measures.

Results

When assignment to high-, medium-, or low-achievement groups was based on within-classroom reading achievement, ANOVAS yielded significant group differences in mean composite self-concept scores $F(2,153) = 5.32$, $p < .007$, and significant group differences on all of the six cluster scores. Results of these analyses are summarized in Table 1. Newman-Keuls tests indicated significant pair-wise comparisons between high- and low-achievement groups on the composite self-concept score and on all six cluster scores. In addition, the medium- and high-achievement groups differed significantly on the Intellectual and School Status cluster score, and the low- and medium-reading-achievement groups differed significantly on the Anxiety cluster score. On all seven dependent measures, the high-reading-achievement group obtained the highest mean self-concept score, the low-reading-achievement group obtained the lowest mean self-concept score,

TABLE 1

Mean Self-Concept Scores for Three Reading-Achievement Groups

	ACHIEVEMENT										
	LOW			MEDIUM			HIGH				
PARTITION/CRITERIA	*M*	*SD*	*n*	*M*	*SD*	*n*	*M*	*SD*	*n*	*F*	*p*<
Within classroom											
Composite	51.0	13.0	46	55.3	12.2	64	60.0	14.5	46	5.32	.007
Behavior	11.8	3.5		12.7	3.3		13.5	3.8		3.01	.05
Intellectual and School Status	11.7	3.8		12.4	3.5		14.1	3.4		5.47	.005
Physical Appearance and Attributes	7.6	3.1		8.5	2.9		9.2	2.7		3.52	.05
Anxiety*	6.4	2.7		7.8	2.6		8.3	2.6		6.98	.005
Popularity	7.4	2.6		7.7	2.5		8.6	2.6		3.12	.05
Happiness and Satisfaction	6.2	1.9		6.8	2.0		7.2	2.0		3.46	.05
Irrespective of classroom											
Composite	53.3	11.2	52	56.1	15.0	52	56.6	14.0	52	1.09	*ns*
Behavior	11.7	3.3		13.0	3.4		13.4	3.8		3.46	.05
Intellectual and School Status	12.4	3.3		13.0	3.6		12.7	3.4		<1	*ns*
Physical Appearance and Attributes	8.6	1.8		8.5	3.1		8.1	3.2		<1	*ns*
Anxiety*	6.9	2.7		8.0	2.9		7.8	2.6		2.41	
Popularity	7.6	2.3		7.6	3.0		8.4	2.4		1.97	
Happiness and Satisfaction	6.5	1.8		6.6	2.3		7.0	1.9		<1	*ns*

*High scores indicate low anxiety.

and the mean for the medium-achievement group was intermediate in magnitude.

When the reading achievement trichotomization was conducted irrespective of within-classroom standing, on the other hand, an ANOVA indicated no significant differences among groups in terms of mean composite self-concept scores, $F(2,153)=1.09$. Moreover, there were no significant differences on five of the six cluster scores. Group differences were manifest on the Behavior cluster score, where both medium- and high-reading-achievement groups exhibited means significantly greater than the low-achievement group but did not differ from one another.

When the partition into achievement groups was conducted without considering within-classroom standing, the mean composite self-concept discrepancy between the high- and low-achievement groups was only 3.3 points. On the other hand, this discrepancy was 9.0 points when the partition was made on the basis of relative within-classroom reading achievement. The test for linear trend on composite self-concept for the within-classroom partition was highly significant, $F(1,153)=10.62$, $p < .01$, whereas a similar test for the classroom-irrespective partition was nonsignificant, $F(1,153)=1.56$, *ns*.

When high, medium, and low groups were formed on the basis of math achievement, analyses of composite self-concept scores yielded significant group differences for both the within-classroom partition, $F(2,156)=12.02$, $p < .0001$, and for the classroom-irrespective partition, $F(2,156)=4.17$ $p < .025$. Results of the analyses based on math achievement are summarized in Table 2.

TABLE 2

Mean Self-Concept Scores for Three Math-Achievement Groups

	ACHIEVEMENT										
	LOW			*MEDIUM*			*HIGH*				
PARTITION/CRITERIA	*M*	*SD*	*n*	*M*	*SD*	*n*	*M*	*SD*	*n*	*F*	*p*<
Within classroom											
Composite	48.4	11.4	46	56.6	12.6	67	61.2	14.1	46	12.02	.0001
Behavior	10.7	3.4		13.5	3.2		13.8	3.4		13.14	.0001
Intellectual and School Status	11.3	3.6		13.0	3.5		13.9	3.5		6.36	.005
Physical Appearance and Attributes	7.9	2.8		8.4	2.9		9.3	3.0		2.85	*ns*
Anxiety*	6.2	2.5		7.7	2.6		8.7	2.5		11.89	.001
Popularity	6.9	2.3		8.0	2.5		8.8	2.7		6.17	.005
Happiness and Satisfaction	6.0	1.9		6.9	1.8		7.4	2.0		6.51	.0025
Irrespective of classroom											
Composite	51.5	10.1	53	56.2	14.9	53	58.9	14.5	53	4.17	.025
Behavior	11.5	3.1		12.9	3.6		13.9	3.5		6.48	.0025
Intellectual and School Status	12.6	2.8		12.4	4.1		13.3	3.8		<1	*ns*
Physical Appearance and Attributes	8.8	2.2		8.0	3.3		8.6	3.1		<1	*ns*
Anxiety*	6.4	2.5		7.9	2.6		8.3	2.7		8.53	.001
Popularity	7.5	2.0		7.7	2.9		8.6	2.7		2.64	*ns*
Happiness and Satisfaction	6.0	1.8		7.1	1.9		7.2	2.0		6.44	.0025

*High scores indicate low anxiety.

When the partition was based on within-classroom performance, pair-wise comparisons revealed that low math achievers obtained significantly lower composite self-concept scores than either medium or high math achievers but medium and high groups did not differ. The mean discrepancy between high- and low-achievement groups was 12.8 points. Significant group differences were obtained on five of the six cluster scores. Both medium- and high-achievement group means differed significantly from the low-achievement group means on the five scores that yielded significant F ratios. In addition, the medium and high groups differed significantly on the Anxiety cluster score.

In the trichotomization irrespective of within-classroom achievement, only low and high groups differed significantly on composite self-concept, with a mean difference of 7.4 points. Three of the six cluster score analyses indicated significant group differences for the classroom-irrespective partition: Behavior, Anxiety, and Happiness and Satisfaction. In each case, both medium- and high-achievement groups obtained significantly greater mean scores than the low-achievement group, but they did not differ significantly from each other.

Tests for linear trend among composite self-concept scores produced significant results for both the within-classroom partition, $F(1,156)=23.28$, $p < .01$, and the classroom-irrespective partition, $F(1,156)= 8.15$, $p < .01$.

Since previous research has indicated a positive relationship between IQ and self-concept (for example, Coopersmith, 1967; Piers, 1969), the differential results found here for the two methods of examining the academic achievement/self-concept relationship might have been the result of greater concomitant variation of IQ and achievement when participants were grouped on the basis of within-classroom reading achievement standing. To test this alternative explanation, we conducted two further ANOVAS, using IQ scores available for 118 of the participants from a previous administration of the Wechsler Intelligence Scale for Children—Revised as the dependent variable and high-, medium-, and low-reading achievement groupings as the independent variable. The results of these analyses are summarized in Table 3. The first analysis, with groupings derived from within-classroom achievement standing, yielded significant group differences, $F(2,115)=3.32$, $p < .05$, with low reading achievers exhibiting significantly lower IQs than high achievers and medium reading achievers not differing in IQ significantly from either low or high achievers. The second analysis, with the achievement groupings derived without concern for within-classroom achievement standing, also yielded a significant group difference, $F(2,115)=7.70$, $p < .001$. Low reading achievers had significantly lower IQs than medium or high achievers, but medium and high achievers did not differ significantly in IQ. These results tend to rule out the IQ/self-concept hypothesis as an alternative explanation, expecially given that the IQ discrepancy between the high and low reading achievers was only 6.25 points when trichotomization occurred within classrooms but was 8.23 points when the trichotomization occurred irrespective of within-classroom achievement standing.

DISCUSSION

These results strongly supported our basic hypothesis that the relationship between academic achievement and self-concept is manifest most strongly within

TABLE 3

Mean WISC-R IQs for Three Reading-Achievement Groups

	ACHIEVEMENT									
	LOW			MEDIUM			HIGH			
PARTITION	M	SD	n	M	SD	n	M	SD	n	F
Within classroom	84.53	10.33	32	87.46	10.68	46	90.78	9.76	40	3.32*
Irrespective of classroom	81.67	9.00	30	89.89	11.33	47	89.90	9.13	41	7.70†

Note. WISC-R = Wechsler Intelligence Scale for Children—Revised.
*$p < .05$.
†$p < .01$.

the context of the social comparison group or classroom. When participants were assigned to either a high-, medium-, or low-achievement group within their particular classroom on the basis of either reading or math achievement test results, a strong positive relationship was found between academic achievement and self-concept. This relationship appears to be not only statistically significant but substantial as well, with an average composite self-concept score difference between low and high achievers of 9 points for math achievement. In contrast, when this trichotomization was conducted irrespective of within-classroom achievement standing, no relationship was found between reading achievement and self-concept, and although a significant relationship was found between math achievement and self-concept, the strength of this relationship was substantially less than when trichotomization was conducted within the classroom.

Analyses of subdimensions of self-concept, as measured by the Piers-Harris cluster scores, also strongly supported the hypothesized social comparison bases of self-concept maintenance. For example, when the within-classroom partitions were made on the basis of reading achievment, the cluster-score means uniformly were ordered high achievement>medium achievement>low achievement, and all six ANOVAS were significant. This pattern of mean scores is in sharp contrast to the classroom-irrespective partition, in which the high>medium>low pattern was manifest on only two cluster scores and only one of these reflected significant group differences.

This investigation was predicated upon the theoretical premise that an individual's self-concept is based in part on an edifice of social comparisons. This viewpoint assumes that the group(s) available to the individual are appropriate for making self-concept relevant social comparisons. A child could well be a member of a classroom, however, and never utilize his/her classmates for comparison purposes with regard to some dimensions of self-concept. For example, a child's self-concept of himself/herself as a gymnast might be based minimally, if at all, on school classmates but rather on the members of the evening gymnastics class at the Y.

In the context of the present study, the dimension of self-concept that should be most sensitive to within-classroom social comparisons is self-concept of academic ability. While the child's classmates might be inappropriate as a social comparison group for some dimensions of self-concept, this group should be salient and optimally appropriate for forming and maintaining the self-concept of academic ability.

The Piers-Harris scale used in this study yields an Intellectual and School Status cluster score that conceptually appears to tap the self-concept of academic ability construct. (Representative items: I am good in my schoolwork. I am a good reader. My classmates think I have good ideas.) This cluster score was extremely sensitive to within-classroom and classroom-irrespective partitions on both reading and math achievement indexes. Significant group differences on this variable were obtained for both reading and math achievement within-classroom partitions, but no group differences were obtained when the partitions on achievement were made irrespective of relative within-classroom performance. Thus, the social comparison basis of self-concept maintenance seems especially clear when the subdimension of self-concept conceptually most relevant to the classroom peer group is examined closely.

While the results of this study seem relatively clear, a number of factors do potentially limit their generalizability to other settings. First, participants in this study were academic underachievers attending special classrooms. Although we have no reason to believe that these results originate in the unique characteristics of the sample, replication of our findings with a more normative setting would be desirable. Second, our decision to consider the average of Math Computation and Math Concepts grade equivalents for children taking the MAT Primary I conceivably may have led to a confounding of results for math achievement analyses. This was not thought to be a serious problem, however, since the Total Mathematics score on the Primary I consists of a combination of computation and concepts components. Therefore, the Primary I Total Math and an average of the Primary II Math Computation and Math Concepts should be at least roughly comparable. Third, we have made no effort to differentiate between self-concept and self-report, notwithstanding widespread recognition that the reported self-concept (what the individual willingly divulges about himself/ herself) and what an individual truly thinks of himself/herself may not correspond exactly. The measurement of self-concept is fraught with problems of social desirability, systematic response bias, response restriction, contextual effects, and myriad other pitfalls (Wylie, 1974). Numerous indirect, unobtrusive, and projective self-concept assessment instruments have been developed over the years (Robinson & Shaver, 1973; Wylie, 1974) in efforts to avoid the pitfalls inherent in the administration of self-report inventories. We realize the drawbacks and limitations to self-report inventories, yet we believe the administration of a well-standardized self-report instrument is preferable to the projective or less obtrusive alternatives. Our philosophy of self-concept measurement was succinctly summarized by Nunnally (1975, pp. 106–7): "Long ago the author came to the conclusion that generally the most valid, economical, sometimes the only, way to learn about a person's sentiments is simply to ask him."

Despite the possible limitations of generalizability, our findings clearly support the hypothesis derived from social comparison theory that the most meaningful way to understand the relationship between academic achievement and self-concept is within the context of the social comparison group or classroom. When information regarding relative academic standing within the classroom was considered, a strong relationship between both reading and math achievement with self-concept was found; but when information regarding relative academic standing within the classroom was not considered, reading achievement showed no relationship to self-concept, and the observed relationship between math achievement and self-concept was substantially less robust. Our results suggest that one basic way in which academic achievement influences self-concept is through the process of social comparison: The child compares his/her own level of achievement to the achievement levels of others in the classroom, and to the extent that the results of such a comparison are favorable, his or her self-concept is enhanced, but if the comparison is unfavorable, his or her self-concept may be diminished.

NOTES

1 Kohr, R. L. "A longitudinal study of self-concept from grade 5 to 9." Paper presented at the meeting of the National Council on Measurement in Education, Chicago, April 1974, p. 7.

2 Gecas, V., Calonico, J., & Thomas, D. "The development of self-concept in the child: mirror theory versus model theory." Paper presented at the meeting of the American Sociological Association, New Orleans, November 1972.

3 For all reading-achievement analyses, $N=156$ subjects. Three of the 159 subjects failed to complete the reading-achievement subtests.

REFERENCES

Black, F. W.

1974 "Self-concept as related to achievement and age in learning-disabled children." Child Development 45: 1137–40.

Bledsoe, J.

1967 "Self-concept of children and their intelligence, achievement, interests, and anxiety." Child Education 43: 436–83.

Coopersmith, S.

1959 "A method of determining types of self-esteem." Journal of Abnormal and Social Psychology 59: 87–94.

1967 The Antecedents of Self-Esteem. San Francisco: Freeman.

Festinger, L.

1954 "A theory of social comparison processes." Human Relations 2: 117–40.

Fink, M. B.

1962 "Self-concept as it relates to academic underachievement." California Journal of Educational Research 13: 57–62.

Hyman, H. H. and Singer, E.

1967 "An introduction to reference group theory and research." In E. P. Hollander & R. G. Hunt (eds.), Current perspectives in social psychology, 2d ed. New York: Oxford University Press.

Lamy, M. L.

1965 "Relationships of self-concept of early primary children to achievement in reading." In I. J. Gordon (ed.), Human development: Readings in research, Glenview, Ill.: Scott Foresman.

Lewis, R. W.

1972 "The relationship of self-concept to reading achievement." Unpublished doctoral dissertation. University of Virginia.

Nunnally, J. C.
1975 "The study of change in evaluation research: principles concerning measurement, experimental design, and analysis." In E. L. Struening & M. Guttentag (eds.), Handbook of Evaluation Research. Vol. 1. Beverly Hills, Calif: Sage.
Piers, E. V.
1969 Manual for the Piers-Harris Children's Self-Concept Scale. Nashville, Tenn.: Counselor Recordings and Tests.
Purkey, W. W.
1970 Self-Concept and Academic Achievement. Englewood Cliffs, N.J.: Prentice-Hall.
Robinson, J. P. and Shaver, P. R.
1973 Measures of Social Psychological Attitudes, Rev. ed. Ann Arbor, Mich.: Institute for Social Research.
Smith, M. D., S. A. Zingale, and J. M. Coleman
In press. "The influence of adult-expectancy/child performance discrepancies upon children's self-concepts." American Educational Research Journal.
Warner, W. L., M. Meeker, and K. W. Eels
1949 Social Class in America. Chicago: Science Research Associates.
Wattenberg, W. W. and C. Clifford
1964 "Relation of self-concepts to beginning achievement in reading." Child Development 35: 461–67.
Williams, J. H.
1973 "The relationship of self-concept and reading achievement in first-grade children." Journal of Educational Research 66: 378–81.
Williams, R. L. and S. Cole
1968 "Self-concept and school adjustment." American Personnel and Guidance Journal 46: 478–81.
Wylie, R. C.
1974 The Self-Concept, Rev. ed., Vol. 1. Lincoln: University of Nebraska Press.

FOUR

SOCIAL INSTITUTIONS

Every society must somehow ensure that certain essential functions are performed if it is to survive (Aberle, Cohen, Davis, Levy, and Sutton, 1950; Merton, 1968). The chief functions are fulfilled within the framework of social institutions. In this section, we are concerned with the interaction of these social institutions with individual self-concepts. In some cases, the focus is on how the institution helps to shape the self-concept; in other cases, on how the self-concept influences institutional functioning and behavior; and in still other cases, on the mutual influence of the two. This section considers the family, educational institution, political institution, economic institution, and military institution.

FAMILY INSTITUTION

The family is a universal institutional system whose fundamental social function is the care, rearing, and socialization of the new generation. It is within this framework that the uncivilized human animal is converted into a civilized, effectively functioning, truly human being. The family is the chief agency of socialization, a coauthor of personality, and, to use Rainwater's (1966) felicitous expression, "the crucible of identity." The self-concept is first formed within this context.

Psychoanalytic theory has assigned critical importance to the family in the formation of personality, contending that every child goes through a series of developmental stages which must be successfully completed before he or she can master the next one on the route to maturity. Failure to resolve the conflicts inherent in each of these stages may lead to fixation at an earlier stage of development; current behavior is, therefore, frequently explained as a symbolic recapitulation of earlier experiences. Various family dramas and conflicts—the oedipal conflict being the most critical—are played out in moving through the necessary stages of personality development.

But a radically different approach to family and personality structure may also be advanced. If one views the self-concept as the thoughts and feelings that the individual has about himself or herself, then its formation is subject to the same principles that govern all attitude formation. Three of these principles are particularly relevant in the present context. The first is that it is easier to affect uncrystallized or nonschematic attitudes than firmly fixed and structured schemata. The second is that highly respected sources of communication will more powerfully affect attitudes than low prestige sources. The third principle is that messages frequently communicated tend to have a stronger impact than those presented rarely.

Herein may rest the significance of the family for the self-concept. Since it is the influence that comes first, its effect is particularly powerful because, at this point, the self-concept is so uncrystallized. There is no self-concept at birth; only gradually, in the course of maturation and interaction, does the self-concept emerge. At this critical juncture, when the structure is the weakest it will ever be, the child's parents (and perhaps siblings) hold a virtual monopoly on communication. In the absence of any previous attitudes or seriously contending viewpoints, the child has little else but the family's opinions to go on. If they think well of the child, then the child is likely to think well of him or herself. Parental attitudes are important, then, because they come first, before a firmly structured self-concept has emerged and crystallized. Later in life, the most vigorous psychoanalytic efforts may be impotent in changing an established self-schema.

A second principle is that highly valued and respected sources will have more powerful attitude effects than others. This fact has long been shown to be the case with regard to attitudes in general (especially unstructured ones) and has also been demonstrated with reference to self-attitudes (Bergin, 1962; Gergen, 1971; Rosenberg, 1973). With regard to the family, one point which may not be evident to the casual observer, but which is vividly demonstrated in child development studies (Piaget, 1948; Flavell, 1974; Schantz, 1975; Damon, 1977) is the enormous respect of young children for adults. This level of respect, to be sure, is not always apparent in the child's behavior. Although children may violate the rules laid down for them, they do not challenge either their validity or the wisdom of their adult propagators. Children may not like what their parents tell them—parental don'ts are never welcome—but they do not challenge the adults' judgments (Damon, 1977). This, then, is the second reason for the importance of the family for self-concept formation—that the adults with whom children have the most sustained interaction and who judge and evaluate them are those whose assessment of the children are most respected.

The third point is that repeated communications are likely to have a more powerful impact than occasional ones. In the family, the child is in constant and sustained interaction with parents day after day, week after week, year after year, so that any general or consistent attitudes they hold toward him or her are inevitably communicated. It is indeed a dictum of communications research that repetition of a message with variation is a highly effective technique of attitude formation and change; and this the child gets in the family. Family members communicate thousands of times in thousands of ways what they think of, and how they view, the child. Such ceaseless propaganda can hardly be without effect.

We thus share with psychoanalysis the view that the early years are important for personality development but our reasons differ. We agree with Epstein (1973), Lecky (1945), and McGuire and Padawer-Singer (1976) that the one's self-concept is the fundamental structure or theory that guides one through life; it is persistent, omnipresent, inescapable, powerful. Because it is not present at birth, emerging only in the course of social interaction, it is especially susceptible to influence by others in the early years because, at that point, the child has nothing else to go on. But this self-concept, once formed, becomes the individual's fundamental frame of reference. The individual adheres to it, particularly its central elements, with great tenacity. Although peripheral or uncrystallized aspects of the self-concept are easily changed, the central components change only with the greatest difficulty. The critical importance of the family, then, is that it exerts its influence precisely at the time of life when the self-concept is most subject to influence.

Actual research on the relationship of parental attitudes or behavior to the child's self-esteem has confirmed certain common expectations but has contradicted others. Coopersmith (1967) found that parental acceptance of the child was positively related to the child's self-esteem, Rosenberg (1963,1965) found parental interest in the child and closeness to the father were positively related to self-esteem, and Sears (1970) found that children of mothers and fathers described as warm when the child was five proved to have substantially higher self-esteem when measured seven years later.

But there are also unexpected findings. One of the most interesting of these is reported in Selection 26, by Coopersmith. The special merit of this study is that it relates the information derived from parents and children independently. Coopersmith interviewed parents to ascertain their attitudes toward childrearing practices, feelings about their children, and reported behavior in family interaction and related these responses to the global self-esteem of their children. Contrary to a powerful child-rearing ideology which has had wide influence over the past quarter century, Coopersmith shows that increasing permissiveness is not associated with higher self-esteem. Firmness and strictness are not inconsistent with parental love and interest and are so interpreted by the child.

That parent-child relations are likely to have an impact on personality development—especially self-esteem—is thus an article of faith of most social scientists. But how much of an impact? This question can best be answered by comparing it to other putative influences. This is the issue addressed by Bachman in his nationwide study of tenth-grade boys (Selection 27). Compared to such variables as socioeconomic level, sibling structure, religious preference, and IQ, how effectively does the youth's perceived relationship with his parents predict his global self-esteem? Bachman's results impressively document the importance of such parent-child relationships.

EDUCATIONAL INSTITUTION

The primary function of the educational institution is the transmission of knowledge to the new generation in order to prepare it for the effective performance of adult social roles. (The term knowledge is used in a broad sense to include not only facts or objective truth but also norms, values, attitudes, and orientations.) Schools are the primary settings within which teachers, principals, pupils, and other personnel carry out their assigned functions.

A depiction of the diverse ways in which this institutional structure may interact with the individual's self-concept far exceeds the scope of this work. We have elected to focus on one aspect of the educational system which bears very directly on self-esteem—the individual's school marks. Marks are important because they are one of the very few public, objective, and unequivocal indications of an important aspect of the child's worth. These letters or numbers are explicit statements by a recognized authority—the teacher—of how good one is, and this public information is transmitted to other authorities—the parents.

Yet the relationship between school marks and self-esteem, as Rogers et al. (Selection 25) have noted, have been rather inconsistent. In considering these findings, it is necessry to direct attention to four issues: part-whole influences, independent effects, direction of causal influence, and changes across time.

The first question is whether, insofar as the self-concept does bear on school performance, it is the broad dimension of global self-esteem or the specific component of academic self-concept that is responsible. Each of these aspects of the self-concept is important but they are conceptually distinct. Many of the studies cited by Purkey (1970) which examine the relationship between global self-esteem and school marks show correlations ranging between 0.15 and 0.25.

On the other hand, the study by Brookover, Thomas, and Paterson, presented as Selection 28, shows correlations of 0.57 between the specific academic self-*concept component and grade point average (see also Mintz and Muller, 1977). The obvious policy implication of such a finding is that, if one were to attempt to improve academic performance by changing self-concepts, efforts should be directed toward changing academic self-concepts rather than global self-esteem. Indeed the general principle extends beyond the particular case. Although some generalization between the specific and the global exists, Wylie (1979) has shown that behavior in a particular area tends to be more strongly associated with the pertinent self-concept component than with global self-esteem.*

The second issue relates to the specification of the effective influence. In arguing that the academic self-concept influences school performance, it is important to ensure that it is the self-concept, not the actual person, *that is responsible for the performance. For example, assume that more intelligent students think they are more academically talented and also earn better marks. Their better marks may not be due to their* belief *that they are academically talented but to their* actual *academic talent. The meaningful question is:* Among those of equivalent ability, *are favorable self-attitudes conducive to superior performance? (Wylie, 1979).*

When Brookover et al. examine the relationship between the self-concept and academic performance, then, they control on the individual's measured intelligence. As noted earlier, among seventh graders, grade point average and the self-concept of ability scale show a correlation of 0.57 for both boys and girls. Controlling on IQ, the correlations still remain 0.42 and 0.39, respectively. Good school performance, then, appears to be due not simply to the fact that the pupil actually is intelligent but also—and this is critical from the self-concept viewpoint—because the pupil has a high opinion of his or her academic ability.

The third problem connected with the interpretation of the relationship between grades and self-esteem is the causal connection between these variables: Are grades responsible for self-esteem? Or is self-esteem responsible for grades? These questions have both theoretical and practical implications. On the theoretical side, the finding that self-esteem has a greater impact on school marks than school marks have on self-esteem would lend support to self-consistency theory. As noted in Section One, this theory holds that people behave in such a fashion as to maintain and reinforce their pictures of self, whether positive or negative. Behavior and its outcomes are thus seen as products of the motive to be true to an established self-picture. On the other hand, the finding that school marks affect self-esteem more than the other way around would lend empirical support to self-attribution *theory. By taking note of one's correct answers or good marks, one comes to view oneself—as one might view some other person—with respect and admiration. One thus draws conclusions about one's own worth by observing what one has done.*

Different policy implications also inhere in the question of whether self-esteem or school marks has the greater effect on the other. Some educators have contended that the poor performance of certain minority group children is attributable to their socially induced inferiority feelings, and that, insofar as motivation bears on performance, achievement can be enhanced by efforts directed toward raising their self-esteem. If the data show that self-esteem does have the predominant effect on marks, then the wisdom of such a policy would acquire empirical support; if the reverse were the case, then such efforts (for the purposes at hand) would appear to be misplaced, however laudatory they might be on other grounds.

Research by Calsyn and Kenny (1977) using the cross-lagged panel correlation technique, attempts to answer the question of which variable—self-esteem or school marks—has the greater effect on the other. Among their findings are data showing that the student's academic achievement affects self-concept of academic ability more than the other way around; this is true, however, for females but not for males. The data for females, then, are consistent with self-perception or self-attribution theory. Why this finding does not hold for males remains an unanswered question.

In directing attention to a relationship, such as that between school performance and self-esteem, it is necessary to recognize the time and culture-boundedness of most empirical generalizations in social psychology. As Cronbach (1975) has observed, empirical generalizations decay; a finding that holds true at one time and place cannot necessarily be assumed to hold true at another. This is not to suggest that the abstract principles underlying the data are in error but that the same principles may produce different empirical results under different conditions.

The relationship between academic performance and self-esteem is an apt case in point. If the academic values of a new cohort of students changes, will the relationship between educational variables and self-esteem also change? This is the question that O'Malley and Bachman address in Selection 29, drawing upon two carefully selected nationwide surveys to compare the relationships among high school seniors in 1969 with high school seniors in 1977.

POLITICAL INSTITUTION

Every society must somehow ensure that people follow certain essential social rules; must arrange for the arbitration and settlement of conflicts among its members or groups; and must organize activities concerned with collective action, whether they are related to internal or external affairs. In fulfilling these functions, a number of institutional agencies, such as political parties, courts, government units, and legislatures, represent settings for the playing of relevant social roles: politicians, civil servants, judges, police, and citizens.

Over the years, a number of political scientists, interested in understanding how personality factors might bear upon such behavior as political participation among citizens or power-seeking among aspiring leaders, have turned their attention to the self-concept as an explanatory variable. Some of the more prominent explanations of the striving for political power can be traced to Alfred Adler's earlier ideas on compensation for feelings of inferiority. In Adler's view, individuals afflicted with organ inferiority will seek to compensate for their deficiencies in order to overcome their low feelings of self-worth. Demosthenes stuttered as a boy: In order to overcome his handicap, he placed pebbles in his mouth and sought to shout down the waves. Napoleon's drive for power was said to stem from inferiority feelings about his height.

Developing the ideas adumbrated by Adler, the pioneering political scientist Harold Lasswell (1948) advanced the general hypothesis that the power seeker pursues power as a means of compensation for deprivation. Power is expected to overcome low estimates of the self by changing either the traits of the self or the environment within which it functions. "The accentuation of power is to be understood as a compensatory reaction against low estimates of the self. . . ." Individuals strive to validate a self-hypothesis, seeking to convince others of their worth basically in order to convince themselves. In fairly direct intellectual descent from Lasswell, Robert Lane (1959) has attempted to spell out this position. "One of the common sources of the need for power is a deeper need for reassurance about the self—'I am not weak,' 'I am not insignificant,' 'I am not dependent.' This need for reassurance is, of course, related to lack of self-confidence, feelings of unworthiness, and low self-esteem" (p. 127). Political biographers, such as Alexander L. George (1968), have addressed the issue of power-seeking as a compensatory value among political leaders.

Some theorists, however, have suggested that the self-concept may inhibit political behavior, representing a major source of political apathy. Lasswell himself pointed out, "At the same time adverse estimates of the self must not be overwhelming, or the resort to power will be blocked by sentiments of utter hopelessness." Similarly, Goldhamer (1950), viewing low self-esteem as a major problem in neurosis, suggests that people may be so exhausted by inner conflicts that they have no time or energy left for public affairs. Horney's concept (1950) of neurotic egocentricity is also in accord with this conclusion. In this view, the individual suffering from crippling or incapacitating emotional problems is so wrapped up in his or her inner world that remote matters of broad scope are felt as unreal or irrelevant.

Empirical evidence showing that low self-esteem may influence political attitudes, participation, interests, and involvement has been presented by Rosenberg (1962), Sniderman and Citrin (1971), Sniderman (1975), and Abramson (1977). In addition, Carmines, in Selection 30, provides evidence that adolescents with low self-esteem have more vague and inaccurate pictures of political and governmental authorities; feel they can do little to influence the government; and are more disposed to engage in protest activity against government policies. Carmines' paper ingeniously takes account of the widely overlooked fact that personality factors affect political behavior only among those to whom political issues are salient. The most psychologically healthy people in the world will not be politically active if they are uninterested in politics—nor should they be. It is primarily among those who are politically interested that the self-concept exercises its political effect.

It would be inappropriate to assume, incidentally, that the self-concept only affects political attitudes and has no bearing on political behavior. Fromm (1941) has argued persuasively that many of the people who supported Adolf Hitler were those who felt insignificant, impotent, and isolated (low self-esteem, low efficacy, high individuation) and who, in order to gain a sense of pride, power, and efficacy, submerged themselves in a mass political movement directed by a powerful leader preaching their racial superiority and promising them national aggrandizement and glory. The social consequences of disturbed self-concepts may be profound indeed.

ECONOMIC INSTITUTION

Among vocational counselors, one idea that has exercised widespread influence has been Super's (1953) self-concept implementation theory of occupational choice. *This theory, which holds that occupational choice involves the matching of self-concept and occupational role, has been consistently supported by research (Morrison, 1962; Oppenheimer, 1966; Marks and Webb, 1969; Leonard, Walsh, and Osipow, 1973). Subsequent research (Korman, 1967; Dipboye, Zaltowski, Dewhirst, and Arvey, 1978; Inskon, 1978) generally suggests that such matching influences occupational adjustment as well. This fact has immense importance both for the individual and for society. There are actually few more fateful decisions in life than an occupational choice—decisions involving long-term commitments which influence the individual's chances of leading a rich, satisfying life. Furthermore, although the decision is not necessarily irrevocable, current occupational specialization is so extreme that the possibilities of change are definitely limited. Therefore, for most people a vocational choice is not simply a decision about what one will be doing tomorrow but about what one will be doing 30 years from now. The self-concept (true or false, accurate or distorted) which governs one's occupational choice thereby structures one's fate.*

But the significance of the occupational decision is no less critical for society. The chief dynamic component of a social structure consists of people fulfilling their occupational roles. Incorrect occupational choices (based, for example, on distorted self-concepts) thus affect the entire system. As an obvious example, when girls are taught that girls lack mathematical or scientific talent and, on grounds of these self-concepts, eschew such fields as physics and engineering, the society is deprived of an important pool of scientific talent.

Super's self-concept implementation theory of vocational choice underwent an important modification when Korman (Selection 31) suggested that self-esteem was a moderator variable conditioning the relationship between self-concept and occupational choice. The springboard for this argument is that, although the self-concept bears on occupational choice, it is not the only determinant. Some people choose occupations in response to other influences (for example, the advice or pressure of parents, peers, or teachers) or on the basis of concern with extrinsic rewards (money, security). What distinguishes those who implement the self-concept from those who do not? Korman suggests that the critical factor is global self-esteem. And, indeed, he is able to demonstrate that, among those with high self-esteem, the self-concept and occupational choice are closely matched, but among those with low self-esteem, they are not. A number of other studies have examined this observed conditional relationship (Dipboye, Zultowski, Dewhirst, and Arvey, 1978; Inkson, 1978) and have generally confirmed the postulate. People with high self-esteem tend to choose occupations which fit their self-concepts whereas those with low self-esteem tend to make their choices on other grounds.

In all societies, different occupations command different levels of social respect. There is impressive agreement across diverse segments within societies regarding which occupations are higher or lower, better or worse, superior or inferior (Hodge and Treiman, 1968; Simmons and Rosenberg, 1971); in fact, the same is true across societies (Inkeles and Rossi, 1956; Treiman, 1977). The principle of reflected appraisals would thus suggest that, in the long run, people's self-esteem will come to correspond more or less to their occupational prestige.

But, given the self-esteem motive, one can hardly expect those in low-status positions to accept passively the social definition of their lesser worth without a struggle. The question addressed by Simpson and Simpson in Selection 32, then, is: How do people in low status occupations attempt to salvage their self-esteem in the face of these facts? Simpson and Simpson focus on the plight of the psychiatric attendant, the person occupying the lowest status in the mental hospital. Although attendants do many things in the mental hospital, Simpson and Simpson found that they tend to focus on those activities most highly valued in this setting—patient therapy and care—rather than on those activities in which they are primarily engaged, such as housekeeping and related chores. In these and other ways, these people attempt to cope with those social forces which assault their cherished feelings of self-worth.

In the economic realm, the activities of individuals playing out their occupational roles are primarily directed toward the production and distribution of goods and services in the society. But all this requires the participation of another actor in the economic process—the consumer. It is he who is the ultimate target of all this hectic occupational activity. Cox and Bauer (Selection 33) suggest that the self-concept may also influence the consumer's behavior. Evidence has been adduced (Janis and Field, 1959) to suggest that people with lower self-confidence tend to be more persuasible, although the generalization appears to apply to men but not to women (see McGuire, 1968). But, as we observed in Section One, the self-confidence dimension exists both as a general disposition and also as a specific self-dimension. That someone is confident of his or her ability to perform well on the basketball court does not guarantee that he or she is self-confident about success in a wide range of other endeavors, nor vice versa. The purpose of Cox and Bauer's investigation is to understand how this fact influences the consumer's tendency to accept a sales message regarding the merits of a product. They emerge with the interesting finding that the people most persuaded by the salesgirls' message are those with medium general self-confidence. People with low self-confidence are probably suspicious of the other's motives whereas those high in self-confidence are sure of their own judgment; their consumer orientations follow from these premises. But this generalization is conditional upon specific self-confidence. Among those women who strongly believed that they were knowledgeable in the consumer area under consideration, general self-confidence played no role. It was only among those less sure of their specific expertise that global self-confidence made a difference.

MILITARY INSTITUTION

Whether the military organization should be treated as an independent institution or as an institutional agency of the political order is a definitional issue that need not be settled for the present purposes. Suffice it to say that the military is an organization serving as an instrument for the exercise of violence, and that, like all institutions, it implements this purpose through the distribution of roles assigned to different positions. But how these tasks are performed depends on the definition of appropriate role behavior and on the individual's self-concept judged in the light of that image.

The case of the Greek military officer (Selection 34) serves to exemplify the concept of a role standard. Associated with most social identity elements is a social expectation, shared by the individual, that incumbents of particular statuses will possess appropriate qualities or characteristics and will behave in appropriate ways. The role standard may be thought of as a socially defined idealized image. Everyone has a picture of the "perfect mother," "ideal teacher," "model officer," and "ideal doctor." These models represent standards by which the individual is socially evaluated and in terms of which he or she evaluates himself or herself. Thus, a mother may not neglect her baby, a man may not cry, a nurse should be sympathetic, a woman compassionate, a man a good provider, and so on.

Such role standards may, however, change with historical circumstances. Indeed, at a particular point in time, competing role models may be found. Kourvetaris' study of the Greek Army officer corps is a good case in point. In an earlier work on American military officers, Janowitz (1960) suggested that, as a consequence of new military technology, a shift had occurred from a heroic self-image to a managerial self-image. Using this work as a springboard, Kourvetaris presents a typology of Greek Army officers' self-images: the hero-image, built around such virtues as courage, adherence to lofty principle, loyalty, honor, self-reliance, self-esteem, and others. The second is the technical specialist self-image, built around efficiency, knowledge, competence, and managerial skills. The third type is a synthesis of the two. Kourvetaris examines the difference in military attitudes of these types and investigates certain social background factors that might underlie these differences.

Such competing standards may represent a source of strain both to the individual and society. At a given historical period, many social roles may include competing images (the kindly personal family practitioner image versus the impersonal, scientific, up-to-date young doctor; the traditional intellectual professor discoursing on philosophy with students in a book-lined study versus the high-powered professorial consultant and grant-getter spending more time on planes than in libraries). One problem faced by occupational incumbents is that the course of historical events may produce a shift in the occupational role definition while the individual's self-concept remains the same.

REFERENCES

Aberle, D., A. Cohen, A. Davis, M. Levy, and F. Sutton.
1950 "The functional prerequisites of a society." Ethics 60: 100–11.
Abramson, P. R.
1977 The Political Socialization of Black Americans. New York: Free Press.
Bergin, A. E.
1962 "The effect of dissonant persuasive communications upon changes in self-referring attitudes." Journal of Personality 30: 423–38.
Calsyn, R. J. and D. A. Kenny
1977 "Self-concept of ability and perceived evaluation of others: cause or effect of academic achievement?" Journal of Educational Psychology 69: 136–45.
Coopersmith, S.
1967 The Antecedents of Self-Esteem. San Francisco: Freeman.
Cronbach, L. J.
1975 "Beyond the two disciplines of scientific psychology." American Psychologist 30: 116–27.

Damon, W.
1977 The Social World of the Child. San Francisco: Jossey-Bass.
Dipboye, R. L., W. H. Zultowski, H. D. Dewhirst, and R. D. Arvey
1978 "Self-esteem as a moderator of the relationship between scientific interests and job satisfaction of physicists and engineers." Organizational Behavior and Human Performance 63: 289–94.
Epstein, S.
1973 "The self-concept revisited: or a theory of a theory." American Psychologist 28: 404–16.
Flavell, J.
1974 "The development of inferences about others." In T. Mischel (ed.), Understanding Other Persons. Oxford: Blackwell.
Fromm, E.
1941 Escape from Freedom. New York: Rinehart.
George, A. L.
1968 "Power as a compensatory value for political leaders." Journal of Social Issues 24: 29–49.
Gergen, K.
1971 The Concept of Self. New York: Holt, Rinehart, & Winston.
Goldhamer, H.
1950 "Public opinion and personality." American Journal of Sociology 55: 346–54.
Hodge, R. W. and D. J. Treiman
1968 "Class identification in the United States." American Journal of Sociology 73: 535–47.
Horney, K.
1950 Neurosis and Human Growth. New York: Norton.
Inkeles, A. and P. H. Rossi
1956 "National comparisons of occupational prestige." American Journal of Sociology 61: 329–39.
Inskon, J. K.
1978 "Self-esteem as a moderator of the relationship between job performance and job satisfaction." Journal of Applied Psychology 63: 243–47.
Janis, I. L. and P. B. Field
1959 "Sex differences and personality factors related to persuasibility." Pp.55–68 in C. I. Hovland and I. L. Janis (eds.), Personality and Persuasibility. New Haven: Yale University Press.
Janowitz, M.
1960 The Professional Soldier: A Social and Political Portrait. New York: Free Press.
Korman, A. K.
1967 "Self-esteem as a moderator of the relationship between self-perceived abilities and vocational choice." Journal of Applied Psychology 51: 65–67.
Lane, R. E.
1959 Political Life. New York: Free Press.
Lasswell, H. D.
1948 Power and Personality. New York: Norton.
Lecky, P.
1945 Self-Consistency: A Theory of Personality. New York: Island Press.
Leonard, R. L., W. B. Walsh, and S. H. Osipow
1973 "Self-esteem, self-consistency, and second occupational choice." Journal of Counseling Psychology 20: 91–93.
Marks, E. and S. C. Webb
1969 "Vocational choice and professional experience as factors in occupational image." Journal of Applied Psychology 53: 292–300.

McGuire, W. J.
1968 "Personality and susceptibility to social influence." Pp. 1130–87 in E. F. Borgatta and W. W. Lambert (eds.), Handbook of Personality Theory and Research. Chicago: Rand McNally.
McGuire, W. J. and A. Padawer-Singer
1976 "Trait salience in the spontaneous self-concept." Journal of Personality and Social Psychology 33: 743–54.
Merton, R. K.
1968 Social Theory and Social Structure. Enlarged edition. New York: Free Press. Chapter 5.
Mintz, R. and Muller, D.
1977 "Academic achievement as a function of specific and global measures of self-concept." Journal of Psychology 97: 53–57.
Morrison, R. L.
1962 "Self-concept implementation in occupational choices." Journal of Counseling Psychology 9: 255–60.
Oppenheimer, E. A.
1966 "The relationship between certain self-constructs and occupational preference." Journal of Counseling Psychology 13: 191–97.
Piaget, J.
1948 The Moral Judgment of the Child. Glencoe, Ill. Free Press.
Purkey, W. W.
1970 Self-Concept and School Achievement. Englewood Cliffs, Prentice-Hall.
Rainwater, L.
1966 "Crucible of identity: the Negro lower-class family." Daedalus 95: 172–216.
Rosenberg, M.
1962 "Self-esteem and concern with public affairs." Public Opinion Quarterly 26: 201–11.
1963 "Parental interest and children's self-conceptions." Sociometry 26: 35–49.
1965 Society and the Adolescent Self-Image. Princeton, N.J.: Princeton University Press.
1973 "Which significant others?" American Behavioral Scientist 16: 829–60.
Schantz, C.
1975 "The development of social cognition." In E. M. Hetherington (ed.), Review of Child Development Theory and Research., Vol. 5. Chicago: University of Chicago Press.
Sears, R. R.
1970 "Relation of early socialization experiences to self-concepts and gender role in middle childhood." Child Development 41: 267–89.
Simmons, R. G. and M. Rosenberg
1971 "Functions of children's perceptions of the stratification system." American Sociological Review 36: 235–49.
Sniderman, P.
1975 Personality and Democratic Politics. Berkeley: University of California Press.
Sniderman, P., and J. Citrin
1971 "Psychological sources of political belief: self-esteem and isolationist attitudes." American Political Science Review 65: 401–17.
Super, D. E.
1953 "A theory of vocational development." American Psychologist 8: 185–90.
Treiman, D.
1977 Occupational Prestige in Comparative Perspective. New York: Academic Press.
Wylie, R.
1979 The Self-Concept: Theory and Research on Selected Topics. Vol. 2 (rev. ed.). Lincoln, Nebr.: University of Nebraska Press

Parental Permissiveness and Children's Self-Esteem

Stanley Coopersmith

26

[The following selection examines the relationship between parental attitudes and practices and the child's self-esteem. Coopersmith devised a 50-item Self-Esteem Inventory (SEI) which he administered to 1,748 fifth and sixth graders attending public schools in central Connecticut. From this pool a small sample of 85 subjects was selected whose members could clearly be classified as high, medium, or low in self-esteem. The mother of each subject was interviewed for about 2½ hours and filled out an 80-item questionnaire dealing with parental attitudes and practices. In addition, information on these issues was obtained from the children themselves. In this selection, Coopersmith examines the relationship between parental permissiveness, as reported by both mother and child, and the child's self-esteem. — Editors]

The concept of permissiveness received its most forceful advocacy by early adherents of psychoanalytic theory. They argued that children would develop into better adjusted and more secure adults if they were reared under open, flexible schedules that were geared to their needs. They proposed that the use of such schedules would result in more immediate gratification and relief and hence provided the child with a sense of trust in himself and confidence in others. Parents who employed such flexible, self-demand procedures, and who thus accepted the onerous obligations of ready and obedient response, were presumed to be more devoted to their children. The commitment, devotion, and presumably greater sensitivity of these permissive parents were assumed to indicate greater acceptance of their children, and were likely to eventuate in healthy—that is, nonneurotic—personality development. The advocates of permissive rearing pointed to the adverse effects of repressive treatment and concluded that nonrestrictive, self-demand procedures would permit greater self-expression and self-trust. This uncritical extension of psychoanalytic theory was based on the implicit assumption that greater impulse expression and gratification was associated with more favorable development, greater happiness, and better adaptation. Structuring of the environment by regular schedules and definite restrictions and demands was assumed to be repressive in effect and to manifest too little concern and acceptance of the child. Parents who employed such procedures were presumably seeking to exclude their own sources of anxiety and were thus more likely to be unaware of their motives and to be extreme in their actions. This view led to the general proposition that less permissive parents were likely to employ harsher forms of punishment and to employ them more frequently than did those who favored impulse expression. In this context parental permissiveness or restrictiveness was taken as an indication of parental mental health, acceptance of the child, and concern for his present and future well-being.

Though this position is no longer expressed with the same vehemence or extremity as it was in the period between 1930–1950, its decline is associated with changes in styles of childrearing rather than with clarification or disproof. The term *permissiveness* remains a vague one, generally associated with the absence of demands and restrictions, and indicative of greater parental acceptance, love, and democratic practices. Such interpretations, however, are connotative rather than denotative meanings of a term that has remained vague despite extended usage, and permissiveness as a procedure remains of uncertain consequences. In the present context, we shall employ the term *permissive* as characterizing the demands and firmness of management procedures employed by parents in regulating and satisfying the requirements of their children. This usage refers solely to the structuring of the child's world of rules and demands and carries no connotations of acceptance or democratic practices—in effect, a philosophy of management that may be carried out with varying sentiments of goodwill and affection. The consequences of that philosophy for the child's self-esteem is a question to which we shall now seek empirical solution.

Our study provided information on three aspects of parental permissiveness: the strictness of training, the demands that children meet (parental) standards, and the consistency with which rules were enforced and violations punished. This information was obtained from each mother and child, utilizing both interview and questionnaire procedures. Before turning to the specific findings, we should note that all our results indicate that the parents of children with high self-esteem are significantly *less* permissive than are the parents of children with less self-esteem. We shall discuss this surprising finding after the results have been presented.

The first aspect of permissiveness, the strictness of parental training, indicates the extent to which parents require that their children act in close conformity to the procedures that parents have established. Such strictness would be contrary to the open, flexible system of demands and gratification espoused by advocates of permissiveness. In our own definition, strictness represents a clearly defined, structured, and enforced set of demands. We determined the mother's attitude toward strictness by her response to the questionnaire item, "Children are actually happier under strict training." The mothers' responses of agreement or disagreement are summarized in Table 1, which reveals that mothers of children with high self-esteem are much more likely to agree with this statement than are mothers of other children. The actual percentages indicate that more than six times as many mothers in the high self-esteem group believe that strictness has beneficial consequences (38.7 percent) as mothers in the medium (6.3 percent) and low (5.9 percent) esteem groups. Thus it appears that permissiveness is *negatively* related to feelings of personal worth or, to state in it reverse, greater strictness is associated with greater self-esteem. In this same vein we note that more mothers of children with high self-esteem regard discipline as very important (84.8 percent) than do the mothers of children with medium (64.7 percent) and low (66.7 percent) self-esteem. This information came from the mother's interview and furnished a corroboration of the mothers' consistency of responses to questionnaire and interview. Other indications were the larger percentage of mothers in the high self-esteem groups who agreed with the statements, "Children who are held to firm rules grow up to be the best adults" and "No child should ever set his will against his parents."

TABLE 1

"Children Are Actually Happier Under Strict Training"

	SUBJECTIVE SELF-ESTEEM					
REPLY	*LOW*		*MEDIUM*		*HIGH*	
Agree	5.9%	(2)	6.3%	(1)	38.7%	(12)
Disagree	94.1	(32)	93.7	(15)	61.3	(19)
Totals	100.0	(34)	100.0	(16)	100.0	(31)

$x^2 = 13.57$ df = 2 $p < .01$

Source: Mother's questionnaire.

A second way of gauging permissiveness, and another aspect of its occurrence, is the number of parental demands imposed upon the child. Under extreme permissiveness, the environment provides gratifications for the child, whose needs are expected to be freely expressed. The needs presumably arise from the child rather than the expectations and requirements of the parent. Parental demands presumably represent restrictions upon the child's freedom and limit the extent to which he might seek alternative or lower levels of gratification. By imposing greater demands, parents imply that a given level of performance must be achieved before they will judge their child as competent. Lesser demands or the complete absence of demands presumably imply that whatever level the child did achieve, so long as it was not markedly below par, would be acceptable. Our appraisal of the level of demands made upon persons who differed in self-esteem was based upon the responses of our subjects. They were asked whether their parents regarded the meeting of high standards or personal enjoyment as more important guides of conduct. The figures in Table 2 indicate the number of children in each group who reported that their parents favored high standards as against personal enjoyment. If these reports are taken as indexes of parental value preference, we would conclude from Table 2 that the parents of children with low self-esteem place less importance on high standards (40.0 percent) than do the parents of children with medium and high self-esteem (71.4 percent and 80.0 percent, respectively). Or, in reverse terms, the parents of children with low self-esteem are more than twice as likely to endorse immediate gratification (60.0 percent) as are the parents of children with medium (28.6 percent) or high (20.0 percent) self-esteem. That lesser demands are associated with lower self-esteem, like the previous finding on strictness, runs counter to assertions regarding the presumed effects of permissive treatment.

TABLE 2

Relative Importance to Parents: Child Enjoying Himself or Meeting High Standards

	SUBJECTIVE SELF-ESTEEM		
IMPORTANT PARENTAL VALUES	*LOW*	*MEDIUM*	*HIGH*
Enjoying himself	60.0% (9)	28.6% (2)	20.0% (3)
Meeting high standards	40.0 (6)	71.4 (5)	80.0 (12)
Totals	100.0 (15)	100.0 (7)	100.0 (15)

$x^2 = 5.40$ df = 2 $p < .08$

Source: Subject's questionnaire.

The third and final aspect of permissiveness we shall consider is the consistency with which regulations are enforced. That is, whereas the prior two findings indicated the firmness and extent of demands, the present variable deals with the question of whether these demands are backed up by supervision and control. Our information on parental enforcement was obtained during the course of the mother interview. The mothers were asked to indicate the care and consistency with which they supervise the rules they had established and their responses are summarized in Table 3. From these responses, it is clear that the mothers of children with high self-esteem are more zealous in their enforcement of familial rules than are the parents of children with medium and low self-esteem. Comparison of the groups reveals that almost nine out of ten (87.9 percent) of the mothers of

TABLE 3

"Care and Consistency with which Rules are Enforced"

	SUBJECTIVE SELF-ESTEEM		
DEGREE OF ENFORCEMENT	*LOW*	*MEDIUM*	*HIGH*
Relatively careful and consistent enforcement	60.0% (18)	58.8% (10)	87.9% (29)
Moderate or little enforcement of rules	40.0 (12)	41.2 (7)	12.1 (4)
Totals	100.0 (30)	100.0 (17)	100.0 (33)

$x^2 = 7.59$ df = 2 $p < .05$

Source: Mother's interview.

children with high self-esteem carefully and consistently enforce established rules, and only approximately six out of ten (60.0 and 58.8 prcent) of the low and medium group mothers are as attentive. Thus the mothers of children with high self-esteem are apt to be more zealous both in enforcing the regulations they establish and in being stricter and more demanding in their requirements. In effect, the level of demands and the degree of enforcement are both greater for children with high self-esteem.

The negative relationship between permissiveness and self-esteem revealed in Tables 1, 2, and 3 runs counter to theoretical expectations and popular belief. Inasmuch as it appears to be a reliable finding, confirmed by both parent and child, its interpretation is all the more intriguing and significant. Our discussion will focus upon two questions that appear to underlie the surprising results obtained: 'Why should strict and demanding regulatory procedures be associated with high self-esteem?" and "How firm or demanding are the nonpermissive conditions associated with high self-esteem?" The first question is the real nub of the discussion because it requires an analysis of the particular effects of firm and open management procedures. The second represents an attempt to determine the operational meaning of the terms *strict and demanding* and the extent to which the mothers of children with high self-esteem can be placed at the polar opposite of *permissiveness*.

It is evident that the mothers of the high self-esteem group are stricter and set higher demands, but should these conditions have an enhancing effect upon the children? Although the findings are clear and consistent, our interpretation will, of necessity, be more tentative and exploratory. The results not only go counter to the usual assertions on the effects of permissiveness; they also extend beyond previously presented theoretical formulations relating to the antecedents of self-esteem. . . . In that context, we concluded that the sources of self-esteem could be subsumed under the general concepts of defenses, successes, values, and aspirations—without, however, specifying how these applied to the actual practices of childrearing. A more specific consideration of the practices associated with permissive and restrictive practices suggests that the relevant concepts are defenses and successes, particularly since the concept of success is associated with parental concern and affection. Turning first to the concept of defenses, we may propose that firmer management will tend to result in more effective inner controls and greater confidence in one's definition of a situation. Parents who establish rules and enforce them are presenting their children with a definition of reality that they believe to be objective and functional. They are establishing a set of beliefs that there are certain ways of acting toward parents, siblings, tasks, and other elements of the environment that are preferable to other ways. By their verbal statements and their actions, these parents lead their children to believe that there is a shared world and that there are preferred solutions for the tasks which they encounter. There are preferred methods of expressing respect and appreciation; preferred resolutions on how and when aggression should be expressed; and preferred answers on the meaning and sources of failure and how it can be avoided. On each of these and other issues, parental resolutions provide the child with answers that diminish doubt and anxiety. To the child these answers are not merely one resolution among many but, coming as they do from the major authoritative force in his life, they assume the weight of Biblical injunction to the fundamentalist believer. These are the methods, the correct ways, the answers, and the goals by which love, peace, and success can be achieved and all doubts put to rest. The firm, demanding parent who is establishing rules and enforcing them is providing definitions to his children and indicating how to interpret the world so as to maximize success and minimize anxiety. When these definitions and solutions are internalized and applied to problematic situations, they are customarily referred to as controls and defenses.

A second basis of the relationship between nonpermissive regulation and self-esteem lies in the greater self-definition that results from consistently enforced rules. Such rules compel the individual to acknowledge forces outside of himself and to recognize the needs and powers of other persons. The resulting distinction between internal experiences and external events brings with it an awareness of the social environment and the difference between wish and reality. The extremely permissive environment in which no demands are made and no rules are enforced provides little basis for distinguishing between personal and social events, and presents only a limited definition of what is valued or functional. In its extreme manifestation such an environment presents a picture of life that is distant from that encountered in other areas of living as well as blind to the intervention and direction practiced by even the most beneficent of parents. Parents who proclaim they they advance no rules and exercise no authority are likely to confuse the child about the existence, significance, and benefits of (even legitimate) authority or to cause him to be suspicious of parental statements and motives. In any event such conditions make for poorer, less distinct differentiation between self and nonself and provide a less accurate and realistic picture of the importance of rules, no matter how disguised they may be. Over an extended series of events, children who can distinguish self and nonself, who are sufficiently reality-oriented to appreciate the needs and demands of others, and who are aware that some rules are always operating are likely to achieve greater and more enduring successes.

The third basis by which strict and demanding procedures may enhance esteem is that they symbolize parental attention. We have already presented evidence that attention of even a negative nature has a more enhancing effect than lack of concern. Hence it seems that the very posing and enforcement of rules necessarily leads to greater interaction between parent and child. This interaction need not be expressed as concern or affection, it need only occur to present an enhancing effect. It is also worth noting that the favorable effects of permissiveness, whatever they are, are more likely to occur during infancy and early childhood than during subsequent development. During these early periods, the major foci are bodily processes, which cannot be hastened or drastically altered without great pressures or the possibilities of aberrant development. Beyond these early stages guidance toward familial and cultural norms is a valid and important function, which at the same time provides enhancing attention to the child. In sum, this increased attention, the more frequent (social and academic) successes provided by a more accurate reality orientation, and the more established controls and resolutions provided by parental norms would appear to underlie the higher self-esteem of children reared under firmer regulatory procedures.

Having suggested how nonpermissive procedures may enhance self-esteem, we now consider the *extent* of demands made by the parents of children with high self-esteem. For, though we have indicated that the parents of these children establish and enforce more regulations than do the parents of children with low self-esteem, our data provide relative rather than absolute indexes of permissiveness. To give a broader perspective on the total range of this dimension, we shall examine the results of other studies of permissiveness and attempt to gauge that portion from which our sample was drawn. There are studies[1,2] that indicate that either extreme method of management, be it complete permissiveness or rigid and inflexible control, have equally poor consequences for the child. Children reared under either extreme regimen are more likely to suffer from difficulties in adjustment and in behavior problems. Less extreme methods of management have equally favorable effects upon personality development. What is important for our purposes is that truly extreme regulatory procedures are associated with *higher* levels of *maladjustment*, but the children in our high self-esteem group have *fewer* symptoms and behavior disorders. This suggests that the procedures employed by the parents of these children are not extreme but only appear to be so when compared to those of the other parents we studied. In this same vein we may note another study,[3] which reveals that children who come from restrictive homes have greater difficulty in relating to their peers and academic settings. But again, the children with high self-esteem whom we are studying have more congenial and successful relationships with their siblings, peers, and schoolmates. From all this, it appears that the regulatory procedures employed by the parents of children with high self-esteem are firm, clear, and demanding but cannot be termed rigid, inflexible, or unduly restrictive. Although we cannot delineate the specific operational meaning of less extreme management procedures, we can conclude that they establish firm, structured rules and demands that are consistently enforced by reasonable persons.

NOTES

1 E. H. Klatskin, E. B. Jackson, and L. C. Wilkin. "The influence of degree of flexibility in maternal child care practices on early child behavior." American Journal of Orthopsychiatry 26 (1956): 79–93.

2 E. H. Klatskin. "Shifts in child care practices in three social classes under an infant care program of flexible methodology." American Journal of Orthopsychiatry 22 (1952): 52–61.

3 M. J. Radke. The Relation of Parental Authority to Children's Behavior and Attitudes. Minneapolis, University of Minnesota Press, 1946.

Family Relationships and Self-Esteem

Jerald G. Bachman

27

[*The following selection was prepared for this volume and was based on data from the Youth in Transition project. The project sampled 2,213 tenth grade boys in 87 high schools throughout the country and then followed most of them in a longitudinal design spanning eight years. The research reported in this selection examines the relationship between nine background predictors and global self-esteem, with special attention to a measure of "family relations."* — Editors]

This selection deals with dimensions that have been of great interest to social scientists for a long time. Self-esteem, happiness, depression, anomie—these and a number of other dimensions all have something to do with an individual's general satisfaction with life. And satisfaction, of one sort or another, has consistently appeared as an important criterion dimension when the impacts of social environments are studied.

While there has been much interest in such dimensions, there has not been a great deal of consistency in their measurement or in their conceptualization. A major step toward improving this situation has . . . been taken by Robinson and Shaver (1969) in their extensive review and documentation of social psychological attitude measures. . . . Robinson and Shaver have noted that life satisfaction and happiness measures have consistently correlated with each other and with other psychological attitudes. "Particularly significant is the finding that persons of high self-esteem or personal competence express more satisfaction with life. Satisfaction

Source: Jerald G. Bachman. "Family Relationships and Self-Esteem." Adapted largely from Jerald G. Bachman, Youth in Transition, Volume 2: The Impact of Family Background and Intelligence on Tenth Grade Boys. Ann Arbor, Michigan: Institute for Social Research, 1970. Additional material adapted from Volume 3, (1971) and Volume 6 (1978) in the Youth in Transition series. Copyright 1970, 1971, and 1978 by the Institute for Social Research. Adapted by the author and reprinted by permission.

has also been found to be greater among people who are better socially adjusted, who demonstrate more trust in people, who feel less alienated, and who suffer less from anxiety, worry, and psychosomatic symptoms" (Robinson and Shaver, 1969, p. 35).

This general finding is replicated in our data collected from tenth-grade boys. Table 1 . . . presents product-moment correlations among [several such measures]. As the table indicates, self-esteem shows fairly strong relationships with each of the other scales having to do with affective states. . . .

TABLE 1
Product-Moment Correlations Among Self-Esteem and Other Affective States Dimensions

	1	2	3	4
1. Self-Esteem				
2. Negative Affective States	–.52			
3. Happiness	.54	–.51		
4. Somatic Symptoms	–.34	.54	–.28	
5. Impulse to Aggression	–.34	.54	–.33	.32

THE MEANING OF SELF-ESTEEM

Self-esteem has been defined in many ways by previous writers. Within our own program of research a variety of meanings have been associated with this term. French and Kahn mention self-esteem among affective states, but they also define it in self-identity terms:

Self-esteem may be defined as the average evaluation of the attributes of the self-identity, where each attribute is weighted according to its centrality. Another measure of self-esteem may be derived from discrepancies between the person's perceived attributes and the attributes of his ideal self, where the ideal self is conceived as the most desirable positions on the dimensions of self-identity (French and Kahn, 1962, p. 21).

Except for our measure of school ability self-concept, we have found it difficult to measure self-identity dimensions through interview techniques; thus for the present at least, we cannot operationalize self-esteem in terms of self-identity.

The definitions provided by Rosenberg and by Coopersmith are quite consistent with the above views, although not linked so explicitly to self-identity dimensions:

When we speak of high self-esteem, then, we shall simply mean that the individual respects himself, considers himself worthy; he does not necessarily consider himself better than others, but he definitely does not consider himself worse; he does not feel that he is the ultimate in perfection but, on the contrary, recognizes his limitations and expects to grow and improve.

Low self-esteem, on the other hand, implies self-rejection, self-dissatisfaction, self-contempt. The individual lacks respect for the self he observes. The self-picture is disagreeable, and he wishes it were otherwise (Rosenberg, 1965, p. 31).

By self-esteem we refer to the evaluation which the individual makes and customarily maintains with regard to himself: it expresses an attitude of approval or disapproval, and indicates the extent to which the individual believes himself to be capable, significant, successful, and worthy. In short, self-esteem is a personal judgment of worthiness that is expressed in the attitudes the individual holds toward himself (Coopersmith, 1967, pp. 4-5).

These several definitions share a common theme which is basic to our use of the term: high self-esteem consists of favorable perceptions and evaluations of oneself.

Our measure of *self-esteem,* summarized in Table 2, is very close to that used by Rosenberg (1965). Six of the ten items were adapted directly from Rosenberg's scale; the others, developed in a study of individuals changing jobs (Cobb et al., 1966), are quite similar to the Rosenberg items. It was on the basis of high intercorrelations in a pilot study that we decided there was no reason to keep the two sets of items separate (Bachman, Kahn, Mednick, Davidson, and Johnston, 1967, p.73). The response scale ranging from "almost always true" to "never true" was used to maintain consistency with other portions of our questionnaire and to permit the embedding of self-esteem items within a much larger set of affective states items. . . .

TABLE 2

Self-Esteem Scale

SELF-ESTEEM (Rosenberg)

I feel that I'm a person of worth, at least on an equal plane with others.
I feel that I have a number of good qualities.
I am able to do things as well as most other people.
*I feel I do not have much to be proud of.
I take a positive attitude toward myself.
*Sometimes I think I am no good at all.

SELF-ESTEEM (Cobb)

I am a useful guy to have around.
*I feel that I can't do anything right.
When I do a job, I do it well.
*I feel that my life is not very useful.

*Reversed scoring

A factor analysis of the self-esteem items (measured in tenth grade) revealed a strong first factor which explained 64 percent of the common variance. Coefficient alpha was 0.75. Reliability data based on the four additional Youth in Transition surveys equal or exceed the tenth-grade reliability (see Bachman, O'Malley, and Johnston, 1978, pp. 97-98).

The response distributions . . . suggest a fairly high level of self-esteem in tenth-grade boys. Two-thirds of our respondents say that they often or almost always feel they have a number of good qualities and feel they are able to do things as well as most other people.

The item which elicits the highest proportion of low self-esteem responses, "Sometimes I think I am no good at all," may be just the sort of statement which captures some adolescents' uncertainty about themselves. It is worth noting that the proportion of boys checking this statement as often or almost always true drops from 17 percent to 10 percent as they go from the start of tenth grade to the end of twelfth grade; similarly, the seldom or never-true responses increase from 53 percent to 66 percent. This is part of a substantial rise in overall self-esteem which we observed from tenth grade to a point five years after most had graduated from high school (Bachman, O'Malley, and Johnston, 1978).

THE MEASURE OF FAMILY RELATIONS

We set out initially to measure several dimensions of family relations using indexes based on questionnaire items. One index, termed parental control, can be disposed of quickly; in preliminary analyses this measure did not show any sort of relationship (linear or curvilinear) with criterion dimensions. The four remaining indexes deal with closeness to mother, closeness to father, parental consultation with son, and parental punitiveness; these indexes were moderately intercorrelated in preliminary analyses (absolute values of product-moment correlations ranged from 0.28 to 0.43), and they related in parallel ways to a number of criterion variables. Given this interrelationship, we explored the possibility of constructing a single general-purpose measure of family relations. Our rationale [was that] it is a great deal simpler both theoretically and analytically if we can use a single dimension to capture most of the predictive power of its separate ingredients. Our conclusion was that a composite measure would indeed prove useful. The composite score was computed directly from the questionnaire items, as shown in Table 3.

TABLE 3

A Composite Measure of Family Relations

A total of 21 questionnaire items, listed below, were used to compute the measure of family relations. The total score on this scale consists of the mean of the scores for all available items, with up to five missing data cases allowed; in other words, a respondent had to provide answers to at least 16 of the 21 questions in order for a scale score to be computed.

CLOSENESS TO FATHER

When you were growing up, how did you feel about how much affection you got from your father (or male guardian)?

How often do you and your father (or male guardian) do things together that you both enjoy—things like playing sports, or going to sporting events, or working on things together?

How close do you feel to your father (or male guardian)?

How much do you want to be like your father (or male guardian) when you're an adult?

CLOSENESS TO MOTHER

When you were growing up, how did you feel about how much affection you got from your mother (or female guardian)?

How close do you feel to your mother (or female guardian)?

How much do you want to be like the kind of person your mother (or female guardian) is?

AMOUNT OF REASONING WITH SON

How much influence do you feel *you* have in family decisions that affect you?

Next we would like to get some idea of how often your parents (or guardians) do each of the following things:

Listen to your side of the argument
Talk over important decisions with you
Act fair and reasonable in what they ask of you

PARENTAL PUNITIVENESS

Next we would like to get some idea of how often your parents (or guardians) do each of the following things:

Completely ignore you after you've done something wrong
Act as if they don't care about you any more
Disagree with each other when it comes to raising you
Actually slap you
Take away your privileges (TV, movies, dates)
Yell, shout, or scream at you
Blame you or criticize you when you don't deserve it
Threaten to slap you
Disagree about punishing you
Nag at you

The resulting scale of family relations was computed for 98 percent of all respondents (with the remaining 2 percent not available due to missing data). The scores were found to approximate a normal distribution. As an aid to later analyses, a bracketed version was developed by dividing the continuum of scores into eight categories.

The scale contains 10 items having to do with parental punitiveness, and 11 items having to do with closeness to parents and the feeling that parents are reasonable. The scale is thus fairly evenly balanced between positively worded and negatively worded items. The scoring of the negative items was reversed; accordingly, a high score indicates a predominance of favorable items. As we mentioned earlier, the measurement of family relations is much less straightforward than the measurement of other family background characteristics that have less emotional involvement for the respondent. The subjective impressions of respondents concerning matters in which they have a very large emotional stake are always suspect. There is much room here for subtle distortion and misinterpretation of response scales, and all of this can occur quite innocently and unintentionally. For these reasons, in our subsequent analyses . . . questions of validity [were] focused particularly on the measure of family relations. . . .

BACKGROUND FACTORS RELATED TO SELF-ESTEEM

Table 4 summarizes relationships between self-esteem and the eight dimensions of family background plus the Quick Test of intelligence. As we examine a number of these relationships we will note similarities to the findings of Rosenberg (1965) and Coopersmith (1967).

TABLE 4

Multiple Classification Analysis of Background Factors Predicting to Self-Esteem

	PREDICTING FROM EACH CHARACTERISTIC SEPARATELY		*PREDICTING FROM 8 BACKGROUND CHARACTERISTICS SIMULTANEOUSLY*		*PREDICTING FROM QUICK TEST AND 8 BACKGROUND CHARACTERISTICS SIMULTANEOUSLY*	
BACKGROUND PREDICTORS:	*ETA*	*ETA²*	*BETA*	*BETA²*	*BETA*	*BETA²*
Socioeconomic Level	.15	.023	.12	.014	.10	.009
Number of Siblings	.07	.005	.03	.001	.03	.001
Broken Home	.04	.002	.03	.001	.03	.001
Family Relations	.36	.133	.36	.128	.35	.124
Religious Preference	.12	.014	.09	.008	.08	.007
Family Political Preference	.06	.003	.04	.002	.04	.002
Community Size	.08	.006	.05	.002	.04	.002
Race (Five-Category)	.07	.005	.10	.010	.14	.019
Quick Test of Intelligence	.14	.021			.12	.016
			$R = .393$		$R = .406$	
			$R^2 = .155$		$R^2 = .165$	
			Percent Variance Explained= 17.0		Percent Variance Explained= 18.1	

Eta is the correlation ratio unadjusted.
Eta² is the explained sum of squares unadjusted.
Beta is the correlation ratio adjusted for effects of other predictors.
Beta² is the explained sum of squares adjusted for effects of other predictors.
R is the multiple correlation coefficient corrected for degrees of freedom.
R^2 indicates the proportion of variance in the dependent variable explained by all predictors together after correcting for degrees of freedom.
The *Percent Variance Explained* is the percentage of variance in the dependent variable explained by all predictors together with no correction for degrees of freedom.

Looking briefly at the data for intelligence, we find a small positive association with self-esteem (Eta = 0.14). A comparison of R^2 with and without the Quick Test (in Table 4) indicates that the QT adds only about 1 percent to the ability of background factors to account for variance in self-esteem.

Coopersmith (1967) found a similar but much larger relationship between measured intelligence and self-esteem in his sample of fifth- and sixth-grade students. He also found self-esteem to be related to self-reports of grades and school ability. Our measure of school ability self-concept does show a positive relationship with self-esteem (r = 0.33). And our respondents' reports of grades also relate positively to self-esteem (r = 0.23).

Turning next to socioeconomic level (SEL), our findings are essentially the same as those of Rosenberg (1965) and Coopersmith 1967); we find a weak positive relationship between SEL and self-esteem (Eta = 0.15).

We find, as did Rosenberg (1965), a tendency for only children to be slightly higher than others in self-esteem. Once we adjust for SEL (through Multiple Classification Analysis), this is the only difference in self-esteem that relates to family size, and it amounts to only one-tenth of a standard deviation. By far the largest relationship between self-esteem and the dimensions of family background involves family relations (Eta = 0.36). Table 4 displays the substantial positive association between self-esteem and good relations with parents. This is consistent with Rosenberg's (1965) finding that adolescents with high self-esteem report that their parents show relatively high interest in their friends, their academic performance, and their contributions to mealtime conversation.

Our findings in this area, and those of Rosenberg as well, suffer from lack of objective data concerning parental behavior. We have had to rely on the subjective assessments of respondents, and . . . such assessments may be colored by tendencies to portray oneself in a favorable light. Coopersmith (1967), on the other hand, did have objective data concerning parental behaviors. Ratings of maternal affection and interest, obtained from interviewer reports and responses by mothers, were positively related to self-esteem in Coopersmith's sample of preadolescents. These findings corroborate our own and leave us less inclined to dismiss our subjective data on relations with parents. . . .

IMPLICATIONS FROM LONGITUDINAL ANALYSES OF SELF-ESTEEM

It is beyond the scope of this chapter to review the full range of longitudinal findings from the Youth in Transition study which relate to self-esteem; however, several findings which bear directly on the data reported above are summarized here.

Our analyses of educational attainment revealed fairly substantial links with the measure of family relations, particularly that portion of the measure dealing with parental punitiveness. Thus, for example, dropping out of high school was more common—and college entrance less frequent—among young men who had earlier reported high levels of parental punitiveness (eta = 0.23, see Bachman, Green, and Wirtanen, 1971, pp. 33-36). This predictive validity heightens our confidence in the family relations measure, although the pattern of causation may be a complex one.

Another finding which heightens our confidence in the parental punitiveness measure is the fact that punitiveness reported in tenth grade shows a moderate correlation with later self-esteem. The linear relationship between punitiveness and tenth-grade self-esteem was -0.30 (product-moment correlation); punitiveness (measured in tenth-grade) correlated -0.23 with eleventh-grade self-esteem, -0.18 with twelfth-grade self-esteem, and -0.12 with self-esteem five years beyond high school (O'Malley, Bachman, and Johnston, 1977, Appendix G). The pattern of declining correlations was certainly consistent with expectations; later family relationships are only partially predictable from those in tenth grade; furthermore, such factors are likely to become less central to a young man's self-esteem as he approaches and reaches adulthood. What is particularly relevant for present purposes is the fact that reports of parental punitiveness at the start of tenth grade showed an appreciable relationship with self-esteem at the end of high school, thus providing another sort of predictive validation.

Further longitudinal analyses of other background dimensions linked to self-esteem across time, including a path analytic treatment, are reported by Bachman and O'Malley (1977). One of the key findings was that a variety of factors having to do with educational success seem to become less important—i.e., show a reduction in *centrality*—as young men proceed through high school and beyond. It may well be the case that such a diminution in the importance of educational success for self-esteem is already underway prior to tenth grade. If so, that would help to account for the discrepancy, noted above, between Coopersmith's relatively larger correlations between intelligence and self-esteem in his sample of fifth- and sixth-grade students, compared with our findings for tenth graders.

REFERENCES

Bachman, J. G., S. Green, and I. D. Wirtanen

1971 "Dropping out—problem or symptom." In Youth in Transition, Vol. 3. Ann Arbor: Institute for Social Research.

Bachman, J. G., R. L. Kahn, M. T. Mednick, T. N. Davidson, and L. D. Johnston

1967 "Blueprint for a longitudinal study of adolescent boys." In Youth in Transition, Vol. 1. Ann Arbor: Institute for Social Research.

Bachman, J. G., and P. M. O'Malley

1977 "Self-esteem in young men: a longitudinal analysis of the impact of educational and occupational attainment." Journal of Personality and Social Psychology 35: 365–80.

Bachman, J. G., P. M. O'Malley, and J. Johnston

1978 Adolescence to adulthood—change and stability in the lives of young men. In Youth in Transition, Vol. 6. Ann Arbor: Institute for Social Research.

Cobb, S., G. H. Brooks, S. V. Kasl, and W. E. Connelly

1966 "The health of people changing jobs: A description of a longitudinal study." American Journal of Public Health 56: 1476–81.

Coopersmith, S.

1967 The Antecedents of Self-Esteem. San Francisco: W. H. Freeman.

French, J. R. P., Jr., and R. L. Kahn

1962 "A programmatic approach to studying the industrial environment and mental health." Journal of Social Issues 18: 1–47.

O'Malley, P. M., J. G. Bachman, and J. Johnston

1977 "Five years beyond high school: causes and consequences of educational attainment." Document No. ED 136 007, ERIC Document Reproduction Service, Arlington.

Robinson, J. P., and P. R. Shaver
1969 "Measures of social psychological attitudes." Appendix B to Measures of Political Attitudes. Ann Arbor: Institute for Social Research.
Rosenberg, M.
1965 Society and the Adolescent Self-Image. Princeton: Princeton University Press.

Self-Concept of Ability and School Achievement

Wilbur B. Brookover

Shailer Thomas

Ann Paterson

28

The interactionist theories of self and role performance based on the work of G. H. Mead and C. H. Cooley have been increasingly accepted in social psychology but have seldom been considered relevant to learning in a school situation. A formalized statement of the relevant theory has been made by Kinch,[1] and postulates concerned with classroom learning have been developed by Brookover.[2] Briefly, the general theory states that self-concept is developed through interaction with significant others which in turn influences his behavior. When applied to the specific school learning situation, a relevant aspect of self-concept is the person's conception of his own ability to learn the accepted types of academic behavior; performance in terms of school achievement is the relevant behavior influenced. The student role is composed of several subroles including one involving academic achievement; the student self-concept similarly is a complex of several segments including self-concept of ability. This study focuses on these particular aspects: self-concept of ability in school and academic achievement.[3]

The study tests three major hypotheses: (1) Self-concept of ability in school is significantly and positively related to the academic performance of students even

Source: Wilbur B. Brookover, Shailer Thomas, and Ann Paterson, "Self-Concept of Ability and School Achievement," Sociology of Education 37 (1964): 271–78.

with an ability dimension controlled. (2) Self-concept of ability in school is differentiated into specific self-concepts which correspond to specific subject areas in the school program, and these specific self-concepts are better predictors of academic performance in the relevant area than is the general self-concept of ability. (3) Self-concept of ability is significantly and positively correlated with the evaluation that one perceives significant others to hold of one's ability.

A number of studies have demonstrated that various types of behavior are related to self-assessment as determined by instruments designed to give a gross or total measure of self.[4] There is some evidence that school achievement is related to such criteria of self,[5] but previous studies have not attempted to measure the academic ability segment of self-concept and test its relationship to achievement and to the perception of others' evaluation.

METHOD OF RESEARCH

Sample

The sample consisted of 1,050 seventh-grade students (513 males and 537 females) in an urban school system. Negro students were excluded from this analysis on the assumption that their self-concept of ability and its relation to achievement would differ from those of the white population. Subsequent analysis verified this assumption.[6]

Instruments

In order to measure self-concept of ability or how the subjects perceived their ability to perform in the academic setting, an eight-item multiple-choice questionnaire was utilized. These items formed a Guttman scale with a reproducibility coefficient of 0.95 for males and 0.96 for females. The scale has an internal reliability of 0.82 for males and 0.77 for females.[7] This "Self-Concept of Ability Scale" was administered in two parallel forms: the first was designed to measure the student's self-concept of ability in general; the second, to measure self-concept of ability in each of four specific school subject areas—arithmetic, English, social studies, and science. Though the references were changed, the substance of the questions remained the same in both forms.

Since it has often been said, particularly in the school situation, that "innate ability" determines performance, IQ was controlled, even though it may be affected by self-concept of ability. Intelligence scores were obtained from the "California Test of Mental Maturity" administered in the fourth and sixth grades. Since an average of IQ scores for two test administrations would tend to be more stable than a single assessment, an average of two total scores on the CTMM was used in this study. Grade point average (GPA) in the four subjects, arithmetic, English, social studies, and science was used as an index of academic performance.

ANALYSIS AND RESULTS

The product-moment correlations between variables of this study and the correlations of pairs of these variables with the effect of the third variable partialed out are presented in Table 1. Even with the effect of IQ partialed out, self-concept and GPA (the index of performance) remain significantly and positively correlated. The correlation between self-concept and IQ is low (though significantly different from zero) when the effect of achievement is statistically controlled. If the IQ—GPA correlation (with the effect of self-concept partialed out) is compared to the multiple correlation of IQ plus self-concept to predict GPA, the correlation increases from 0.48 to 0.69 for males, and from 0.53 to 0.72 for females. Such increases approximately double the variance accounted for. These multiple correlations have, for the males, beta weights of 0.44 for IQ and 0.37 for self-concept; for females, beta weights are 0.49 for IQ and 0.34 for self-concept. Although IQ is weighted slightly higher than self-concept for both sexes, this is more evident for females than for males. It is concluded that there is a significant relationship between self-concept and GPA even with the "ability" factor controlled.

TABLE 1

Correlations Between Seventh Grade GPA, Intelligence, and Self-Concept of Ability*

	CORRELATION COEFFICIENTS				
	NO VARIABLE CONTROLLED		*THIRD VARIABLE CONTROLLED*		
VARIABLES CORRELATED	*MALES* N = 513	*FEMALES* N = 537	*VARIABLE CONTROLLED*	*MALE* N = 513	*FEMALE* N = 537
7th GPA—IQ	.61	.65	S-C	.48	.53
7th GPA—S-C	.57	.57	I.Q.	.42	.39
Self-concept—IQ	.46	.48	GPA	.17	.17

*The Multiple Correlation (R 1.23) of Self-Concept and I.Q. with GPA is 0.69 for males and 0.72 for females.

The second hypothesis stated that the self-concepts which relate to specific areas of performance in school would be differentiated from the general self-

TABLE 2

Mean Self-Concept of Ability Scores and Mean Grade Point Averages in all Subjects and for Each of Four School Subjects; (The Higher the Self-Concept Score the More Positive the Self-Concept. Range Possible, 8–40)

	MALES (N=513)		*FEMALES (N=537)*	
	MEAN SELF-CONCEPT	*MEAN GPA*	MEAN SELF-CONCEPT	*MEAN GPA*
General S-C	27.35*	2.07	28.25*	2.43
Mathematics	26.97	2.10	27.47†	2.36†
English	25.45†	2.00†	28.17	2.61†
Social Studies	25.63†	1.99†	26.58†	2.29†
Science	27.18	2.21†	27.73	2.49†

*Mean general self-concept of ability score, not mean of specific subject self-concept of ability scores.

†Significantly different ($p < .05$) from the mean score for all subjects using a two-tailed "t" test for correlated data.

concept of ability and would be better predictors of specific subject achievement than would the general self-concept of ability. The means of general self-concept of ability scores and specific subject self-concept of ability scores, and the corresponding GPA's are presented in Table 2. The general self-concept score is higher than any of the specific subject scores. This may indicate that the student's general self-concept is closer to his areas of successful academic performance than to his areas of failure. (The general self-concept of ability score is *not* an average of the other scores but was obtained from a separate assessment of self-concept.)

To test the hypothesis that the specific subject-matter self-concept is a better predictor of achievement in that subject than is general self-concept, the correlation of general self-concept of ability and achievement in a specific subject was compared with the correlation of specific subject self-concept of ability and specific subject achievement. These correlations are shown in Table 3. The specific self-concept of ability correlations are significantly higher for males in mathematics, social studies, and science; for the females the correlation is significantly higher in social studies. On the other hand, the correlation between specific self-concept and achievement in English is lower (although not significantly so) than the correlation between general self-concept of ability and achievement in English.

TABLE 3

Correlation Among General Self-Concept of Ability, Self-Concept of Ability in Specific Subjects, and Seventh Year Grades in Four Subjects for 513 Males and 537 Females

VARIABLES CORRELATED	*CORRELATION COEFFICIENTS*							
	MATH		*ENGLISH*		*SOCIAL STUDIES*		*SCIENCE*	
	M	*F*	*M*	*F*	*M*	*F*	*M*	*F*
General S–C and grade	.50	.52	.44	.52	.51	.50	.52	.48
Specific S–C and grade	.59	.54	.43	.47	.56*	.58*	.61*	.51
General S–C, Specific S–C, and grade (R 1.23)	.60	.59	.48	.55	.60	.61	.63	.57

*Significantly greater than correlation between general S–C and grade on one-tailed "t" test.

While the findings indicate that specific self-concept is a significantly better predictor of GPA in mathematics, social studies and science for males, the same does not hold for females except in social studies. Although these sex differences may be a reflection of factors in this particular community and school system, it is interesting that math and science are subjects usually defined as important areas of achievement for males. By the same argument it might have been expected that self-concept in English would have been a better predictor among females. Why social studies alone is so distinguished among females is not clear. Since this is the subject in which females have the lowest achievement (see Table 2), it may be that social studies is important only because it is an area of concern—perhaps girls cannot tolerate a nonuniform achievement pattern.

The last row of Table 3 contains the multiple correlation of general self-concept and specific self-concept with grades. All of the multiple correlations account for significantly more variance than the correlations in row one.

The third hypothesis stated that an individual's self-concept of ability is significantly correlated with the images that he perceives significant others to have of his ability. This hypothesis has been tested on data from interviews with 110 over- and under-achievers and the test, therefore, does not reflect all achievement and ability levels.[8] It is expected, however, that the same relationships would hold in a sample of normal achievers.[9]

The "significant others" in this research were mother, father, favorite teacher, and best friend. A list of significant others was obtained by administering two open-ended questions: "List the people who you feel are important in your life" and "List the people who you feel are concerned about how well you do in school." All students mentioned at least one parent as a significant other and approximately 90 percent mentioned a teacher as someone who was concerned about their achievement. Peers were mentioned as significant others by slightly less than half of the group. These four categories of significant others (mother, father, teacher, peer) were thus the most frequently mentioned by the subjects.

The questions which were asked about the student's perception of significant others were directly parallel to the questions the student had answered earlier about himself. Table 4 shows the correlations between the over- and under-achieving student's general self-concept of ability and the evaluations of his ability that he perceives the four significant others to hold. All correlations are moderately high and roughly comparable. The highest correlation is with a composite (a sum) of the perceived evaluations of ability of all significant others. In the last column of Table 5 are found the correlations of the composite conceptions of specific subject ability held by the significant others and the over- and under-achieving student's self-concept of ability in that subject. The correlations in this column of Table 5 are much lower than the correlations between general self-concept of ability and perceived evaluations by significant others. This may indicate that significant others contribute heavily to an individual's general self-concept of ability, but that the interaction between a specific significant other and the student does not specify evaluations in specific areas of the student role. Such an interpretation gains support when we examine the remainder of Table 5. Here

TABLE 4

Correlations Between the Student's Self-Concept of His General Ability And the Images That He Perceives Each of Four Significant Persons To Hold of His Ability (Males and Females Combined: N = 110)

STUDENT'S PERCEPTION OF	*CORRELATION WITH SELF-CONCEPT*
Mother's image	.50
Father's image	.52
Teacher's image	.55
Peers' image	.47
Student's self-concept and a combination of the images of all four significant others	.58

are presented the correlations between specific subject self-concept of ability and perception of specific significant others' evaluations; these correlations are generally lower than the correlations in the last column, and three of them are so small as to not be significantly different from zero for this sample.

TABLE 5

Correlations of the Student's Self-Concept of Ability in Four School Subjects with the Image He Perceives Four Significant Others to Hold of His Ability in Four Subjects (Males and Females Combined: N = 110)

	SIGNIFICANT OTHERS				
SUBJECT	MOTHER	FATHER	FAVORITE TEACHER	BEST FRIEND	COMPOSITE OF FOUR SIGNIFICANT OTHERS
Arithmetic	.31	.22	.25	.28	.31
English	.29	.15*	.18*	.30	.27
Social Studies	.38	16*	.34	.38	.37
Science	.29	.28	.29	.26	.32

*Correlation is *not* significantly different from zero.

Such a pattern of correlations may be an indication that self-concept is not a reflection of a specific significant other but rather it may reflect a community of opinion. If it is accepted that self-concept is not a reflection of or a result of evaluations made by an individual significant other but corresponds more closely to the evaluations made by a community of "significant others," then it may be more accurate to speak in Mead's terms of the "generalized other" rather than individual significant others. This may be taken as additional support of the findings of Miyamoto and Dornbusch that an individual's self-concept is more closely related to his estimate of general attitudes toward him than it is to the perceived responses of a particular group.[10]

When the correlations of the students' self-concepts of ability in each of the four subjects with the perceived evaluations of each of the four significant others were examined, it was found that there are some differences in the correlations for each of the significant others. The student's self-concept was generally more highly correlated with the images that he perceived his mother and best friend held of him than it was with the images he felt his father and teacher held of him.

Summary

Using seventh-grade students in an urban school system, it was found that (1) There is a significant and positive correlation between self-concept and performance in the academic role; this relationship is substantial even when measured IQ is controlled. (2) There are specific self-concepts of ability related to specific areas of academic role performance, which differ from the general self-concept of ability. These are, in some subjects, significantly better predictors of specific subject achievement than is the general self-concept of ability. (3) Self-concept is significantly and positively correlated with the perceived evaluations that significant others hold of the student; however, it is the composite image rather than the images of specific others that appear to be most closely correlated with the student's self-concept in specific subjects.

NOTES

1 John W. Kinch, "A formalized theory of self-concept (Research Note)," American Journal of Sociology 68 (January 1963): 481–86.

2 Wilbur B. Brookover, "A social psychological conception of classroom learning," School and Society 87 (February 28, 1959): 84–87, and Wilbur B. Brookover and David Gottlieb, A Sociology of Education (New York: American Book Co., 1964), chapter 16.

3 See Wilbur B. Brookover, Ann Paterson, and Shailer Thomas, Self-Concept of Ability and School Achievement (East Lansing, Michigan: Bureau of Research and Publications, Michigan State University, 1962), for a more detailed report of this research. U.S. Office of Education Cooperative Research Project No. 845.

4 Joseph C. Bledsoe and Karl C. Garrison, The Self-Concepts of Elementary School Children in Relation to their Academic Achievement, Intelligence, Interests, and Manifest Anxiety, U.S. Office of Education Cooperative Research Project No. 1008, Athens, Georgia, University of Georgia; Thomas S. McPartland, John H. Cumming, and Wynona S. Garretson, "Self-conception and ward behavior in two psychiatric hospitals," Sociometry 24 (June 1961): 111–24; Walter C. Reckless, Simon Dinitz, and Ellen Murray, "Self-concept as an insulator against delinquency," American Sociological Review 21 (December 1956): 744–46; Ruth Wylie, The Self Concept (Lincoln, Nebraska: University of Nebraska Press, 1961).

5 See Bledsoe and Garrison, Self-Concepts of Elementary School Children; Bernard Borislow, "Self-evaluation and academic achievement," Journal of Counseling Psychology 9 (Fall 1962); Helen H. Davidson and Gerhard Lang, "Children's perceptions of their teachers' feelings toward them related to self-perception, school achievement and behavior," Journal of Experimental Education 29 (1960): 107–18; G. A. Renzaglia, "Some correlates of the self structure as measured by an index of adjustment and value" (Ph.D. Thesis, University of Minnesota, 1952); Thelma Adams Reeder, "A study of some relationships between level of self-concept, academic achievement and classroom adjustment" (Ph.D. Thesis, Denton: North Texas State College, 1955).

6 Richard J. Morse, "Self-concept of ability, significant others and school achievement of eighth grade students: a comparative investigation of Negro and Caucasian students" (M.A. Thesis, Michigan State University, 1963).

7 See Brookover, Paterson, and Thomas, Self-Concept of Ability, for detailed data.

8 See Brookover, Paterson, and Thomas, Self-Concept of Ability, for material on selection and definitions of over- and under-achievers. Limited resources necessitated the use of these smaller selected groups.

9 The assumption that the hypothesis would be supported in a sample of normal achievers was tested in a replication of the study one year later. The correlations of general self-concept with perception of significant others are for males (N=731): parents 0.64, teachers 0.49, peer 0.50, total 0.60. For females (N=751) the eight-grade correlations are parents 0.75, teachers 0.63, peer 0.58, total 0.74.

10 Frank Miyamoto and Sanford Dornbusch, "A test of the interactionists' hypotheses of self-conception," American Journal of Sociology 61 (March 1956): 399–403.

Self-Esteem and Education: Sex and Cohort Comparisons Among High School Seniors

Patrick M. O'Malley
Jerald G. Bachman

29

A recent analysis by Bachman and O'Malley (1977), based on a sample of about 1,600 young men from the high school class of 1969, showed that self-esteem is positively correlated with educational success. The study also showed that educational accomplishments seem to have greater importance or centrality for self-esteem during the high school years than during the five years beyond high school. Although the data for that study were nationally representative and covered an eight-year longitudinal span, there remained at least two important limitations on the generalizability of the findings. First, and most obviously, the study was limited to young men, thus leaving it unclear whether the findings are applicable to young women. Second, the study spanned the interval from 1966 to 1974, a period in which there were important social changes, including changes in public views about the value of education. Therefore, the data left some uncertainty about whether the changing link between educational success and self-esteem

Source: Patrick M. O'Malley and Jerald G. Bachman, "Self-Esteem and Education: Sex and Cohort Comparisons Among High School Seniors," Journal of Personality and Social Psychology 37 (1979): 1153–59.

reflected a genuine developmental process in late adolescence or a secular trend that affected the society as a whole.

The present article, reporting new data from a nationwide cross section of male and female seniors from the high school class of 1977, provides a partial replication and extension of the study of the class of 1969. The new data permit us to overcome both of the limitations noted above. Unlike the previous study, the findings reported here are not longitudinal; therefore, we will not be concerned with relating self-esteem to later (post-high school) educational and occupational attainments. Instead, we will see how self-esteem among seniors relates to recent educational success (high school grades), self-ratings of academic ability, college plans, and parental education. We will examine these relationships in parallel fashion for three distinct groups: senior males in the class of 1969, senior males in the class of 1977, and senior females in the class of 1977.

One of the basic conclusions from the previous study was that

> *those things having to do with a self-concept of educational success—things such as academic skills, past classroom performance, future aspirations, and the like—undergo some reduction in salience or "centrality" for the overall self-esteem of young men as they move through the final years of high school and go on to other experiences (Bachman & O'Malley, 1977, p. 377).*

The study recognized the possibility of different interpretations.

> *The first interpretation, and the one which we have emphasized, is that this shift in centrality is a fairly typical part of the developmental sequence followed by young people in this society. During the late high school years and the period which follows, the young person in the process of becoming an adult increasingly anticipates and experiences situations in which self-evaluation depends on factors quite different from success in school; and this means that academic things become less dominant in shaping self-esteem. An alternative interpretation of our findings is that they reflect a particular secular trend or cultural change during the late sixties and early seventies—a general decline in the importance or value that society places upon education and educational success. Trust in government declined dramatically during this period, and some would argue that faith in education as the pathway to success has also suffered a setback (Bachman & O'Malley, 1977, pp. 378–379).*

The present analysis, by comparing data for males in the classes of 1969 and 1977 provides a means of testing whether one of the alternative interpretations outlined above is more valid than the other. First, it must be understood that the earlier longitudinal study revealed a gradual and continuing change from 1966 (start of 10th grade) through 1974 (5 years postgraduation); across a sequence of five data collections, correlations between self-esteem and educational factors grew progressively smaller (Bachman & O'Malley, 1977; Bachman, O'Malley, & Johnston, 1978). Now suppose that this gradual change reflected a substantial secular trend or cultural change affecting the relationship between self-esteem and educational success; then, unless the trend dramatically reversed during the past several years, correlations between educational factors and self-esteem should be substantially lower for seniors in 1977 compared with seniors in 1969. But suppose, on the other hand, that the earlier findings were due solely to developmental changes occurring during late adolescence; then, unless such developmental patterns were somehow different a decade later, the correlations for seniors in 1977 should be similar to those found for seniors in 1969.

A different point of interest in the present analysis is how males and females compare in the extent to which self-esteem is determined by (correlated with) various educationally relevant dimensions. Douvan and Gold (1966), in reviewing the literature on self-esteem more than a decade ago, concluded that the self-esteem of boys and girls depended to some extent on different components. Also, Rosenberg and Simmons (1975) found evidence that indicated that adolescent boys emphasized the importance of competence and achievement more than did girls. If this is true, we may expect that to the extent that boys' needs for competence and achievement depend on educational experiences, correlations of educationally relevant variables with self-esteem should be higher for boys than for girls.

A final point of interest is whether boys have higher levels of self-esteem than girls do. There have been reports that adolescent females' self-images are less favorable than males' (Rosenberg & Simmons, 1975), although others have not found differences (Drummond, McIntire, & Ryan, 1977; Rosenberg, 1965). There are good reasons why females' self-esteem should be lower than that of males, feminists would argue. The females' less advantageous position in society could easily result in lower self-esteem. Simmons and Rosenberg (1975) in their study of adolescent girls found that "at least in 1968, girls appeared to have a more unfavorable self-picture than did boys" (p. 233). As implied in the quote, an interesting question is whether that was still true in 1977. Perhaps the upheaval in women's rights and roles in the period from 1968 to 1977 resulted in an erasure of those differences.

In fact, a comparison has already been made between the findings from the 1968 study (Simmons & Rosenberg, 1975) and findings from a later, similar study conducted from 1974 to 1975 (Bush, Simmons, Hutchinson, & Blyth, 1977–1978) "to see if the new feminist ideology and movement could have had an effect on girls' self-esteem" (p. 472). Like the 1968 study, this more recent study found that girls' self-esteem in the sixth and seventh grades averaged slightly lower than boys'. The present study extends the time period to 1977 and looks at seniors, rather than sixth and seventh graders.

In sum, this article employs data from two studies to address three theoretically important questions about self-esteem. First, are the patterns of correlation between self-esteem and educational factors essentially the same for males in the high school classes of 1969 and 1977? Second, are these patterns of correlation similar for males and females (in 1977)? Third, are there differences in levels of self-esteem between males and females (in 1977)?

METHOD

Sample

One source of data is the Youth in Transition sample of young men from the high school class of 1969, described in detail by Bachman et al. (1978). Briefly, this is a nationally representative sample of 2,277 sophomores in 87 schools in the 48 contiguous states. Data collections were made in 1966 when they were sophomores and again in 1968, 1969 (when they were seniors), 1970, and 1974. In the 1969 data collection, the one mose relevant here, 1,799 participated (79 percent of the original target sample)

The second source of data is the Monitoring the Future project being conducted by the University of Michigan's Institute for Social Research. The study is described in detail by Bachman and Johnston;[1] only a brief overview is given here. The project consists of a series of annual questionnaire surveys of male and female seniors in high school. In addition, annual follow-up surveys are mailed to a subset of each sample for six years following their graduation. The initial base-year data collection is conducted in about 125 schools selected to provide an accurate cross section of high school seniors throughout the United States. The 1977 base-year survey of over 18,000 seniors provided the data to be reported here.[2] The measure of primary interest, self-esteem, was included in only one of the five forms used in the study, so analyses in this report were based on an essentially random 20 percent of the total. The number of respondents with complete data on the self-esteem index was 3,183.

Measures

Self-esteem measures in the two studies were similar but not identical. The Monitoring the Future measure was an eight-item index similar to that used by Rosenberg (1965). Respondents were asked to indicate on a five-point scale the extent of their agreement or disagreement with the items. The response categories—disagree, mostly disagree, neither, mostly agree, agree—were coded from 1 to 5, with higher values assigned to responses indicating higher self-esteem. The first four items were positively worded, and the second four were negatively worded. Table 1 shows the eight items, with their means, standard deviations, and item-index correlations, separately for males and females. Coefficient alphas were 0.79 for males and 0.83 for females.

The measure of self-esteem used in the Youth in Transition study differed slightly from the Monitoring the Future measure. A different five-point scale was used; respondents were asked to indicate how often each item was true for them, with responses ranging from almost always true to never true. There were 10 items, 7 of which were virtually identical to those used in the 1977 Monitoring the Future study (Items 1–3 and 5–8 in Table 1). (See Bachman & O'Malley, 1977, for the Youth in Transition item wordings, means, standard deviations, and item-index correlations.) Coefficient alpha for males in the class of 1969 was 0.79, the same as the value for males in the class of 1977.

Because the two studies employed different response scales, and some different items, it is difficult to compare means and standard deviations directly. However, because the two measures are very similar in their basic content as well as index characteristics (coefficient alphas and item-index correlations), their correlations with other measures should be comparable. (The comparability can be heightened by using subscales based on the seven common items. The present article includes correlations based on these subscales. To maintain comparability with other reports using these data, however, we focused primarily on the complete 10-item and 8-item measures.)

Unless otherwise stated, the remaining measures listed below are the same in the two studies.

TABLE 1

Self-Esteem Items and Item-Index Correlations

ITEM	1977 HIGH SCHOOL SENIORS: MALES *n*	*M*	*SD*	*	FEMALES *n*	*M*	*SD*	*	*t* TEST BETWEEN MEANS
I take a positive attitude toward myself.†	1,568	4.13	.93	.54	1,736	3.98	.99	.56	***
I feel I am a person of worth, on an equal plane with others.†	1,555	4.27	.85	.49	1,727	4.21	.90	.55	
I am able to do things as well as most other people.†	1,560	4.41	.75	.39	1,733	4.30	.81	.50	***
On the whole, I am satisfied with myself.†	1,539	4.06	1.05	.48	1,718	4.06	1.03	.57	
I feel I do not have much to be proud of.‡	1,519	4.03	1.14	.54	1,707	4.05	1.15	.60	
Sometimes I think that I am no good at all.‡	1,506	3.63	1.32	.51	1,701	3.47	1.39	.50	***
I feel that I can't do anything right.‡	1,498	4.07	1.11	.41	1,695	4.11	1.08	.53	
I feel that my life is not very useful.‡	1,501	4.18	1.05	.60	1,687	4.18	1.10	.62	
Self-esteem index	1,494	4.10	.66	.79§	1,689	4.04	.72	.83§	*

*Item-index correlation, corrected for part-whole.
†Response of "agree" coded 5 (high self-esteem).
‡Response of "disagree" coded 5 (high self-esteem).
§Coefficient alpha.
**$p < .05$. ***$p < .01$.

Father's education and mother's education were measured on a six-point scale ranging from grade school or less to graduate or professional school. Parental education is a mean of father's and mother's education. Grades were self-reported on a nine-point scale. In the Youth in Transition sample, the grades for junior and senior years were averaged together; in the Monitoring the Future sample respondents were asked for "your average grades so far in high school."

College plans is a dichotomy indicating whether the respondent planned to enter college or not. Self-concept of school ability is a mean of two items that asked respondents to compare themselves, on a seven-point scale, with others of the same age on school ability and intelligence. For the class of 1969, the measure was obtained as of junior year; for the class of 1977, the measure was made as of senior year.

Statistical Significance

In reporting statistical significance levels, we made no adjustment for the clustered sampling design used for both samples. One reason for not adjusting for design effect was that we did not have good estimates of the design effect for self-esteem and its correlations with other variables. We are confident, however, that these design effects are small because there is little clustering of self-esteem by school. Since the nominal probability levels are nevertheless likely to be slightly inflated, we report statistical significance at both the 0.01 and the 0.05 levels.

RESULTS AND DISCUSSION

Class of 1977: Male Versus Female Levels of Self-Esteem

Table 1 shows that responses to the self-esteem items for males and females in the class of 1977 indicated a generally high level of self-acceptance. The average response was just above "mostly agree" for the positive items and about "mostly disagree" for the negative items. On six of the eight items, males were higher in self-esteem than females (three of these significantly so); for the total index, males were significantly higher ($p < .05$). Females were more internally consistent, however, as indicated by the higher item-index correlations for all but one item, and the higher coefficient alpha.

The fact that self-esteem was slightly lower for females than for males is consistent with Simmons and Rosenberg (1975) and Bush et al. (1977–1978). Apparently, the recent activities aimed at upgrading women's position in society have not resulted in a total elimination of the differences in self-esteem for high school seniors. But perhaps more important is the fact that the difference in Table 1 is small indeed—less than 0.09 of a standard deviation. This very small difference is statistically significant given a large number of cases, but studies that use smaller samples would be unlikely to show statistically significant differences. This may explain why Maccoby and Jacklin (1974) reported that statistically significant sex differences were seldom found. They commented that "the similarity of the sexes in self-esteem is remarkably uniform across age levels through college age" (p. 153). But their review was based on a number of studies, most of which involved small samples.

There is another large-scale study of a nationally representative sample of high school seniors that included a measure of self-esteem similar to those used in the present articles, namely, the "National Longitudinal Study of the High School Class of 1972." Using these data, Conger, Peng, and Dunteman[3] reported that female seniors were statistically significantly lower in self-esteem than males by about 0.10 of a standard deviation.

A further note of consistency in the finding of slightly lower scores on self-esteem for females than for males comes from the Monitoring the Future data collections from seniors in 1975 and 1976. In those years, an abbreviated four-item self-esteem scale was used. In each year, the females averaged slightly lower than the males.

One other point should be made. Our discussion thus far has taken these self-reports of self-esteem at face value and dealt only with bivariate relationships. It is possible that a more substantial difference between sexes in self-esteem—or even a reversal of the difference reported here—is being masked or suppressed by other related variables that we have not controlled (Rosenberg, 1973). There are several likely candidates for such suppressor variables. Maccoby and Jacklin (1974) noted that boys score higher on lie or defensiveness scales. Thus, boys might defensively overrate themselves on the self-esteem measures. If so, girls may actually have higher self-esteem than boys. A related possible suppressor is social desirability, the tendency to present oneself in as favorable a light as possible. Bush et al. (1977–1978) included such a measure in their study and found that girls were higher than boys in social desirability. Thus, their findings that females were slightly lower in self-esteem could not be due to a social desirability effect. If anything, the differences would be greater if social desirability were controlled. But the correlations among all the variables in their study were low, and controlling actually made little difference in relationships; the zero-order and partial correlations were similar.

Finally, in the Monitoring the Future data, grades could be suppressing a sex effect on self-esteem. We demonstrate that grades and self-esteem are positively correlated; further, females report higher grades than males (data not shown here). Therefore, one would expect females to show higher self-esteem. The fact that they showed lower self-esteem indicates that self-esteem differences would be greater if grades were controlled. But again the differences between zero-order and partial relationships were small. The zero-order correlation of 0.04 between sex and self-esteem becomes a standardized regression coefficient of only 0.08 when grades are controlled, and the substantive significance of a regression coefficient of 0.08 is dubious indeed.

In sum, the data on sex differences in self-esteem among adolescents showed some consistency across studies and across time. Females scored slightly lower than males, but so slight were the differences that relatively large samples were required to achieve statistical significance. Such differences—on the order of 0.10 of a standard deviation or less—are of dubious substantive significance. As Maccoby and Jacklin (1974) pointed out, it is the similarity, not the difference, that is remarkable. Although there remains the logical possibility of substantively important effects of sex on self-esteem, the various suggested controls—some of which serve to heighten self-esteem differences between the sexes and some of which serve to lessen differences—do not appear to be sufficiently strong to alter the conclusion that self-esteem scores are distributed similarly among males and females.

Classes of 1969 and 1977: Educational Variables and Self-Esteem

Now we turn to correlations between self-esteem and measures of parental education, grades, college plans, and self-concept of school ability. We compare these correlations, obtained separately for males and females, with those in the Youth in Transition sample of boys in the high school class of 1969.[4] Table 2 shows these correlations. The basic import of Table 2 is that the correlations of self-esteem with the various measures of background, achievement, and aspirations are all similar among the three groups. None of the pairwise comparisons between groups showed a statistically significant difference. In other words, (a) the correlations for male seniors were stable across the 8 years from 1969 to 1977 and (b) the correlations were similar for both males and females in the class of 1977.

This second finding is rather important. As noted earlier, Douvan and Gold (1966) concluded that the self-esteem of boys and girls depended to some extent on different components. The data in Table 2 suggest that the self-esteem of male and female seniors does not depend differentially on the components listed there.

The first correlational finding—that the self-esteem of male seniors correlates with educationally relevant measures about equally for the classes of 1969 and 1977—provides an extension and replication of part of the findings of the previous report. Although it does not deal with the longitudinal aspects of that report, by replicating the cross-sectional aspects it provides some added support for the conclusions reached there.

It appears that self-esteem in high school does depend to some extent on factors of background, achievement, and aspiration. All correlations in Table 2 are positive, and some are at least moderately high (i.e., grades and self-concept of school

TABLE 2

Correlations of Self-Esteem with Educational Measures for Seniors in 1969 and in 1977

MEASURE	YOUTH IN TRANSITION (CLASS OF 1969) MALES (n = 1,715)*	MONITORING THE FUTURE (CLASS OF 1977) MALES (n = 1,494)*	MONITORING THE FUTURE (CLASS OF 1977) FEMALES (n = 1,689)*
Father's education	.09 (.10)	.08 (.09)	.11 (.11)
Mother's education	.06 (.07)	.07 (.07)	.08 (.08)
Parental education	.08 (.10)	.08 (.09)	.11 (.11)
Grades	.21 (.21)	.25 (.26)	.24 (.26)
College plans	.18 (.19)	.18 (.20)	.14 (.16)
Self-concept of school ability	.27 (.26)	.28 (.29)	.29 (.30)

Note. All correlations are significantly different from zero at the 0.01 level, except that between self-esteem and mother's education, for the 1977 senior males, which is significant at the 0.05 level. The correlations in parentheses are based on the subscale that consists of the 7 items common to both studies (Items 1–3 and 5–8 in Table 1). In no case does a subscale correlation differ from the corresponding full scale correlation by more than 0.02. The 7-item subscale correlates 0.95 with the 10-item Youth in Transition measure, 0.98 with the 8-item Monitoring the Future measure for males, and 0.99 for females. Subscale coefficient alphas are 0.76, 0.76, and 0.80 for the three samples, respectively.

*The number of cases varies slightly for each correlation, with up to 8 percent missing data.

ability). (All of the correlations in Table 2 are significantly different from zero.)

As discussed above, the earlier longitudinal analysis found that "educational success and its correlates seemed to grow less central to the self-esteem of young men . . . as they moved through high school and beyond," and this was interpreted as "a fairly typical part of the developmental sequence followed by young people in this society" (Bachman & O'Malley, 1977, p. 378). But an alternative explanation was that there was an overall secular trend involving a lessening importance of education for self-esteem—a pattern that would be reflected in reduced correlations between education and self-esteem in later cohorts of students. If the data presented in Table 2 had shown lower correlations for the 1977 seniors (male) than for those from the class of 1969, the secular trend interpretation would have been supported. In fact, however, Table 2 shows a striking degree of similarity in the relationships for the two cohorts; certainly the correlations for the class of 1977 are not at all lower than those for the class of 1969.

Thus, by failing to confirm the secular trend interpretation, the present replication and extension provides additional, albeit indirect, support for a basic conclusion from the earlier study: Educational success becomes less central to self-esteem during late high school and the years that follow. Furthermore, given the high degree of similarity between male and female self-esteem data in the class of 1977, it is likely that this process holds true for both sexes.

NOTES

1 Bachman, J. G., & Johnston, L., "The Monitoring the Future project: Design and Procedures." Unpublished manuscript, 1978. (Available from the Institute for Social Research, University of Michigan, P.O. Box 1248, Ann Arbor, Mich. 48106).

2 The study began with the class of 1975; however, 1977 was the first year that included all of the eight self-esteem items presented in this article.

3 Conger, A. J., Peng, S. S., and Dunteman, G. H., "National Longitudinal Study of the High School Class of 1972: Group Profiles on Self-Esteem, Locus of Control, and Life Goals." Unpublished manuscript, 1977. (Available from Research Triangle Institute, Research Triangle Park, N.C. 27709).

4 Because the Monitoring the Future sample design eliminated high school dropouts, the present computations for the Youth in Transition sample also eliminate dropouts. The number of cases is therefore slightly different from the earlier report that included dropouts (Bachman & O'Malley, 1977).

REFERENCES

Bachman, J. G. and P. M. O'Malley
1977 "Self-esteem in young men: a longitudinal analysis of the impact of educational and occupational attainment." Journal of Personality and Social Psychology 35: 365–80.

Bachman, J. G., P. M. O'Malley, and J. Johnston
1978 Adolescence to adulthood—change and stability in the lives of young men. In Youth in Transition, Vol. 6. Ann Arbor, Mich.: Institute for Social Research.

Bush, D. E., R. G. Simmons, B. Hutchinson, and D. A. Blyth
1977–1978 "Adolescent perception of sex-roles in 1968 and 1975." Public Opinion Quarterly 41: 459–74.

Douvan, E. and M. Gold
1966 "Modal patterns in American adolescence." In L. W. Hoffman and M. L. Hoffman (eds.), Review of Child Development Research. New York: Russell Sage Foundation.

Drummond, R. J., W. G. McIntire, and C. W. Ryan
1977 "Stability and sex differences on the Coopersmith self-esteem inventory for students in grades two to twelve." Psychological Reports 40: 943–46.

Maccoby, E. E. and C. N. Jacklin
1974 The Psychology of Sex Differences. Stanford, Calif.: Stanford University Press.

Rosenberg, F. and R. G. Simmons
1975 "Sex differences in the self-concept in adolescence." Sex Roles 1: 147–59.

Rosenberg, M.
1965 Society and the Adolescent Self-Image. Princeton, N.J.: Princeton University Press.
1973 "The logical status of suppressor variables." Public Opinion Quarterly 37: 359–72.

Simmons, R. G. and F. Rosenberg
1975 "Sex, sex roles, and self-image." Journal of Youth and Adolescence 4: 229–58.

Psychological Origins of Adolescent Political Attitudes: Self-Esteem, Political Salience, and Political Involvement

Edward G. Carmines

30

Much of the recent research in political socialization has sought to identify and explore those factors which are related to the learning of political orientations, attitudes, and behavioral patterns. Socioeconomic status, race, sex, and cognitive ability are just a few of the many variables which seem to influence this learning process. These factors are supposedly related to the kind of political phenomenon learned, the rate at which it is acquired, and the degree to which it is retained as an element in the individual's political makeup.

However, the political influence of personality characteristics—that set of characteristics which define each of us most distinctively—has been largely overlooked in recent research. The relevance of personality predispositions to an understanding of political behavior is based on a fundamental though sometimes

Source: Edward G. Carmines, "Psychological Origins of Adolescent Political Attitudes: Self-Esteem, Political Salience, and Political Involvement," Reprinted from "Psychological Origins of Adolescent Political Attitudes," American Politics Quarterly 6: 167–86, © Sage Publications, Beverly Hills, by permission of the publisher.

neglected fact: that human behavior (including political behavior) "is a function of both the *environmental situations* in which actors find themselves and the *psychological predispositions* they bring to those situations" (Greenstein, 1969:7).

While environmental constraints and personal factors jointly explain political behavior, these two sets of influences are not always of equal importance. Rather, personal factors are likely to be especially important in ambiguous situations. According to Greenstein (1969: 50, 51), these instances include the "completely new situation in which there are no familiar cues," the "complex situation in which there are a great number of cues to be taken into account," and the "contradictory situation in which different elements suggest different structures." The political learning of preadults occurs largely under such ambiguous circumstances, for it typically involves the grasping of unfamiliar, contradictory cues from a multiplicity of socialization agents. Therefore, the political implications of personality should be an important concern to those interested in understanding the political attitudes of preadults.

ROSENBERG'S CONCEPTION OF SELF-ESTEEM

The present study focuses on the personality dimension often referred to as self-esteem. The social and political importance of self-esteem stems from the belief that "since the individual's perceptions of the world are always filtered through the lens of his private motivational system, it follows that how a man sees himself will bear a relationship to how he sees the world" (Rosenberg, 1962: 201). It is reasonable to assume, then, that an individual's perception of self has a distinct though probably complex and selective influence on the way in which he perceives and interprets political stimuli.

Most studies of self-esteem focus primarily on the psychological implications of this personality trait. In contrast, Rosenberg's (1965, 1967) research not only focuses on the psychological implications of self-esteem, but also on its social and political importance. Rosenberg defines self-esteem as a person's attitude toward a particular object—the self. Self-esteem, therefore, has all of the properties that are possessed by attitudes in general. They can be described in terms of direction, intensity, salience, importance, clarity, stability, consistency, content, and verifiability.

Self-esteem, however, does possess certain properties which are not typical of attitudes in general. Among the most important of these are the following: (1) self-esteem is relatively fixed and stable, (2) it is invariably salient and important, (3) it is highly emotive, and (4) it is reflexive—an attitude held toward one's self rather than toward an external object (Coopersmith, 1967; Rosenberg, 1965).

Self-esteem, in sum, is a construct located squarely within the realm of attitudinal theory while simultaneously remaining distinct from other attitudes. If this is the nature of self-esteem, as conceptualized by Rosenberg, how shall we describe its content? Put more directly, what does it mean to say that one individual has high self-esteem while another has low self-esteem? High self-esteem indicates that an individual has a favorable perception and evaluation of himself whereas low self-esteem signifies an unfavorable evaluation of the self.

Recent research has indicated that persons with low self-esteem manifest a variety of adverse personality traits (for an excellent review of this evidence see Sniderman, 1975: 64–115). For example, they tend to be "guilt-ridden, cautious, morbidly afraid of a failure, chronically anxious, and psychologically vulnerable." Conversely, persons with high self-esteem "feel a sense of command over themselves and their immediate environment; they are well-integrated, candid, and willing to take risks" (DiPalma and McClosky, 1970: 1065).

The influence of self-esteem on specific political attitudes and behavior has been explored in several recent studies (Sniderman, 1975; Sniderman and Citrin, 1971). In his study of the causes and consequences of self-esteem in adolescence, Rosenberg (1965:211, 212) drew the following political portrait of the adolescent with low self-esteem:

He expresses a relative lack of interest in matters of national or international import, he is less likely to follow such questions in the press and on the air, and he manifests greater ignorance of such subjects on an objective test of knowledge. In addition, he appears to participate less frequently than others in discussions of national or international questions; he is unlikely to assume a forceful or dominant role in such discussions; and he is unlikely to be called upon by others for his advice and opinion on such matters.

Rosenberg examined the effects of self-esteem on a fairly narrow range of political orientations. Theoretically, however, the impact of self-esteem need not be so limited. The purpose of this paper, therefore, is to examine the relationship between self-esteem and a variety of political attitudes held by adolescents.

SELF-ESTEEM AND POLITICAL ATTITUDES OF ADOLESCENTS

In the first place, self-esteem should have an impact on adolescents' cognitive orientation toward politics. Those adolescents with low self-esteem should be more inhibited in their learning and understanding of political phenomena than those with high self-esteem. Adolescents with damaged egos are likely to be characterized by a variety of adverse, personal problems, and it is unlikely that they will be able to move beyond these into a clear and accurate conception of social and political realities.

Because of its direct and considerable influence on key intellectual processes, low self-esteem should also indirectly affect the acquisition and understanding of political stimuli. This is because personality traits affect basic processes of perception, judgment, and learning inherent in any phenomenological domain, including the domain of politics. Consequently,

by influencing an individual's cognitive processes, psychological dispositions such as anxiety or low self-esteem partially determines his level of political awareness, his capacity to perceive and interpret political stimuli accurately, and the way he organizes and interrelates his ideas [Sniderman and Citrin, 1971:402].

Low self-esteem not only impairs cognitive efficiency in general, it hampers social learning in particular (see Sniderman, 1975: 136–162). Low self-esteem characteristically reduces one's level and focus of attention. This is partly due to the fact that social withdrawal is a common response for those with low self-regard. But the more important reason that low self-esteem diminishes attentiveness is that the habits of avoidance and social inattention tend to be self-reinforcing. As a consequence, the absence of self-acceptance affects not only the likelihood of exposure, but its efficacy as well. This is an important way that low self-esteem lessens a person's understanding of politics, for exposure to political stimuli often occurs during interpersonal communications.

In summary, there are three psychological processes which link low self-esteem to a lack of comprehension of politics. First, persons with low self-esteem tend to be so preoccupied with their own personal problems that they have little energy to devote to matters of political import. Second, feelings of low self-esteem, like other adverse personality traits, measurably impair the functioning of cognitive processes. Finally, a lack of self-regard has a detrimental effect on one's ability to profit from social interactions.

Self-esteem should also influence adolescents' level of political cynicism and political efficacy. In particular, adolescents with high self-esteem should feel less distrustful toward political authorities and evidence a higher sense of political effectiveness than those with low self-esteem. To adolescents with low self-esteem, the world often appears to be a bewildering and threatening place. Plagued by constant feelings of self-doubt and vulnerability, they are unlikely to develop feelings of interpersonal trust. Without trusting people in general, it would be exceedingly difficult for those with low self-regard to trust political authorities in particular.[1] Futhermore, since adolescents with low self-esteem do not have confidence in their own abilities and do not have a high regard of their own worthiness, they are not apt to see these qualities in others, including government officials.

For somewhat similar reasons, self-esteem should influence adolescents' degree of political efficacy. Since the adolescent with high self-esteem not only considers himself worthy but also believes that he can act capably within his immediate environment, he is likely to maintain a similar conception of his potential political role. Consequently, a high self-estimate should provide the psychological basis for developing feelings of political efficacy. On the other hand, since adolescents with low self-esteem are unsure of themselves and evidence little confidence in their ability to deal successfully with immediate environmental demands, they are not likely to believe that they will become effective participants in the political arena.

Self-esteem should also have an effect on adolescents' propensity to become involved in political activities. It is not difficult to see how low self-esteem can dampen inclination to become involved in politics. Lacking self-confidence and feeling that their weak egos will be exposed and further damaged in interpersonal relationships, adolescents with low self-esteem find it more comfortable simply to avoid becoming involved with others. Politics, however, not only involves a great deal of interpersonal contact, but it often requires that the individual himself initiates such contact. From this, it is but a short step to see that those with low self-esteem are psychologically unprepared to pursue political activities.

Quite apart from the negative impact of low self-esteem on political participation is the propensity toward involvement which is associated with high self-esteem. That is, as Sniderman (1975: 151) has argued, high self-esteem is a positive stimulus, not merely the absence of a negative one. High self-esteem is a psychological trait which motivates one to become active in all areas of life—politics included (for evidence, see Rosenberg, 1965; Coopersmith, 1967; and Mussen and Porter, 1959).

However, those adolescents high in self-esteem should be less likely to engage in protest activity than those low in self-esteem. Because they feel politically efficacious and trusting toward political authorities, adolescents with high self-esteem are likely to eschew protest activity. In effect, they are more likely to believe that their political demands would be met without having to engage in such activity. On the other hand, since adolescents with low self-estimates feel neither politically efficacious nor trusting, they should be more favorably disposed toward protest actions if inclined to participate at all.

THE MEDIATING INFLUENCE OF POLITICAL SALIENCE ON THE LINKAGE BETWEEN SELF-ESTEEM AND POLITICAL ATTITUDES

Up to this point, it has been argued that there is a relationship between adolescents' self-esteem and certain political attitudes. Before evaluating the empirical validity of this connection, however, it is necessary to introduce the notion of political salience to extend the theoretical formulation. Political salience refers to the importance, interest, and psychic energy that individuals invest in and attach to political phenomenon. It is assumed that this is not a constant, but that the relative centrality of politics varies across individuals as well as occasions and lifespan. Specifically, it is hypothesized that the linkage between self-esteem and political attitudes is substantially stronger among those adolescents for whom politics represents an important dimension of their life-space than among those who have little interest in political affairs.

Why should political salience structure the relation between adolescents' self-esteem and their political attitudes? The answer lies in the nature of the personality disposition itself. Personality dispositions like self-esteem exert their primary influence on those areas and objects which the individual has defined as being meaningful. For other, less central concerns, the individual's self-esteem tends to be less thoroughly engaged and thus less influential. Therefore, it is not assumed that self-esteem affects the political attitudes and beliefs of all adolescents equally; rather, that if an individual perceives politics to be salient, then his level of self-esteem will more significantly influence the way in which he responds to political stimuli. Although self-esteem influences the perception and evaluation of political stimuli generally, *it is brought to bear most forcefully and most consistently only among those adolescents for whom politics is salient.* This line of reasoning is consistent with Levinson's (1958: 10) dictum that "the more politics 'matters,' the more likely it is that political behavior will express enduring inner values and dispositions."

The theoretical connection between adolescents' self-esteem and their political attitudes can be summarized in propositional form as follows:

1. Self-esteem should be positively related to comprehension of politics.
2. Self-esteem should be negatively related to political cynicism.
3. Self-esteem should be positively related to political efficacy.

4. Self-esteem should be positively related to involvement in conventional political activities.
5. Self-esteem should be negatively related to involvement in protest activities.

More important, it is predicted that each of these relationships will be substantially stronger among those adolescents for whom politics is salient than among those who have little interest in political affairs.

SAMPLE

The data for this study were obtained by Roberta Sigel as part of a large project to investigate the political orientations of rural adolescents. In the spring of 1971, 346 high school students, mainly sophomores and seniors, in two small rural Western New York communities (population under 2,500 each) were interviewed. Both communities are located in a county belonging to the Appalachian tier and have been characterized as economically depressed. In one school, each student in the sophomore and senior class was interviewed; in the second school a sample had to be drawn (roughly one-third of the total population) because the classes were too large for complete enumeration. All 346 students were given two paper-and-pencil questionnaires; 217 among them were also individually interviewed by professional interviewers.

MEASUREMENT OF VARIABLES

Self-esteem, the independent variable of this study, is measured by a scale developed and reported by Rosenberg (1965). Three properties of the measure are worth noting. First, the scale is designed to measure the respondent's global self-esteem. The items do not specify particular areas of activity or qualities which the individual must take into consideration in judging himself. The scale attempts to gauge the adolescent's basic attitude toward his own worth by allowing him to invoke his own frame of reference.

The second important property of the scale is closely related to the first: namely, that the scale is designed to capture the respondent's enduring, longstanding self-estimate. The emphasis here is not on the adolescent's immediate or momentary self-perception; rather, the scale stresses the more permanent, more stable components of the self-image.

Finally, the exact meaning of scoring high on this scale should be emphasized. It does not mean that the adolescent stands in awe of himself, nor does it mean that he expects others to stand in awe of him. As Rosenberg (1965: 31) says, the high self-esteem individual "does not necessarily consider himself superior to others." High self-esteem, as reflected in the scale items, means simply that the individual considers himself "good enough" (for a more extensive discussion of Rosenberg's self-esteem scale, see Carmines and Zeller, 1974).

Cognitive orientations toward politics are measured by two indicators: (1) a four-item index requiring the identification of the names of five very prominent federal officeholders (Bachman, 1970), and (2) a ten-item index measuring adolescents' ability to differentiate between principles and practices which are essential to a democracy and those which, although practiced in the United States, are not essential democratic features.[2] These indicators will be referred to as the "Knowledge of Political Authorities Index" and the "Essentials of Democracy Index," respectively. Respondents were give a score on each of these measures according to the number of items they correctly identified. Because the measures intercorrelate only weakly (Gamma = 0.14), they will be analyzed separately.

Adolescents' political cynicism or distrust is measured by the Bachman et al. (1969) six-item cynicism scale. The manifest content of the scale pertains to attitudes toward the honesty, trust, benevolence, and competency of the governmental structure and those who run it. The adolescents' political efficacy is measured by a five-item scale developed by Easton and Dennis (1967). The

TABLE 1
Factor Loadings of the Political Participation Acts Extracted by the Principal Component Procedure and Rotated to a Quartimax Solution

	ROTATED COMPONENTS		
POLITICAL ACTS	*PROTEST ACTIVITY*	*POLITICAL ACTIVISM*	*VOTING PARTICIPATION*
Organize a demonstration or protest march	800*	103	117
Form an organization to pressure the government to do something about the matter	700	178	192
If all else fails, engage in violent action to get the decision changed	779	-248	-115
Go to the government office and try to get the decision changed	268	440	193
Write a letter about the problem to the government	-011	863	-061
Get friends and neighbors to help you write letters and talk to people in the government	-060	872	103
Vote against the persons who made the decision in the next election	214	064	630
Accept the government's decision; they may have information that I don't have	-003	098	846
Percent of Total Variance	27	22	13
Percent of Explained Variance	44	35	21

*The underlined factor loadings specify the items that were used in constructing each of the three participation scales. Decimal points have been omitted from this table.

scale measures the degree to which the adolescent feels that citizens are politically effective and the corresponding degree to which governmental authorities are felt to be responsive to citizen demands.[3]

The measurement of political participation poses the most acute problem. This is due to the fact that adolescence is generally characterized by an absence of direct political involvement. Therefore, the measure of political participation used in this study focuses on attitudes toward different political acts rather than actual involvement in politics. Specifically, the adolescents were asked if they would engage in eight different political acts if the government enacted a policy which they thought was bad for the country. A principal component analysis of the correlations among these political acts indicates that they measure three distinct modes of participation (see Table 1). These modes of political participation will be referred to as protest activity, political activism, and voting participation, respectively.[4]

The degree to which politics is salient for the respondents is operationally defined by a standard political interest item. The item and its response categories are as follows: "Some people think about what's going on in the government very often and others are not that interested. How much of an interest do you take in government and current events?" (1) No interest, (2) Very little interest, (3) Some interest, (4) A lot of interest, (5) A very great interest. Respondents who choose response 1 to 3 will be considered low/medium in political interest—adolescents for whom politics is not especially salient; choice or response 4 or 5 indicates high interest—politics is salient for those adolescents.

FINDINGS[5]

Table 2 presents the contingent relationship between self-esteem and the Knowledge of Political Authorities Index while controlling for political interest. Among those for whom politics is salient, a clear and consistent relationship emerges (Gamma = 0.51) between self-esteem and political knowledge. For the less interested the comparable statistic falls to 0.13.

TABLE 2

Self-Esteem by the Knowledge of Political Authorities Index, Controlling for Political Interest

	HIGH POLITICAL INTEREST			LOW POLITICAL INTEREST		
	SELF-ESTEEM			SELF-ESTEEM		
KNOWLEDGE OF POLITICAL AUTHORITIES INDEX	LOW	MEDIUM	HIGH	LOW	MEDIUM	HIGH
Low	59%	32%	14%	54%	53%	44%
Medium	23	40	36	35	34	42
High	18	28	50	11	13	14
Totals	100%	100%	100%	100%	100%	100%
$N =$	22	25	36	85	74	85
	Gamma = .51			Gamma = .13		

A similar pattern characterizes the relationship between self-esteem and the Essentials of Democracy Index (see Table 3). Again, the predicted relationship is substantially stronger among adolescents for whom politics is salient (Gamma = 0.33) than among their less interested counterparts (Gamma = 0.12). Results from both these tables point to the same conclusion: adolescents' self-esteem is related to comprehension of politics, but the relationship is much more pronounced among those adolescents who are interested in politics than among those who are not.

TABLE 3
Self-Esteem by the Essentials of Democracy Index, Controlling for Political Interest

	HIGH POLITICAL INTEREST			*LOW POLITICAL INTEREST*		
	SELF-ESTEEM			*SELF-ESTEEM*		
ESSENTIALS OF DEMOCRACY INDEX	*LOW*	*MEDIUM*	*HIGH*	*LOW*	*MEDIUM*	*HIGH*
Low	30%	24%	16%	37%	28%	31%
Medium	48	36	31	42	37	37
High	22	40	53	21	35	32
Totals	100%	100%	100%	100%	100%	100%
$N =$	23	25	36	87	74	85
		Gamma = .33			Gamma = .12	

As Table 4 reveals, self-esteem is also strongly related to political cynicism among those adolescents who are high in political interest (Gamma = –0.42). However, the corresponding relationship is very weak (Gamma = –0.10) among those low in political interest.

TABLE 4
Self-Esteem by Political Cynicism, Controlling for Political Interest

	HIGH POLITICAL INTEREST			*LOW POLITICAL INTEREST*		
	SELF-ESTEEM			*SELF-ESTEEM*		
POLITICAL CYNICISM	*LOW*	*MEDIUM*	*HIGH*	*LOW*	*MEDIUM*	*HIGH*
Low	17%	24%	53%	22%	27%	31%
Medium	26	32	19	34	38	32
High	57	44	28	44	35	37
Totals	100%	100%	100%	100%	100%	100%
$N =$	23	25	36	87	74	85
		Gamma = –.42			Gamma = –.10	

Similarly, among those adolescents for whom politics is salient there is a moderately strong relationship between self-esteem and political efficacy (Gamma = 0.33). For the less interested the comparable statistic is 0.16 (see Table 5). As with the Knowledge of Political Authorities Index, the Essentials of Democracy

Index, and political cynicism, so with feelings of political effectiveness—the influence of self-esteem is substantially stronger among those adolescents high in political interest than among those low in interest.

TABLE 5

Self-Esteem by Political Efficacy, Controlling for Political Interest

	HIGH POLITICAL INTEREST			*LOW POLITICAL INTEREST*		
	SELF-ESTEEM			*SELF-ESTEEM*		
POLITICAL EFFICACY	*LOW*	*MEDIUM*	*HIGH*	*LOW*	*MEDIUM*	*HIGH*
Low	39%	32%	25%	41%	29%	27%
Medium	35	28	14	30	39	35
High	26	40	61	29	32	38
Totals	100%	100%	100%	100%	100%	100%
N =	23	25	36	87	74	85
	Gamma = .33			Gamma = .16		

The relation between adolescents' self-esteem and attitudes toward different modes of political participation presents a picture strikingly different from that just described. In particular, the anticipated relationship holds only with respect to protest activity (see Table 6). As hypothesized, among adolescents high in political interest, those high in self-esteem are less likely to approve of protest activities than those low in self-esteem (Gamma = –0.35). Also, as predicted, the relationship is considerably weaker among those low in political interest (0.01). However, self-esteem is *not* highly related to attitudes toward political activism and voting participation (tables not shown). These weak relationships (Gammas = 0.08 and 0.03, respectively) are to be expected among those adolescents who have little interest in political affairs, but the fact that self-esteem also makes relatively little difference even among those highly interested in politics is surprising and indeed, on face value, perplexing (Gammas = 0.09 and 0.08, respectively). Consequently, considerable attention will be devoted to this finding later.

TABLE 6

Self-Esteem by Protest Activity, Controlling for Political Interest

	HIGH POLITICAL INTEREST			*LOW POLITICAL INTEREST*		
	SELF-ESTEEM			*SELF-ESTEEM*		
PROTEST ACTIVITY	*LOW*	*MEDIUM*	*HIGH*	*LOW*	*MEDIUM*	*HIGH*
Low	17%	32%	37%	39%	47%	42%
Medium	18	36	34	30	27	20
High	65	32	29	31	26	38
Totals	100%	100%	100%	100%	100%	100%
N =	23	25	35	85	74	85
	Gamma = –.35			Gamma = –.01		

Table 7 shows the relationship between self-esteem and these political attitudes while controlling for four variables: grade, sex, intelligence, and socioeconomic status. The table includes only that subset of adolescents for whom politics is salient, and only those political attitudes which showed substantial bivariate relationships with self-esteem. The magnitude of the partial gammas indicates that the political significance of self-esteem is a stable and pervasive phenomenon, for this personality trait continues to be related to adolescents' political attitudes after controlling for each of these other factors.

TABLE 7

Partial Gamma Correlations Between Self-Esteem and Political Attitudes Controlling for Grade, Sex, Intelligence, and Socioeconomic Status

	CONTROLLING FOR			
	GRADE	*SEX*	*INTELLIGENCE*	*SOCIOECONOMIC STATUS*
Knowledge of Political Authorities Index	.48	.41	.40	.50
Essentials of Democracy Index	.32	.30	.27	.24
Political Cynicism	–.41	–.36	–.39	–.40
Political Efficacy	.31	.27	.29	.25
Protest Activity	–.34	–.30	–.32	–.34

*For a discussion of partial gamma, see Davis (1967).

†Socioeconomic status is a composite score based on father's occupation and education and mother's education.

CONCLUSIONS AND IMPLICATIONS

The purpose of this paper has been to illuminate the influence that personality characteristics have on adolescents' political attitudes by examining the political implications of self-esteem. The main finding of the paper is that self-esteem exerts a significant influence on the political orientations, attitudes, and beliefs of those adolescents for whom politics is salient but has little effect on those for whom politics is not salient. The specific relationships discovered among those adolescents interested in politics can be summarized as follows:

1. Adolescents with a diminished sense of self-worth are more likely to hold a vague, unclear, and inaccurate view of the political world than those with high self-esteem.
2. Those with low self-esteem are also more politically cynical or distrustful than those with high self-esteem. Previous research has suggested that persons low in self-esteem find it extremely difficult to trust others; this analysis suggests that this is not only the case with respect to interpersonal relationships, but that a lack of self-regard also undercuts an individual's capacity to trust political authorities and the government generally.
3. Similarly, low self-esteem is linked to feelings of political ineffectiveness. Adolescents with low self-esteem seem to believe that neither they nor

citizens generally can effectively influence the course of governmental action. As a consequence, adolescents with low self-esteem are unlikely to assume that governmental policy is responsive to citizen demands.

4. Adolescents who are high in self-esteem seem less likely to engage in protest activity than those low in self-esteem. This relationship seems to reflect an underlying belief on the part of adolescents with high self-esteem that their political demands will be met without having to engage in protest actions. On the other hand, adolescents with low self-esteem seem to conceive of protest activity as a more necessary means by which to influence governmental policy.

But while it is reasonable that self-esteem and protest activity are negatively related, it is more difficult to understand the relatively weak connection between self-esteem and conventional political activity. It could be a function of the community in which the study was conducted. Rural, small towns do not, as a rule, emphasize the efficacy or desirability of vigorous political activity. To the degree that this attitude becomes embedded in the local political culture, it tends to reduce and standardize the participant orientation of the members of the community. Under these circumstances the high level of involvement which is usually characteristic of those with high self-esteem may be counterbalanced by their greater tendency to acquire the modal values of the political culture. More generally, this line of reasoning suggests that cultural norms channel and in some cases can dampen the effect of individual differences in personality makeup.

Alternatively, the weak connection between self-esteem and attitudes toward conventional political activity may be an artifact of the participation measures. Unlike the other political attitudes, the measures of political participation used in this study are hypothetical in the extreme. Moreover, the students have had little or no experience to bring to bear in answering questions about participation. Hence, it is entirely possible that the hypothesized relationship between self-esteem and conventional political activity will emerge at a later point in the life cycle.[6]

This paper has both methodological and theoretical implications. Methodologically, it has stressed the importance of controlling for political interest when investigating the linkage between personality traits and political attitudes. The evidence contained in this paper clearly suggests that personality traits like self-esteem exert a much greater influence on the political attitudes of those adolescents high in political interest than those low in political interest. The political consequences that flow from self-esteem thus seem to vary greatly in magnitude depending on the salience that politics has for adolescents.

This observation should not lead to the conclusion that personality plays only a minor role in shaping adolescents' political orientations. Rather, it suggests that the influence of personality is not invariant—it is not the same for all aspects of political behavior under all circumstances for all individuals. As Greenstein (1975: 72) has argued, "the effects of any psychological variable on political behavior may be moderated or enhanced by structural factors that cause psychological dispositions to have different behavior consequences in one setting than another and by other individual dispositions that may interact with the variable of interest."

Elaborating Greenstein's observation, this paper suggests that the extent to which people perceive politics to be a salient aspect of their life-space is a crucial mediating factor which acts either to strengthen or weaken the connection between personality and political behavior. Thus, the almost nonexistent relationship found between self-esteem and the political attitudes of adolescents for whom politics is *not* salient is consistent with the idea that for these persons "politics rarely takes on sufficient psychological importance for it to acquire the symbolic and affective associations necessary to engage some basic personality characteristic" (Sniderman, 1975: 263). Conversely, self-esteem is seen to have a more powerful influence on the political attitudes of those for whom politics is salient because politics then becomes an appropriate and meaningful arena for the exercise of individual differences in personality.

Theoretically, these findings have important implications for democratic citizenship. They suggest that the level of self-esteem found in adolescence foreshadows the development of differential modes of adult political beliefs and behavior. That is, high self-esteem in adolescence may well set in motion a developmental sequence which culminates with the emergence of an active, informed citizen. Conversely, the set of political attributes which characterize the adolescent with low self-esteem has the distinctive earmark of an apathetic citizen. Moreover, the fact that adolescents with low self-esteem show a propensity to become involved in protest activities suggests that they may become disaffected citizens as well. Yet, it must be emphasized that the likelihood of either of these developments depends on a number of other factors—not the least of which is the power that politics has to engage adolescents' deep-seated personality needs.

NOTES

1 This is not to argue, of course, that personality dispositions are the only influences which lead citizens to distrust political leaders. For a discussion of this distinction see Fraser (1971).

2 The exact items are available from the author.

3 A principal component analysis of the political cynicism and political efficacy scales indicates that they are unidimensional. The cynicism scale has an alpha reliability coefficient of 0.776, while the efficacy scale's reliability is 0.715.

4 These participation scales have alpha reliability coefficients of 0.660, 0.615, and 0.472, respectively. These were considered reasonable due to the small number of items in each scale.

5 These hypotheses were also tested using product-moment correlations and ordinal measures based on the complete distribution of the variables. In both cases the results confirm the interpretation offered here in all essential respects.

6 This interpretation was suggested by an anonymous reviewer of this paper.

REFERENCES

Bachman, J. G.
1970 Youth in Transition: The Impact of Family Background and Intelligence on Tenth-Grade Boys. Ann Arbor: Institute for Social Research.

Bachman, J. G., R. L. Kahn, M. T. Mednick, T. N. Davidson, and L. D. Johnson
1969 Youth in Transition, Ann Arbor: Institute for Social Research.
Carmines, E. G. and R. A. Zeller
1974 "On establishing the empirical dimensionality of theoretical terms: an analytical example." Political Methodology 1: 75-96.
Coopersmith, S.
1967 The Antecedents of Self-Esteem. San Francisco: W. H. Freeman.
Davis, J. A.
1967 "A partial coefficient for Goodman and Kruskal's gamma." Journal of American Statistical Association 62: 971-77.
DiPalma, G. and H. McClosky
1970 "Personality and conformity: the learning of political attitudes." American Political Science Review 64: 1054-73.
Easton, D. and J. Dennis
1967 "The child's acquisition of regime norms: political efficacy." American Political Science Review 61: 25-38.
Fraser, J.
1971 "Personal and political meaning correlates of political cynicism." Midwest Journal of Political Science 15: 347-64.
Greenstein, F. I.
1975 "Personality and politics." Pp. 1-92 in F. I. Greenstein and N. W. Polsby (eds.), The Handbook of Political Science, Vol. 2. Reading, Mass.: Addison-Wesley.
1969 Personality and Politics. Chicago: Markham.
Levinson, D. J.
1958 "The relevance of personality for political participation." Public Opinion Quarterly. 22: 3-10.
Mussen, P. H. and L. W. Porter
1959 "Personal motivation and self-conceptions associated with effectiveness and ineffectiveness in emergent groups." Journal of Abnormal and Social Psychology 59: 23-27.
Rosenberg, M.
1962 "Self-esteem and concern with public affairs." Public Opinion Quarterly 26: 201-11.
1965 Society and the Adolescent Self-Image. Princeton, N.J.: Princeton University Press.
1967 "Psychological selectivity in self-esteem formation." Pp. 26-50 in C. W. Sherif and M. Sherif (eds.), Attitude, Ego-Involvement, and Change. New York: John Wiley.
Sniderman, P.
1975 Personality and Democratic Politics. Berkeley: University of California Press.
Sniderman, P. and J. Citrin
1971 "Psychological sources of political belief: self-esteem and isolationist attitudes." American Political Science Review 65: 401-17.

Self-Esteem as a Moderator of the Relationship Between Self-Perceived Abilities and Vocational Choice

Abraham K. Korman

31

The predictive power of "self-implementation" theory as an explanatory principle underlying the vocational choice process has received a considerable amount of support from various investigators in recent years (cf. Englander, 1960; Holland, 1963). Despite such support, however, it is also well accepted that there are a considerable number of other influences in this process, among the most important of which are social pressures from family and friends. It is also apparent that these influences may frequently be at variance with the wishes of the individual making the choice.

In an effort to reconcile these differing viewpoints into a common theoretical framework, the hypothesis has been proposed and tested elsewhere (Korman, 1966) that self-esteem operates as a moderator on the vocational choice process in that individuals high in self-esteem would seek those vocational roles which

Source: Abraham K. Korman, "Self-Esteem as a Moderator of the Relationship Between Self-Perceived Abilities and Vocational Choice," Journal of Applied Psychology 51 (1967): 65–67.

would be congruent with one's self-perceived characteristics, whereas this would less likely be the case for those individuals with low self-esteem. This hypothesis stemmed from two major theoretical assumptions:

1. All other things being equal, individuals will engage in those behavioral roles which will maximize their sense of cognitive balance or consistency;
2. An individual's self-esteem or general evaluation of himself is part of his cognitive structure (self-esteem is defined as a persons' characteristic evaluation of himself as an individual; low self-esteem is characterized by a sense of personal inadequacy and an inability to achieve need satisfaction in the past; high self-esteem is defined by a sense of personal adequacy and a sense of having achieved need satisfaction in the past).

From these assumptions it was predicted and verified that individuals high in self-esteem would be more likely to choose those occupations which they perceived to be likely to satisfy their specific needs and to be in keeping with their self-perceived characteristics than those individuals with low self-esteem. Such choice patterns were predicted to be consistent with the high-self-esteem individual's cognition of himself as an adequate, need-satisfying individual and the lack of such cognitions in the low-self-esteem person.

The major purpose of the research to be reported here was to generalize these findings to the area of abilities by testing a number of hypotheses which postulated similar relationships between self-esteem, perceptions of the ability requirements of the chosen occupation, and perceptions of one's own abilities. In particular, the following hypotheses were tested:

Hypothesis 1

Individuals with high self-esteem are more likely to see themselves as having high abilities in those areas where their chosen occupation calls for high abilities than are those with low self-esteem likely to see themselves as having high abilities in those areas where their chosen occupation calls for high abilities;

Hypothesis 2

For those areas where the chosen occupation is perceived to call for low abilities, the individual with low self-esteem is as likely to see himself as having high abilities as is the person with high self-esteem.

This latter hypothesis provides a control on the results of the first hypothesis in that, if supported, it would suggest that the high-self-esteem person does not describe himself in terms of a "set" to be more adequate in everything but rather as being more adequate just in those areas which are called for by the role.

METHOD

Subjects

The basic sample for the research consisted of 126 lower-division students at a large eastern private university, who had claimed to have made a fairly definitive occupational choice. Of these, 70 were male and 56 female. Each sex was analyzed separately.

For the two hypotheses, each sample was split into high- and low-self-esteem groups on the basis of approximately top one-third and bottom two-thirds, in line with previous research.

Measuring Instruments

"Self-Esteem" was measured by the self-assurance scale of the Ghiselli Self-Description Inventory.[1] Evidence for the construct validity of this instrument is available in a number of publications (cf. Ghiselli, 1963).

"Self-Perceived Abilities" was measured by the Ability-Assessment Questionnaire. This is an instrument designed to indicate the extent to which the person sees himself as possessing various abilities which have been isolated in different factor-analytic studies. Examples of the abilities tapped by this 13-item questionnaire are "the ability to visualize or perceive objects in space and place them in relation to one another," "the ability to work rapidly and quickly with numbers," and "the ability to produce a large number of ideas in a short period of time." Using a rough classification, three of the items deal with numerical abilities, three with perceptual abilities, and the rest concern themselves with more verbal self-perceived skills. The test-retest item reliability of the questionnaire has a median of 0.81 (about 3 weeks apart).

"Occupationally Required" abilities, as perceived, were measured by the Career Description Questionnaire. This instrument is similar in format to the Ability Assessment Questionnaire, but differs in that the subject is asked to describe his chosen occupation. In addition, the items appear in a different order.

"Vocational Choice" was measured by a questionnaire procedure found to have high concurrent validity and reliability in the previous study (Korman, 1966). As before, all individuals who had received psychological counseling were eliminated as a control.

Procedures

The questionnaires were administered in at least two different sessions to the subjects during regular class meetings of introductory psychology classes.[2] In a few cases the Career Description Questionnaire and the Ability Assessment Questionnaire were administered at the same meeting since previous work by the author has found this to be a permissible procedure. However, generally, these were administered in separate sessions.

The average time between classes was about 2 weeks, with some considerably longer.

Discrepancy scores were computed between the two highest occupationally required abilities and the corresponding self-perceptions, and the two lowest occupationally required abilities and the corresponding self-perceptions. (In case of ties, either the top three and/or bottom three abilities were utilized.) Each individual's discrepancy score was computed as follows:

(a) For high abilities

Discrepancy = Occupationally Required Abilities — Self-Perceived Abilities

(b) For low abilities

Discrepancy = Self-Perceived Abilities — Occupationally Required Abilities

Thus, Hypothesis 1 predicted that the mean discrepancy would be less for the high-self-esteem group than for the low-self-esteem group for the "high abilities" analysis, while Hypothesis 2 predicted there would be no differences for "low abilities."

RESULTS

The results of the investigation are summarized in Table 1 and indicate that all hypotheses received support. That is, the high-self-esteem person sees himself as more likely to meet the ability requirements of his chosen occupation than does the low-self-esteem male.

A further check was made on these results as to whether there was any differential systematic tendency for the low-self-esteem individual to see himself as low in

TABLE 1

Summary of Results-Discrepancies between Self-Perceived Abilities and Abilities Called for in Chosen Occupation

	HYPOTHESIS 1: HIGH ABILITIES		*HYPOTHESIS 2: LOW ABILITIES*	
MODERATOR	*MALES*	*FEMALES*	*MALES*	*FEMALES*
High self-esteem				
M	.67	.72	.97	.73
SD	.67	.91	.97	.75
N	27	19	27	19
Low self-esteem				
M	1.23	1.09	1.10	1.10
SD	.46	.42	1.10	.74
N	43	37	43	43
t	3.73‡	1.68†	.50	1.70*

Note. All tests are one-tailed tests.

*This would have been significant at the .05 level in the opposite direction from that predicted for a one-tailed test.

†$p < .05$.

‡$p < .01$.

self-perceived ability, compared to occupational requirements when matched against high self-esteem. Utilizing a random sample of 53 cases from the overall sample, this was found not to be the case. The mean discrepancy between required ability and self-perceived ability, when summed over for all items (high, medium, and low), was exactly the same for the high- and low-self-esteem groups when carried out to two decimal points.

DISCUSSION

These results support quite strongly the notion that individuals with high self-esteem are more likely to seek out and accept the situations which seem to be in keeping with their own self-percept, that is, a "balance" situation. Hence, a person who thinks of himself/herself as being adequate and competent is more likely to wind up in these situations where he thinks he will be adequate and competent. Such situations are not, however, "balance" situations for those who feel they are inadequate and incompetent and hence appear to be less of an incentive for them. In fact, as the results for the females show here (and as trends in the previous research indicated), they may even tend to choose an occupation which calls more for their low abilities than their high.

Since one's own self-perceived abilities are related to one's actual abilities to at least a modest level (Arsenian, 1942) and since self-esteem results from one's self-perceived adequacy in given roles, an interesting possibility for a closed-loop system presents itself here in that the low-self-esteem individual is more accepting of situations where he does not think he will be adequate and where he actually will tend not to be adequate. This will lower his self-esteem even further and lead him even further to choose roles where he does not think he will be adequate. However, just the opposite would take place for the high-self-esteem person.

A similar closed-loop situation would present itself in the noncognitive areas in that low-self-esteem people would be more likely to accept social roles that are non-need-satisfying. This would lead to non-need satisfying situations and thus a further lowering of self-esteem.

NOTES

1 The author wishes to thank Edwin E. Ghiselli for granting permission to use the Self-Description Inventory, undated.

2 The author is indebted to James Kirkpatrick and Donald Davis for allowing the use of their classes in obtaining subjects.

REFERENCES

Arsenian, S.
1942 "Own estimate and objective achievement." Journal of Educational Psychology 33: 291–302.

Englander, M.

1960 "A psychological analysis of vocational choice: teaching." Journal of Counseling Psychology 7: 257–64.

Ghiselli, E.

1963 "The validity of management traits related to occupational level." Personnel Psychology 16: 109–13.

Holland, J. C.

1963 "Explorations of a theory of vocational choice and achievement: II. A four-year prediction study." Psychological Reports 12: 547–94.

Korman, A. K.

1966 "Self-esteem variable in vocational choice." Journal of Applied Psychology 50: 479–86.

The Psychiatric Attendant: Development of an Occupational Self-Image in a Low-Status Occupation

Richard L. Simpson

Ida Harper Simpson

32

Members of occupational groups often develop occupational self-images: sets of beliefs, attitudes, and evaluations regarding their work.[1] By stressing certain highly valued aspects of the work—the skill it requires, its social utility, the prerequisites it affords—an occupational self-image can provide work motivation and work satisfaction.[2] The person in a high-status occupation is aided in maintaining a flattering self-image by the social prestige of his occupation. Occupations such as those of the physician and the business executive are widely known to require skill and to carry high income and pleasant working conditions. Low-ranking

Source: Richard L. Simpson and Ida Harper Simpson, "The Psychiatric Attendant: Development of an Occupational Self-Image in a Low-Status Occupation," American Sociological Review 24 (1959): 389–92.

occupations, however, do not command favorable society-wide evaluations; the public evaluates many jobs as unappealing or, oftentimes, distasteful.

How then do people in low-status occupations maintain favorable self-images? A number of plausible answers may be suggested. One is that they do *not* maintain favorable self-images, but are dissatisfied with their work and would leave it if they could. Another is that they are dissatisfied with their work but project their aspirations onto their children.[3] Still another is that they reject or fail to internalize the value of occupational success, perhaps seeking personal fulfillment in activities off the job.[4] Probably all of these patterns are to be found; yet it also seems likely that many low-status workers are satisfied with their jobs and have favorable occupational self-images. In this paper we try to show one way in which work satisfaction among low-status occupational groups can come about.

Our hypothesis is that people in low-status occupations may seize upon some aspect of their work which is highly valued, either throughout the society or in the work subculture, and build a self-image around it. We present data showing the basis on which workers in a low-status occupation—psychiatric attendants—may maintain a favorable occupational self-image. Attendants tend to minimize the less glamorous features of their work and focus upon the most highly valued element in the hospital's subculture: care of the patient.

SOURCE OF DATA

The findings grew out of a study of psychiatric nursing practices in North Carolina hospitals. Attendants were interviewed about their reasons for choice of the job, their duties, and their attitudes toward work. Interviews were conducted with 81 men and 63 women, selected randomly to include 15 percent of the attendants in each of five hospitals: a state mental hospital for whites, a state mental hospital for Negroes, a Veterans' Administration mental hospital for both races, a private mental hospital for whites, and a psychiatric in-patient clinic for whites in a general hospital affiliated with a medical school.[5] The findings presented below hold for all five hospitals: there are no differences between hospitals significant at the 0.05 level on a chi-square test.

CHOICE OF THE JOB AND WORK SATISFACTION

Each attendant was asked, in open-ended questions, why he had chosen the job, and why he had remained in the job of attendant. The answers to each question were classified as either intrinsic (pertaining to the work itself) or extrinsic (pertaining to the externals of the job).[6] Answers which incorporated more than one reason were coded according to the first reason given.[7] *Intrinsic reasons* included such explanations as interest in understanding mental illness through contact with patients, humanitarian interest in patients' welfare, satisfaction of working with people rather than things, and affection or sympathy for patients. *Extrinsic reasons* included such explanations as better salary than for former job, not qualified for anything else, spouse or relatives worked in the hospital, convenient transportation from home to hospital, and friendship with co-workers.

As Table 1 indicates, the majority of attendants (82.6 percent) gave extrinsic reasons for taking their jobs but less than half (46.5 percent) of the entire group offered the same type of reason for remaining. Thus there is a marked overall shift in the kind of reason emphasized: from extrinsic to intrinsic. More particularly, about half of those who took their jobs for extrinsic reasons changed their outlook and said that they remained for intrinsic reasons. Among the 17.4 percent who took their jobs for intrinsic reasons, less than one-third (4.9 percent) changed to extrinsic reasons for remaining. Despite the fact that this small group shifted in a contrary direction, a general trend toward the intrinsic rather than the extrinsic as reasons for remaining in the job seems to be clear. A chi-square test shows the overall shift in pattern of the responses, from reasons for taking the job to reasons for staying in the job, to be statistically significant at the 0.001 level for men and women considered separately and for both sexes combined.[8]

TABLE 1

Reasons for Taking and Remaining in the Job of Attendant

REASONS	*MEN* (N=81)	*WOMEN* (N=63)	*ALL ATTENDANTS* (N=144)
Took job for extrinsic reason, remained for extrinsic reason	46.9%	34.9%	41.6%
Took job for extrinsic reason, remained for intrinsic reason	38.3	44.5	41.0
Took job for intrinsic reason, remained for intrinsic reason	12.3	12.7	12.5
Took job for intrinsic reason, remained for extrinsic reason	2.5	7.9	4.9
Total	100.0	100.0	100.0

For men, $x^2 = 25.48$, d.f. = 1, $p < .001$; for women $x^2 = 16.03$, d.f. = 1, $p < .001$; for all attendants, $x^2 = 40.96$, d.f. = 1, $p < .001$.

The intrinsic reasons for remaining in their jobs, offered by 53.5 percent of the attendants, focus on their personal relationships with patients. Except for one individual whose purpose was to gain intellectual understanding of mental illness, the reasons given by these attendants appear to reflect an occupational self-image of the kind hypothesized: one which places heavy emphasis on the importance of the attendant in patient care. Their reasons for taking the job are mainly extrinsic, suggesting that no such self-image existed before they began work. These findings suggest that many attendants acquired a favorable self-image, not from the society at large as people in high-status occupations often do, but from the subculture of the hospital.[9]

The quotations below illustrate the kinds of reasons the attendants gave for taking and keeping their jobs.

Extrinsic Reasons for Taking the Job of Attendant

Negro male attendant at the Negro state hospital: "I got to where I couldn't conduct the farm as I wanted to, because of my health and high blood pressure. Some of my friends had always worked here, and they pointed me here."

White male attendant at the white state hospital: "I wanted to quit farming; it's all work and no money and you're old before your time. My brother worked here and he told me about it. I had no notion what it was like when I started, but I liked it so I have stayed on."

Negro female attendant at the Negro state hospital: "The lady I worked for as a maid wanted me to find a better job. I didn't know of another job I could do. If I had, I would have chosen it instead."

White male attendant at the veterans' hospital: "The pay looked all right and I wasn't trained for much else, so I thought I'd give it a try."

Intrinsic Reasons for Remaining in the Job of Attendant

White female attendant at the private hospital: "Somebody has to help these people get well, and I feel it's our mission to do that."

White male attendant at the veterans' hospital: ". . . I ask myself how I would want my mother or my wife or my kids treated if they got mentally sick, and that's how I try to treat these people here. It could happen to anybody."

Negro male attendant at the Negro state hospital: ". . . They get to feeling so bad they'll just brood all day long unless somebody shows an interest in them. We try to talk to them and cheer them up when they are like that."

White female attendant at the white state hospital: "I have a real interest in the psychiatric nursing [sic] we do. The patients see us more than they see anyone else, and how we act with them is very important to their welfare."

ATTENDANTS' PERCEPTIONS OF THEIR DUTIES

A further indication of the attendants' self-image is the way in which they perceive their duties. They were asked, in open-ended questions, to name the *most important* and *most time-consuming* aspects of their work. The activities mentioned as most important differ somewhat from the activities cited as most time-consuming. Chi-square tests show the patterns of responses to the two questions to differ significantly at the 0.001 level, for men and women separately and for both sexes combined. The attendants' answers tend to stress activities directly connected with patient care as most important, although housekeeping tasks such as cleaning floors and making beds may be more time-consuming. Table 2 shows these findings. When the attendants were asked to name the most important duties, 73.8 percent of the 141 who responded mentioned care of patients or interaction with them as most important; only 7.8 percent referred to housekeeping and miscellaneous tasks. But when they were asked to name the most time-consuming duties, 52 percent of the 144 indicated housekeeping and miscellaneous tasks while only 34.8 percent cited care of patients or interaction with them.

TABLE 2

Activities Mentioned as Most Important and Most Time-Consuming

TYPE OF ACTIVITY (IN ORDER OF MOST PATIENT-CENTERED TO LEAST PATIENT-CENTERED)	PERCENTAGE OF ATTENDANTS MENTIONING ACTIVITY AS MOST IMPORTANT			PERCENTAGE OF ATTENDANTS MENTIONING ACTIVITY AS MOST TIME-CONSUMING		
	MEN (N=79)	WOMEN (N=62)	ALL ATTENDANTS (N=141)	MEN (N=81)	WOMEN (N=63)	ALL ATTENDANTS (N=144)
Interaction with patients	25.3%	32.3%	28.4%	6.2%	3.2%	4.9%
Physical care of patients	40.5	51.6	45.4	33.3	25.4	29.9
Supervision and observation of patients' behavior	24.1	11.3	18.4	12.4	14.3	13.2
Housekeeping and miscellaneous	10.1	4.8	7.8	48.1	57.1	52.0
Total	100.0	100.0	100.0	100.0	100.0	100.0

Chi-squares computed from contingency tables including data on most important and most time-consuming activities: for men, $x^2 = 32.64$, d.f. = 3, $p < .001$; for women $x^2 = 48.22$, d.f. = 3, $p < .001$; for all attendants, $x^2 = 76.00$, d.f. = 3, $p < .001$.

DISCUSSION

The data support the hypothesis that people in a low-status occupation can develop or maintain a favorable occupational self-image by focusing upon some highly valued aspect of the work situation. In the case of psychiatric attendants, emphasis is placed on care of the patient.

Professional training, such as that which doctors and nurses receive, not only provides technical competence but usually leads to an occupational self-image. The psychiatric attendant, however, has not undergone such extensive training. Therefore when attendants develop favorable occupational self-images, they are apt to be based on the workers' direct role in the primary function of the hospital, patient care.[10] Cleaning floors and supplying linen closets have only an ancillary relation to patient care—understandably, most attendants do not regard these duties as their most important tasks although they are time-consuming.

This is not to imply that all attendants are entirely happy in their work. In our sample, 46.5 percent of the attendants gave extrinsic reasons for staying in their jobs, and some of those who gave intrinsic reasons may have felt ambivalent about their work. It seems, however, that a self-image based on patient care brings a measure of job-satisfaction to many attendants. Further research would be needed to determine the factors associated with intrinsic or extrinsic reasons for remaining on the job.

The self-image developed among psychiatric attendants serves the same functions as the ideologies of other occupations. It furnishes ego-enhancement and motivation. It appears likely that other low-status groups may develop self-images similarly, each grasping at whatever symbols of skill or social utility the situation affords.

NOTES

1 For a survey and selected bibliography of studies of occupational self-images and ideologies, see Theodore M. Caplow, The Sociology of Work (Minneapolis: University of Minnesota Press, 1954), pp. 124–41.

2 For a recent treatment of the ego-enhancing functions of occupational self-images, see Harvey L. Smith, "Contingencies of professional differentiation," American Journal of Sociology 63 (January 1958): 410–14.

3 Both Chinoy and Guest find that automobile workers tend to be dissatisfied with their work. Reactions to this dissatisfaction include day-dreaming about starting businesses of their own, hoping that their children will find better work, and a sense of futility and resignation. See Ely Chinoy, "The tradition of opportunity and the aspirations of automobile workers," American Journal of Sociology 57 (March 1952): 453–59; and Robert H. Guest, "Work careers and aspirations of automobile workers," American Sociological Review 19 (April 1954): 155–63.

4 See Allison Davis, "The motivation of the underprivileged worker," in William Foote Whyte (ed.), Industry and Society (New York: McGraw-Hill, 1946), pp. 84–106. See also Robert K. Merton's discussion of "ritualism" and "retreatism" in his Social Theory and Social Structure (Glencoe, Ill.: Free Press, 1949), pp. 125–49.

5 The North Carolina Psychiatric Nursing Survey was conducted in the summer of 1955 by the Social Research Section, Division of Health Affairs, University of North Carolina, under the direction of Harvey L. Smith, director, and Harry W. Martin, project coordinator. Martin drew the sample, arranged for interviews, and with Alvin M. Katz, constructed the interview schedule; the authors of this paper interviewed the attendants. The study was sponsored by the American Nursing Association, the North Carolina State Nurses' Association, and the School of Nursing and the Institute for Research in Social Science of the University of North Carolina. The larger study, focused on nurses rather than attendants, is reported in Harry W. Martin and Ida Harper Simpson, Patterns of Psychiatric Nursing, New York: American Nurses' Foundation, Inc., 1956. The authors are indebted to Harvey L. Smith and Harry W. Martin for critical reading of the manuscript and to James M. Beshers, Morton B. King, Jr., Robert E. Clark, and Berton H. Kaplan for suggestions and advice.

6 The intrinsic-extrinsic dichotomy is an adaptation of the classifaction of goals presented in E. R. Hilgard and D. H. Russell, "Motivation in school learning," 49th Yearbook, National Society for the Study of Education, 1950.

7 A justification for coding open-ended responses in this manner is reported by Zeisel, who states that tests have shown high correlations between item-mentioned-first tabulations and tabulations based on all items mentioned. Hans Zeisel, Say It With Figures (New York: Harper, 1957), pp. 79–81.

8 The method used for assessing the significance of changes is taken from Quinn McNemar, Psychological Statistics (New York: Wiley, 1955), pp. 228–30.

9 Comparable situations, in which occupational groups maintain favorable self-images not shared by the general public but based rather on the values of work subcultures, are reported in Becker's discussion of the dance musician and Goodrich's discussion of the coal miner. "Art for art's sake" and sturdy independent skill are the values emphasized in the self-images described, respectively, by Becker and Goodrich. Howard S. Becker, "The Professional Dance Musician and His Audience," American Journal of Sociology 57 (September 1951): 136–44. Carter Goodrich, The Miner's Freedom (Boston: Marshall Jones Company, 1925).

10 On the possible importance of a group's relation to the primary function of an organization in establishing the prestige of the group within the organization, see Raymond W. Mack, "The prestige system of an air base: squadron rankings and morale," American Sociological Review 19 (June 1954): 281–87.

Self-Confidence and Persuasibility in Women

Donald F. Cox
Raymond A. Bauer

33

A well-established finding in the literature on personality and persuasibility is that males low in self-esteem, or *generalized* self-confidence, are on the whole more readily persuaded than males high in self-confidence.[1] Generally, this finding has not held for females.[2] One of the purposes of this paper will be to test the hypothesis that, at least in some situations, there is a relationship between generalized self-confidence (a personality variable) and persuasibility in women.

Another well-established finding is that people low in *specific* self-confidence with regard to a particular influence situation (i.e., confidence in performing a specific task or in solving a specific problem) are more readily persuaded in that influence situation than are people high in specific self-confidence.[3] This finding apparently holds for both males and females.

Although research in both these traditions has found an inverse linear relationship between self-confidence, and persuasibility,[4] the behavioral explanations that have been advanced in each case are vastly different. In the case of general self-confidence, the explanation is based on a desire to solve problems of social relations or ego defense. That is, those low in self-esteem comply with the suggestions of others in order to avoid social disapproval,[5] or, as in an alternate

Source: Donald F. Cox and Raymond A. Bauer, "Self-Confidence and Persuasibility in Women." Reprinted by permission of the publisher from "Self-Confidence and Persuasibility in Women," by Donald F. Cox and Raymond A. Bauer, Public Opinion Quarterly, Vol. 28, No. 3, pp. 453–66. Copyright 1964 by the Trustees of Columbia University.

explanation that has been advanced, to utilize preferred ego-defense mechanisms that vary according to the level of self-esteem.[6] With specific self-confidence, it might be argued that subjects are motivated by a desire to make a correct judgment, i.e., to solve the problem presented by the task. The argument is that those low in specific self-confidence accept help in order to deal better with the problem, and hence are more persuasible. Those high in specific self-confidence know they can handle the problem properly, do not accept help, and are less persuasible.

As long as the two research traditions are considered separately, the explanations that have been advanced to explain the relationship between two types of self-confidence and persuasibility cause no theoretical difficulty. But what happens when the two types of self-confidence are studied simultaneously, in relation to the same influence situation? What happens, for instance, when people high in specific self-confidence but low in general self-confidence are given an opportunity to alter a previously made judgment in a problem-solving situation? Do they change their judgment in the direction advocated by the communicator in the hope of avoiding social disapproval or solving ego-defense problems? Or do they tend to stick to their original judgment because they feel confident that the judgment was correct and they want to solve the problem presented by the task? As far as we know, the two types of self-confidence have never been studied together.

Our intention is to attempt to join the two research traditions by examining the relationship of both specific and generalized self-confidence to persuasibility among one set of subjects in one particular influence situation. A major purpose of this examination will be to test the hypothesis that, in certain specifiable situations, the desire to perform properly in the task is a more reasonable explanation of the self-confidence-persuasibility relationship than is the desire to avoid social disapproval or to indulge in one's favorite defense mechanism.

The empirical basis of this paper is a study of the relationship between self-confidence (both specific and generalized) and persuasibility in lower- and middle-class women.

METHOD

Subjects

A total of 297 lower- and middle-class housewives were divided into three groups, composed of members of the "Ladies' Sodality" of three Roman Catholic churches in the Boston area. Most subjects were between 35 and 50 years of age, had completed high school, had family incomes of $400 to $800 monthly, and were married. All were Catholic.[7] A donation of $2 per subject was made to the Sodality to which the subject belonged, as a means of securing the cooperation of the group.

Procedure

Before being informed of the nature of the primary task, subjects were asked to indicate how good they generally were at judging people, colors, fashions, fabrics, and nylon stockings. Subjects were then asked to evaluate "two brands" of nylon stockings and to indicate how confident they were about their evaluation. The stockings were in fact identical, except for the identifying letters R and N. After making the evaluations on 18 attributes, subjects heard a tape-recorded "salesgirl's" opinion that Brand R stockings were better on 6 attributes—feel, weight, texture, fit, weave, and versatility. Subjects then reevaluated the nylons; evaluated the salesgirl; indicated how confident they were about their evaluations of the salesgirl; answered some questions on stocking-buying habits and attitudes; completed three personality tests (one of which was a measure of self-confidence); and, finally, provided information on their age, education, marital status, and income. The same procedure was followed with each group, providing three replications of the experiment.[8]

MEASURES

Change in Evaluation

For each of the six attributes mentioned by the salesgirl, a comparison was made of each subject's before and after evaluations of the nylons. One point was given for a change of one point on the nine-point scale (for example, a change of a particular attribute from "neither brand better:" to one brand "slightly better" was worth one point). If the change on an attribute was in the direction advocated by the salesgirl, the score for that attribute was given a positive sign; if in the opposite direction, a negative sign. Each subject therefore had six change scores (one for each attribute mentioned by the salesgirl). These six scores were then summed algebraically to provide an index of change in evaluation— an index that measures both the amount and the direction of the change. Inclusion of magnitude as well as net direction does not affect the conclusions but vastly complicates the presentation of data. This analysis, therefore, will be based only on *direction* of change.

Generalized Self-Confidence

The measure of generalized self-confidence consisted of 9 items from the 23-item Janis and Field measure of feelings of inadequacy.[9] Because of the time required for the entire procedure, it was not possible to use the full 23 items. For reasons that will be discussed below, it was necessary to administer the self-confidence test about ten minutes after the subjects had rerated the stockings. This sequence was used by Janis and Rife,[10] using the same 23-item Janis and Field measure of self-confidence, in studying the relationship of self-confidence and persuasibility, with no apparent undesirable effects.

A preferred procedure, used in some but not all experiments, is to obtain personality measurements under circumstances removed as far as possible from the actual experiment. This was physically impossible in our situation. Furthermore, our expectation, which proved to be warranted, that the personality items might cause problems of rapport prompted us to administer these items after the experiment with the stockings. (In two of the three groups, the subjects were told that the two parts of the procedure—the stocking experiment and the personality data—were two separate, unrelated marketing studies.) In all groups, a series of questions requiring about ten minutes to answer, which included two other personality tests of cognitive needs and styles, intervened between the stocking-judgment questions and the self-confidence test.

It is possible that ratings of generalized self-confidence might have been contaminated by the subjects' experience in the preceding experiment. However, the fact that this measure correlated with prior measures of ability to judge people, colors, fabrics, fashion, and nylon stockings indicates that it tapped some generalized aspect of personality rather than a momentary reaction to success or failure in the experiment. More to the point, some of the patterns of data that emerged were too complex to be explained in terms of contamination resulting from administering the personality test after the experiment.

Specific Self-Confidence (Degree of Confidence in a Judgment)

Subjects could be divided into three groups according to whether they were (1) more confident in judging the nylons than in judging the salesgirl, (2) less confident in judging the nylons than in judging the salesgirl, or (3) equally confident in both judgments. There is a special reason for using this particular system of categorization. An integral feature of the major work of which this is a part[11] is the concept of preferred cues. In the major study it was predicted that, given more than one cue, a cue rated with a relatively high degree of confidence would be more likely to be used than another cue rated with less confidence, even if the second cue was considered more important. Both with respect to these particular data and to the data of the broader study, analyses have been made incorporating both relative confidence and evaluation of cues. Including evaluation (*how* competent was the salesgirl?) strengthens all the conclusions we present here. However, for the sake of simplicity, we will confine ourselves to employing relative level of confidence (which cue did the subject have more confidence in rating?), since it operates with sufficient power independently of the actual evaluation given to the cue, and the presentation of data, naturally, is vastly simplified.

FINDINGS

Generalized Self-Confidence and Persuasibility in Women

With the possible exception of Maslow's study,[12] no relationship has been found between such "personality" variables as self-esteem or self-confidence and persuasibility among female experimental subjects. They have generally been found to be more persuasible than male subjects but this greater persuasibility exhibited itself independently of the personality dimensions of self-confidence. As an interpretation of this lack of relationship, Janis and Hovland suggest that "the culture seems to demand of girls greater acquiescence in relation to prestigeful sources of information . . . , with the result that girls on the whole are more susceptible to influence regardless of their personality traits."[13] In other words, the cultural pressures for compliance are so great that level of general self-confidence is either inoperative or becomes smothered.

Two conditions may affect the generality of this explanation: (1) the population of subjects studied and (2) the nature of the issue or problems involved. In previous studies of female subjects, the populations have been high school or college girls, who may represent a relatively small range of self-confidence levels compared with women from the general population. In connection with the problem involved, it seems likely that in some situations women might be more concerned with the substance of the issue than with "conforming." In fact, Janis and Hovland anticipate such a possiblity by pointing out that certain responses are "content bound."[14]

We anticipated that, if there was a relationship between generalized self-confidence and following the salesgirl's suggestion, it would take the form of the simple negative correlation between self-confidence and persuasibility that had been found with male subjects. To our surprise, we found the relationship to be curvilinear, and quite pronounced (see Table 1). These data depart from previous findings, therefore, on two dimensions: (1) the establishment of a relationship between self-confidence and persuasibility in women, and (2) the establishment of a curvilinear relationship where all previous relationships had been roughly linear. (Correspondence with Janis established the fact that he and Field actually plotted their data, and that their "zero" correlation among female subjects did not result from suppressed curvilinearity.)

As Table 1 reveals, among subjects high in self-confidence, 45 percent changed in the direction advocated by the salesgirl, among subjects of medium self-confidence 62 percent changed, and among subjects low in self-confidence only 37 percent changed.[15] The relationship is significant beyond the 0.01 level. Furthermore, the curvilinear pattern was replicated in each of the three experimental groups.

TABLE 1

Change in Evaluation in Relation to Feelings of Generalized Self-Confidence (in Percent)

DEGREE OF GENERALIZED SELF-CONFIDENCE	*CHANGE IN EVALUATION*				
	POSITIVE	*NONE*	*NEGATIVE*	*TOTAL*	*(BASE)*
High	45	42	13	100	(121)
Medium	62	27	11	100	(74)
Low	37	34	29	100	(102)

$x^2 = 16.8 \quad p < .01$

A possible and plausible explanation of the behavior of the low self-confidence group is that they are reacting in a defensive manner. These are people whose ego defenses are so brittle that they cannot stand the strain of contradictions or even implied criticism by another person. They lash back in an effort to maintain a precariously protected ego. Fortunately, a test of this explanation is available. If the defensive-reaction hypothesis is valid, then very low self-confidence subjects should not only be less likely to exhibit positive change, they should also be more likely than any other group to change in the direction opposite to that advocated by the salesgirl. Table 1 shows this to be the case. Only 13 percent of the high and 11 percent of the medium self-confidence groups changed in the negative direction, but more than double those proportions, 29 percent, of the low self-confidence group showed negative change. When the high and medium group data are pooled, the difference between the proportion of negative changes among high-medium subjects and the proportion among lows is significant beyond the 0.003 level (two-tailed test).

A way of looking at these data that makes them less neatly curvilinear is to consider *total change*, i.e. change in either direction. Viewed thus, the data indicate that there was almost as much total change in the low self-esteem group (66 percent) as in the medium group (73 percent). This view assumes that a systematic move counter to the suggested direction is also "persuasion," though possibly of a perverse form.

Thus, a variant of the relationship between self-confidence and persuasibility holds for our lower- and middle-class housewives. The curvilinear relationship may be due to the types of subjects used in this study; for example, we may have had a substantial group of subjects who were markedly less self-confident than those used in other experiments. If this is not the explanation of the curvilinear relationship, then we still do not know why other investigations failed to find a relationship of any sort among female subjects.

Preferred Defense Mechanisms vs. Desire to be Correct

Cohen preposes differences in preferred defensive mechanisms as an explanation of differential persuasibility.[16] According to Cohen's scheme, situational factors should affect the relative persuasibility of people with different levels of self-esteem. For example, he hypothesizes that threatening appeals are more likely to be rejected by people high in self-esteem, while appeals that enhance the individual's self-picture are more likely to be accepted by them than by the lows. Leventhal and Perloe present data that can be interpreted as supporting Cohen's hypothesis.[17]

Since the salesgirl definitely favored Brand R, her message should have been self-enhancing to subjects who initially favored Brand R.[18] According to Cohen, the subjects high in self-confidence should be especially persuasible in this situation because of their propensity for ego-enhancing defense mechanisms. Because of the curvilinear pattern of our data, it is not clear *exactly* what prediction Cohen's hypothesis would lead to; in general, however, the highs who favored Brand R should be more persuasible than than the mediums or lows. In any event, the *pattern* should be different among the group who initially preferred Brand R than among those initially preferring Brand N. Table 2 shows that the pattern is identical in both the "ego-enhancing" and the more threatening situation, though the absolute level of influence is greater across the board in the ego-enhancing condition. In both conditions, subjects with medium self-confidence were considerably more persuasible and those with low self-confidence exhibited the greatest negative reaction.

Although ego enhancement and "threat" do not produce the pattern of differential ego defense that Cohen predicted, these factors do not seem to be trivial on an across-the-board basis. Note that those subjects who initially favored Brand R had

TABLE 2
Change in Evaluation as a Function of Generalized Self-Confidence and Initial Brand Preference (in Percent)

DEGREE OF GENERALIZED SELF-CONFIDENCE	CHANGE IN EVALUATION POSITIVE	NONE	NEGATIVE	TOTAL	(BASE)
Initially preferred Brand R:					
High	59	31	10	100	(39)
Medium	77	12	11	100	(26)
Low	59	11	30	100	(27)
Initially preferred Brand N or neither:					
High	39	48	13	100	(82)
Medium	54	36	10	100	(48)
Low	30	42	28	100	(75)

the least possibility to shift in the direction advocated by the salesgirl, since their own judgment of the variables was already on the average in closer agreement with her judgment than was the average judgment of all other subjects. Yet, at each level of self-confidence, at least 20 percent more subjects were persuaded among those who initially preferred Brand R. The salesgirl's statement apparently was ego-enhancing to those who initially preferred Brand R. Hence, it is all the more interesting that these data do not exhibit the *difference in pattern* between the two situations that is implied by Cohen's specific notion of differential ego defenses among persons of varying levels of self-confidence. However, the *general* notion of different patterns of ego defense at varying levels of self-confidence is bolstered by the counter-suggestibility of the low self-confidence group under *both* conditions.

Social Approval vs. Desire to be Correct

Janis places emphasis on desire for social approval as a factor that makes persons of lesser self-esteem more persuasible.[19] Even considering the curvilinear nature of our data, Janis's hypothesis could still be made consistent with the analysis to this point. It would be reasonable to interpret the counter-suggestibility as a reaction formation to an extreme desire for social approval. However, the hypothesis that subjects are motivated to avoid social disapproval is couched only in terms of the subjects' relationship to the source of influence. Our analysis considers also the subjects' relationship to the object being judged, i.e., specific self-confidence.

Perhaps the study that bears most clearly on the issue of specific self-confidence and persuasibility is that of Hochbaum, in which he argues that "a person's dependence on social referents is inversely related to his confidence in his competence to judge the issue in question."[20] In support of this argument, Hochbaum demonstrates that when male and female college students were told that they were good at performing a particular type of judgment (predicting the behavior of a person described in a case history), they were less likely to change their judgment to conform to a group judgment.

This general notion that people are likely to accept help when they need it could be extended across a wide range of psychological findings reaching back over many decades. (Such findings range from conclusions that may be drawn from the classical experimental work of Asch to the recent conclusion of London and Lim that the "influence of one's peers over his decisions in a group problem solving situation increases directly as the problem becomes more complex.")[21] But it does not tell us what to expect when specific and general self-confidence are considered simultaneously.

Deutsch and Gerard come closest to dealing with this issue in a paper in which they distinguish between "normative social influence" (an influence to conform with the positive expectation of another) and "informational social influence" (an influence to accept information obtained from another as obtained from reality). Their data led them to conclude that groups can exert normative or informational social influence on individuals, and that informational influence ("in the sense that the judgments of others are taken to be a more or less trustworthy source of information about the objective realities with which [the subject is confronted]") can occur even if the subject is not normatively influenced.[22]

It is our intention to carry this line of reasoning further and, in effect, through the mechanism of self-confidence measurement, specify those situations in which informational influence is most likely to occur. Our hypothesis is that in those situations in which people are confronted with a task of reasonable importance to them, and for which there is presumably a "correct" answer,[23] they are more likely to be motivated by a desire to achieve such a correct answer than by a desire for social approval or ego defense. This position is not necessarily "competitive" with that of either Janis or Cohen. Our faith in the existence and importance of ego defense and desire for social approval as motives is high. Rather than deprecate these motives in any sense, we shall end by arguing that they are better understood and their operation better predicted if we are *simultaneously* aware of subjects' perceived confidence in handling the specific task.

As will be recalled, subjects not only were categorized on the basis of general self-confidence but also were divided into three groups according to the degree of confidence they had in their *initial* judgments of the nylons relative to the degree of confidence they had in their judgments of the salesgirl. The "social approval" explanation would have nothing to say about differential persuasibility under these conditions. Our prediction was that subjects relatively more confident in judging nylons than in judging the salesgirl would, in their effort to make a correct judgment, tend to follow their own inclinations. Among this group, therefore, level of generalized self-confidence should be less of a factor. Or, to put it somewhat differently, when *specific* self-confidence is relatively high, generalized self-confidence will play a reduced role.

We see in Table 3 that this prediction is borne out more cleanly than one might have hoped. Among subjects relatively more confident in their ability to judge nylons, general self-confidence plays practically no role.[24] Changes in the direction of adopting the salesgirl's views are 35 percent among the high self-confidence group, 37 percent among the medium, and 33 percent among the low. True, those low in self-confidence in this group continue to show a greater rate of counter

TABLE 3

Change in Evaluation as a Function of Generalized Self-Confidence and Relative Degree of Confidence in Evaluating Cues (in Percent)

DEGREE OF GENERALIZED SELF-CONFIDENCE	CHANGE IN EVALUATION				
	POSITIVE	NONE	NEGATIVE	TOTAL	(BASE)
Subjects *more* confident in evaluating the stockings:					
High	35	49	16	100	(37)
Medium	37	48	15	100	(27)
Low	33	41	26	100	(42)
Subjects equally confident in evaluating the stockings and the salesgirl:*					
High	30	63	7	100	(27)
Medium	50	42	8	100	(12)
Low	16	58	26	100	(19)
Subjects *less* confident in evaluating the stockings:†					
High	60	28	12	100	(57)
Medium	86	6	8	100	(35)
Low	51	17	32	100	(41)

*It will be noted that the "equally confident" group falls out of line in that *as a whole* this group shows less change than the "more confident" group. It appears that this group is contaminated by a subgroup of subjects who were not "playing the game" but used the same scale point for all ratings. This accounts for their being equally confident *and* unchanged. This dilution by apparently spuriously homogeneous data depresses the apparent rate of change in this group. $x^2 = 6.2 \quad p < .05$.

†$x^2 = 17.7 \quad p < .01$.

persuasibility. But, in general, the pattern for this group is extemely flat compared with the other two groups.[25]

Among subjects who were less confident about judging nylons or who evaluated the two cues with equal confidence, level of general self-confidence was definitely related to persuasibility. In both groups medium self-confidence subjects were most likely to change their evaluations; subjects high or low in self-confidence were least likely to change. Furthermore, the degree of change is regularly greater among those subjects who were less confident in evaluating stockings than among those who were equally confident in evaluating the stockings and the salesgirl. As a matter of fact, of those 35 subjects who were less confident in judging the stockings and had medium self-confidence, 86 percent changed in the direction advocated by the salesgirl.

These data do not constitute a negation of Janis's hypothesis. Unquestionably the desire for social approval is overriding in some situations. The discussion by Janis and Hovland certainly lays adequate theoretical ground for such variation. However, in this instance, the hypothesis that our subjects were seeking a "correct" judgment fits the data better than either of the theories of persuasibility that have heretofore been put forth to explain the role of self-confidence.

DISCUSSION

Contrary to most previous findings, our data strongly support the notion of a relationship between self-confidence and persuasibility in women *under some conditions.* The requisite condition may be that women be genuinely involved in the task at hand. The generality of this needs testing.

Furthermore, the results suggest that the linear relationship previously found among male subjects requires modification. The results of the present study, showing that under some conditions, at least, women very low in self-confidence become counter-persuasible, were significant beyond the 0.01 level. Furthermore, the curvilinear pattern was replicated in each of three experimental groups. It is, therefore, doubtful that these results are accidental.

The existence of a curvilinear relationship even under special circumstances calls into question the implied condescension found in most discussions of persuasibility. A reasonable interpretation of our data is that the subjects, confronted with a difficult task, generally went about handling it in a reasonable way. The task, incidentally, was not too far removed from real-life situations. The fact that the two stockings were identical was a matter of experimental convenience: it kept the design clean. Choices between nearly similar, or even among dissimilar, objects varying on a number of dimensions can be just about as difficult as the choice between Brand N and Brand R. Hence, it is scarcely unreasonable that persons lacking confidence in their own judgment should make use of available "expert testimony." As a matter of fact, it might well be argued that the counter-suggestible low self-confidence subjects were the ones who were psychologically victimized, but they were victimized not so much by the salesgirl as by their own defensiveness. Although it is true that the experimental situation involved factual deception, the bulk of the subjects apparently took it on face value, and it is in this context that we say they acted reasonably. We should not make the error of assuming that, because the experimental deception was successful, the subjects were dupes.

In the most general fashion, we believe that the introduction of the problem-solving orientation in relationship to personality factors is the crucial differentiating factor in our experiment. The range of human tasks that may be engaged in at any one time can be grouped into three convenient categories: (1) solution of an immediate external problem, (2) management of social relations, (3) ego defense. The solution of immediate problems is not a task foreign to psychology, but in studies of persuasibility it has seldom been related to the other two tasks. A previous study has already suggested quite strongly that the amount of risk involved in handling the immediate task affects the subject's handling of interpersonal relations. Specifically, physicians faced with more risky decisions are less likely to comply with the wishes of drug company salesmen.[26]

While the trio of "tasks" referred to above would be generally recognized, they have been treated as competitive explanations in various areas of the social sciences. The solution of immediate problems is the type of "rational" activity favored by proponents of "economic man." Psychologists and sociologists, on the other hand, have favored social adjustment and ego defense as preferred explanatory principles. This, we believe, has taken place largely because it has fallen to the social scientist to explain behavior that appeared to be "irrational" when considered from the point of view of the traditional "rationalist." The deliberate inclusion of the problem-solving aspect in the study of persuasion promises to throw additional light on the problems of social relations and ego defense.

NOTES

1 See S. E. Asch, "Effects of group pressure upon the modification and distortion of judgments," in E. E. Maccoby, T. M. Newcomb, and E. L. Hartley (eds.), Readings in Social Psychology (New York, Holt, 1958), pp. 174-82; L. Berkowitz and R. M. Lundy, "Personality characteristics related to susceptibility to influence by peers or authority figures," Journal of Personality 25 (1957): 306–16; I. L. Janis "Personality correlates of susceptibility to persuasion," Journal of Personality 22 (1954): 504–18; I. L. Janis, "Anxiety indices related to susceptibility to persuasion," Journal of Abnormal and Social Psychology 51 (1955): 663–67; I. L. Janis and D. Rife, "Persuasibility and emotional disorder," in C. I. Hovland and I. L. Janis (eds.), Personality and Persuasibility (New Haven, Yale University Press, 1959), pp. 121–37; G. S. Lesser and R. P. Abelson, "Personality correlates of persuasibility in children," pp. 187–206 in Hovland and Janis, (eds.), Personality and Persuasibility; H. Linton, "Rorschach correlates of response to suggestions," Journal of Abnormal and Social Psychology 49 (1954): 75–83; H. Linton and E. Graham, "Personality correlates of persuasibility," pp. 69–101 in Hovland and Janis, (eds.), Personality and Persuasibility; A. L. Messer, E. D. Hinkley, and C. I. Mosier, "Suggestibility and neurotic symptoms in normal subjects," Journal of General Psychology 19 (1938): 391–99; H. A. Witkin et al., Personality through Perception, (New York: Harper, 1954).

2 For example, see I. L. Janis and P. B. Field, "Sex differences and personality factors related to persuasibility," pp. 55–68 in Hovland and Janis, (eds.), Personality and Persuasibility. An exception appears in the work of A. H. Maslow, "Dominance, personality and social behavior in women," Journal of Social Psychology 10 (1939): 3–39, who reported that "prestige suggestibility has a fairly high negative correlation with dominance feeling." Dominance feeling, which includes high self-confidence, was assessed by personal interviews. The sample included 130 college women. However, no quantitative data were reported.

3 Examples of research in this tradition includes: S. E. Asch, "Studies of independence and conformity: I. A minority of one against a unanimous majority," Psychological Monographs 70 (1956); G. M. Hochbaum, "The relation between group members' self-confidence and their reactions to group pressures to uniformity," American Sociological Review 19 (1954): 678–87; P. London and H. Lim, "Yielding reasons to social pressure: task complexity and expectations in conformity," Journal of Personality, Spring (1964): 75–89; J. F. Coleman, R. R. Blake, and J. S. Mouton, "Task difficulty and conformity pressures," Journal of Abnormal and Social Psychology 57 (1958): 120–22.

4 We shall use the term "persuasibility" to mean just that—regardless of whether the subject is persuasible in only one situation or in a set of situations.

5 I. L. Janis, "Anxiety indices related to susceptibility to persuasion," Journal of Abnormal and Social Psychology 51 (1955): 663–67.

6 A. R. Cohen, "Some Implications of Self-esteem for Social Influence," pp. 102–20 in Hovland and Janis, (eds.), Personality and Persuasibility.

7 A comparison of the results of Catholic with 22 non-Catholic subjects (used in the pretest) on other variables in the large study revealed no patterned differences.

8 In the analyses to follow, the results for each group were pooled to provide larger cell sizes.

9 Hovland and Janis, (eds.), Personality and Persuasibility, pp. 300–1.
10 Janis and Rife, "Persuasibility and Emotional Disorder."
11 D. F. Cox, "Information and uncertainty: their effects on consumers' product evaluations." Unpublished doctoral dissertation, Boston: Harvard University Graduate School of Business Administration, 1962.
12 A. H. Maslow, "Dominance, personality and social behavior in women."
13 I. L. Janis and C. I. Hovland, "Summary and implications for future research," in Hovland and Janis, (eds.), Personality and Persuasibility.
14 Janis and Hovland, "Summary and implications."
15 It will be noted in Table 1 that the high, medium, and low groups are not of exactly equal size. The groups were split at the natural inflection points indicated by the data. We recognize that splitting the groups in this fashion can be controversial. Obviously, the pattern would hold in a slightly attenuated fashion if we took "top third," "middle third," and "lower third." But there is no conceivable theoretical or empirical argument to support the notion that the inflection points should occur at any particular point on this particular scale. Further work with this or another scale might establish some proper "break points," but, in the meantime, we defend our division on the simple ground that it gives a more accurate description of what happened with these particular data.
16 Cohen, "Some implications of self-esteem for social influence."
17 H. Leventhal and S. I. Perloe, "A relationship between self-esteem and persuasibility," Journal of Abnormal and Social Psychology 64 (1962): 385–88.
18 On the other hand, subjects who preferred R only slightly might have felt that the salesgirl was too pro-R, in which case the message would be less self-enhancing and more threatening.
19 Janis and Hovland, Personality and Persuasibility.
20 Hochbaum, "The relation between group members' self-confidence," p. 679.
21 London and Lim, "Yielding Reason."
22 M. Deutsch and H. Gerard, "A study of normative and informational social influences upon individual judgment," Journal of Abnormal and Social Psychology 51 (1955): 629–36.
23 By a correct answer, we mean the solution to a problem that has only one answer, or a situation in which subjects assume that a correct answer could be supplied by a competent judge.
24 The distinction between *specific* and *general* self-confidence is made with the realization that it is theoretically possible to make and measure further gradations in self-confidence level, e.g., intermediate self-confidence or an even more general level of self-confidence than that used in this study. We used the most specific and the most general measures available to us. An intermediate measure was also used: "How good a judge of nylons (in general) are you?" vs. "How good a judge of salesgirls (in general) are you?" This measure was less useful than either the general self-confidence measure or the specific measure in predicting probability of change in the direction advocated.
25 For the benefit of those who are curious about what is contributed by adding the *evaluation* of the salesgirl to the relative degree of confidence in rating her, the following can be reported: for those subjects who are more confident in rating the stockings *and* have a low opinion of the salesgirl's ability, the *net* change is approximately zero.
26 R. A. Bauer, "Risk handling in drug adoption: the role of company preference," Public Opinion Quarterly 25 (1961): 546–59.

Professional Self-Images and Political Perspectives in the Greek Military

George Andrew Kourvetaris

34

INTRODUCTION

An analysis of the military profession should begin with the consideration of some model of military professionalism along both subjective and objective dimensions. The study of the military profession, as exhibited most fully by its officers, is a study of a close to ideal type of the managerial profession. Thus whether one sees military professionalism as essentially internally generated (Huntington, 1957), or "forced" through outside pressure from the state (van Doorn, 1965), or paralleling broader societal developments (Janowitz, 1960), there is general agreement that the prototypic and distinct sphere of military officership has been characterized by the management of the institutionalized means of violence.

Although there is some convergence of professional attributes between military and civilian occupational structures, the differences are still the more salient (Huntington, 1957; Janowitz, 1960, Lasswell, 1962; van Doorn, 1965, Feld, 1968; Moskos, 1970). Qualities which serve to differentiate military from civilian professionals include: (1) the military profession by its very nature is the sole client of the state which it is pledged to support and defend; (2) military professionalization is predicated upon an elaborate system of authority which

Source: George Andrew Kourvetaris, "Professional Self-Images and Political Perspectives in the Greek Military," American Sociological Review 36 (1971): 1043–57.

combines elements of both bureaucracy and feudalism; (3) a military profession is not a "free" profession in the civilian sense of the term inasmuch as its goals and objectives are externally defined by civil authority; and (4) ethics and "character" are considered essential ingredients in an officer's professional career advancement. In brief, a constellation of characteristics serve to differentiate military professionalism quite markedly from nearly all civilian professions.

A leading issue in the sociological study of the military has to do with the relationship between military professionalism and political intervention.[1] Two major interpretations of the genesis of military interventionism have been set forth in the literature. One regards the internal structure of the military organization as the primary factor in predisposing the armed forces to intervene in the sociopolitical arena, for example, the level of military professionalism or perceived threats to the military's corporate identity (Janowitz, 1964; Fidel, 1970). The other stresses external conditions, especially the political sector, as the determining condition of military interventionism, for example, political decay or breakdowns in public order (Finer, 1962; Terrebery, 1968; Huntington, 1968).

This paper seeks to throw light on this issue by analyzing the military's assumption of political power in Greece on April 21, 1967. The present analysis focuses mainly on military professional self-images and the relation of these self-images to social and military background factors and to the officer's political attitudes toward military intervention.

Throughout, the term *professional self-images* is used interchangeably with the term *professionalism*, defined by Vollmer and Mills (1966:126) as the "advocacy of a set of attitudes and behaviors believed to be appropriate to a particular occupation." Correspondingly, our focus is on attitudes regarded as appropriate to the military and its corps of professional officers. The term *political perspectives* is taken to mean the officers' political attitudes on various national issues, particularly the factors leading to military intervention in politics.[2]

That military organizations are often socially and politically significant in countries undergoing the "stress of transition" has been noted by a number of writers (Lissak, 1964; Janowitz, 1964; Pye, 1961; Needler, 1966; Rustow, 1963; Johnson, 1962; Germani and Silvert, 1961; Lerner and Robinson, 1960; Lovell, 1969). Greek society finds itself in this state of change from a traditional society to one more socially differentiated and economically developed (Sanders, 1967) and provides a test of the foregoing hypothesis.

As with the armies of recently emerging nations, the development, organization and the subsequent professionalization of the Greek military were not solely indigenous phenomena. Both indigenous and exogenous political and military influences have contributed to the present character of the military in modern Greece. Following World War II, particularly since the "Truman Doctrine" and the creation of the NATO alliance, the Greek military has become a *bona fide* member of the professional armies of the West. Its professionalism is based on an elaborate system of what one might call *competitve professionalism*. Because the Greek military is a member of an international military organization, it has had to maintain certain universal criteria of soldiery and military professionalism to be accorded a full and equal professional status among its fellow NATO members.

As compared with other NATO armies, the Greek officer's training is more closely related to various political, social, and national processes and affairs. His training and education involve a specialized, as well as broad, range of subjects. Career advancement is a slower process among the Greek officers, particularly in time of peace. This "promotional freeze" generated much dissatisfaction among certain ranks, particularly prior to the 1967 military coup.

RESEARCH PROCEDURES

To investigate the impact of these factors on the 1967 coup, personal interviews were conducted with 100 middle and upper ranking army career officers in the winter months of 1968–1969. Since an officer's career in the Greek military for all practical purposes begins when he reaches the rank of major, officers below that rank were omitted from the sample. Officers included in the sample were selected from the 1968 officer's directory, made available by the Statistical Service of the Greek Army Headquarters.

At the first stage of sampling, 200 names were selected from the listing of middle and upper ranking army officers as given in the aforementioned directory. Of this lot, 106 were selected for interviewing, according to their location in more or less strategic military garrisons. Included in this final sample were 5 generals, 13 colonels, 29 lieutenant colonels, and 59 majors. Branches of service represented were Infantry, Artillery, Armor, and the support branches—Corps of Engineers, Signal Corps, and Services (Supply and Transportation only).

From the 106 officers thus selected, 100 interviews were completed. The interview schedule consisted of 44 questions concerning professional self-images, political attitudes, social background and career characteristics of the officers. Most of the interviews were conducted while the officers were on duty and ran from one to two hours.

Because the military in Greece had assumed political power at the time this research was being conducted, one cannot say conclusively that the responses to the questions reflected differences in attitudes or differing degrees of conformity to a perceived "party line." However, the author is confident that the officers' responses were honest.

PROFESSIONAL SELF-IMAGES

In his pioneer study, *The Professional Soldier*, Janowitz (1960: 21–36) has noted a decline in heroic attitudes among American professional officers. Although heroic self-images and attitudes are by no means absent from contemporary American professional officers, Janowitz suggests that a gradual transformation from a heroic self-image to that of a managerial self-image has taken place. In a later writing, Janowitz (1965: 233-237) argues that the introduction of nuclear weapons has fundamentally changed the self-image of the professional soldier. He sees a gradual transformation of the old models of professionalism to new ones in which political, intellectual, as well as professional considerations must be taken into account. The emphasis on scientific precision and scientific management has made the military profession aware of the new limits of force and increasingly more aware and capable of tolerating and managing change. In view of the latter, Janowitz also suggests a transformation of the military profession from an "absolutist" position in which war is inevitable to a more "pragmatic" position in which war is problematic.

Following Janowitz' lead, Lovell (1964:125) investigated the professional socialization of West Point cadets and found no significant decline in heroic attitudes during the socialization process of the cadets when these attitudes were functional for their preferred branch of service. Thus, those attracted to branches where the traditions of personal charisma, valor, and leadership continue to be emphasized were more likely to have a heroic orientation than those in branches where technical skill was the dominant prerequisite for success.

Furthermore, it has been noted (Janowitz 1960: 228) that an officer's self-image is a reflection of social and cultural processes as well. As a professional, the officer acquires both general and specific knowledge pertinent to his corresponding role and rank. He must learn his "ideal" and "real" roles by incorporating into his self-image those values, attitudes, concepts, beliefs, actions, and rationalizations which both set him apart from other members of social groups and make him an integral member of the general social structure. Because he is a product of his military and social structures, he comes to develop a "higher" sense of mission, a commitment, and a "consciousness of kind" as a member of a national army and a professional corps of officers.

How does the Greek army officer perceive himself? What changes have transpired in his self-image over the years? Has there been a managerial transformation or does he still maintain his heroic qualities? From the officers' responses, it was possible to construct a typology[3] of their self-images.

The self-images of the Greek Army officer corps can best be depicted and analyzed in terms of two main types composed of Greek versus Western European/American influences (see Figure 1). Each of the two types consists of three components. On the one hand, there is the *pallikar-leventis-philotimo* self-image syndrome; on the other, there is the technical-specialist-managerial self-image syndrome. The former is a product of indigenous societal/cultural values and ideals, as well as Greek military virtues that lend themselves to the more heroic/primitive aspects of the officer's self-conceptions. The latter is a product of exogenous professional/managerial military influences emanating from countries of Western Europe and the United States. These latter influences address themselves to a more competitive/professional self-image of the officer based primarily on more universalistic criteria and expertise. It seemed that a fusion or synthesis of both of these self-images was reflected in the attitudes of most of the officers.

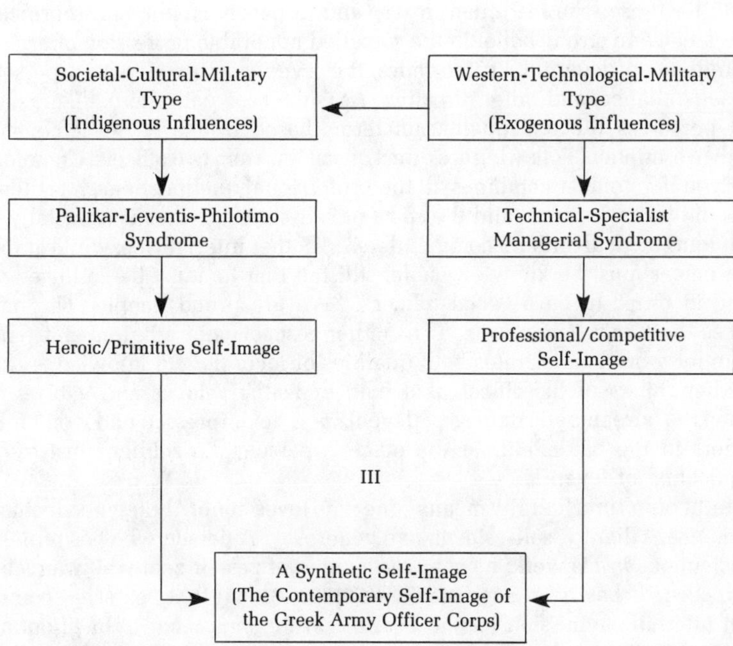

Fig. 1 **Self-Images of the Greek Army Officers.**

Self-Image I: Pallikar-Leventis-Philotimo Syndrome

These ideals have been incorporated into the normative value system of the modern Greek social structure from the time of the War of Greek National Independence against the Ottoman Empire. The concept of *pallikar*, for example, was part of the Greek legend carried over from Byzantine frontier days to the present. It portrays the "hero-image" of a person who fights for a cause or an ideal such as liberty or social justice. In its ideal form, a *pallikar* confronts death itself and only death can bring about a catharsis of his soul and of his agonistic spirit. For him social structure is based on a system of social equality in a *gemeinschaft* type of communal life. Stratification is conceived only in terms of social honor, social values, and deference. His incentive to fight does not derive from material gain, but from an inner compulsion and moral imperative for something that transcends the "self."

The concept of *leventis* is related to military virtues and physical manliness, stature, graciousness of movement and glamor, as well as the moral qualities of a magnanimous and brave man. As with *pallikar*, the person who possesses the quality of *leventia* has something intrinsic and unique about him, an attitude which he acquires through training and which has potential for further development and growth. It is a product of culture and social structure as well as of specific character training and is both a moral and existential quality. It is a desirable attribute for those who lead men in war and in peace. Honor, self-sacrifice for a noble ideal, and strong belief in the so-called honorable profession of arms are all ingredients of *leventia*. Furthermore, the *leventis*-image depicts a person of pride, self-reliance, and inner direction. As is the case with the *pallikar*, such a person perceives life on equalitarian terms based primarily on achievement rather than ascription. Following are direct quotations from two officers. Commented one: "Even if an officer combines all the professional qualifications, he still must possess the *leventia* image and the spirit of self-sacrifice. This is especially true for the young tactical military commanders." Another interviewee, while granting that an officer must be knowledgeable, still felt that he must be endowed with *leventia* in order to be a "good officer": "We are proud people. The officer possesses the Greek *leventia* . . . The soldier respects and admires that type of commander who demonstrates both qualities of *leventia* and knowledge . . . . If the soldier thinks of his officer as a man of leather gloves and a brief case (meaning the bureaucratic managerial type), he is not impressed and won't follow his orders in the battlefield. In the officer's person, the soldier must see the personification of *leventia*."

The term *philotimo* literally means "one who loves honor" but, synecdochically defined, means dignity, self-esteem, and generosity. A person who has *philotimo* is conscientious in his work; he is a worthy man of zest or zeal who wants to be distinguished. It has been suggested (Lee, 1953: 81–84) that "external coercion without internal submission has no bearing on the maintenance of *philotimo*," and "warmth within firmness, exuberance within austerity and discipline are also indispensable traits of Greek *philotimo*." Ideally, every Greek must possess it to be a Greek; it is what one might call a national character trait.

Philotimo finds its fullest expression in the self-image of the Greek officer. The greater the intensity of one's *philotimo*, the greater the degree of one's Hellinicity. It is according to the *philotimo* quality that an officer perceives himself as fundamentally different from other social groups and professions. In the officer's opinion, when a Greek loses his *philotimo* he ceases to function as a social and constructive human being. It is this trait of *philotimo* that gives the Greek his uniqueness and his cultural identity and exhorts him toward self-sacrifice, self-enhancement, and self-realization. Some officers held that the army was prompted to intervene in the political processes both in the present and in the past because Greek politicians and other leaders had lost this quality of *philotimo*. According to the officers the military revolution of April 1967 was a crisis of Greek *philotimo* in general and of political civilian elites in particular.

It must be emphasized that the *pallikar-leventis-philotimo* syndrome and especially the first two components are most prevalent among the combat forces, particularly the infantry. Although these qualities are not unique to the military profession, one might expect these attributes to find their fullest expression in the military because of the nature of the profession and the personality characteristics of the military man. Also, it must be stressed than these qualities are closer to the emotional-sentimental side of one's personality than to the mental-rational side.

Self-Image II: Technical-Specialist-Managerial Syndrome

Following World War II, one witnessed the development of a new managerial and professional ideology that has affected the Greek military self-image. The technical-specialist-managerial syndrome constitutes an equally important aspect of the officer's self-image, especially in light of modern technological and scientific development. The heroic self-image was not sufficient for the technological change, sociopolitical developments and economic events that had been taking place both within and outside of the military organization. In order for the contemporary Greek Army officer to be accorded full professional and managerial status and to become an equal and full-fledged NATO partner, a transformation of the officer's role and a readjustment of his military self-image to a more rational, organizational and professional one were necessary.

Despite the fact that the degree of technological and professional sophistication of the military organization reflects the technological and industrial level of the society at large, it can be argued that smaller armies (such as that of Greece), more than any other social organization, are replicas of larger armies as long as they are attached to supranational military organizations or pacts—i.e., NATO, SEATO, Warsaw, etc. This is especially true of those nations that are considered strategically and militarily attached to such superpowers as the United States and Soviet Union.

Viewed in this respect and regardless of the industrial/technological level of development of the country concerned, the smaller army and its officer corps must follow the professional model of the larger army. For a military to be accorded professional status, there must be structural and behavioral criteria of professional competence above and beyond national standards. Furthermore, the efficiency and competence of a modern army depends upon its technical equipment as well as the kind of leadership provided by its officer corps.

That the officers were aware of the need for a broader dimension to their self-image was reflected in their statements. For example, one respondent said that the "present officer is more modern (meaning more educated). He is not the *Karavana* (an officer who thinks of the messpot and food only) type of earlier times; he does not lack anything compared with the professional soldiers of other countries. The officers are among the best of NATO and the allied schools. The Greek officer has something of an additional air about him." Another officer summarized these changes in a more direct way: "Up to 1940, the officer was more of a *pallikar* type and less of the managerial/professional type . . . . The nature of modern military warfare and technology changed the training of the officer corps . . . ."

Self-Image III: A Synthetic Self-Image

While the officer has readjusted his self-image from a *pallikar-leventis-philotimo* type, it must be emphasized that the Greek officer has not lost his traditional heroic qualities. Both elements, the officers argued, are present in a new fusion or synthesis of military virtues and professional competence. Most of the officers felt that not only are these qualities present in the senior army officer whose military virtues were tested on the battlefield, but that they are also found among the younger army officers, although in a more incipient stage.

One might hypothesize that because some nations have not reached high levels of industrialization and managerial development, their armies are expected to retain the heroic qualities, especially in those nations occupying a low or semideveloped industrial and managerial status. Greece is considered a Western nation, but it occupies an intermediate position of industrial development; therefore, one should expect its army to retain its heroic qualities. There are also specific geographic, historic, and strategic factors that cannot be altered, and, in this sense, the army and its officer corps cannot be completely transformed into a technological type army.

In support of this line of reasoning was the finding that the synthetic type is the most prevalent self-image in the contemporary Greek Army officer corps. This synthesis is reflected in the statement by one of the officers: "The heroic is present in the Greek officer, but it is enriched by us—the younger officers—who have enhanced and brightened the *pallikar-leventis* image more prevalent of the older officer, with more education and training. The soldier of earlier times preferred the *leventis* type and the heroic fighter while the present ones prefer that type of officer who combines both the heroic and managerial." Another officer perceived his balanced self-image in this manner: "Knowledge is absolutely indispensable for the officer since his responsibilities are many. Knowledge is intertwined with

TABLE 1

Distribution (Percentage) of Types of Professional Self-Images by Selected Military Attitudes

MILITARY ATTITUDES	*MANAGERIAL*	*HEROIC*	*SYNTHETIC*	*TOTAL*	*(N)*
Career Motivation*					
Family/Friends or Personal Advancement	36%	25%	39%	100%	(28)
Social Values	28	22	50	100	(72)
	$x^2 = 0.988$, 2 df, $p > .05$				
Differentiating Qualities†					
Military Qualities or Virtues	12	27	61	100	(33)
Institutional/Organizational Qualities or Virtues	37	21	42	100	(67)
	$x^2 = 6.861$, 2 df, $p < .05$				
Primary Qualities of a Good Officer‡					
Ethics and Character	21	22	57	100	(73)
Managerial and Technical Skill	51	26	23	100	(27)
	$x^2 = 11.9$, 2 df, $p < .05$				

*Percentages obtained by analyzing responses to the question: "How did you decide to make the military your career?"

†Percentages obtained by analyzing responses to the question: "What are the qualities that make the military different from civilian structures?"

‡Percentages obtained by analyzing responses to the question: "What are the qualities which make a good officer?"

life and death. We are undergoing a change. We are engaged in continuous study and research. But the heroic type has not disappeared from the self-image of the Greek officer; neither will it in the future under any development of the army. The war is won 75 percent of the time by psychic and moral power and 25 percent by material means. You must have a heart to effectively use the means; the military commander has to make decisions. Such types made the military revolution; they combined both professional competence and heroic qualities."

The nature of the officers' professional self-images was consistent with the officers' responses to questions concerning career motivation, military versus civilian institutional differences, and their perceptions of a "good officer." For purposes of discussion, the *pallikar-leventis-philotimo* self-image syndrome will be referred to simply as "heroic," the specialist-technical-managerial as "managerial," and the combination or fusion of the above two as "synthetic." (Table 1 shows the officers' responses to these questions as related to their professional self-images.)

Career Motivation

The overwhelming majority of officers reported that the most significant motivating factor(s) for choosing the military profession as their career was some social value or societal ideal rather than some material/personal or family/kinship consideration(s) or influence(s).

What Makes the Military Different

Officers stressed the differentiating aspects of their profession, not only in response to specific questions but throughout the interviews generally. The majority of the officers cited institutional factors as well as military virtues in differentiating military professionals from their civilian counterparts. The tendency to stress both military qualities or virtues and institutional/organizational qualities as differentiating attributes was most evident among those officers who held a synthetic self-image.

Primary Qualities of a "Good Officer"[4]

From the officer's point of view, "ethics and character" constitute the primary qualities of a good officer. For, although managerial and professional skills are important aspects of a good officer, the officers argued that they could not adequately function as good professional soldiers without the qualities of ethics and character. It is in this light that a Greek Army officer sees himself as more than and different from a professional man in the civilian sense.

SOCIAL-MILITARY CORRELATES AND PROFESSIONAL SELF-IMAGES

The relationship between professional self-images and selected social military background variables was also examined. Variables used in this analysis of social background include father's social class, place of birth, region, age, and foreign language competency of the officers. The analysis of military background variables included rank, branch, higher military education, and combat experience. (Table 2 gives a cumulative profile of the social background characteristics of the officers.)

Social Background: Father's Social Class[5]

Table 2 shows little or no relationship between father's social class and the officer's own professional self-images. Almost one half of those from middle-class backgrounds and exactly one-half from lower-class backgrounds identified with a synthetic type of professional self-image, suggesting that the father's class background was not an influential factor in the officer's own attitudes toward professional self-images.

TABLE 2

Distribution (Percentage) of Types of Professional Self-Images by Selected Social Background Characteristics

SOCIAL CHARACTERISTICS	MANAGERIAL	HEROIC	SYNTHETIC	TOTAL	(N)
Father's occupation*					
Upper-middle and middle class	32%	21%	47%	100%	(66)
Lower or working class	24	26	50	100	(34)
	$x^2 = 0.844$, 2 df, $p > .05$				
Place of Birth†					
Urban	27	18	55	100	(22)
Semi-urban	35	29	36	100	(37)
Rural	27	20	53	100	(41)
	$x^2 = 3.444$, 4 df, $p > .05$				
Religion‡					
Southern	31	18	51	100	(61)
Central	12	47	41	100	(17)
Northern and Islands	40	20	40	100	(20)
Not ascertained	—	—	—	—	(2)
	$x^2 = 8.056$, 4 df, $p > .05$				
Age					
44–45	23	33	44	100	(43)
35–43	38	17	45	100	(57)
	$x^2 = 4.12$, 2 df, $p > .05$				
Foreign Language					
Fluency or some competence in at least one language	47	16	37	100	(47)
Little or none	16	34	50	100	(44)
Not ascertained	—	—	—	—	(9)
	$x^2 = 10.443$, 2 df, $p < .05$				

*Upper-middle and middle class includes career officers, civilian professionals, owners and operators of small businesses, white collar and technical employees; Lower or working class includes owners and operators of small farms, skilled and manual workers.

†Urban: all cities with a population of 50,000 or over; semiurban: 5,000–50,000 population; rural: below 5,000.

‡Southern Greece includes Peloponnese, Crete, Attica and greater Athens, Sterea Greece, and Euboea; central Greece refers to Thessaly only; northern Greece includes Macadonia, Epirus, and Thrace; and the Islands refer to those in the Ionian and Aegean Seas. (Source: National Statistical Service of Greece, *Yearbook of Greece,* 1967 [Census 1961]:131).

Place of Birth and Region

Little or no relationship exists between place of birth and perceptions of professional self-image. For example, a rural background was no more conducive to an heroic self-image than an urban one. Whether an officer came from a rural or urban background, he tended to perceive himself as a synthetic professional type. Officers from semiurban backgrounds exhibited the three self-images with almost equal frequency. These findings might lead one to hypothesize that the professional ideology and socialization of the Greek army career officer corps produce officers similar in life style and professional self-image, irrespective of place of birth.

Relationships between regional origin of the officers and professional self-images were also not significant. However, officers from the southern regions of Greece most often perceived themselves as the synthetic type officer; those from central Greece pictured themselves as either the heroic or synthetic type, and those from the northern parts of Greece and the Greek islands tended to be of either the managerial or synthetic type.

Age

Table 2 shows that older officers tend to perceive themselves as the heroic types while younger officers tend to perceive themselves as managerial. However, this relationship was not statistically significant. Despite the fact that the older officers were viewed as more heroic and less managerial than their younger counterparts, nonetheless both young and old officers saw themselves with approximately equal frequency as synthetic professional types. Within this mixed type, the data do not allow one to determine the extent to which a younger officer was more managerial and less heroic or, conversely, the older officer was more heroic and less managerial.

Foreign Language Competency

The relationship between a foreign language competency and the officer's professional self-image was found to be statistically significant. Speaking, or being competent in, a foreign language was directly associated with a managerial self-image. Almost one-half of those who reported competency in at least one foreign language (or some competence) tended to be of this type, whereas only 16 percent who had little or no knowledge of a foreign language could be classified as such.

From the foregoing discussion, one concludes that standard social background variables do not explain differences among officers in their professional self-images. The second line of analysis was related to a number of military background variables with the officers' professional self-images. (Table 3 gives us a cumulative profile of the officers' military background characteristics and their professional self-images.)

Military Background: Rank

The lower the rank of the officer, the more likely he was to view himself as managerial or synthetic rather than heroic. Among the majors, 35 percent perceived

TABLE 3

Distribution (Percentage) of Types of Professional Self-Images by Selected Military Background Characteristics

MILITARY CHARACTERISTICS	MANAGERIAL	HEROIC	SYNTHETIC	TOTAL	(N)
Rank					
Generals and Colonels*	24%	35%	41%	100%	(17)
Lt. Colonels	21	24	55	100	(29)
Majors	35	19	46	100	(54)
	x^2 = 3.692, 4 df, p > .05				
Branch					
Infantry	26	19	55	100	(51)
Artillery	25	38	37	100	(16)
Armoured	10	20	70	100	(10)
Support Branches	48	17	35	100	(23)
	x^2 = 9.05, 6 df, p > .05				
Combat Experiences					
Combat Experience	25	25	50	100	(67)
Noncombat Experience	42	9	49	100	(33)
	x^2 = 5.007, 2 df, p > .05				
Higher Military Education					
War College Graduate	18	37	45	100	(38)
Nonwar College Graduate	37	23	40	100	(62)
	x^2 = 4.560, 2 df, p > .05				

*This category contains 4 generals and 13 colonels. At the time this study was conducted, the highest ranking officer was a three-star general. Recently however, a four-star general was introduced in all branches of the Armed Forces.

Generals were included in the support branches along with corps of engineers, signals, and supply/transportation officers.

themselves as managerial, 19 percent as heroic, and 46 percent as synthetic. One explanation of this relationship is that the lower the officer's rank the more likely he is to have had more education and the less likely he was to have had combat experience. However, this relationship was not statistically significant.

Branch

One might anticipate that the army branch in which an officer served could influence his professional self-image. For example, one might expect that the Infantry officer would perceive himself more as the heroic type because his branch stresses military valor or because he could be expected to have more direct combat experience than other officers. However, this was not the case. Among Infantry officers, 25 percent viewed themselves as managerial, 19 percent as heroic, and 55 percent as synthetic.

Combat

Regardless of combat experience, the majority of the officers viewed themselves as synthetic. However, those officers with no combat experience more frequently chose a managerial self-image than those with combat experience.

Higher Military Education

Among the war college graduates, 18 percent were managerial, 37 percent were heroic, and 45 percent were synthetic in self-image. Among nongraduates, 37 percent were managerial, 23 percent heroic, and 40 percent synthetic. Higher military education thus contributed more to heroic than managerial self-images among officers. The relationship, however, was not statistically significant.

In summary, as with social background variables, military background did not account for differences among the officers' professional self-images. In concluding this section, it should be noted that whether an officer perceived himself as managerial, heroic, or synthetic, and regardless of his social and military background, he displayed a strong career commitment and a belief in the calling of his profession. Self-images are attitudinal attributes and may or may not co-vary with structural attributes.

If we place the officers on a conservative-liberal continuum, we can see that their conservatism is more cultural than political and is one of form rather than substance. In Greece, however, it is unlikely that one can apply the Western European or American model of political conservatism. The officer is an advocate of and contributor to the modernization and change of Greek society. At the same time he upholds those traditional forms which he feels are germane to the maintenance of cultural continuity and national existence. The officers believed the army to be the embodiment of national ideals, identity, and consciousness. The army, the Greek nation, and its history, in the words of the chief of the armed forces, are "A testament to Greece's struggles and sacrifices, its epics and tragedies, its triumphs and failures, its exaltations and falls . . . ."

The officer's self-image and political orientation contained an underlying element of puritanism—a religious moral certainty. Officers felt that they represented and lived by a set of superior social values. To them the military profession was a repository of Greco-Christian ideals. This attitude was reflected in most of their political attitudes.

One officer expressed feelings about "puritanism" in the following manner: "The officer is popular; he represents the real Greek. The revolution spoke to the hearts of the Greeks. The officer commands souls and dies in the fire; his profession is unique." A second officer: "Due to his mission, the officer must abide by a high ethical code. He makes no compromise with his conscience. Whatever he does is visible to everyone. Society expects him to possess a high moral code, to be the incarnation of the ideal." From the very early stages of professional socialization, the officer is nourished with such values and ideals as faith in country, God, and family honor.

SUMMARY AND CONCLUSION

This study focusing on the professional and political orientations of the Greek Army officer corps indicates that the shift from heroic to managerial styles of military leadership noted in the United States and other Western industrialized countries has not been paralleled in Greece. Rather, the modal self-image of the Greek officer is a synthesis of a primitive and indigenous heroic value system with a managerial ethic derived from the contemporary Western model.

Social origins and class distinctions were deemphasized among the officers. Officers as a group perceived themselves to be middle class economically and upper middle class socially. Unlike Western European armies, the social recruitment of the Greek army officers did not evolve from a feudal or aristocratic model. In fact, the social recruitment in the Greek military followed patterns similar to those found in the armies of the emerging nations rather than to those characteristic of the Western European armies. Furthermore, one might tentatively suggest than professionalism and social background variables operated to diminish social class differentials in that they provided and encouraged an equalitarian ideology not only within the military subsociety but for Greek society as a whole. Greek military stratification was based on criteria of achievement and deference rather than ascriptive criteria.

NOTES

1 For a fuller explanation of the relationship between military professionalism and military intervention in politics, see Huntington, 1957 and 1968; Bienen 1968; Finer, 1962; Germani and Silvert, 1961; Horowitz, 1967; Janowitz, 1964; Needler, 1966; van Doorn, 1968 and 1969; Ambler, 1966; McWilliams, 1967; Johnson, 1962; Hurewitz, 1969; Riddleberger, 1965; Feld, 1968.

2 The term *intervention* or *interventionism* is more of a descriptive than an analytical concept. In a more general military context, it might mean overt as well as covert forms of military intervention. Actual military intervention in politics might include the initial act of intervention (i.e., coups, rebellions, revolts, conspiracies, espionage), the period after the seizure of power, and the institutionalized intervention of the regime (Bienen, 1968). In a different context, *intervention* might refer to the actual or potential military operation by one state or group of states against another. The concept of *military intervention* presupposes that the military acts as if it were outside the social system or society of which it is a part. But in the majority of cases where the military intervenes in the sociopolitical processes of its society, it is considered an integral part of that society. In the present analysis, *intervention* or *interventionism* of the Greek military refers to the active role of the military or the reasons given by professional officers for military political leadership both in diachronic as well as synchronic contexts.

3 The construction of the typology of the officers' professional self-images given here is derived, but differs, from Janowitz's (1960) typology of managerial/heroic images. While Janowitz's typology was useful as a research tool, it was only partially applicable to the Greek case. The formulation and the subsequent analysis of the typology were partially based on the officer's responses and partially on sociocultural and historical data. Some pertinent questions asked were: "Do you think that the professional orientation of the Greek career officer is undergoing a transformation of his self-image?" "Could you briefly trace such a transformation?" "Looking ahead 20 years from now, what trends do you see for the Greek military profession?" "Do you think that most soldiers would like to serve under a man who never had combat experience?"

4 The official evaluation sheet of an officer's traits lists six main prerequisites of personal, charismatic, professional, and organizational qualifications (Antigraphon Diadohikon Simioseon Axiomatikon—An Evaluation Sample Sheet for the Officer, 1965). In order of importance these qualities were: (a) *Ethical* and *psychic qualities* including criteria of military virtues (decisiveness, steadfastness, courage, discretion, initiative, honesty, sincerity, justice, responsibility, discipline, cooperativeness); (b) *Command and leadership qualities* (personality, effectiveness of authority, judgment,

primary group relations with subordinates, managerial ability; (c) *Professional competence or expertise* (this included items such as general knowledge, technical competence, educational ability, ability to absorb new developments, methods, effort to improve his professional experience, diverse experience and ability in administration; (d) *Health and bodily qualities* (e) *Other qualifications or disqualifications* were also included concerning the officer's personality characteristics and the quality of his family life, the kinds of relationships with his fellow officers, and in general his attitudes toward his profession and the military institution; and (f) *Combat experience.*

5 Although occupation is not synonymous with one's social class, the occupation of the officer's father was used as a rough index of the officer's social background. Those officers whose fathers were engaged or had been engaged for most of their lives in some white collar occupation (i.e., professional, managerial, business, etc.) were designated as middle class. Likewise, those officers whose fathers were engaged or had been engaged in some blue-collar occupation (i.e., foremen, small farmers, craftsmen) were designated as working class. In terms of the officer's personal perceptions of social class, almost all of them perceived themselves as being upper-middle class socially and middle class economically.

REFERENCES

Ambler, John S.

1966 The French Army in Politics. Columbus: Ohio State University Press.

Bienen, Henry (ed.)

1968 The Military Intervenes. New York: The Russell Sage Foundation.

Feld, M. D.

1968 "Professionalism, nationalism, and the alienation of the military." Pp. 55–70 in J. van Doorn (ed.), Armed Forces and Society: Sociological Essays. The Hague: Mouton.

Fidel, Kenneth

1970 "Military organization and conspiracy in Turkey." Studies in Comparative International Development 6: 19–43.

Finer, S. E.

1962 The Man on Horseback: The Role of the Military in Politics. New York: Fred A. Praeger.

Germani, Gino and Kalman Silvert

1961 "Politics, social structure and military intervention in Latin America." Archives Européennes de Sociologie 2: 62–81.

Horowitz, Irving L.

1967 "The military elites." In Lipset and Solari (eds.), Elites in Latin America. New York: Oxford University Press.

Huntington, Samuel P.

1957 The Soldier and the State: The Theory and Politics of Civil Military Relations. Cambridge: Harvard University Press.

1968 Political Order in Changing Societies. New Haven: Yale University Press.

Hurewitz, J. C.

1969 Middle East Politics: The Military Dimension. New York: Fred A. Praeger.

Janowitz, Morris

1960 The Professional Soldier: A Social and Political Portrait. New York: Free Press.

1964 The Military in the Political Development of New Nations: A Comparative Approach. Chicago: University of Chicago Press.

1965 "The armed forces and society in Western Europe." European Journal of Sociology 6 (August): 225–37.

Johnson, John J. (ed.)
1962 The Role of the Military in Underdeveloped Countries. Princeton: Princeton University Press.
Lasswell, Harold D.
1962 "The Garrison-State hypothesis today." Pp. 51–70 in Samuel P. Huntington (ed.), Changing Patterns of Military Politics. New York: Free Press.
Lee, Dorothy D.
1953 "Greece." In Margaret Mead (ed.), Cultural Patterns and Technical Change. Paris: UNESCO.
Lerner, D. and R. D. Robinson
1960 "Swords and ploughshares: the Turkish army as a modernizing force." World Politics 13: 19–44.
Lissak, M.
1964 "Social change, mobilization, and exchange of services between the military establishment and civil society: the Burmese case." Economic Development and Cultural Change 13: 1–19.
Lovell, John
1964 "The professional socialization of the West Point cadet." In Morris Janowitz (ed.), The New Military. New York: Russell Sage Foundation.
Lovell, John P., Mun Hui Sok, and Young Ho Lee
1969 "Professional orientation and the policy perspectives of military professionals in the Republic of Korea." Midwest Journal of Political Science 13 (August): 415–38.
McWilliams, Wilson C. (ed.)
1967 Garrisons and Government: Politics and the Military in New States. San Francisco: Chandler Publishing.
Moskos, Charles C., Jr.
1970 The American Enlisted Man. New York: Russell Sage Foundation.
Needler, Martin C.
1966 "Political development and military intervention in Latin America." American Political Science Review 60 (September): 616–26.
Pye, Lucien W.
1961 "Armies in the process of political modernization." European Journal of Sociology 2: 82–92.
Riddleberger, Peter B.
1965 Military Roles in Developing Countries: An Inventory of Past Research and Analysis. Washington, D.C.: Special Operations Research Office, The American University.
Rustow, D. A.
1963 "The military in Middle Eastern society and politics." In S. N. Fisher (ed.), The Military in the Middle East: Problems in Society and Government. Columbus, Ohio: State University Press.
Sanders, Irwin T.
1967 "Greek society in transition." Balkan Studies 8: 317–32.
Terreberry, S.
1968 "The evolution of organizational environments." Administrative Science Quarterly 12 (March): 590–613.
van Doorn, Jacques
1965 "The officer corps: a fusion of profession and organization." European Journal of Sociology 6 (August): 262–82.
van Doorn, Jacques (ed.)
1968 Armed Forces and Society: Sociological Essays. The Hague: Mouton.
1969 Military Profession and Military Regimes. The Hague: Mouton.
Vollmer, Howard M. and Donald L. Mills
1966 Professionalization. Englewood Cliffs: Prentice-Hall.

FIVE

DEVIANCE

Although both deviance and the self-concept may affect one another, some investigators have focused on the self-concept as a cause of deviance whereas others have looked at deviance as a cause of the self-concept. The selections in this section are intended to illustrate both viewpoints.

The self-concept might bear upon deviance in many ways. The person whose self-values or pride system centers on morality, goodness, or conformity may be less likely to engage in deviant behavior than one emphasizing independence, daring, or nonconformity. Another possibility is that a youth may turn to deviance in order to overcome his or her low self-esteem. For example, a young man lacking academic, athletic, or social distinction, who commands little respect from parents, teachers, or peers, may turn to delinquency in order to enhance his feeling of self-worth. This enhancement is achieved in several ways. First, the youth gains the approval, acceptance, and respect of delinquent others, thereby increasing his self-respect. Second, he may achieve success in various forms of delinquent endeavor—fighting, pilfering, vandalism—thus demonstrating the virtues of strength, courage, and cunning. These qualities, at which he may excel, however, gain him no kudos in the conforming society, which values skill at reading, manners, and verbal facility. Third, a shift to a delinquent subculture creates a change in significant others. The evidence is clear that the opinions of those who matter to us have a stronger impact on our self-concepts than the opinions of others who do not matter. When young people shift over to a delinquent environment, they may still continue to believe that their parents, teachers, and school mates have little respect for them, but they now no longer care. Their delinquent mates, who appreciate their virtues, become the new significant others. Finally, it has been suggested that such youngsters may attempt to restore their damaged self-esteem by striking back at the society which has denigrated or disregarded them.

Other forms of deviance may fulfill different self-esteem functions. Among adults, alcohol or drugs are sometimes used to escape from the unbearable feelings of insignificance or self-hatred that afflict the individual. In some cases these chemical agents provide a temporary feeling of euphoria, efficacy, and significance that enhance the individual's feeling of self-esteem and self-confidence.

Conversely, deviance, in its turn, may influence the self-concept. Since people deplore and condemn those who violate the norms of the culture, the deviant, seeing himself from their perspectives, might be expected to condemn himself. But particular others' viewpoints aside, deviants are also members of their culture, and they have internalized its norms and values. Homosexuals, alcoholics, or drug addicts may thus despise themselves for the violation of social rules to which they, too, subscribe.

According to some theorists, it is not deviant behavior, but deviant labeling, that bears upon the self-concept. In this view, it is society's application of a pejorative tag to the individual (delinquent, convict, drug addict, alcoholic, mental patient), often by some official certifying agency, such as the school, the courts, or hospital officials, that affects the self-concept. First, these labels become elements of social identity; like most such elements, they are socially evaluated; and, because they are associated with norm violation, they are deplored and condemned. Second, deviants are stereotyped and treated accordingly. A mental patient labeled dangerous may be treated that way by others even though his or her last aggressive act was ten years ago; the labeled delinquent is assumed to be dishonest;

the convict, dangerous; the homosexual, effeminate; and so on. The point is that society responds to the individual in terms of the label, not in terms of the actual person. Third, the labeled individual comes to develop a corresponding self-concept and behaves accordingly. Therefore, if one sees oneself as a delinquent, and is so viewed by others, then the theory of self-consistency obliges one to behave as a delinquent. Finally, social labeling may affect the structure of the self-concept, when the officially certified label, instead of being one of many social identity elements, becomes central to it. The deviant label achieves identity salience or role primacy.

Deviant behavior and the self-concept are thus connected, as the following selections demonstrate. Because of space limitations, we confine our discussion to three types of deviance: delinquency, alcoholism, and homosexuality.

DELINQUENCY

Martin Gold (Selection 35) examines the relationship between particular institutional contexts, self- attitudes, and the coping functions of deviant patterns. In the context of educational institutions, Gold links failure in the role of student and its adjunct school roles to a consequent derogated self-image. Delinquent behavior is used as a device to enhance self-esteem. He further draws the implications that educational programs which facilitate experiences of success and more personal student-teacher relationships may thereby reduce the provocation toward delinquency and strengthen the controls against delinquency.

As noted earlier, a critical problem in research in this area is the causal connection between the variables. If one discovers a relationship between low self-esteem and deviance, one does not know whether the self-esteem is responsible for the deviance or vice versa. Howard B. Kaplan (Selection 36) employs a longitudinal design to establish the causal independence of the self-concept. His strategy is to examine the self-esteem of nondeviants in the seventh grade and then to determine one year later whether those with low self-esteem were more likely than those with high self-esteem to engage in deviant acts. Since later behavior cannot be the cause of earlier attitudes, his positive findings suggest that self-esteem may be a causal force in delinquency. The data further suggest that the influence of self-esteem on deviance is not a narrow and specific one but, rather, applies to a very wide range of deviant acts, most of which are largely uncorrelated with one another. Self-esteem thus appears to have a general bearing on deviance.

In another study (Selection 37), Kaplan, continuing to test aspects of his general theory of deviant behavior, addresses the hypothesized relationship between antecedent performance of deviant patterns and subsequent reduction of self-derogating attitudes. For a number of deviant patterns, and particularly among males, such self-enhancing consequences of deviant patterns are indeed observed. However, the self-enhancing consequences of deviant patterns are clearly contingent upon a number of factors, such as compatibility with gender-related roles.

ALCOHOLISM

Pearlin and Radabaugh (Selection 38) report analyses of survey data suggesting linkages between experiences in the economic sphere, self-esteem, and the coping functions of alcohol. The data are compatible with the model that economic hardship leads to anxiety and that people turn to alcohol in order to alleviate their psychological distress. This mechanism is used, however, primarily by those with low self-esteem and low feelings of efficacy (mastery). The authors suggest that, among those with higher self-esteem and self-confidence, those with economic problems are no more likely than people who are well-to-do to resort to alcohol in order to alleviate stress.

HOMOSEXUALITY

The final selection (39), by Hammersmith and Weinberg, deals with a different form of deviance, namely, homosexuality. At the time their study was conducted, homosexuality was a highly derogated sexual orientation, especially in American society. Psychoanalysts treated it as a pathology, and society frequently responded to it with shock, horror, or disgust. Much of the literature took it for granted that homosexuals had low self-esteem, either because their self-hatred drove them to homosexuality in the first place, because they shared the derogating attitudes of the broader society toward this abnormality, or because they were exposed to the scorn and derision of other people.

But there is a different theoretical tradition which holds that the problem is that of accepting the deviant social identity. For example, Lecky has argued that people seek self-consistency, a clear-cut stable way of defining themselves and living according to that self-definition. From this point of view, the self-concept problem arises not because individuals see themselves as deviants but because they reject themselves as deviants.

Hammersmith and Weinberg find that self-esteem and self-concept stability depend on whether the homosexual accepts himself as a homosexual or whether he continues to try to overcome this disposition. It is those with the poorest prognoses, the least disposition to change, the strongest commitment to a deviant identity who are most likely to accept and respect themselves. Self-esteem thus depends not so much on the deviance as on the individual's attitude toward it.

Scholastic Experiences, Self-Esteem, and Delinquent Behavior: A Theory for Alternative Schools

Martin Gold

35

A major conclusion of this paper is that the schools as an institution may have the capacity to prevent and reduce delinquency, independently from other institutions in their community. The school itself may be in control of major social psychological forces that generate delinquency. While other social institutions—the family, the economy, the juvenile justice system, the media, and, to a small degree, the peer group—play a part in producing delinquency, the schools may effectively grasp the opportunity to implement ameliorative programs.

A PARTIAL THEORY OF DELINQUENT BEHAVIOR

The focal phenomenon of the theory is *delinquent behavior—the deliberate commission by a juvenile of an act he knows violates the juvenile code in such*

Source: Martin Gold, "Scholastic Experiences, Self-Esteem, and Delinquent Behavior: A Theory for Alternative Schools," Crime and Delinquency 24 (1978): 290–308. Reprinted by permission.

a way that, if caught, he is liable to judicial response. Since this definition has been discussed in some detail elsewhere, I will elaborate on it here only briefly.[1]

Delinquent behavior differs a great deal from *juvenile delinquency,* that is, officially recorded alleged offenses by juveniles. Delinquent behavior is more than thirty times greater in volume and is distributed differently in the population—for example, it occurs at the same rate among juveniles from all social classes.[2] The methods by which it is measured are also quite different; while self-reports are the most appropriate means of data collection, the reports of direct observers, preferably peers but also teachers and others who see young people often and closely, often provide good data. The records of delinquent behavior begin to become invalid precisely at that point where the definition of juvenile delinquency enters, that is, where observations on which records are based have been made by the police. These official records are least distorted when they reflect observations made during the commission of delinquent acts and become increasingly invalid as the discretionary authority of the police, juvenile judges, court workers, and others affect the record. But even street contacts with the police have been shown to be subject to some discretion,[3] so they too must be regarded cautiously as observations of delinquent behavior. Therefore, to test the theory, I rely as much as possible upon self-report data and the observations of people other than agents of the juvenile justice system. I assume that delinquent behavior itself, rather than juvenile delinquency as defined above, constitutes both the theoretical and the social problem at issue. I will occasionally use the term *delinquency* to mean *delinquent behavior.*

I do not intend to present a comprehensive theory of delinquent behavior in this article, even if I were able to. Rather, I will present only that part of a more complete theory that involves the institution of the schools. I will argue that the function of the school in determining delinquent behavior may be treated independently, for both theoretical and practical purposes. This part of the theory does not necessarily have to take into account other determinants because the schools are a determinant in their own right. The schools can mount an ameliorative effort whose effectiveness would not be contingent upon other influences.

James Short and Fred Strodtbeck made this point in drawing implications from their study of peer processes in delinquent behavior:

> *The old message that delinquency begins in the home is more disavowed than reaffirmed by our analysis. Insofar as it is present, it emerges in a new form. We firmly believe that need dispositions which are requited by gang membership arise in the interactions between the lack of preparation for school-type achievement in the home and the absence of access to alternative adaptations to failure in the schools.*[4]

The theory is social-psychological in the sense that its object is to explain individuals' disruptive and delinquent behavior (juveniles' delinquency) by means of psychological variables, certain attitudes, and motives, which are shaped mainly by conditions in the individuals' social environment—in this case, the ordinary practices of their schools.

The theory posits that delinquent behavior is an ego defense, in the psychoanalytic meaning of that term,[5] against the external realities that threaten a young person's self-esteem. Since the theory will come finally to prescribe an external remedy—an institutional change—rather than a psychodynamic therapy that aims to alter internal states, it is important to note that the defense is against the recognition of an external threat, not against an internal conflictful impulse. Delinquent behavior is conceptualized as a form of ego restriction[6]; it is a way of avoiding situations which endanger self-esteem and of engaging in experiences that promise a form of self-enhancement. The theory assumes that a derogated self-image is naturally aversive and that it will set in motion psychic forces to dispel it. Delinquent behavior is interpreted as a manifestation of these forces.

The reality particularly relevant to the present discussion is failure in playing important social roles, and the role of student is particularly germane. No other role incumbent upon young people in our society is so fraught with failure as studenthood.[7] Insofar as any role entails clear and pressing standards for achievement, it creates the conditions for success and failure. Achievement stands at the core of the student role. Constant testing, grading, and comparing are indicative of the salience of striving. Experiences of success and failure pervade scholastic life, especially at the secondary school level. In no other setting—at home, on the job, among friends—are the standards of achievement so clear or the means to attain them so narrow. The only adolescent role comparable in this respect to being a student is being an athlete; and today, the athlete role during adolescence is so closely tied to the schools as an institution that it may be said to be a role within it.[8]

Two terms central to the theory are provocations and controls.

By *provocations* I mean the experiences that motivate a person to be disruptive and delinquent.

By *controls* I mean the *goals and values* that constrain a person from being disruptive and delinquent.

Provocation

The theory of delinquent behavior as a defense is linked to the concept of the schools as an institution through the hypothesis that a major provocation for delinquent behavior is incompetence in the role of student and its adjunct roles in the school. The youth falls short of his aspirations for scholastic achievement. Furthermore, he experiences few if any other successes in school: He is not particularly popular or well-known among classmates and has no close friends; he does not excel in any extracurricular activities; and he has no special interest or hobby in school or elsewhere at which he can demonstrate particular competence. The consequence of these experiences is a derogated self-image, a feeling that one is not worth much and will not ever be. Delinquent behavior, particularly disruptive behavior in school, is a defense against self-derogation.

Such disruptive behavior consists of attacks on school property and personnel, including fellow students; theft; dealing in drugs; noisy and distracting behavior; violation of rules, such as smoking; and truancy. Disruptive behavior in school is especially appropriate as a way of coping with low self-esteem for several reasons. First, inasmuch as the derogation is generated by scholastic experiences, the behavior occurs at the time and in the place where the pain is felt. Second, the appreciative audience that enhances its effectiveness as a coping mechanism is more readily found at school than elsewhere. This point deserves some elaboration.

Disruptive, delinquent behavior is conceived to be a public *performance*, a mode of self-presentation. It is hypothesized that such behavior is motivated by a desire to enhance the self by the approval of others. Disruptive behavior leads fairly easily to self-aggrandizement since it is not difficult to accomplish if one "has guts" (that is, if one is sufficiently provoked). In addition, the school creates a ready audience of peers with similar problems, who will not only observe and applaud but will often participate as well. And typically there is an undercurrent of adolescent negativity toward school even among those who would not behave badly themselves, which will result in an even wider audience. This conjunction of elements at school makes it a likely stage for a disruptive, self-aggrandizing performance.

A third reason for coping by means of disruptive and delinquent behavior lies in the message it conveys. While functioning as a performance, the behavior is also a declaration of revolt against the criteria by which the person has come to regard himself as a failure. It defies the exercise of authority over both deportment and standards for scholastic achievement, devalues the devaluations, and rejects the devaluators.[9]

Control

Not every youth who is failing as a student finds disruptive delinquent behavior an appropriate way to rescue self-esteem. The element of control must be taken into account. Some youngsters are so closely attached to people who would disapprove of such behavior that the appreciation of disruption by a peer audience is offset. Where there are warm parent-adolescent relationships that might be ruptured, where there is love that might be withdrawn, where there are affectional, material, and other resources that might be withheld, disruptive behavior bears more costs than benefits and therefore is not displayed.

When strong controls effectively counter strong provocations to be disruptive, then delinquency is not a strong defense against a derogated self-image. Unable to cope by engaging in disruptive and delinquent behavior, a youth is likely to feel great anxiety or may take flight from reality, depending on his other coping skills and the other forces in his life. That is, alternatives to disruptive and delinquent behavior may be various forms of mental illness. Thus, the theory generates a hypothesis that the intensity (frequency and seriousness) of delinquent behavior will vary inversely with symptoms of mental illness, particularly pervasive anxiety.

EVIDENCE

Evidence that gives credence to the theoretical model can be found scattered in the social science literature. No one study provides data on all the hypothetical links. So we must draw upon the literature piecemeal, as it casts some light on one hypothetical link or another or as it demonstrates the effect of one or another component of an alternative school program.

Scholastic Achievement and Self-Esteem

Research findings leave little doubt that better students tend to have higher self-esteem. Studies using a variety of measures of both scholastic competence and self-esteem have demonstrated this relationship.

Jerald Bachman[10] employed a combination of items from batteries developed by Morris Rosenberg[11] and by Cobb, Brooks, Kasl, and Connelly[12] to measure the self-esteem of a representative sample of tenth-grade American boys. The self-esteem scale is a transparent measure—almost all respondents would realize its intent—and includes items such as "I take a positive attitude toward myself," "I feel I do not have much to be proud of," and "I am a useful guy to have around." Boys' responses correlated ($r = 0.23$, $p < 0.01$) with their reports of recent school grades.

Mary Prendergast and Dorothy Binder[13] administered the Tennessee Self-Concept Scale and the Rosenberg Self-Esteem Scale to 366 urban ninth graders and correlated their scores with measures of scholastic proficiency obtained from the Houghton Mifflin Test of Academic Progress. Self-esteem as measured by the Tennessee Self-Concept Scale was unusually well correlated with reading proficiency (0.98), and it related moderately well (0.32) with math proficiency. The Rosenberg Self-Esteem score was correlated with reading and math scores at 0.35 and 0.57, respectively.

Edgar Epps measured scholastic achievement and self-esteem among black students in eight urban high schools.[14] Rosenberg's index of self-esteem was correlated with the students' total scores on the School and College Abilities Test (SCAT) in the four northern high schools, on the Otis IQ Test in the four southern high schools, and with their grades in all the schools. The correlation with self-esteem was nearly the same for test scores and for grades ($r = 0.24$ and $r = 0.25$, respectively).

Studies of upper elementary school pupils, which correlated the California Achievement Test with the Tennessee Self-Concept Scale,[15] with Bills' Index of Adjustment,[16] or with an adaptation of the Stephenson Q-sort technique,[17] all yielded positive correlations between self-esteem and scholastic achievement.

Scholastic Achievement and Disruptive Behavior

One must be aware of the inadequacy of most of the data on the relationship between scholastic achievement and disruptive, delinquent behavior. Research on delinquency, in the past and, for the most part, today as well, has relied on official records of apprehended, adjudicated, and sometimes incarcerated youths for indirect measures of the degree of delinquent behavior. But a relationship of delinquency to scholastic achievement is built into the data by the process of creating official records, for it is more likely that an apprehended youth will acquire an official record if an inquiry determines that he is doing poorly in school. Whether the actual commission of delinquent acts is related to scholastic achievement will not, therefore, be conclusively demonstrated by official data. For this reason, we will review here studies that measure delinquent behavior by means of unofficial observation and self-reports.

John Feldhusen, John Thurston, and James Benning[18] had third- and sixth-grade teachers in a semirural Wisconsin county nominate two boys and two girls in their classes who demonstrated exemplary behavior (e.g., "industrious," "productive") and an equal number who characteristically display disruptive behavior (e.g., "disrupts class," "bullies others," "tardy or absent without excuse"). A sample of 256 boys and girls was then randomly selected from each category for intensive study. The researchers found that disruptive pupils scored significantly lower in the reading and arithmetic sections of the Sequential Tests of Education Progress (STEP) than did the "good citizens," and that the difference between categories of nominees was greater at the sixth-grade than at the third-grade level. Follow-up studies five and eight years later by the same authors showed that the difference in scholastic achievement persisted through high school.[19]

Carl Weinberg asked seventh- and eighth-grade teachers to identify the boys in their classes who (1) "contributed most to the solidarity of the classroom group by their outstanding efforts, excellent cooperation, demonstration of leadership abilities, and general all around willingness to help," or (2) "contributed most to the disunity or conflict present in the classroom through disobedience, lack of effort, and general nonconformity to school and classroom expectations."[20] Teachers' nominations were checked with principals, vice-principals, office staff, and school records to assemble two categories of students who were clearly quite different in their reputations. Then student's STEP scores for reading, writing, and arithmetic were compared, and the disruptive boys' achievement was found to be markedly lower ($p<0.001$). This was true among sons of both white-collar and blue-collar workers.

In a study of a representative sample of American boys and girls, the present author collected data on self-reported delinquent behavior and on self-reported grades in school. A reliable negative relationship ($p<0.01$) was found among the fifteen- through eighteen-year-olds, but not among the eleven- through fourteen-year-olds.

In sum, then, several studies employing different measures have established a correlation between disruptive or delinquent behavior and scholastic achievement. Of course, correlation is not causation; the relationship supports but does not confirm the hypothesis of a causal link between the two. The idea that scholastic failure causes disruptive and delinquent behavior would be more certainly confirmed by an experiment in which scholastic achievement is raised and disruptive, delinquent behavior subsequently declines.

Self-Esteem and Delinquent Behavior

A study by this author and David Mann makes a distinction in the concept of self-esteem that is especially relevant to the concept of delinquency as a psychological defense.[21] Measures were taken of both conscious and unconscious levels of self-esteem. Conscious self-esteem was measured by the described self versus ideal self-discrepancy method: Each subject rated fourteen bipolar items (e.g., "slow-quick," "tough-mild," "smooth-rough") on a seven-point scale for both "myself" and "myself as I would like to be now." The discrepancy scores between identical items under the two different headings were summed, without regard to their direction. A high sum—large discrepancy—was taken as indicative of low conscious self-esteem. To measure self-esteem at a relatively unconscious level, each respondent was presented with a vertical array of eight circles and instructed to write "me" in the circle in which he felt he belonged; the respondent's unconscious self-esteem was determined by the circle in which he wrote "me," the topmost circle representing the highest self-esteem.[22]

Among eighth-grade boys from a lower-class, rural Michigan junior high school, no significant difference in conscious self-esteem was found between highly delinquent high achievers and highly delinquent low achievers, although there was a difference ($p<0.10$) between high achievers and low achievers among boys who were not highly delinquent. But the low achievers who were highly delinquent registered the lowest *unconscious* self-esteem, significantly different from that of the high achiever ($p<0.002$). These data were interpreted to mean that delinquent behavior served a defensive function, elevating the boys' conscious but not their unconscious level of self-esteem.

Mann has replicated this finding among fifteen- through eighteen-year-old boys representaive of all the boys in the age group residing in the contiguous 48 states.[23] Fifteen- to eighteen-year-old boys whose unconscious self-esteem was markedly lower than their conscious self-esteem also confessed to significantly more delinquent acts than did other boys. This was not true among younger adolescent boys.

Another study points to the causal relationship between self-esteem and delinquent behavior.[24] Twenty fifteen- to seventeen-year-old boys were identified by their histories of antisocial behavior, repeated truancy, chronic problems of school adjustment, failing grades, aggressive acts, and reputations with attendance officers, courts, or police; and they were at the point of leaving school, voluntarily or involuntarily. Ten boys were selected at random from these 20 and offered the services of a clinician from the Judge Baker Child Guidance Clinic, primarily to help them find employment. They received comprehensive services for ten months, while the other ten boys did not. At the end of that time, only three of the ten boys in treatment had been placed on juvenile probation, compared with seven of the control group ($p<0.10$).

To measure self-esteem in this study, a clinical psychologist rated pairs of stories elicited by Thematic Apperception Test cards. Five stories were told at the beginning and five at the end of treatment. The ratings were done in a triple-blind design, the rater not knowing which story was the first one of a pair, which boys told which pairs of stories, or which pairs were told by the same person. Improvement in self-esteem was observed more frequently among the boys in treatment than among the untreated group ($p<0.01$). Its causal relationship to changes in delinquent behavior is suggested by the authors: "The results indicate that the first area of change is in attitude toward self."[25] It is also notable that the Metropolitan Achievement Test scores of the boys in treatment improved in reading, vocabulary, and arithmetic, while the scores of the control boys declined ($p<0.01$). This occurred even though no special attempt was made to get the boys in treatment back into school or to tutor them.

A follow-up study testified to the importance of self-esteem in the change process:

Of great interest is that comparison of the follow-up stories with those given immediately after treatment indicated the same course of change as in the before and after treatment comparisons. That is, self-image changed most, control of aggression next, and attitude toward authority least. No boy showed a change in control of aggression who had not first changed in self-image, and no changes were shown in attitude toward authority unless there were changes in the other two areas.[26]

Howard B. Kaplan has reported a predictive study that also causally links low self-esteem to delinquent and disruptive behavior.[27] Over 4,000 junior high school students were asked on a questionnaire about their attitudes toward themselves (e.g., "On the whole, I am satisfied with myself" and "I feel I do not have much to be proud of") and about their deviant behavior in the previous year (e.g., "Sold narcotic drugs," "Cheated on exams"). These data were collected twice, about a year apart. For each of the 22 deviant acts in the questionnaire, Kaplan identified those students who had denied ever doing that act up to the first administration; he divided these students into those who had reported high, medium, and low self-esteem. Then he compared their later reports of deviant acts. As hypothesized, for each of the 22 acts, more of those who had given evidence of low self-esteem at the start of the year reported having committed the act during the ensuing year than did those who had indicated high self-esteem.

Finally, with a still different measure and research strategy, Elliot Aronson and David Mettee demonstrated how low self-esteem can generate delinquency.[28] The researchers created differential levels of self-esteem among women enrolled in an introductory psychology course by giving them randomly predetermined reports of their profiles on a personality test they had just taken. A subject was told either that her profile indicated that she has "a stable personality and is not given to pronounced mood fluctuations of excitement or depression" or that her profile showed that she has "a rather unstable personality and is given to. . . ." Following this experimental induction, the women participated in a blackjack game, during which an apparently malfunctioning card-dealing apparatus gave them what they thought was an unobtrusive opportunity to cheat. Significantly more women cheated whose self-esteem was threatened ($p>0.03$).

Thus, several studies support the hypothesis that low self-esteem leads to delinquent behavior. . . .

A PROMISING EDUCATIONAL PROGRAM

With this partial theory of the etiology of delinquent behavior before us, we can now offer a promising remedy that can be effected by the schools.

There are many variations in alternative educational programs, depending on the students they are meant to serve, the unmet needs these students are assumed to have, and the educational theory that links the program to the needs of the students. Our concern is with students who are disruptive in the school and in the community and whose behavior may plausibly be supposed to stem from their failure as students. The theory outlined above suggests the nature of an alternative school program that might reduce disruptive behavior.

We believe that there are two essential ingredients of effective alternative education: a significant increase in the proportion of a youth's successful—versus unsuccessful—experiences, and a warm, accepting relationship with one or more adults. Both of these point to the need for an individualized program.

In the first place, we hypothesize that an effective program tailors the educational process to the juvenile in several ways. First, the educational materials and tasks are appropriate to the student's present level of skills. Second, their content appeals to the student's own interests. Third, the student is allowed to master them at his own pace. And fourth, evaluation is based on individual progress—comparisons being made with the student's own previous performance, not with norms for age or grade.

In the second place, the social norms that typically govern teacher-student formal role relationships are largely suspended and replaced by more informal, more interpersonal relations. The differences between role relationships and interpersonal relations have to do with their affective components and with the personalities revealed in the relationship. Ordinarily, secondary school teachers are encouraged to assume a routine pleasantness toward their students that, in effect, amounts to affective neutrality. In the interests of fairness, teacher-student relationships are relatively constant from one student to another. Neither teachers nor students are supposed to take one another's peculiarities into account; rather, peculiarities must be submerged in the enactment of formal roles. Interpersonal relations, in contrast, are affectively loaded, participants demonstrating their changing feelings toward one another. And each takes into account the other's individuality in their interactions, rather than holding the other strictly to the rules of a formal relationship. We hypothesize that an effective teacher will help create a unique relationship with each student, a relationship into which he infuses a genuine liking and acceptance of the student but, on the other hand, does not conceal genuine revulsion for some kinds of behavior.

By providing successful experiences and thus reducing the provocation of school failure, a program can break the etiological chain that is identified in the partial theory of delinquent behavior. The warm, accepting relationship with teachers also enhances the student's self-image. Furthermore, this kind of relationship is conducive to the formation of social bonds that strengthen the individual's controls over his behavior.

Such programs have already evolved, independently of any explicit theory. One finds, in descriptions of alternative school programs for delinquent youths, emphasis on individualized curricula, ungraded classrooms, personal evaluation, and warm teacher-student relationships. A recent report on the Woodward Day School in Worcester, Massachusetts, is typical:

> *. . . other programs [for aggressive and other emotionally disturbed children in the Worcester school system have] adopted many of the Woodward Day School features: a controlled small environment, location outside of public school walls, individualized attention, acceptance of deviant behavior, and emphasis on improving the students' self-image.*[29]

Ann Swidler describes two alternative high schools in Berkeley, California, in similar terms:

> *Group High and Ethnic High avoided teaching students about achievement, about success and failure. They concentrated instead on teaching students self-confidence and self-respect. The first element in increasing students' self-confidence was reducing the inequality of status between teachers and students. Casual, friendly relations between teachers and students lessened students' fear, and made the teachers seem approachable, nonintimidating friends. Students felt important precisely because, as one student put it, "The teachers were*

really friends with students." A second way to avoid evaluating students, and to build self-confidence, is to construct assignments with few possibilities for failure. . . . [At Group High] students were praised and rewarded for sharing their ideas with the group; not for having the right answers. Indeed, right or wrong answers, correct or incorrect facts and ideas, were subordinated to psychological and socio-emotional considerations. Students were not judged; they were encouraged to develop their individual potential.[30]

But in these alternative programs, as in other efforts to reduce delinquency, data are rarely collected to test either the effectiveness of the programs or their theoretical assumptions. So one has to glean hints from the empirical literature on how separate components of the program might work if they were integrated.

One study already reviewed is relevant here. The services offered by Joseph Massimo to ten disruptive and delinquent boys[31] included the two components present in an effective alternative school program: an increased ratio of success to failure experiences, and warm relationships with norm-abiding adults. The worker made particular efforts to ensure that his clients were adequately prepared for the jobs they took, that they received guidance and assistance in keeping their jobs, and that remedial education was tailored to each boy's needs. Furthermore, personal support was available at all times, day or night, and the worker avoided role rigidity. While this program was not a school program, it points a way to effective teacher behavior.

More pertinent perhaps is the Quincy, Illinois, alternative school program described by Paul Bowman.[32] Sixty eighth graders who were performing poorly at their schoolwork were selected for study; most of them were discipline problems at school and 41 percent had police or court records. Three groups of 20 youngsters each were defined randomly, two of these groups becoming special classes, the third continuing in the conventional junior high school program. The special classes differed in several ways from the traditional program. The students spent a larger share of their school day with one teacher who had volunteered to lead the class, who knew the students well, and who was sympathetic toward them. The children were not pushed to achieve; the pace was slow, tailored to their current levels of functioning.

The efforts of the teachers were aimed at making school a pleasant experience; helping pupils learn the basic skills of reading, writing, and arithmetic; helping them learn the practical things they would use in their daily lives; and providing experiences in which they could find some success.[33]

Clearly it was the intent of the program to maximize success experiences and provide warm teacher-student relationships.

The effects of the special classes were mixed but promising. The students in the alternative program showed neither more nor less gain in achievement scores than did the randomized controls. But their attitudes toward school improved along with their attendance, relative to the controls. About two years after the program began, official delinquency records were checked again; these revealed that the students in the alternative program had had fewer contacts with the police and that the offenses for which they were apprehended had become less serious. The control group was exhibiting the opposite trend. It is not clear from the published reports just what produced the positive changes. It appears not to have been real advances in scholastic abilities, although it seems likely that the students felt that they were making better progress, which psychologically may be more crucial than the objective fact. It also seems likely that social bonds with their teachers grew stronger and were thus able to provide some constraint against antisocial behavior.

The importance of warm interpersonal relations with a socializing adult in the effective treatment of delinquents is underlined by Roy Persons and Harold Pepinsky.[34] Eighty-two boys incarcerated in a state reformatory were selected as appropriate for a combination of group and individual psychotherapy. Half of them were randomly assigned to the treatment group. The authors write that

> *one of the major objectives of every therapist was to encourage in each boy the development of warm, interpersonal relationships, both with the therapist and with the other boys in his group.*[35]

One of the more immediate effects of the therapeutic program was to raise the level of participants' scholastic performance in the reformatory school: Significantly more participants than controls ($p<0.05$) made the scholastic honor roll. Another effect was improvement in the participants' behavior so that fewer of them were reported to be disciplinary problems ($p<0.01$) and more were granted passes that permitted greater freedom at the institution ($p<0.01$).[36] Yet one might be skeptical about measures of effectiveness taken within the institution where personnel who make decisions are also aware of who is receiving treatment and who is not. More impressive are the differential records compiled by the randomized groups after they were released: After the same amount of time on the outside, 61 percent of the controls were reinstitutionalized for delinquent behavior compared with 32 percent of those treated ($p<0.01$).[37]

SUMMARY

A partial theory of delinquent behavior has been presented that conceptualizes delinquency as a psychological defense against a derogated self-image. The theory identifies failure in the role of student as a major threat to the self-image. Thus, it implicates the schools as an institution as a significant provoker of delinquent behavior. Concomitantly, the schools are recognized as having great potential for reducing delinquency. A specific alternative educational program is described that might effectively draw upon the schools' potential.

What needs to be done now is experimentation. The effective ingredients hypothesized for alternative school programs have to be realized in concrete programs. Administrative orientations have to be changed, teachers selected and trained, learning materials assembled, sites established, and students identified. The programs have to be permitted a period for consolidation before they are evaluated.

Then evaluation should take the form of rigorous field experiments that not only assess the degree to which the programs reach their goals of delinquency reduction but also test whether the theory is valid. That is, an experiment must first determine whether a program actually establishes warmer interpersonal relationships between students and teachers than the relationships established in the conventional schools. The research should then determine whether these elements actually affect students' self-esteem. Finally, the research should observe whether raising levels of self-esteem, especially unconscious feelings of self-esteem, lowers delinquent behavior. . . .

These questions are obviously beyond the immediate scope of the theory. But the theory sets some conditions for appropriate answers. Solutions conducive to reform, of individuals and of institutions, will take into account their effect on youngsters' self-esteem and their potential for helping youths find a respectable place in the community and society. These goals can guide the designs of alternative school programs.

NOTES

1 Martin Gold, Delinquent Behavior in an American City (Belmont, Calif.: Brooks/Cole, 1970); and Martin Gold and David Mann, "Delinquency as defense," American Journal of Orthopsychiatry, April 1972, pp. 463–79.

2 Gold, Delinquent Behavior in an American City.

3 Irving Piliavin and Scott Briar, "Police encounters with juveniles," American Journal of Sociology, September 1964, pp. 206–14.

4 James F. Short and Fred L. Strodtbeck, Group Process and Gang Delinquency (Chicago: University of Chicago Press, 1965), p. 275.

5 Anna Freud, The Ego and Mechanisms of Defense (New York: International Universities Press, 1946).

6 This, in turn, is a refined member of that family of defenses based on primitive denial. Ibid., see also E. Jacobson, "Denial and repression," Journal of the American Psychoanalytic Association 1 (1957): 61–92.

7 William Glasser, Schools without Failure (New York: Harper & Row, 1969).

8 James S. Coleman, The Adolescent Society (New York: Free Press, 1961).

9 Albert K. Cohen, Delinquent Boys: The Culture of the Gang (New York: Free Press, 1955).

10 Jerald G. Bachman, The Impact of Family Background and Intelligence on Tenth Grade Boys, vol. 2, Youth in Transition (Ann Arbor, Mich.: Institute for Social Research, 1970).

11 Morris Rosenberg, Society and the Adolescent Self-Image (Princeton, N.J.: Princeton University Press, 1965).

12 S. Cobb et al., "The health of people changing jobs: a description of a longitudinal study," American Journal of Public Health, September 1966, pp. 1476–81.

13 M.A. Prendergast and D. Binder, "Relationships of selected self-concept and academic achievement measures," Measurement & Evaluation in Guidance, July 1975, pp. 92–95.

14 Edgar G. Epps, Family and Achievement: A Study of the Relations of Family Background to Achievement Orientation and Performance among Urban Negro High School Students (Ann Arbor, Mich.: Institute for Social Research, 1969).

15 R. L. Williams and S. Cole, "Self-concept and school adjustment," Personnel and Guidance Journal, January 1968, pp 478–81.

16 J. C. Bledsoe, "Self-concepts of children and their intelligence, achievement, interests, and anxiety," Journal of Individual Psychology, May 1964, pp. 55–58.

17 V. D. C. Bennett, "An investigation of the relationships among children's self-concept, achievement, intelligence, body size and the size of their figure drawing" (Unpublished manuscript, no date).

18 John F. Feldhusen, John R. Thurston, and James J. Benning, "Classroom behavior, intelligence, and achievement," Journal of Experimental Education, Winter 1967, pp. 82–87.

19 John F. Feldhusen, John R. Thurston, and James J. Benning, "Prediction of academic achievement of children who display aggressive-disruptive classroom behavior" (Paper presented at the annual meeting of the American Educational Research Association, New York, 1971).

20 Carl Weinberg, "Achievement and school attitudes of adolescent boys as related to behavior and occupational status of families," Social Forces, May 1964, pp. 462–66.

21 Gold and Mann, "Delinquency as defense."

22 This method was adapted from R. Ziller et al., "Self-esteem: a self-social construct," Journal of Consulting and Clinical Psychology, February 1969, pp. 84–95.

23 David W. Mann, "When delinquency is defensive: self-esteem and deviant behavior" (PhD. diss., The University of Michigan, 1976).

24 Joseph L. Massimo and Milton F. Shore, "The effectiveness of a comprehensive, vocationally oriented psychotherapeutic program for adolescent delinquent boys," American Journal of Orthopsychiatry, July 1963, pp. 634–42.

25 Massimo and Shore, "Effectiveness of a comprehensive, vocationally oriented psychotherapeutic program," p. 641.

26 Milton F. Shore and Joseph L. Massimo, "Comprehensive vocationally oriented psychotherapy for adolescent delinquent boys: a follow-up study," American Journal of Orthopsychiatry, July 1966, pp. 609–15.

27 Howard B. Kaplan, "Self-attitudes and deviant response," Social Forces, June 1976, pp. 788–801.

28 Elliot Aronson and David R. Mettee, "Dishonest behavior as a function of differential levels of induced self-esteem," Journal of Personality and Social Psychology, June 1968, pp. 121–27.

29 J. Kennedy et al., "A day school approach to aggressive adolescents," Child Welfare, December 1976, pp. 712–24.

30 Ann Swidler, "What free schools teach," Social Problems, December 1976, pp. 214–27.

31 Massimo and Shore, "Effectiveness of a comprehensive, vocationally oriented psychotherapeutic program"; Shore and Massimo, "Comprehensive vocationally oriented psythotherapy for adolescent delinquent boys"; Milton F. Shore and Joseph L. Massimo, "Five years later: a follow-up study of comprehensive vocationally oriented psychotherapy," American Journal of Orthopsychiatry, October 1969, pp. 769–73, and Shore et al., "Studies of psychotherapeutic change in adolescent delinquent boys."

32 Paul H. Bowman, "Effects of a revised school program on potential delinquents," Annals of the American Academy of Political and Social Science, March 1959, pp. 53–62.

33 Bowman "Effects of a revised school program," p. 59.

34 Roy W. Persons and Harold E. Pepinsky, "Convergence in psychotherapy with delinquent boys," Journal of Counseling Psychology, May 1966, pp. 329–34.

35 Ibid., p. 530.

36 Roy W. Persons, "Psychological and behavioral change in delinquents following psychotherapy," Journal of Clinical Psychology, July 1966, pp. 337–40.

37 Roy W. Persons, "The relationship between psychotherapy with institutionalized boys and subsequent community adjustment," Journal of Consulting Psychology, April 1967, pp. 137–41.

Self-Attitudes and Deviant Response

Howard B. Kaplan

36

This paper examines the proposition that negative self-attitudes increase the probability of later adoption of each of a range of different types of deviant responses.

The hypothesis is part of an emerging general theory of deviant behavior that explains why individuals lose motivation to conform to, or acquire motivation to deviate from, the normative expectations of the person's predeviance membership group(s), and in fact so behave as to contravene such expectations. The theory is a general one in the sense that it suggests explanatory factors common to the adoption of any of a range of deviant responses rather than those that are specific to the adoption of one particular deviant pattern.

According to the theory under consideration, the development of negative self-attitudes in the course of membership group experiences influences deviant responses by two routes: first, by leading to the experience of conformity to membership group patterns as intrinsically distressing; and, second, by influencing the person's need to seek alternatives to the now intrinsically disvalued normative patterns in order to satisfy the self-esteem motive. A detailed statement of the theoretical orientation along with citations of supporting empirical studies are presented elsewhere (Kaplan, 1972, 1975).

Many studies have suggested associations between negative self-attitudes and particular patterns of deviant responses including cheating (Aronson and Mettee, 1968) dishonesty (Graf, 1971), delinquency (Hall, 1966; Scarpitti, 1965; Schwartz and Tangri, 1965), felonies involving personal assault or property crimes (Wood, 1961), drug abuse (Brehm and Back, 1968; Kaplan and Meyerowitz, 1970), alcoholism (Berg, 1971; Carroll and Fuller, 1969), homicide (Leon, 1969; Miller, 1968) suicidal behavior (Braaten and Darling, 1962; Miller, 1968; Wilson et al., 1971), and

Source: Howard B. Kaplan, "Self-Attitudes and Deviant Response," Social Forces 54 (1976): 788–801.

psychiatric disorders (Harrow et al., 1968; Long et al., 1970; Wilson et al., 1971; Wylie, 1961). However, these reports cannot be accepted as adequate support for the proposition for three reasons. First, each of the studies considers only one or a few rather than a broader range of deviant response patterns. Second, although most findings tend to support the thesis, important exceptions have been noted which require explanation—whether owing to differences in methods or to other factors (Kaplan, 1975). Third, with few exceptions these investigations did not use longitudinal research designs. Therefore, the findings could be explained in terms other than those that assert the influence of negative self-attitudes on the adoption of deviant responses. The observed association, for example, might be interpreted as showing that deviants tend to develop negative self-attitudes.

A longitudinal research design that encompasses data on a broad range of deviant behaviors would provide a more appropriate means to examine the relationship between antecedent negative self-attitudes and the probability of subsequent deviant responses.

HYPOTHESIS

The hypothesis was stated as follows: *Among persons presumed not to have already adopted the deviant response patterns in question, those with more negative self-attitudes will be significantly more likely to perform subsequently each of a range of specified deviant acts.* For two reasons, no such relationship was expected for persons who apparently had already adopted the deviant responses. First, prior performance of the act in question might imply that it was not *deviant* in the context of the person's current membership groups. Since the theoretical statement implicates antecedent negative self-attitudes in the subsequent adoption of *deviant* responses there was no reason to anticipate the relationship if the act was not in fact deviant. Second, whether or not the acts were truly deviant, the relationship between self-attitudes and subsequent performance might be obscured by the self-enhancing/self-derogating implications of consequences of prior performance of the acts.

METHODS

The hypothesis was tested using data collected in the course of a longitudinal research project.

Sample

The target sample was all of the 7th grade students in 18 of the 36 junior high schools in the Houston Independent School District as of March 1971. The schools were selected by use of a table of random numbers. The registered 7th grade students in the selected schools numbered 9,459 or 49.8 percent of the 7th grade students in all 36 schools.

To test the hypothesis, it was necessary to consider all students who were present for both the first test administration and the follow-up testing conducted approximately one year later. These 4,694 students were 61.6 percent of those providing usable tests at the first administration and 49.6 percent of all 7th grade students enrolled in the sample schools at that time.

The attrition of the sample was disproportionately accounted for by subjects who had already engaged in deviant behavior by the time of the first test administration as indicated by self-reports of having recently performed the acts in question. For each of the 22 deviant acts under consideration, students who reported having performed the act during the specified period prior to the first test administration were appreciably less likely than the others to have been present for the second test administration. The relationship was significant ($p < 0.05$) for 15 of the 22 acts by chi-square analysis. Depending on the act, between 9 and 55 percent of the students reporting performance of the act prior to the first testing compared to between 61 and 68 percent of those reporting not performing the deviant act were present for the second testing. Subjects were least likely to continue participation in the study if they indicated performance of presumably more serious acts, such as selling or using narcotics and breaking and entering. Since the hypothesis presumed that the students had not yet adopted deviant response patterns, those reporting the performance of the act during the month prior to the first testing would have been excluded from the analysis in any event. Therefore, the lesser representation of these students did not constitute as serious a bias in the sample as would have been the case were they to be included in the analysis.

No significant bias with regard to the measure of negative self-attitudes (self-derogation score) was introduced by the attrition of the baseline sample. The observation that dropping out of the study was related to prior performance of the deviant acts but was not significantly related to self-attitudes confirmed the expectation that the earlier performance of the act would not have the same significance in relationship to negative self-attitudes as initial adoption of the deviant responses.

Data Collection

The students who were to take the test generally met at one or two common locations (lunchroom or auditorium) in each school during the morning of a school day where they responded to a 209-item structured self-administered questionnaire. The test was administered three times, during March or April of 1971, 1972, and 1973.

A face sheet requested identifying information. Although self-reports of delinquent behavior are known to be somewhat more candid under conditions of anonymity, observed differences under the two conditions have been reported as small and more pronounced for less serious violations (Kulik et al., 1968). Further, subjects have shown basically the same rankings on antisocial behavior and displayed equally high validation of self-report scores (using other criteria of delinquency) under the two conditions. Thus it was not anticipated that the condition of nonanonymity in the present study in itself would seriously compromise the validity of the data.

Operational Definitions

The major terms of the hypothesis are "Self-attitudes" and "Deviant-responses."

Self-attitudes refer to the affective component of self-responses—that is, the person's emotional responses to his perceptions and evaluations of his own traits and behaviors. Self-attitudes are conceptualized as varying from positive to negative (pleasurable to painful) and, in intensity, from strong to weak. The person's characteristic self-attitude over a specified period of time thus would be a function of the frequency distribution of his experiences of more or less intense positive and negative self-attitudes during that period.

Self-attitudes were measured by scores on a self-derogation scale. The seven items of the scale were those with appreciable loadings on the self-derogation factor derived in an earlier study (Kaplan and Pokorny, 1969) of correlates of self-derogation among a representative sample of adults in Houston, Texas. The self-derogation scores showed strong relationships as predicted with measures of depressive affect and psychophysiological indicators of anxiety (Kaplan and Pokorny, 1969) and otherwise showed good construct validity (Kaplan, 1970a, 1970b, 1971; Kaplan and Pokorny, 1971, 1972). These items were used earlier by Rosenberg in a ten-item Guttman scale to measure adolescents' self-esteem.

The component items of the self-derogation measure, the inter-item correlations, and the test-item correlations are presented in Table 1. The self-derogation score was computed by assigning a weight of 2 to self-derogating responses to items 109, 180, 184, and a weight of 1 to self-derogating responses to the remaining items. The weights were added, and the sum divided by the number of units for which scores were available (maximum of 10), and the result multiplied by 100.

The inter-item correlations generally were low but statistically significant. The test-item correlations were moderate to high with the greatest magnitudes as would be expected manifested for the double-weighted items. The weighting of the items as described resulted in a pattern of test-item correlations strikingly similar to the item loadings on the self-derogation factor derived in the earlier study (Kaplan and Pokorny, 1969). The two patterns are presented in Table 1.

Deviant responses are conceptualized as acts occurring in circumstances by which a person, previously motivated to conform to a group's normative expectations (viewed as applicable to him by both the subject and the group membership at large), comes to lose motivation to conform and/or acquires motivation to violate the normative expectations, and in fact does so. Thus conceptualized, behavior is deviant specifically with reference to the standards of one or more of the groups in which a person holds membership. Excluded from consideration are those instances of *de facto* violations of normative expectation to which the person was motivated, but unable to conform owing to force of circumstance as when equally legitimate but conflicting expectations are imposed or when inability to conform to subjectively accepted standards is due to circumstances of birth.

Deviant responses were indicated by self-reports of various acts (see Table 3) of the kind investigated in a number of studies of undetected crime and delinquency. Many of these studies are cited by Clark and Tifft (1966) and Gold (1970). At the first test administration, students were asked to indicate whether they performed the deviant behavior in question during a specified period prior to the test. The

TABLE 1

Self-Derogation Score Inter-Item and Test-Item Correlations

ITEM		INTER-ITEM CORRELATIONS 109	113	118	142	152	180	184	$\overline{X}$ INTER-ITEM CORRELATION	TEST-ITEM CORRELATIONS	ITEM LOADING ON SELF-DEROGATION FACTOR: HOUSTON ADULT STUDY (KAPLAN & POKORNY, 1969)
109* I wish I could have more respect for myself	(true)†	—	16‡	21	18	−06	20	21	17	62	61
113 On the whole, I am satisfied with myself	(false)	—	—	−15	−18	17	−20	−16	17	42	44
118 I feel I do not have much to be proud of	(true)	—	—	—	28	−12	17	17	18	44	37
142 I'm inclined to feel I'm a failure	(true)	—	—	—	—	−14	19	15	19	41	46
152 I take a positive attitude toward myself	(false)	—	—	—	—	—	−11	−07	11	31	41
180 At times I think I'm no good at all	(true)	—	—	—	—	—	—	45	22	72	76
184 I certainly feel useless at times	(true)	—	—	—	—	—	—	—	20	70	76

*Numbers refer to student questionnaire items.

†Indicates a self-derogating response.

‡All correlations were significant at the $p < .001$ level. The correlations were observed for students tested on all three occasions. These correlations refer to the score on the first test. The smallest N for any correlation from this study presented here is 3,056. Decimal points are omitted.

Signs are corrected to give the high value to the self-derogating response.

specified period in question was "within one month" for all of the items except the following where the time period is as indicated parenthetically: 26 (during the last nine weeks period); 28 (within the last week); and 29 (during the last exam period). At the second and third testings the time reference was "within the last year" except for item 28 which retained the same ("within the last week") time reference.

The relatively brief time period reference at the first administration was employed in an attempt to differentiate between students who had already adopted deviant response patterns and those who had not done so. It was noted above that prior performance of the act might imply acceptability of the act by the person's current membership groups. Since the theory attempts to account for the motivated adoption of responses that are *deviant* in the actor's membership groups, persons who had already adopted a deviant response pattern are not appropriate subjects in a test of the theory. It was assumed that the probability was greater that students indicating performance of the act during that brief period would already have adopted a deviant response pattern than would students not indicating recent performance of the act and, conversely, the probability was greater that students indicating nonperformance of the act relative to those indicating recent performance of the act would not already have adopted a motivationally relevant deviant response pattern.

To use a more extended time period, so excluding subjects whose performance of the act did not imply motivated deviant responses would introduce factors that might obscure the hypothesized relationship. For example, while the use of the prior year as a time reference might exclude persons for whom the deviant act was a normative pattern, it would also exclude persons who only occasionally—perhaps as an experiment, or by accident—performed the deviant act. The result would be the overrepresentation in the sample of persons who conform out of timidity rather than out of the lack of motivation to deviate or the positive motivation to conform.

Two issues were considered with regard to the validity of the measure of deviant behavior: (1) whether the item content truly reflects *deviant* responses, that is failure to conform to the normative expectations of one or more membership groups; and, (2) whether self-reports of behavior are adequate indexes of the actual performance of the behaviors.

On the first question, although subgroup variation in the definition of deviant behavior was anticipated it was assumed that there was general consensus as to the nature of deviant behavior in the population at large. This assumption appears warranted based on such findings as those reported by Rossi and his associates (1974: 224) indicating "that norms concerning crime seriousness are widely diffused throughout subgroups of our society." However it remained to be determined if there was agreement that the specific acts under consideration are deviant.

This problem was tackled by hypothesizing relationships which should be observed if the items indeed reflect deviant behavior as it is conceptualized in the present study. These predictions were derived from the same general theory of deviant behavior from which the hypothesis under investigation was derived (Kaplan, 1972, 1975). It was reasoned that if the items do reflect deviant behavior as defined above then affirmative responses should be less characteristic of people who had found satisfaction in and lacked motivation to leave their membership groups (family, school) than of people who had adverse experiences in and desired to leave these groups. Affirmative responses also should be less in evidence for those who did not anticipate greater gratification from contranormative than normative patterns. Finally, affirmative responses should be less in evidence among those who have not experienced such deviance as standard responses in their environment. Although space limitations preclude a detailed report of the procedure for testing these expectations, the results were that each hypothesis was supported thereby suggesting construct validity of the items said to indicate deviant behavior.

The second issue was the relationship between the self-reports of behavior and the actual behavior. For various reasons the only available external validating criteria were reports of vice-principals or school counselors about the students' behavior. Either the vice-principal or appropriate grade school counselor in each school, whichever in their judgment was best informed about the students, was asked to fill out a form on which they responded to the following instruction: "Based on available records or any other knowledge you may have of the student please indicate whether or not the student has done any of the following things during the preceding twelve months." The forms were administered during the six-week period following the second student testing and referred to student behavior during the preceding 12 months, that is, the year between the first and second student testings. Three response categories were presented for each of the deviant behavior items: reasonably certain he (she) has done so, suspect he (she) has done so, no reason to believe he (she) has done so. Data were collected from school personnel regarding all but three modes of deviant response for which student self-report data were available: getting angry and breaking things; using wine, beer or liquor; and, getting failing grades.

These reports constitute a less than ideal validating criterion particularly because of the general lack of familiarity with student behavior on the part of the school personnel.

Table 2 summarizes the findings of the relationship between student self-reports and school personnel reports using chi-square analysis to test the hypothesis of no relationship ($df = 2$). The null hypothesis is rejected in 18 of the 19 instances ($p < .001$ for 14 relationships; $p < .01$ for 1 relationship; $p < .05$ for 3 relationships). Students are appreciably and significantly more likely to report performing each deviant act (with the exception of cheating on exams) during the preceding year in instances where school personnel have indicated that they are reasonably certain the student has performed the act during the same time period than in instances where the school personnel "suspect" or "have no reason to believe" that the student has done so.

However, although for a number of the items substantial percentages of students in the "reasonably certain" category report performance of the behavior, for a large number of the deviant behaviors appreciable portions of this category do not report doing so. Thus, varying degrees of underreporting may be suspected depending on the deviant behavior. This observation is congruent with other validation studies of self-reports of deviant behavior (Clark and Tifft, 1966; Gold, 1970). These studies, although reporting a high degree of overall accuracy, indicated appreciable underreporting for a number of items such as those employed in the present study. It should be noted, however, that these investigations differ from

TABLE 2

Percentage of Students Reporting Deviant Behavior by School Personnel Reports of Students Behavior

	SCHOOL PERSONNEL REPORTS OF STUDENT BEHAVIOR		
	HAS	*MAY HAVE*	*NO KNOWLEDGE*
3 Took things worth between $2 & $50	35	20	12***†
	(51)*	(138)	(4243)
7 Took things worth less than $2	45	36	27***
	(88)	(248)	(4059)
10 Thought about or threatened to take your own life	100	40	18**
	(2)	(15)	(4388)
17 Carried a razor, switch blade, or gun as a weapon	50	29	12***
	(14)	(58)	(4310)
24 Sold narcotic drugs (dope, heroin)	33	15	04***
	(12)	(33)	(4297)
29 Cheated on exams	42	40	41
	(106)	(308)	(3943)
31 Attempted suicide	100	09	10***
	(2)	(32)	(4365)
33 Started a fist fight	25	24	17*
	(95)	(139)	(4124)
38 Took narcotic drugs	60	35	11***
	(30)	(110)	(4189)
44 Skipped school without an excuse	53	28	16***
	(324)	(210)	(3837)
50 Took part in gang fights	21	17	10*
	(24)	(81)	(4287)
57 Used force to get money or valuables	30	14	05***
	(10)	(72)	(4284)
61 Broke into and entered a home, store or building	60	07	05***
	(10)	(60)	(4287)
64 Damaged or destroyed public or private property on purpose	27	15	09***
	(26)	(181)	(4130)
69 Stole things from someone else's desk or locker	23	20	15*
	(43)	(194)	(4138)
72 Used a car without owner's permission	50	12	06***
	(4)	(48)	(4297)
75 Beat up someone who did nothing to you	32	10	08***
	(19)	(90)	(4249)
78 Took things worth $50 or more	30	09	04***
	(10)	(44)	(4305)
82 Smoked marijuana	74	50	14***
	(39)	(153)	(4127)

*Indicates number of students receiving that response from school personnel.

†Indicates significant chi-square relationship between school personnel and student reports of deviant behaviors: * = $p < .05$; ** = $p < .01$; *** = $p < .001$.

the present one in a number of ways including subject characteristics, validating criterion, consideration of frequency (as opposed to presence or absence) of deviant acts, and time reference.

The extent of student overreporting cannot be estimated in view of the general unfamiliarity with student behavior on the part of school personnel. These people could not assert that the student did not perform the act but rather only that they had no reason to believe the student had done so. However, instances of overreporting apparently constitute a relatively small portion of self-report errors (Clark and Tifft, 1966).

The data were interpreted as justifying the use of self-reports as a rough indicator of deviant behaviors in the sense that the probability is far greater that a student who reports the act will have in fact committed the act (by the criteria of school personnel reports) than that a student who denies the act will have done so; or, conversely, that the probability is far greater that externally validated cases of deviant performers will so identify themselves than will performers whose deviant behavior is unknown. However, the self-report data should not be used to estimate the absolute number of deviant actors in a population.

Analysis

The hypothesis asserted a relationship between self-derogation level at the time of the first testing and self-reports (at the time of the second testing) of performance of deviant behaviors during the year interval between the first and second testings. The self-derogation scores were thus temporally prior to the behaviors reported on at the second testing.

Self-derogation levels were determined by arbitrarily dividing the distribution of self-derogation scores of the students responding to the first test into three groupings: low (0–20), medium (21–50), and high (above 50).

The hypothesis was tested for all students present for the first two testings for whom the appropriate data (self-derogation level at the first administration and self-reports of the deviant behavior in question) were available *and who reported not performing the deviant behavior during the specified period prior to the first testing*. Students who were "high," "medium," or "low," respectively in self-derogation at the time of the first administration were compared with regard to the relative frequency with which they reported (at the time of the second administration) performing each of the deviant behaviors under consideration between the first and second test administrations. Chi-square analysis was used to test the hypothesis of no relationship. Gamma was employed as a measure of association (Goodman and Kruskal, 1954).

The decision was made to initially examine the relationship between self-derogation and each of the 22 deviant acts separately in view of two simultaneous considerations: the low magnitudes of intercorrelations among the deviant behaviors, and the theoretical orientation that views self-attitudes as a common antecedent of the adoption of any of a broad range of deviant responses.

Only 29 percent of the 231 Pearsonian correlations were significant at the 0.01 level (49 percent of the correlations were signficant at the 0.05 level). The mean intercorrelation (disregarding sign) was 0.11. Thus, the observation of significant relationship between self-derogation and each of a broad range of essentially uncorrelated deviant behaviors would lend support to the assertion that self-derogation predisposes a person to adopt any of a range of deviant responses rather than of one or a few modes of deviant behavior that imply performance of other deviant patterns.

RESULTS

The findings relating to the test of the hypothesis are summarized in Table 3. For each of the 22 deviant acts the hypothesis of no relationship between antecedent self-derogation and subsequent performance of deviant behavior may be rejected ($p < .001$ in 15 instances, $p < .01$ in 3 instances, and $p < .05$ in the remaining 4 instances). For each of the deviant behaviors in question, among students reporting nonperformance of the deviant behavior during the specified period prior to the first testing, students in the low self-derogation category at the first testing relative to those in the medium and high self-derogation groupings were appreciably less likely to report (at the second testing) having performed the deviant behavior during the period between the first and second testing. For example, 8 percent of the low, 11 percent of the medium, and 14 percent of the high self-derogation subjects (at the time of the first testing) reported (at the time of the second testing) having taken things worth between $2 and $50 during the preceding year. It will be recalled that these figures are for those students who reported that they did not perform this behavior during the specified period prior to the first testing. Corresponding figures for having thought about or threatened to take your own life were 9, 14, and 23 percent. For using narcotic drugs the corresponding percentages were 8, 11, and 15 percent. Corresponding percentages of students indicating damaging or destroying public or private property were 5, 9, and 10 for the three self-derogation groupings.

For 19 of the 22 behaviors the observed relationship was linear with low, medium, and high self-derogation subjects respectively manifesting an increasing percentage of subsequent self-reports of deviant behavior. In the remaining three instances (items 17, 61 and 78), although the medium and high self-derogation subjects were both more likely than the low self-derogation subjects to report performing the deviant behavior, the high self-derogation category was somewhat less likely than the medium group to report performance of the deviant behavior.

The degree of association (gamma) between each item and self-derogation category are reported parenthetically following each item in Table 3. Although all of the gammas are statistically significant ($p < .001$ in 16 instance, $p < .01$ in 5 instances, and $p < .05$ in 1 instance), the magnitudes are generally low to moderate ranging from 0.09 to 0.34 with a mean of 0.18. Perhaps more impressive than the magnitudes of the associations is the consistency of the pattern of associations by which antecedent self-derogation was observed to be related to subsequent reports of each of a range of essentially uncorrelated deviant acts, thus lending strong support to the hypothesis.

For reasons stated above, it was not anticipated that antecedent self-derogation would be related to subsequent deviant responses for subjects who reported the deviant acts during the specified periods prior to the first testing. Therefore, these relationships will not be reported here in detail. However, since these data were

TABLE 3

Percentage of Students Reporting Performance of Deviant Behaviors During the One-Year Interval Between the First and Second Test Administration by Self-Derogation Level at First Administration Among Students Indicating Nonperformance of the Behavior During a Specified Period Prior to the First Test Administration

	SELF-DEROGATION LEVEL AT FIRST ADMINISTRATION		
DEVIANT BEHAVIOR	*LOW*	*MEDIUM*	*HIGH*
3 Took things worth between $2 & $50 (.22)*** *	7.8 (1672)†	10.7 (1452)	14.2***‡ (1265)
7 Took things worth less than $2 (.09)**	19.5 (1547)	21.9 (1248)	24.1* (1022)
10 Thought about or threatened to take your own life (.34)***	9.4 (1624)	13.9 (1306)	22.9*** (1025)
14 Became angry and broke things (.17)***	21.0 (1462)	27.3 (1185)	30.8 (917)
17 Carried a razor, switch blade or gun as a weapon (.15)***	7.3 (1626)	11.5 (1397)	11.1*** (1217)
24 Sold narcotic drugs (dope, heroin) (.18)**	3.1 (1661)	4.4 (1461)	5.3 (1279)
26 Received a failing grade in one or more school subjects (.16)***	15.9 (1408)	22.8 (1047)	23.0*** (831)
28 Used wine, beer or liquor more than two times (.12)***	18.2 (1574)	23.1 (1318)	23.8*** (1143)
29 Cheated on exams (.16)***	31.7 (1528)	37.7 (1283)	42.6*** (1043)
31 Attempted suicide (.30)***	5.0 (1688)	7.5 (1390)	11.5*** (1163)
33 Started a fist fight (.11)**	11.5 (1536)	12.8 (1296)	15.5*** (1104)
38 Took narcotic drugs (.19)***	8.1 (1638)	11.1 (1455)	13.5*** (1250)
44 Skipped school without an excuse (.15)***	13.9 (1637)	19.8 (1427)	20.0*** (1212)
50 Took part in gang fights (.14)**	6.1 (1651)	8.2 (1410)	9.1** (1228)
57 Used force to get money or valuables (.25)***	3.0 (1651)	5.7 (1427)	6.4*** (1243)
61 Broke into and entered a home, store or building (.16)**	3.2 (1656)	5.6 (1464)	5.2** (1295)
64 Damaged or destroyed public or private property on purpose (.24)***	5.3 (1652)	9.1 (1414)	10.4*** (1213)
69 Stole things from someone else's desk or locker (.18)***	10.0 (1608)	12.3 (1374)	16.4*** (1155)
72 Used a car without the owner's permission (.21)***	4.3 (1666)	5.9 (1457)	7.9*** (1279)
75 Beat up someone who did nothing to you (.19)***	5.0 (1633)	7.3 (1393)	8.5*** (1198)
78 Took things worth $50 or more (.14)*	2.6 (1677)	4.6 (1471)	3.9* (1297)
82 Smoked marijuana (.12)***	11.8 (1617)	13.8 (1430)	16.3** (1222)

*Indicates Goodman and Kruskal's gamma: $*p < .01$; $**p < .01$; $***p < .001$.
†Indicates number of students in cell.
‡Indicates significant level for chi-square analysis ($df = 2$); $*p < .05$; $**p < .01$; $***p < .001$.

a by-product of the computer analysis used to test the hypothesis it is noted in passing that, as expected, for these subjects antecedent self-derogation was generally unrelated to subsequent reports of deviant responses. For only one item (14) was the chi-square statistic significant, permitting rejection of the null hypothesis.

DISCUSSION

To test the hypothesis, subjects were used who were presumed not to have previously adopted the deviant pattern under consideration, as indicated by the student's denial that he had performed the deviant act during a specified period (usually a month) prior to the first testing. Of course, the denial of deviant performance during that period is no guarantee that the student had not already adopted the behavior pattern. He may already have performed the act repeatedly prior to the specified period. Furthermore, even if he had not previously performed the act, the behavior in question might not constitute deviant behavior for some subjects. Rather the student might have learned the behavior as an appropriate one to be performed at some future time, that is, by the way of anticipatory socialization. However, the probability is greater that he has not already adopted the behavior as a normatively endorsed membership group response if he indicates prior nonperformance than if he indicates prior performance of the act during the period in question. By this assertion it would be appropriate to speak of the *adoption* of a deviant response to preexisting self-derogation associated with past experiences in the membership group. The fact that this relationship was observed for persons who had not reported prior performance of the act but was not observed for persons who had reported prior performance of the act fits this assumption.

An alternative explanation of the observed relationship between antecedent self-derogation and subsequent adoption of deviant responses might assert that self-derogation influences not the *performance* of deviant behavior so much as the willingness to confess it, perhaps by way of self-reproach or as a reflection of the absence of self-protective patterns. However, such an explanation would have to account for the fact that the student used in this analysis reported *not* performing the act during the period prior to the first testing.

These considerations notwithstanding the observation of significant associations between antecedent self-derogation on the one hand and the subsequent performance of each of several virtually uncorrelated, manifestly dissimilar deviant patterns, on the other hand, lends strong support both to the thesis that negative self-attitudes are a common predisposing influence in the adoption of a range of deviant response patterns and to the general theory of deviant behavior from which it was derived.

REFERENCES

Aronson, E. and D. R. Mettee
1968 "Dishonest behavior as a function of differential levels of induced self-esteem." Journal of Personality and Social Psychology 9: 121–27.

Berg, N. L.
1971 "Effects of alcohol intoxication on self-concept: studies of alcoholics and controls in laboratory conditions." Quarterly Journal of Studies on Alcohol 32: 442–53.
Braaten, L. J. and C. D. Darling
1962 "Suicidal tendencies among college students." Psychiatric Quarterly 36: 665–92.
Brehm, M. L. and K. W. Back
1968 "Self-image and attitudes toward drugs." Journal of Personality 36: 299–314.
Carroll, J. L. and G. B. Fuller
1969 "The self and ideal-self-concept of the alcoholic as influenced by length of sobriety and/or participation in alcoholics anonymous." Journal of Clinical Psychology 25: 363–64.
Clark, J. P. and L. L. Tifft
1966 "Polygraph and interview validation of self-reported deviant behavior." American Sociological Review 31: 516–23.
Gold, Martin
1970 Delinquent Behavior in an American City. Belmont: Brooks/Cole.
Goodman, L. and W. Kruskal
1954 "Measures of association for cross-classifications, I." Journal of the American Statistical Association 49: 732–64.
Graf, R. G.
1971 "Induced self-esteem as a determinant of behavior." Journal of Social Psychology 85: 213–17.
Hall, P. M.
1966 "Identification with the delinquent subculture and level of self-evaluation." Sociometry 29: 146–58.
Harrow, M., D. A. Fox, K. L. Markhus, R. Stillman, and C. B. Hallowell
1968 "Changes in adolescents' self-concepts and their parents' perceptions during psychiatric hospitalization." Journal of Nervous and Mental Disease 147: 252–59.
Kaplan, H. B.
1970a "Self-derogation and adjustment to recent life experiences." Archives of General Psychiatry 22: 324–31.
1970b "Self-derogation and childhood family structure: family size, birth order and sex distribution." Journal of Nervous and Mental Disease 151: 13–23.
1971 "Social class and self-derogation: a conditional relationship." Sociometry 34: 41–64.
1972 "Toward a general theory of psychosocial deviance: the case of aggressive behavior." Social Science and Medicine 6: 593–617.
1975 Self-Attitudes and Deviant Behavior. Pacific Palisades: Goodyear.
Kaplan, H. B. and J. H. Meyerowitz
1970 "Social and psychological correlates of drug abuse: a comparison of addict and non-addict populations from the perspective of self-theory." Social Science and Medicine 4: 203–25.
Kaplan, H. B. and A. D. Pokorny
1969 "Self-derogation and psychosocial adjustment." Journal of Nervous and Mental Disease 149: 421–34.
1971 "Self-derogation and childhood broken home." Journal of Marriage and the Family 33: 328–38.
1972 "Sex-related correlates of adult self-derogation: reports of childhood experiences." Developmental Psychology 6: 536.
Kulik, J. A., K. B. Stein, and T. R. Sarbin
1968 "Disclosure of delinquent behavior under conditions of anonymity and nonanonymity." Journal of Consulting and Clinical Psychology 32: 506–9.
Leon, C. A.
1969 "Unusual patterns of crime during La Violencia in Columbia." American Journal of Psychiatry 125: 1564–75.

Long, B. H., R. C. Ziller, and J. Bankes
1970 "Self-other orientations of institutionalized behavior-problem adolescents." Journal of Consulting and Clinical Psychology 34: 43–47.
Miller, D. H.
1968 "Suicidal careers." Dissertation Abstracts 28A: 4720.
Rosenberg, Morris
1965 Society and the Adolescent Self-Image. Princeton: Princeton University Press.
Rossi, P. H., E. Waite, C. E. Bose, and R. E. Berk
1974 "The seriousness of crimes: normative structure and individual differences." American Sociological Review 39: 244–37.
Scarpitti, F. R.
1965 "Delinquent and non-delinquent perceptions of self, values, and opportunity." Mental Hygiene 49: 399–404.
Schwartz, M. and S. S. Tangri
1965 "A note on self-concept as an insulator against delinquency." American Sociological Review 30: 922–26.
Wilson, L. T., N. G. Braucht, R. W. Miskimins, and K. L. Berry
1971 "The severe suicide attempter and self-concept." Journal of Clinical Psychology 27: 307–9.
Wood, A. L.
1961 "A socio-structural analysis of murder, suicide and economic crime in Ceylon." American Sociological Review 26: 744–53.
Wylie, Ruth C.
1961 The Self-Concept. Lincoln: University of Nebraska Press.

Deviant Behavior and Self-Enhancement in Adolescence

Howard B. Kaplan

37

INTRODUCTION

The following considers the thesis that the adoption of deviant patterns by individuals who have self-rejecting attitudes will decrease their level of self-rejection. Numerous reports have suggested that self-rejection is associated with the adoption of a broad range of deviant patterns and/or that the adoption of such deviant patterns follows or accompanies the *subjective expectation* of outcomes associated with self-enhancement whether the mode of deviance in question be drug abuse (Anhalt and Klein, 1976; Davis and Brehm, 1971; Davis, 1972; Sadava, 1973; Segal, Rhenberg, and Sterling, 1975; Smith and Fogg, 1975; Stokes, 1974), alcoholism or alcohol abuse (Berg, 1971; Carroll and Fuller, 1969; Williams, 1965), dishonesty (Aronson and Mettee, 1968; Graf, 1971), delinquency or criminality (Gough and Peterson, 1952; Scarpitti, 1965; Wood, 1961), any of numerous functional psychiatric disorders (Arieti, 1967; Kaplan, 1977, 1978a; Wylie, 1961, pp. 205–218); violence (Miller, 1968; Leon, 1969; Toch, 1969), radical social protest (Isenberg, Schnitzer, and Rothman, 1977) or suicide (Glaser, 1965; Hattem, 1964; Miller, 1968; Wilson et al., 1967). However, that deviant patterns *in fact* have self-enhancing consequences has not been demonstrated with any consistency. Although a few studies have suggested such self-enhancing consequences of deviant patterns, these investigations have either considered only one or a few (rather than a broad range of) modes of deviance and/or used questionable research procedures such as small unrepresentative and improperly controlled samples or designs that

Source: Howard B. Kaplan, "Deviant Behavior and Self-Enhancement in Adolescence," Journal of Youth and Adolescence 7 (1978): 253–77.

militate against conclusions regarding temporal relationships between self-attitudes and deviant behavior. Even in the few instances which established a temporal relationship between antecedent deviant responses and subsequent self-attitudes, other studies were observed to report conflicting findings, differences that could be attributed to variable research operations. A case in point is the observation by Berg (1971) of alcoholics' more favorable self-attitudes while intoxicated in contrast to the observation by Vanderpool (1969) of more negative self-attitudes while under the influence of alcohol. A detailed discussion of the literature relevant to a consideration of the hypothesized self-enhancing consequences of diverse modes of deviant behavior is presented elsewhere (Kaplan, 1972, 1975b).

Unlike the studies referred to above, the present report considers the relationship between deviant behavior and self-enhancing consequences in the context of a prospective longitudinal research design that simultaneously considers the influence of diverse modes of deviance upon changes in self-attitudes among a large sample of adolescents. Earlier reports from this study have been concerned with testing other aspects of a general theory of deviant behavior including the postulate of the self-esteem motive (1975d), and hypothesized antecedents of negative self-attitudes (Kaplan, 1976a), relationships between antecedent level of (and increases in) self-derogation and subsequent adoption of deviant responses (Kaplan, 1975a, 1976b, 1977b, 1978b), and factors said to intervene between self-derogation and subsequent deviant response patterns (Kaplan, 1975c, 1977a). The analysis that follows is the first report of results concerning another major aspect of the general theory to be outlined below—the hypothesized relationship in highly self-rejecting individuals between antecedent deviant response patterns and subsequent decreases in self-rejecting attitudes.

HYPOTHESIS

It was anticipated that diverse modes of deviant behavior by highly self-rejecting individuals would be generally associated with subsequent decreases in self-rejection—particularly under conditions that imply mitigation of adverse responses (that is, negative sanctions) by others to the subject occasioned by the adoption of the deviant pattern(s). Such mitigating circumstances might include approval by self and others of attributes of the act as consistent with roles to which the subject feels a commitment, although the act itself might be defined as deviant (as when the successful exercise of power, risk-taking behavior, and active manipulation of the environment associated with certain forms of delinquency are viewed as compatible with the masculine role). However, where the act is judged by valued others and self as incompatible with the requirements of roles to which the person feels a commitment, self-enhancement is less likely to follow adoption of the deviant pattern.

Insofar as such circumstances in association with particular patterns of deviant behavior are concomitants of specified social positions (such as those based upon differentiations of gender) the self-enhancing consequences of particular deviant patterns should be a function of the deviant actor's various social positions.

The hypothesis and more specific expectations regarding the self-enhancing consequences of particular deviant patterns were derived both from a recent statement of a general theory of deviant behavior and from empirical studies, some of which tested other aspects of this theory. Specifically, deviant behaviors were more likely to have self-enhancing consequences among males than among females, and males were more likely to experience self-enhancing consequences from modes of deviance associated with activity, power needs, and externalization of blame, while female subjects were expected to experience self-enhancing consequences of deviant responses—if any—as a consequence of more passive patterns of deviance and those that facilitate distortion of affective significance.

Theoretical Basis

The hypothesis was derived from a general theory of deviant behavior (Kaplan, 1975b). The theory is general in that it seeks to explain the common origins of multiple modes of deviance rather than the unique history leading to one deviant pattern. Deviant behaviors are defined as responses which do not conform to the normative expectations of the person's (predeviance) membership group(s) and which derive from the loss of previous motivation to conform or from the development of a new motivation to deviate from normative expectations. The definition excludes behaviors which, although defined as deviant by other groups, are compatible with the normative expectations of the subject's membership/reference groups, as well as behaviors to which the person was motivated to conform but was incapable of doing so because of conflicting expectations or physical incapacity.

Briefly, the theoretical model is based upon the postulate of the self-esteem motive whereby, universally and characteristically, a person is said to behave so as to maximize the experience of positive, and to minimize the experience of negative, self-attitudes. Self-attitudes refer to the person's (more or less intense) positive and negative emotional experiences upon perceiving and evaluating his own attributes and behavior.

Intense self-rejecting attitudes are said to be the end result of a history of membership group experiences in which the subject was unable to defend against, adapt to, or cope with circumstances having self-devaluing implications (that is, disvalued attributes and behaviors, and negative evaluations of the subject by valued others). By virtue of the (actual and subjective) association between past membership group experiences and the development of intensely distressful negative self-attitudes the person loses motivation to conform to, and becomes motivated to deviate from membership group patterns (those specifically associated with the genesis of negative self-attitudes, and, by a process of generalization, other aspects of the membership groups' normative structures). Simultaneously, the unfulfilled self-esteem motive prompts the subject to seek alternative (that is, deviant) response patterns which offer hope of reducing the experience of negative (and increasing the experience of positive) self-attitudes. Thus, the person is motivated to seek and adopt deviant response patterns not only because of a loss of motivation to conform to the normative structure (which has an earlier association with the genesis of negative self-attitudes) but also because the deviant patterns represent the only motivationally acceptable alternatives that might effectively serve self-enhancing functions. Which of several deviant patterns is adopted, then, would be a function of the person's history of experiences influencing the visibility and subjective evaluation of the self-enhancing/self-devaluing potential of the pattern(s) in question.

Adoption of the deviant response has self-enhancing consequences if it facilitates intrapsychic or interpersonal avoidance of self-devaluing experiences associated with the predeviance membership group, serves to attack (symbolically or otherwise) the perceived basis of the person's self-rejecting attitudes (that is, representations of the normative group structure), and/or offers substitute patterns with self-enhancing potential for behavior patterns associated with the genesis of self-rejecting attitudes. To the extent that the person experiences self-enhancing consequences and is able to defend against anticipated or unanticipated adverse consequences of the behavior, he will be confirmed in the deviant pattern. If self-devaluing consequences outweigh self-enhancing outcomes, the person is likely to experiment with alternative modes of deviance, since normative patterns would continue to be motivationally unacceptable. . . .[1]

Change in Self-Derogation[1] Self-enhancing consequences were conceptualized in terms of the degree of reduction in self-derogation scores between the second and third test administrations. Change in self-derogation from the second to the third testing was measured by a residual gain score. A gain is said to be residualized "by expressing the posttest score as a deviation from posttest-on-pretest regression line" (Cronbach and Furby, 1970, p. 68). The raw residual change in self-derogation between the second and third testing (Rch SD 2–3) is defined as Rch SD 2-3 $= Y - \overline{Y} - \beta\, y \bullet x\,(X - \overline{X})$, where $Y =$ time 3 score, $\overline{Y} =$ mean time 3 score, $X =$ time 2 score, $\overline{X} =$ mean time 2 score, $\beta\, y \bullet x =$ the regression coefficient $[r_{yx}\sigma y/\sigma x]$. The effect of residualizing is to remove "from the posttest score, and hence from the gain, the portion that could have been predicted linearly from the pretest. The residualized score is primarily away of singling out individuals who changed more or less than expected" (Cronbach and Furby, 1970, p. 74).

The decision to use such a measure of self-attitude change was necessary, since the adoption of deviant response patterns is accompanied or preceded by increases in self-rejection (Kaplan, 1975a, 1976c, 1977b). Thus, although at T_1 all of the subjects under consideration (high self-derogation subjects) were similar in having relatively high self-rejection scores, by T_2 those who had adopted a deviant pattern could be expected to have relatively higher scores on self-rejection than their nondeviant counterparts. Since subjects with initially higher self-derogation scores are known to manifest greater subsequent decreases in self-rejection (Kaplan, 1975d), it was necessary to extract the confounding influence of initial level of self-derogation in order to consider the relationship between deviant response patterns and subsequent decreases in self-derogation.

Deviant Response Patterns Deviant responses were defined operationally in terms of self-reports of the 28 acts listed in Table 1. At the first test administration, the students were asked to indicate whether or not they performed the deviant behavior during a specified period prior to the test. The specified period in question was "within one month" for all of the items except the following, where the time period is as indicated parenthetically: items 5 (ever), 11 (ever), 26 (during the last nine weeks period), 28 (within the last week), 29 (during the last exam period), 56 (ever), 68 (within the last year). At the second and third testings, the time reference was "within the last year" except for item 28, which retained the same ("within the last week") time reference. Six of these variables were not considered in earlier analyses, since the deviant nature of two of the variables (items 48, 84) was more questionable than that of the others and the occurrence of the four others (items 5, 11, 56, 68) depend in part upon the behavior of others. In analyses in which subject characteristics were used to predict the adoption of deviant response patterns, it was advisable to exclude the items that were dependent for their occurrence upon others' responses. However, it is appropriate to consider such items in the present analysis, where the consequences of the deviant behavior (including coming to the attention of the authorities) are under investigation. . . .

Subjects were characterized as having adopted a deviant response pattern if they reported the deviant pattern at both T_1 and T_2. Subjects who denied the deviant act at both T_1 and T_2 were said to have not adopted the pattern in question. . . .

Analysis

The relationship between deviant patterns and subsequent decreases in self-derogation among initially self-rejecting subjects was considered for each of four subgroupings. The subjects' self-reports were used to differentiate them in terms of gender and socioeconomic status (mother graduated from high school versus mother did not graduate from high school) into (1) higher socioeconomic status males, (2) lower socioeconomic status males, (3) higher socioeconomic status females, and (4) lower socioeconomic status females.

The initially (T_1) high self-derogation subjects in each subgrouping who adopted each of the 28 deviant patterns (that is, affirmed the deviant act at T_1 and T_2) were compared with the initially high self-derogation subjects who did not adopt the deviant pattern (that is, denied the deviant act at T_1 and T_2) with regard to mean residual change in self-derogation T_2-T_3. Significance of difference between means was determined by a *t* test (one-tailed) assuming unequal variances (Welch, 1947).

These procedures permitted the establishment of a temporal relationship between deviant response patterns (defined as prior to T_1 and between T_1 and T_2) and subsequent base-free decreases in self-derogation (between T_2 and T_3) among initially high self-derogation subjects.

RESULTS AND DISCUSSION

It was found that the hypothesized relationship between antecedent patterns of deviance and subsequent reduction of self-derogation was generally a function of the interaction between gender and mode of deviance, and that the observed interaction tended to be compatible with the more specific expectations reviewed above. The findings are summarized in Table 1. The results will be considered for each of the four population subgroupings.

TABLE 1

Change in Self-Derogation (Mean Residual Gain Scores) T_2-T_3 by Adoption of Deviant Patterns and Gender × Socioeconomic Status Among Initially (T_1) High Self-Derogating Subjects

	HIGHER SOCIOECONOMIC STATUS MALES		LOWER SOCIOECONOMIC STATUS MALES		HIGHER SOCIOECONOMIC STATUS FEMALES		LOWER SOCIOECONOMIC STATUS FEMALES	
	REPORTED DEVIANT ACT AT T_1 AND T_2	DENIED DEVIANT ACT AT T_1 AND T_2	REPORTED DEVIANT ACT AT T_1 AND T_2	DENIED DEVIANT ACT AT T_1 AND T_2	REPORTED DEVIANT ACT AT T_1 AND T_2	DENIED DEVIANT ACT AT T_1 AND T_2	REPORTED DEVIANT ACT AT T_1 AND T_2	DENIED DEVIANT ACT AT T_1 AND T_2
(3) *Took things worth between $2 and $50	5.7†	7.5	−0.7	3.4	0.7	4.4	28.3§	6.6
	22.3	26.1	18.3	24.3	23.2	24.5	0.0	25.6
	10	189	7	63	2	319	1	92
(5) Suspended or expelled from school	−10.3‡**	7.0	7.5	2.5	15.1	4.9	31.1**	5.5
	1.4	26.1	24.8	24.2	33.4	24.7	9.1	27.1
	2	225	5	59	5	308	2	92
(7) Took things worth less than $2	3.4	6.8	−8.8*	6.2	4.1	5.4	11.1	6.9
	21.7	26.1	19.8	23.9	22.3	24.5	20.9	26.5
	51	121	15	46	25	251	11	70
(10) Thought about or threatened suicide	13.2	5.2	−1.0	3.5	9.5	3.6	0.5	4.8
	23.0	26.2	19.6	23.6	26.6	24.1	23.3	28.0
	21	164	6	55	49	209	13	59
(11) Contact with police, sheriff or juvenile officers	−2.1*	6.1	−20.9*	3.6	1.1	4.8	34.8§	6.1
	12.9	25.5	21.7	22.5	20.0	24.6	0.0	25.6
	12	168	5	56	3	320	1	96
(14) Became angry and broke things	3.0	7.2	−1.4	8.3	8.7	4.9	9.2	4.9
	24.0	26.1	25.0	24.4	23.0	24.6	26.2	26.0
	56	103	17	36	49	199	20	62

TABLE 1 (Continued)

Change in Self-Derogation (Mean Residual Gain Scores) T_2-T_3 by Adoption of Deviant Patterns and Gender × Socioeconomic Status Among Initially (T_1) High Self-Derogating Subjects

	HIGHER SOCIOECONOMIC STATUS MALES		LOWER SOCIOECONOMIC STATUS MALES		HIGHER SOCIOECONOMIC STATUS FEMALES		LOWER SOCIOECONOMIC STATUS FEMALES	
	REPORTED DEVIANT ACT AT T_1 AND T_2	DENIED DEVIANT ACT AT T_1 AND T_2	REPORTED DEVIANT ACT AT T_1 AND T_2	DENIED DEVIANT ACT AT T_1 AND T_2	REPORTED DEVIANT ACT AT T_1 AND T_2	DENIED DEVIANT ACT AT T_1 AND T_2	REPORTED DEVIANT ACT AT T_1 AND T_2	DENIED DEVIANT ACT AT T_1 AND T_2
(17) Carried a razor, switch blade, or gun as a weapon	–4.9*	8.1	–3.0	4.6	38.3§	4.4	–24.3§	6.5
	25.0	26.7	16.2	24.3	0.0	24.1	0.0	25.9
	20	175	7	59	1	330	1	98
(24) Sold narcotic drugs (dope, heroin)	11.5	6.4	–8.9§	2.5	0.0§	2.5	0.0§	6.5
	20.4	25.4	0.0	24.0	0.0	24.5	0.0	25.8
	2	222	1	71	0	338	0	99
(26) Received a failing grade in one or more school subjects	11.1	6.0	4.8	1.4	10.5**	1.4	10.7	2.3
	25.4	27.2	24.3	21.6	23.7	23.4	19.2	29.0
	45	117	17	34	43	216	25	44
(28) Used wine, beer, or liquor more than two times	–10.8***	7.4	1.2	3.5	3.3	4.9	14.3	8.6
	19.8	25.1	26.1	24.8	13.9	24.4	30.1	25.5
	21	153	9	53	15	254	4	84
(29) Cheated on exams	0.6	5.8	–8.6	7.4	4.4	5.0	13.3	4.8
	18.6	26.7	21.5	21.3	25.3	23.5	27.0	25.6
	30	119	4	47	67	142	13	58
(31) Attempted suicide	17.7*	4.9	1.8	2.2	5.2	4.1	3.3	5.4
	10.6	25.3	13.4	21.5	24.7	24.1	27.9	26.1
	5	202	4	59	21	286	8	75

TABLE 1 (Continued)

Change in Self-Derogation (Mean Residual Gain Scores) T_2-T_3 by Adoption of Deviant Patterns and Gender × Socioeconomic Status Among Initially (T_1) High Self-Derogating Subjects

	HIGHER SOCIOECONOMIC STATUS MALES		LOWER SOCIOECONOMIC STATUS MALES		HIGHER SOCIOECONOMIC STATUS FEMALES		LOWER SOCIOECONOMIC STATUS FEMALES	
	REPORTED DEVIANT ACT AT T_1 AND T_2	DENIED DEVIANT ACT AT T_1 AND T_2	REPORTED DEVIANT ACT AT T_1 AND T_2	DENIED DEVIANT ACT AT T_1 AND T_2	REPORTED DEVIANT ACT AT T_1 AND T_2	DENIED DEVIANT ACT AT T_1 AND T_2	REPORTED DEVIANT ACT AT T_1 AND T_2	DENIED DEVIANT ACT AT T_1 AND T_2
(33) Started a fist fight	1.9	7.0	7.9	0.5	11.6	5.1	27.4***	6.8
	25.4	24.7	14.6	22.0	14.7	24.3	12.6	24.9
	36	147	7	50	7	300	8	86
(38) Took narcotic drugs	26.0	6.9	0.0§	2.2	-11.4*	5.7	10.0	6.0
	30.5	25.5	0.0	23.0	25.7	24.3	24.6	26.1
	3	194	0	67	7	305	4	90
(44) Skipped school without an excuse	-3.2	7.8	-2.3	1.6	3.6	5.0	20.2**	6.4
	26.8	25.7	23.2	20.8	25.8	24.5	8.3	26.3
	10	183	5	60	8	287	5	85
(48) Participated in social protest	20.4	6.0	4.1	2.8	2.3	5.0	10.6	5.3
	28.0	25.6	34.0	23.5	25.4	24.1	15.2	23.5
	6	196	7	55	14	280	5	73
(50) Took part in gang fights	3.8	7.6	7.3	3.3	4.5	5.3	45.2***	4.2
	26.5	25.5	13.0	23.2	16.5	24.2	10.4	26.3
	10	202	4	60	4	320	2	94
(56) Sent to a psychiatrist, psychologist, or social worker	3.2	6.8	0.0§	4.8	40.2§	5.7	0.0§	7.4
	24.6	26.2	0.0	22.4	0.0	24.4	0.0	25.4
	4	199	0	64	1	323	0	98

TABLE 1 (Continued)

Change in Self-Derogation (Mean Residual Gain Scores) T_2-T_3 by Adoption of Deviant Patterns and Gender × Socioeconomic Status Among Initially (T_1) High Self-Derogating Subjects

	HIGHER SOCIOECONOMIC STATUS MALES		LOWER SOCIOECONOMIC STATUS MALES		HIGHER SOCIOECONOMIC STATUS FEMALES		LOWER SOCIOECONOMIC STATUS FEMALES	
	REPORTED DEVIANT ACT AT T_1 AND T_2	DENIED DEVIANT ACT AT T_1 AND T_2	REPORTED DEVIANT ACT AT T_1 AND T_2	DENIED DEVIANT ACT AT T_1 AND T_2	REPORTED DEVIANT ACT AT T_1 AND T_2	DENIED DEVIANT ACT AT T_1 AND T_2	REPORTED DEVIANT ACT AT T_1 AND T_2	DENIED DEVIANT ACT AT T_1 AND T_2
(57) Used force to get money or valuables	-12.7	-2.2	-40.0*	-4.3	18.7	-5.4	0.0§	-6.9
	23.6	29.7	0.0	28.9	32.7	26.3	0.0	29.8
	6	201	2	69	3	331	0	95
(61) Broke into and entered a home, store or building	-10.3**	6.5	-15.2§	2.6	13.9§	5.4	0.0§	5.7
	1.4	25.9	0.0	24.0	0.0	24.3	0.0	26.2
	2	216	1	70	1	341	0	103
(64) Damaged or destroyed public or private property on purpose	-1.5*	7.5	14.8*	2.3	-5.0	5.2	0.0§	5.3
	16.6	25.3	15.4	23.5	30.0	24.0	0.0	26.8
	14	172	6	60	4	316	0	96
(68) Taken to office for punishment	9.3	5.4	13.4	-0.5	11.2*	4.7	2.8	2.9
	23.7	23.6	24.8	18.3	20.9	24.0	28.3	26.4
	55	110	9	40	35	233	12	68
(69) Stole things from someone else's desk or locker	-1.2	6.7	-5.3*	7.3	8.6	6.2	14.8§	5.8
	23.0	25.4	19.4	23.8	21.2	23.9	0.0	25.5
	20	156	9	47	8	293	1	96

TABLE 1 (Continued)
Change in Self-Derogation (Mean Residual Gain Scores) T_2-T_3 by Adoption of Deviant Patterns and Gender × Socioeconomic Status Among Initially (T_1) High Self-Derogating Subjects

	HIGHER SOCIOECONOMIC STATUS MALES		LOWER SOCIOECONOMIC STATUS MALES		HIGHER SOCIOECONOMIC STATUS FEMALES		LOWER SOCIOECONOMIC STATUS FEMALES	
	REPORTED DEVIANT ACT AT T_1 AND T_2	DENIED DEVIANT ACT AT T_1 AND T_2	REPORTED DEVIANT ACT AT T_1 AND T_2	DENIED DEVIANT ACT AT T_1 AND T_2	REPORTED DEVIANT ACT AT T_1 AND T_2	DENIED DEVIANT ACT AT T_1 AND T_2	REPORTED DEVIANT ACT AT T_1 AND T_2	DENIED DEVIANT ACT AT T_1 AND T_2
(72) Used a car without the owner's permission	−5.3**	5.9	0.0§	3.1	0.0§	5.3	0.0§	5.0
	3.6	26.2	0.0	24.4	0.0	24.4	0.0	25.7
	2	212	0	65	0	333	0	99
(75) Beat up someone who did nothing to you	8.5	6.1	−15.2§	3.2	25.7§	5.0	24.8§	6.2
	24.8	26.1	0.0	24.8	0.0	24.4	0.0	26.2
	20	181	1	61	1	322	1	104
(78) Took things worth $50 or more	−8.9§	6.7	0.0§	1.7	12.0§	5.3	0.0§	6.6
	0.0	25.9	0.0	22.6	0.0	24.3	0.0	26.2
	1	224	0	74	1	348	0	105
(82) Smoked marijuana	−3.0*	6.6	8.1	2.0	8.5	6.1	0.5	5.6
	8.3	26.2	16.8	24.2	30.4	24.1	36.2	25.3
	6	185	3	56	8	296	4	88
(84) Participated in strike, riot, or demonstration	20.2§	6.6	−11.2*	−0.2	20.2	4.8	31.1§	7.4
	0.0	25.7	4.1	22.8	24.8	24.1	0.0	25.5
	1	210	2	61	4	333	1	97

*Numbers refer to questionnaire items.

†The series of three entries in each column indicates the mean of the residual change score, the standard deviation and the *N*. The asterisks indicate significance level: * = $p < 0.05$, ** = $p < 0.01$, *** = $p < 0.001$, for difference between adjacent means by *t* test (one-tailed), assuming unequal variances (Welch, 1947).

‡Positive signs indicate relative increases in self-derogation from T_2 to T_3. Negative signs indicate relative decreases in self-derogation from T_2 to T_3.

§Differences between means could not be computed due to paucity of cases.

Among *higher socioeconomic status males,* as expected, initially high self-derogation subjects who adopted several modes of deviance (that is, affirmed performing the behavior at both T_1 and T_2) relative to those who did not adopt the pattern (that is, denied performance at T_1 and T_2) manifested greater decreases in self-derogation between T_2 and T_3. In 18 of the 26 instances in which comparisons were possible, those who adopted the deviant patterns tended to manifest more negative and less positive residual gain scores on the self-derogation measure than those who did not adopt the pattern. The comparisons were statistically significant for 8 of the deviant patterns. Significantly greater subsequent (T_2-T_3) decreases (smaller subsequent increases) in self-derogation were associated with antecedent (T_1 and T_2) reports of being suspended or expelled from school; having anything to do with police, sheriff, or juvenile officers for something the subject had done or was suspected of doing; carrying a razor, switchblade, or gun as a weapon; using wine, beer, or liquor more than two times during the preceding week; breaking into and entering a home, store, or building; purposely damaging or destroying public or private property; taking a car for a ride without the owner's knowledge; and smoking marijuana. Also noted was a nonsignificant ($p = 0.08$) tendency for initially high self-derogation subjects who stole from someone's desk or locker at school to display greater subsequent decreases in self-derogation. For only one item (attempted suicide) was the deviant response associated with a significant increase in self-derogation ($p = 0.01$). In this connection a nonsignificant tendency ($p = 0.08$) for subjects who thought about or threatened suicide to manifest subsequent increases in self-rejection was also noted. These findings suggest that unlike the other patterns for higher socioeconomic status males, suicidal responses are reflections of, rather than functional responses to, self-rejecting attitudes.

Although the data are not presented here, deviant behavior was not associated with subsequent decreases in self-derogation among initially medium and low self-derogation subjects with the same consistency that it was among initially high self-derogation subjects. This observation provides support for the thesis that deviant behaviors are adopted in response to high levels of self-derogation and are more or less functional in reducing self-rejecting attitudes. Among initially medium self-derogation subjects none of the items significantly associated with the subsequent decreases in self-derogation among initially high self-derogation subjects were similarly associated with subsequent decreases in self-rejection, and indeed, only 1 of the 25 items for which comparisons could be made (took things worth $50 or more) was significantly associated with subsequent decreases in self-rejecting attitudes. On the other hand, several items (thought about or threatened suicide, became angry and broke things, carried a weapon, received a failing grade, took narcotic drugs, breaking and entering) were significantly associated with subsequent *increases* in self-derogation among initially medium self-derogation subjects. Similarly, among initially low self-derogation subjects only 2 of the 24 items for which comparisons could be made (contact with police, sheriff, or juvenile officers; breaking and entering) were associated with subsequent decreases in self-derogation. However, only one pattern (social protest) was associated with a subsequent increase in self-derogation. Perhaps for *low* self-derogation subjects who adopted deviant patterns the "deviance" represents behavioral responses which the subjects learned in the course of their socialization.

This would account for both the performance of the "deviant" responses by low self-derogation subjects as well as the paucity of significant changes in self-derogation subsequent to adoption of the pattern.

Among *lower socioeconomic status males,* as among higher socioeconomic status males, initially high self-derogation subjects who adopted each of several modes of deviance relative to those who did not adopt the pattern manifested greater subsequent base-free decreases in self-derogation. For 13 of the 21 instances in which comparisons were possible, those who adopted the deviant patterns tended to manifest more negative and fewer positive residual gain scores on the self-derogation measure than those who did not adopt the pattern. The comparisons were statistically significant for 5 of the deviant patterns. Significantly greater subsequent (T_2-T_3) decreases (smaller subsequent increases) in self-derogation were associated with antecedent (T_1 and T_2) reports of stealing things worth less than $2; having contact with police, sheriff, or juvenile officers; using force to get money or valuables; stealing things from someone else's desk or locker; and participating in a strike, riot, or demonstration. A tendency was also noted for initially high self-derogation subjects who became angry and broke things ($p = 0.10$), carried weapons ($p = 0.15$), and cheated on exams ($p = 0.11$) to display greater subsequent decreases in self-derogation. For only one item (purposely damaged or destroyed public property) was antecedent deviant response significantly associated with a subsequent increase in self-derogation.

Although a relationship between antecedent deviant patterns and subsequent decreases in self-derogation was hypothesized only for initially *high* self-derogation subjects, it is noted again (as it was for higher socioeconomic status males) that this relationship was *not* consistently observed among initially low and medium self-derogation subjects. Among the initially medium self-derogation subjects only 2 of the 15 items for which comparisons could be made (stole things worth less than $2, stole things worth between $2 and $50) were significantly associated with subsequent decreases in self-derogation, and only one other item (took part in gang fights) was related at a nonsignificant level ($p = 0.12$). All of the remaining items were (nonsignificantly) associated with subsequent increases in self-derogation. Similarly, among the initially *low* self-derogation subjects only one item (skipped school without an excuse) was significantly associated with subsequent decreases in self-derogation. However, of the 17 items for which comparisons could be made, 12 deviant patterns were associated with subsequent *increases* in self-derogation, 3 of them significantly so (stole things worth between $2 and $50; used wine, beer, or liquor more than two times during the preceding week; was taken to the office for punishment).

The lower socioeconomic status males under consideration were those who remained in the study; perhaps they represented those for whom leaving the system would be particularly costly. By implication, they might also represent those vulnerable to adverse responses by system representatives evoked by deviant patterns; this could account for the more numerous instances among *lower* socioeconomic status males in which deviant patterns were associated with subsequent increases in self-derogation. In support of this reasoning, it is again noted that among all the patterns, only for those skipping school without an excuse (suggesting loose affective ties to the school) was the deviant response associated with a subsequent decrease in self-rejection. In any case, the observation of a more consistent relationship between antecedent deviant responses and subsequent decreases in self-rejection among initially high (compared to initially medium or low) self-derogation subjects for lower socioeconomic status males once again supports the general position that deviant patterns are responses to self-derogation and are (under specifiable conditions) functional in reducing self-rejecting feelings.

The deviant patterns observed to be associated with subsequent decreases in self-derogation generally might have been predicted on the basis of the literature cited above. The deviant patterns that tended to be associated with male deviants and that were interpretable as compatible with features of the masculine role (activity, aggressiveness, potency, etc.) tended to be associated with subsequent decreases in self-derogation.

The findings for female subjects were also compatible with the theoretical issues and empirical reports reviewed above. On the basis of the female's greater vulnerability to interpersonal sanctions and her observed lesser tendency to adopt deviant responses, female subjects were expected to be less likely to experience self-enhancing consequences from the range of deviant responses. The particular deviant responses that had self-enhancing consequences were more likely to be passive, nonaggressive responses that facilitated reinterpretation of the affective significance of life events. Specifically, the expectation that drug abuse would have self-enhancing consequences among females was compatible with observations of a female-specific association of increase in alienation (e.g., sense of isolation from others) with adoption of marijuana use (Jessor, Jessor, and Finney, 1973); higher self-esteem among drug-taking females than among drug-taking males (Burke and Eichberg, 1972); a female-specific increase in perceived positive functions of marijuana associated with the adoption of marijuana use (Jessor, Jessor, and Finney, 1973); low denial of effects in combination with self-dissatisfaction as a predictor of females' inclination to drug use (Brehm and Back, 1968); and male drug users rejecting the culturally prescribed assertive male role and female users identifying with the unassertiveness of the traditional female role (Fitzgibbons, Berry, and Shearn, 1973).

As expected, among initially high self-derogating females, few deviant patterns were associated with subsequent decreases in self-derogation, and these patterns related to drug abuse. Among *higher socioeconomic status females*, only one deviant pattern was significantly associated with subsequent decreases in self-derogation. High self-derogation females who reported using narcotics at T_1 and T_2, relative to those who denied use at those times, manifested significantly greater subsequent (T_2-T_3) decreases in self-derogation. One other pattern was appreciably but not significantly associated with subsequent decreases in self-derogation. High self-derogation females who reported marijuana use at T_1 and T_2, relative to those who denied using marijuana at T_1 and T_2, manifested appreciably greater ($p = 0.10$) subsequent (T_2-T_3) decreases in self-derogation. On the other hand, receiving failing grades and being taken to the office for punishment were associated with significant subsequent *increases* in self-derogation. This finding suggests a particular sensitivity to negative sanctions related to school failure (higher socioeconomic status females in the present study were least likely to receive high scores on a measure of perceived self-devaluing experiences in the school environment); and a number of other patterns were appreciably, if not significantly, related to subsequent increases in self-derogation.

Among *lower socioeconomic status females* none of the deviant patterns was significantly related to subsequent decreases in self-derogation among initially high self-derogation subjects. These findings, again, are in accord with the expectations (based on the literature and findings reviewed above) that the related factors of more negative responses to female as opposed to male delinquency, the greater inhibition imposed on the expression of a broad range of delinquent patterns during the female socialization process, and—perhaps most significantly—the greater vulnerability of females to interpersonal sanctions would in large measure preclude the experience of self-enhancing consequences of the deviant response patterns under consideration. In this connection, let us recall that the lower socioeconomic status females, who were just noted to be least likely to enjoy self-enhancing consequences of deviant patterns, were observed above to be most likely to receive high scores on the defenselessness/vulnerability index. In general, then, the observed gender-related differences with regard to self-enhancing consequences of deviant responses (among initially high self-derogating subjects) were in accord with expectations.

The major findings from this study, particularly with regard to the association between multiple modes of deviance and subsequent decreases in self-derogation among initially high self-derogating males (regardless of socioeconomic status) question the frequently drawn conclusions and assumptions concerning the adverse consequences on self-attitudes of repeated deviant behavior, institutionalization, and—more generally—coming to the attention of the authorities (Fitts and Hammer, 1969; J. R. Williams, 1976). Also called into question are the conclusions that apprehension has no consequences for level of self-esteem (Jensen, 1972), conclusions that are all too often drawn in the face of conflicting findings and are based on inappropriate research designs. In the present study it has been observed that under certain conditions deviant (including delinquent) behavior—whether or not it is known to have attracted the attention of the authorities—has self-enhancing consequences. Individuals who have developed relatively high levels of self-derogating attitudes in the course of their membership group experiences and who have adopted deviant patterns (relative to those who have not adopted such patterns) were observed to subsequently decrease their level of self-rejecting attitudes. This decrease occurred particularly under conditions in which the patterns could be assumed to be compatible with, or symbolic extensions of, valued social roles (presumably unrelated to the genesis of the self-rejecting attitudes) so that the subjects were therefore (or for other reasons) more protected from occasions for self-devaluation and from negative responses by valued others as a consequence of the deviant responses. These observations lend support to the general theory of deviant behavior from which the hypothesized relationships between antecedent deviant patterns and subsequent self-enhancement are derived.

NOTES

1 The sample, data, and methods used in this report are described in the previous article by Howard Kaplan, "Self-Attitudes and Deviant Responses."

REFERENCES

Anhalt, H. S. and M. Klein
1976 "Drug abuse in junior high school populations." American Journal of Drug and Alcohol Abuse 3: 589-603.
Arieti, S.
1967 "Some elements of cognitive psychiatry." American Journal of Psychotherapy 124: 723-36.
Aronson, E. and D. R. Mettee
1968 "Dishonest behavior as a function of differential levels of induced self-esteem." Journal of Personality and Social Psychology 9: 121-27.
Berg, N. L.
1971 "Effects of alcohol intoxication on self-concept." Quarterly Journal of Studies on Alcohol 32: 422-53.
Bogo, N., C. Winget, and G. Gleser
1970 "Ego defenses and perceptual styles." Perceptual and Motor Skills 30: 599-604.
Brehm, M. L. and K. W. Back
1968 "Self image and attitudes toward drugs." Journal of Personality 36: 299-314.
Burke, E. L. and R. H. Eichberg
1972 "Personality characteristics of adolescent users of dangerous drugs as indicated by the Minnesota Multiphasic Personality Inventory." Journal of Nervous and Mental Disease 154: 291-98.
Carroll, J. L. and G. B. Fuller
1969 "The self and ideal self-concept of the alcoholic as influenced by length of sobriety and/or participation in Alcoholics Anonymous." Journal of Clinical Psychology 25: 363-64.
Cronbach, L. J. and L. Furby
1970 "How we should measure change—or should we?" Psychological Bulletin 74: 68-80.
Davis, G. C. and M. L. Brehm
1971 "Juvenile prisoners: motivational factors in drug use." Proceedings of the American Psychological Association 6 (Part 1): 333-34.
Davis, K. E.
1972 "Drug effects and drug use." Pp. 517-45 in Wrightsman, L. S. (ed.), Social Psychology in the Seventies. Monterey, Calif.: Brooks-Cole.
Fitts, W. H. and W. T. Hammer
1969 The Self-Concept and Delinquency. Nashville, Tenn.: Counselor Recordings and Tests.
Fitzgibbons, D. J., D. F. Berry, and C. R. Shearn
1973 "MMPI and diagnosis among hospitalized drug abusers." Journal of Community Psychology 1: 79-81.
Glaser, K.
1964 "Attempted suicide in children and adolescents: psycho-dynamic observations." American Journal of Psychotherapy 19: 220-27.
Gough, H. G. and D. R. Peterson
1952 "The identification and measurement of predispositional factors in crime and delinquency." Journal of Consulting Psychology 16: 207-12.
Graf, R. G.
1971 "Induced self-esteem as a determinant of behavior." Journal of Social Psychology 85: 213-17.
Hattem, J. V.
1964 "The precipitating role of discordant interpersonal relationships in suicidal behavior." Dissertation Abstracts 25: 1135-36.
Isenberg, P., R. Schnitzer, and S. Rothman
1977 "Psychological variables in student activism: the radical triad and some religious differences." Journal of Youth and Adolescence 6: 11-24.

Jensen, G. F.
1972 "Delinquency and adolescent self-conceptions: a study of the personal relevance of infraction." Social Problems 20: 84–103.
Jessor, R., S. L. Jessor, and J. Finney
1973 "A social psychology of marijuana use: longitudinal studies of high school and college youth." Journal of Personality and Social Psychology 26: 1–15.
Kaplan, H. B.
1972 "Toward a general theory of psychosocial deviance: the case of aggressive behavior." Social Science and Medicine 6: 593–617.
1975a "Increase in self-rejection as an antecedent of deviant responses." Journal of Youth and Adolescence 4: 281–92.
1975b Self-Attitudes and Deviant Behavior. Pacific Palisades, Calif.: Goodyear Publishing.
1975c "Sequelae of self-derogation: predicting from a general theory of deviant behavior." Youth and Society 7: 171–97.
1975d "The self-esteem motive and change in self-attitudes." Journal of Nervous and Mental Disease 161: 265–75.
1976a "Antecedents of negative self-attitudes: Membership group devaluation and defenselessness." Social Psychiatry 11: 15–25.
1976b "Self-attitudes and deviant response." Social Forces 54: 788–801.
1976c "Self-attitude change and deviant behavior." Social Psychiatry 11: 59–67.
1977a "Antecedents of deviant responses: predicting from a general theory of deviant behavior." Journal of Youth and Adolescence 6: 89–101.
1977b "Gender and depression: a sociological analysis of a conditional relationship." Pp. 81–113 in W. E. Fann, I. Karacan, A. D. Pokorny, and R. L. Williams (eds.), Phenomenology and Treatment of Depression. New York: Spectrum Publishing Company.
1977c "Increase in self-rejection and continuing/discontinued deviant response." Journal of Youth and Adolescence 6: 77–87.
1978a "Self-attitudes and schizophrenia." Pp. 241–91 in W. E. Fann, I. Karacan, A. D. Pokorny, and R. L. Williams (eds.), Phenomenology and Treatment of Schizophrenia. New York: Spectrum Publishing Company.
1978b "Social class, self-derogation and deviant response." Social Psychiatry 13: 19–28.
Leon, C. A.
1969 "Unusual patterns of crime during La Violencia in Columbia." American Journal of Psychiatry 125: 1564–75.
Miller, D.
1968 "Toward a symbolic interaction theory of suicide." Dissertation Abstracts 28: 4720A.
Sadava, S. W.
1973 "Patterns of college student drug use: a longitudinal social learning study." Psychological Reports 33: 75–86.
Scarpitti, F. R.
1965 "Delinquent and non-delinquent perceptions of self, values and opportunity." Mental Hygiene 49: 399–404.
Segal, B., G. Rhenberg, and S. Sterling
1975 "Self-concept and drug and alcohol use in female college students." Journal of Alcohol and Drug Education 20: 17–22.
Smith, G. M. and C. P. Fogg
1975 "Teenage drug use: a search for causes and consequences." Pp. 279–98 in D. J. Lettieri, (ed.), Predicting Adolescent Drug Abuse: A Review of Issues, Methods and Correlates. Washington, D.C.: National Institute of Drug Abuse.
Stokes, J. P.
1974 "Personality traits and attitudes and their relationship to student drug using behavior." International Journal of Addictions 9: 267–87.
Toch, H.
1969 Violent Men. Chicago: Aldine Press.

Vanderpool, J. A.
1969 "Alcoholism and the self-concept." Quarterly Journal of Studies on Alcohol 30: 59–77.

Welch, B. L.
1947 "The generalization of 'student's' problems when several different population variances are involved." Biometrika 34: 28–35.

Williams, A. E.
1965 "Self-concepts of college problem drinkers: (1) A comparison with alcoholics." Quarterly Journal of Studies on Alcohol 26: 589–94.

Williams, J. R.
1976 Effects of Labeling The "Drug Abuser": An Inquiry. Rockville, Md.: National Institute on Drug Abuse.

Wilson, L. T., G. N. Braucht, R. W. Miskimins, and K. L. Berry
1971 "The severe suicide attempter and self-concept." Journal of Clinical Psychology 27: 307–9.

Wood, A. L.
1961 "A socio-structural analysis of murder, suicide, and economic crime in Ceylon." American Sociological Review 26: 744–53.

Wylie, R. C.
1961 The Self Concept. Lincoln: University of Nebraska Press.

Economic Strains and the Coping Functions of Alcohol

Leonard I. Pearlin
Clarice W. Radabaugh

38

Drinking is a multidimensional behavior, varying in such respects as frequency, quantity, the setting in which it is typically done, the occasions that give rise to it, and its many social and psychological consequences. In this paper our interest is confined to the use of alcohol as a mechanism for controlling anxiety. Of the innumerable conditions that potentially contribute to anxiety, we shall be concerned with but one: insufficient financial resources. Because so many life chances depend on the possession of economic resources, the scarcity of the latter can be an especially potent antecedent of anxiety.

The view that consumption of alcohol may serve as a mechanism for coping with anxiety aroused by economic conditions has a variety of conceptual and empirical underpinnings in the vast literature on drinking. Pivotal among them is the repeated finding from both the laboratory (Greenberg 1963) and the clinic (Alexander 1963) that alcohol in moderate amounts can alleviate the stressful impact of environmental threats through the metabolic and perceptual effects it produces in the organism (Washburn 1955; Chavetz, Demone, and Solomon 1962, pp. 6–8). The fact that alcohol can act as a tranquilizer for individuals should be reflected in broader relationships between the intensity of strains existing in a society and the level of alcohol consumption in that society. Such relationships, indeed, have been observed (Horton 1943, pp. 261–81), although it has been

Source: Leonard I. Pearlin and Clarice W. Radabaugh, "Economic Strains and the Coping Functions of Alcohol," American Journal of Sociology 82 (1976): 652–63. Reprinted by permission of the authors and publisher.

argued (Bales 1945, pp. 480–99) that the volume of alcohol consumption depends not only on extant strains, but also on the number of alternatives a society provides for dealing with tensions.

Such broad overviews of the interrelationships between cultural strains, anxiety, and drinking have been supplemented by more recent systematic large-scale sample surveys of drinking practices (Riley and Marden 1947; Cahalan, Cisin, and Crossley 1969). One of the most important contributions of these surveys has been to establish that variations in drinking patterns correspond to lines of social structural demarcation. Such findings strongly suggest that if social strains do, in fact, help to regulate the use of alcohol, they will not be found to exist equally among people located differentially in society.

These findings and perspectives converge on the present study and help to bring into focus its purpose: to determine empirically whether drinking does function as a means for controlling and alleviating anxiety, especially that which arises from economic problems. It should be emphasized that it is not our intention to account for as many sources of anxiety as possible or to assemble all the possible reasons for drinking. Instead we intend to illustrate how the meaning and functions of drinking may be bound up in experiences and feelings that have their roots in basic features of social and economic organization.

BACKGROUND AND METHODS

The data analyzed in this paper are part of a larger investigation into the social origins of personal stress. The information was gathered through scheduled interviews with a sample of 2,300 people representative of the census-defined urbanized area of Chicago (U.S. Bureau of the Census 1972), which includes sections of northwestern Indiana as well as some of the suburban areas of Chicago.[1] . . .

Two criteria were used in choosing respondents within sampled households. First, anyone younger than 18 or older than 65 did not qualify, for it was desired to have a sample weighted in favor of those actively engaged in occupational life. Where more than one person in a household qualified as a respondent under the age limitations, the older candidate was systematically chosen. A second restriction concerned respondent's sex. The sex of the person to be interviewed in each household was predesignated so that the final sample would have as equal a number of males and females as possible. This restriction could be ignored only in instances where all age-qualified respondents were of the same sex. Because females typically head such households, the final sample contained more women than men.

The interview schedule was designed to yield several distinct types of information. First, it asked people about potential strains—that is, conflicts, frustrations, and threats—that earlier exploratory interviews had revealed to be commonly experienced. It was particularly concerned with the strains that occur in the major social role areas of occupation, marriage, child rearing, and economic life. Second, the interview included a number of questions about the coping strategies and coping resources people employ in dealing with the strains they experience in these roles. And third, it inquired into the emotional stresses that they feel and the extent to which they experience symptoms of various states of psychological disturbance, such as depression and anxiety. The present report, although it brings together only a small portion of the data, cuts across several of these areas.

DISTRESS CONTROL AS A FUNCTION OF DRINKING

The fact that the inquiry into drinking practices is part of a more inclusive study of social stress had considerable influence on the questions asked about drinking. As we noted earlier, drinking is a complex behavior that can be approached from many directions and described at many levels. In surveys dealing exclusively with drinking, considerable time is required simply to gather information pertaining to its elementary aspects, such as what, when, where, with whom, and how much people drink. It was necessary to be more selective here. In keeping with the broader goals of the inquiry, our questions were limited to learning whether respondents were abstinent or not and, if not, the extent to which drinking was part of their social lifestyle, how often in the past month they had drunk to inebriety and, finally, some of the manifest consequences that individuals attributed to their own drinking behavior. It is with the last mentioned data that this paper is primarily concerned, particularly those consequences indicative of the control of anxiety.

It is difficult to determine when drinking is used by people to control psychological distress, for there is nothing about alcohol consumption itself that indicates the reasons for or consequences of its use. In this respect it is similar to a variety of behaviors, such as television viewing (Pearlin 1959), that may be employed as coping devices by some people but not by others. Since the behavior alone cannot provide a clear indication of how it is being used, it is necessary to ask the subject himself what drinking "does for him." A question adapted from the work of Cahalan et al. (1969, p. 242) was used for this purpose. Respondents, except those who had indicated previously that they were teetotalers (614, or 27 percent of the total sample), were presented with this item: "Here are different reasons people have for drinking. Thinking of yourself and your reasons, how true are [*sic*] each of these reasons for you personally?" Eight statements were then given, each answered by "very true," "true," or "not true." Only two statements will figure in this analysis: "A drink helps me to forget my worries" and "A drink helps cheer me up when I am in a bad mood."[2] A score of distress control was created simply by according a value from one to three to the response categories. Thus, people who responded "very true" to both statements have a score of six, and those answering "not true" to both have a score of two.

It needs to be recognized that the thrust of the questions is aimed at consequences of drinking about which the person himself has some consciousness. The measure, therefore, deals only with a single manifest function of drinking and encompasses neither latent functions outside the awareness of drinkers nor manifest functions other than the use of alcohol to assuage emotional distress. It is difficult to be certain, of course, whether the functions an individual recognizes are among those actually performed by his drinking. In this connection, however, it is relevant to note that there is a substantial rise in the frequency of reported inebriation as the disposition to use alcohol for the control of distress increases ($P < .001$).

Finally it should be emphasized that the index reflects the use of alcohol as a means for the temporary containment or diminution of an existing noxious emotional state. This coping behavior is thus an effort to control distress after it emerges and is very different from behaviors aimed at eliminating conditions underlying the distress. Clearly, the use of alcohol is at most a means of appeasing unpleasant emotions currently being experienced and probably leaves intact the situations out of which such emotions have grown.

ECONOMIC STRAINS AND ANXIETY

In concentrating on economic antecedents of distress, we are being very selective, for there is a plethora of conditions with the potential for arousing emotional disturbance. However, there are strategic advantages in emphasizing economic circumstances. One is that problems in this area have an extraordinary capacity to provoke distress. Because so many fundamental activities and life chances depend on the economic resources people possess, deprivations and difficulties in this domain are not likely to be borne without emotional repercussions. Also, economic life circumstances typically resist efforts toward rapid improvement; problems that exist here, therefore, are often more persistent and durable than ones stemming from other sources. As a consequence of the persistent quality of economic problems, people tend to develop equally persistent ways of coping with them, such as habitual reliance on alcohol. If environmental strains, inner distress, and drinking behavior are interrelated, their connections should be especially stable and amenable to observation when the strains involve economic problems.

We assess a family's economic resources in two ways, one of them being total family income. Income information, however, is at best incomplete, for it does not take into account the fact that the same level of income reflects a different resource for families differing in size and age composition. The second indicator avoids problems of equivalence by focusing on the actual economic strain people experience, without regard to their incomes. It involves a three-part question: "How often does it happen that you do not have enough money to afford: (1) the kind of food you (your family) should have? (2) the kind of medical care you (your family) should have? (3) the kind of clothing you (your family) should have?" Each item was answered by "never," "once in a while," "fairly often," or "very often," and a total score was formed by adding the values of the three responses. This measure taps the intensity of the effort in which one has to engage simply to meet the fundamental economic requirements of life. There are families with fairly substantial incomes whose scores on the measure reveal severe economic strain, especially families with three or more children. Nevertheless, there is a close association between family income and our direct measure of strain, with strain intensifying as income declines.

How do these indicators of economic hardship relate to psychological distress, anxiety in particular? Anxiety is measured here by a set of items that is fairly standard in surveys. They ask respondents how frequently they experience 12 common psychophysiological symptoms of anxiety (Lipman et al. 1969; Derogatis et al. 1971). Table 1 is divided into two parts, showing separately the relationship of income and of economic strain to anxiety among nonteetotalers. The difference in the total number of respondents reporting in each part results from over 300 respondents having been either unable or unwilling to provide income information. It is apparent from the results of the table that economic hardships, whether gauged by income or by felt strain, are significantly associated with anxiety. This element of psychological distress, therefore, does not arise simply from chance events impinging on the lives of people randomly located in the society, but is in part a consequence of distinctive circumstances experienced at different economic levels.

TABLE 1

Economic Hardships and Anxiety (Percent)

	ANXIETY				
	INTENSE	*MODERATE*	*LOW*	*N*	*TOTAL*
Family income per year ($):					
Less than 6,000	33	27	40	221	100
6,000– 9,999	18	29	53	265	100
10,000–13,999	19	29	52	427	100
14,000–17,999	17	29	54	274	100
Over 18,000	13	26	61	309	100
	$x^2 = 66.9$; 8 df; $P < .001$				
Economic strain:					
Severe	41	27	32	99	100
Moderate	35	32	33	145	100
Little	24	34	42	234	100
None	16	26	58	1,191	100
	$x^2 = 84.8$; 6 df; $P < .001$				

ANXIETY AND DISTRESS CONTROL

We have seen that limited incomes and economic strains contribute to anxiety. Once this psychological state is aroused, how do people deal with it? Drinking, we have been assuming, is one mechanism that may be employed to control anxiety, and the more intense the anxiety, the greater will be the tendency to use alcohol in this way.

In Table 2 we see how anxiety is associated with the use of alcohol for distress control. The table reveals two findings of interest. First, there are many anxious people who do not place drinking in the service of distress management, and this is something we shall consider in depth shortly. The second finding is apparent in spite of the first: the more intensely one experiences anxiety, the more likely one is to use alcohol to control the anxiety.

These results, then, together with earlier findings, suggest the presence of a set of interlocking conditions converging on drinking behavior: because of the crucial

TABLE 2

Level of Anxiety and Use of Alcohol for Control of Distress (Percent)

DISPOSITION TO USE ALCOHOL FOR DISTRESS CONTROL	ANXIETY		
	INTENSE (336)	MODERATE (470)	LOW (865)
Strong	23	14	12
Weak	18	16	16
Minimal	59	70	72
	$x^2 = 24.4$; 4 df; $P < .001$		

Note. Ns in parentheses.

stakes that depend on economic resources, hardship in this area is likely to generate a high level of anxiety, and once they are host to intense anxiety, people become more disposed to use alcohol as a temporary escape from the unpleasant burdens of their distress. Thus drinking has meanings and functions traceable to the life circumstances of people and to the threats to their psychological well-being posed by these circumstances.

ANXIETY AND THE FUNCTIONS OF ALCOHOL: INTERVENING CONDITIONS

We noted concerning Table 2 that in spite of the significant relationship between anxiety and drinking for distress control there is a substantial number of drinkers whose anxieties are at an intense level but who do not use alcohol to allay their tensions. Obviously, drinking has no coping functions for many imbibers who harbor intense anxiety. In order to understand more fully the use of alcohol for the control of distress, therefore, it is necessary to take into account conditions that serve to make drinking an attractive coping technique for some distressed people but not for others.

Some of the factors influencing the ways people attempt to cope with anxiety are rooted in personality. Especially crucial in this regard are personality characteristics that reflect self-attitudes. One of these concerns mastery, which here refers to the extent to which people see themselves, at one extreme, as being in control of the important circumstances of their lives or, at the other extreme, as having to submit fatalistically to external forces. One's standing on this dimension, we submit, can have a great deal to do with where he directs his coping efforts. When confronting distressing circumstances, a person in possession of a sense of mastery will attempt to deal with his distress by manipulating the circumstances. A person lacking this attribute is more likely to rely on devices that help him live with distress and to accept as inevitable the circumstances causing it. Let us see whether drinking may be one such device whose use varies according to a sense of mastery.

Table 3 is arranged to show how the relationship between anxiety and the use of alcohol for distress control is regulated by different conditions of mastery.[3]

TABLE 3

Mastery, Anxiety, and Disposition to Use Alcohol for Distress Control (Percent)

	LIMITED MASTERY			MODERATE MASTERY			GREAT MASTERY		
DISPOSITION TO USE ALCOHOL FOR DISTRESS CONTROL	INTENSE ANXIETY (95)	MODERATE ANXIETY (67)	LOW ANXIETY (111)	INTENSE ANXIETY (169)	MODERATE ANXIETY (229)	LOW ANXIETY (356)	INTENSE ANXIETY (72)	MODERATE ANXIETY (174)	LOW ANXIETY (398)
Strong	39	22	19	17	16	12	14	8	10
Weak	10	13	14	23	18	21	18	16	12
Minimal	51	64	67	60	66	67	68	77	78
	$x^2 = 11.5$; 4 df; $P < .02$ Gamma = .24			$x^2 = 4.6$; 4 df; N.S. Gamma = .09			$x^2 = 5.8$; 4 df; N.S. Gamma = .09		

Note. Ns in parentheses.

TABLE 4

Self-Esteem, Anxiety, and Disposition to Use Alcohol for Distress Control (Percent)

	LOW SELF-ESTEEM			MODERATE SELF-ESTEEM			HIGH SELF-ESTEEM		
DISPOSITION TO USE ALCOHOL FOR DISTRESS CONTROL	INTENSE ANXIETY (114)	MODERATE ANXIETY (83)	LOW ANXIETY (98)	INTENSE ANXIETY (81)	MODERATE ANXIETY (115)	LOW ANXIETY (145)	INTENSE ANXIETY (141)	MODERATE ANXIETY (272)	LOW ANXIETY (622)
Strong	37	29	17	20	20	17	13	7	10
Weak	18	14	26	22	18	15	15	16	14
Minimal	45	57	57	58	62	68	72	77	76
	$x^2 = 12.0$; 4 df; $P < .02$ Gamma = .20			$x^2 = 2.6$; 4 df; N.S. Gamma = .11			$x^2 = 5.2$; 4 df; N.S. Gamma = .02		

Note. Ns in parentheses.

Although we know from Table 2 that this use of alcohol is most apt to be found among people who are intensely anxious, Table 3 shows that the level of anxiety is especially closely related to distress control under conditions of limited mastery. Indeed, the gamma coefficients, which are presented to facilitate the comparison of the three conditional relationships, indicate that anxiety has no significant or appreciable association with drinking for distress control among people possessing either a moderate or a great sense of mastery. When people are both intensely anxious and lacking in mastery, it is readily apparent that they are outstandingly more disposed to use drinking as a coping mechanism than are people with similarly intense anxiety who see their world as amenable to their control. Clearly, the relationship between anxiety and the coping functions of alcohol is mediated by sentiments of personal efficacy.

This kind of sentiment, futhermore, is connected to economic circumstances in a way that has crucial implications for the entire process of distress arousal and coping repertoires. We find, specifically, that the sense of mastery declines as income declines ($P < .001$) and as economic strain rises ($P < .001$). It should also be noted that mastery is even more substantially related to the level of educational attainment than to the level of income, suggesting that mastery probably does not result directly from the possession of money but indirectly from opportunities and achievements that are concomitants of economic resources. Whatever the linkages between economic factors and mastery, the central point of the findings is that the people who are most exposed to conditions provocative of strain and distress may also be those least in possession of an important psychological coping resource. Thus, it is the poor who are most likely to have to bear the burdens of anxiety that result from economic threat, and it is also the poor who are least likely to have the experiences and opportunities that contribute to a sense of mastery, a characteristic that serves to reduce potential reliance on alcohol as a distress management device. These interlocked circumstances impose a double penalty on those with restricted economic resources, first, by exposing them more fully to anxiety-producing conditions and, second, by providing them with fewer psychological resources that would help orient them directly toward the alteration of these conditions. The deprivations of the poor occur on many levels of experience.

Similar results appear with a second self-attitude, self-esteem. For our assessment of self-esteem, we have adopted the Rosenberg scale (1965, pp. 305–7), a measure of the extent to which one holds a positive attitude toward himself. Table 4 shows that the largest proportion of those strongly disposed to put drinking in the service of distress control are those who have both intense anxiety and low self-esteem. Even the disposition of intensely anxious people to use drinking as a coping device diminishes as self-esteem rises. Thus, as in the case of mastery, the relationship between anxiety and drinking practices is greatest among those whose self-esteem is lowest. As the level of self-esteem rises, the magnitude of this relationship shrinks. It is apparent that self-esteem enables one to bear a burden of anxiety without turning to practices that blunt awareness of the burden. Self-esteem may not always succeed in allaying anxiety, but it does appear to help one to tolerate the distress without the same need to escape from an awareness of it that is suggested by the drinking practices of highly anxious people with low self-esteem.

Self-esteem also has a close relationship to the level of income, just as mastery does. Similarly, we find that self-esteem varies closely with educational attainment, as it did with mastery. Consequently, once more the group most lacking in economic resources and the achievement opportunities associated with such resources is also most lacking in a personal characteristic that helps to provide coping options. The very people most entrapped by the process leading to the use of alcohol to control distress are also least in possession of a personality attribute that could aid their discovery of alternative ways of dealing with distress.

Intense anxiety, in sum, is especially likely to result in the use of alcohol as a tranquilizer if a sense of personal efficacy is lacking and self-esteem is low. Each of these conditions, furthermore, is related to the economic circumstances that impinge on people. Indeed, because of the network of interrelationships among the conditions we have been examining, it is probable that they have an overlapping influence on ultimate drinking practices. Through regression analysis, it is possible to evaluate more directly the separate contribution that each of the major conditions we have been examining makes to the dependent variable.

The original zero-order correlation between economic strain and drinking is 0.09. By itself it is rather modest, though significant. But as the mediating conditions are added sequentially to the regression equation, the multiple correlations increase. Thus, when economic strain and anxiety are found together, as we know is likely, their joint correlation with drinking for distress control rises to 0.15. By adding to the regression equation mastery and self-esteem, the two personality resources that have been shown to act as barriers to drinking for the control of anxiety, the multiple correlations are elevated to 0.21 and 0.25, respectively. Two interaction terms, mastery with anxiety and self-esteem with anxiety, provide an additional small increment, together raising the correlation to 0.27. When anxiety is aroused by economic hardship, then, the chances that escape drinking will result are substantially increased; when economic deprivations and anxiety are in the presence of limited mastery and low self-esteem, these chances are further advanced to three times the original correlation.

It is readily apparent from the magnitude of these correlations that conditions other than those examined here also have a major part in accounting for escape drinking. But from those that were considered, it is equally apparent that there is an interlocking set of economic, social, and psychological conditions that both contribute to the arousal of anxiety and channel behavior to drinking as a means of coping with it.

NOTES

1 We would like to acknowledge the assistance of Leslie Edelhoch in analyzing these data. [A description of the sample is presented in Selection 20 by Rosenberg and Pearlin — EDITORS]

2 The remaining six statements are as follows: a drink helps me to relax; I drink to be sociable; a drink helps me when things go wrong; a drink helps me gain self-confidence; a drink helps me when I am lonesome; and I drink when I am bored. Drinking for relaxation and for sociability are so common that responses to these two items have very little variation. It should also be noted that the antecedent conditions for the statements above are for the most part different from those underlying responses to the two statements used in our index of distress control.

3 The measure of mastery is derived from seven items, each responded to by "strongly agree," "somewhat agree," "somewhat disagree," or "strongly disagree." The scores ranged from 4 to 28, with people scoring from 4 to 17 classified as having limited mastery, from 18 to 23 as having moderate mastery, and from 24 to 28 as having great mastery. The seven items are: There is really no way I can solve some of the problems I have; Sometimes I feel that I'm being pushed around in life; I have little control over the things that happen to me; I can do just about anything I really set my mind to do; I often feel helpless in dealing with the problems of life; What happens to me in the future mostly depends on me; and There is little I can do to change many of the important things in my life.

REFERENCES

Alexander, F.

1963 "Alcohol and behavior disorder." Pp. 130–41 in Salvatore P. Lucia, (ed.), Alcohol and Civilization. New York: McGraw-Hill.

Bales, R. F.

1945 "Cultural differences in rates of alcoholism." Quarterly Journal of Studies on Alcohol 6: 480–99.

Cahalan, D., I. Cisin, and H. M. Crossley

1969 American Drinking Practices. New Brunswick, N.J.: Rutgers Center of Alcohol Studies.

Chavetz, M. E., H. W. Demone, Jr., and H. Soloman

1962 Alcoholism and Society. New York: Oxford University Press.

Derogatis, L. R., R. S. Lipman, L. Covi, and K. Rickles

1971 "Neurotic symptom dimensions." Archives of General Psychiatry 24: 454–64.

Greenberg, L. A.

1963 "Alcohol and emotional behavior." Pp. 109–21 in Salvatore P. Lucia, (ed.), Alcohol and Civilization. New York: McGraw-Hill.

Horton, D.

1943 "The function of alcohol in primitive societies: a cross-cultural study." Quarterly Journal of Studies on Alcohol 4: 199–320.

Lipman, R. S., K. Rickles, L. Covi, R. Derogatis, and E. H. Uhlenhuth

1969 "Factors of symptom distress." Archives of General Psychiatry 21: 328–38.

Pearlin, L. I.

1959 "Social and personal stress and escape television viewing." Public Opinion Quarterly 23: 256–59.

Riley, J. W., Jr. and C. F. Marden

1947 "The social pattern of alcohol drinking." Quarterly Journal of Studies on Alcohol 8: 265–73.

Rosenberg, M.

1965 Society and the Adolescent Self-Image. Princeton, N.J.: Princeton University Press.

U.S. Bureau of the Census

1972 Census of Housing: 1970 Block Statistics. Financial Report HC(3)–68, Chicago, Illinois-Northwestern Indiana Urbanized Area. Washington, D.C.: U.S. Government Printing Office.

Washburne, C.

1955 "Alcohol, self and the group." Quarterly Journal of Studies on Alcohol 17: 108–23.

Homosexual Identity: Commitment, Adjustment, and Significant Others

Sue Kiefer Hammersmith

Martin S. Weinberg

39

Central to the symbolic interactionist perspective is the notion that through the social interaction in which they engage, people seek to establish and maintain stable identities and to evaluate them positively (Schwartz and Stryker, 1971). It has also been pointed out that a person accomplishes this by commitment to "socially recognized and meaningful categories" and that one's identity may be attained by commitment not only to "nondeviant" categories but to "deviant" ones as well (Cohen, 1965).

With regard to this conception of "deviant identity," several points become salient. The deviant, like the so-called conformist, is seen as engaged in establishing his identity and receiving validation through social interaction. Thus, deviant identities may reflect not personal disintegration or failure, as is often supposed, but rather success in establishing an identity. We would also expect that the more committed one is to any socially meaningful category, even if it is generally evaluated as deviant, the more "settled" the question of identity will be and thus the more stable his self-conception.

Source: Sue Kiefer Hammersmith and Martin S. Weinberg, "Homosexual Identity: Commitment, Adjustment, and Significant Others," Sociometry 36 (1973): 56–79.

Symbolic interactionism also suggests that one seeks to evaluate himself positively and that one derives his self-evaluation from incorporating the perceived evaluations of "significant others" (Schwartz and Stryker, 1971). We would further expect, then, that the more committed a person is to any category of identity (compared to those not so committed), the more his significant others will support such an identity. Thus, the easier it will be for him to incorporate a positive self-conception and to attain psychological well-being.

With regard to deviant identities, Schwartz, Fearn and Stryker (1966) tested some of these notions with a sample of emotionally disturbed children. Using therapists' prognoses for cure as an indicant of the child's commitment to the emotionally disturbed role (poorest prognosis representing greatest commitment), they found those more committed to the deviant role (1) had the most stable and positive self-concepts, and (2) seemed primarily influenced in their self-concept by those most supportive of their deviance (i.e., the therapist) while those less committed seemed influenced by others as well. It must be noted, however, that the measure of commitment is very indirect and that the conclusions are based on a sample of only nine children with a poor prognosis for cure.

This article is a continuation of Schwartz, Fearn, and Stryker's work. Our intention is to demonstrate how symbolic interactionist models can be explicitly formulated and systematically tested. This is in contradistinction to the more common practice of leaving one's model implicit, and the practice illustrated by Schwartz et al. of simultaneously implying a number of different causal models. Hence this paper can be regarded as an exercise explicitly delineating and then statistically testing the various causal models that are implicit in the hypotheses which Schwartz et al. propose.

With data from a large sample of male homosexuals in three Western societies, we test the following general hypothesis and a number of causal models associated with it: commitment to a deviant identity is positively correlated with a report of significant others supportive of that identity, a stable, positive self-concept, and good psychological adjustment; by the same token, those not so fully committed have less support, less stable and positive self-concepts, and more symptoms of psychological strain.

HOMOSEXUAL IDENTITY: HYPOTHESES AND MODELS

What is meant by commitment to homosexuality? In Western society, it is taken for granted that children will become heterosexual adults and that their lives will be ordered accordingly. Family and friends operate on the seemingly natural assumption that a child will develop heterosexual interests, date, and settle into family life. In this milieu the child also sees his future in these terms.

Surely few if any homosexuals, then, focus in their youth on homosexuality as their goal and thereupon set about to achieve that identity. Rather, it would seem, homosexuality is a sexual orientation that emerges despite contrary social expectations and cultural condemnation and which, if not merely a transitory stage, the person must reckon with as a stable part of his social and psychological being.

It has been noted that the young homosexual experiences guilt and shame, anxiety, depression and feelings of worthlessness, but that he is largely relieved of these feelings when he "accepts" his homosexuality. Association with other homosexuals, who take the particular sexual orientation to be a matter of course, often contributes to this process (cf. Weinberg, 1970a; Weinberg and Williams, 1974).

Accepting one's homosexuality may involve redefining one's self as a homosexual rather than as a temporarily variant heterosexual (cf. Dank, 1971). It may involve revising one's expectations for the future and giving up attempts to approximate a heterosexual role by dating, marrying, or in other ways upholding a pretense of heterosexuality.

The person who defines himself as homosexual may still regret the identity. The homosexual may resign himself to his homosexuality as a fact of life and yet feel that he would really rather be "a heterosexual."

One's identity has a future as well as a present, underlying not only today's interaction, but also future interaction. It is, therefore, important to examine the person's satisfaction with his present identity as a future identity—in short, his commitment to that identity. The highly committed homosexual would by definition elect to remain that way if given a choice between homosexuality and heterosexuality. Hence the highly committed homosexual can be considered as "settled down" in his deviant identity. Thus, we would expect homosexual commitment to be positively associated with stability of self-concept. Furthermore, since commitment involves a preference for that identity, we would expect it to be positively associated with self-esteem. In the same way, we would expect homosexual commitment to be negatively associated with symptoms of psychological maladjustment such as anxiety and depression.

Finally, we are interested in the extent to which others support the homosexual in his deviant identity. Schwartz, Fearn, and Stryker (1966) imply that the highly committed deviant evaluates the significance of others' opinions of him, in light of that commitment, in order to perceive maximum support for it—viz., to devalue the opinions of others who are or would be intolerant of the deviance, and likewise to attach more importance to any who support it. Conversely, of course, it could be argued that the deviant whose significant others support him in that identity is more likely, because of this support, to become highly committed to that identity.

We would suggest, however, that except for fellow homosexuals, the significant others of the homosexual rarely support that identity in the sense of encouraging it. In general, parents, friends, relatives, and other associates at most amicably accept his homosexuality (and are so perceived by the homosexual). This may take the form of (1) efforts to relate normally in realms where sexual orientation is not directly relevant, and (2) withdrawal of pointed or subtle pressure regarding the expectation of heterosexuality in other realms.

We are proposing then, that commitment to a deviant identity indicates self-affirmation, hence adjustment, on the part of the deviant and that it is associated with social validation, or support, of that identity by others. Thus we hypothesized that commitment to homosexuality would be:

1. Positively related to stability of self-concept.
2. Positively related to self-esteem.

3. Negatively related to symptoms of maladjustment (such as anxiety symptoms or depression).

4. Positively related to perceived support of significant others.

These hypotheses, it must be noted, suggest correlational rather than causal relationships. Indeed, many different causal relationships could produce the hypothesized correlations between psychological adjustment, homosexual commitment, and support. (While *perceived* support is not to be considered equivalent to *actual* support, the former is hereafter referred to as "support" for the sake of brevity. In others words, we recognize that perceptions of support can be inaccurate due to misreadings, projecting one's own increased acceptance of homosexuality, etc.) A number of models underlying the hypothesized correlations are suggested by the symbolic interactionist perspective. In presenting and discussing these models, the term *adjustment* is used to refer to high stability of self-concept and self-esteem, and to low anxiety symptoms and depression.

$$\text{(M1) } X_1\text{: Commitment} \xrightarrow{+} X_2\text{: Adjustment} \xrightarrow{+} X_3\text{: Support}$$

It may be suggested that commitment to an identity positively influences adjustment and that adjustment influences the choice of significant others who are supportive. The logic producing this model is roughly as follows. The search for a socially meaningful, continuing identity is basic to the human process. Until or unless one settles upon such an identity, one suffers anxiety and uncertainty. This anxiety is motivational in the person's continuing search for an identity.

As one becomes committed to a deviant identity (i.e., as one settles upon that identity as the present and future foundation for self-regard and relating to others), anxiety about identity decreases. Having found a socially meaningful identity, the deviant's self-concept stabilizes; he finds it intrinsically rewarding to have an established identity, and his self-esteem and psychological adjustment increase.

As part of this "settling in" process, the deviant, now more sure of himself, elicits validation from his social environment. This is accomplished by devaluating the opinions of those who do not support the deviant identity and by attaching importance to the opinions of those who do support it.

According to the first model, the less committed deviant, by contrast, is socially and psychologically less sure of himself and his worth. Anxious about and unstable in his identity, he reaches in many directions for social validation, including evaluating as significant the opinions of those who do not support the deviant identity.

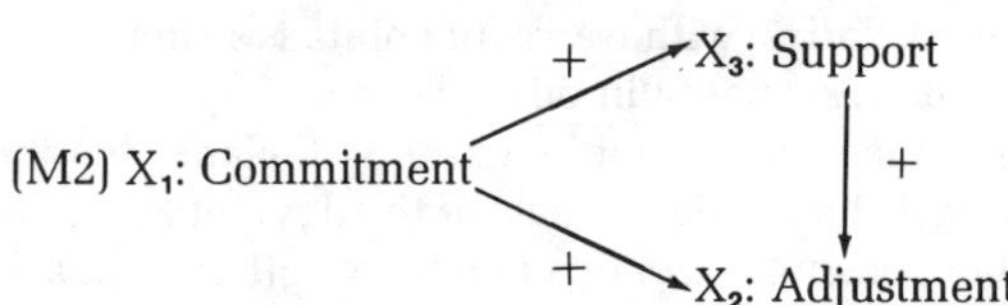

Again emphasizing the independence of the person's commitment to a deviant identity, the second model suggests that commitment increases psychological adjustment—i.e., that it increases self-esteem and stability of self-concept and decreases anxiety and depression. The rationale for this assertion was explored in the discussion of Model 1.

Likewise, the highly committed homosexual is seen to focus on those who most support that identity, consequently increasing psychological adjustment by finding validation. Thus, for the highly committed deviant an improvement in adjustment is obtained both by his commitment and by his success in finding support from others.

$$\text{(M3) } X_3\text{: Support} \xrightarrow{+} X_1\text{: Adjustment} \xrightarrow{+} X_1\text{: Commitment}$$

The third model highlights the importance of social validation in making an identity rewarding or not, suggesting that support of significant others influences psychological adjustment, which in turn influences commitment. This model, one of the models implicit in the Schwartz, Fearn, and Stryker study, suggests that the person derives his self-concept from others' reactions to him. If others support the deviant identity, then the deviant's adjustment improves as he (a) is relieved of the anxiety accruing from an "unsettled" identity and (b) experiences the pleasure intrinsic to an identity and its validation. Through such positive reinforcement, he becomes highly committed to the deviant identity.

If, however, he perceives the people he considers important as questioning the validity and worth of the identity, the deviant is likely to remain in an identification limbo, unstable in his self-concept, unsure of his worth, not highly committed to that identity.

Thus, whereas the first, voluntaristic model suggests that the significance a person attaches to another's evaluation of him *follows from* commitment, this model suggests that the significance one attaches to various others' opinions is largely given *before* he settles into an identity, and that significant others' opinions, as the person perceives them, influences the degree of commitment to that identity. Thus, commitment to a deviant identity, which in the first model is the social psychological determinant of electing significant others who are supportive, is, in this model, the product of support of significant others.

$$\text{(M4) } X_3\text{: Support} \xrightarrow{+} X_1\text{: Commitment} \xrightarrow{+} X_2\text{: Adjustment}$$

It also could be argued that support of significant others directly influences commitment. If significant others support one's deviant identity as it develops, or if he can find new supportive others whose opinions are respected, the deviant is likely to become highly committed to his deviant identity. Thus, he settles into that identity, which in turn produces higher self-esteem, stability of self-concept, and psychological well-being. If significant others do not support the identity, the deviant regrets that identity, has low commitment to it, and consequently suffers with feelings of maladjustment. In Model 4, then, deviant commitment intervenes between support of significant others and psychological adjustment.

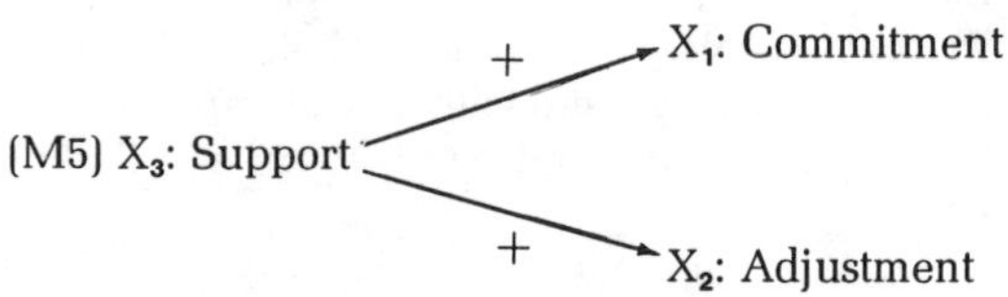

One could argue, quite simply, that support of the deviant's significant others determines both his level of commitment to homosexuality and, independently, his adjustment. That is to say, the deviant's perception of significant others as supportive influences positively the degree of satisfaction with, and commitment to, the identity. Independently, Model 5 proposes, the deviant's perception of his significant others as supportive also increases his adjustment. This model indicates that neither is commitment the result of adjustment, nor adjustment the result of commitment. Rather, it suggests that one's adjustment and commitment both follow, somewhat deterministically, from support by significant others.

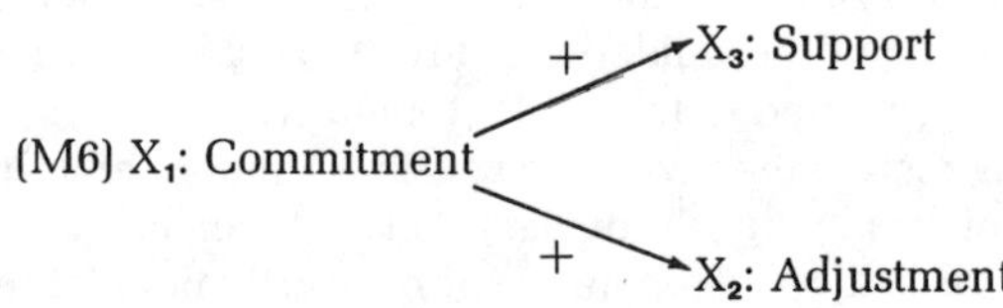

Finally, it could be suggested that commitment is the crucial factor that influences, independently, both the validation one elicits from one's social environment—i.e., significant others who are supportive—and one's adjustment. This suggests, again, that as a person becomes more committed to his homosexual identity, he tends to attach more importance to the opinions of those who are supportive of him in that identity and less to those who are not.

Model 6 also proposes that the more committed homosexual is better adjusted because he has settled into an identity with which he is satisfied; it suggests, however, that support of his significant others does not directly affect the homosexual's psychological adjustment or his homosexual commitment.

METHOD

A test of these models is provided with data from a larger study on the social and psychological adjustment of homosexuals in which questionnaires were completed by 2,497 respondents from the United States, the Netherlands, and Denmark (Weinberg and Williams, 1974). These particular countries were included in the study for several reasons. First, the larger study is oriented around social reaction theory, or more specifically, how different degrees of social rejection affect the homosexual's social and psychological adjustment. Weinberg and Williams provide data which demonstrate that the Netherlands and Denmark are more tolerant of homosexuality than is the United States. Since societal differences in social reaction to homosexuality are not a focus of this paper, data from homosexuals in the two European countries are used for purposes of replication (as they also are in the larger study). Finally, since Dutch and Danish represent different linguistic traditions, the probability of obtaining replicated findings due to an artifact of translation is minimized by including both countries.

Sample

Respondents were contacted in each society through mail organizations (organizations whose purpose is the betterment of the homosexual situation and whose contact with members is primarily by mail), private homosexual social clubs, and bars that cater primarily to homosexuals.

The questionnaires were distributed in the following ways. Questionnaires were mailed to 2,700 persons on the mailing list of the Mattachine Society of New York, a mail organization, the stated goal of which is "changes in the prevailing attitudes of society toward homosexuality and the removal of legal sanctions and public discrimination against homosexuals." Females on the mailing list were omitted. Approximately 950 of the addressees resided in New York City; another 350 resided in New York State, Connecticut, or New Jersey. The remaining persons represented 44 states. An additional 200 questionnaires were mailed to San Francisco residents on the mailing list of the Mattachine Society of San Francisco.

Two hundred fifty-eight questionnaires were handed out at the Society for Individual Rights (SIR) in San Francisco. This organization is engaged in many of the same activities as Mattachine, although it functions more as a social club than does the Mattachine Society. SIR's premises are used for dances, relaxation, shows, and discussion groups, and it conducts various athletic activities and participates in various community programs. A questionnaire was given to every male at the club or at a club function during a period of ten days. Fifty questionnaires were also distributed among males attending private homosexual clubs in Manhattan.

A questionnaire was handed to every seventh male in a random sample of 20 homosexual bars in Manhattan, with 225 questionnaires being so distributed. Two hundred thirty-four questionnaires were similarly distributed in a random sample of 25 homosexual bars in San Francisco. Each of these distributions took place during two consecutive weekends.

Altogether, 3,667 questionnaires were distributed in the United States, of which 1,117 were completed and returned. The response rate, computed with a correction for the number of persons receiving more than one questionnaire and for undeliverable mailed questionnaires, is 38.7 percent.

European respondents were obtained in a similar manner. Questionnaires were mailed to every other person on the mailing list of *Cultuuren Ontspanningcentrum* (COC) in Amsterdam and to every person on the mailing list of *Forbundet* in Copenhagen. These are mail organizations similar to the Mattachine Society in the United States. Altogether, 1,859 questionnaires were sent out in the Netherlands and 962 in Denmark. Females were excluded.

In Amsterdam, a questionnaire was handed to every male at the COC club over a period of nine days. In this way, 547 questionnaires were given out. In Copenhagen, a similar procedure was employed for handing out 558 questionnaires to males in attendance at *Forbundet's* two clubs: Club 48 and the Pink Club.

Finally, the questionnaire was handed to every male in all 30 homosexual bars in Amsterdam. As in the United States, the distribution was done in two consecutive weekends. This resulted in 388 questionnaires being distributed. The same procedure was utilized for handing out 396 questionnaires in Copenhagen's 15 bars.

Of the 2,794 questionnaires distributed in the Netherlands, 1,077 were returned; the corrected response rate is 45.1 percent. In Denmark, only 303 questionnaires were returned of the 1,916 which were estimated to have been distributed, providing an apparent corrected response rate of 24.2 percent.

In summary, questionnaires were completed and returned by 1,117 respondents in the United States, 1,077 in the Netherlands, and 303 in Denmark.

While it may be argued that samples from these sources are not representative of the entire male homosexual population, they do seem representative of those homosexuals whom the researcher is likely to obtain from nonclinical and noninstitutional sources with regard to the psychological scales used in this paper (see Weinberg, 1970b).

Measures

From the 145-item questionnaire, the items listed below were used as indicants of our variables. Except those items for which other response categories and values are presented, all items had these response categories: strongly agree, agree, not sure, disagree, and strongly disagree. Values of 1 through 5 were attached to these categories according to the direction of the item, so that a higher value indicates higher homosexual commitment, stability of self-concept, self-esteem, anxiety symptoms, or depression. The score for each scale was obtained by summing the values attached to the responses for each item in that scale. The reliability of the scale was tested in terms of coefficient alpha, which provides a measure of internal consistency taking into account the number of items. Its computation is a generalized form of the Kuder and Richardson formulas 20 and 21 (Cronbach, 1951).

I. Homosexual Commitment (Alpha Coefficient = 0.78):
   A. I wish I were not homosexual.
   B. I would not want to give up my homosexuality even if I could.

II. Stability of Self-Concept (Alpha Coefficient = 0.70):
   A. I have noticed that my ideas about myself seem to change very quickly.
   B. I feel that nothing, or almost nothing, can change the opinion I currently hold of myself.
   C. Some days I have a very good opinion of myself; other days I have a very poor opinion of myself.
   D. Do you ever find that on one day you have one opinion of yourself and on another day you have a different opinion? (Yes, this happens often, 1; yes, this happens sometimes, 2; yes, but this rarely happens, 3; no, this never happens, 4.)

E. Does the opinion you have of yourself tend to change a good deal? (Changes a great deal, 1; changes somewhat, 2; changes very little, 3; does not change at all, 4.)

III. Self-Esteem (Alpha Coefficient = 0.86):
A. I feel that I have a number of good qualities.
B. I take a positive attitude toward myself.
C. On the whole, I am satisfied with myself.
D. I feel that I'm a person of worth, at least on an equal plane with others.
E. All in all, I am inclined to feel that I am a failure.
F. I certainly feel useless at times.
G. I am able to do things as well as most other people.
H. I wish I could have more respect for myself.
I. I feel I do not have much to be proud of.
J. At times I think I am no good at all.

IV. Anxiety Symptoms (Alpha Coefficient = 0.85):
A. Do you ever have trouble getting to sleep or staying asleep? (Nearly all the time, 4; pretty often, 3; not very much, 2; never, 1.)
B. Have you ever been bothered by nervousness, feeling fidgety and tense? (Nearly all the time, 4; pretty often, 3; not very much, 2; never, 1.)
C. Are you ever troubled by headaches or pains in the head? (Nearly all the time, 4; pretty often, 3; not very much, 2; never, 1.)
D. Do you have loss of appetite? (Nearly all the time, 4; pretty often, 3; not very much, 2; never, 1.)
E. How often are you bothered by having an upset stomach? (Nearly all the time, 4; pretty often, 3; not very much, 2; never, 1.)
F. Do you find it difficult to get up in the morning? (Nearly all the time, 4; pretty often, 3; not very much, 2; never, 1.)
G. Have you ever been bothered by shortness of breath when you were not exercising or working hard? (Many times, 4; sometimes, 3; hardly ever, 2; never, 1.)
H. Have you ever been bothered by your heart beating hard? (Many times, 4; sometimes, 3; hardly ever, 2; never, 1.)
I. Do you ever drink more than you should? (Many times, 4; sometimes, 3; hardly ever, 2; never, 1.)
J. Have you ever had spells of dizziness? (Many times, 4; sometimes, 3; hardly ever, 2; never, 1.)
K. Are you ever bothered by nightmares? (Many times, 4; sometimes, 3; hardly ever, 2; never, 1.)
L. Do you tend to lose weight when you have something important bothering you? (Many times, 4; sometimes, 3; hardly ever, 2; never, 1.)
M. Do your hands ever tremble enough to bother you? (Many times, 4; sometimes, 3; hardly ever, 2; never, 1.)
N. Are you troubled by your hands sweating so that you feel damp and clammy? (Many times, 4; sometimes, 3; hardly ever, 2; never, 1.)
O. Have there ever been times when you couldn't take care of things because you just couldn't get going? (Many times, 4; sometimes, 3; hardly ever, 2; never, 1.)

V. Depression (Alpha Coefficient = 0.88):
   A. I am not as happy as others seem to be.
   B. In general, I feel in low spirits most of the time.
   C. I get a lot of fun out of life.
   D. I often feel downcast and dejected.
   E. On the whole, I think I am quite a happy person.
   F. Taking all things together, how would you say things are these days—would you say you are very happy, 1; pretty happy, 2; not too happy, 3; very unhappy, 4?

The measure of support of significant others was constructed using two sets of items. In the first set, the respondent was presented with this list of persons: mother, father, brother(s), sister(s), most of your aunts and uncles, best male heterosexual friend, most other male heterosexual friends, wife, best female heterosexual friend, most other female heterosexual friends, most of your work associates, your employer, most of your neighbors, heterosexuals in general. Where such a relationship exists (or existed before the listed party's death), the respondent was asked to rate each of the person(s) on a seven-point scale as to how important it is to him that each has (or had, if deceased) a "good" opinion of him; the scale ran from "1" which signifies "very important" to "7" which signifies "very unimportant."

In the second set of items, the respondent was presented with the same list and asked how each of the persons would respond, or has responded, to finding out about the respondent's homosexuality—whether they are or would be accepting, understanding but not accepting, tolerant but not understanding, intolerant but not rejecting, or rejecting. For each respondent, the measure of support of significant others (those categories rated "1" or "2" in the first set of items) who are rated as accepting of the respondent's homosexuality was derived by computing the proportion of significant others.

Given the sampling sources (homosexual bars, clubs, and mail organizations), we may infer that, by and large, the subjects all receive some degree of support for their homosexual identity from other homosexuals. We have no measure of this support; thus, our data deal only with the support which the subject receives from other significant persons.

Analysis

Zero-order and partial Pearsonian correlation coefficients, regression coefficients, beta weights, and Fs were computed to test the adequacy of the various models previously presented.

RESULTS

As hypothesized, commitment to homosexuality is found to be positively related to stability of self-concept and to self-esteem, and negatively related to measures of psychological maladjustment (Table 1). Thus, the association which Schwartz, Fearn, and Stryker found between commitment to a deviant role and a stable, positive self-concept is replicated among adult male homosexuals in the United States and the Netherlands. (For Denmark, the correlations were in the predicted direction; due to the weaker correlations and smaller sample size for Denmark, however, statistical significance was obtained only for self-esteem and depression.)

TABLE 1

Zero-order Correlation between Commitment (c) and Adjustment (a)

	r_{ca}		
MEASURE OF ADJUSTMENT	*UNITED STATES*	*NETHERLANDS*	*DENMARK*
Stability of self-concept	.30‡	.21‡	.14
Self-esteem	.35‡	.32‡	.29‡
Anxiety symptoms	–.18‡	–.13‡	–.12
Depression	–.36‡	–.39‡	–.32‡

NOTE: * indicates statistical significance at the 0.05 level, † at the 0.01 level, and ‡ at the 0.001 level.

Our models delineate adjustment as the result of either commitment, support of significant others, or a combination of the two. In order to determine whether the zero-order correlation between commitment and adjustment is produced either entirely or in part by support of significant others, the zero-order correlations

TABLE 2

Zero-order and Partial Correlations between Commitment (c) and Adjustment (a), Controlling for Support of Significant Others (s)

UNITED STATES		
Measure of Adjustment	r_{ca}	$r_{ca\text{-}s}$
Stability of self-concept	.30‡	.31‡
Self-esteem	.35‡	.34‡
Anxiety symptoms	–.18‡	–.17‡
Depression	–.36‡	–.35‡
NETHERLANDS		
Measure of Adjustment	r_{ca}	$r_{ca\text{-}s}$
Stability of self-concept	.21‡	.20‡
Self-esteem	.32‡	.30‡
Anxiety symptoms	–.13‡	–.12‡
Depression	–.39‡	–.37‡
DENMARK		
Measure of Adjustment	r_{ca}	$r_{ca\text{-}s}$
Stability of self-concept	.14	.13
Self-esteem	.29‡	.32‡
Anxiety symptoms	–.12	–.10
Depression	–.32‡	–.38‡

NOTE: * indicates statistical significance at the 0.05 level, † at the 0.01 level, and ‡ at the 0.001 level.

are compared with partial correlations which control for support of significant others (Table 2).

If adjustment is a direct product of commitment only, as specified by Models 1, 4, and 6, then we would expect the correlation between commitment and adjustment not to be affected by controlling for the support of others. (Figure 1 contains a composite of the models.) If, alternatively, commitment and adjustment are both independent products of support of significant others (M5), then the correlation between commitment and adjustment should disappear or substantially decrease when support is controlled. Likewise, if the relationship between commitment and adjustment in any way involves the support of others as an intervening variable (as in M2), then the relationship between commitment and adjustment should disappear or substantially decrease when support is controlled.

Referring to Table 2, we see that the partial r's between commitment and the various measures of adjustment, controlling for support of significant others, do not differ significantly from the zero-order ones. Thus we see that the models which hold support of significant others to be the determining background variable of commitment and adjustment, or an intervening variable between them, are not supported (viz., M5 and M2). Rather, commitment and adjustment are related directly, positively, and independently of support of significant others (as suggested by Models 1, 3, 4, and 6).

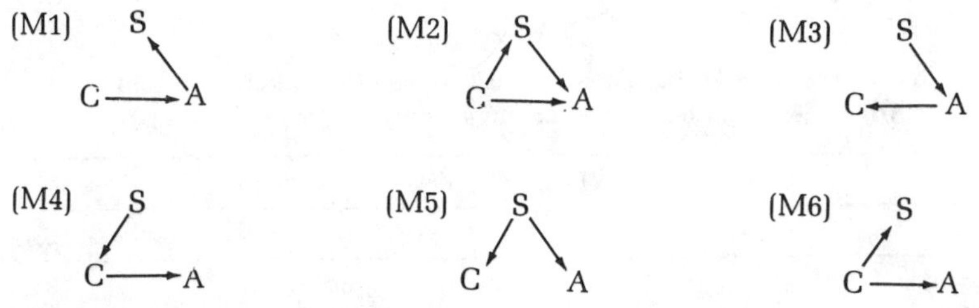

Fig. 1. Graphic summary of the models tested where C indicates homosexual commitment; S, support of significant others; A, psychological adjustment, viz., high self-esteem and stability of self-concept and low anxiety symptoms and depression.

A number of models (M2, M3, M5, and the Schwartz, Fearn, and Stryker study) contain the common-sense assumption that persons with more supportive significant others will be more psychologically adjusted because of it, but this assumption is not given much support by our data. For such a direct relationship, the partial correlation between adjustment and support, controlling for commitment, would have to meet two criteria. (1) It would have to be statistically significant (a probability level of 0.05 was used). (2) The actual value of the correlation would have to be large enough to be substantively important (any coefficient less than 0.10 was considered negligible). Schwartz, Fearn, and Stryker infer this direct relationship among emotionally disturbed children. But in general, the partial correlations in Table 3 show the relationship between adjustment and support, controlling for commitment, to be negligible among homosexual males in each country.

TABLE 3

Zero-order and Partial Correlations Between Support of Significant Others (s) and Adjustment (a), Controlling for Commitment (c)

UNITED STATES		
Measure of Adjustment	r_{sa}	$r_{sa\text{-}c}$
Stability of self-concept	.05	.02
Self-esteem	.15‡	.08‡
Anxiety symptoms	–.07*	–.03
Depression	–.15‡	–.08*
NETHERLANDS		
Measure of Adjustment	r_{sa}	$r_{sa\text{-}c}$
Stability of self-concept	.07*	.03
Self-esteem	.22‡	.07*
Anxiety symptoms	–.08*	–.05
Depression	–.17‡	–.11†
DENMARK		
Measure of Adjustment	r_{sa}	$r_{sa\text{-}c}$
Stability of self-concept	.04	–.07
Self-esteem	.17*	.11
Anxiety symptoms	–.11	.13
Depression	–.27‡	–.22†

NOTE: * indicates statistical significance at the 0.05 level, † at the 0.01 level, and ‡ at the 0.001 level.

This indicates that generally, among male homosexuals, support and adjustment are not related directly (as proposed by M1, M2, M3, M5, and by Schwartz, Fearn, and Stryker). Rather, support seems to influence adjustment only through the intervening variable of commitment. The common-sense assumption that support promotes adjustment is thus shown in this instance to be incorrect—viz., support enhances adjustment only to the extent that it increases the homosexual's commitment to his deviant identity.

Thus, any direct effect of the support of significant others on psychological adjustment may have to be regarded as specific to those situations and deviant identities where it is found. Such an effect may be contingent on a number of factors. For example, whether or not a significant other supports one's deviant identity may be more consequential for psychological adjustment when that identity is more relevant to the particular relationship with the other and when the relationship encompasses more of the deviant's everyday life.

We would expect, then, that the therapist's support or nonsupport of an institutionalized emotionally disturbed child's identity would be more important for psychological adjustment than the support or nonsupport of one's homosexual identity by the significant others we list. First, the deviant identity is the very focus of the therapist-child relationship. Thus support or nonsupport of the deviant identity is more likely to be expressed or perceived in any particular encounter between child and therapist than between a homosexual and the significant others we consider.

Second, the relationship between a homosexual and various significant others may be of relatively narrow scope. Thus, his parents' opinion of him may be very important to a homosexual. Yet if relatively little time is spent with them (for instance, because of geographical separation), the parents' acceptance or rejection of their son's homosexuality may not affect his general psychological adjustment very much. For the institutionally confined child, however, the therapist's support of the child's emotionally disturbed identity may have many more consequences for psychological adjustment, as that relationship encompasses, or in large part determines much more of the child's daily life.

M1 proposes alternatively that adjustment determines the selective evaluation of others as significant. Again, however, the negligible partial correlations between support and our measures of adjustment (controlling for commitment) indicate no direct relationship between support and adjustment, thereby disconfirming M1 as well.

Moreover, the weak zero-order correlations between support of significant others and adjustment decrease even further when commitment is controlled. This indicates that, for our sample at least, support and adjustment are both related to commitment, but are not directly related to each other—i.e., that commitment is either an intervening variable or a background variable affecting both support and adjustment, as suggested by M4 and M6.

As hypothesized, commitment to homosexuality is positively related to support of significant others, with a zero-order r of 0.22 in the United States and 0.21 in the Netherlands and Denmark. All the models predict that commitment and support of significant others will be positively related. Some models (M1 and M3) suggest, however, that adjustment is an important intervening variable. The deterministic version of such a model (M3) suggests that if support of significant others is high, psychological comfort in the deviant role is high, and therefore, there will be high commitment to that role (as suggested by Schwartz, Fearn, and Stryker). The more voluntaristic version (M1) suggests that once a person has chosen an identity, psychological comfort increases, and that in order to reinforce his certainty in this identity, the person thereafter evaluates more highly the opinions of those who support, and less highly the opinions of those who do not support, that identity.

We can again test the adequacy of models M1 and M3 by seeing if the relationship between commitment and support is significantly affected when we control for adjustment, as it would be if adjustment were an intervening variable (Table 4).

In none of the three countries does the relationship between commitment and support of significant others disappear or significantly decrease when we control for adjustment. Again, rejection of M1 and M3 is indicated, along with the conclusion that as far as the variables included in this study are concerned, commitment is related to support of significiant others directly, and only directly.

In sum, then, commitment is directly related to both adjustment and support but the latter variables do not directly affect each other in any significant way. Thus, based on data from three countries, it appears that, among the models proposed, the Support of Significant Others-Commitment-Adjustment Model (M4)

TABLE 4

Zero-order and Partial Correlations Between Commitment (c) and Support of Significant Others (s), Controlling for Adjustment (a)

Measure of Adjustment	r_{cs}	$r_{cs\text{-}a}$
UNITED STATES		
Stability of self-concept	.22‡	.21‡
Self-esteem	.22‡	.17‡
Anxiety symptoms	.22‡	.21‡
Depression	.22‡	.18‡
NETHERLANDS		
Stability of self-concept	.21‡	.20‡
Self-esteem	.21‡	.18‡
Anxiety symptoms	.21‡	.20‡
Depression	.21‡	.15‡
DENMARK		
Stability of self-concept	.21†	.22†
Self-esteem	.21†	.17*
Anxiety symptoms	.21†	.23†
Depression	.21†	.13

NOTE: * indicates statistical significance at the 0.05 level, † at the 0.01 level, and ‡ at the 0.001 level.

and the Voluntaristic Independent Effects Model (M6) best represent the probable relationships between homosexual commitment, adjustment, and support of significant others (Figure 2).

(M4) S, + / (S → C), C —+→ A

(M6) S, + / (C → S), C —+→ A

Fig. 2. **Models supported which relate support of significant others for the deviant identity (S), commitment to that identity (C), and psychological adjustment (A).**

Our data provide no basis for preferring one of these models over the other, i.e., we cannot determine the direction of the relationship between commitment and support (cf. Blalock, 1972: 445–448). It may be that each model best represents a particular type of homosexual. Indeed, although we could not deal with nonrecursive models in this paper, it seems likely that both processes are at work—that the level of homosexual commitment is determined in part by perceived support of one's significant others, while the evaluation of various others as being significant or not depends in part on one's commitment. It is, in fact, just such feedback mechanisms that are suggested by symbolic interactionism.

SUMMARY

A number of models suggested by the symbolic interactionist perspective relating deviant commitment, psychological adjustment, and perceived support of the deviant identity by significant others were tested with data gathered from a large sample of male homosexuals from the United States, the Netherlands, and Denmark. Homosexual commitment was found to be positively related to psychological adjustment and support of significant others. Adjustment and support were not found to be directly related to each other and were found to be only weakly related through commitment.

Of the six models tested, two were supported. Both of these models propose that, for homosexuals, commitment—i.e., having "settled into" a homosexual identity—leads to better psychological adjustment as indicated by a more stable, positive self-image, fewer anxiety symptoms, and less depression. In addition, one model proposes that support of his homosexual identity by significant others positively influences the homosexual's commitment to that identity. Alternatively, the other supported model suggests that the homosexual's commitment influences his selective evaluation of the importance he attaches to others' opinions of him. The model implicit in the Schwartz, Fearn, and Stryker work on emotionally disturbed children in which psychological adjustment follows from support was not corroborated by this study.

REFERENCES

Blalock, Hubert M., Jr.
1972 Social Statistics, 2nd ed. New York: McGraw-Hill.
Cohen, Albert K.
1965 "The sociology of the deviant act." American Sociological Review 30 (Feburary): 5-14.
Cronbach, L. J.
1951 "Coefficient alpha and the internal structure of tests." Psychometrika 16: 297–334.
Dank, Barry M.
1971 "Coming out in the gay world." Psychiatry 34 (May): 180–97.
Schwartz, M., G. F. N. Fearn, and S. Stryker
1966 "A note on self conception and the emotionally disturbed role." Sociometry 29 (September): 300–5.
Schwartz, Michael and Sheldon Stryker
1971 Deviance, Selves and Others. Washington: American Sociological Association.
Weinberg, Martin S.
1970a "The male homosexual: age-related variations in social and psychological characteristics." Social Problems 17 (Spring): 527–37.
1970b "Homosexual samples: differences and similarities." The Journal of Sex Research 6 (November): 312–25.
Weinberg, Martin S. and Colin J. Williams
1974 Male Homosexuals: Their Problems and Adaptations. New York: Oxford University Press.

SIX

DEFENSE MECHANISMS

One of the outstanding products of Freud's genius was his discovery of the so-called defense mechanisms. But although Freud (and Anna Freud, 1946) clearly demonstrated how frequently we employ these defense mechanisms, the question remains: What are these defense mechanisms intended to defend? We agree with Freud that they are intended to defend against anxiety, but not necessarily with his view of the source of the anxiety. For example, what fear underlies the boy's alleged desire to remove the father and possess the mother? Is it castration anxiety or is it the unbearable shame of a self that would have these desires? Or consider the Don Juan who engages in sexual conquests in order to avoid an underlying homosexual panic. What is so terrifying about allowing into consciousness the truth about one's homosexual desires? Is it simply the consciousness of negative social consequences or superego punishment or the much more shattering effects on the self-concept?

Several distinguished psychologists (Allport, 1961; Hilgard, 1949; Murphy, 1947) have concluded that the central objective of the defense mechanisms is the defense and protection of the self-concept. These mechanisms, furthermore, are not simply invoked in the face of massive psychological threat but represent a constant, pervasive, omnipresent feature of moment-to-moment existence. Since a wide range of circumstances, events, or conditions involve self-concept threats, the mechanisms are constantly mobilized in its defense.

The selections in this section are, first of all, intended to call attention to the amazing inventiveness and vigilance of the human mind to protect and defend the self-concept. Faced with threats to self-esteem or self-consistency, a variety of mechanisms, techniques, or devices are employed, simultaneously or sequentially. Just as no military force depends exclusively on a single weapon but uses all appropriate weapons, so the individual engaged in self-protection employs an array of weapons to defend the self-concept. (cf., Frenkel-Brunswick, 1939; A. Freud, 1946; Sykes and Matza, 1957; Kaplan, Boyd, and Bloom, 1964; Scott and Lyman, 1968; Hewitt and Stokes, 1975; Rosenberg, 1979.) To take a simple example, when we do poorly on a test, we may conclude that the test was stupid or unfair, that the room was hot and stuffy, that the subject was not one that interested us, that we never really tried to do well, and so on.

Second, the following selections are intended to make the point that individuals not only deal with the threats that assail the self but also act to ward off these threats in the first place; we might call this practice anticipatory defense. *People may set low expectations for themselves in order to ensure that, when put to the test, they will succeed. The study by Wortman, Costanzo, and Witt (Selection 41) showed that when the subjects were told that a future test was in the offing, they reduced the ego-enhancing attributions they would otherwise have made. By denying that their success was due to their ability, they forestalled the potentially damaging self-esteem consequences of subsequent failure. Self-esteem defense may thus take unexpected forms. Individuals may temper the ego-enhancing implications of their performance in order to avoid the ego-deflating implications of defeat; they play down their abilities in order to protect their self-esteem (Epstein, 1973; Jones, 1973). Hewitt and Stokes (1975) have described an array of devices used by people to forestall threats to their self-esteem in interactional situations.*

Finally, our selections have been chosen to counteract a perspective of individuals as passive, docile, malleable products of their environment. This is not to say that people are uninfluenced by their social experiences but that these experiences are mediated by the human mind within a given system of motives. This section illustrates the active, creative, inventive component of the human intellect operating to protect self-esteem.

Gordon W. Allport (Selection 40) deals with the psychoanalytic defense mechanisms. Probably no single idea was more successful in stimulating general interest in psychoanalysis than these mechanisms, many of which struck the public as immediately and intuitively true. Allport demonstrates how each of these mechanisms operates in the service of the self-esteem motive. This is not to say that self-esteem protection is the sole motive underlying these psychological devices but that it is the primary one.

Selection 41 derives from attribution research. Attribution is concerned with the process of inferring dispositions or underlying characteristics (for example, cause, motive, intention, ability) of entities on the basis of observable characteristics. How do naive individuals explain or account for people's behavior? For example, does the individual characteristically explain his or her own behavior primarily in terms of internal factors (an ability, need, or attitude) or external factors (situational or contextual conditions)? One answer is that it depends on whether he or she has succeeded or failed. Like most other studies, Selection 41, by Wortman, Costanzo, and Witt find that those who have succeeded tend to ascribe their performance to inner qualities, whereas those who have failed are more likely to attribute this outcome to external circumstances. Both methods protect self-esteem. This study provides an unusually rich description of the range of external causes that may be blamed for one's failure. Those who failed were more likely to say they had bad luck, that the instructions were confusing, that the task was very difficult, and that the information given was inadequate. Even when internal attributions were used, they were also protective of self-esteem. Those who failed denied that they had worked hard at the task or that doing well mattered very much to them.

Selection 42, by Rosenberg, deals with certain processes of psychological selectivity protective of self-esteem. Beginning with an interest in perception, psychologists came to realize that a wide range of sensory and cognitive processes—hearing, attending, remembering, interpreting—were influenced by such inner factors as attitudes, values, needs, and so on. In a famous study, Bruner and Goodman (1947) found that poorer children saw a half dollar as larger than richer children did. Similarly, Levine and Murphy (1947) found that communists and noncommunists, exposed to certain political communications, remembered the arguments on their side better than the arguments on the other side. There is ample evidence to indicate that people selectively perceive or remember in terms of inner needs or frames of reference (Erdelyi, 1974). Selection 42 illustrates that the self-esteem motive also governs diverse selective processes. Five such selectivity mechanisms are discussed, and evidence is presented to indicate that they operate in the service of self-esteem protection.

The authors of the selections in this section, although stemming from widely divergent theoretical traditions and animated by a wide range of interests, nevertheless are compelled to take account of the self-concept. Thus, Allport's selection is based on a consideration of Freudian theory; Wortman, Costanzo, and Witt base their work on attribution theory; and Rosenberg follows a tradition originally stemming from the area of social perception. Other authors (Hewitt and Stokes, 1975; Scott and Lyman, 1968), following the symbolic interactionist tradition, have directed attention to certain verbal mechanisms of self-esteem protection, and Secord and Backman (1965), rooting their work in Heider's balance theory and Festinger's cognitive consistency theory, specify devices people use to maintain interpersonal congruency. Despite the diversity of theoretical orientations, there is a convergence in recognition of the importance of the self-concept. This is not to say, of course, that other motives—the wish to avoid anxiety or to avoid the disruption of the social interaction—are not also served by these mechanisms. The self-concept motives are pervasive, but they are not of exclusive importance.

REFERENCES

Allport, G.
1961 Pattern and Growth in Personality. New York: Holt, Rinehart, & Winston.
Bruner, J. S. and C. C. Goodman
1947 "Value and need as organizing factors in perception." In T. M. Newcomb and E. L. Hartley (eds.), Readings in Social Psychology. New York: Holt.
Epstein, S.
1973 "The self-concept revisited: or a theory of a theory." American Psychologist 28: 404–16.
Erdelyi, M.
1974 "A new look at the new look: perceptual defense and vigilance." Psychological Review 81: 1–25.
Frenkel-Brunswick, E.
1939 "Mechanisms of self-deception." Journal of Social Psychology 10: 409–20.
Freud, A.
1946 The Ego and the Mechanisms of Defense. New York: International Universities Press.
Hewitt, J. P. and R. Stokes
1975 "Disclaimers." American Sociological Review 40: 1–6.
Hilgard, E. R.
1949 "Human motives and the concept of the self." American Psychologist 4: 374–82.
Jones, S. C.
1973 "Self and interpersonal evaluations: esteem theories versus consistency theories." Psychological Bulletin 79: 185–99.
Kaplan, H., I. Boyd, and S. Bloom
1964 "Patient culture and the evaluation of self." Psychiatry 7: 116–26.
Levine, J. M. and G. Murphy
1947 "The learning and forgetting of controversial material." In T. M. Newcomb and E. L. Hartley (eds.), Readings in Social Psychology. New York: Holt.
Murphy, G.
1947 Personality. New York: Harper.
Rosenberg, M.
1979 Conceiving the Self. New York: Basic Books.
Scott, M. and S. Lyman
1968 "Accounts." American Sociological Review 33: 46–62.

Secord, P. F. and C. W. Backman
1965 "An interpersonal approach to personality." Pp. 91–125 in B. Maher (ed.), Progress in Experimental Personality Research. Vol. 2. New York: Academic Press.

Sykes, G. and D. Matza
1957 "Techniques of neutralization: a theory of delinquency." American Sociological Review 22: 664–70.

Mechanisms of Defense

Gordon W. Allport

40

MECHANISMS OF DEFENSE

It is not necessary to accept Freud's theories of motivation and of the unconscious in order to appreciate his brilliant account of the protective strategies we all employ in order to guard our self-esteem. Self-love and pride are universal in human nature, even though in mature personalities they are not necessarily sovereign. Every day we experience grave threats to our self-esteem: we feel inferior, guilty, insecure, unloved. Not only big things but little things put us in the wrong: we trip up in an examination, we make a social boner, we dress inappropriately for an occasion. The ego sweats. We suffer discomfort, perhaps anxiety, and we hasten to repair the narcissistic wound.

The mechanisms of ego-defense (Freud's term) are sly devices by which we try to circumvent discomfort and anxiety. These self-protective strategies are common, but they do not by any means constitute the normal person's entire repertoire of adjustive actions. Often he faces up to his weaknesses and failings and proceeds to cope with them realistically. He meets his guilt, his fears, his blunders head on and works out a way of life that fully and consciously takes them into account and makes of them building blocks for a more integrated personal edifice. The opposite of *defense*, then, is *coping*. The neurotic shows much defense, less coping. In the healthy personality coping ordinarily predominates.

Many philosophers prior to Freud have dealt with our human tendency to sidestep or prettify our failings—among them Hobbes, Nietzsche, Bentham—but to Freud goes the credit for permanently inscribing this chapter in the science of psychology.

What is the nature of this pervasive self-protective motive? Older philosophers were wont to say, "Self-defense is nature's oldest law," or "By whatever name we call the ruling tyrant, self is all in all." For Freud it is a matter of the ego defending itself against anxiety. Among psychologists, Koffka speaks of "a force which propels the ego upward."[1] McDougall finds at the center of every personality a sentiment of self-regard which plays "the most powerful all-pervasive role in the higher life of man."[2] Psychoanalysts speak of "basic narcissism."...

What are some of the chief strategies of ego-defense? Freud rightly gives first place to repression.

Repression

The individual frequently denies conscious outlet to unwelcome wishes and thoughts. "Everything contradictory to the ruling tendencies of the conscious personality, to its wishes, longings and ideals, and everything which would disturb the good opinion one likes to have of oneself is apt to be repressed."[3]

Repression has first place on our list because all other mechanisms of defense seem to depend on it in one way or another. If all our wishes, memories, and conflicts were fully available to consciousness, we would normally employ *coping* rather than defense. It is precisely because we find coping too difficult that we resort to repression. and when the true nature of the conflict is no longer clearly understood, we are ripe for new strategies of self-deception.

To take an example, deans and departmental chairmen in colleges are often astonished by the number of academically deficient students who "forget" that they have received letters of warning about their college work. To them the threat of separation from college is unwelcome and the simplest thing to do is to repress the thought. Having conveniently "forgotten"the threat, the student is then free to have a good time, and also to build up his self-esteem in a variety of minor ways. He can excuse his previous failures, blame his instructors, rationalize his laziness—until the tragic reality finally catches up with him. Even if he has not really forgotten the warning, he has at least dulled its significance and assured himself that it was for some reason not applicable to him.

Denial

Even if one does not actually forget a threat, one may still deny its existence.[4] A common example occurs after the sudden news of a catastrophe or a bereavement. We are likely to say and believe, at least for the time being, "It just can't be so."

A child of three was told that his mother was to have another baby. His jealousy aroused, the child said, "No baby," and kept repeating this formula for many weeks. When the infant arrived he persisted in overlooking its presence and still kept up his chant, "No baby, no baby."

Let us return to the theory of repression. Sometimes the attempt to repress is ineffective, but sometimes it succeeds. In the neuroses it is ineffective for it causes compulsive and not-understood behavior. But there is another kind of repression which is wholly benign, serving well the normal function of coping. Every day we deliberately suppress much material, banishing what is not useful and what does not square with our chosen style of life—and we suffer no ill consequences.

An experiment illustrates the point. McGranahan warned his subjects that they would receive an electric shock if they gave the name of any color in a word-association test. A person who could not inhibit the tendency to say "green" to the stimulus word "grass" was given an uncomfortable shock. The experimenter, by the very nature of his negative instructions, was in effect inviting a mental set for color, but he was also asking the subjects to repress this set. Most of his subjects had no difficulty with the task. They suppressed the color set by adopting a noncolor set. Thus, they might set themselves to give superordinate terms, or synonyms, or contrasting words. By adopting a safe mental set, they avoided the dangerous and unwanted set. They repressed it, and the repression was all to the good.[5] They escaped the shock. Others, however, could not effectively suppress the tabooed idea of color, even though repeatedly punished by receiving an unpleasant shock.

Repression, then, is the process of excluding from consciousness all or part of a conflict situation. (If the process is deliberate, as in this experiment, we speak of *suppression;* if not deliberate, of *repression.*) When the suppression or repression serves the interests of coping by banishing irrelevant and unwanted impulses and memories, it is benign. Sometimes, however, as we have seen, the banishment is unhealthy; suppressed impulses and memories continue to disturb the personality. The flaming wastebasket cannot safely be put into a closet and the door closed.[6]

Rationalization

The term *rationalization* applies broadly to any form of self-deception.[7] It is an absurdity of the English language that the term signifies the *opposite* of "rational" or "reason." Reason is the capacity to shape one's belief and conduct to accord with one's knowledge of the world, and if one's knowledge is insufficient, the capacity to acquire more knowledge pertinent to the issue in hand. Reason fits one's impulses and beliefs to the world of reality; rationalization fits one's concept of reality to one's impulses and beliefs. As someone has said, reasoning discovers *real* reasons, rationalization *good* reasons for what we do.

In one experiment people were confronted with uncomplimentary opinions about themselves. Sometimes they were told that a stranger gave a harsh judgment of them, sometimes that a friend did so. A few people took this information to heart and seriously considered whether they ought not revise their own self-judgments in a downward direction. But more frequently they saved face through rationalization. The stranger, they said, "is a poor judge of people," or "he just doesn't know me." The friend gave more trouble; but some people claimed, "He couldn't have said that," or "He really meant something different." And after a time many subjects distorted their memories of what the friend had said, and reported that the judgment was more favorable than in fact it was.[8]

Rationalizations range from the trivial to the grandiose. On impulse we jump to justify our misdeeds. As Emerson said, "That which we call sin in others is experiment for us." Our irritability or laziness we readily blame on the heat or the humidity. When our child breaks a neighbor's window we minimize the deed by calling it "kid stuff." A dozen times a day we find ways of defending our good opinion of ourselves and our families.

At a more complex level we build up elaborate fictions and ideologies. According to Lotze, a man's philosophical creed is more often than not an attempt to justify a fundamental view of things adopted once for all early in life. Belief in the innate inferiority of the Negro is a comfortable rationalization for white people whose self-esteem and economic advantage depend on keeping Negroes "in their place." One historian has gone so far as to say that nearly all of the writing of the past in social sciences, politics, and ethics "may be brushed aside by future generations as mainly rationalizing."[9]

But this line of thinking becomes dangerous. To reduce all theory to rationalization cuts the ground from under us all. Is Darwin's theory of the survival of the fittest a mere rationalization of nineteenth-century cutthroat economic competition? Is Freudian psychology nothing more than a rationalization of his "decadent, sex-ridden" life? Was Kant's emphasis on the role of reason only a comforting escape from his lack of success in his emotional and active life? One may admit that thinking is often tendentious without concluding that it never has objective validity. Reason transcends rationalization; its function is to distinguish the false from the true; and unless we believe this fact we cannot hope to establish a science of psychology—or of anything else. Rationalization is certainly common in human thought, but its role should not be exaggerated.

Projection

The important defense mechanism of projection is a special type of rationalization. It is basically the form of self-deception wherein one ascribes one's own unwelcome thoughts, wishes, and shortcomings to another person.

If we can blame others, we are saved from the pain of blaming ourselves. Somehow we feel especially righteous and free from sin when we comfortably talk about our own shortcomings in others. Do I tell lies? Well, look at Tony. He is an inveterate liar! This particular form of projection Ichheiser has called the "mote-beam mechanism." The other fellow has evil impulses, so too do I; but thanks to projection I behold only the mote in his eye and overlook the beam in my own.[10]

Sometimes, of course, the other fellow hasn't even a mote—he is wholly innocent. Yet I can "see" my failures in him. An extreme example would be the psychotic who thinks that everyone except himself is crazy. A more common example is groundless gossip which tells nothing true about the victim but a great deal about the inner conflicts of the gossiper.

In *complementary projection*, we do not ascribe our own states of mind to others, but rather ascribe to them motives and behavior that would explain (or complement) our own distress.[11] The timid child thinks that the dog, or the boy next door, or the Chinese laundryman has aggressive designs against him. The paranoiac believes that others are plotting his destruction. Through complementary projection our fears, guilt, or worries receive an "explanation." Do I feel depressed? Well, it is because other people don't treat me fairly.

Displacement is a special form of projection. A disgruntled workman is much irritated by his foreman, but he can neither retaliate nor directly cope with the issue; and so at night he vents his annoyance on his wife and children. Bottled-up humiliations for defeat in World War I, plus an array of social disorders and personal conflicts, led Nazi Germany to make scapegoats of the Jews. It is particularly interesting that Hitler's bill of particulars against the Jews contained the very items of which he himself was guilty (greed for power, war-mongering, sexual perversion). Prejudice against minority groups often takes the form of blaming Jews, Negroes, politicians—almost any group—for frustrations in our own lives. It seems easier to blame them than to seek out and cope with true causes.[12]

Fixation and Regression

A not infrequent defense mechanism is to avoid being one's true age. No one expects much from a baby, a child, or a young person. And so the child may remain babyish, the young person childish, and the adult adolescent in behavior. This infantile drag betokens an attempt to avoid the responsibilities appropriate to one's age.

In time of crisis some people regress. The bride who finds married life too exacting may return to her mother. The husband, not fully mature, confronts his wife with a recital of his own mother's virtues as cook, homemaker, comforter. Temper tantrums in an adult are regressive in nature.

Neurasthenia (habitual invalidism), too, may be a regressive self-protection. If I am ill no one can expect me to cope with my problems at an adult level. Imaginary invalidism thus becomes a safe defense.

Reaction Formation

Reaction formation is an odd form of defense. To hide the source of conflict from others and even from himself, a person may vigorously pretend the exact opposite to what he feels. He does not hate his offspring, but loves them passionately; he is not fearful, but an adventurous daredevil. Extreme priggishness may by a reaction formation to hide lewd impulses. A mother who dislikes her child may actually smother it with devotion. "Usually a reaction formation is marked by extravagant showiness—the person protests too much—and by compulsiveness."[13]

Sublimation

In Freudian theory, the process by which repressed instinctual impulses are expressed in socially and personally acceptable channels is called *sublimation.* Since sex and agression cannot often be expressed directly they remain as "aim-inhibited wishes," and they seek substitute outlets. By becoming a nurse, a woman may sublimate her desire for maternity; a boys' club leader may by this activity sublimate repressed homosexuality; a surgeon sublimates his repressed sadism by carving people in a socially approved way. The poet finds that he can "chew and suck beautiful lines" rather than his mother's breast. Psychoanalysis says that such adult interests as these are "transparent substitutions" for the true (but now unconscious) wishes that the individual harbors.

Although there may be occasional (neurotic) cases that fit such formulation, the doctrine of sublimation implies far too much. It implies that all our mature desires are nothing more than a "cover up" for repressed instinctual wishes. The primary process remains supreme, the structure of the id never changes, and what we regard as a mature socialized person is little more than a wolf in sheep's clothing. . . .[14]

Compensation

The concept of compensation . . . is Adlerian and not Freudian. It does, however, overlap the present discussion of defense mechanisms. Compensation is a counteractive measure taken against a person's feelings of inferiority. Some compensations, however, are clearly of the coping variety. Demosthenes the orator, Roosevelt the Rough Rider, the immigrant who became a tycoon are all instances of compensation by coping. The nonathletic youth who substitutes brains for brawn is also manifesting coping rather than defense. But many compensations are genuine instances of ego-defense. Daydreams, bluster and bullying, sour-grapes and sweet-lemon rationalizations, neurasthenic invalidism can with perfect propriety be considered to be both compensations and instances of ego-defense.

NOTES

1 K. Koffka, Principles of Gestalt Psychology (New York: Harcourt, Brace, 1935), pp. 670ff.

2 W. McDougall, Energies of Men (New York: Scribner, 1933), p. 233.

3 F. Alexander, The Medical Value of Psychoanalysis (New York: Norton, 1932), p. 79.

4 Anna Freud, The Ego and the Mechanisms of Defense (New York: International Universities Press, 1946), Chap. 7.

5 D. V. McGranahan, "A critical and experimental study of repression," Journal of Abnormal and Social Psychology 35 (1940): 212–25. See also L. Belmont and H. G. Birch, "Re-individualizing the repression hypothesis," Journal of Abnormal and Social Psychology 46 (1951): 226–35.

6 Although Freud himself was much more concerned with ineffective and unhealthy repression than with benign, he does not deny the possibility that unwelcome wishes may be "actually destroyed or annulled." Not every impulse lingers in the unconscious. See E. Jones, The Life and Work of Sigmund Freud (New York: Basic Books, 1957), Vol. 3, p. 259.

7 The term was first used in 1908 by Ernest Jones, "Rationalisation in every-day life," Journal of Abnormal Psychology 3 (1908): 161–69. The process itself, however, has been recognized under many names: *fictions* and *fallacies* (Bentham), *ideology* (Mannheim), *derivations* (Pareto), *hypocrisy* (Le Dantec), *myth, folklore, thobbing,* and the like. See G. W. Allport, "Historical background of modern social psychology" in G. Lindzey (ed.), Handbook of Social Psychology (Cambridge, Mass.: Addison-Wesley, 1954), Vol. 1, Chap. 1.

8 O. J. Harvey, H. H. Kelley, and M. M. Shapiro, "Reactions to unfavorable evaluations of self made by other persons," Journal of Personality 25 (1957): 393–411.

9 J. H. Robinson, The Mind in the Making (New York: Harper, 1921), p. 47.

10 G. Ichheiser, "Projection and the mote-beam mechanism," Journal of Abnormal and Social Psychology 42 (1947): 131–33.

11 Cf. G. W. Allport, The Nature of Prejudice (Cambridge, Mass.: Addison-Wesley, 1954), Chap. 24.

12 Allport, Nature of Prejudice, Chap. 21.

13 Calvin S. Hall and Gardner Lindzey, Theories of Personality (New York: Wiley, 1957).

14 For a more detailed analysis of the concept of sublimation see G. W. Allport, Personality: A Psychological Interpretation (New York: Holt, Rinehart & Winston, 1937), p. 185.

In replying to this critique, Sappenfield argues that Freud's conception of sexuality can be broadly interpreted to cover all instances of positive cathexis (satisfaction of a person as a whole), and that in this sense all forms of adult motivation are genuine sublimations. B. R. Sappenfield, Personality Dynamics (New York: Knopf, 1954), pp. 356–62. It is a serious question whether Freud's concept of sexuality can with propriety be so far extended.

Effect of Anticipated Performance on the Attributions of Causality to Self and Others

Camille B. Wortman
Philip R. Costanzo
Thomas R. Witt

41

The purpose of this experiment was to explore some factors that are likely to affect an individual's attributions of causality for his task performance. While theorists have speculated on the process by which individuals make attributions about the intentions and dispositions of others (Jones & Davis, 1965), about entities in the environment (Kelley, 1967), and about beliefs and attitudes (Bem, 1967), the process by which individuals draw inferences about their performance has received little attention.

Although there is little theoretical work on this topic, a number of empirical studies have focused on this problem. Several investigators (see, e.g., Fitch, 1970; Johnson, Feigenbaum, & Weiby, 1964; Medow & Zander, 1965; Streufert & Streufert, 1969) have examined the causal attributions of individuals who received false

Source: Camille B. Wortman, Philip R. Costanzo, and Thomas R. Witt, "Effect of Anticipated Performance on the Attributions of Causality to Self and Others," Journal of Personality and Social Psychology 27 (1973): 372–81.

feedback that they had succeeded or failed at a task. These studies have generally found that individuals attribute causality to themselves when they succeed while attributing causality for their failures to factors in the environment or situation. These findings suggest that an individual's attributions of causality following task performance are affected by a motivation to view himself positively (cf. Festinger, 1954)—possessing the talents and abilities that make one a desirable person and not possessing characteristics that are negative or undesirable. Some authors (see, e.g., Bem, 1972) have argued that these results do not necessarily demonstrate the existence of a self-enhancing motive and have suggested that subjects make these attributions because success feedback is more consistent with their self-concept than failure feedback. However, a few investigators (see, e.g., Eagly, 1967; Steiner, 1968) have asked subjects to rate themselves on a certain dimension and have given the subjects feedback that was either more positive or more negative than their self-rating. Even though the positive and negative feedback were equally discrepant from the subjects' self-view, subjects attributed the positive feedback to their own personal characteristics while assigning the negative feedback to external causes.

Beyond this initial step, however, little has been learned about the process by which individuals assign causality to themselves for their performance. It seems clear that individuals do not always exaggerate their personal causality for success while denying it for failure. It is important, therefore, to test the generality of previous findings and to determine those factors that lead individuals to deviate from the strategy of making positive self-attributions.

The purpose of this study was to examine the role of one such factor: whether the individual expects to continue the task on which he is asked to make a self-attribution. In each of the studies mentioned previously, subjects were asked to make a self-attribution after completing a task. One wonders whether an individual's self-attributions would be positive if he expected to continue performing a task. The results of a few previous studies suggest that they would not. In a recent experiment by Feather and Simon (1971), pairs of subjects were asked to work independently on a series of anagrams. Prior to performing the anagrams, subjects were asked how confident they were that they would do well and how confident they were that the other would do well. It was found that subjects expressed more confidence in the other's ability than in their own. Radloff (1966) also found that individuals who anticipated continued performance were very conservative in attributing ability to themselves.

These studies suggest that when an individual expects to continue performing a certain task, he is somewhat reluctant to make self-enhancing attributions. In order to test this reasoning, an experiment was conducted in which both an individual's performance (success versus failure) and his anticipation about continuing to perform the task (anticipation versus nonanticipation) were manipulated. As in previous experiments, subjects were expected to exaggerate personal causality for successful outcomes and situational causality for failure outcomes. However, subjects in the anticipation condition were expected to be more negative in their self-attributions of ability than subjects in the nonanticipation condition.

In addition to examining the effects of these variables on self-attribution, the authors wished to determine whether they would affect an individual's attribution about the performances of another. The authors reasoned that if individuals are motivated to view themselves positively, they may under certain circumstances feel threatened by the successful performance of another, since another's success may convey to them that they do not compare favorably with the other. Unfortunately, the research literature concerning individuals' attributions about others has not been particularly clear. While a few experiments have suggested that individuals are reluctant to attribute causality to others when they succeed (see e.g., Beckman, 1970; Shaw & Sulzer, 1964), others have produced contradictory findings (see, e.g., Feather & Simon, 1971; Weiner & Kulka, 1970). For this reason, the present experiment was designed to obtain information about other attribution as well as self-attribution. In addition to assigning causality for their own behavior, subjects in the current experiment were faced with a successful other and were asked to assign causality for the other's performance. The authors were not sure whether an individual's attributions about another would be affected by his own success or failure or by his expectations about continuing with the task. However, they hoped that the data collected from this experiment would suggest some interesting hypotheses for future research on attribution of causality to others and on self—other attributional disparities.

METHOD

Overview

The subjects were requested to help the experimenters by working with a partner and evaluating two "case studies" which were part of a social perceptiveness test. Each case study was followed by 5 "sample" questions and 10 "official" questions. All subjects were asked to complete the sample questions of one case. Subjects in the success condition were informed that they had done very well on these questions, while subjects in the failure condition were told that they have done poorly. Crosscutting this variable was a manipulation of anticipated future performance: Subjects in the anticipation condition were led to expect that they would be completing the official questions, while subjects in the nonanticipation condition were told that they would not. In order to expose the subject to a successful other, the subjects were led to believe that their partner had been asked to complete the official questions and that he had done quite well on both the sample questions and the official questions. Finally, the subjects were asked to evaluate their own case study and their partner's case study and to make attributions of ability and causality to both themselves and their successful partner. This resulted in a 2 × 2 × 2 factorial design with two between-subjects factors (Success—Failure and Anticipation—Nonanticipation) and one within-subjects factor (Self—Other).

Subjects

Forty male high school students[1] from the junior and senior classes were randomly selected from their study halls to take part in the experiment. Four subjects were eliminated from the analysis because reading difficulties prevented them from completing the dependent measures.

Procedure

The experiment was conducted in a large high school classroom. The subjects entered the classroom in groups of about 10 and were randomly assigned to desks widely separated from one another. The experimenter introduced herself and explained that she was a psychologist from Duke University. She told the subjects that they were going to take part in a study designed to gain information about a new psychological test, the Social Perceptiveness Scale. They were told that this test had been developed by psychologists to measure a person's ability to deal with people. It was explained to the subjects that the test contained several case studies about real individuals and that people taking the test were required to read each case study and answer questions about the person described in each one.

The subjects were told that although psychologists were enthusiastic about the test, it had one major shortcoming—its length. It was explained to them that psychologists at Duke were interested in shortening the test to just one or two case studies so that it could be administered more quickly and easily. The experimenter explained, however, that the psychologists were not sure which case studies to include. They felt that some of the cases might contain easier questions than others and that some might provide more information about the person described than others. The subjects were told that they would be asked to help evaluate the cases.

The subjects were then informed that they would be working with a partner and that for purposes of anonymity they would not know who their partner was. They were told, "You and your partner will be evaluating two cases. Each of you will get a chance to look at your own case and your partner's case and then evaluate both of them on forms that we will distribute to you." In reality, the purpose of telling the subjects that they would be working with a partner was to provide a convenient rationale for exposing each subject to a successful other and asking him to make attributions about himself and the other. And the real purpose of having anonymous partner was so that the attributions made to the partner would not be affected by the subject's knowledge of the partner's personal characteristics.

The subjects were told that the experimenters needed different people to do different things during the course of the experiment and that for this reason all of the remaining instructions would be given in written form. At this point each subject was given a case study. These case studies were enclosed in impressive, professionally printed folders labeled Social Perceptiveness Scale. Each case study contained some personal information about a young man. This information included descriptions of the young man's social behaviors, achievements, and attitudes as well as friends' descriptions of him. Following this information, there were a series of 5 sample questions and 10 official questions. The subjects were asked to read the case description and go on to fill out *only* the sample questions. Both the sample and the official questions were constituted as multiple-choice items and included inquiries as to the described person's considerateness of others, his likely mode of child discipline, his personality, his concern for monetary attainment, and his tendency to brag about his accomplishments. The subjects were instructed to raise their hand when they finished the sample questions.

At this point in the experimental procedure, the two experimental inductions were introduced. The subject was first given bogus feedback as to his success or failure on the sample questions and was then led to either anticipate or not anticipate completing the official questions.

Success—Failure Manipulations Once a subject had raised his hand indicating completion of the sample questions, the experimenter or an assistant approached him, picked up his paper, and pretended to score it. Half of the subjects were randomly assigned to the success condition and found that they got all five items right. The remaining subjects were assigned to the failure condition and found that they got only one of the five items right.

Anticipation—Nonanticipation Manipulation After the experimenter or assistant scored the subject's sample questions, she gave him a sheet of written instructions describing what would occur next in the study. While the first part of these instructions was the same for all subjects, the second part contained the manipulation of anticipated performance. The first part stated,

In this study we need people to do all sorts of different things for us. For some of the cases we need people to just take the sample questions, and not bother answering the official questions. For other cases we need people to complete the official questions as well as the sample questions so that we can score their case and see how well they do.

For the subjects who had been randomly assigned to the anticipation condition, the second part of the instructions read, "For the case that you took we do need people to answer the official questions so we want you to answer them for us later. . . ." Instructions for subjects who had been assigned to the nonanticipation condition stated, "For the case you took we do not need people to answer the official questions, so you will not have to answer them . . . ."

All of the subjects were told that their partner was requested to complete the official questions. The subjects were led to believe that their partner had been asked to work on his official questions immediately because there were some additional tasks that the experimenters wanted him to do. The subjects were asked to help the experimenters by scoring their partner's questions. The request to score the partner's questions was actually made in order to expose the subjects to the partner's successful performance. After a few minutes, subjects were given a scoring key for their partner's case. They were then given an answer sheet presumably completed by him. In reality, the answer sheet had been falsified by the experimenter to indicate a high degree of success on both the sample questions and the official questions.

After the subject had scored what he thought was the partner's answer sheet, the experimenter gave him a copy of the case study that his partner presumably had worked on, an instruction sheet, and a case evaluation form. Of course, the subjects still had copies of their own case study. The instruction sheet asked the subject,

Please read through your partner's case. You don't have to answer the questions in your partner's case, but please look at them carefully. Then look at your own case and the

questions again. As soon as you have looked through both of these cases, we would like you to fill out the Case Evaluation Form given to you by the experimenter.

The case evaluation forms contained all of the dependent measures, including questions about the difficulty of the cases, the adequacy of the case material, and the subject's attributions of causality for both his own performance and his partner's performance. Subjects in the anticipation condition were additionally told, "As soon as you have finished the Case Evaluation Form, we want you to complete the official questions for your case. Then we will ask your partner to score your questions so that we can determine how well you did .... Then you may leave," Nonanticipation subjects were told, "As soon as you finish the Case Evaluation Form, you may leave; you do not have to answer the official questions in your case or any other case." At the conclusion of the experimental sessions, the subjects met in a group and were probed for suspicion. None of the subjects appeared to be suspicious about any aspect of the procedure. At this point the true purpose of the study was revealed to the subjects. Great care was taken to demonstrate that the scores received on the sample questions were unrelated to the subjects' social perceptiveness and to explain why the hypothesis of the study could not have been revealed prior to the collection of the data.

Dependent Variables

On the case evaluation form, subjects were asked to indicate how many of the sample questions they got right, how many questions their partner got right, and whether or not they anticipated completing the official questions. They were also asked how well they thought they would do on the official questions. These questions were included in order to check the effectiveness of the manipulations. Following these questions, subjects were asked to evaluate their partner's case and performance on the series of 11-point scales ranging from 0 to 10. They were asked to assess: (*a*) the difficulty of the questions the partner received on a scale ranging from "his questions are pretty easy" to "his questions are very difficult"; (*b*) the adequacy of the information in his case on a scale ranging from "doesn't provide very much information" to "provides plenty of information"; and (*c*) the clarity of the information on a scale ranging from "clear and easy to understand" to "somewhat confusing." They were asked to assess the role that luck played in their partner's score on a scale ranging from "he received the score that he did primarily because of luck" to "he received the score that he did primarily because of his social perceptiveness." They were also asked to evaluate their partner's social perceptiveness on a scale ranging from "not very socially perceptive" to "extremely socially perceptive."

The subject's attention was then focused on his own case. He was asked to evaluate his own case on 11-point scales identical to those used to evaluate his partner's case. In addition to evaluating the difficulty of the questions, the adequacy of the information, the clarity of the material, the role of luck, and his social perceptiveness, he was asked to assess his motivation (how hard he tried to do well) on a scale ranging from "not at all hard" to "extremely hard." He was also asked to assess how important it was to him to do well on the test on a scale ranging from "not at all important. I don't care how I do" to "extremely important."

In summary, subjects were given a case study from a social perceptiveness scale containing 5 sample questions and 10 official questions. Half of the subjects were led to believe that they had done well on the sample questions; half were led to believe that they had done poorly. Half of the subjects anticipated completing the official questions and having them evaluated; half did not. All of the subjects were exposed to a partner who had done well on both the sample and official questions. Subjects were asked to make attributions of causality and ability to both their partners and themselves.

RESULTS

Because of the large number of dependent variables employed in this study, the decision was made to perform a multivariate analysis of the data and to examine the univariate analyses only if the multivariate tests reached significance. This technique was thought to be advisable under the present circumstances because (*a*) it takes into account any intercorrelations which may exist between the dependent measures and (*b*) it precludes the possibility of focusing on "significant" results which have in fact occurred by chance because of the large number of tests performed (see Overall & Klett, 1972, for a more detailed discussion of multivariate analysis).

Analysis of the Case Variable

While the subjects were led to believe that there were about as many case studies as there were subjects, there were only two cases circulated. Half of the subjects were given Case A and were led to believe that their partner received Case B, while the remaining subjects received Case B and were led to believe that their partner had been given Case A. Although these case studies focused on different individuals, they were very similar to each other and were purposely constructed to be equivalent in all respects. However, counterbalancing was undertaken to insure that self—other differences in the assessment of difficulty, clarity, etc., could not be attributed to actual differences in the case studies. In order to test the possibility that the cases were not in fact equivalent, a 2 × 2 × 2 × 2 analysis of variance was performed in which Case was used as a factor. A multivariate analysis testing the main effects and interactions for the Case variable revealed no significant effects. Since Case did not appear to have a systematic effect on the subjects' responses, the results were collapsed across the Case variable.

Checks on the Manipulations

Success—Failure Manipulations Except for one subject in the failure condition who stated that he got two of the five sample problems correct, all of the subjects correctly reported the score they "achieved" on the sample problems. That the subjects understood the implications of their score on the sample questions may be surmised from their answers to the question, "How well do you think you will (would) do on the official questions?" Subjects in the success condition clearly anticipated that they would do better on the official questions than subjects in the failure condition ($F = 17.497$, df $= 1/28$, $p < .001$).

Anticipation—Nonanticipation Manipulation Subjects' answers to the question, "Will you be completing the official questions?" revealed that this manipulation had the desired effect on the subjects. All of the subjects correctly reported whether or not they would be completing these questions.

Major Analyses

Cell means for each of the dependent measures are presented in Table 1. A multivariate analysis was performed in which the subjects' responses to the dependent measures were combined to yield a single F value. The multivariate analysis revealed significant main effects for Success—Failure ($F = 5.527$, df $=$ $16/17$, $p < .001$), Anticipation—Nonanticipation ($F = 2.429$, df $= 16/17$, $p < .04$), and Self—Other ($F = 8.078$, $df = 5/28$, $p < .001$). In addition, there was a significant Success—Failure × Self—Other interaction ($F = 3.109$, $df = 5/28$, $p < .03$) and a marginal Anticipation—Nonanticipation × Self—Other interaction ($F = 2.043$, $df = 5/28$, $p < .11$).

TABLE 1

Cell Means for Each of the Dependent Measures

MEASURE	SUCCESS				FAILURE			
	ANTICIPATION		NONANTICIPATION		ANTICIPATION		NONANTICIPATION	
	SELF	OTHER	SELF	OTHER	SELF	OTHER	SELF	OTHER
Luck	5.33	8.00	8.11	8.22	3.11	6.67	4.22	6.44
Social perceptiveness	5.67	8.00	7.33	7.11	4.44	6.89	6.11	7.00
Difficulty	6.61	4.67	5.11	4.44	8.00	4.33	6.22	5.89
Amount of information	6.94	7.11	8.67	7.89	3.56	6.89	4.88	7.33
Clarity	4.94	2.06	3.33	2.44	7.22	3.89	7.22	4.00
Motivation*	8.00		7.56		5.78		4.11	
Importance*	7.50		6.67		5.00		4.11	
	($n = 9$)		($n = 9$)		($n = 9$)		($n = 9$)	

NOTE: The higher the mean, the less the role of luck, the greater the social perceptiveness, the greater the difficulty, the greater the amount of information, the more confusing the material, the greater the motivation, and the greater the importance.

*Subjects were not asked to assess motivation and importance for the other.

Success—Failure Variable Since the multivariate analysis revealed a number of significant effects, univariate analyses of variance were conducted on the subjects' responses to each of the dependent measures. The results of the univariate analyses dealing with self-attribution are summarized in Table 2. The Success—Failure manipulation was found to have a strong effect on subjects' self-attributions. Consistent with previous research, subjects who failed attributed their performance to luck significantly more than successful subjects ($F = 16.069$, $df = 1/32$, $p < .001$). They also indicated that the information given to them was inadequate ($F = 29.984$, $df = 1/32$, $p < .001$) and that their case was confusing ($F = 13.206$, $df = 1/32$, $p < .001$), relative to subjects in the success condition and showed a nonsignificant tendency to view their case as more difficult than successful subjects ($F = 2.738$, $df = 1/32$, $p < .11$). In addition, failing subjects denied that they had tried to do well ($F = 8.075$, $df = 1/32$, $p < .001$) and denied that the task was important to them ($F = 13.087$, $df = 1/32$, $p < .001$) in comparison with subjects who succeeded.

TABLE 2

***F* Values for Dependent Measures Dealing with Self-Attribution**

SOURCE	LUCK	SOCIAL PERCEP-TIVENESS	DIFFICULTY	AMOUNT OF INFORMATION	CLARITY	MOTIVATION	IMPORTANCE
Between subjects							
Success–Failure (A)	16.069†	2.965	2.738	29.984†	13.206‡	8.075†	13.087§
Anticipation–Nonanticipation (B)	6.508*	5.513*	4.707*	5.451	<1	<1	1.817
A × B	1.195	<1	<1	<1	<1	<1	<1
Within subjects							
Self–Other (C)	12.588†	8.447†	11.230†	10.573†	20,375‡		
A × C	1.548	<1	<1	16.168‡	1.472		
B × C	2.601	4.816*	5.463*	1.331	<1		
A × B × C	<1	<1	1.081	<1	<1		

* $p < .05$.
† $p < .01$.
‡ $p < .001$.

An examination of the cell means in Table 1 reveals that the subjects' attributions about the other's behavior were not nearly as strongly affected by the Success—Failure manipulation as self-attributions were, and this accounts for the significant Success—Failure × Self—Other multivariate interaction. However, the data suggest that an individual's performance had some effect on how he viewed the other's task and the other's ability. Subjects who failed viewed the other's case materials as significantly less clear than successful subjects ($F = 4.255$, $df = 1/32$, $p < .05$) and tended to view the other's questions as more difficult. Perhaps subjects who failed showed a general tendency to view the kind of task that they had just completed as a hard one and for this reason viewed the other's material, as well as their own material, as relatively difficult and unclear. Another interpretation is that subjects were attempting to exaggerate the positive qualities of their successful partner and therefore exaggerated the task at which he had just succeeded. However, this second interpretation is refuted by the fact that subjects who failed attributed their successful partner's performance to luck significantly more than subjects who succeeded ($F = 5.058$, $df = 1/32$, $p < .03$). Failing subjects also tended to view the successful other as less socially perceptive than successful subjects, although this latter result did not approach reliability.

Anticipation—Nonanticipation Variable As expected, this variable had a strong and significant effect on subjects' self-attributions. The analyses of variance (see Table 2) indicate that subjects in an anticipation condition attributed significantly less social perceptiveness to themselves ($F = 5.513$, $df = 1/32$, $p < .03$) than subjects in the nonanticipation condition. And when asked to attribute their performance to social perceptiveness or to luck, these subjects attributed their score to luck ($F = 6.508$, $df = 1/32$, $p < .02$) significantly more than subjects in the nonanticipation condition. In addition, subjects who expected to complete the official questions viewed their questions as more difficult ($F = 4.707$, $df = 1/32$, $p < .04$) and their information as less adequate ($F = 5.451$, $df = 1/32$, $p < .03$) than those who did not.

An examination of the cell means in Table 1 reveals that although the anticipation variable strongly affected the subjects' self-attributions, it produced no reliable effects on their attributions about their successful partners.

Self—Other Variable As noted previously, one reason for asking subjects to rate another as well as themselves was to provide some exploratory data on self—other disparities in attribution.[2] The results revealed that subjects viewed their own case as significantly more difficult than the other's ($F = 11.230$, $df = 1/32$, $p < .01$), and their material as less clear ($F = 20.375$, $df = 1/32$, $p < .001$). However, they viewed the other as more socially perceptive than themselves ($F = 8.447$, $df = 1/32$, $p < .01$). And when asked to attribute their performance to social perceptiveness or to luck, they tended to attribute their own performance to luck while attributing the other's to his social perceptiveness ($F = 12.588$, $df = 1/32$, $p < .01$).

It is not surprising that an individual's self-attributions differ from his attributions about another when the other succeeds and he fails. The conclusion that his case materials are more difficult and that the other is more socially perceptive is perfectly logical under the circumstances. More interesting is the subject's tendency to manifest this same pattern of results when both they and the other succeed (multivariate $F = 2.816$, $df = 5.28$, $p < .04$). However, examination of the cell means in Table 1 suggests that self—other differences in attribution produced by successful subjects are due primarily to those who anticipated future performance. If success—anticipation subjects are considered separately, they are found to view their case as more difficult than the other's ($F = 3.886$, $df = 1/32$, $p < .06$) and their material as more confusing ($F = 6.370$, $df = 1/32$, $p < .02$). They also attributed more social perceptiveness to the other than to themselves ($F = 6.206$, $df = 1/32$, $p < .02$) and attributed their own successful performance significantly more to luck ($F = 4.892$, $df = 1/32$, $p < .04$). In contrast, successful subjects who did not anticipate future performance produced no self—other differences in attribution (all $Fs < 1$).

DISCUSSION

Consistent with the results of previous studies, subjects in the present experiment showed a strong tendency to attribute more causality to external causes under failure than under success. Subjects who failed attributed their performance to luck significantly more than successful subjects. In addition, failing subjects exaggerated the difficulty of their questions, minimized the amount of information available to them, and exaggerated how confusing their case was, relative to successful subjects. Of course, the conclusion that their case was difficult is consistent with the notion that failing subjects attribute causality for their performance to external causes. However, the authors would also expect successful subjects to view their task as relatively difficult since the conclusion that one succeeded at an easy task is not particularly enhancing to one's self-esteem. Successful subjects did tend to view their task as more difficult ($F = 3.504$, $df = 1/32$, $p < .07$) and their material as less clear ($F = 5.447$, $df = 1/32$, $p < .03$) than their successful partners, suggesting that their assessment of these factors was affected by their motive to view themselves positively.

In addition to his attributions of causality for performance, an individual's conclusions about the performance itself may be influenced by his motivation to view himself positively. For example, failing subjects can avoid the negative implications of failure by viewing the outcome as trivial or unimportant or by maintaining that they were not trying their best. In the present experiment, subjects showed a clear tendency to adopt such a strategy. Failing subjects attributed less importance to doing well than successful subjects and denied that they had tried to do well in comparison with successful subjects.

The present authors have suggested that differential attributions as a function of success and failure stem from the motivation of an individual to view himself positively. However, Bem (1972) has maintained that what appear to be motivational distortions can often be explained by looking at an individual's knowledge of his past history. Bem has suggested that if past experience has convinced an individual of his capability on some dimension, then he is likely to dismiss information that is inconsistent with this self-knowledge by attributing causality to external factors. Bem's reasoning suggests that in the present experiment, subjects may have attributed their failure to external causes not in order to maintain their self-esteem but because such self-information was discrepant with their self-view.

Although this explanation cannot be ruled out completely, there are two reasons why it is unlikely to account for the results of the present study. First, the authors conducted rather extensive pretesting to determine how individuals evaluated themselves on the dimension of social perceptiveness—the ability to deal with people effectively. This pretesting revealed that individuals are highly uncertain about their ability to deal with people. Furthermore, most people rated themselves about average on social perceptiveness, and there was relatively little variability. In fact, this rating is why the investigators chose social perceptiveness—they wanted to avoid a trait on which subjects had firmly anchored or extreme self-ratings. Second, an attempt was made during the experiment itself to assure subjects that people don't know how socially perceptive they are. This was mentioned as one of the advantages of being able to measure social perceptiveness. Subjects were specifically told that "individuals who think they are very socially perceptive are often not very good at dealing with people. And individuals who think they are terrible at it are often much better than they think." These statements were intended to minimize the influence of the subject's past history, but they probably did not eliminate it entirely. A challenge for future experimenters is to devise methodological techniques that completely eliminate differences in past history as an explanation for differences in attribution (see, e.g., Storms, 1971).

The most important finding to emerge from this experiment is that anticipated performance at a task has a strong effect on subjects' self-attributions. Subjects who anticipated future performance attributed less ability to themselves than subjects who did not. They also viewed their task as significantly more difficult and the resources available to them as significantly less adequate. How are these attributions likely to serve an individual's motive to view himself favorably? By structuring the situation in this way, individuals can view themselves positively, regardless of their performance on the task. If they do poorly, they have the satisfaction of having predicted it and can view the disadvantages under which they were working as the cause of their poor performance. If they do well, they are pleasantly surprised. And the fact that they were working on a difficult task with inadequate resources should make their success even more impressive. A recent experiment by Feather (1969) suggested that individuals are more disturbed by unexpected failure than by expected failure and more rewarded by unexpected success than by expected success. Subjects who anticipate performance can both avoid unexpected failure and insure unexpected success by making a relatively low estimate of their ability. The tendency of subjects to exaggerate the difficulty of their task prior to performance is quite striking when contrasted with prior research. Previous studies suggested that individuals adopt esteem-maintaining strategies after succeeding or failing at a certain task (see, e.g., Fitch, 1970). However, the findings of this experiment suggest that an individual begins to construct such strategies before he even undergoes the task.

In addition to exaggerating the difficulty of the task and the inadequacy of one's resources, there are probably other strategies that an individual can adopt before performing a task that will enhance his self-image. For example, if the task involves an opponent, one can exaggerate the positive characteristics of the opponent. This strategy seems to be adopted quite frequently by athletic coaches and may explain why subjects who expected to answer the official questions rated their partner as more socially perceptive than they rated themselves. Such a strategy should make it possible for an individual who is outperformed by his opponent to attribute this to his opponent's good qualities, rather than to his own bad ones. And of course, an individual who outperforms a very able opponent is more impressive than one who outperforms a mediocre or untalented one.

Since anticipation has been shown to have a strong effect on an individual's self-attributions, it is important that experimenters interested in other variables take care not to manipulate it inadvertently. Such manipulation is likely to produce rather ambiguous results. For example, Bem (1972) cited an unpublished study by Ross, Bierbrauer, and Polly in which both professional teachers and college students attempted to teach spelling to a student. Bem argued that the results of this study are contrary to theories of self-esteem maintenance, since the teachers accepted more blame when the student failed and less credit when he succeeded than college students did. Bem reasoned that since teaching ability is presumably more central to the self-concept of teachers than students, the teachers should have tried harder to take credit when the student succeeded and to avoid blame when he failed. Of course, ego involvement in the task is not the only difference between the students and the professional teachers. Professional teachers presumably anticipate that they will be teaching in the future, while students do not. This fact may explain the tendency of teachers to be more negative in their self-attributions than students.

In conclusion, the results of this study suggest that anticipation of future performance has a strong effect on an individual's self-attributions as well as his attributions about the task in question. Clearly, this is a variable that should receive serious consideration from attribution theorists in the future.

NOTES

1 The authors would like to thank L. S. Dockery and John A. Cox of the Guilford County School System in North Carolina for their help in obtaining subjects.

2 The results on the Self-Other variable should be interpreted with some caution, since subjects always rated their partner first and themselves second.

REFERENCES

Beckman, L.
1970 "Effects of students' performance on teachers' and observers' attributions of causality." Journal of Educational Psychology 61: 82.

Bem, D. J.
1967 "Self-perception: an alternative interpretation of cognitive dissonance phenomena." Psychological Review 74: 183–200.
1972 "Self-perception theory." In L. Berkowitz (ed.), Advances in Experimental Social Psychology. Vol. 6. New York: Academic Press.

Eagly, A. H.
1967 "Involvement as a determinant of response to favorable and unfavorable information." Journal of Personality and Social Psychology Monograph 7: (3, Pt.2).

Feather, N. T.
1969 "Attribution of responsibility and valence of success and failure in relation to initial confidence and task performance." Journal of Personality and Social Psychology 13: 129–244.

Feather, N. T. and J. G. Simon
1971 "Attribution of responsibility and valence of outcome in relation to initial confidence and success and failure of self and other." Journal of Personality and Social Psychology 18: 173–88.

Festinger, L. A.
1954 "A theory of social comparison processes." Human Relations 7: 117–40.

Fitch, G.
1970 "Effects of self-esteem, perceived performance, and choice on causal attributions." Journal of Personality and Social Psychology 16: 311–15.

Johnson, T. J., R. Feigenbaum, and M. Weiby
1964 "Some determinants and consequences of the teacher's perception of causation." Journal of Educational Psychology 55: 237–46.

Jones, E. E. and K. E. Davis
1965 "From acts to dispositions." In L. Berkowitz (ed.), Advances in Experimental Social Psychology. Vol. 2. New York: Academic Press.

Kelley, H. H.
1967 "Attribution theory in social psychology." Nebraska Symposium on Motivation 15: 192–238.

Medow, H. and A. Zander
1965 "Aspirations for the group chosen by central and peripheral members." Journal of Personality and Social Psychology 1: 224–28.

Overall, J. E. and C. J. Klett
1972 Applied Multivariate Analysis. New York: McGraw-Hill.

Radloff, R.
1966 "Social comparison and ability evaluation." Journal of Experimental Social Psychology (Suppl. 1), 6–26.

Shaw, M. E. and J. L. Sulzer
1964 "An empirical test of Heider's levels in attribution of responsiblity." Journal of Abnormal and Social Psychology 69: 39–46.

Steiner, I. D.

1968 "Reactions to adverse and favorable evaluations of oneself." Journal of Personality 36: 553–64.

Storms, M. D.

1971 "Videotape and the attribution process: reversing the perspective of actors and observers." Unpublished doctoral dissertation, Yale University.

Streufert, S. and S. C. Streufert

1969 "Effects of conceptual structure, failure, and success on attribution of causality and interpersonal attitudes." Journal of Personality and Social Psychology 11: 138–47.

Weiner, B. A. and A. Kulka

1970 "An attributional analysis of achievement motivation." Journal of Personality and Social Psychology 15: 1–20.

Psychological Selectivity in Self-Esteem Formation

Morris Rosenberg

42

Although Freud almost totally disregarded the self-image in his theoretical work, his famous defense mechanisms, as both Murphy (1947) and Allport (1961) observed, are primarily designed to maintain a favorable self-attitude. Concepts such as repression, denial, rationalization, projection, regression, sublimation, compensation—"these concepts," Allport observed, "are of value in understanding our strategies for guarding our own self-esteem (1961, p. 163)." In this discussion we wish to illustrate just one principle that is peculiarly relevant to the defense and enhancement of the self, namely, the principle of psychological selectivity. How does selectivity enable a person to defend, maintain, and enhance his ego or self?

. . . . One problem in many discussions of psychological mechanisms is that it is difficult to stipulate the *conditions* under which they will find expression. This is much less true of the mechanism of selectivity. Selectivity, we suggest, is particularly free to operate under two conditions: (1) where the situation is unstructured or ambiguous, and (2) where the range of options is wide. These conditions will vary with the particular attitude under consideration. With regard to self-attitudes, we suggest, ambiguity is particularly great and the range of options unusually wide. For these reasons, the principle of selectivity operates

Source: Morris Rosenberg, "Psychological Selectivity in Self-Esteem Formation," from Attitude, Ego-Involvement and Change, Carolyn W. Sherif and Muzafer Sherif (editors), 1967: 26–50.

with particular force in regard to self-evaluation. Without claiming to be exhaustive, we wish to point to five types of selectivity that may influence self-attitudes, namely, selectivity of values, of interpretation, of standards, of interpersonal relations, and of situations.

SELECTIVITY OF SELF-VALUES

Just as a [person] may hold political, religious, and other social values, so he may hold values regarding himself. Although widely overlooked in self-esteem studies, it is fairly obvious that a [person's] global self-esteem is not based solely on his assessment of his constituent qualities. His self-esteem is based on his self-assessments of qualities that *count*. This point was emphasized with characteristic felicity by William James as far back as 1890. He observed:

I, who for the time have staked my all on being a psychologist, am mortified if others know much more psychology than I. But I am contented to wallow in the grossest ignorance of Greek. My deficiencies there give me no sense of personal humiliation at all. Had I "pretensions" to be a linguist, it would have been just the reverse ....
Yonderpuny fellow, ... whom everyone can beat, suffers no chagrin about it, for he has long ago abandoned the attempt to "carry that line," as the merchants say, of self at all. With no attempt, there can be no failure; with no failure no humiliation. So our self-feeling in this world depends entirely on what we back ourselves to be or do (1950, p. 310).

The relevances of self-values is easily demonstrated from our adolescent study. Consider the quality "likeable." Some students think they are very likeable whereas others think they are not. As we would anticipate, those who consider themselves likeable are more likely to think well of themselves in general, to have high global self-esteem. *But the strength of this relationship depends upon the importance attached to being likeable* (Rosenberg, 1965).

As Table 1 shows, among those who *care* about being likeable, the relationship of the self-estimate to global self-esteem is very strong, whereas among those to whom this quality matters little, the relationship is much weaker.

TABLE 1

Self-Estimate as "Likeable" and Global Self-Esteem According to Value Attached to Being "Likeable"

GLOBAL SELF-ESTEEM	CARE ABOUT BEING "LIKEABLE" (SELF-VALUE): CARE A GREAT DEAL			CARE SOMEWHAT, LITTLE, OR NOT AT ALL		
	ACTUALLY CONSIDER ONESELF LIKEABLE (SELF-ESTIMATE)					
	VERY	FAIRLY	LITTLE OR NOT AT ALL	VERY	FAIRLY	LITTLE OR NOT AT ALL
High	54%	45%	17%	46%	49%	31%
Medium	39	42	33	39	43	50
Low	7	13	50	15	8	19
Total percent	100	100	100	100	100	100
N	(345)	(569)	(52)	(41)	(133)	(34)

It is especially interesting to consider those students who said they were "little" or "not at all" likeable. Among those who did *not* care about whether they were likeable, only 19 percent had low global self-esteem, whereas among those who cared a great deal, fully 50 percent had low self-esteem.

Lest one assume that this result is unusual, we have chosen the 16 qualities out of the 44 in our study which were most highly valued. Consider just those people who feel they are *poor* with regard to these qualities, that is, they do *not* consider themselves likeable, or dependable, or intelligent, or conscientious. How many of these people have global low self-esteem? The answer is that it depends on how important each of these qualities is to the individual. Table 2 shows that with regard to 15 of these 16 qualities, those who *cared* about the quality had lower self-esteem than those who considered the quality unimportant. Yet these people ranked themselves the same way with respect to their possession of the qualities in question. To know that someone considers himself deficient with regard to a particular quality is plainly an inadequate indication of what he thinks of himself. We must also know how much he *values* this quality.

TABLE 2
Low Self-Estimates and Low Self-Esteem According to the Importance of Qualities Rated

	CARE ABOUT QUALITIES LISTED	
	GREAT DEAL	*LITTLE OR NOT AT ALL*
RATE SELF POOR ON QUALITIES BELOW	*PERCENT WITH LOW SELF-ESTEEM*	
Good student in school	32	18
Likeable	50	19
Dependable and reliable	36	23
Intelligent, good mind	34	26
Clear-thinking, clever	34	22
Hard-working, conscientious	28	17
Easy to get along with	38	23
Realistic, able to face facts	30	17
Friendly, sociable, pleasant	29	24
Honest, law-abiding	42	21
Mature, not childish	29	31
Good sense, sound judgment	33	26
Kind and considerate	28	22
Get along well	39	21
Well-liked by many different people	35	23
Stand up for rights	27	26
Moral and ethical	32	25

Now, with regard to self-values, the principle of selectivity is free to operate because the range of options is so inordinately wide. Many years ago, Allport and Odbert (1936) compiled a list of over 17,000 adjectives by which objects could be characterized. Not all of them, to be sure, are applicable to individuals, but an enormous number are. There scarcely seems to be any limit to the types of qualities an individual may consider important in evaluating himself. He may consider it important to be generous, good at working with his hands, a third generation American, popular, nonconformist, hip, daring, moral, thoughtful, good at dancing, cute, ruthless, imaginative, and so forth.

Given this enormous range of options, which values will the individual tend to select as important? One obvious hypothesis is that he will be disposed to value *those things at which he considers himself good and to devalue those qualities at which he considers himself poor.* As one illustration, consider the quality "good at working with your hands." Table 3 shows that among those who felt they possessed this skill, 68 percent valued the quality highly, whereas among those who believed they lacked this quality, only 6 percent attached that much importance to it. Indeed if we consider the same 16 qualities mentioned above, we find, *without exception,* those who considered themselves good in terms of these qualities were more likely to value the qualities than those who considered themselves poor. Self-values, we see, tend to be selected in such a way as to enable the individual to maintain a congenial self-picture.

TABLE 3

Self-Estimate and Self-Value for Quality "Good at Working with Your Hands"

	SELF-ESTIMATE: ACTUALLY CONSIDER SELF "GOOD AT WORKING WITH HANDS"		
SELF-VALUE: CARE ABOUT WORKING WITH HANDS	*VERY*	*FAIRLY*	*LITTLE OR NOT AT ALL*
Care a great deal	68%	27%	6%
Care somewhat or little	32	73	94
Total percent	100	100	100
N	(224)	(392)	(533)

If people are reasonably free to choose their own values, then we are led to a interesting paradox of social life, namely, that almost everyone can consider himself superior to almost everyone else as long as he can choose *his own* basis for judgment. For instance, take four boys. One is a good scholar, the second a good athlete, the third very handsome, and the fourth is a good musician. So long as each focuses upon the quality at which he excels, each is superior to the rest. At the same time each person may blithely acknowledge the superiority of the others with regard to qualities to which he himself is relatively indifferent.

The freedom to select one's values in a fashion congenial to one's self-image is not, of course, without limit. . . . The selection of self-values does, however, have wide latitude because of the enormous range of alternatives available and the private nature of self-values. Under these circumstances, psychological selectivity will play its anticipated role.

SELECTIVE INTERPRETATION

Let us now consider how the principle of selectivity may operate to influence the interpretation of evidence about the self. Our contention is that, since the meaning of the evidence regarding the self is generally so ambiguous, the likelihood will be considerable that the interpretation of the evidence will be selective in the interests of psychological comfort.

In judging oneself, one must take account of the "facts." But "facts," as everyone knows, are amenable to highly varying interpretations. Take a soldier who, in the heat of battle, rushes into the enemy stronghold; taking them by surprise, he destroys or captures them. What he has done is an objective fact. But how shall his act be interpreted? Does it prove that he is a man of utmost courage, fearless to the core? Or does it mean that he is simply too stupid to recognize obvious danger when it stares him in the face? The man's act is clear, but whether the act reflects the quality of "courage" or of "foolhardiness" is a matter of interpretation.

Now let us consider an example closer to the high school student's experience—his grade average. Grades are an objective measure of performance. But what do grades mean? This, to a substantial extent, is up to the individual to decide. Consider a number of characteristics that reflect intellectual qualities: good student in school; intelligent, a person with a good mind; clear-thinking and clever; imaginative and original; knowing quite a bit about many different things; a person with good sense and sound judgment; a logical, reasonable type of person. Table 4 reveals striking differences in the *degree* of association between grade average and self-estimations on these qualities. The association of objective grades to the belief that one is a good student in school is 0.52, but the association of grades to the conviction that one is clear-thinking and clever is only 0.16, and the association of grades to the belief that one is imaginative and original is only 0.08.

TABLE 4
Association Between School Grades and Self-Estimates with Regard to Various Aspects of Intellectual Competence

RELATIONSHIP BETWEEN SCHOOL AVERAGE AND ESTIMATE OF ONESELF AS . . .	*COEFFICIENT OF CONTINGENCY (C)*
A good student in school	.52
Intelligent	.40
Clear-thinking and clever	.16
Logical and reasonable	.16
Know quite a bit about many different things	.15
A person with good sense and sound judgment	.14
Imaginative and original	.08

In other words, most people agree that grades are a good indication of whether they are good students, but they are by no means convinced that grades tell much about whether they are "clear-thinking and clever" or "imaginative and original." Table 5 shows that nearly three fourths of the students with D or F averages consider themselves as very or fairly likely to be imaginative and original, and the same is true with regard to having good sense and sound judgment.

This need not reflect a denial of reality. A student averaging D or F knows that he has poor grades. But there are many aspects of intelligence, and there is nothing in the objective situation to compel the student to interpret his poor grades as relevant to these aspects of intelligence.

TABLE 5

Grade Average and Self-Estimate as "Imaginative and Original"

SELF-ESTIMATE: CONSIDER SELF "IMAGINATIVE AND ORIGINAL"	*GRADE AVERAGE IN SCHOOL*			
	A	B	C	D-F
Very	26%	26%	25%	32%
Fairly	56	49	49	41
A little	17	23	22	24
Not at all	1	2	3	3
Total Percent	100	100	100	100
N	(77)	(438)	(485)	(148)

If the relevance of grades to intellectual abilities is so vague, how much more ambiguous must be the relevance of evidence regarding such characteristics as "moral," "interesting," "easy to get along with," and the like. Here there are no report cards, no test scores, no class percentile ranks. There are no General College Entrance Examination scores for tact, consideration, or independence. Under these circumstances, the inflation of the self-estimates (reflected in extremely skewed distributions of the estimates) is to be anticipated.

Another factor introducing ambiguity into the interpretation of evidence is the nature of trait language. Traits are the main dimensions by which individuals are characterized (Murphy, 1947, p. 506). Yet the language of traits is simply permeated with evaluative overtones. Even a superficial glance at a list of adjectives shows that the vast majority are not simply descriptions but imply negative or positive judgments. To call a person kind is not a description; it is an accolade. To call him cruel is not to describe him, but to condemn him.

The nature to trait language, therefore, [produces] the anomaly that *opposite* linguistic patterns are entirely appropriate to the description of the *same* behavior. For example, if one man calls us clever and thoughtful whereas another calls us shrewd and calculating, are they really describing anything different? If a friend says we are kind, warm, and generous and an enemy says we are maudlin, syrupy, and prodigal, is there really any disagreement about what we are like? Indeed both I and my critic may agree that I am Bohemian and nonconformist, a term he employs to condemn a quality in which I take the utmost pride. Even though people may agree on the evidence, then, they assuredly do not agree on its evaluation.

The fact that this process is so extreme and yet so common highlights the nature of self-evaluation more sharply than perhaps any other single thing. *There is scarcely any behavior which cannot be interpreted as admirable in some way* (the last resort is to say that "at least" one is not the opposite appalling extreme). Furthermore, the individual who engages in "reverse interpretation" cannot clearly be proved wrong. . . .

In the silence of our minds, generally unimpeded by the intrusion of alternative interpretations, we are free to review and evaluate the evidence as our biases dictate, to shift perspectives until a congenial one emerges, and to emerge with a comfortable conclusion.

Just as selectivity holds sway with regard to interpreting the meaning of evidence pertaining to the self, so it has free rein when it comes to the choice of evidence in the first place. The type of evidence relevant to a given characteristic is widely varied. On what basis shall a man judge his generosity—whether he has contributed to the Community Chest, whether he has recently given money to a beggar, whether he bought his wife or child a birthday present, whether he loaned money to a friend, whether he picked up the check at a restaurant for a party, or what? He is not obliged to consider all these criteria; he can choose one—any one he wants, any one that fits. And he is right at least in one respect: the situation is so unstructured that *there is no way to prove him wrong.* The same is obviously true of the vast range of qualities that characterize a person.

Thus from the mass of experiences or communications available to the individual, he will tend to select those best suited to providing a congenial interpretation. To the outside observer these interpretations may appear bizarre or ludicrous. They are not, however, necessarily pathological. Selective interpretation of evidence is easy in this area, both because there is actually little clear objective evidence about the self and because there are so few generally accepted criteria of evaluation.

A high level of ambiguity and wide range of options thus makes possible selectivity of interpretation, linguistic selectivity, and selectivity of evidence. That these mechanisms are effective is suggested by the data from our adolescent study. In this investigation the students were asked to rate themselves on 48 qualities that are generally considered desirable and that are not sex-linked. With regard to every quality but one, the subjects were more likely to rank themselves favorably than unfavorably. This result is clearly consistent with people's preferences for positive self-attitudes.

SELECTIVITY OF STANDARDS

In his trailblazing discussion of the self in 1890, William James (1950, p.310) devised a most ingenious formula: Self-esteem equals success over pretensions. It was but a small step for him to point out that it may be as blessed a relief for the individual to reduce the denominator as to increase the numerator.

The truth of this observation is apparent from the fact that it is not simply how good a person thinks he is with regard to some quality but how good he *wants to be* that counts. In the realm of standards, too, the range of options is wide, and the situation is extremely unstructured.

How good is "good enough"? Assume that people are satisfied to be fairly good students in school, a choice they can make unhindered. By this criterion, as Table 6 shows, all of the A students, almost all of the B students, seven tenths of the C students, and even nearly half of the D or F students qualify as fairly or very good students. Using this moderate standard, most people meet it very well.

This is all the more true of standards with regard to more ambiguous qualities. A man may want to be "considerate" or "dependable and reliable," but he is under no pressure to be *extremely* considerate or dependable. It is perfectly satisfactory if he is reasonably so. In view of the ease with which evidence can

TABLE 6
Grade Average and Self-Estimate as Student in School

SELF-ESTIMATE: CONSIDER SELF "A GOOD STUDENT IN SCHOOL"	GRADE AVERAGE IN SCHOOL			
	A	B	C	D–F
Very	82%	31%	6%	9%
Fairly	18	63	64	36
A little	—	5	24	38
Not at all	—	1	5	17
Total Percent	100	100	100	100
N	(73)	(439)	(498)	(154)

be selected and interpreted in a congenial way, we can reasonably assume that most people can meet the moderate standards they select for themselves.

People have a wide range of options in setting standards for themselves. One can aspire to the pinnacle of achievement, to a good level of performance, to moderate accomplishment, or even to modest success. A man may aim to be a dominant figure in the world of business or politics or to be a competent plumber or carpenter. This principle is all the more true of nonoccupational goals. One person may aspire to be the ultimate in sweetness, goodness, and kindness, whereas another is content just to be a decent fellow. One person may set a goal of being absolutely punctual and of never making an error, whereas another may be satisfied to be reasonably reliable. There is thus a great choice available in the setting of standards of performance in the great sweep of areas pertaining to the self.

Given these options, what standards do people select for themselves? If any single conclusion is suggested by the great body of literature concerning level of aspiration appearing in the forties, it is that most people tend to set goals that they interpret as falling within a reasonable range of their potential accomplishments. When college students were told that WPA workers, college students, and authors and literary critics had made certain scores on a test of literary acquaintance and were asked how well they expected to do, their estimates centered about the hypothetical college students' average (Chapman and Volkman, 1939). Similarly, when individual students were "graded" on a task and then asked how well they expected to do next time, their estimates changed to conform to a new realistic assessment.

Gordon Allport has summarized the level of aspiration studies in a sentence. He commented: "The history of ten years' research on the Lewinian problem is too intricate to trace here, but, unless I am mistaken, every investigation has directly or indirectly confirmed Hoppe's initial claim that the subject behaves in such a manner as to maintain his self-esteem at the highest possible level" (1943, pp. 470-471).

More recent surveys of occupational aspirations tend to confirm the laboratory findings. In a study of college students' values (Rosenberg, 1957), a sample of respondents was asked: "What business or profession would you *most like* to go into?" and "What business or profession do you realistically think you are most apt to go into?" Although in an abstract sense each student might ideally like to be a surgeon, corporation lawyer, or millionaire, these young people did not choose these aspirations. Seventy-six percent said they realistically expected to enter the occupation they most desired, and the course of time had the effect of bringing occupational aspirations and expectations still closer together. Most of the students had scaled down their aspirations to correspond to what they considered within the range of realistic fulfillment. The individual thus tends to select goals (standards and levels of performance) in accord with his assessment of his qualities. This selectivity enables him to achieve his personal goals, to consider himself "good enough," and to maintain a favorable opinion of himself.

It may be noted that many standards are normatively determined and that the principle of selectivity of standards characterizes groups as well as individuals. One might call these "societal coping mechanisms." Such standards, it should be noted, are not always high.

For example, the occupational achievements of people of working-class origins are considerably lower than those raised in a middle-class environment. Does their lower success result in lower self-esteem? Not necessarily, because their aspirations (or "pretensions") are much lower. It is not necessary to repeat here Hyman's (1953) ample documentation of this fact. It is sufficient to observe that a working-class boy who wants to become a plumber is as likely to achieve his goal as a middle-class boy who wants to become a doctor.

It is thus both apparent and important that groups have normative aspirations that are internalized by individuals as their private standards. These normative aspirations tend to be within realistic range of fulfillment.

INTERPERSONAL SELECTIVITY

One of the most consistent findings in mass communications research, as noted earlier, is that people elect to expose themselves to communications with which they agree. With regard to self-esteem, of course, the mass media are largely irrelevant. What is most important is the communications we get from other people. But selectivity operates in interpersonal communications as well as impersonal communications. We may advance as a fundamental principle of social life that people, when given the choice, will tend to associate with those who think well of them and to avoid those who dislike or despise them, thereby biasing the communications about themselves to which they are exposed in a favorable direction.

The outstanding case in point is *friendship*. Friendship is the purest illustration of picking one's propaganda. It is characteristic of a friend that not only do we like him but that he also likes us. To some extent, at least, it is probable that we like him *because* he likes us. Indeed, it is well-nigh impossible to be friends with someone who hates us, not only because we would have no taste for such a friendship but because *he* would not allow the friendship to exist. The upshot of friendship selection is thus to expose people to implicit and explicit interpersonal communications that reflect well on themselves. They hear much less from people who dislike them.

All friendship, then, is at least to some extent a "mutual admiration society," whereby each partner helps to sustain the desired self-image of the other. If Mead

(1934) and Cooley (1912) were correct in assuming that our self-evaluations are largely dependent upon the evaluations others have of us, then the principle of selectivity involved in friendship helps to explain why people are more likely to hold favorable than unfavorable attitudes toward themselves.

Perhaps one of the most important appeals of *romantic love* is the great intensity with which the mutual admiration is held. To be sure, love may be unrequited, but where it is mutually held, it is surely a great prop to self-esteem. To find that someone considers us the most beautiful girl in the world or the most wonderful boy is to find a source for the kind of communication that we select to hear.

What is true of friends and lovers is equally true of *groups*. The avid search for social acceptance is one of the prime enterprises of youth. Young people are constantly in quest of environments where they will be accepted, whether it be the peer group, the beatnik group, Greenwich Village, or whatever. They rebel against their parents, who disapprove of their behavior, characteristics, or qualities—a disapproval offensive to self-esteem—and gravitate toward groups that accept and approve of them, thereby enhancing their self-esteem.

In addition to the individual's selection of interpersonal communications, a social selection with a normative character holds sway. We might say there exists a worldwide social conspiracy designed to elevate the general level of self-esteem. We are all part of that conspiracy. The secret, of course, is *tact*. "Tact is everything, talent nothing," it has been said. One of Webster's definitions of tact is a "peculiar ability to deal with others without giving offense." A person devoid of tact is rejected as a boor or a clod.

[People] living in society are thus under pressure to protect one another's self-esteem. To imply that someone is stupid, immoral, or disagreeable is to give offense. This behavior is not only punished by the object of attack, but by everyone else as well, since it threatens a social norm that protects the self-esteem of all. Under certain social conditions, such as in the search for scientific truth, it is functionally indispensable to violate the norm. In ordinary social relations, however, it is acceptable to express our admiration and regard for another (although even this must be done in a normatively acceptable way) but not to express our disdain and disrespect. To censor our disdain for another person is also the better part of valor, for we can be assured that the expression of such sentiments will stimulate their object to make observations ill-designed to enhance our own self-esteem.

There is one further point about interpersonal communication that merits attention, namely, that its ambiguity permits the principle of selective interpretation to operate with great freedom. Cooley expressed most vividly the point that our attitudes toward ourselves are importantly influenced by the views others hold of us. "Each to each a looking glass, Reflects the other that doth pass" (1902, p. 152). But Cooley was careful to stress that it was not what others *actually* thought of us but our *imagination* of their thought that was decisive. When we read a newspaper or book, we can usually read the lines; but when we read the mind of another human being, particularly his attitudes toward us, we must usually read between the lines. In this great blank white space it is relatively easy to see a message that is congenial.

The communications about ourselves are thus either biased in a generally favorable direction or are sufficiently ambiguous that our own biases are free to operate. That this is the case is suggested by the responses of our adolescent subjects to the question: "What do most people think of you?" Nearly 97 percent said that most people thought very well or fairly well of them, and only 3 percent said fairly poorly or very poorly. Even two thirds of those with low self-esteem attributed such benevolent attitudes to others. They may, of course, be right. It is possible that a vast wave of mutual love and good will engulfs the world. One cannot, however, evade at least the suspicion that with the ambiguity inherent in appraising another's attitudes toward us, a great many people are giving themselves the benefit of the doubt.

We cannot, of course, completely control our interpersonal environments . . . However, to the extent that we have the option . . . we tend to expose ourselves and to be exposed to interpersonal communications of a favorable sort. The communications we thereby receive are heavily biased in a favorable direction.

SITUATIONAL SELECTIVITY

Finally, we may briefly consider the phenomenon of situational selectivity. In a complex, multifaceted society, [people] are not always able to *make* their environments, but they are often able to *select* their environments. A major motivation in such selectivity, we would suggest, is the desire to maintain a congenial self-image. In other words, the individual will be disposed to expose himself to situations in which he excels rather that to those in which he is found wanting.

Occupational choice is a prime example of situational selectivity. In their study of *Occupational Choice*, Ginzberg, Ginsburg, Axelrad, and Herma (1951) accept it as axiomatic that a student will not select an occupation unless he expects to be good at it. When given the choice, then, [people] gravitate toward situations in which their skills will find expression and their talents elicit appreciation.

In speaking of this issue of selectivity, we have at the same time been illustrating the pervasiveness and centrality of the self-esteem drive. It directs thought and action in a wide variety of areas. To an important extent it determines our selection of our values, our memory processes, our perspectives and interpretations of facts, our standards of evaluation and reference points, our goals, our choice of friends, marital partners, groups, associations, occupations, or environments generally. As a pervasive influence, there are few factors that can match self-esteem. The maintenance of self-esteem is thus a continuing and omnipresent aspect of our daily lives as well as of our longer-range aims.

REFERENCES

Allport, G. W.
1943 "The ego in contemporary psychology." Psychological Review 50: 451–78.
1955 Becoming. New Haven: Yale University Press.
1961 Pattern and Growth in Personality. New York: Holt, Rinehart & Winston.
Allport, G. W. and H. S. Odbert
1936 "Trait-names: a psycholexical study." Psychological Monographs. No. 211.

Chapman, D. W. and J. Volkmann
1939 "A social determinant of the level of aspiration." Journal of Abnormal Psychology 34: 225–38.
Cooley, C.H.
1902 Human Nature and the Social Order. New York: Scribner's.
Ginzberg, E., S. W. Ginsburg, S. Axelrad, and J. L. Herma
1951 Occupational Choice. New York: Columbia University Press.
Hyman, H. H.
1953 "The value systems of different classes: a social psychological contribution to the analysis of stratification." Pp. 426–42 in R. Bendix and S. M. Lipset (eds.), Class, Status and Power. Glencoe, Ill.: Free Press.
James, W.
1950 The Principles of Psychology. New York: Dover.
Mead, G. H.
1934 Mind, Self and Society. Chicago: University of Chicago Press.
Murphy, G.
1947 Personality. New York: Harper.
Rosenberg, M.
1957 Occupations and Values. Glencoe, Ill.: Free Press.
1965 Society and the Adolescent Self-Image. Princeton: Princeton University Press. Social

Name Index

Pages set in boldface indicate a selection by the author.

Subject Index